MARATHI

Marathi, the language of Maharashtra, is one of the major Indo-Aryan languages of India. This descriptive grammar provides a comprehensive and sophisticated account of the syntax, morphology and phonology of the Marathi language.

Marathi bridges the long-standing gap between the traditional descriptions of Marathi and contemporary linguistic analyses. It includes in-depth discussion on topics of cross-linguistic interest, such as phrase structure, anaphora and reflexives, subordination, coordination, relativization, causativization, negation, and word order. Regional, dialectal and stylistic variations are also covered, together with significant sociolinguistic and functional aspects of the various structures of Marathi.

Marathi is presented in a broad, universally intelligible linguistic framework which makes it accessible to linguists and non-linguists, and native speakers and non-native speakers alike. It provides a rich resource for those interested in language typology, language variation, language geography and language contact.

Rajeshwari V. Pandharipande is Professor of Linguistics, Religious Studies and Comparative Literature at the University of Illinois and a native speaker of Marathi. Her publications include *Sociolinguistic Dimensions of Marathi: Multilingualism in Central India* (forthcoming) and over fifty articles on South Asian sociolinguistics, the syntax and semantics of South Asian languages, and the language of religion.

DESCRIPTIVE GRAMMARS

Series Editor: Bernard Comrie

University of Southern California

ADVISORY BOARD
W.S. Allen, Cambridge University
J.T. Bendor Samuel, Summer Institute of Linguistics
D.C. Derbyshire, Summer Institute of Linguistics
R.M.W. Dixon, Australian National University
M.E. Krauss, University of Alaska
B. Krishnamurti, Osmania University
Y. Lastra, National Autonomous University of Mexico
S.A. Wurm, Australian National University

ABKHAZ
B.G. Hewitt

KOBON
J. Davies

MANGARAYI
F. Merlan

TAMIL
R.E. Asher

WEST GREENLANDIC
M. Fortescue

JAPANESE
J. Hinds

RUMANIAN
G. Mallison

MODERN GREEK
B.D. Joseph and
I. Philippaki-Warburton

AMELE
J. Roberts

BASQUE
M. Saltarelli

GULF ARABIC
Clive Holes

KANNADA
S.N. Sridhar

FINNISH
H. Sulkala and M. Karjalainen

CATALAN
José Ignacio Hualde

PUNJABI
Tej K. Bhatia

MAORI
Winifred Bauer

KOREAN
Ho-min Sohn

NDYUKA
George L. Huttar and
Mary L. Huttar

RAPANUI
Veronica Du Feu

NIGERIAN PIDGIN
Nicholas G. Faraclas

WARI'
Daniel L. Everett and
Barbara Kern

EVENKI
Igor Nedjalkov

MALTESE
Albert Borg and
Marie Azzopardi-Alexander

KASHMIRI
Kashi Wali and
Omkar N. Koul

KOROMFE
John R. Rennison

PERSIAN
Shahrzad Mahootian

MALAYALAM
R.E. Asher and T.C. Kumari

EDITORIAL STATEMENT

Until quite recently, work on theoretical linguistics and work on language description proceeded almost entirely in isolation from one another. Work on theoretical linguistics, especially in syntax, concentrated primarily on English, and its results were felt to be inapplicable to those interested in describing other languages. Work on describing individual languages was almost deliberately isolationist, with the development of a different framework and terminology for each language or language group, and no feeding of the achievements of language description into linguistic theory. Within the last few years, however, a major rapprochement has taken place between theoretical and descriptive linguistics. In particular, the rise of language typology and the study of language universals have produced a large number of theoreticians who require accurate, well-formulated descriptive data from a wide range of languages, and have shown descriptive linguists that they can both derive benefit from and contribute to the development of linguistic theory. Even within generative syntax, long the bastion of linguistic anglocentrism, there is an increased interest in the relation between syntactic theory and a wide range of language types.

For a really fruitful interaction between theoretical and descriptive linguistics, it is essential that descriptions of different languages should be comparable. The *Questionnaire* of the present series (originally published as *Lingua*, vol. 42 (1977), no. 1) provides a framework for the description of a language that is (a) sufficiently comprehensive to cover the major structures of any language that are likely to be of theoretical interest; (b) sufficiently explicit to make cross-language comparisons a feasible undertaking (in particular, through the detailed numbering key); and (c) sufficiently flexible to encompass the range of variety that is found in human language. The volumes that were published in the predecessor to the present series, the *Lingua Descriptive Studies* (now available from Routledge), succeeded in bridging the gap between theory and description: authors include both theoreticians who are also interested in description and field-workers with an interest in theory.

The aim of the Descriptive Grammars is thus to provide descriptions of a wide range of languages according to the format set out in the *Questionnaire*. Each language will be covered in a single volume. The first priority of the series is grammars of languages for which detailed descriptions are not at present available. However, the series will also encompass descriptions of better-known languages with the series framework providing more detailed descriptions of such languages than are currently available (as with the monographs on West Greenlandic and Kannada).

Bernard Comrie

MARATHI

Rajeshwari V. Pandharipande

Routledge
Taylor & Francis Group
LONDON AND NEW YORK

First published 1997
by Routledge
2 Park Square, Milton Park, Abingdon, Oxon, OX14 4RN

Simultaneously published in the USA and Canada
by Routledge
270 Madison Ave, New York NY 10016

Transferred to Digital Printing 2010

British Library Cataloguing in Publication Data
A catalogue record for this book is available from the British Library

Library of Congress Cataloguing in Publication Data
Pandharipande, Rajeshwari.
Marathi / Rajeshwari V. Pandharipande.
p. cm. – (Descriptive grammar)
1. Marathi language–Grammar. I. Title. II. Series.
PK2356.P36 1997
491.4'65–dc21 96–38089

ISBN10: 0–415–00319–9 (hbk)
ISBN10: 0–415–59148–1 (pbk)

ISBN13: 978–0–415–00319–3 (hbk)
ISBN13: 978–0–415–59148–5 (pbk)

Publisher's Note
The publisher has gone to great lengths to ensure the quality of this reprint but points out that some imperfections in the original may be apparent.

For my parents
who gave me the precious gift of the Marathi language

CONTENTS

Acknowledgements xxviii
Key to abbreviations xxx
Maps xxxiii
Introduction xxxv

SYNTAX 1
1.1 **GENERAL QUESTIONS** 1
1.1.1 SENTENCE TYPES 1
1.1.1.1 Direct speech and indirect speech 1
1.1.1.2 Interrogative sentences 7
1.1.1.2.1 Yes-no questions 7
1.1.1.2.1.1 Neutral yes-no questions 7
1.1.1.2.1.2 Leading questions 8
1.1.1.2.1.2.1-2 Degree of certainty of answers to leading questions 10
1.1.1.2.1.3 Alternative questions 10
1.1.1.2.2 Question-word questions 11
1.1.1.2.2.1 Constituents of the sentence that can be questioned 16
1.1.1.2.2.1.1 Constituents of the main clause that can be questioned 16
1.1.1.2.2.1.2 Constituents of the subordinate clause that can be questioned 20
1.1.1.2.2.1.2.1 Non-finite clauses 21
1.1.1.2.2.1.2.1.1 Infinitival clauses 21
1.1.1.2.2.1.2.1.2 Participial clauses 22
1.1.1.2.2.1.2.1.3 Nominalized clauses 22
1.1.1.2.2.1.3 Constituents of noun phrases that can be questioned 23
1.1.1.2.2.1.4 Constituents of postpositional phrases that can be questioned 28

1.1.1.2.2.1.5 Constituents of coordinate structures that can be questioned 29
1.1.1.2.2.1.6 Number of sentence constituents that can be questioned 31
1.1.1.2.2.2 - 1.1.1.2.2.2.1 Status of the questioned element 32
1.1.1.2.3 Echo questions 32
1.1.1.2.3.1 Yes-no echo questions 32
1.1.1.2.3.2 Question-word echo questions 35
1.1.1.2.3.3 Yes-no question echo questions 36
1.1.1.2.3.4-7 Elements of the sentence that can be questioned in echo questions 36
1.1.1.2.4 Answers 37
1.1.1.2.4.1 - 1.1.1.2.4.1.3 Answers not marked as distinct speech acts 37
1.1.1.2.4.2 Answers in the form of incomplete sentences 37
1.1.1.2.4.2.1 Minimum answers to yes-no questions 38
1.1.1.2.4.2.1.1 Response particles 'yes' and no' 39
1.1.1.2.4.2.1.2 Answers to leading questions 40
1.1.1.2.4.2.2 Answers to question-word questions 41
1.1.1.3 Imperatives 42
1.1.1.3.1 Positive imperative 42
1.1.1.3.1.1 Possible person-number combinations 42
1.1.1.3.1.1.1 The direct imperative 42
1.1.1.3.1.1.2 The optative 44
1.1.1.3.1.1.3 The suggestive 47
1.1.1.3.1.1.4 The obligative 48
1.1.1.3.1.1.5 The future obligative 51
1.1.1.3.1.1.6 The future 52
1.1.1.3.1.1.7 Prohibitive 53
1.1.1.3.1.2 Degrees of imperative 53
1.1.1.3.1.2.1 Use of *pāhū* and *bara* in imperative sentences 54
1.1.1.3.2 - 1.1.1.3.2.2 The negative imperative 55
1.1.1.3.3 Other devices of expressing imperatives 57
1.1.1.3.3.1 Yes-no questions as imperatives 57
1.1.1.3.3.2 Question-word questions as imperatives 58
1.1.1.3.3.3 Statements as generic imperatives 58
1.1.1.3.3.4 Parallel statements as negative imperatives 58
1.1.1.3.3.5 Performatives as imperatives 59
1.1.1.3.3.6 Contingent forms as negative imperatives 59
1.1.1.3.3.7 Imprecation (cursing) 59
1.1.1.3.3.8 Statements (implying advice) as imperatives 60
1.1.1.3.3.9 Questions as imperatives 61

1.1.2 SUBORDINATE CLAUSES 61
1.1.2.1 General markers of subordination 61
1.1.2.2 Noun clauses 62
1.1.2.2.1 Marking of noun clauses 62
1.1.2.2.2 Types of noun clauses 63
1.1.2.2.2.1 Finite noun phrase complements 63
1.1.2.2.2.2 Non-finite noun phrase complements 64
1.1.2.2.2.3 Finite verbal complements 65
1.1.2.2.2.3.1 Complementizer *kī* construction 65
1.1.2.2.2.4 Non-finite verbal complements 66
1.1.2.2.3 Indirect statements 67
1.1.2.2.4 Indirect questions 69
1.1.2.2.5 Indirect commands 71
1.1.2.2.6 - 1.1.2.2.6.7 Non-finite noun clauses 72
1.1.2.3 Adjective clauses (relative clauses) 76
1.1.2.3.1 Marking the sentential relative clause 76
1.1.2.3.2 Restrictive and non-restrictive relative clauses 80
1.1.2.3.3 - 1.1.2.3.3.3 Position of the head noun 84
1.1.2.3.4 - 1.1.2.3.4.4 Form of the relativized element 84
1.1.2.3.5 - 1.1.2.3.5.3 Position of relativized element 85
1.1.2.3.6 Headless relative clauses 86
1.1.2.3.7 Elements of the sentence that can be relativized 88
1.1.2.3.7.1 Constituents of the main clause that can be relativized 88
1.1.2.3.7.1.1 Constituents of the main clause that can be relativized by finite/sentential relative clauses 88
1.1.2.3.7.1.2 Constituents of the main clause that can be relativized by participial clauses 89
1.1.2.3.7.2 Constituents of the subordinate clause that can be relativized 92
1.1.2.3.7.2.1 Constituents of the subordinate clause that can be relativized by the sentential relative clause 92
1.1.2.3.7.2.2 Constituents of subordinate clauses that can be relativized by the participial relative 94
1.1.2.3.7.3 Elements of noun phrases that can be relativized 97
1.1.2.3.7.4 Elements of postpositional phrases that can be relativized 100

1.1.2.3.7.5 Elements of coordinate structures that can be relativized....100
1.1.2.4 Adverb clauses....103
1.1.2.4.1 Marking and position....103
1.1.2.4.2 Different types of adverb clauses....103
1.1.2.4.2.1 Adverb clauses of time....103
1.1.2.4.2.1.1 Finite clauses with relative clause-like time markers....103
1.1.2.4.2.1.2 Participial non-finite constructions....105
1.1.2.4.2.2 Manner....109
1.1.2.4.2.2.1 Relative clause-like manner adverbial clauses....109
1.1.2.4.2.2.2 Participial constructions as manner adverbials....110
1.1.2.4.2.3 Purpose....111
1.1.2.4.2.4 Cause....112
1.1.2.4.2.4.1 Finite clause marked with *kāraṇ* 'because'....112
1.1.2.4.2.4.2 Gerund....113
1.1.2.4.2.4.3 Infinitive....114
1.1.2.4.2.4.4 Participles....114
1.1.2.4.2.4.5 Conjunctive particle āṇi 'and'....115
1.1.2.4.2.5 Conditional and concessive clauses....115
1.1.2.4.2.5.1 Conditional clauses....115
1.1.2.4.2.5.2 Concessive clauses....119
1.1.2.4.2.6 Results....120
1.1.2.4.2.7 Degree....121
1.1.2.4.2.7.1 Clauses of comparative degree....121
1.1.2.4.2.7.2 Equative....122
1.1.2.4.3 Non-finite comparative clauses....124
1.1.2.5 - 1.1.2.5.1 Sequence of tenses....124

1.2 **STRUCTURAL QUESTIONS**....125
1.2.1 INTERNAL STRUCTURE OF THE SENTENCE....125
1.2.1.1 Copular sentences....125
1.2.1.1.1-3 Copular sentences with nominal, adjectival, and adverbial complements....125
1.2.1.1.4-5 Retention and deletion of copula....126
1.2.1.1.6 Different types of copula....127
1.2.1.2 Verbal sentences....129
1.2.1.2.1 Subject....129
1.2.1.2.2 Direct object....133
1.2.1.2.3 Indirect object....136

1.2.1.2.4 Other types of verbal arguments/oblique objects....137
1.2.1.2.5 Combination of arguments....137
1.2.1.2.6 Order of arguments....138
1.2.1.3 Adverbials....138
1.2.1.3.1 - 1.2.1.3.1.1-2 Types of adverbials....138
1.2.1.3.1.3 Cases of noun phrases....140
1.2.1.3.1.4.1-2 Adverbial clauses....140
1.2.1.3.2 Position of adverbials....140
1.2.1.3.3 Optionality of adverbs....141
1.2.2 ADJECTIVE PHRASES....141
1.2.2.1 Definition....141
1.2.2.1.1 Operational definition of adjective phrases....142
1.2.2.2 Adjectivals with arguments....143
1.2.2.3 Adverbial modification of adjectives....144
1.2.3 ADVERBIAL PHRASES....144
1.2.3.1 Definition....144
1.2.3.2 Adverbial modifiers of adverbials....146
1.2.4 - 1.2.4.3.5 POSTPOSITIONAL PHRASES....147
1.2.4.4 Cases governed by postpositions....148
1.2.5 NOUN PHRASE (NOMINAL CONSTITUENT)....149
1.2.5.1 Definition....149
1.2.5.2 Modifiers in noun phrases....150
1.2.5.2.1 Attributive adjectives....150
1.2.5.2.2 Relative clauses....150
1.2.5.2.3 Possessive adjectives....150
1.2.5.2.4-5 Articles and demonstrative objects....151
1.2.5.2.6 Quantifiers and numerals....151
1.2.5.2.7 Adverbials....153
1.2.5.2.8 Emphatic markers and limiters....154
1.2.5.2.9 Comparative/superlative/equative structures....154
1.2.5.2.10 Other elements....155
1.2.5.3-4 Co-occurrence and combination of modifiers....156
1.2.5.5 Order of constituents in the noun phrase....157

1.3 **COORDINATION**....158
1.3.1.1 Sentence coordination....158
1.3.1.1.1 'and' coordination....159
1.3.1.1.2 'but' coordination....160
1.3.1.1.3 'or' coordination....162
1.3.1.2 - 1.3.1.2.3 Number of coordinators....163
1.3.1.3 Coordination of major categories....163
1.3.1.3.1 'and' coordination....163

1.3.1.3.2 'but' coordination 164
1.3.1.3.3 'or' coordination 165
1.3.1.4 Coordination and accompaniment 168
1.3.1.5 Structural parallelism and coordination 169
1.3.1.5.1 Adjectives and participial constructions 170
1.3.1.5.2 Nouns and nominalized constructions 171
1.3.1.5.3 Different types of adverbials 172
1.3.1.5.4 Active and passive verbs 174
1.3.1.5.5 Coordination of different categories of verbs 175
1.3.2.1 - 1.3.3.3 Elements of the sentence that can be omitted under identity in coordination 175
1.3.3.4 Verb agreement in coordination 176

1.4 **NEGATION** 182
1.4.1 SENTENCE NEGATION 182
1.4.1.1 Negation as a finite/auxiliary verb 186
1.4.1.2 Negation in modals 188
1.4.1.3 Negation and tense 188
1.4.2 CONSTITUENT NEGATION 189
1.4.3 MULTIPLE NEGATIVES 190
1.4.4 NEGATION AND COORDINATION 191
1.4.5 NEGATION AND SUBORDINATION (NEG RAISING) 192
1.4.6 UNIVERSAL NEGATION 193

1.5 **ANAPHORA** 195
1.5.1 - 1.5.1.2 MEANS OF EXPRESSING ANAPHORA 195
1.5.1.3 Personal pronouns 197
1.5.1.4 Reflexive pronouns 197
1.5.1.5-6 Other means of expressing anaphora 198
1.5.2 ANAPHORA IN DIFFERENT SYNTACTIC CONTEXTS 198
1.5.2.1 Anaphora within the clause 198
1.5.2.2 Anaphora in coordinate structures 199
1.5.2.3 Anaphora between superordinate and subordinate clauses 201
1.5.2.3.1 Anaphora between a superordinate and a following subordinate clause 201
1.5.2.3.2 Anaphora between a superordinate and a preceding subordinate clause 202
1.5.2.3.3 Anaphora between a non-finite subordinate clause and a superordinate clause 204

1.5.2.4 Anaphora between different subordinate clauses.......206
1.5.2.5 Anaphora between different sentences.......................207

1.6 **REFLEXIVES**...207
1.6.1 MEANS OF EXPRESSING REFLEXIVITY.................207
1.6.2 SCOPE OF REFLEXIVITY...207
1.6.3 POSITION OF THE REFLEXIVE PRONOUN.............211
1.6.4-5 POSSIBLE RELATIONS BETWEEN ANTECEDENT AND REFLEXIVE.....212
1.6.6 REFLEXIVE RELATIONS WITHIN NOMINALIZED CLAUSES...216
1.6.7 REFLEXIVE RELATIONS WITHIN ORDINARY NOUN PHRASES...............................217
1.6.8 REFLEXIVES WITHOUT OVERT ANTECEDENTS...............................217
1.6.9 OTHER USES OF REFLEXIVE FORMS.....................218
1.6.9.1 Reflexive pronouns as emphatic pronoun.................218
1.6.9.2 Reflexive as an adverb..219
1.6.9.3 Codependency of the coreferential referents.............219

1.7 **RECIPROCALS**...219

1.8 **COMPARISON**...222
1.8.1-3 MEANS OF EXPRESSING COMPARISON..............222
1.8.4 ELEMENTS THAT CAN BE OMITTED UNDER IDENTITY.......................................225
1.8.5 TWO TYPES OF COMPARATIVE STRUCTURE........225
1.8.6 CORRELATIVE COMPARISON...............................226
1.8.7 SUPERLATIVE...226

1.9 **EQUATIVES**...227

1.10 **POSSESSION**...229
1.10.1 SENTENCE TYPES EXPRESSING POSSESSION.....229
1.10.2 ALIENABLE AND INALIENABLE POSSESSION....231
1.10.3 TEMPORARY AND PERMANENT POSSESSION....231
1.10.4-5 POSSESSION OF DIFFERENT TYPES OF ENTITIES...231
1.10.6 OTHER...233

1.11 **EMPHASIS**...234
1.11.1 SENTENCE EMPHASIS..234

1.11.1.1 Non-contradictory emphasis....234
1.11.1.2 Contradictory emphasis....237
1.11.2.1 Constituent emphasis....238
1.11.2.1.1 Emphatic stress....238
1.11.2.1.2 Emphatic particles....239
1.11.2.1.3 Movement of emphasized element....243
1.11.2.1.4-5 Clefting and pseudoclefting....244
1.11.2.1.6 Emphasis by dislocation....245
1.11.2.1.7 Repetition....247
1.11.2.1.8 Inversion....248
1.11.2.1.9 Combinations of devices to express emphasis....249
1.11.2.2.1 - 1.11.2.2.2.4 Elements that may be emphasized....249
1.11.2.2.2.5 Emphasis of more than one constituent simultaneously....250
1.11.3 FOCUS OF YES-NO QUESTIONS....250

1.12 **TOPIC**....252
1.12.1 MEANS OF INDICATING THE TOPIC OF A SENTENCE....252
1.12.2 ELEMENTS THAT CAN BE TOPICALIZED....254
1.12.3 OBLIGATORY / OPTIONAL STATUS OF TOPICALIZATION....254

1.13 **HEAVY SHIFT**....254
1.13.1 HEAVY SHIFT PROCESSES....254
1.13.2 STRUCTURES SUBJECT TO HEAVY SHIFT....255
1.13.2.1 Adjective phrases....255
1.13.2.2 Noun phrases....255
1.13.2.3 Adverb phrases....258
1.13.3-4 LANDING SITES OF HEAVY STRUCTURES....258
1.13.5 HEAVY SHIFT WITH ELEMENTS ADJACENT TO COMPLEMENTIZERS....260

1.14 **OTHER MOVEMENT PROCESSES**....260

1.15 **MINOR SENTENCE TYPES**....260
1.15.1 VOCATIVES....261
1.15.2 EXCLAMATIONS....263
1.15.3 GREETINGS....265
1.15.4 TOPIC QUESTIONS....265
1.15.5 SHORT ANSWERS....266

1.15.6 INFINITIVE SENTENCES 267
1.15.7 NONCHALANT EXPRESSIONS 267

1.16 **OPERATIONAL DEFINITIONS OF WORD CLASSES** 268
1.16.1 NOUN 268
1.16.2 PRONOUN 268
1.16.3 VERB 269
1.16.4 ADJECTIVE 269
1.16.5 POSTPOSITION 270
1.16.6 NUMERAL AND QUANTIFIER 270
1.16.7 PARTICLE 272

MORPHOLOGY 273
2.1 **INFLECTIONAL MORPHOLOGY** 273
2.1.1 NOUN INFLECTION 273
2.1.1.1 Means used to express syntactic and semantic functions of noun phrases 273
2.1.1.2 Expression of syntactic functions 283
2.1.1.2.1 Subject of intransitive verbs 283
2.1.1.2.2 Subject of transitive verbs 284
2.1.1.2.3 Subject of copular constructions 285
2.1.1.2.3.1 Subject of 'dative subject constructions' 285
2.1.1.2.4 Direct object 286
2.1.1.2.5 Indirect object 292
2.1.1.2.6 Object of comparisons 293
2.1.1.2.7 Object of equation 293
2.1.1.2.8 Other objects governed by verbs 295
2.1.1.2.9 Complement of copula constructions 297
2.1.1.2.10 Subject complement 298
2.1.1.2.11 Object complement 299
2.1.1.2.12 Objects governed by adjectives 300
2.1.1.2.13 Agent in passive/pseudopassive/impersonal constructions 301
2.1.1.2.14 Topic 303
2.1.1.2.15 Emphasized elements 304
2.1.1.3 - 2.1.1.3.4 Syntactic functions in non-finite or nominalized constructions 304
2.1.1.4 Means of expressing non-local semantic functions 305
2.1.1.4.1 Benefactive 305
2.1.1.4.2 Source 306
2.1.1.4.3 Instrumental 308
2.1.1.4.4 Comitative 310

2.1.1.4.5 Circumstance..311
2.1.1.4.6 - 2.1.1.4.6.3 Possessive....................................312
2.1.1.4.7 Possessed..312
2.1.1.4.8 Quality..312
2.1.1.4.9 Quantity..315
2.1.1.4.10 Material..316
2.1.1.4.11 Manner..317
2.1.1.4.12 Cause..319
2.1.1.4.13 Purpose..320
2.1.1.4.14 Function..321
2.1.1.4.15 Reference..321
2.1.1.4.16-17 Essive and translative....................................322
2.1.1.4.18 Part-whole..323
2.1.1.4.19 Partitive..324
2.1.1.4.19.2 & 2.1.1.4.19.4 Non-partitive numerals and quantifiers....................................325
2.1.1.4.19.5 Partitive negative quantifiers....................................326
2.1.1.4.19.6 Non-partitive negative quantifier....................................326
2.1.1.4.20 Price..326
2.1.1.4.21 Value..327
2.1.1.4.22 Distance..327
2.1.1.4.23 Extent..328
2.1.1.4.24 Concessive..329
2.1.1.4.25 Inclusion..330
2.1.1.4.26 Exclusion..330
2.1.1.4.27 Addition..331
2.1.1.4.28 Vocative..331
2.1.1.4.29 Citation form..334
2.1.1.4.30 Label form..334
2.1.1.5 Local Semantic functions....................................335
2.1.1.5.1 General location..335
2.1.1.5.2 Proximate location..337
2.1.1.5.3 Interior..339
2.1.1.5.4 Exterior..341
2.1.1.5.5 Anterior..342
2.1.1.5.6 Posterior..344
2.1.1.5.7-8 Superior and superior-contact location....................................345
2.1.1.5.9-10 Inferior and inferior-contact location....................................347
2.1.1.5.11-12 Lateral and lateral-contact location....................................348
2.1.1.5.13-14 Citerior and citerior-contact location....................................350
2.1.1.5.15-16 Ulterior and ulterior-contact location....................................351
2.1.1.5.17-18 Medial location..351

2.1.1.5.19 Circumferential location 352
2.1.1.5.20 Citerior-anterior location 352
2.1.1.5.21-29 Motion past long objects 352
2.1.1.5.30 Other directional locations 353
2.1.1.5.31 Locational precision 353
2.1.1.6 Location in time 355
2.1.1.6.1 General time expression 355
2.1.1.6.1.1 Time of day 355
2.1.1.6.1.2 Period of day 357
2.1.1.6.1.3 Day of the week 358
2.1.1.6.1.4 Month of the year 358
2.1.1.6.1.5 Year 359
2.1.1.6.1.6 Festivals 359
2.1.1.6.1.7 Seasons 359
2.1.1.6.2 Frequentatives 360
2.1.1.6.3 Punctual future 361
2.1.1.6.4 Punctual past 361
2.1.1.6.5 Duration 362
2.1.1.6.6-7 Anterior duration-past and future 362
2.1.1.6.8 Posterior duration-past 363
2.1.1.6.9 Posterior duration-future 364
2.1.1.6.10 Anterior-general 364
2.1.1.6.11 Posterior-general 365
2.1.1.6.12 Point in period-past 365
2.1.1.6.13 Point in period-future 365
2.1.1.7 Double case-marking 366
2.1.1.8.1 The number-marking system in nouns 366
2.1.1.8.2-3 The extent to which the system of number-marking is obligatory 366
2.1.1.8.4 Collective and distributive plural 367
2.1.1.8.5 Collective nouns 367
2.1.1.8.6 Manner of realization of the number distinction 368
2.1.1.8.7 Number-marking of foreign words 368
2.1.1.9 Noun classes 368
2.1.1.9.1 Gender 368
2.1.1.9.2 Meaning of noun classes 369
2.1.1.9.3-4 Classifiers 369
2.1.1.9.5 Assignments of loan words to noun classes 370
2.1.1.10 - 2.1.1.10.6 Definiteness marking in noun phrases 370
2.1.1.11 - 2.1.1.11.6 Indefiniteness marking on noun phrases 373

2.1.1.12 - 2.1.1.12.4 Referential and non-referential indefiniteness.....374
2.1.1.13 - 2.1.1.13.2 Genericness.....374
2.1.1.14 - 2.1.1.14.4 Degree of importance of actors.....375
2.1.2 PRONOUNS.....375
2.1.2.1 Personal pronouns.....375
2.1.2.1.1 Free pronouns.....376
2.1.2.1.1.1 - 2.1.2.1.1.5 Obligatory/optional status of pronouns.....378
2.1.2.1.2 - 2.1.2.1.3.7 Person distinctions in pronouns.....381
2.1.2.1.4 - 2.1.2.1.5.2 Number marking in pronouns.....381
2.1.2.1.6 - 2.1.2.1.6.1 Proximity marking in pronouns.....382
2.1.2.1.7 Special anaphoric pronouns.....382
2.1.2.1.8 Gender distinctions in pronouns.....382
2.1.2.1.9 - 2.1.2.1.9.1 Other relationships.....382
2.1.2.1.10 Lists of pronominal forms.....382
2.1.2.1.11 Tense marking in pronouns.....382
2.1.2.1.12 Status distinctions in pronouns.....383
2.1.2.1.13-14 Special non-specific indefinite pronouns.....384
2.1.2.1.15 - 2.1.2.1.15.3 Special emphatic pronouns.....385
2.1.2.1.16 Complex pronouns.....385
2.1.2.1.17 Pronoun-noun constructions.....386
2.1.2.1.18 Pairs of pronouns.....386
2.1.2.1.19 Secondary pronoun system.....386
2.1.2.1.20 - 2.1.2.1.20.1.5 Case system in pronouns.....387
2.1.2.2 - 2.1.2.2.7 Reflexive pronouns.....389
2.1.2.3 Reciprocal pronouns.....391
2.1.2.4 - 2.1.2.4.11.1 Possessive pronouns.....391
2.1.2.5 - 2.1.2.5.8.1 Demonstrative pronouns.....391
2.1.2.6 - 2.1.2.6.1 Interrogative pronouns.....391
2.1.2.6.2 Other question words.....393
2.1.2.7 - 2.1.2.7.3 Relative pronouns.....394
2.1.3 VERB MORPHOLOGY.....394
2.1.3.1 Voice.....394
2.1.3.1.1 - 2.1.3.1.1.1.3 Passive.....394
2.1.3.1.1.2 - 2.1.3.1.2.3 Impersonal passive.....399
2.1.3.1.2 - 2.1.3.1.2.2 Means of decreasing the valency of a verb.....400
2.1.3.1.3 Means of increasing the valency of a verb.....401
2.1.3.1.3.1.1 Verbal causativization.....401
2.1.3.1.3.2 Agentivity of the causee.....405
2.1.3.1.3.3 Omission of causee.....407

2.1.3.2 Tense 407
2.1.3.2.1 Tenses distinguished formally 408
2.1.3.2.1.1 Universal time reference....................................408
2.1.3.2.1.2 Present 409
2.1.3.2.1.3 - 2.1.3.2.1.3.2 Past 410
2.1.3.2.1.4 Future 413
2.1.3.2.3 Absolute/relative tense...414
2.1.3.3 Aspect..414
2.1.3.3.1 Perfective aspect...414
2.1.3.3.1.1-2 Form of perfective aspect...............................415
2.1.3.3.1.3 - 2.1.3.3.1.3.4 Situations indicated by the perfect aspect...........................416
2.1.3.3.1.4 Similarity between expression of perfect aspect and recent past tense.................418
2.1.3.3.2 Aspect and duration 418
2.1.3.3.2.1 Nature of marking..418
2.1.3.3.2.1.1 Perfective 418
2.1.3.3.2.1.1.1 *dzā* 'to go'..419
2.1.3.3.2.1.1.2 *pāh/bagh* 'to see'..420
2.1.3.3.2.1.1.3 *de* 'to give'...420
2.1.3.3.2.1.1.4 *ṭāk* 'to drop'..420
2.1.3.3.2.1.1.5 *ghe* 'to take'..421
2.1.3.3.2.1.1.6 *tsuk* 'to make a mistake'................................421
2.1.3.3.2.1.2 Imperfective aspect 421
2.1.3.3.2.1.3 Habitual aspect..422
2.1.3.3.2.1.4-5 Continuous and progressive aspects 423
2.1.3.3.2.1.6 Ingressive aspect 425
2.1.3.3.2.1.7 Terminative aspect 425
2.1.3.3.2.1.7.1 Prior completion 426
2.1.3.3.2.1.8 Iterative aspect 426
2.1.3.3.2.1.9-10 Semelfactive and punctual aspects..............427
2.1.3.3.2.1.11 Durative aspect...428
2.1.3.3.2.1.12 Simultaneous aspect 429
2.1.3.3.2.1.13 Other aspects 430
2.1.3.3.2.2.2 Restriction on the combination of different aspectual values 431
2.1.3.4 Mood..431
2.1.3.4.1 Indicative..432
2.1.3.4.2 Conditional 432
2.1.3.4.3 Imperative...433
2.1.3.4.4 Subjunctive/optative..434
2.1.3.4.5 Intentive..434

2.1.3.4.6 Debitive 435
2.1.3.4.7 Potential 436
2.1.3.4.7 - 2.1.3.4.7.1 Potential and permission 438
2.1.3.4.8 Degree of certainty 439
2.1.3.4.9 Authority for assertion 440
2.1.3.4.10 Hortatory 441
2.1.3.4.11 Monitory 441
2.1.3.4.12-13 Narrative and consecutive 442
2.1.3.4.14 Contingent 442
2.1.3.5 Finite and nonfinite forms 443
2.1.3.5.1 Infinitive 443
2.1.3.5.2 Gerund 444
2.1.3.5.2.1 Relative participles 445
2.1.3.5.2.2 Adverbial participles 445
2.1.3.5.2.3 Conjunctive/absolutive participles 445
2.1.3.5.2.4 Agentive participle 446
2.1.3.6 Agreement 446
2.1.3.6.1-2 Categories which must / may be coded in6
the verb 446
2.1.3.6.3 Conditioning factors 446
2.1.3.6.4 Features of subject coded in verb 447
2.1.3.6.5 Effect on coding of incompatible features 447
2.1.3.6.5.1 Discrepancies between syntactic and semantic
features 448
2.1.3.6.6 Environment in which there is no verb
agreement 449
2.1.3.6.7 Identity between subjects of different verbs 449
2.1.3.6.8-9 Reflexive form of the verb 450
2.1.3.6.10 Orientation of actions and incorporation 450
2.1.3.7 Change or loss of features in a string of verbs 450
2.1.4 ADJECTIVES 450
2.1.5 -2.1.5.4 POSTPOSITIONS 452
2.1.6 NUMERALS/QUANTIFIERS 452
2.1.6.1 Forms of numerals 452
2.1.6.2 Cardinal numerals as attributes 455
2.1.6.3 Counting different kinds of objects 455
2.1.6.4-5 Ordinal numerals 455
2.1.6.6 Quantifiers 456
2.1.6.6.1-2 Quantifier compounds and other means of
quantification 458
2.1.7 - 2.1.7.2.4 ADVERBS 459
2.1.8 CLITICS AND PARTICLES 459

2.2 **DERIVATIONAL MORPHOLOGY** 459
2.2.1 DERIVATION OF NOUNS 460
2.2.1.1 Nouns from nouns 460
2.2.1.2 Nouns from verbs 468
2.2.1.2.1 Syntax of deverbal nouns and non-derived nouns 479
2.2.1.3 Nouns from adjectives 480
2.2.1.4 Nouns from adverbs 483
2.2.1.5 Nouns from other categories 484
2.2.1.5.1 Postpositions 484
2.2.1.5.2 Reflexive pronoun 484
2.2.2 DERIVATION OF VERBS 484
2.2.2.1 Verbs from nouns 484
2.2.2.2 Verbs from verbs 486
2.2.2.3-5 Verbs from other categories 486
2.2.3 DERIVATION OF ADJECTIVES 487
2.2.3.1 Adjectives from nouns 487
2.2.3.2 Adjectives from verbs 494
2.2.3.3 Adjectives from adjectives 496
2.2.3.4 Adjectives from adverbs 501
2.2.3.5 Adjectives from other categories 503
2.2.4 DERIVATION OF ADVERBS 504
2.2.4.1 Adverbs from nouns 504
2.2.4.2 Adverbs from verbs 509
2.2.4.3 Adverbs from adjectives 511
2.2.4.4 Adverbs from adverbs 512
2.2.4.5 Adverbs from other categories 514
2.2.5 POSTPOSITIONS 514
2.2.5.1 Order of suffixes 515
2.2.6 DERIVATION OF POSTPOSITIONS 515
2.2.6.1 Complex postpositions 515
2.2.6.2 Simple derived postpositions 516
2.2.6.2.1 De-nominal 516
2.2.6.2.2 De-verbal 517
2.2.6.2.3 De-adjectival 517
2.2.6.2.4 De-adverbial 517
2.2.6.3 Compound morphology 517
2.2.6.3.1 Nouns 518
2.2.6.3.1.1 Noun-noun compounds 518
2.2.6.3.1.2 Superordinate compounds 519
2.2.6.3.1.3 Complex compounds 520
2.2.6.3.1.4 Hyponymous compounds 520

2.2.6.3.1.5 Attributed compounds....521
2.2.6.3.1.6 Emphatic compounds....521
2.2.6.3.1.7 Reduplicative compounds....522
2.2.6.3.1.8 Echo-words/Partially reduplicative compounds....523
2.2.6.3.1.9 Adjective-noun compounds....524
2.2.6.3.1.10 Noun + *gaṇīk*....525
2.2.6.3.2.1 Noun-verb compounds....526
2.2.6.3.2.2 Participle-noun compounds....526
2.2.6.3.3.1 Adjective-numeral compounds....527
2.2.6.3.3.2 Reduplicated and echo-compounds....527
2.2.6.3.4 Verbs....529
2.2.6.3.4.1 Conjunct verbs....529
2.2.6.3.4.2 Verb-verb compounds/serial verbs....531
2.2.6.3.4.3 Reduplicative verb compounds....533
2.2.6.3.5 Hybrid compounds....535

PHONOLOGY....537
3.1 **PHONOLOGICAL UNITS (SEGMENTAL)**....537
3.1.1 DISTINCTIVE SEGMENTS....537
3.1.2 DESCRIPTION OF DISTINCTIVE SEGMENTS....538
3.1.2.1 Non-syllabics (consonants)....538
3.1.2.1.1 Plosives and africates....538
3.1.2.1.2 Fricatives....541
3.1.2.1.3 Nasals....541
3.1.2.1.4 Liquids....542
3.1.2.1.5 Semi vowels....542
3.1.2.2 Syllabics....542
3.1.2.2.1 Vowels....542
3.1.2.2.1.2 Diphthongs....544
3.1.2.2.1.3 Nasal vowels....544
3.1.2.2.2 Nasal diphthongs....545
3.1.2.2.3 Nasalization of glides....546
3.1.2.2.4 Vowel assimilation....546
3.1.2.3 Consonants and vowels occurring in loan words....546
3.1.2.4 Restrictions on phonological segments by grammatical categories....547

3.2 **PHONOTACTICS**....547
3.2.1 DISTRIBUTION OF SEGMENTS....547
3.2.1.1 Word-final consonants....547
3.2.1.2 Word-initial consonants....547

3.2.2 CONSONANT CLUSTERS 547
3.2.2.1 Distribution of consonant clusters....................547
3.2.2.2 Possible consonant clusters..............................548
3.2.2.2.1 Possible word-initial consonant clusters..............548
3.2.2.2.2 Possible word-medial consonant clusters 549
3.2.3 DISTRIBUTION OF VOWELS 552
3.2.3.1 Word-final vowels...552
3.2.3.2 Word-initial vowels...552
3.2.3.3 Sequences of (syllabic) vowels..........................552
3.2.4 CORRESPONDENCE BETWEEN THE STRUCTURE OF LEXICAL MORPHEMES AND WORD STRUCTURE 552
3.2.5 SYLLABLES 553
3.2.5.1 Assignment of medial clusters to syllables 553
3.2.5.2 Canonical Syllable...553
3.2.6 RESTRICTIONS BETWEEN CONSONANTS AND VOWELS 553
3.2.6.1 Restrictions between syllable-initial units and following vowels..............................553
3.2.6.2 Restrictions between word/syllable-final units and preceding vowels..............................553
3.2.6.3-5 Restrictions between syllable-initial and syllable-final units 554
3.2.6.6 Phonotactic patterns in different word classes............554

3.3 **SUPRASEGMENTALS** 554
3.3.1 DISTINCTIVE DEGREES OF LENGTH.....................554
3.3.1.1-2 Vowels..554
3.3.1.3 Semivowels...554
3.3.1.4 Stops...555
3.3.1.5 Liquids..555
3.3.1.6 Nasals...555
3.3.1.7 Affricates...555
3.3.1.8 Fricates...555
3.3.2 STRESS 555
3.3.3 TONES/PITCH..559
3.3.4 INTONATION...559
3.3.4.1 Major intonation patterns 559

3.4 **MORPHOPHONOLOGY (SEGMENTAL)**...........................562
3.4.1 ALTERNATIONS 562
3.4.1.1 Assimilatory processes.......................................562

3.4.1.1.1 Consonant assimilation....563
3.4.1.1.1.1 Nasal assimilation....563
3.4.1.1.1.2 Retroflexion....563
3.4.1.1.1.3 Palatalization....563
3.4.1.2 Dissimilatory processes....564
3.4.1.3 Other alternations between segments....564
3.4.1.3.1 Vowel shortening....564
3.4.1.3.1.1 High vowel shortening....564
3.4.1.3.1.2 Low vowel shortening....566
3.4.1.3.2 Glide formation....566
3.4.1.3.3 Vowel raising....567
3.4.1.3.4 Vowel lowering....567
3.4.1.3.5 Vowel lengthening....569
3.4.2 METATHESIS....569
3.4.3 COALESCENCE AND SPLIT....570
3.4.4 DELETION AND INSERTION....570
3.4.4.1 Deletion processes....570
3.4.4.1.1 Degemination....570
3.4.4.1.2 Word-final schwa deletion....570
3.4.4.1.3 Stem-final /ā/ deletion....571
3.4.4.1.4 Stem-final /e/ deletion....571
3.4.4.1.5 Deletion of long high vowels in non-final position....571
3.4.4.1.6 Deletion of short vowels....572
3.4.4.2 Insertion processes....572
3.4.4.2.1 The increment vowel....572
3.4.4.2.2 Glide insertions....573
3.4.4.2.3 Vowel insertion for cluster simplification....573
3.4.4.2.4 Apparent schwa insertion....575
3.4.4.2.5 Gemination....575
3.4.5 REDUPLICATION....575

3.5 **MORPHOPHONOLOGY (SUPRASEGMENTAL)**....576

IDEOPHONES AND INTERJECTIONS....577
4.1 **IDEOPHONES**....577

4.2 **INTERJECTIONS**....582

LEXICON....583
5.1 **STRUCTURED SEMANTIC FIELDS**....583
5.1.1 KINSHIP TERMINOLOGY....583

5.1.1.1 Kin related by blood ... 583
5.1.1.1.1 Own generation ... 583
5.1.1.1.2 First ascending generation ... 584
5.1.1.1.3 Second ascending generation ... 584
5.1.1.1.4 First descending generation ... 584
5.1.1.1.5 Second descending generation ... 584
5.1.1.1.6 Other relatives ... 585
5.1.1.2 Kin by partial blood ... 585
5.1.1.3 Kin by marriage ... 586
5.1.1.4 Kin by adoption ... 587
5.1.1.5 Kin by fostering ... 587
5.1.2 COLOR TERMINOLOGY ... 588
5.1.3 BODY PARTS ... 589
5.1.4 COOKING TERMINOLOGY ... 592
5.1.4.1 Methods of cooking ... 592
5.1.4.2 Cooking implements ... 593
5.1.4.3 Typical dishes ... 594
5.1.5 AGRICULTURE ... 595
5.1.5.1 Crops grown in the area ... 595
5.1.5.2 Agricultural implements ... 595
5.1.5.3 Agricultural activities ... 596

5.2 **BASIC VOCABULARY** ... 596

BIBLIOGRAPHY ... 602

INDEX ... 614

ACKNOWLEDGMENTS

Writing this grammar has been a long journey full of many challenges. Although only one name goes on the cover of the book, the project is a product of the encouragement, labor, care, and support of many: my colleagues, friends, and family, to whom I owe my deep appreciation.

First, I express my sincere thanks to Bernard Comrie, the editor of this series, for his patience, expert advice, suggestions, and comments, which constantly made me strive for precision and accuracy of presentation (responsibility fot the shortcomings which remain is my own).

It was my good fortune to have Dr. Karen Dudas as editor of this book. Karen has read earlier versions of this book and meticulously corrected them with her expert editorial skills, unfailing patience and, most of all, with utmost care.

I am greatly indebted to Mithilesh Mishra for his constant help as an uncompromising linguist, a sincere friend, and an extremely careful editor from the inception to the completion of this project. His meticulous evaluations, and insightful and constructive comments on various versions of this book have sharpened my views on various issues in the grammar.

My heartfelt thanks are due to Patricia Gallagher for typing several versions of this book and patiently accommodating various changes in the format as well as the contents without any complaints. She has helped much beyond the call of duty.

My special thanks are due to Wen-ying Lu who, with patience and care, helped me check the manuscript for references, diacritics, and many other errors of typing and format. I cannot thank her enough for her unfailing commitment to the project. I would like to express my sincere appreciation to Devin Casenhiser who helped me prepare the index for this book with patience and care.

I am also indebted to Robert Jones, Geoffrey Muckenhirn (Language Learning Laboratory at UIUC), and Vijay Patel for their help with various technical aspects of word-processing. I am especially grateful to Vijay Patel for creating the laser font for the old bitmap font used in preparing the first camera-ready copy of this book. My thanks are also due to Larry Vance (Department of Physics at UIUC) for preparing the maps for this book.

I gratefully acknowledge the Research Board of the University of Illinois for providing financial assistance for this project during the academic year of 1994-95.

Writing this grammar has made me appreciate the enormous work of the grammarians such as M. K. Damle, K. Chiplunkar, S. G. Tulpule, J. Bloch, A. R. Kelkar and many others, who provided extremely important insights into the Marathi language. I respectfully acknowledge their contribution to this grammar. Similarly, I have benefited from the work on Marathi done by K. Wali, M. Dalrymple, V. Khokle, I. Junghare, S. M. Gupte, R. V. Dhongde, C. P. Masica, P. E. Hook, F. C. Southworth, A. M. Ghatge, and others.

I am grateful to my colleagues and friends, Braj and Yamuna Kachru, Hans Hock, Gary Porton, Manindra Verma, Tej Bhatia, and S. N. Sridhar, who have always been consistent sources of encouragement, guidance and support.

I am also thankful to Narindar Aggarwal, Siva Monrad (Asian Library at UIUC), and Pam Lindell (Modern Languages and Linguistics Library at UIUC) for providing extensive help with library materials over a long period of time.

The staff at Routledge, especially, Louisa Semlyen and Miranda Filbee, have provided excellent support and cooperation throughout the preparation of the manuscript. I am truly appreciative of their generous help.

I would like to thank my parents and my parents-in-law who consistently supported my career. Their deep love and admiration for Marathi is perhaps only faintly reflected in this grammar of the language. I cannot close this statement without acknowledging the love, encouragement, and support of my husband Vijay and my children Rahul and Pari, who have shared with me the joys and pains of writing this book.

KEY TO ABBREVIATIONS

ABBREVIATIONS

ø	nominative/deleted noun phrase
1/1p	first person
2/2p	second person
3/3p	third person
abl	ablative
acc	accusative
adj	adjective
adv	adverb
adv.part	adverbial participle
ag	agent
asp.	aspirated
aux	auxiliary
caus	causative
clt	clitic
comit	comitative
comp	complementizer
compr	comparative particle
compr	comparison
conc	concessive
cond	conditional
conj	conjunction
conj.part	conjunctive participle
cont	contingent
cor	correlative marker
cor-eq	correlative equative
dat	dative
def	definite
dem	demonstrative
DO	direct object
emph	emphatic

eq	equative
erg	ergative
excl	exclusive
f/fem	feminine
fut	future
gen	genitive
ger	gerund
H	Hindi
hab	habitual
hon	honorephic
hum	human
i	subscript/coreference
imp	imperative
imperf	imperfective
incl	inclusive
incr	increment vowel
indef	indefinite
inf	infinitive
inst	instrumental
intr	intransitive
intens	intensifier
irr	irrealis
IO	indirect object
lit	literally
loc	locative
M	Marathi
m/mas	masculine
n/neut	neuter
neg	negative
nom	nominative
obl	oblique
oblig	obligative
opt	optative
ord	ordinal
part	participle
pass	passive
perf	perfect
perf.part	perfective participle
pl	plural
pl.f	plural singular
pl.m	plural masculine
pl.n	plural neuter

poss	possessive
pot	potential
pp	postposition
PRC	participial relative clause
pres	present
pres.part	present participle
prog	progressive
proh	prohibitive
prox	proximate
pst	past
pst.part	past participle
pt	particle
Q	question
quot	quotative
redu	reduplicated item
refl	reflexive
rel	relative marker
rel-eq	relative equative
rel.part	relative participle
rem	remote
sf	singular feminine
s/sg	singular
S/Skt	Sanskrit
sm	singular masculine
sn	singular neuter
SRC	sentential relative clause
sug	suggestive
top	topic
tr	transitive
uhon	ultra honorephic pronoun
unasp.	unaspirated
vd.	voiced
vl.	voiceless
voc	vocative

MAP 1

INDIA

MARATHI AND ITS NEIGHBOURING LANGUAGES

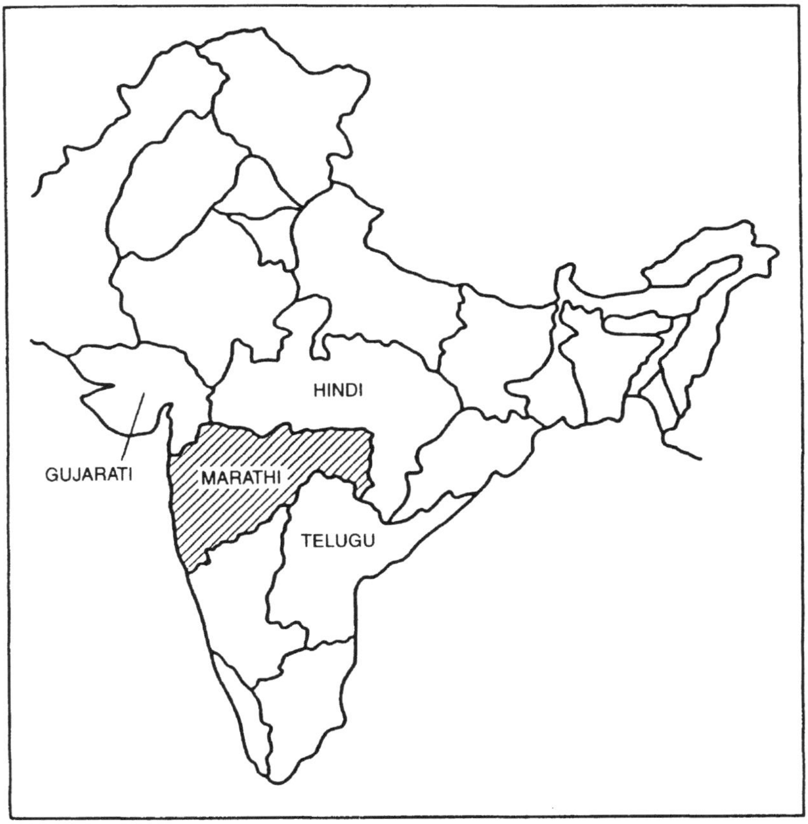

Note: Boundaries are neither political nor to scale. Adapted from Schwartzberg (1978). Plate X.B2. p101.

MAP 2

MAJOR DIALECTS OF MARATHI

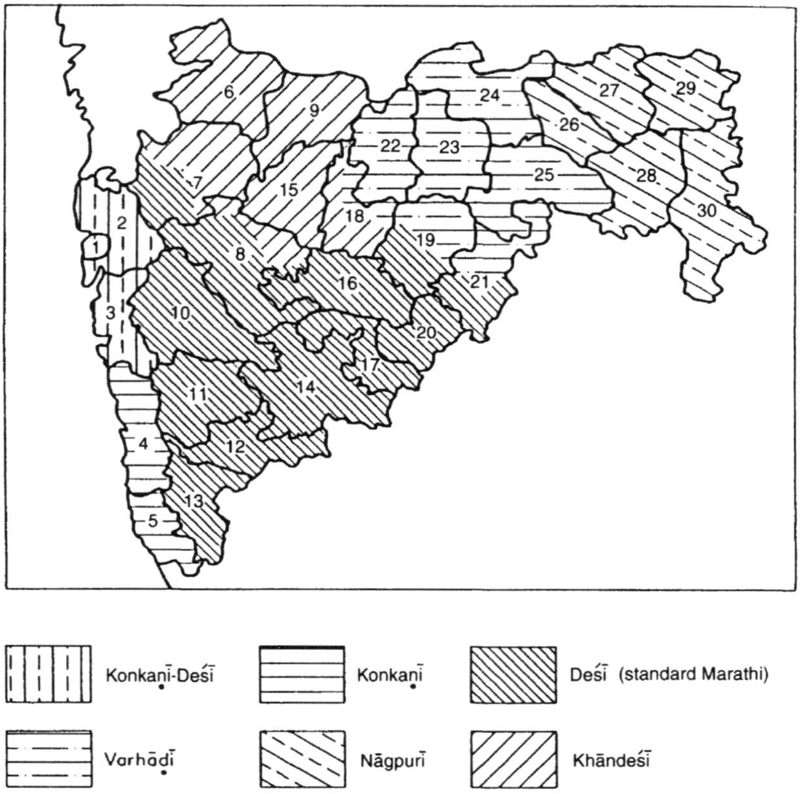

1. Bombay 2. Thane 3. Raygad 4. Ratnagiri 5. Sindhudurg
6. Dhule 7. Nashik 8. Ahamadnagar 9. Jalgaon 10. Pune
11. Satara 12. Sangli 13. Kolhapur 14.Solapur 15. Aurangabad
16. Bid 17. Usmanabad 18. Jalna 19. Parbhani 20. Latur
21. Nanded 22. Buldhana 23. Akola 24. Amaravati 25. Yavatmal
26. Vardha 27. Nagpur 28. Chandrapur 29. Bhandara 30. Gadchiroli

INTRODUCTION

Marathi, etymologically derived from Mahārāṣṭrī '(the language) of the great (*mahā*) land/nation (*rāṣtra)*, is one of the major modern Indo-Aryan languages. Marathi is one of the eighteen official languages in India and the language of the Maharashtra state. The state covers a large area of 118,758 square miles which include thirty districts (see Map 2 on p. xxxiv) grouped in six socio-linguistic regions. The districts of Bombay, Thana, Raygad, Ratnagiri and Sindhudurg are grouped under Konkan region, Dhule, Nashik, Ahamadnagar and Jalgaon are grouped under Khandesh, Pune, Satara, Sangli, Kolhapur and Solapur are grouped under Desh, Aurangabad, Bid, Usmanabad, Jalna, Parbhani, Latur and Nanded are grouped under Marathwada, Buldhana, Akola, Amravati, Yawatmal and Vardha are grouped under Varhad, and Nagpur Chandrapur, Bhandara and Gadchiroli are grouped under Vidarbha. (Varhad, and Vidarbha are generally viewed as two divisions of Mahavidarbha.) There are approximately sixty two million speakers of Marathi, including speakers outside the native state of Maharashtra. Marathi occupies a geographically unique position since it is spoken in the area which links two major language families—Indo-Aryan in the north, and Dravidian in the south.

Maharashtra, traditionally called *dakṣiṇāpath* "the avenue to the south"(Kulkarni, K. P. 1969: 197), clearly has been viewed as a geographic, cultural, and linguistic link between the north and the south. Marathi is surrounded by Indo-Aryan languages such as Gujarati in the north and Hindi in the north and northeast, and Dravidian languages such as Kannada and Telugu in the south. (See Map 1 on page xxxiii.) It is therefore not surprising that Marathi shares features of both Indo-Aryan and Dravidian languages. Additionally, within its native state of Maharashtra, Marathi has had sustained contact with politically dominant languages such as Telugu and Kannada (during the Yadav period 1000-1300 C.E.), Persian

(Mughal period 1300-1700 C.E.), and English (British period 1700-1947 C.E.). This contact has resulted in large scale borrowings from these three languages into Marathi.

Although Marathi is a descendent of Sanskrit, Mahārāṣṭrī Prākṛt and Apabhraṃśa mark the two major chronological stages between Sanskrit and Marathi. The stages of the development of Marathi are generally recognized as Old Marathi (1000-1300 C.E.), Middle Marathi (1300-1800 C.E.), and Modern Marathi (1800-). The genetic roots of Marathi (i.e., Sanskrit> Mahārāṣṭrī Prākṛt> Mahārāṣṭrī Apabhraṃśa) are well known. However, the link between Marathi and the Jain Mahārāṣṭrī Apabhraṃśa was not known until the scholars like Gune, Jacobi, and Hiralal Jain edited literary works like *Nāyakumāracariya* and *Bhavisayattakahā* (for details see Tulpule 1960: 9). On the basis of the oblique base of Marathi and its synthetic structure (i.e., case-suffixes, as opposed to postpositions), scholars linked Marathi with its immediate predecessor Jain Mahārāśṭrī Apabhraṃśa. (See Figure 1 for the origin and development of Marathi.) The first Marathi sentence, dated 1117 C.E., appears in the inscription on the statue of Gomateshwar at Shrāvan Belgola in the Mysore state. Additionally, the inscriptions of Parel (1187 C.E.), Patan (1206 C.E.), Pandharpur (1213 C.E.) and Pur (1285 C.E.) are some of early specimens of Marathi. However, based on the other inscriptional evidence, Tulpule (1969: 313) claims that the first attested record of Marathi may be earlier than 1200 C.E. Although it is difficult to assess the exact dates of early Marathi texts, the earliest literary text in Marathi is considered to be *Wiwekasindhu* of Mukundaraja in 1188 C.E.

Figure 1

The Origin and Development of the Marathi Language

(Only the directly relevant brancnes are represented in the following figure to show the origin and development of Marathi.)

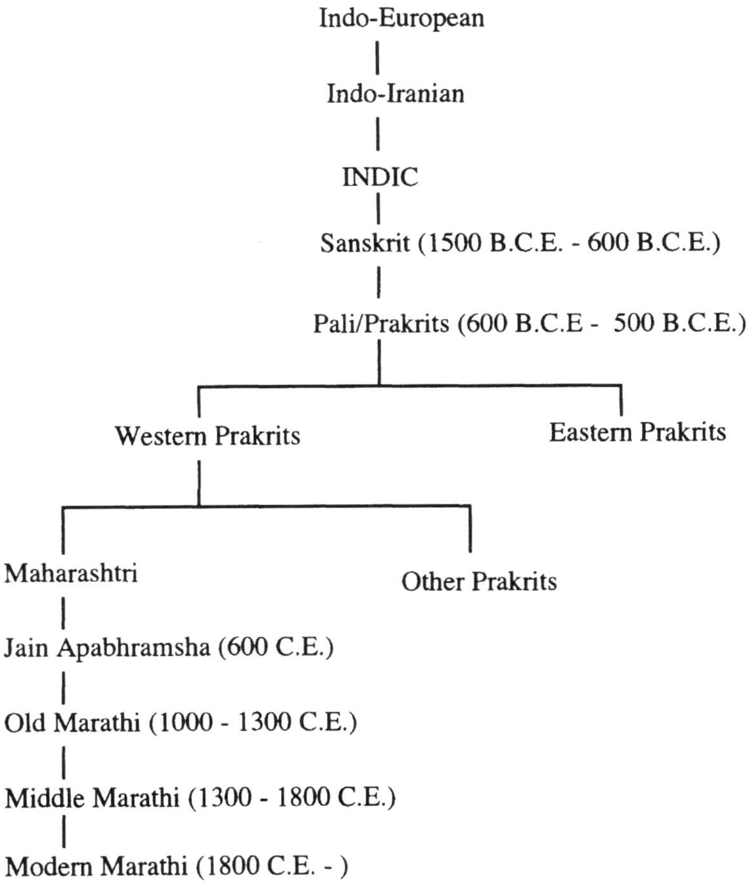

Marathi shares features of Indo-Aryan languages such as SOV word order, a large number of Sanskrit words in the lexicon, and the gender and number systems.However, there are also present in Marathi some features which typically mark Dravidian languages, such as the quotative marker, a complex participial system, and extensive borrowings from Kannada and Telugu. Since Marathi shows a blending of the features of these two language families, it has been claimed to be a pidgin by Southworth (1971).

Like Hindi, Marathi uses the Devanagari script, locally known as *bāḷbodh* (understood by children, i.e., simple), with additional characters for */ḷ/* and */r-/* in */r/-* conjuncts. Historically, word-final */ẽ/* has changed to */a/* and is reflected in the orthography by the replacement of the original */ẽ/* by *anuswār*. Similarly, unpronouned nasals are dropped in Modern Marathi. The use of *moḍī*, an alternative cursive form of Devanāgarī for handwriting, is no longer common.

Marathi has retained some Old Indo-Aryan features, e.g., the distinction between aspirated and unaspirated voiceless stops and retroflection. Vowels */a/*, */i/* and */u/* contrast in length, and the contrast between oral and nasal vowels of Old Marathi is lost in standard Marathi and is marginally maintained only in some southern dialects of Marathi in certain contexts (e.g., *dzāḍā-var* 'tree-on' vs. *dzāḍā̃-var* 'trees-on', *gharā-tSyā* 'house-of' vs. *gharā̃-tSyā* 'trees-of', etc.). The retroflex flaps */ṛ/* and */ṛh/* are absent, while the */ḷ/* of Dravidian and Old Sanskrit is present. Affricates are a salient feature of Marathi. However, the contrast between alveolar and palatal affricates (not reflected in the orthography) is neutralized before */y/* and */i/* and optionally before */e/*. Although heavy syllables are generally stressed, stress is not distinctive in Marathi. Marathi has two numbers (singular and plural) and three genders (masculine, feminine, and neuter), similar to Old and Middle Indo-Aryan. Inflectional and derivational morphology is mostly affixal. However, the morphophonemic alternation of *guṇa* and *vṛddhi* vowels is also maintained. Nouns are classified according to gender and endings (vocalic or consonantal) and are declined for gender, number, and case.Syntactic and semantic functions of noun phrases are expressed by case-suffixes and postpositions. Marathi has three morphological cases: direct, oblique, and vocative. The oblique form occurs when a noun or a noun phrase is followed by a case-suffix or a postposition. Verbs occur in finite and non-finite forms. Marathi is set off from

Hindi and brought closer to Dravidian by a much larger range and greater use of participles (Bloch 1920). Causatives are formed by adding *-aw* to the verb stem. Characteristically, *lāw-ṇe* 'to apply' can be added to any verb to form a coersive causative. Similar to other Modern Indo-Aryan languages such as Hindi, Punjabi, and Gujarati, Marathi has compound verbs (verb + verb) as well as conjunct verbs (nominal + verb). Nouns and adjectives borrowed from Sanskrit and English freely participate in the latter sequence. Reduplication of nouns, pronouns, adjectives, verbs, and adverbials are commonly used to convey intensive, distributive, and indefinite meanings. The verb in Marathi agrees with the subject in number, gender, and person, except when it is followed by a postposition */-ne/* in transitive perfective, optative, and obligational, where it agrees with the direct object. If both the subject and the direct object are followed by a case-suffix or a postposition, the verb remains in its unmarked form (i.e., third person, singular, neuter). Unlike Hindi, the agentive postposition *-ne* in Marathi is restricted to the third person only, and the postposition *-lā* (accusative/dative) does not always block agreement. Negation is expressed by a particle *-na* 'not' as well as by the verbs (like Gujarati and Tamil) *nas* 'to be not', *nako* 'don't' (prohibitive) and 'do not want', and *naye* 'should not'. The characteristic feature of Marathi is that these negative verbs agree with their subjects in person and number.

The earliest grammars of Konkaṇī (which was viewed as a variety of Marathi,) were written in Portuguese by Christian missionaries in Goa in the 17th century. Thus Father Stephens' *Arte da Lingua Canarim* (1640), a grammar of the Southern Konkani, and *Arte Canarina da Norte*, a grammar of the Northern Konkaṇī, written by a Franciscan Christian missionary (published in 1857, see Arjunwadkar 1987: 2) mark the first grammars of of Marathi.

The Marathi grammatical tradition has been rich and varied. The three major influences on the development of the Marathi grammatical tradition are: a) the European tradition (primarily of the Latin grammars), b) the native Sanskrit grammatical tradition, and c) the current western linguistic tradition. The grammars of Marathi written within these three traditions differ considerably from each other in their audiences, goals, and methodological frameworks. The grammars written within the European tradition were in English and primarily aimed at educating 19th-century Christian missionaries in regional languages of India (including Marathi) in order to enable them to successfully carryout their missionary activities. The notable grammars written within this tradition are: (Carey's *The Grammar of the Mahrattā Language* (1805), Stevenson's *The Principles of Murathee Language* (1883), Ballentine's *A Grammar of the Mahratta Language (1839),* and Burgess' *Grammar of the Marathi Language (1854).* Those grammars analyzed and described Marathi within the model of Latin and Latin-based languages. For example, eight parts of speech , active and passive voice, past, present, and future tense-system, etc., which are important features of Latin grammar, were assumed to be important tools for analyzing Marathi grammar as well. On the other hand, the aspect-based system of Marathi (similar to the Indo-Aryan languages) was ignored in these studies. However, these grammars provided tremendous impetus for analyzing Marathi within a new framework. Navalkar's *The Student's Manual of Marathi Grammar* (1925), and Kher's *A Higher Marathi Grammar* (1895) are two notable examples of the impact of this new tradition on Marathi grammars written in English.

The second and the most influential grammatical tradition which remains dominant till today is that of the Sanskrit grammars. Although some of the grammars of Marathi (Damle 1966 [1911]) do reflect some influence of the European tradition, most of the grammars actually written in Marathi abide by the Sanskrit grammatical tradition. The first two grammars in this tradition are *Pancawārtik* of Bhismacarya (1300-1400 C.E.) and *Mahārāṣtraprayog Candrikā* (1827, published in 1970) by Venkatmadhav which are modeled on Panini's *Siddhāntakaumudī.* Some of the prominent grammars in this tradition are Tarkhadkar's *Maharaṣṭra Bhāṣetse Vyākraṇ* (1836, 1850, 1879), Godbole's *Marathi Bhāṣete Nawīn Wyākraṇ* (1867), Joshi's *Prauḍhabodh Marathi Wyākraṇ* (1889), Damle's *Shastrīya Marathi Vyākraṇ* (1911), and Sabnis' *Ādhunik Marāīṭhse Vyākraṇ* (1951). The major contribution of these grammars was that they explained the patterns of Marathi (e.g., the case-system, word-compounds, verbal and nominal derivations, sandhi-rules, agreement, etc.) within the framework of the Sanskrit grammars and thereby highlighted some salient features of Marathi which differ significantly from Latin-based languages. Some of these grammarians, such as Damle, were familiar with both, the English/Latin-based tradition and the Sanskrit tradition, and therefore, brought to light and discussed the relative validity of the two approaches toward the analysis of Marathi.

The third, and currently the most influential theoretical framework of Marathi grammar, is based on the western linguistic tradition—notably Chomsky's (originally transformational generative grammar, and its following incarnations, as well as other theoretical frameworks). The two grammars written in this tradition are Apte's *A Sketch of Marathi Transformational Grammar* (1962), and Kelkar's *The Phonology and Morphology of Marathi* (1958). Additionally, several studies are available in the form of individual articles and dissertations (see bibliography for details) on diverse aspects of Marathi grammar. The most valuable contribution of these works is that they provide methodological frameworks which allow the authors to understand the issues in Marathi grammar (e.g., the ergative pattern of agreement, variation in the properties of subject, etc.) within the context of universal/language-independent linguistic patterns and thereby provide a method for cross linguistic comparison.

As compared to the extensive work on synchronic grammar, the historical grammar of Marathi has not received adequate attention. Bloch's *The formation of the Marathi language* (1920, 1970 (translated into English from French by Chanana)), and Master's *A Grammar of Old Marathi* (1967) are the only two comprehensive studies on this topic. There is a definite need for studies on the diachronic grammar of Marathi which takes into account not merely internal historical developments in Marathi (from the early 20th century) but also give adequate attention to the impact of Marathi-Persian and Marathi-English contact on the structure and function of Marathi—in particular on the development of new styles, and registers. Some of the studies on Marathi dialects, such as Ghatge's *A Survey of Marathi Dialects* (1963) and Grierson's *Linguistic Survey of India*, Volume VII (1905) are useful for tracing the diachronic development of Marathi.

The tradition of linguists/grammarians needs a special mention here. These grammarians did not write grammars; rather, they raised specific issues related to the phonology, morphology, syntax, and semantics of Marathi, as well as sociolinguistic issues such as the standardization of the language, the emergence of new varieties, sociocultural goals of grammar, etc. These studies examined the relative validity of the grammars of diverse theoretical motivations in resolving the issues. This tradition goes back to Chiplunkar's work *Marathī Wyākraṇāwar Nibandha(1893).* Other notable studies in this tradition include Gunjikar's *Marathi Wyākraṇāwar WitSār* (1867-1890, first published in 1942), Mangrulkar's *MarathitStyā Wyākraṇātsā PunarwitSār* (1964), Dikshit's *Marathi Wyākraṇ: Kāhī Samsyā* (1980), and Arjunwadkar's *Marathi Wyākraṇ: Wād āṇi Prwād* (1987).

Marathi has consistently maintained a very rich literary tradition from its earliest beginnig to the present. Throughout the turbulent history of Mughal (13th through the 18th centuries) and then British rule (18th till the 20th century), Marathi has gone through various "incarnations." During the Mughal rule the official language of the state was Persian, while it was English during the British rule. During these periods, Marathi was sidetracked, and at best, overshadowed by the influence of Persian and English respectively. Thus the history of the Marathi language is permeated with the struggle to survive under severe adverse socio-political conditions. This linguistic history of Marathi is interesting from the point of view of understanding the crucial role of social context(s) in the development of the form and function of Marathi. Thus,a brief look at the forces which contributed toward the survival of the language might prove useful to understand the present form of Marathi.

The first attested poetic composition in Marathi is *Abhiṣṭārtha Chintāmaṇī* by Soma Deva, a Chalukya prince (1129 C.E.). Before its contact with the west, the early Marathi literature primarily focuses on religious themes and issues in continuation of the classical Sanskritic tradition. However, those early literary/religious works, specifically of the Mahānubhāva, Adināth and Adinārāyaṇa sects, reflect as well as critique the linguistic, social, and religious climate of their time. Jñāneśwar's monumental contribution to Marathi is *Jñāneśwarī* (also known as *Bhāvārthadīpikā*), which is a commentary on the Hindu religious classic, the Bhagavadgītā. That commentary served two major roles, one religious and the other linguistic. It brought to the masses who did not have access to Sanskrit, the philosophy/religion of the Bhagavadgītā (in Marathi, their own language). Secondly, it established and authenticated a strong literary tradition in Marathi and thereby elevated Marathi to the status of literary Sanskrit. In the centuries following Jñāneshwar, poet-devotees(*bhakta-kavī*) such as Nāmdev (1270 C.E.), Tukārām (1598 C.E.), Rāmdās (1608 C.E.), and Eknāth, (1615 C.E.), sustained the vitality of the literary tradition in Marathi through their emphasis on the practice of the "socially realistic religion and linguistic tradition". Other group of poets, such as Wāman Paṇḍit (16th century), Raghunāth Paṇḍit (17th century), and Moropant (18th century) who tailored their diction and themes after classical Sanskrit epic poetry, was influential during the Mughul/British rule of the 16th through the18th centuries in educating the masses of their religious, cultural, and linguistic heritage and thereby sustained the growth of the Marathi literary tradition. Those poets harbored an enormous awareness of the need to maintain the linguistic identity of Marathi in the wake of internal as well as external forces. They not only raised a heightened confidence regarding the ability of Marathi to communicate the traditional religious/philosophical knowledge, which hitherto had been confined to Sanskrit, but they also cultivated a strong sense of national cultural identity in the face of foreign rule. (For details, see Tulpule 1979.)

One of the most fascinating events in the history of Marathi took place during the 17th century under the political rule of the Marāṭhā king Shivaji (in Maharashtra). History tells us that Marathi had been replaced by Persian in all official, formal correspondence and education. The number of Marathi words in the lexicon was reduced to 14.4 percent compared to 80 percent Persian (Gramopadhye 1941: 11). Shivaji entrusted a poet-grammarian, Raghunath Paṇḍit, from Tanjavur with the responsibility of compiling a Persian-Sanskrit dictionary of administrative and political terminology, in order to allow the Persian lexicon to be replaced with Sanskrit counterparts. In addition, Shivaji implemented the policy of using Marathi, as opposed to Persian, as the official language. This dictionary, named *Rājyawyawahār koś,* marked the first attempt in the history of India to preserve the linguistic identity of a language. Sanskrit was used extensively as a source from which to borrow or derive new vocabulary Although this venture could not entirely wipe out the influence of Persian, it certainly arrested its spread, and more importantly, it reinstated the cultural roots of Marathi into its grammar. A similar situation recurred during almost two hundred years of the British rule. At that time, English was the official language of the government, education, and, as a result, the technical terminology was entirely English regardless of whether the language of communication was Marathi. After 1947, the government of India, the newspapers, and the education department of Maharashtra worked toward developing a Marathi lexicon to replace English words in the language. The UNESCO report (1953: 65, quoted in

Śāsanwyawahārāt Marathi: 115) says, "the planned vocabulary development should make the best possible use of the natural tendencies of the language." In the case of Marathi, as in other modern Indian languages, Sanskrit was once again used as the reservoir from which the appropriate vocabulary was borrowed or derived. It should be mentioned here that neither Persian nor English influence has been completely wiped out from Marathi; rather, it has become restricted to certain registers and/or styles of Marathi.

Marathi belongs to the 'outer circle' of Indo-Aryan languages (Grierson 1905). There are six major dialects of Marathi (see Map 2 on page xxxiv) *Konkaṇī Deśī* (in the north-Konkan), (2) *Konkaṇī* (in the south-Konkan), 3) *Deśī* (around Pune and surrounding districts), 4) *Varhāḍī* (in the north), 5) *Nagpurī* (Nagpuri in the text, spoken in the four districts around Nagpur, the north-east), 6) *Khāndeśī* (in the north-west). While *Khāndeśī* is significantly influenced by Yujarati, *Varhāḍī* and *Nāgpurī* on the north-east show a distinct influence of Hindi. As opposed to these, the *Deśī* spoken in the south-east depicts a close connection with Kannada and Telugu. In spite of the differences, the dialects of Marathi show a remarkably high level of mutual intelligibility as has been already noted by Grierson (1905). Additionally, there are several local dialects of Marathi such as *Ghāṭī* (in the south Kulaba district), *Varhāḍī* (in the Buldhana, Amaravati, Akola districts), etc. Similarly, there are various caste dialects particular to different regions (for example, *Koḷī* (the fisherman's dialect of the coastal area), *Kuṇbī* (the farmer's dialect, *Dhangarī* (the cowherd's dialect in Janjira district), *Karhāḍī* (the brāhmin dialect spoken around the river Kṛṣṇā (now spoken in Bombay, Satara, Ratnagiri districts) etc. (For details see Grierson (1905), Ghatge (1963), Agnihotri (1983)).

The two major Marathi styles are *grānthik* 'written /literary' (marked by Sanskrit borrowings) and *bolbhaṣā* 'spoken/colloquial' (with Perso-Arabic and English borrowings). Although the use of the English lexicon has increased decidely in the last 100 years in the spoken language, the use of the Sanskrit lexicon marks formal Marathi speech from its colloquial counterpart.

It is evident from the above discussion that Marathi has been in contact with diverse languages throughout its history and including the present. This contact has resulted in changes in the structure of Marathi and thereby in the emergence of various styles and registers of Marathi. At present, the style/registral repertoire of the Marathi speech community includes three well-defined styles/registers: Sanskritized, Persianized and Englishized. These are used in mutually exclusive domains. The Sanskritized style/register (which is marked by the extensive use of Sanskrit vocabulary and syntax) is used in the religious domain and the formal speech. The Persianized style/register is used in courts of law, police stations, etc. In contrast to these, the Englishized style/register marks the colloquial educated speech and is used at social gatherings, in business transactions, etc. (For further discussion on style repertoire, see Pandharipande (forthcoming).)

The Marathi speech community in Maharashtra is largely bi/multilingual. Its linguisitc repertoire is large, generally including a local dialect, the Standard dialect, and Hindi. The Marathi speech community is largely diglossic. The functional distribution of these codes is given below:

Linguistic Repertoire of Marathi Speech Community

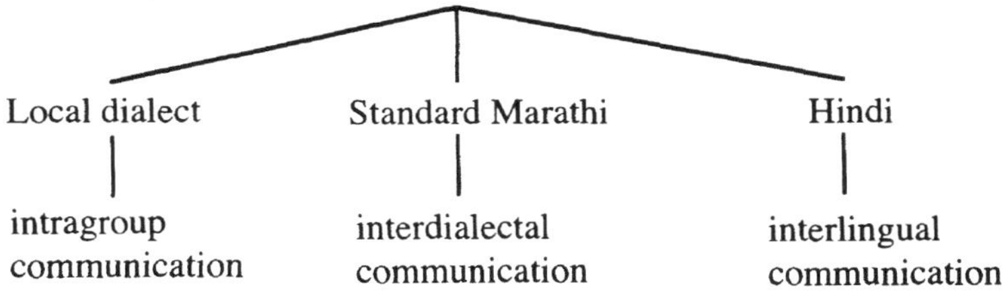

It is necessary to note here that in those areas of Maharashtra which intersect with other states, the languages of those states (such as Gujarati, Kannada, Telugu) are included in the repertoire (in addition to the above three codes) of Marathi speakers. Thus the functional distribution of the codes varies in various parts of Maharshtra, depending upon the role of the codes in that area. (For details, see Gumperz's discussion on the case of the Kupwar village at the border of Maharashtra and Karnataka.)

The present work is based on the standard variety of Marathi spoken around Pune. However, significant variation across dialects is also discussed wherever necessary.

Lingua questionnaire

This volume is part of the *Croom Helm Descriptive Grammars Series*. The goal of this series is to provide comprehensive descriptions of a wide variety of languages across the world. The format used in those descriptions is uniform and is flexible enough to include adequately the range of variation across genetically and typologically unrelated languages and thereby allows crosslinguistic comparison of the structures/grammars. In order to accomplish this goal in the best possible way, this volume has followed the format outlined in the *Questionnaire* developed by Comrie and Smith (1977) and originally published in *Lingua*, vol. 42. The *questionnaire* has served as a comprehensive and useful index to this volume.

Transcription

Though the transcription used in this volume follows most of the conventional practices in the linguistic literature on Marathi and other Indo-Aryan languages, there are a few notable exceptions to make the pattern (of transcription) fairly transparent. Thus, the distinction between the alveolar and alveo-palatal affricates is represented by the symbols */ts/*, */dz/*, and */dzh/* (alveolar affricates) and */ts/*, */tsh/*, */dʒ/*, and */dʒh/* (alveo-palatal affricates) respectively. (For detail see Table 2 on page 539).

Table 1 (on page 537) provides specific information about the conventions followed for transcribing short and long vowels and diphthongs. Since Marathi (and perhaps other Indo-Aryan languages as well) does not have the labio-dental fricative */v/*, the labial glide */w/* is used instead. In transcribing proper names, */v/* is retained in the English glosses and translations.

Chart of Marathi Alphabet

Vowels: ***Independent***

a	ā	i	ī	u	ū	e	ai
अ	आ	इ	ई	उ	ऊ	ए	ऐ
o	au						
ओ	औ						

Consonants: ***Independent***

k	kh	g	gh	ŋ		
क	ख	ग	घ	ङ		
ts tS	tSh	dz ʤ	dzh ʤh	ñ		
च	छ	ज	झ	ञ		
ṭ	ṭh	ḍ	ḍh	ṇ		
ट	ठ	ड	ढ	ण		
t	th	d	dh	n		
त	थ	द	ध	न		
p	ph	b	bh	m		
प	फ	ब	भ	म		
y	r	l	w	ś		
य	र	ल	व	श		
ṣ	s	h	ḷ	kṣ	dñy	ṛ
ष	स	ह	ळ	क्ष	ज्ञ	ऋ

Vowels: *Dependent* (following consonants)

a	ā	i	ī	u	ū	e	ai
none	ा	ि	ी	ु	ू	े	ै
o	au						
ो	ौ						

Homorganic nasal or nasalized vowel:

ं

Consonants (first) in a consonant cluster:

k	kh	g	gh	ŋ	
क्	ख्	ग्	घ्	ङ्	
ts tS	tSh	dz ʤ	dzh ʤh	ñ	
च्	छ्	ज्	झ्	ञ्	
ṭ	ṭh	ḍ	ḍh	ṇ	
ट्	ठ्	ड्	ढ्	ण्	
t	th	d	dh	n	
त्	थ्	द्	ध्	न्	
p	ph	b	bh	m	
प्	फ्	ब्	भ्	म्	
y	l	w	ś	r	
य्	ल्	व्	श्	र्‍	
ṣ	s	h	ḷ	kṣ	dñy
ष्	स्	ह्	ळ्	क्ष्	ज्ञ्

r (variants: after consonant): ्र and ^

ṛ (after consonant): ृ

SYNTAX

1.1 GENERAL QUESTIONS

1.1.1 SENTENCE TYPES

1.1.1.1 *Direct speech and indirect speech*

Direct and indirect speech is generally marked by one of the two quotative markers, *mhaṇūn* 'having said' or *asa* 'thus'. These markers always follow direct and indirect speech as shown in (1) and (2). Note that *mhaṇūn* occurs elsewhere in the language as the usual conjunctive participle form of the verb *mhaṇ* 'say' and *asa* 'thus' as an adverbial relative particle (see examples (16) - (17)).

(1)

āī,	lawkar	ye,	lawkar	ye
mother	quickly	come-imp-2s	quickly	come-imp-2s

{mhaṇūn / asa}	to	orḍat	hotā
quot	he	shout-prog	was-3sm

'He was shouting, "Mother, come quickly, come quickly." '

(2)

to	orḍat	hotā	āī	lawkar
he	shout-prog	was-3sm	mother	quickly

ye	lawkar	ye	{mhaṇūn / asa}
come-imp-2s	quickly	come-imp-2s	quot

'He was shouting, "Mother, come quickly, come quickly." '

As is evident in (1) and (2), *mhaṇūn/asa* follow the quoted material irrespective of whether the matrix clause follows (1), or precedes (2) the subordinate clause. Consider example (3) below, which is ungrammatical because *mhaṇūn/asa* precedes the quoted material.

(3)*	to	orḍat	hotā	{mhaṇūn / asa}
	he	shout-prog	was-3sm	quot

āī	lawkar	ye	lawkar	ye
mother	quickly	come imp-2s	quickly	come imp-2s

'He was shouting, "Mother, come quickly, come quickly." '

Additionally, quoted and indirect speech may be introduced by the complementizer *kī,* in which case the occurrence of both *mhaṇūn* and *asa* is optional as in (3a) below:

(3a)	anū	mhaṇte	kī	tī/mī	hindī
	Anu	say-pres-3sf	comp	she/I	Hindi

śikel	(asa/mhaṇūn)
learn-fut-3s	(quot)

'Anu says that she will learn Hindi.'

mhaṇūn and *asa* may never precede quoted material either in the unmarked word order (quoted material + quotative marker + matrix clause, and matrix clause + quoted material + quotative marker, as in (1) and (2) respectively) or in the two other possible variant word orders as shown below in (4) and (5).

quoted material + matrix clause + quotative marker

(4)	malā	te	māhīt	āhe	to	sāŋgat
	I-dat	that	know	aux	he	tell-prog

hotā	{*mhaṇūn / asa}
was 3sm	quot

' "I know that", thus was he telling.'

It is important to note here that the quotative marker *asa* may occur either immediately following the quoted material (as in (1) and (2)) or it may be separated from the quoted material by an intervening matrix clause (as in (4)) but, *mhaṇūn* must occur immediately following the quoted material (as in (1) and (2)). Additionally, the material which is under focus in the matrix clause can precede the quoted material. The phrase under focus in the matrix clause occurs sentence-initially (and before the quoted material) and the rest of the matrix clause occurs in the usual sentence-final position (after the quoted material). Example (5) illustrates this point.

(5)	mohan	mitrālā	mī	te	kām	karīn
	mohan	friend-dat	I	that	work	do-fut-1s

{asa / mhaṇūn}	sāŋgat	hotā
quot	tell-prog	was-3sm

'Mohan was telling (his) friend, "I will do that work." '

When the quoted material is not under focus in the discourse, the word order is matrix clause + quoted material + quotative marker, as shown in (6) below.

(6)	to	sāŋgat	hotā	malā	te	māhīt
	he	tell-prog	was-3sm	I-dat	that	know

āhe	{asa / mhaṇūn}
aux	quot

'He was telling, "I know that." '

The use of the quotative markers is optional when the verb in the matrix clause is one of the speech verbs, e.g., *mhaṇ* 'say', *bol* 'speak', and *sāŋg* 'tell', etc.

asa and *mhaṇūn* are also used to introduce subordinate (complement) clauses of verbs such as wāṭ 'feel', *samadz* 'understand', and *witSār kar* 'think', as illustrated in the following examples.

(7) *wāṭ* 'feel':

to	punhā	parat	yeṇār	nāhī	{asa / mhaṇūn}
he	again	back	come-fut	not	quot

tilā	wāṭla
she-dat	feel-pst-3sn

'She felt that he would not return again.' (lit: ' "He will not come back", she felt.')

(8) *samadz* 'understand':

mī	kām	kela	pāhiʤe	{asa / mhaṇūn}
I	work	do-pst-3sn	must	quot

tyālā	samadzla
he-dat	understand-pst-3sn

'He understood that he had to do the work.' (lit: ' "I must do the work", he understood.')

(9) *witSār kar* 'think':

mīnālā	mādzha	spaṣṭa	bolṇa	āwḍel
Meena-dat	my	straight	talk-3sn	like-fut-sn

kā	{asā / mhaṇūn}	to	witSār karat	hotā
Q	quot	he	think-prog	was

'He was thinking whether or not Meena would like his straight talk.' (lit: ' "Will Meena like my straight talk?" he was thinking.')

One of the most interesting features of the quotative markers *asa* and *mhaṇūn* is that these two can be used to introduce both direct and indirect speech. Consider example (10).

(10)	{mādzhī / tyātSī}	badlī	dzhālī	{asa / mhaṇūn}	to
	{my / his}	transfer	happen-pst	quot	he

sāŋgat	hotā
tell-prog	was

'He was telling (them) that he had been transferred.' (lit: 'He was telling, "My/his transfer happened." ')

When the quotative markers introduce indirect/reported speech, they seem to function like the usual complementizer *kī*. However, while *kī* always precedes the subordinate clause (i.e., matrix clause + *kī* + subordinate clause), *asa* and *mhaṇūn* always occur after the subordinate clause (recall examples (1) and (2)).

asa and *mhaṇūn* are interchangeable only when they function as quotative markers or complementizers. When the subordinate clause denotes the purpose (11) or reason (12) of the action in the matrix clause, only mhaṇūn (and not asa) is used.

(11)	to	yeṇār	{mhaṇūn / *asa}	mī	sagḷa	ghar
	he	come-fut	therefore	I	entire	house

sadzawla
decorate-pst-3sn

'I decorated the entire house because he was coming.'

(12)	khūp	abhyās	kelā	{mhaṇūn / *asa}	to
	a lot	study	do-pst-3sm	therefore	he

pās	dzhālā
pass	become-pst-3sm

'He passed because he studied a lot.'

Additionally, *mhaṇūn* (but never *asa*) can be used as an identifier of a proper noun (13).

(13)	tyā	gāwāt	wiʤay	{mhaṇūn / *asa}	ek
	that	town-loc	Vijay	ident	one

	mulgā	malā	bheṭlā
	boy	I-dat	meet-pst-3sm

'In that town I met a boy named Vijay.'

Another interesting fact about the Marathi quotatives is that *asa* and *mhaṇūn* occur even with direct (as in (14)) and indirect (as in (15)) questions in subordinate clauses:

(14)	mohan ne	witSārle	sudhā	kuṭhe
	Mohan-ag	ask-pst-3sn	Sudha	where

	gelī	{asa / mhaṇūn}
	go-pst-3sf	quot

'Mohan asked, "Where did Sudha go?" '

(15)	mohan ne	witSārle	kī	sudhā	kuṭhe
	Mohan-ag	ask-pst-3sn	comp	Sudha	where

	gelī	{asa / mhaṇūn}
	go-pst-3sf	quot

'Mohan asked where Sudha went.'

It should be noted here that *mhaṇūn* and *asa* function as conjunctive participle and relative particle respectively elsewhere in the language as shown in (16) and (17) below.

mhaṇūn : conjunctive participle of the verb *mhaṇ* 'to say'

(16)	tī	he	mhaṇūn	gharī	gelī
	she	this	say-conj.part	home-loc	go-pst-3sf

'Having said this, she went home.'

asa : adverbial relative particle

(17)

tū	asa	moṭhyāne	bolū	nakos
you	like this-3sn	loudly	talk	neg-imp-2s

'Do not talk loudly like this.'

1.1.1.2 *Interrogative sentences*

There are two types of interrogative sentences: yes-no questions (see 1.1.1.2.1) and different types of question-word questions (see 1.1.1.2.2). Additionally, a change in intonation is used to mark an interrogative sentence. In question-word questions, the occurrence of question words in different positions denotes different types of interrogatives.

1.1.1.2.1 *Yes-no questions*

Yes-no questions can be either neutral or leading. The purpose of yes-no questions is to seek information regarding a proposition and thus they are open to either answer (i.e., yes or no). On the other hand, leading questions seek confirmation or denial of the stated proposition.

1.1.1.2.1.1 *Neutral yes-no questions*

In neutral yes-no questions, the question-word *kā(y)* 'what' occurs at the end of the sentence usually with a rising intonation. Additionally, a rising intonation on the verb (which is usually sentence-final) by itself (i.e., without the particle *kāy*) also denotes a neutral yes-no question. Except for the occurrence of *kā(y)* in the first type, and the rising intonation in the second, the structure of the interrogative remains identical to its declarative counterpart. Consider (18) and (19) below.

(18) Declarative sentence:

to	kāl	parat	ālā
he	yesterday	back	come-pst-3sm

'He came back yesterday.'

(19) Question:

to	kāl	parat	ālā	kā(y) ?
he	yesterday	back	come-pst-3sm	Q

'Did he come yesterday?'

Note that (18), without the sentence-final question particle *kā(y),* is a declarative sentence while (19) is a question because of the sentence-final *kā(y).* The sentence-final position is obligatory for *kā(y)* in neutral yes-no questions because in all other positions *kā(y)* denotes only an information or question word question. Note that in neutral yes-no questions the sentence-final *kāy* may be optionally reduced to *kā,* which is not possible when *kāy* occurs elsewhere in the sentence to denote an information question. The following examples (20) and (21) show the difference between yes-no and information questions.

(20)

tī	phula	toḍte	kā/kāy ?
she	flowers	picks	Q

'Does she pick flowers?'

(21)

tī	kāy *kā	toḍte ?
she	Q	picks-pres-3sf

'What does she pick?'

Note that when in an information question (21) *kāy* is reduced to *kā,* the resulting sentence is ungrammatical. If *kā* is not interpreted as the abbreviation of *kāy,* but rather as the question word *kā* 'why', then (21) is grammatical and the meaning of (21) in this case is 'Why does she pick (flowers)?'. (See section 1.1.1.2.2 for more discussion.)

1.1.1.2.1.2 *Leading questions*

Leading questions are used to elicit confirmation or denial of the proposition, which may be expressed in a declarative affirmative or declarative negative. Leading questions are typically marked by the negative particle *na* 'is it not true'. *na* with a rising intonation always occurs sentence-finally in a leading question and there is no change in the word order. Consider examples (22) and (23).

(22)

to	gharī	gelā	na ?
he	home-loc	go-pst-3sm	tag

'He went home, didn't he?' (i.e., is it not true?)

(23)

to	gharī	gelā	nāhī	na ?
he	home-loc	go-pst-3sm	neg	tag

'He did not go home, did he?' (i.e., is it not true?).

When *na* occurs elsewhere (i.e., in non-sentence-final position) in the sentence, it functions only as a negative particle, as in example (24).

(24)

to	na	gharī	ālā	na
he	neg	home-loc	come-pst-3sm	neg
śāḷet		gelā		
school-loc		go-pst-3sm		

Additionally, leading questions can be marked by the compound particle *ho na* (literally, 'yes-no'), meaning 'Is it not true?'. Similar *to na, ho na* also occurs in both declarative affirmative and declarative negative. Consider examples (25) and (26).

(25) Declarative affirmative:

to	gharī	gelā,	ho na?
he	home-loc	go-pst-3sm	Q

'He went home, didn't he?' (i.e., is it not true?)

(26) Declarative negative:

to	gharī	gelā	nāhī,	ho na?
he	home-loc	go-pst-3sm	neg	Q

'He did not go home, did he?' (i.e., is it not true?)

The third marker for leading questions is the compound particle *nāhī kā* (lit: 'not what'), meaning 'is it not true?'. Consider examples (27) and (28).

(27) Declarative affirmative:

to	ālā,	nāhī	kā
he	come-pst-3sm	neg	Q

'He came, didn't he?' (i.e., is it not true?)

(28) Declarative negative:

to	mumbaīlā	gelā	nāhī,	nāhī	kā?
he	Bombay-dat	go-pst	neg	neg	Q

'He did not go to Bombay, did he?' (i.e., is it not true?)

1.1.1.2.1.2.1-2 *Degree of certainty of answers to leading questions*

Though Marathi has three different markers for leading questions, these are not used interchangeably and certain pragmatic factors determine the choice of the particles. The use of these three particles reflect different degrees of truth value of the propositions, according to the speaker's belief. While *ho na* marks the highest degree of the truth value of the proposition (from the speaker's point of view), *nāhī kā* marks the lowest degree of certainty about the proposition, and *na* falls between the two. This is schematically shown in figure 2.

Figure 2

Truth Value of the Proposition

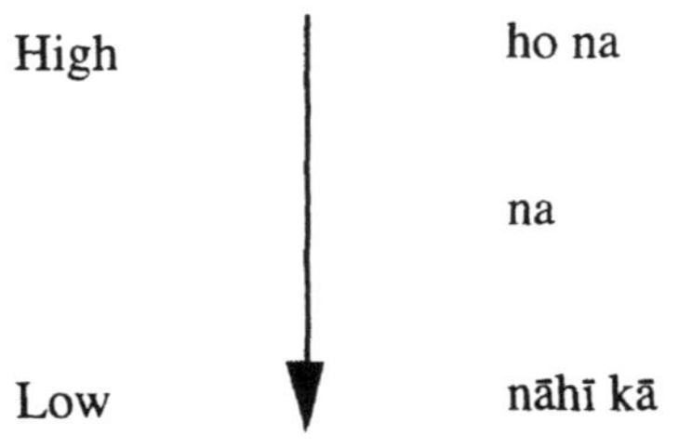

1.1.1.2.1.3 *Alternative questions*

Alternative questions are formed by placing the particle *kī* 'or' between two clauses.

(29)	to	ā̃mbā	khāto	kī	sāntra	(khāto)
	he	mango	eat-pres-3sm	or	orange	(eat-pres-3sm

'Does he eat a mango or (does he eat) an orange ?'

In this case, the repeated verb in the second clause is optionally deleted. However, in the following example where the alternative actions are questioned, verbs in both clauses are retained.

(30)	to	gharī	gelā	kī	(to)	ɔfis
	he	home-loc	go-pst-3sm	or	(he)	office

madhe	baslā
in	sit-pst-3sm

'Did he go home or did he sit in the office ?'

1.1.1.2.2 *Question-word questions*

Question-word questions (generally known as information questions) are formed by substituting a question-word for a constituent in a sentence. The question-word generally occupies the position of the questioned constituent in a sentence ((31) - (39c)) (although, the question-word may occur in other positions as well). The usual word order of the sentence is generally unaffected by the introduction of a question word (though variations in word order are possible (39d)). Question-words can be categorized depending upon the types of constituents they question: (i) pronominal question-words—*koṇ* 'who', *kā̃y* 'what'; (ii) adjectival question-words—*kasa* 'what kind', *koṇtā* 'which one', and *kitī* 'how much'; and (iii) adverbial question-words—*kẽmwhā* 'when', *kuṭhe* 'where', *kadhī* 'when', *kaśālā* 'what for', and *kā* 'why'.

(i) Pronominal questions

Pronominal question-words generally occur in the positions usually occupied by nouns and pronouns; namely, subject and direct (DO) and indirect (IO) objects. (31) and (31a) illustrate the use of *koṇ* 'who' in the subject position, while (32a) and (33a) show the use of *kā̃y* 'what' and *koṇālā* 'to whom' in the direct and indirect postions respectively.

(31) to gāṇa mhaṇto
he song sing-pres-3sm

'He sings a song.'

(31a) koṇ gāṇa mhaṇta/ mhaṇto?
who song sing-pres-3sn sing-pres-3sm

'Who sings a song?'

(32) mohan ā̃mbe khāto
Mohan mangoes eat-pres-3sm

'Mohan eats mangoes.'

(32a) mohan kāy khāto ?
Mohan what eat-pres-3sm

'What does Mohan eat?'

(33) mohan dīpālā paise deto
Mohan Deepa-dat money give-pres-3sm

'Mohan gives money to Deepa.'

(33a) mohan koṇālā paise deto
Mohan who-dat money give-pres-3sm

'To whom does Mohan give money ?'

When the verb agrees with the question-word constituent, the expected person, number, and gender features on the verb may vary depending upon the speaker's expectation, knowledge, and belief about the possible referent of the question word. The unmarked agreement feature on the verb remains the third person, neuter, singular. Consider examples (34a), (34b), and (34c), which illustrate the variations in agreement with the question-word *koṇ* 'who'.

(34a) koṇ gharī āla ?
who home-loc come-pst-3sn

'Who came home ?' (No knowledge about gender)

(34b) koṇ gharī ālā ?
who home-loc come-pst-3sm

'Who came home ?' (Knowledge that person is a male)

(34c) koṇ gharī ālī ?
who home-loc come-pst-3sf

'Who came home?' (Knowledge that person is a female)

If the speaker has no clues about the person (e.g., the person's gender, number, etc.), then the verb has the unmarked agreement features (i.e., third person, singular, neuter) as in (34a). In contrast to this, if the speaker knows that person who arrived was a man (34b) or a woman (34c) and the purpose of the question is to seek more information about him/her, then the verb shows corresponding agreement features (i.e., third person, singular, masculine, in (34b) and third person, singular, feminine in (34c)).

The question-word *kāy* 'what' is similar to *koṇ* 'who', except that *kāy* 'what' is used for [-animate] nouns/pronouns while *koṇ* 'who' is used for [+animate] and [+ human] nouns. The use of *koṇ* is optional for animals. Also, the variation in the verb agreement is similar to the pattern noted above in the case of *koṇ* 'who'. Consider examples (35a), (35b), and (35c).

(35a) tyāne kāy āṇla ?
he-ag what bring-pst-3sn

'What did he bring ?' (No knowledge about gender/number)

(35b) tyāne kāy āṇle ?
he-ag what bring-pst-3pl.m

'What did he bring ?' (Knowledge that object is masculine, plural)

(35c) tyāne kāy āṇlyā
he-ag what bring-pst-3pl.f

'What did he bring ?' (Knowledge that object is feminine, plural)

When the speaker does not have any knowledge of what was brought, the third person, singular neuter agreement is in order, as in (35a). However, when the speaker knows the item(s) (i.e., its gender, and number) and the question is aimed at seeking more specific information about the item(s), then the agreement varies accordingly, as in (35b) and (35c).

(ii) Adjectival questions

Adjectival question-words occur in the prenominal position (like adjectives) and agree with the following nouns in gender, number, person and case. Consider example (36a), which shows the occurrence of *kaśi* 'what kind' in the position of the adjective *lāl* 'red' in (36), and its agreement with the following noun *sāḍī*.

(36)	tine	lāl	sāḍī	wikat	ghetlī
	she-ag	red-3sf	saree-3sf	buy	take-pst-3sf

'She bought a red saree.'

(36a)	tine	kaśī	sāḍī	wikat	ghetlī ?
	she-ag	what kind-3sf	saree-3sf	buy	take-pst-3sf

'What kind of saree did she buy?'

In the following examples (37a) and (38a), the use of different adjectival question-words is illustrated.

(37)	tsaurastyāwartsa	niḷa	ghar	titsa	āhe
	intersection-on-of	blue-3sn	house-3sn	her-3sn	is

'The blue house at the intersection is hers.'

(37a)	titsa	koṇta	ghar	āhe ?
	her-3sn	which-3sn	house-3sn	is

'Which one is her house?'

(38)	tyāne	don	ā̃mbe	khālle
	he-ag	two	mangoes-3pl.m	eat-pst-3pl.m

'He ate two mangoes.'

(38a)	tyāne	kitī	ā̃mbe	khālle
	he-ag	how many	mangoes-3pl.m	eat-pst-3pl.m

'How many mangoes did he eat?'

(iii) Adverbial questions

Adverbial question-words usually occur before the verb—either immediately before the verb or in other preverbal position(s) as shown in (39a - 39c).

(39)	to	kāl	śikāgolā	nāṭak	baghāylā
	he	yesterday	Chicago-dat	play	watch-dat

gelā
go-pst-3sm

'He went to Chicago yesterday to watch a play.'

(39a)	to	kāl	kuṭhe	gelā ?
	he	yesterday	where	go-pst-3sm

'Where did he go yesterday?'

(39b)	to	kāl	śikāgolā	kā/kaśālā	gelā ?
	he	yesterday	Chicago-dat	why/what for	go-pst-3sm

'Why/what for did he go to Chicago yesterday?'

(39c)	to	kẽmwhā	śikāgolā	nāṭak	baghāylā	gelā
	he	when	Chicago-dat	play	see-dat	go-pst-3sm

'When did he go to Chicago to see the play?'

To summarize, the unmarked word order of sentences with adverbial question words is given below:

Subject + (DO) + (IO) + adv Q + verb

However, as in Hindi and other Indo-Aryan languages, the question word may occur postverbally to denote emphasis, stress or other discoursal clues (e.g., negative entailment, frustration of the speaker, etc.). Consider example (39d) in which *kuṭhe* emphasizes the speaker's desire to find the exact location as well as his frustration about someone's going away.

(39d)	to	kāl	gelā	kuṭhe ?
	he	yesterday	go-pst-3sm	where

'Where exactly did he go yesterday?'

1.1.1.2.2.1 *Constituents of the sentence that can be questioned*

Consituents of both main and subordinate clauses can be questioned.

1.1.1.2.2.1.1 *Constituents of the main clause that can be questioned*

Constituents of the main clause that can be questioned are subjects, objects, indirect objects, adjectives, adverbs (of time, place, and manner), object of postposition and verbs. However, when a verb is questioned, the verb stem *kar* 'do' (in its appropriate tense and aspect) must co-occur with the question-word *kāy* 'what'. The following examples (40a - 43) illustrate the questioning possibilities with respect to the constituents of the sentence (40). Also, examples (44a) and (45a) show that the objects of postposition can also be questioned.

(40)	mohan	anūlā	udyā	śāḷet
	Mohan	Anu-dat	tomorrow	school-loc

hindītsa	pustak	deīl
Hindi-of	book	give-fut-3s

'Mohan will give the Hindi book to Anu tomorrow.'

(40a) subject:
koṇ anūlā udyā śāḷet hindītsa pustak deīl ?

'Who will give Anu the Hindi book tomorrow ?'

(40b) Direct object:
mohan anūla udyā śāḷet kāy deīl ?

'What will Mohan give to Anu in school tomorrow ?'

(40c) Indirect object:
mohan koṇālā udyā śāḷet hindītsa pustak deīl ?

'To whom will Mohan give the Hindi book tomorrow ?'

(41) Time adverbial:
mohan anūlā kẽmwhā śāḷet hindītsa pustak deīl ?

'When will Mohan give the Hindi book to Anu in school ?'

(42) Place adverbial:
mohan anūlā udyā kuṭhe hinditsa pustak deīl ?

'Where will Mohan give the Hindi book to Anu tomorrow?

(43) Verb:

mohan	(udyā)	(śāḷet)	kāy	karel ?
mohan	(tomorrow)	(school-loc)	what	do-fut-3s

'What will Mohan do (tomorrow) (in school) ?'

Benefactive object of postposition:

(44)

to	kuṭumbāsāṭhī	paise	kamawto
he	family for	money	earn-3sm

'He earns money for the family.'

(44a)

to	koṇāsāṭhī	paise	kamawto ?
he	who-for	money	earn-pres-3sm

'Who does he earn money for ?'

Instrument:

(45)	tī	penne	lihite
	she	pen-inst	write-pres-3sf

'She writes with pen.'

(45a)	tī	kaśāne	lihite ?
	she	with what	write-pres-3sf

'With what does she write ?'

Notice that when the verb is questioned (43), the entire predicate is deleted (while adverbs may optionally occur) and the verb *kar* 'do' co-occurs with the question-word *kāy* 'what'. Without the verb *kar* 'do', the question is ungrammatical, as shown in (43a).

(43a) Verb:

Mohan	(udyā)	(śāḷet)	kāy	karel/ *ø ?
mohan	(tomorrow)	(school-loc)	what	do-fut-3s

'What will Mohan do (tomorrow) (in school)?'

Note that a noun of possession within the possessive phrase may not be questioned if the noun of possession is followed by a postposition. This is illustrated by the following ungrammatical sentences (46a), (47a), and (48a).

(46)	mohan	sudhātSyā	gāḍīne	ālā
	Mohan	Sudha-poss	car-inst	come-pst-3sm

'Mohan came by Sudha's car.'

(46a)	*mohan	sudhātSyā	kaśāne	ālā ?
	Mohan	Sudha-poss	what-inst	come-pst-3sm

'By what of Sudha did Mohan come?'

(47)	madhūne	tyātSyā	bhāwālā	paise
	Madhu-ag	he-poss	brother-dat	money-3pl.m

dile
give-pst-3pl.m

'Madhu gave money to his brother.'

(47a)*	madhūne	tyātSyā	koṇālā	paise	dile ?
	Madhu-ag	he-poss	who-dat	money	give-pst-3pl.m

'To his whom did Madhu give money?'

(48)	tyātSyā	gharāt	diwā	dzaḷto	āhe
	he-poss	house-loc	lamp	burn-prog	is

'A lamp is burning in his house.'

(48a)*	tyatSyā	kaśāt	diwā	dzaḷto	āhe
	he-poss	what-loc	lamp	burn-prog	is

'In his what a lamp is burning ?'

However, the possessor in (46), (47), and (48) can be readily questioned, as shown in (46b), (47b), and (48b).

(46b) mohan koṇātSyā gāḍīne ālā ?

'By whose car did Mohan come?'

(47b) madhūne koṇātSyā bhāwālā paise dile ?

'To whose brother did Madhu give money ?'

(48b) koṇātSyā gharāt diwā dzaḷto āhe ?

'In whose house is a lamp burning ?'

Examples (46c), (47c), and (48c) show that the entire possessive phrase can readily be questioned.

(46c)	mohan	kasā/kaśāne	ālā ?
	Mohan	how/by what	come-pst-3sm

'How did Mohan come?/By what (transportation) did Mohan come ?'

(47c)

madhūne	koṇālā	paise	dile ?
Madhū-ag	who-dat	money	give-pst-3pl.m

'To whom did Madhu give money ?'

(48c)

kuṭhe	diwā	dzaḷto	āhe ?
where	lamp	burn-prog	is

'Where is a lamp burning?'

1.1.1.2.2.1.2 *Constituents of the subordinate clause that can be questioned*

All major constituents (subject, object, indirect object, and verb) of a subordinate clause can be questioned. Such questions, though grammatical, are not frequently used by speakers. The questioning possibilities in the subordinate clause are illustrated in the following sentences (in (49a) - (49d)).

(49)

kāl	sudhā	anūla	phula	det
yesterday	Sudha	Anu-dat	flowers	give-prog

hotī	he	mohanne	pāhila
was	this	Mohan-ag	see-pst-3sn

'Yesterday Mohan saw that Sudha was giving flowers to Anu.'

(49a) Subject:
kāl koṇ anūlā phula det hotī he mohanne pāhila ?

'Yesterday, who did Mohan see giving flowers to Anu ?'

(49b) Direct object:
kāl sudhā anūlā kāy det hotī he mohanne pāhila?

'Yesterday, what did Mohan see Sudha giving to Anu ?'

(49c) Indirect object:
kāl sudhā koṇālā phula det hotī he mohanne pāhila ?

'Yesterday, to whom did Mohan see Sudha giving flowers ?'

(49d) Adverb:
kẽmwhā sudhā anūlā phula det hotī he mohanne pāhila ?

'When did Mohan see Sudha giving flowers to Anu ?'

1.1.1.2.2.1.2.1 *Non-finite clauses*

Non-finite clauses consist of infinitival, participial, and gerundive forms of the verb and except participial clauses, non-finite clauses typically lack tense and aspect markers.

1.1.1.2.2.1.2.1.1 *Infinitival clauses*

Any constituent of an infinitival clause can be questioned. Consider examples (50), (51), and (52).

(50) Direct object:

tū	koṇālā	bheṭāylā	dillīlā	gelā(s) ?
you	who-acc	meet-inf-dat	Delhi-dat	go-pst-2sm

'In order to meet whom did you go to Delhi ?' (lit: 'Who did you go to Delhi to meet ?')

(51) Indirect object:

tū	koṇālā	paise	dyāylā	mumbaīlā
you	who-dat	money	give-inf-dat	Bombay-dat

gelā(s) ?
go-pst-3sm

'In order to give money to whom did you go to Bombay ?' (lit: 'Who did you go to Bombay to give money to ?')

(52) Object of postposition:

sudhāne	tulā	koṇābarobar	pustaka
Sudha-ag	you-dat	who-with	books

pāṭhwāylā	sāŋgitla ?
send-inf-dat	tell-pst-3sn

'With whom did Sudha ask you to send the books ?'

1.1.1.2.2.1.2.1.2 *Participial clauses*

Any consituent of a participial clause can be questioned as shown in examples (53) - (55) below.

(53) Direct object:

kāy	pāhūn	to	hasāylā	lāglā ?
what	see-conj.part	he-dat	laugh-inf	begin-pst-3sm

'On seeing what did he begin to laugh ?'

(54) Indirect object:

koṇālā	paise	deūn	to	gharī
who-dat	money	give-conj.part	he	home-loc

gelā ?
go-pst-3sm

'After having given money to whom did he go home?

(55) Object of postposition:

koṇādzawaḷ	basūn	to	pustak	wātsat
who-next to	sit-conj.part	he	book	read-

hotā ?
be-pst-3sm

'Seated next to whom was he reading the book ?'

It should be noted that in the infinitival and participial clauses in which subjects are coreferential to the matrix subject lack overt subjects.

1.1.1.2.2.1.2.1.3 *Nominalized clauses*

Any constituent of a nominalized clause can be questioned, including its subject, as in (56) and (57).

(56) Subject:

koṇātsa	bolṇa	tulā	hasawta ?
who-poss	talk-inf	you-dat	laugh-caus-3sn

'Whose talk(ing) makes you laugh ?'

(57) Direct object:

tyātsa	*kāy*	deṇa	tulā	āwḍat	nāhī ?
he-poss	what	give-inf	you-dat	like	neg

'His giving what do you not like ?'

(57a) Indirect object:

tyātsa	*koṇālā*	baghṇa	tulā
his	who-dat	see-inf-3sn	you-dat

āwḍat	nāhī?
like-pres	neg

'His seeing whom do you not like ?'

An important difference between finite and non-finite clauses should be noted here; namely, in the latter a noun of possession followed by a postposition can be questioned (as in (57)), but this is not the case in the former (as in (47a) and (48a)).

1.1.1.2.2.1.3 *Constituents of noun phrases that can be questioned*

The Marathi noun phrase may consist of a number of elements, including:

(i) demonstrative,
(ii) quantifier,
(iii) descriptive adjective,
(iv) classifier,
(v) possessive,
(vi) adverbial,
(vii) emphatic element,
(viii) relative clause, and
(ix) comparative/superlative/equative structures.

The following examples illustrate the questioning possibilities of these structures.

Demonstrative:

(58)

hī	huśār	mulgī
this	intelligent	girl

'This intelligent girl'

(58a) *koṇtī* huśār mulgī ?

'Which intelligent girl ?'

Quantifier:

(59)	titSyā	sahā	kawitā
	her	six	poems

'Her six poems.'

(59a) titSyā *kitī* kawitā ?

'How many of her poems ?'

(60)	titSī	tisrī	mulgī
	her	third	daughter

'Her third daughter'

(60a)	titSī	*kitwī*	mulgī ?
	her	which-numbered	daughter

'Her which numbered daughter ?'

Classifier:

Classifiers such as *ranga* 'color', *lākūḍ* 'wood', and words of measuring weight (e.g., 1 lb., 1 kilogram, etc.) or volume (1 gallon, 1 litre, etc.) cannot be questioned. Classifiers such as *ranga* 'color' and *lākūḍ* 'wood', etc., typically follow adjectives or adjectival elements. The measure words follow numerals. The following examples show that the classifiers cannot be questioned.

(61)	gulābī	*rangātse*	phūl
	pink	color-poss	flower

'Pink colored flower'

(61a)*	gulābī	*kaśātse*	phūl ?
	pink	what-poss	flower

'Pink what of flower ?'

(62) ṭhisūḷ lākḍātsa ṭebal
soft wood-poss table

'Table of soft wood'

(62a)*ṭhisūḷ *kaśātsa* ṭebal ?
soft what-poss table

'Table of soft what ?'

(63) don kilo ḍāḷ
two kilogram lentils

'Two kilograms of lentils'

(63a)*don *kāy* ḍāḷ ?
two what lentils

'Two what of lentils?'

In the above cases (in (61) - (63a)) the entire nominal can be questioned, as in the following examples.

(61b) *koṇta* phūl ?
which flower

'Which flower ?

(62b) *koṇta/kasa* ṭebal ?
which/what kind table

'Which/what kind of table ?'

(63b) *kitī* ḍāḷ ?
how much lentil

'How much lentils ?'

Possessor noun:

(64) mohantse bhāū
Mohan-poss brothers

'Mohan's brothers.'

(64a) *koṇātse* bhāū ?
who-poss brothers

'Whose brothers ?'

Noun of possession:
(65) mohantse koṇ?
Mohan-poss who

'Who of Mohan's ?'

Adverbial:
(66) gharātlī khurtSī
house-loc-def chair

'Chair (which is) in the house.'

(66a) *kuṭhlī* khurtSī?
where-def chair

'Chair (which is in) where ?' (lit: 'Chair belongs to where ?')

Benefactive:
(67) tyātSyāsāṭhī paise
he-poss-for money

'Money for him'

(67a) *koṇāsāṭhī* paise ?
who-for money

'Money for whom?'

Emphatic element:
(68) titSīts goṣṭa
hers-emph story

'Only/indeed her story'

(68a) *titSī-kāy goṣṭa ?

'What her story ?'

Relative clause:

There are two types of relative clauses in Marathi—the participial and sentential. The major difference between these two is that the main verb in the former is in the relative (adjectival) participle form, while the main verb in the latter is finite.

Any constituent of a participial relative clause can be questioned, while no constituent of a sentential relative clause can be questioned. Consider the following examples:

(69a) subject of a participial relative clause:

koṇ	karat	aslela	kām	sāmpla ?
who	do-prog	be-pst rel.part-3sn	work-3sn	finish-pst-3sn

'The work being done by whom got finished?' (lit: 'The work that who was doing (got) finished?')

(69b) Direct object of a participial relative clause:

mohanne	lihilela	*kāy*	phekla ?
Mohan-ag	write-pst-rel.part-3sn	what	throw-pst-3sn

'What did Mohan throw that was written?'

(69c) Indirect object of a participial relative clause:

koṇālā	paise	dilelā	diwas	tulā
who-dat	money	give-pst-rel.part-3sm	day-3sm	you-dat-3sm

āṭhwat	nāhī ?
remember	not

'The day you gave money to whom that you do not remember ?'

(69d) Subject of a sentential relative clause:

*dzo	*koṇ*	itha	rāhto	to	mulgā
rel	who	here	live-pres-3sm	cor	boy

tudzhā	bhāū	āhe ?
your-3sm	brother	is

'Who lives here that boy is your brother ?'
(lit: 'The boy that who lives here is your brother ?')

(69e) Direct object of a sentential relative clause:

**koṇālā*	kāl	tsorāne	mārle	to
who-acc	yesterday	thief-ag	beat-pst-3sn	who

ādz	hospiṭalmadhe	āhe ?
today	hospital-in	is

'Who$_i$ did the thief beat yesterday who$_i$ is in the hospital today?'
(lit: 'He that who the thief beat yesterday is in the hospital ?')

(69f) Indirect object of a sentential relative clause:

*rāmne	*koṇālā*	pustak	dile	to
Ram-ag	who-dat	book	give-pst-3sn	who

śāleṭ	śikawto ?
school-loc	teach-pres-3sm

'Whom did Ram give a book who teaches in school ?'
(lit: 'He that whom Ram gave book teaches in a school ?')

1.1.1.2.2.1.4 *Constituents of postpositional phrases that can be questioned*

A postpositional phrase consists of a noun followed by a postposition. The postposition assigns oblique case to the noun. The noun (oblique) phrase elements in the postpositional phrase (in (70) and (71)) can be readily questioned, as shown in (70a) and (71a) respectively.

(70)

to	mīnābarobar	ālā
he	Meena-with	come-pst-3sm

'He came with Meena.'

(70a)	to	*koṇābarobar*	ālā ?
	he	who-with	come-pst-3sm

'Who did he come with ?'

(71)	tyāne	tuʤhyāsāṭhī	phula	āṇlī
	he-ag	you-for	flowers	bring-pst-3pl.m

'He brought flowers for you.'

(71a)	tyāne	*koṇāsāṭhī*	phula	āṇlī ?
	he-ag	who-for	flowers	bring-pst-3pl.n

'For whom did he bring flowers ?'

1.1.1.2.2.1.5 *Constituents of coordinate structures that can be questioned*

The two modes of coordination are juxtaposition (72a) and lexical coordination (shown in (73a)). Juxtaposition does not allow questioning of its constituents as shown in (72b) below. However, constituents within lexically coordinated structures may be readily questioned as shown in (73b), (74b), (75b) and (76b).

(72) Juxtaposition:

(72a)	mohanne	sãntrī	keḷī	āṇlī
	Mohan-ag	oranges	bananas	bring-pst-3pl.n

'Mohan brought oranges and bananas.'

(72b)	*mohanne	sãntrī	*kāy*	āṇlī ?
	Mohan-ag	oranges	what	bring-pst-3pl.n

'What did Mohan bring (and) oranges ?'

(73) Lexical coordination: Noun phrase

(73a)	mohan	āṇi	madhū	āle
	Mohan	and	Madhu	come-pst-3pl.m

'Mohan and Madhu came.'

(73b)	mohan	āṇi	*koṇ*	āle ?
	Mohan	and	who	come-pst-3pl.m

'Mohan and who came ?'

(74)	sudhā ne	rāʤūlā	āṇi	raghūlā	śikawla
	Sudha-ag	Raju-dat	and	Raghu-dat	teach-pst-3sn

'Sudha taught Raju and Raghu.'

(74a)	sudhāne	*koṇālā*	āṇi	raghūlā	śikawla ?
	Sudha-ag	who-dat	and	Raghu-dat	teach-pst-3sn

'Who and Raghu did Sudha teach ?'

(75) Lexical coordination: verb phrase

(75a)	to	ʤewlā	āṇi	tSahā	pyālā
	he	eat-pst-3sm	and	tea	drink-pst-3sm

'He ate (food) and (then) drank tea.'

(75b)	to	ʤewlā	āṇi	*kāy*	pyālā ?
	he	eat-pst-3sm	and	what	drink-pst-3sm

'What (food) did he eat and drink ?'

It should be noted here that (73b), (74c), (74a), (74b), and (76b) are not frequently used but are acceptable in appropriate contexts. In fact, these are often understood as echo questions. Moreover, in a coordinate structure, questioning of the second constituent is more readily acceptable than questioning of the first one (compare (74a) and (74b)). In all cases the question word must be marked with a postposition identical to the one borne by the questioned constituent. Examples (76a) and (76b) illlustrate this. (76a) is ungrammatical because the question word *koṇ* does not have the appropriate postpositional ending.

(76)	sudhā ne	madhūlā	āṇi	mīnālā	pāhila
	Sudha-ag	Madhu-acc	and	Meena-acc	see-pst-3sn

'Sudha saw Madhu and Meena.'

(76a)	*sudhā ne	madhūlā	āṇi	*koṇ*	pāhila ?
	Sudha-ag	Madhu-acc	and	who	see-pst-3sn

'Who did Sudha see Madhu and ?'

(76b)	sudhā ne	madhūlā	āṇi	*koṇālā*	pāhila ?
	Sudha-ag	Madhu-acc	and	who-acc	see-pst-3sn

'Who did Sudha see Madhu and ?'

Disjunctive elements in lexically coordinated structures may not be questioned.

(77)	*anū	kīmwā	*koṇ*	ālī / āla ?
	Anu	or	who	come-pst-3sf/3sn

'Anu or who came ?'

1.1.1.2.2.1.6 *Number of sentence constituents that can be questioned*

There are no grammatical restrictions on the number of constituents in a sentence that can be questioned simultaneously. Thus all or any subset of the constituents of (78) can be questioned, as shown in (78a) - (79e).

(78)	mohan ne	sudhālā	parwā
	Mohan-ag	Sudha-acc	day before yesterday
	bādzārāt	pāhila	
	market-in	see-pst-3sn	

'Mohan saw Sudha day before yesterday in the market.'

Subject:

(78a)	*koṇī*	sudhālā	parwā
	who	Sudha-acc	day before yesterday

bādzārāt	pāhila ?
market-in	see-pst-3sn

'Who saw Sudha in the market the day before yesterday ?'

Direct object and place adverbial:

(78b)	mohan ne	*koṇālā*	parwā	kuṭhe
	Mohan-ag	whom	day before yesterday	where

pāhila ?
see-pst-3sn

'Whom did Mohan see where the day before yesterday ?'

Time adverbial:

(78c)	mohan ne	sudhālā	*kẽmwhā*	bādzārāt	pāhila ?
	Mohan-ag	Sudha-acc	when	market-in	see-pst-3sn

'When did Mohan see Sudha in the market ?'

Subject, time and place adverbial:

(78d)	*koṇi*	sudhālā	*kẽmwhā*	*kuṭhe*	pāhila ?
	who	Sudha-acc	when	where	see-pst-3sn

'Where did who see Sudha when ?'

Subject, direct object, time, and place adverbial:

(78e)	*koṇī*	*koṇālā*	*kẽmwhā*	*kuṭhe*	*pāhila ?*
	who	whom	when	where	see-pst-3sn

'Who saw whom when where ?'

1.1.1.2.2.2 - 1.1.1.2.2.2.1 *Status of the questioned element*

There is no change in the status of the questioned element.

1.1.1.2.3 *Echo questions*

1.1.1.2.3.1 *Yes-no echo questions*

A yes-no echo question generally asks for clarification or confirmation of information which has already been given to the questioner by the speaker. The question usually repeats (e.g., (79a) and (79b)) one or more elements of the statement (e.g., (79)). In this case, the verbal element is generally repeated along with some or all of the constituents of the noun phrase. The subject, in most cases, is deleted and the verb has the same gender and number endings as that of the (deleted) subject.

Speaker A:

(79)	to	ãŋgṇāt	baslā	āhe
	he	courtyard-loc	sit-pst-3sm	is-3s

'He is sitting in the courtyard.'

Speaker B:

(79a)	(to)	ãŋgṇāt	baslā	āhe?
	(he)	courtyard-loc	sit-pst-3sm	is-3s

'(Is he) sitting in the courtyard?'

(79b)	ãŋgṇāt ?
	courtyard-loc

'In the courtyard ?'

(79c)	baslā	āhe?
	sit-pst-3sm	is-3s

'Is sitting?'

Note that in (79a), where the subject is optionally deleted, the markers of third person masculine gender and singular number of the subject are retained on the verb—*baslā āhe* 'is seated/sitting'. The echo question (80a) can be preceded by another question; i.e., *ho kā?* 'Is that so?'.

Speaker A:

(80)	titsa	kāl	lagna	dzhāla
	her	yesterday	wedding-3sn	happen-pst-3sn

'Her wedding took place yesterday.'

Speaker B:

(80a)	(titsa)	kāl	lagna	dzhāla ?
	(her)	yesterday	wedding-3sn	happen-pst-3sn

'Did she get married yesterday ?' (lit: 'Did her wedding happen yesterday ?')

(80b)	*ho kā*	titsa	kāl	lagna
	Is that so?	her	yesterday	wedding-3sn

dzhāla ?
happen-pst-3sn

'Is that so? Her wedding took place yesterday ?

It is important to note here that in a yes-no echo question, the complete sentence, subjectless sentence, or only the questioned element is repeated. This is illustrated in (80) - (81b). (80a) shows that the whole sentence is repeated in the echo question. In (81) the subject is deleted; in (81a) the time adverbial, along with the subject, is deleted; in (81b) only the questioned word (i.e., the verb *dzhāla* 'happened') is repeated.

(81)	kāl	lagna	dzhāla ?
	yesterday	wedding	happen-pst-3sn

'Did the wedding take place yesterday ?'

(81a)	lagna	dzhāla ?
	wedding	happen-pst-3sn

'Wedding happened ?'

(81b)	dzhāla ?
	happen-pst-3sn

'took place ?'

1.1.1.2.3.2 *Question-word echo questions*

In echo questions, the question-word is accompanied by the verb and, optionally, by other elements. Consider the following examples.

Speaker A:

(82)	mohan	dukānāt	kām	karto
	Mohan-3sm	shop-loc	work	do-pres-3sm

'Mohan works in the shop.'

Speaker B:

(82a)	kuṭhe	kām	karto ?
	where	work	do-pres-3sm

'Where (does he) work ?'

In (82) the sentence contains more than one element and, therefore, more than one type of echo questions are possible. This is illustrated in (83) - (83b).

Speaker A:

(83)	mohan	dukānāt	kām	karto
	Mohan-3sm	shop-loc	work	do-pres-3sm

Speaker B:

(83a)	kā̃y	karto ?
	what	do-pres-3sm

'What does he do ?'

Speaker A:

(83b)	(dukānāt)	kam	karto
	(shop-loc)	work	do-pres-3sm

'(He) works in the shop.'

1.1.1.2.3.3 *Yes-no question echo questions*

These are similar to yes-no questions echoing a statement, mostly with repetition of the subject noun phrase. The conversation in (84) illustrates this point.

Speaker A: yes-no question:

(84)	tū	mūmbaīt	rāhtes	kā ?
	you	Bombay-in	live-pres-2sf	Q

'Do you live in Bombay ?'

Speaker B: yes-no question echo question:

(84a)	mī	mumbaīt	rāhte	kā	ho	mī
	I	Bombay-in	live-pres-1sf	Q	yes,	I

mumbaīt	rāhte
Bombay-in	live-1sf

'Do I live in Bombay ? Yes, I live in Bombay.'

Negative response:

(84b)	mī	mumbaīt	rāhte	kā ?	nāhī	mī
	I	Bombay-in	live-pres-1sf	Q	neg	I

mumbaīt	rāhāt	nāhī
Bombay-in	live-pres	neg

'Do I live in Bombay ? No, I do not live in Bombay.'

1.1.1.2.3.4-7 *Elements of the sentence that can be questioned in echo questions*

The elements of the sentence which can be questioned in echo-questions are the same as for non-echo questions.

Speaker A:

(85)	āī	rodz	sakāḷī	mandirāt
	mother	everyday	morning	temple-in

pūdʒesāṭhī	dzāte
worship-for	go-pres-3sf

'Mother goes to the temple every morning for worship.'

Speaker B:

(85a)	*koṇ*	*kẽmwhā*	*kuṭhe*	*kaśāsāṭhī*	*dzāte ?*
	who	when	where	what for	go-pres-3sf

Who goes where, when, for what ?

(85b)	āī	rodz	*kuṭhe*	dzāte ?
	mother	everyday	where	go-pres-3sf

'Where does Mother go every day ?'

(85c)	āī	*kẽmwhā*	*kaśālā*	mandirāt	dzāte ?
	mother	when	why	temple-in	go-pres-3sf

'Why and when does Mother go to the temple ?'

More than one element can be questioned in echo-questions, as shown in (85) - (85c). Note that (85) is a statement and (85a) - (85c) are the possible echo-questions based on the information in (85).

1.1.1.2.4 *Answers*

1.1.1.2.4.1 - 1.1.1.2.4.1.3 *Answers not marked as distinct speech acts*

Answers are not marked as distinct speech acts. However, some of the responses to yes-no questions uniquely mark answers and separate them from statements, i.e., *ho(y)* 'yes' and other interjection-type responses such as *hũ* 'yes' and *uhũ* 'no'. The negative particle *nāhī* 'no' is used elsewhere in the language in a negative statement. In colloquial Marathi a palatal click is often used as a negative response to a question word.

1.1.1.2.4.2 *Answers in the form of incomplete sentences*

Incomplete sentences are often accepted as possible answers. In the appropriate contexts in a discourse, all constituents of a sentence (individually and/or in combination) are deletable. When the whole statement is questioned (as in 86), the minimum answer is generally the verb as in (86a).

(86)	kāl	to	nāṭkālā	gelā	hotā	kā?
	yesterday	he	play-dat	go-pst-3sm	had	Q

'Had he gone to play yesterday?'

Answer:

(86a)	gelā	hotā
	go-pst-3sm	had

'Yes, he did.' (lit: 'had gone')

It may be noted here that the deletion of the subject (and other major nominal constituents) on the basis of the marking (gender, number, person, etc.) on the verb is very common in the language and is not a unique feature of answers.

1.1.1.2.4.2.1 *Minimum answers to yes-no questions*

The minimum answer to a yes-no question is ho 'yes', *nāhī* 'no', *kadātSit* 'perhaps', *māhīt nāhī* '(I) do not know', as illustrated below.

Question:

(87)	tū	udyā	yeśīl	kā ?
	you	tomorrow	come-fut-2s	Q

'Will you come tomorrow ?'

Answers:

(87a) ho 'yes'

(87b) nāhī 'no'

(87c) kadātSit 'perhaps'

(87d) māhīt nāhī '(I) do not know '

Additionally, the verb with all its affixes can be the minimum answer to a yes-no question. The verb, in this case may be preceded by the particle *ho* 'yes' or *nāhī* 'no' as shown in (88a) and (88b).

Question:

(88)	to	ʤewlā	kā ?
	he	eat-pst-3sm	Q

'Did he eat ?'

Answers:

(88a)	(ho)	ʤewlā
	(yes)	eat-pst-3sm

'Yes, he did.' (lit: 'yes, ate')

(88b)	(nāhī)	ʤewlā	nāhī
	(no)	eat-pst-3sm	neg

'No, he did not eat.' (lit: 'no, not ate')

1.1.1.2.4.2.1.1 *Response particles 'yes' and no'*

The particle *ho(y)* is used for affirmation answers and the particle *nāhī* is used for a negative response. Both *ho(y)* and *nāhī* may be reduplicated for emphasis as in (90a) and (90b).

Question:

(89)	tū	udyā	yeśīl	kā ?
	you	tomorrow	come-ful-2s	Q

'Will you come tomorrow ?'

Answers:

(90a)	ho(y), ho(y)	'yes, yes'
(90b)	nāhī, nāhī	'no, no'
(90c)	*kadātSit, kadātSit	'perhaps, perhaps'

While the affirmative and negative particles are reduplicated, the particle *kadātSit* cannot be reduplicated (90c). Additionally, the use of adverbials *-dzarūr* 'certainly' with the affirmative and *bilkul* 'certainly' with the negative particles respectively mark a yet higher degree of emphasis as shown in.

(91a) ho, ho, dzarūr
'yes, yes, certainly'

(91b) nāhī, nāhī, bilkul nāhī
'no, no, certainly not'

(91c) - (91d) show that the adverbials *dzarūr,* and *bilkul* do not precede the reduplicated particles.

(91c) *dzarūr, ho, ho

(91d) *bilkul nāhī, nāhī

1.1.1.2.4.2.1.2 *Answers to leading questions*

Answers to leading questions are based on whether the speaker agrees with the proposition underlying the question.

Question:

(92)	to	gharī	gelā,	na ?
	he	home-loc	go-pst-3sm	tag

'He went home, didn't he?'

Answers:

(92a)	ho,	to	gharī	gelā
	yes,	he	home-loc	go-pst-3sm

'Yes, he went home.'

(92b)	nāhī,	to	gharī	gelā	nāhī
	neg	he	home-loc	go-pst-3sm	neg

'No, he did not go home.'

Question:

(93)	to	gharī	gelā	nāhī,	na?
	he	home-loc	go-pst-3sm	neg	tag

'He did not go home, did he?'

Answers:

(93a)	ho,	to	gharī	gelā	nāhī
	yes,	he	home-loc	go-pst-3sm	neg

'Yes, he did not go home.'

(93b)	nāhī,	to	gharī	gelā
	neg	he	home-loc	go-pst-3sm

'No, he went home.'

Note that in (93a) and (93b) the affirmative and negative particles indicate agreement and disagreement with the underlying proposition respectively.

1.1.1.2.4.2.2 *Answers to question-word questions*

Answers to question-word questions usually consist of only the constituent required by the question. The rest of the sentence is generally deleted on the assumption that the questioner already has the information conveyed by it. Examples (94a) and (95a) illustrate this point. The question in (94) focuses on the indirect object. Thus the answer in (94a) contains only the indirect object, while the rest of the sentence is deleted.

Question:

(94)	tū	koṇālā	paise	diles ?
	you	to whom	money	give-pst-2s

'To whom did you give money ?'

Answer:

(94a) anūlā
Anu-dat

'To Anu.'

When the focus of the question is on the direct object, (95), the answer contains only the direct object.

Direct Object:

Question:

(95)	tū	anūlā	kāy	diles ?
	you	Anu-dat	what	give-pst-3s

'What did you give Anu ?'

Answer:

(95a) paise
money

'Money'

1.1.1.3 *Imperatives*

Marathi has seven distinct types of imperatives based on morphological/formal and semantic criteria, such as verb form, person possibilities of the subject, emphasis, the degree of politeness, and meaning. These are listed below:

(a) direct imperative
(b) optative
(c) suggestive
(d) obligative
(e) future obligative
(f) future
(g) prohibitive (or negative imperative)

1.1.1.3.1 *Positive imperative*

1.1.1.3.1.1 *Possible person-number combinations*

1.1.1.3.1.1.1 *The direct imperative*

The structure of a typical imperative sentence is illustrated in (96). It is viewed as the canonical imperative form in Marathi. It takes second person subjects, it allows deletion of the subject, and the verb is in its basic/root/uninflected form. This imperative form conveys direct commands.

(96) *deṇe* 'to give':

	(tū)	pustak	de
	you-s	book-sn	give-s

'(You) give the book.'

The singular form of the imperative is the unmarked form. There is no other instance in the language where the bare verb stem (without any suffixes) functions as a finite verb.

The stem serves as the singular imperative form for both vowel (96) as well as consonant-ending verbs (97).

(97) *karṇe* 'to do':

(tū)	kām	kar
(you)	work	do-s

'(You) do the work.'

Examples (98) - (102) show that the plural and/or polite imperative forms vary according to shape of the verb stem. */ā/*-ending verbs have identical singular and plural imperative forms. Compare (98) and (98a).

(98) *khāṇe* 'to eat':

tū	ā̃mbe	khā
you-s	mangoes	eat-s

'You eat the mangoes.'

(98a)

tumhī	ā̃mbe	khā
you-pl	mangoes	eat-pl

'You (pl) eat the mangoes.'

Examples (99), (100), and (101) show that when verb stems are */e/*-ending (99) and (100), and */ū/*-ending (101), the suffix */ā/* is added to the stem. (In this case, the verb stem undergoes certain changes (such as *ye* —> *yā* (99), and *de* —> *dyā* (100)) according to the general phonological rules of the language (for details see sections 3.4.1.3.2 and 3.4.4.1.4).

(99) *yeṇe* 'to come':

tumhī	gharī	yā
you-pl	home	come-pl

'You (pl) come home.'

(100) *deṇe* 'to give'

tumhī	pustaka	dyā
you-pl	books	give-pl

'You (pl) give books.'

(101) *dhūṇe* 'to wash':

tumhī	kapḍe	dhuwā
you-pl	clothes	wash-pl

'You (pl) wash clothes.'

For consonant-ending verb stems, the plural suffix */ā/* occurs in the final position of plural imperative verb forms, as in (102).

(102) *sā̃ŋgṇe* 'to tell':

tumhī	goṣṭa	sā̃ŋgā
you-pl	story	tell-pl

'You (pl) tell the story.'

In addition to the direct imperative, the other forms mentioned in 1.1.1.3 (i.e., (b) -(f)) may also function as imperatives. In these cases (i.e., (b) the optative, (c) the suggestive (d) the obligative, (e) the future obligative, and (f) the future) the imperatives are understood as less direct/more polite compared to the 'true/direct imperative' discussed above. Each of these functional imperatives will be discussed in the following sections.

1.1.1.3.1.1.2 *The optative*

The optative form of the verb is marked by the suffix *-we* (and its various forms according to number and gender) if the verb is */ā/*-ending (as in 103). In all other cases (i.e., when the verb stem ends in a vowel other than /ā/, or if the verb stem is consonant-ending) an infix */ā/* is inserted between the verb stem and the suffix *-we* as in (104) and (105). The optative is understood as a suggestion rather than a command. The meaning of the optative can be paraphrased as, "I suggest that you do X." (X = action denoted by the verb). Consider examples (103), (104), and (105).

(103) *dzāṇe* 'to go':

{tū / tumhī} dzāwe
{you-s / you-pl} go-opt-3sn

'You (s/pl) may go.'

(104) *basṇe* 'to sit':

{tū / tumhī} itha basāwe-3sn
{you-s / you-pl} here sit-opt-s/pl

'You (s/pl) may sit here.'

(105) *sā̃mbhāḷṇe* 'to take care':

bābā, tumhī malā sā̃mbhāḷāwe
father you-pl I-acc take care-opt-3sn

'Father, you may protect me/take care of me.'

Note that examples (103) - (105) show that the optative form of both intransitive (103) - (104) and transitive (105) verbs does not agree with the subject. The verb remains in its unmarked form (i.e., third person, singular, neuter). It is important to note that the optative shows a split pattern of agreement. The optative verb as seen in (103) - (105) does not agree with the subject, but the following examples show that it does agree with the object (if it is not followed by a postposition (106)). Example (107) shows that the verb fails to agree with the object if it is followed by a postposition; in such cases the verb remains in its unmarked form.

(106) {tū / tumhī} kāme/kāma karāwīt
{you-s / you-pl} job-3pl.n do-opt-pl.n

'You-s/pl) may do the jobs.'

(107)	{tū / tumhī}	tilā	baghāwe
	{you-s / you-pl}	she-acc	see-opt-3sn

'{You-s / you-pl} may see her.'

An interesting property of the optative in Marathi is that when the optative verb takes a third person subject ((108) and (109)) it can function as an imperative, although it is generally interpreted as a polite suggestion and not a direct command. The use of the third person instead of the usual second person in these sentences is rooted in the complex network of social relations involving such parameters as power, prestige, authority, etc. between the speaker and the hearer. This form is almost always preferred over the direct imperative when the hearer is higher on the scale of power, prestige, and authority than the speaker. Another interesting aspect of the imperative optative form in this case (i.e., with the third person subject) is that the subject takes the agentive marker/postposition *-ne* regardless of whether the verb is transitive (108) or intransitive (109).

(108)	{tyāne / tyā̃nnī}	gāṇa	mhaṇāwa
	{he-ag / they-ag}	song-3sn	sing-opt-3sn

'He/they may sing a song.'

(109)	{tyāne / tyā̃nnī}	khālī	basāwe
	{he-ag / they-ag}	down	sit-opt-sn

'He/they may sit down.'

Additionally, the optative can also be used with the first person plural subject *āpaṇ* 'we'. In this case, the intended meaning is the speaker's suggestion for a joint action on the part of the speaker and the addressee, as in (110) below.

(110)	āpaṇ	ātā	gharī	dzāwe
	we	now	home-loc	go-opt-sn

'We may go home now.'

1.1.1.3.1.1.3 *The suggestive*

The structure of the suggestive form of the verb is: verb stem + postposition *-lā* + verb *hawa* 'to need, to want'. The main verb in this construction remains in its invariant form (e.g., *dzā-y-lā* 'to go'). The infix */y/* is inserted between the stem and the postposition *-lā*. The ergative (partial) pattern is observed in this case too. The auxiliary verb *hawa* 'need/want' agrees with the object (if it is not followed by a postposition). In other cases, (i.e., when the object is followed by a postposition, or if it is absent) the verb *hawa* remains in its unmarked form regardless of whether the main verb is transitive or intransitive.

The meaning of this form can be paraphrased as 'I think that it is necessary for X to do Y (action).' The verb in this case takes the second, third, and first person subjects, as illustrated in (111), (112), and (113).

The suggestive is used to express the speaker's opinion about the obligation of the hearer, third person, first person, or the joint obligation of the speaker and the hearer, and, furthermore, to indirectly suggest that the obligation may be fulfilled.

2nd person:

(111)	tū	ātā	gharī	dzāylā	hawa
	you-s	now	home-loc	go-to	need-3sn

'You need to go home now.'

3rd person:

(112)	tyāne	paise	dyāylā	hawet
	he-ag	money-pl.m	give-to	need-3pl.m

'He needs to give money.'

1st person:

(113)	{mī / āpaṇ}	katsrā	phekāylā	hawā
	{I / we(you+I)}	garbage-3sm	throw-to	need-3sm

'I/we need to throw the garbage.'

The suggestive construction alternatively allows the postposition *-lā* after the subject. In this case, the speaker indicates that conditions or circumstances external to the agent (subject) require the agent to perform the action expressed by the main verb, and therefore, the speaker suggests that the agent should do it.

As opposed to this, in cases such as (111) - (112), where there is ø-marking on the first and second person subject and *-ne* marking on the third person subject, it is implied that the obligation to perform the act is caused by conditions related to the agent's own sense of will, desire, motivation, etc. Contrast (111) with (114).

(114)	tulā	ātā	gharī	dzāylā	hawa
	you-dat	now	home-loc	go-to	need-3sn

'You need to go home now.'

In (111), the speaker suggests that the hearer should go home because of a known pattern of behavior, that is, he might know, for example, that the agent (in this case, the hearer) generally likes to go home by 5 p.m. and it is 5 p.m. now or that the speaker has guessed the hearer's intention to leave for home, etc. In contrast to this, in (114) the assumed obligations (according to the speaker) are external to the will or volition of the agent/hearer; i.e., the hearer's wife will be upset if he does not go home now, or his/her work is done and therefore there is no need for the hearer to stay any more, etc.

1.1.1.3.1.1.4 *The obligative*

The obligative verb consists of two parts; the verb stem, along with the perfective suffix (which is also the marker of past tense) followed by the appropriate vowel; and, secondly, the appropriate form of the verb *pāhidʒe* 'should'. The obligative does not express a direct command; rather, it expresses a suggestion by the speaker for the agent/patient to perform the action expressed by the main verb. The form of sugestion expressed by the obligative is stronger than that expressed by the optative or the suggestive. The meaning of the obligative verb can be paraphrased in English as, 'X should do Y.' This construction allows first, second, and third person subjects. The subject takes either *-lā* (dative) or *-ne* (the agentive or supposedly ergative) postpositions. When the subject takes the dative postposition *-lā,* the intransitive main verb as well as the obligational verb *pāhidʒe* 'should' remain in their respective unmarked forms, as in (115).

(115)	tulā/tyālā	gharī	gela	pāhidʒe
	you-dat/he-dat	home-loc	go-perf-3sn	oblig-s

'You/he should go home.'

However, if the main verb is transitive, the main verb as well as the obligational verb agree with the direct object (if it is not followed by a postposition), as in (116).

(116)	tulā/tyālā	pustaka	watslī	pāhidʒet
	you-dat/he-dat	book-3pl.n	read-perf-3pl.n	oblig-pl

'You/he should read books.'

If the direct object is followed by a postposition, both the main verb and the obligational verb remain in their unmarked forms, as in (117).

(117)	tulā/tyālā	mohanlā	bheṭla	pāhidʒe
	you-dat/he-dat	Mohan-DO	meet-perf-3sn	oblig-s

'You/he should meet Mohan.'

Note that in (117) the direct object (DO) *Mohan* is followed by the postposition *-lā* and the verbs do not agree with the subject or the object.

When the subject is followed by the (ergative/agentive) postposition *-ne,* the pattern of verb-agreement is similar to the above, i.e., if the main verb is intransitive, both the main verb and the obligational verb remain in their unmarked forms (118). If the main verb is transitive, both verbs agree with the DO (if it is not followed by a postposition (119)). If the DO is also followed by a postposition, both verbs remain in their unmarked forms (120).

(118)	tū ø/rām ne	gharī	gela	pāhidʒe
	you-ø/Ram-ag	home-loc	go-perf-3sn	should-s

'You/Ram should go home.'

(119)	tū-ø/rām ne	patra	lihilī	pāhidʒet
	you-ø/Ram-ag	letters-3pl.n	write-perf-3pl.n	should-pl

'Ram should write letters.'

(120)	tū-ø/rām ne	ḍɔkṭarlā	bheṭla	pāhidʒe
	you-ø/Ram-ag	doctor-DO	meet-perf-3sn	should-s

'You/Ram should see the doctor.'

While the traditional grammars (see Damle 1966 [1911]) treat the postpositions *-lā* and *-ne* as optional in this construction, a close examination of the data points out that these are not semantically identical. The postpositions *-ne* and *-lā* express the speaker's opinion regarding the conditions which induce the obligation for the agent to perform the action. While *-ne* indicates that (in the speaker's opinion) the obligation is caused by conditions pertaining to the agent (e.g., the agent's desire for responsibilities, disposition, needs, etc.), *-lā* indicates that (in the speaker's opinion) the obligation is caused by conditions external to the agent (e.g., the agent's job, the physical context of the event, etc.). The obligation indicated by *-ne* can be called agent-induced obligation, while the obligation indicated by *-lā* can be called externally induced obligation. The obligative shares this feature with the suggestive (secton 1.1.1.3.1.1.3). For example, when the speaker uses the postposition *-ne* (121), he/she implies that in his/her opinion the agent/subject *Sudha* should go home because she (*Sudha*) must feel responsible to be home by midnight.

(121)	rātrītse	bārā wadzle	ātā	sudhāne/sudhā-lā
	night-of	twelve-tolled	now	Sudha-inst/Sudha-dat
	gharī	gela	pāhidʒe	
	home-loc	go-perf-3sn	should-s	

'It is twelve o'clock at night, Sudha should go home now.'

Whereas if the speaker uses the postposition *-lā,* he/she implies that the circumstances (such as her husband is ill, the children are waiting for her, etc.) require *Sudha* to go home. When *pāhidʒe* is used with a second person pronoun, the following pattern occurs:

(122)	tulā	nokrī	kelī	pāhidʒe
	you-dat	job-3sf	do-perf-3sf	should-s

'You should do the job.' (because the circumstances require that you do the job)

(123)	tū	nokrī	kelī	pāhidʒe(s)
	you	job-3sf	do-perf-3sf	should (2s)

'You should do the job.' (because you should feel obligated to do it).

Note that *-lā* and ø marking are alternatively used on the subjects in (122) and (123) respectively. While *-lā* indicates externally induced obligation, the ø-marking indicates internally induced obligation. This obligative construction optionally allows the main verb to be followed by the postposition *-lā* as in (124) and (125). In this case, the degree of imperative is lower than the one expressed with the perfective form of the verb, as in (118) - (123).

(124)	tyālā	gharī	dzāylā	pāhidʒe
	he-dat	home-loc	go-inf-dat	should-s

'He should go home.'

(125)	tyāne	gharī	dzāylā	pāhidʒe
	he-ag	home-loc	go-inf-dat	should-s

'He should go home.'

1.1.1.3.1.1.5 *The future obligative*

The future obligative is used to express an indirect command. In this case, the speaker indicates that the subject of the construction is strongly obligated to perform the action and that he/she does not have any choice (of performing/not performing the action). The construction can be paraphrased in English as "You will have to do X".

The subject is followed by the postposition *-lā,* the main verb is followed by the optative inflection *-wa* (and its various forms *-wā/-we* (singular and plural), *-wī/-wyā* (feminine singular and plural) and *-wa/-wī* (neuter singular and plural) followed by an auxiliary verb *lāg* 'to be attached to', which is inflected for future tense endings. If the main verb is intransitive, both the main and the auxiliary verb remain in their unmarked form (126). When the main verb is transitive, both the main verb and the auxiliary agree with the DO (if it is not followed by a postposition) (127). If DO is also followed by a postposition, both verbs remain in their unmarked forms (128).

(126)	tulā	kām	karāwa	lāgel
	you-dat	work-3sn	do-opt-3sn	will have to-3sn

'You will have to do the work.'

(127)	tulā	dzāwa	lāgel
	you-dat	go-opt-3sn	will have to-3sn

'You will have to go.'

(128)	tulā	madhūlā	bheṭāwa	lāgel
	you-dat	Madhu-acc	meet-opt-3sn	will have to-3sn

'You will have to meet Madhu.'

1.1.1.3.1.1.6 *The future*

Regular verb forms inflected for future tense are also used to indicate a polite suggestion to perform an action. Only second personal pronouns can be the subject of this construction.

(129)	tū	patra	pāṭhawśīl
	you	letter	send-fut-2s

'You will send (a) letter.'

1.1.1.3.1.1.7 *Prohibitive*

See sections 1.1.1.3.2 - 1.1.1.3.2.2.

1.1.1.3.1.2 *Degrees of imperative*

The degrees of imperative force can be viewed as a hierarchy of the force of commands ranging from strong to weak. The grammatical constructions discussed in the preceding sections (1.1.1.3.1.1.1-6) can be viewed as various points on the hierarchy, as illustrated in (130) below.

(130) Stronger command/less polite

1. future obligative
2. direct imperative
3. obligative
4. suggestive
5. optative
6. future

Weaker command/more polite

Degrees of imperative coincide with degrees of politeness. The choice of the appropriate imperative construction is determined on the basis of the degree of politeness which the speaker chooses/intends to indicate.

Different degrees of politeness are expressed by choosing one or more of the following means: (i) the use of the various imperative constructions (as shown in (130)), and (ii) the choice of the singular, plural-honorific, or ultra-honorific second person pronoun subject (*tū, tumhī,* and *āpaṇ,* respectively). The polite (plural) forms *tumhī/āpaṇ* are appropriate in a formal context or in interaction with a stranger, old people, or superiors at the place of work. In contrast to this, the singular second person pronoun *tū* is used when addressing younger relatives, close friends, servants, laborers, etc. When closeness or intimacy is to be expressed, the singular, informal form *tū* (and not the plural, formal forms *tumhī* or *āpaṇ)* is used. For example, while addressing mother, god, or a close friend, *tū* is used and *tumhī/āpaṇ* is viewed as an inappropriate choice in this context. It should be noted here that the conventions of appropriatenes of address terms have undergone a considerable change in the history of the Marathi speech community. For example, up until about 200 years ago, both husband and wife were expected to address each other with the plural-honorific *tumhī.* However, during the last two hundred years, as is evident from the literature, an asymmetrical practice may be observed; i.e., the husband addressing the wife with the informal non-honorific pronoun *tū,* while the wife addressing the husband with the honorific pronoun *tumhī.* Currently, this practice is again changing in favor of using the non-honorific/informal tū reciprocally by the husband and the wife. Parents use second singular pronoun *tū* to address their child. The relationship between mother and child is viewed as more informal/intimate compared to the relationship between father and child. Therefore, a child uses non-honorific *tū* (second singular pronoun) to address his/her mother and the honorific pronoun *tumhī* (second plural) to address his/her father.

Additionally, the use of honorific and ultra-phonorific *tumhī* and *āpaṇ* respectively is commonly used for expressing sarcasm among friends. Similarly, the use of the honorific and ultra-honorific by the elderly with young children also expresses sarcasm. However, the contextual determinants (e.g., context of the situation, age of the participants, etc.) of the choice of second person pronouns need to be examined more in order to better explain choices of pronouns.

1.1.1.3.1.2.1 *Use of pāhū and bara in imperative sentences*

Pāhū (lit: 'we will see') and *bara* (lit: 'all right') are used in imperative sentences following the imperative verb. Both *pāhū* and *bara* intensify the force of command. However, between the two, *pāhū* is stronger than *bara.* Sentences with *pāhū* (e.g., *kām kar pāhū* (lit: 'do the work')) can be paraphrased in English as 'let me see you do the work', while a sentence with *bara* (e.g., *kām kar bara* (lit:) 'do the work, all right ?') can be paraphrased in English as 'Do the work, all right ?'.

(131)	ātā	tū	gharī	dzā	pāhū
	now	you	home-loc	go-imp-2s	intens

'Let me see you go home now.'

(132)	ātā	tū	gharī	dzā	bara
	now	you	home-loc	go-imp-2s	intens

'Be sure to go home now.'

Both *pāhū* (131) and *bara* (132) add an adverbial shade of meaning to the imperative verb. These constructions are similar to the obligative construction in their function of intensifying the force of command. However, they differ from the obligative construction in that force of obligation incumbent on the addressee in constructions with *pāhū* and *bara* is caused by the speaker's view (wish/desire/opinion), while in the obligative as well as suggestive construction, the obligation is viewed from the addressee's point of view. In other words, the strength of command in obligative and suggestive sentences is determined from the addressee's point of view; the strength of command in the constructions with *pāhū* and *bara* is determined from the speaker's point of view.

1.1.1.3.2 - 1.1.1.3.2.2 *The negative imperative*

Negative imperatives are formed by using three devices: (a) the negative verb *nako* (and its variants), (b) *naye* (and its variants, and (c) the negative particle *na*. While *na* is neutral regarding the degree of imperative, *nako* and *naye* are not. *Nako* indicates a strong imperative, directly prohibiting the agent from performing an act. On the other hand, *naye* indicates an indirect prohibition, and can be paraphrased in English as 'In my opinion you/she may/should not perform the action X'. While *nako* and *naye* are used in all contexts where imperatives are used, *na* is restricted to the optative and the obligative construction with *pāhidʒe* (where the main verb is in the perfective form, see section 1.1.1.3.1.1.4)). It is necessary to note here that the use of *na* is disappearing from the language and is being taken over by *nako* and *naye*.

When *naye* is used, the main verb is in its invariant form (i.e., verb stem + *ū)*. Although the main verb generally retains the invariant form (stem + *ū)* with nako (133), example (136) shows that the main verb may take the suffix *-lā*. In this case, the meaning of the negative sentence is different from that in (133). In this case, the speaker is merely expressing his/her opinion and not making any suggestion, and hence *naye* is blocked in this case (136). Consider the following examples.

(133) tū kām karū nako(s)
you work do do not

'Do not do the work.'

(134) tū kām karū naye
you work do do not

'You may not do the work.' (this is my opinion)

When the main verb is in the invariant form (stem + *ū), nako* is exclusively used for second person subjects (see (133) and (135)), while *naye* is used for all persons (137).

(135) *to kām karū nako(s)
he work do do not

'He (should) not do the work.'

(136) tyāne gharī dzāylā {nako / *naye}
he-ag home-loc do-inf-dat {should not / *may not}

'He should not go home.'

(137) {mī / tū / tyāne} kām karū {naye / *nako}
{I / you / he-ag} work do do not

'{I / you / he} may not do the work.' (this is my opinion)

On the basis of the above, it can be claimed that *nako* is the direct negative imperative while *naye* is the indirect (suggestive) negative imperative.

Two points need to be noted here: (a) in (136) and (137) the negative verb *nako* and *naye*, respectively, replace *hawa* in (111) - (114), and *pāhidʒe* in (115). Therefore, the difference in the degree of imperative (maintained in (111) - (114) vs. (115) is lost, and (b) the use of *naye* is blocked in this case.

The above discussion shows that the negative imperatives *nako* and *naye* replace the affirmative imperatives—direct, imperative, optative, suggestive, and obligative. Thus the negative imperatives show only two levels of force of command—the higher (with *nako*) and lower (with *naye*). Examples (138) and (139) illustrate that an alternate device (*na*) is used to negate the obligational imperatives (i.e., optative and obligatives). The use of *na* (instead of *nako/naye*) does not affect the degree of obligation in these sentences since the verb-form which is indicative of the degree of obligation (i.e., optative vs. obligative) is neither deleted nor is it changed. Therefore, in order to distinguish a negative optative from a negative obligative, *na* is used instead of *nako/naye* .

(138)	tyāne	he	kām	na	karāwe
	he-ag	this	work	neg	do-opt

'He may not do this work.'

(139)	tyāne	he	kām	na	kele	pāhidʒe
	he-ag	this	work	neg	do-perf-3sn	should-s

'He should not do the work.'

1.1.1.3.3 *Other devices of expressing imperatives*

The imperative 'meaning' or 'function' can be conveyed by a variety of other constructions. Some of these follow.

1.1.1.3.3.1 *Yes-no questions as imperatives*

Both positive and negative yes-no questions may be used to convey the meaning of a positive imperative:

(140)

malā	thoḍā	bhāt	deśīl	kā ?
I-dat	a little	rice	give-fut-2s	Q

'Will you give me a little rice ? (lit: 'Give me a little rice.')

(141)

koṭ	ghet	nāhīs	kā ?
coat	take	neg-2s	Q

'Aren't you taking a coat ?' (lit: 'Take a coat.')

1.1.1.3.3.2 *Question-word questions as imperatives*

Both positive and negative question-word questions may be used to convey imperatives:

(142)

adzūn	kā	ʤewlā	nāhīs ?
yet	why	eat-pst-3sm	neg-2s

'Why have (you) not eaten yet ? ('You should have eaten by now. Don't waste any more time; eat now'.)

(143)

tā̃mbyā	kuṭha	āhe?
water jug	where	is

'Where is the water-jug?' ('Bring the water-jug.')

1.1.1.3.3.3 *Statements as generic imperatives*

(144)

rodz	pepar	wātslā	tar	bātmī
everyday	newspaper	read-pst-3sm	then	news

kaḷte	
understand	

'If one reads the newspaper every day then one gets/receives the news.' ('You should read the newspaper every day.')

1.1.1.3.3.4 *Parallel statements as negative imperatives*

The imperative meaning may also be expressed by a pair of conjoined sentences where the first clause expresses a positive statement and the second clause conveys a warning. Although the first clause does not contain any overt marker of the conditional construction, it is interpreted as a condition.

(145)	tū	titsā	apamān	kar,	mī
	you	her	insult	do-imp-2s	I

punhā	tuʤhyāsī	kadhīhī	bolṇār	nāhī
again	you-dat	ever	talk-fut	neg

'You insult her, and I will never talk to you again.'

1.1.1.3.3.5 *Performatives as imperatives*

Performative verbs such as *winānti karṇe* 'request', *prārthanā karṇe* 'pray' may be used with a first person subject to express imperative meaning.

(146)	mī	tulā	ātā	gharī	dzāṇyātSī
	I	you-acc	now	home-loc	go-inf-poss-3sf

winānti	karto
request-3sf	do-pres-3sm

'I request you to go home now.' ('Please go home now.')

1.1.1.3.3.6 *Contingent forms as negative imperatives*

The meaning "don't you dare . . . " is conveyed by using the word *khabardār* in the beginning of the sentence. The verb takes the imperfect aspect and is followed by the conditional marker *tar* 'if'.

(147)	khabardār	tethe	gelās	tar!
	beware,	there	go-pst-2s	if

'Don't you dare go there!'

1.1.1.3.3.7 *Imprecation (cursing)*

The speech act of imprecation (cursing) is expressed with a verb of happening *hoṇe* with the optative suffix on it.

(148)	titsā	nāś	howo
	her	destruction	may happen

'May she be destroyed.' (lit: 'May her destruction happen.')

1.1.1.3.3.8 ***Statements*** *(implying advice)* ***as imperatives***

Two types of statements are used to convey imperative meaning (Pandharipande 1981a). The first kind is a statement in the present tense, with third person plural endings on the verb, marked by the obligatory absence of a subject as in (149). Use of the passive is also possible in this construction, as in (150).

(149)	lahān	mulānnā	asa	sārkha
	young	children-acc	like this	continuously
	rāgāwat	nāhīt		
	angry-pres	not-3pl		

'One should not continously get angry at young children' (lit: '(They) do not get continously angry at young children.')

Passive:

(150)	kaḍak	unhāt	aśī	kāma	kelī
	scorching	heat-loc	like this	jobs	do-pst-3pl.n
	dzāt	nāhīt			
	go-pass	not-3pl			

'One should not do such jobs in (such) scorching heat.' (lit: 'Such jobs are not done in (such) scorching heat.')

The statements in this construction are (according to the speaker) propositions of fact(s). The statements are indirect suggestions by the speaker to the addressee to abide by the conditions expressed in those statements, which according to the speaker hold universal validity. The second type of statement which conveys imperative meaning is a statement in the future tense with a second person subject as in (151). Semantically, this construction is similar to the construction with a tag-question, although a tag is typically absent, as in (151). This construction is more frequently used in Nagpuri Marathi than in other varieties of Marathi.

(151) tū udyā malā bheṭśīl
you tomorrow I-dat meet-fut-2s

'You will see me tomorrow.' (Won't you?)

1.1.1.3.3.9 *Questions as imperatives*

Yes-no questions as well as tag-questions are frequently used as requests/suggestions, as in (152) and (153).

(152) tū madzha ewhḍa kām kartes kā?
you I-poss-3sn this much work do-pres-2s Q

'Can you do this much work for me?' (lit: 'Do you do this much of my work?')

(153) tū malā madat karśīl na?
you I-dat help do-fut-2s tag

'You will help me, won't you?'

1.1.2 SUBORDINATE CLAUSES

1.1.2.1 *General markers of subordination*

Subordinate clauses have finite as well as non-finite verbs. There are three major types of subordinate clauses: (i) nominal, (ii) adjectival (relative), and (iii) adverbial. Subordinate clauses are generally marked by one or more of the following markers of subordination: (i) one of the quotative markers (i.e., *asa* or *mhaṇūn*) which may precede or follow the subordinate clause; (ii) the complementizer *kī* which precedes the subordinate clause; (iii) verb-modification: forms of verbal participles, infinitives, and gerunds. Marathi, compared to other Indo Aryan languages such as Hindi and Punjabi, has a much wider range of participles only (to exclusion of infinitives and gerunds), a property that is very similar to Dravidian languages (for discussion on the range of participles in one of the Dravidian langauges—Kannada, see Sridhar 1990); (iv) suffixes, and postpositions (e.g., *-āt* 'in', *-lā* 'for/to', *sāṭhī* 'for', *muḷe* 'because of', *pekṣā* 'compared to', *pāsūn* 'since', etc.) occurring clause-finally; (v) word order: non-finite subordinate clauses generally precede the main clause. However, when a subordinate clause is the focus, it occurs in the post-verbal position (i.e., after the main clause). The latter word order, however, is definitely marked. A finite clause with the complementizer *kī* follows the main clause; (vi) word order within a subordinate clause is relatively more rigid compared to main clauses—especially regarding the clause-final occurrence of the verb, i.e., in subordinate clauses, the verb must occur clause-finally.

Examples of subordinate clauses of different types with different markers of subordination are given below:

Nominal subordinate clause with quotative marker asa:

(154)	rām	udyā	yeīl	asa	madhū	mhaṇālā
	Ram	tomorrow	come-fut-3sm	quot	Madhu	say-pst-3sm

' "Ram will come tomorrow," thus Madhu said.'

Nominal subordinate clause with the complementizer *kī:*

(155)	malā	wāṭta	kī	ādz	pāūs
	I-dat	feel-pres-3sn	comp	today	rain

padel
fall-fut-3s

'I feel that it will rain today.' (lit: 'I feel that the rain will fall today.')

Subordinate clause with the infinitive (non-finite) verb form:

(156)	tyātsa	ugītsats	rāgāwaṇa	malā
	he-poss-3sn	without reason	get angry-inf	I-dat

āwḍat	nāhī
like-pres	not

'I do not like him getting angry without (any) reason.'

1.1.2.2 *Noun clauses*

1.1.2.2.1 *Marking of noun clauses*

Subordinate noun clauses can be finite as well as non-finite. There is no one single marker for all noun clauses. Finite noun clauses are marked by the complementizer *kī* or the quotative marker *asa/mhaṇūn* (cf. 1.1.1.1). Non-finite clauses are marked by verb modification as well as by various suffixes and postpositions. (See sections 1.1.2.2.2.2 and 1.1.2.2.2.4).

1.1.2.2.2 *Types of noun clauses*

Noun clauses can function as subject, direct object, or complement of nouns, verbs, copulas, or postpositions.

1.1.2.2.2.1 *Finite noun phrase complements*

Nouns such as *itStShā* 'desire', *bātmī* 'news', *wiśwās* 'faith', *samdzūt* 'understanding', etc. take noun clause complements. In such cases, the complement noun clause precedes the lexical noun, and it is immediately followed by one of the complementizers (homophonous with the demonstrative pronouns) such as *hī* 'this' (feminine singular), *hyā* 'these' (feminine plural), *hā* 'this' (masculine singular), *he* 'these' (masculine plural). In this case, the finite verb in the clause is inflected for agreement and tense as shown in (157).

(157)	to	gharī	ālā	hī	bātmī
	he	home-loc	come-pst-3sm	this-	news-3sf
	mī	aiklī			
	I-1sf	hear-pst-3sf			

'I heard the news that he came home.'

(158)	tyāne	dɔkṭar	whāwa	hī	(mādʒhī)
	he-ag	doctor	become-opt-3sn	this-3sf	(my-3sf)
	itStShā	āhe			
	desire/wish	is			

'It is my wish that he should be a doctor.' (lit: 'He may become a doctor is my wish/desire.')

A variant of the above construction without a lexical head is often encountered in cases such as the following:

(159) to	tulā	bheṭlā	(he)
he	you-dat	meet-pst-3sm	(this-3sn)

tsāŋgla	dzhāla
good-3sn	happen-pst-3sn

'It was good that he met you.'

1.1.2.2.2.2 *Non-finite noun phrase complements*

Non-finite noun phrase complements are of two types—one with a lexical head and the other without an overt lexical head. Complements with lexical heads usually have gerundive form of the verb followed by the possessive or other case suffix. The verb in complement noun phrases expresses a wide range of tense, aspect, mood, and polarity (negative and positive) distinctions. Also, the verb in the complement noun phrase may be followed by the auxiliary verb *as* 'to be'.

The non-finite complement noun phrase with the gerundive verb form is illustrated in (160) and (161). (161) also shows that when the main verb is marked with a non-perfective marker, verb *as* 'to be' (following the main verb) is used to bear the gerundive marker. For full details of the aspectual categories, see section 2.1.3.3 and sub-sections thereof.

(160) to	paḷūn	gelyatSī	afwā
he	run-conj.part	go-ger-poss-3sf	rumor-3sf

kharī	nāhī
true	not

'The rumor that he ran away is not true.'

(161) to	kām	karṇār	aslyātSī	bātmī
he	work	do-fut	be-ger-poss-3sf	news-3sf

kharī	āhe
true	is

'The news that (lit: of) he is going to do the work, is true.'

Another variant of this construction is shown in (162), in which the complement clause without an overt complementizer precedes the matrix clause and the verb in the complement clause is in its infinitive form.

(162)	tyātsa	wartsewar	rāgāwaṇa	tsāŋgla
	he-poss-3sn	again and again	angry-inf-	good-3sn

	nāhī
	neg

'It is not good that he gets angry very often.' (lit: 'His getting angry over and over again is not good.')

1.1.2.2.2.3 *Finite verbal complements*

There are two types of finite verbal complements. The first type is the quotative clause discussed in section 1.1.1.1. Recall that the matrix verb in such cases is generally a verb of saying. However, verbs expressing various mental states (e.g., *wāṭ* 'feel', *kaḷ* 'come to know', *witSār kar* 'think' (lit: 'do thinking')) also occur in this construction. The second type of finite verbal complement is discussed below.

1.1.2.2.2.3.1 *Complementizer kī construction*

Another construction with finite verbal complements is that with the complementizer *kī* 'that'. Marathi shares this construction with other Indo-Aryan languages such as Hindi, Punjabi, Gujarati, etc. The complementizer *kī* precedes the complement clause and the complement clause obligatorily follows the matrix clause. The verb in the complement clause is inflected for tense and/or aspect and agrees with the appropriate noun (i.e., subject, object, etc.) within the complement clause. This construction is similar to the English construction with the complementizer 'that' (e.g., John said that he would study in India).

(163)	mohan	mhaṇālā	kī	madhū
	Mohan	say-pst-3sm	comp	Madhu

	dillīla	gelā
	Delhi-to	go-pst-3sm

'Mohan said that Madhu went to Delhi.'

The matrix verbs in this construction are typically the verbs such as *sāŋg*, 'tell', *wāṭ* 'seem/feel', *kaḷ* 'come to know', *dis/pāh* 'see', *witSār kar* 'think' (lit: 'do thinking'), *bol* 'speak', *aik* 'hear', and *anumān kar* 'infer'.

Verbs of wanting (wish, desire) and verbs with complement clauses indicating the purpose of the action (expressed by the matrix verb) require the optative verb form in the complement clause as in (164).

(164)	mādʒhī	itStShā	āhe	kī	tyāne
	I-poss-3sf	desire/wish-3sf	aux	comp	he
	yāwe				
	come-opt-3sn				

'I want him to come.' (lit: 'My desire/wish is that he should come')

The non-identical subject of the complement clause blocks its reduction to a non-finite clause.

1.1.2.2.2.4 *Non-finite verbal complements*

Non-finite verbal complements are marked by: (i) verbs with either the infinitive suffix (*-ṇe*) or its variant *-āy* followed by the possessive suffix (*-tsV*) or dative suffix *-lā* or the instrumental suffix (*-ne*); (ii) verbs with the participial suffix *-ūn* (conjunctive participial suffix); (iii) verbs with the gerundive suffix *-lyā* (followed by a case-marker/postposition, etc.). Examples (165) - (170) illustrate non-finite noun phrase complements.

Infinitive:

(165)	titsa	oraḍṇa	tyālā	āwḍat	nāhī
	she-poss	shout-inf	he-dat	like-pres	neg

'He does not like her shouting.'

(166)	mohanne	dillilā	dzāytsa	ṭharawla
	Mohan-ag	Delhi-dat	go-inf-poss	decide-pst-sn

'Mohan decided to go to Delhi.'

Gerund + instrumental suffix *-ne:*

(167)	auṣadh	ghetlyāne	tulā	bara	wāṭel
	medicine	take-ger-inst	you-dat	all right	feel-fut-s

'You will feel all right if you take the medicine.' (lit: 'By taking medicine, you will feel fine.')

Gerund + dative suffix *-lā:*

(168)	tilā	gharī	gelyālā	barets	diwas
	she-dat	home-loc	go-ger-dat	many	day-3pl.m

dzhāle
happen-pst-3pl.m

'Many days have passed since she has gone home.'

Gerund + possessive suffix *tsa:*

(169)	mīnā	ālyātsa	malā	kaḷla
	Meena	come-ger-poss	I-dat	find (out)-pst-3sn

'I found out that Meena had arrived.' (lit: 'I found out about Meena's arrival.')

Conjunctive participle:

(170)	tyālā	gharī	dzāūn	barets	diwas
	he-dat	home-loc	go-conj.part	many	day-3pl.m

dzhāle
happen-pst-3pl.m

'Many days have passed since he has gone home.'

1.1.2.2.3 *Indirect statements*

Indirect statements are introduced by either the quotative marker (*asa* or *mhaṇūn*) or by the complementizer *kī*. Since both the quotative marker (*asa or mhaṇūn*) and the complementizer (*kī*) may also occur in direct statements, the distinction between direct and indirect statements depends on the choice between the first and the third person pronominal subject in the embedded clause and whether or not the matrix and the embedded subjects are coreferential. Examples (171a) and (172a) are direct statements since the first person pronominal subject of the embedded clause must be coreferential to the matrix subject (except in certain pragmatically marked contexts in which case the first person pronominal subject in the embedded clause may refer to the speaker). Examples (171) and (172) are indirect statements since the embedded clause has a third person pronominal subject (which may or may not be coreferential to the matrix subject).

(171)	umā$_i$	mhaṇte	kī	tilā $_{i/j}$	mumbaī
	Uma	say-pres-3sf	comp	she-dat	Bombay-3sf

āwaḍte
like-pres-3sf

'Uma$_i$ says that she$_{i/j}$ likes Bombay.'

(171a)	umā	mhaṇte	kī	malā	mumbaī
	Uma	say-pres-3sf	comp	I-dat	Bombay-3sf

āwaḍte
like-3sf-pres

'Uma says, "I like Bombay." '

(172)	tilā $_{i/j}$	mumbaī	āwaḍte	asa	umā$_i$
	she-dat	Bombay-3sf	like-pres-3sf	quot	Uma

mhaṇte
say-pres-3sf

'Uma$_i$ says that she$_{i/j}$ likes Bombay.' (lit: 'She likes Bombay, thus Uma says.')

(172a)	malā	mumbaī	āwaḍte	asa	umā
	I-dat	Bombay-3sf	like-pres-3sf	quot	Umā

mhaṇte
say-pres-3sf

'Uma says, "I like Bombay." '

A subordinate clause with a nominal head, as in (173) below, may also function as an indirect statement.

(173) tyāne āpla lagna
he-ag self-poss-3sn marriage-3sn

dzhālyātSī bātmī sāŋgitlī
happen-ger-poss-3sf news-3sf tell-pst-3sf

'He told the news of his marriage.' (lit: 'He told the news of having got married.')

Subjectless complements of verbs of 'hearsay' also function as indirect statements as shown in (174).

(174) { aikiwāt āhe / aikṇyāt (āla) āhe } kī to
hear-loc (came) aux comp he

gharūn paḷūn gelā
home-from run-conj.part go-pst-3sm

'It is heard that he ran away from home.'

1.1.2.2.4 *Indirect questions*

Indirect questions generally follow the same pattern as indirect statements, i.e., they precede the matrix clause and are followed by the quotative marker *asa* or *mhaṇūn* as in (175).

Indirect question:

(175) tū kuṭhe dzātos { mhaṇun / asa } to
you where go-2sm quot he

malā witSārat hotā
I-dat ask-prog be-pst-3sm

' "Where are you going ?", he was asking me.'

When indirect questions follow the matrix clause, they are preceded by the complementizer *kī* and involve pronominal substitution as in (175a).

Pronoun substitution in indirect question:

(175a)	to	malā	witSārat	hotā	kī	mī
	he	I-dat	ask-prog	be-pst-3sm	comp	I

	kuṭhe	dzāto	{mhaṇun / asa}
	where	go-pres-3sm	quot

'He was asking me where I was going.'

Notice that though both (175) and (175a) are indirect questions, the question-clause precedes the matrix clause in (175) and fọllows it in (175a). In (175) the question clause is followed by the quotative marker (*asa* or *mhaṇūn*). In (175a) the subject pronoun *tū* 'you' in the subordinate question-clause is replaced by *mī* 'I' and the complementizer *kī* precedes the subordinate question-clause. The quotative marker (*asa/mhaṇūn*) may optionally occur at sentence-final position in (175a).

Indirect questions may also occur in nominalized forms where the question-word in (176) is replaced by a lexical item as in (176a).

(176)	tū	tithe	kā	dzātes?	asa	tine
	you	there	why	go-2sf	quot	she-ag

	malā	witSārle
	I-dat	ask-pst-3sn

'She asked me, "Why do you go there?" '

Lexical substitution and the replacement of the question word:

(176a)	tine	mādʒhyā	tithe	dzāṇyātsa
	she-ag	I-poss	there	go-inf-poss-3sn

	kāraṇ	witSārla
	reason	ask-pst-3sn

'She asked (me) the reason of my going there.'

It is important to note here that if the embedded subject is a question-word, the distinction between direct and indirect question-word is neutralized as in (177) and (178), (i.e., both (177) as well as (178) can be treated as direct or indirect questions.)

(177)	tine	witSārla	kī	koṇ	ʤewāylā	yeīl
	she-ag	ask-pst-3sn	comp	who	eat-inf-dat	come-fut-3s

'She asked, "Who will come to dinner?" ' or 'She asked who would come to dinner.'

(178)	tyāne	witSārla	kī	kāy	bātmī	āhe
	he-ag	ask-pst-3sn	comp	what	news	is

'He asked, "What is the news?" ' or 'He asked what the news was.'

In addition to the above, the following type of questions in (179) and (180) (which apparently are not addressed to any particular person) are used as indirect questions.

(179)	mī	killyā	kuṭha	ṭhewlyā	astīl	bara?
	I	keys	where	keep-pst-3pl.f	be-fut-pl	indeed

'Where indeed might I have kept the keys?'

(180)	dilip	hyāweḷī	kuṭha	asel	bara?
	Dilip	this-time-loc	where	be-fut-3s	indeed

'Where indeed might Dilip be at this time?'

Questions such as those in (179) and (180) are used as an indirect and polite way to seek information. However, since the questions are not directly addressed to anyone in particular, the hearer has the choice to remain silent without offending the questioner.

1.1.2.2.5 *Indirect commands*

Indirect commands are conveyed by one of the following strategies: (i) by using an infinitive followed by the dative marker (-*lā*) embedded under a verb of saying as shown in (181).

(181) gharmālkāne ghar malā soḍāylā
(house-lord) house I-dat leave-inf-dat
landlord-ag

sāŋgitla āhe
say-pst-3sn aux

'The landlord has asked me to vacate the house.'

(ii) by using the complementizer *kī* and the obligative form of the verb as in (182).

(182) to mhaṇālā kī mī hī kāme
he say-pst-3sm comp I these jobs-3pl.n

karāylā hawīt
do-inf-dat need-3pl.n

'He said that I need to do these jobs.'

(iii) Some other possibilities of semantically indirect command have already been discussed in 1.1.1.3.1.1.2 - 1.1.1.3.1.1.6. Example of indirect command by using *asa* is given in (183).

(183) tū dzāylā hawa asa to bollā
you go-inf-dat should quot he say-pst-3sm

'He said, "You should go." '

1.1.2.2.6 - 1.1.2.2.6.7 *Non-finite noun clauses*

It has already been mentioned that Marathi has both types of noun clauses—finite and non-finite. Non-finite clauses typically lack subject-verb agreement. There are three types of non-finite clauses: (a) infinitive, (b) gerund, and (c) participle. Participles encode the full range of tense, aspect, voice, mood, and polarity (positive/negative) distinctions. Non-finite noun clauses of the infinitival type are formed by adding the suffix *-ṇe* to the verb stem. For example, by adding the suffix *-ṇe* to the verb stem *ye* 'come', the infinitive *yeṇe* 'to come' is derived. These derived infinitives lack subject-verb agreement and tense. The infinitival form is treated as a noun and the nominal suffixes/case-markers are added on to it. The infinitives are followed by the dative, possessive, instrumental, and locative suffixes/postpositions (For a detail discussion on infinitive see 2.1.3.5.1). Non-finite clauses of the gerundive type are formed by adding nominal suffixes/case-markers to the perfective form of the verb. Gerunds, similar to infinitives, are also followed by dative, possessive and instrumental suffixes/postpositions, for example: *bol* 'speak': *boll* (perf) + *ne* (instrumental); *bollyāne* 'because of/due to (the act of) speaking'.

Participial non-finite noun clauses are of the types shown below in (184a) - (184e). They primarily have adjectival function and, therefore, they can be called relative participles. The relative participles express the full range of aspect and/or tense, mood, and polarity distinctions.

(184a) Present / habitual participle: *dzā ṇārā* (mas-sg)
go-pres.part

'The one who goes'

(184b) Past / perfective: *ge lelā* (mas-sg)
go-perf.part

'The one who is gone'

(184c) Future: *dzāṇār aslelā* (mas-sg)
go-fut be-perf.part

'The one who is going to go (will go)'

(184d) Progressive: *dzāt aslelā* (mas-sg)
go-prog be-perf.part

'The one who is (in the process) of going'

(184e) Passive: *kelā gelelā* (mas-sg)
do-perf go-perf.part

'That which is done'

All of the above participles have their respective negative counterparts as given below:

(185a)	Present / habitual:	*na dzāṇāra* 'The one who does not go'
(185b)	Past / perfective:	*na gelelā* 'The one who has not gone'
(185c)	Future:	*dzāṇār naslelā* 'The one who will not go'
(185d)	Progressive:	*dzāt naslelā* 'The one who is not in the process of going'
(185e)	Passive:	*na kelā gelelā* 'That which is not done'

Though Marathi allows the use of relative participles (as discussed above) as well as relative clauses, speakers of Marathi show a clear preference for participles over finite relative clauses for communicating the same meaning. In this repect, thus, Marathi is closer to the Dravidian languages as opposed to the Indo-Aryan languages, since the speakers of the former show a preference for participles over relative clauses.

The non-finite markers are listed below. In the following list, V stands for any one of the vowels in parenthesis.

(186a) Infinitives -ṇV(e/a) optionally followed by case-suffixes/postpositions.

(186b)
- (i) present/habitual: ṇā-rV (a/ī/e/yā)
- (ii) perfective (past): -lV (ā/ī/e/a/e/ya)
- (iii) future: ṇār-asle-lV (ā/ī/e/a/e/yā)
- (iv) progressive: t-as-le-lV (ā/ī/e/a/e/yā)
- (v) passive: lā -gele-lV (ā/ī/e/a/e/yā)
- (vi) negative: V-aspect/tense marker + nas (negative) - le-lV (ā/ī/e/a/e/yā)

Similar to finite clauses, participles retain the markers of tense, aspect, voice, and mood.

Infinitive complements of certain classes of verbs require obligatory deletion of their subject under identity with the matrix subject or object.

Identical subject deletion:

(187)	malā	gharī	dzāṇyātSī	itStShā	āhe
	I-dat	home-loc	go-inf-poss-3sf	desire	is-3sf

'I wish to go home.' (lit: 'I have the desire to go home.')

(188)	mī	madhūlā	patra	lihāylā	sāŋgitla
	I	Madhu-dat	letter	write-inf-dat	tell-pst-3sn

'I asked Madhu to write a letter.'

The above-mentioned deletion in non-finite clauses is not different from the deletion of an identical subject, as well as subject-object deletion, in finite clauses. Consider the following examples which are finite counterparts of (187a) and (188a) respectively.

(187a)	mādʒhī	itStShā	āhe	kī	ātā	ø
	I-poss-sf	desire	is	comp	now	(I)
	gharī	dzāwa				
	home-loc	go-opt-sn				

'I wish that I may go home.' (lit: 'My wish is that I may go home now.')

(188a)	mī	madhūlā	sāŋgitla	kī	ø
	I	Madhu-dat	tell-pst-sn	comp	(Madhu)
	patra	lihī			
	letter	write-imp-2s			

'I told Madhu to write a letter.' (lit: 'I told Madhu that (he) write a letter.')

The word order in non-finite clauses is similar to their finite counterparts. However, inversions and other types of scrambling are quite infrequent and awkward (if not ungrammatical) in non-finite clauses. At this point, no systematic study is available of word-order in finite and non-finite clauses in Marathi. Non-finite clauses are generally verb-final. Neither the object nor the adverb can be moved to post-verbal position as shown in examples (189) and (190).

Movement of the direct object to post-verbal position:

(189)	*mī	madhūlā	lihāylā	patra	sāŋgitla
	I	Madhu-dat	write-inf-dat	letter	tell-pst-sn

'I told Madhu to write a letter.'

Movement of the adverb to post-verbal position:

(190)	*mī	madhūlā	dzāylā	gharī	sāŋgitla
	I	Madhu-dat	go-inf-dat	home-loc	tell-pst-sn

'I told Madhu to go home.'

However the indirect object of the matrix clause (and the subject of the non-finite clause) can be readily moved to post-verbal position as shown in (191).

(191)	mī	patra	lihāylā	sāŋgitla	madhūlā
	I	letter	write-inf-dat	tell-pst-sn	Madhu-dat

'I told Madhu to write a letter.'

1.1.2.3 *Adjective clauses (relative clauses)*

There are two types of adjective/relative clauses in Marathi—sentential relative clauses (SRC) and participial relative clauses (PRC). Although both types are equally acceptable to Marathi speakers, the frequency of PRC is decidedly higher than SRC in both the spoken and the written language. Both SRC and PRC show almost equal accessibility vis-a-vis noun phrases (Nps) in relativization. The choice between PRC and SRC is determined by stylistic and contextual factors. No systematic study is available on the factors which determine the choice between PRC and SRC in spoken or written language.

1.1.2.3.1 *Marking the sentential relative clause*

The sentential relative clause (SRC) is marked by the following: (a) the relative marker *dzo* 'who/which' which immediately precedes the relativized element; (b) the correlative marker *to* which is homophonous with the remote demonstrative/third person pronoun to and immediately precedes the head noun; (c) both relative and correlative markers agree with the head noun in gender and number; and (d) the deletion of the coreferential/identical Np in either main or the relative (subordinate) clause is optional. The direct and oblique forms of the relative as well as correlative markers are given below:

(192) Relative markers:

	Masculine	Feminine	Neuter
Direct:			
Singular	dzo	ʤī	ʤe/dze
Plural	ʤe	ʤyā	ʤī
Oblique			
Singular	ʤyā	ʤyā	ʤyā
Plural	ʤyān	ʤyān	ʤyān

(193) Correlative markers:

	Masculine	Feminine	Neuter
Direct:			
Singular	to	tī	te
Plural	te	tyā	tī
Oblique			
Singular	tyā	tyā	tyā
Plural	tyān	tyān	tyān

It is important to note that the relative marker *dzo* 'who/which' is not identical to the question word (*koṇ* 'who' *koṇta* 'which). When the head noun (relativized noun phrase) is not followed by a case-suffix or a postposition, it is in the direct case; however, when it is followed by a case-suffix or a postposition, it is in the oblique case.

In addition to the above, Marathi has a correlative marker *asā* (masculine singular) with its variants (*ase* (masculine plural), *aśī* (feminine singular), *aśā* (feminine plural), *ase* (neuter singular), *aśī* (neuter plural)). This marker is used when the head noun phrase has a hypothetical and not an actual referent as in (203a).

Further, the direct as well as the oblique forms of the correlative marker *to* (and its variants) are identical to the respective demonstrative pronouns in all genders and numbers.

Consider the following example of a sentential relative clause:

(194)	dzo	māṇūs	itha	śikawto	to	ø
	rel	man	here	teach-pres-3sm	cor	(man)

madzhā	bhāū	āhe
I-poss-3sm	brother	is

'The man who teaches here is my brother.'

The symbol ø indicates the site of the head Np prior to its deletion. Example (194) consists of two clauses which share an identical and coreferential noun phrase as shown in (194a) below.

(194a)	Relative clause:	māṇūs	itha	śikawto
		man	here	teach-pres-3sm

'The man teaches here.'

Main clause:	māṇūs	mādzhā	bhāū	āhe
	man	I-poss-sm	brother	is

'The man is my brother.'

The relative clause takes the relative marker *dzo* whereas the main clause takes the correlative marker *to.* When the relative clause precedes the main clause, the resulting sentence is (194). In this case, the second occurrence of *māṇūs* in the main clause is deleted under identity with the preceding occurrence of *māṇūs* in the relative clause.

The other variants of (194) are shown in (194b) - (194g). Sentences (194a) - (194g) differ from one another in terms of the deletion of the head Np, copying and deletion of relative/correlative markers, and the sequential order of the relative and the main clause.

Deletion of the identical Np in the relative clause:

(194b)	dzo ø	itha	śikawto	to	māṇūs
	rel ø	here	teach-pres-3sm	cor	man

mādzhā	bhāū	āhe
I-poss-sm	brother	is

'The man who teaches here is my brother.'

Deletion of the relative marker:

(194c)	ø	itha	śikawto	to	māṇūs
	ø	here	teach-pres-3sm	cor	man

mādzhā	bhāū	āhe
I-poss-sm	brother	is

'The man who teaches here is my brother.'

Main clause preceding the relative clause:

(194d)	to	māṇūs	mādzhā	bhāū	āhe
	cor	man	I-poss-sm	brother	is

dzo	ø	itha	śikawto
rel	ø	here	teaches

'The man who teaches here is my brother.'

Copying the correlative marker and insertion of the relative clause after the head noun:

(194e)	to	māṇūs	dzo	itha	śikawto
	cor	man	rel	here	teach-pres-3sm

to	mādzhā	bhāū	āhe
cor	poss-ms	brother	is

'The man who teaches here is my brother.'

Deletion of the head Np in the relative clause and copying the correlative:

(194f)	to	ø	dzo	itha	śikawto	to
	cor	ø	rel	here	teach-pres-3sm	cor

mā̃ṇūs	mā̃dzhā̃	bhā̃ū	ā̃he
man	I-poss-sm	brother	is

'The man who teaches here is my brother.'

Placement of the head Np after the correlative and relative markers followed by a copy of the correlative:

(194g)	to	dzo	mā̃ṇūs	itha	śikawto
	cor	rel	man	here	teach-pres-3sm

to	mā̃dzhā̃	bhā̃ū	ā̃he
cor	I-poss-sm	brother	is

'The man who teaches here is my brother.'

The participial relative clause is formed by (a) deleting the relativized noun phrase and (b) by changing the verb into its participial form by adding the appropriate suffixes (for examples of various participles, see 1.1.2.2.6).

1.1.2.3.2 *Restrictive and non-restrictive relative clauses*

Sentential relative clauses are usually restrictive, except those with proper nouns as their heads. Participial relative clauses in general are ambiguous between restrictive and non-restrictive interpretation (195) except in those cases when the head noun is either a proper noun or a definite noun phrase marked by the demonstrative adjective *hā̃* (or its variant) or *to* (or its variant), in which case it is always non-restrictive. Consider the various examples of the PRC in (195) - (197).

(195)	paḷūn	gelelā	mulgā	sāpḍlā
	run-conj.part	go-perf.part-sm	boy	find (intr)-pst-3sm

'The boy who had run away was found.'

(195) is ambiguous between restrictive and non-restrictive interpretation, depending upon the extralinguistic context of the utterance. If the speaker assumes that the hearer does not have knowledge of the boy who had run away, then (195) is interpreted as

a restrictive PRC. However, if the speaker assumes that the PRC contains old information (i.e., the boy had run away) and that the hearer knows about it, then the PRC 'the boy who ran away' has a non-restrictive interpretation. In contrast to the above, the PRC is unambiguously interpreted as non-restrictive if the head Np is a proper noun as in (196).

(196)	nāgpurlā	rāhṇārā	mādzhā	bhāū
	Nagpur-acc	live-pres-rel.part-3sm	I-poss-sm	brother

dilip	wakīl	āhe
Dilip	lawyer	is

'My brother Dilip, who lives in Nagpur, is a lawyer.'

In (197) since the head Np is preceded by the demonstrative pronoun *he* 'this', (197) is interpreted as a non-restrictive PRC.

(197)	ṭeblāwar	paḍlela	he	pustak
	table-on	lie-pst-rel.part-3sn	this-3sn	book-3sn

kuṇātsa	āhe
who-poss-	is

'Whose book is this which is lying on the table?'

Examples of restrictive and non-restrictive SRC are given below in (198) - (199).

Sentential relative clause with a restrictive interpretation:

(198)	dzo	mulgā	kāl	ālā	to
	rel	boy	yesterday	come-pst-3sm	cor

uttam	tSitrakār	āhe
excellent	painter	is

'The boy who had come yesterday is an excellent painter.'

Sentential non-restrictive relative clause with a proper noun as the head Np:

(199)	mohan	dzo	sāḷet	śikawto	to
	Mohan	rel	school-loc	teach-pres-3sm	cor

mādzhā	mitra	āhe
I-poss-sm	friend	is

'Mohan, who teaches in the school, is my friend.'

There is no formal distinction between restrictive and non-restrictive SRC. It has been claimed (Kelkar (1973:274-300)) that the two types of SRC differ from each other in terms of word order. If the SRC precedes the head Np, it conveys the restrictive interpretation as in (200). In contrast to this, if the relative clause follows the head Np (as in (201)), it is generally interpreted as non-restrictive.

(200)

dzo	ø	tudzhā	śedzārī	āhe	to
rel	ø	you-poss-sm	neighbor	is	cor

mādhzā	bhāū	gāyak	āhe
I-poss-sm	brother	singer	is

'My brother who is your neighbor is a singer.'

(201)

mādhzā	bhāū	dzo	tudzhā śedzārī	
I-poss-sm	brother	rel	you-poss-sm	neighbor

āhe	(to)	gāyak	āhe
is	(he)	singer	is

'My brother, who is your neighbor, is a singer.'

However, as Gupte (1975:83-93) correctly points out, the above claim is not fully justified since there are cases such as the following (pointed out by Junghare (1973)) where the restrictive interpretation is not blocked despite the fact that the SRC follows the head Np.

(202)

to	mādzhā	bhāū	dzo	mumbaīt
cor	I-poss-sm	brother	rel	Bombay-loc

rāhto	to	wakīl	āhe
live-pres-3sm	cor	lawyer	is

'My brother who lives in Bombay is a lawyer.'

Junghare (1973:253) ascribes the restrictive interpretation to the occurrence of the correlative pronoun *to* before the head Np. According to Junghare (1973), it is the presence or absence of the correlative before the head Np which is responsible for the restrictive or non-restrictive readings respectively. Gupte (1975) correctly argues against this claim by pointing out that the correlative may optionally occur in a non-restrictive clause (as in (202)) without blocking the restrictive interpretation of the sentence. According to Gupte, "Therefore, in the absence of any formal distinction between restrictive and non-restrictive relative clause, their semantic interpretation is determined by the nature and extent of the hearer's knowledge of the referent of the head Np." (Gupte 1975:80). It must be added here that the speaker's assumptions about the hearer's knowledge of the referent of the head Np (i.e, sociocultural factors such as conventions of referring to cousins and friends as brothers and sisters, etc.) are also relevant for determining the restrictive vs. non-restrictive interpretation of an SRC. Therefore, restricting the determinant to one single factor as Gupte does (i.e., hearer's knowledge about the referent of the head Np) is not adequate.

A close examination of relative clauses in Marathi shows that the restrictive vs. non-restrictive interpretation is determined on the basis of the degree to which the head Np is identifiable (through various clues). The higher the degree of identifiability, the higher the possibility of interpreting the relative clause as non-resrictive. In contrast to this, the lower the degree of identifiability of the referent of the head Np, the more likely the restrictive interpretation of the relative clause. This approach allows the blending of both linguistic as well as non-linguistic factors together for identifying the referent of a head Np. It also explains why in many cases (as pointed out by Junghare (1973)) when the head Np is preceded by a correlative, the relative clause is interpreted as non-restrictive while it is interpreted as restrictive when no correlative precedes it. Since the correlative *to* (and its variants) in Marathi is homophonous with the distant demonstrative, it is not surprising that the head Np preceded by the demonstrative has a more definite referent (202) compared to the Np which is not preceded by a correlative (201). Thus the relative clause in the former case is more likely to be interpreted as non-restrictive as opposed to the latter, which is more likely to be interpreted as restrictive. This assumption also explains why a relative clause with a proper noun as head Np is interpreted as non-restrictive, because proper nouns generally have a very high degree of restrictive identification of their referents. However, if more than one individual with the same proper name is known to the speaker and the hearer, then the use of a proper noun as a new Np will not prevent the relative clause from being interpreted as restrictive. There are kinship terms, such as mother and father, which are universally accepted as unambiguous identity markers of their referents. When these terms are head Nps, the relative clauses are interpreted as non-resrictive. Recall (200) where the relative clause precedes the head Np, yielding a non-restrictive interpretation, while (201) where the head Np precedes the relative clause yields a restrictive interpretation. The above assumption explains the role of word order on the basis of the identifiability of the referent of the head Np. When the head Np is placed before the relative clause, it is more likely to be interpreted as old information and thereby provides a high degree of identifiability of the head Np. In such cases, the relative clause is non-restrictive (201). On the other hand, the occurrence of the head Np after the relative clause indicates that the referent of the head Np is not identifiable or its identifiability without the relative clause is lower. Therefore, the relative clause is interpreted as restrictive (202).

It is also to be noted here that relative clauses with first and second person pronouns as their head Nps are non-restrictive while those with the third person pronoun as head Np are generally restrictive. PRC shares with SRC conditions regarding its restrictive vs. non-restrictive interpretation.

1.1.2.3.3 - 1.1.2.3.3.3 *Position of the head noun*

The head noun may precede or follow the relative clause. Non-restrictive sentential relative clauses generally follow the head noun, while restrictive relative clauses generally precede the head noun. Participial relative clauses generally precede the head noun when they are non-restrictive and follow it when they are restrictive.

1.1.2.3.4 - 1.1.2.3.4.4 *Form of the relativized element*

In sentential relativization the head Np (i.e., relativized element) undergoes deletion either in the relative or in the main clause. The occurrence of the head noun twice (in the main and the relative clause) is rare but possible as in (203).

(203)	dzo	māṇūs	tuʤhyā	śedzārī
	rel	man	you-poss	neighborhood-loc

rāhto	to	maṇūs	lekhak	āhe
live-pres-3sm	cor	man	writer	is

'The man who lives in your neighborhood is a writer.'

It has already been shown (examples (194) - (202)) that the head noun may be deleted in either the main or the relative clause. Examples (194b) - (194g) show that the strategy of copying the correlative marker in the main clause is also used. Although the copy of the correlative marker may replace the head noun in the main clause (194e) - (194g), it may be used along with the head Np (194f). In the participial relative clause, the relativized Np is always deleted. The following example (203a) involves the use of the correlative marker *aśī* to suggest the hypothetical referent of the head Np.

(203a)	malā	aśī	widyārthinī	hawī	kī	ʤī
	I-dat	cor	student	want	comp	rel

Hindī	bolte
Hindi	speak-3sf

'I want (such) a student who speaks Hindi.'

1.1.2.3.5 - 1.1.2.3.5.3 *Position of relativized element*

In sentential relative clauses, the relativized element usually does not move to the clause-initial position. However, it may be optionally moved to the initial position of the clause in order to bring the relativized element into focus. Consider the following examples (204) and (205). In (204), the relativized Np is in its original position, while in (205) it is moved to the clause-initial (focus) position.

(204)	madhū	ʤe	pustak	wātsto	āhe
	Madhu	rel	book-3sn	read-pres-prog	aux

te	mādzhe	āhe
cor	poss-3sn	is

'The book which Madhu is reading is mine.'

(205)	ʤe	pustak	madhū	wātsto	āhe
	rel	book-3sn	Madhu	read-pres-prog	aux
	te	mādzhe	āhe		
	cor	I-poss-3sn	is		

'The book which Madhu is reading is mine.'

Note that the relativized element in (204) and (205) is *pustak* 'book' which is the direct object (DO) in both sentences. In Marathi, the DO generally follows the subject. Thus when it is relativized in (204), its position (i.e., following the subject) remains unchanged. In contrast to this, in (205) it is moved to the clause-initial position. Although the English translation does not reflect the difference between (204) and (205), for Marathi speakers, the DO *pustak* 'book' is more in focus in (205) as compared to its counterpart in (204); that is, in (204), the speaker, by placing *Madhū* (subject) in the clause-initial position, emphasizes the significance of *Madhū* (the book which is being read by *Madhū* as opposed to anyone else). In contrast to this, in (205) where the relativized DO *pustak* is in the clause-initial position, there is less emphasis on *Madhū,* and, therefore, the interpretation of the sentence is 'the book which *Madhu* happens to be reading.' The emphasis in (205) is on *pustak* 'book'.

1.1.2.3.6 *Headless relative clauses*

Two types of headless relative clauses are observed in Marathi. The first type is exemplified in the PRC as in (206) where the assumed head Np is generic (e.g., 'the one', 'whosoever', etc.). The second type of relative clause is observed in (207) where an unspecified head Np is deleted. In both cases, the retention of the relativized head Np is possible but not preferred.

(206)	sāŋkaṭāt	madat	karṇārā	(māṇūs)
	calamity-loc	help	do-pres.part-sm	(person)
	kharā	mitra	asto	
	true	friend	be-hab-3sm	

'The person who helps in the time of calamity is a true friend.'

Note that in (206) the participle *madat karṇārā* 'helper' (lit: 'one who does help') assumes a generic Np such as *māṇūs* 'person'. Although the occurrence of māṇūs in (206) immediately following the participle is possible, the use of the participle without the overt head Np is more frequent and preferred. The second type of headless relative clause is exemplified in (207) where the head Np which is deleted is indefinite and its referent is not known to the speaker.

(207)	tyā ne	ʤe	(kāhī)	aikla	te	mī
	he-ag	rel	(something)	hear-pst-3sn	cor	I

aikla	nāhī
hear-pst-3sn	not

'I did not hear what (ever) he heard.'

(207) can easily be considered as conjoining of the following two simple sentences:

(207a)	tyāne	kāhī (tarī)	aikla
	he-ag	something	hear-pst-3sn

'He heard something.'

(207b)	mī	te	aikla	nāhī
	I	cor	hear-pst-3sn	not

'I did not hear that.'

Since the relativized element is indefinite (*kāhī* (*tarī*) 'something'), it is optionally deleted in the relative clause.

The non-occurrence of an unspecific head Np is observed in (208) (where a participial relative clause is used).

(208)	tsukītSyā	weḷī	ālelyā̃nnā
	wrong-poss	time-loc	come-pst.part-acc-3pl

mī	parat	pāṭhawla
I	back	send-pst-3sn

'I sent back (those) who had come at the wrong time.'

1.1.2.3.7 *Elements of the sentence that can be relativized*

1.1.2.3.7.1 *Constituents of the main clause that can be relativized*

1.1.2.3.7.1.1 *Constituents of the main clause that can be relativized by finite/sentential relative clauses*

Any constituent of a main clause, with the exception of the verb, can be relativized in a finite relative clause. Consider examples (209) - (215).

Relativization of subject:

(209)	to	mulgā	[dzo	ø	kāl	ālā]
	cor	boy	rel	ø	yesterday	come-pst-3sm

'The boy who came yesterday . . .'.

Relativization of direct object:

(210)	te	pustak	[ʤe	ø	mī	wātsla]
	cor	book-3sn	rel	ø	I	read-pst-3sn

'The book which I read . . .'

Relativization of indirect object:

(211)	tī	mulgī	[ʤi	ø	lā	mī	goṣṭa	sāŋgitlī]
	cor	girl	rel	ø	dat	I	story	tell-pst-3sf

'The girl whom I told the story'

Relativization of adjunct (object of purposive postposition):

(212)	tī	mulgī	[ʤi	ø	tSyā	sāṭhī	mī
	cor	girl	rel		poss-f-obl	for	I

ṭhā̃mblo . . .]
wait-pst-1sm

'The girl for whom I waited . . .'

Relativization of adjunct (object of locative postposition):

(213)	te	ghar	[ʤyā	ø	-t	mīnā	rāhte]
	cor	house	rel-obl	ø	loc	Meena	live-pres-3sf

'The house in which Meena lives . . .'

Relativization of possessor noun:

(214)	tī	mulgī	[ʤi	ø	tsa	gāṇa	mī
	cor	girl	rel	ø	poss-3sn	song	I

aikla]	
hear-pst-3sn	

'The girl whose song I heard . . . '

Relativization of object of comparison:

(215)	to	mulgā	[ʤyā	ø	tSyāhūn	rām
	rel	boy	rel	ø	than	Ram

lahān	āhe
young	is

'The boy than whom Ram is younger . . .'

1.1.2.3.7.1.2 *Constituents of the main clause that can be relativized by participial clauses*

Except object of the postposition, any constituent of the main clause can be relativized by a PRC. However, the deletion of the relativized noun phrase along with its case marking and postpositions creates ambiguity regarding grammatical relations within the relative clause. Hence, in such cases, the constraints on relativization are not grammatical but pragmatic. Since the relativized Np is absent and the site of deletion is not marked, it is only the pragmatics of the situation which indicates the thematic roles of the constituents. When the relative clause violates the expected selectional restrictions allowed by the pragmatics of the situation, the relative clause is perceived as ungrammatical.

The following examples (216) - (225) exemplify the possibilities of the PRC with regard to the accessibilty of noun phrases in the main clause.

Relativization of the subject:

(216)	gāṇa	mhaṇārī	mulgī	māʤhī	bahīṇ	āhe
	song	sing-pres.part-sf	girl	I-poss-sf	sister	is

'The girl who is singing is my sister.'

Relativization of the direct object:

(217)	tū	pāṭhawlelī	sāḍī	surekh	āhe
	you	send-pst.part-sf	saree-sf	beautiful	is

'The saree which you sent is beautiful.'

Relativization of Indirect object:

(218)	tyāne	āmāntraṇ patrikā	dilelī	sagḷī
	he-ag	invitation card	give-pst.part-pl	all-pl.n
	māṇsa	lagnālā	ālī	
	people-pl.m	wedding-that	come-pst-3pl.m	

'All the people whom he had sent (given) invitation cards, had come to the wedding.'

Relativization of a place adverbial:

(219)	mī	rāhāt	aslela	ghar	khūp
	I	live-pres	he-pst.part-sn	house-sn	very
	dzuna	āhe			
	old	is			

'The house in which I am living, is very old.'

Relativization of a time adverbial:

(220)	raghū	ʤanmalelyā	warṣī	waḍilā̃nnā
	Raghu	born-pst.part-obl	year-loc	father-dat
	khūp	paisā	miḷālā	
	a lot	money	receive-pst-sm	

'The father got a lot of money the year Raghu was born.'

Relativization of an instrumental phrase:

(221)	mī	patra	lihilelī	pensīl	māḍīwartSyā
	I	letter	write-pst.part-sf	pencil-sf	upstairs-of
	kapāṭāt	āhe			
	closet-loc	is			

'The pencil with which I wrote the letter is in the closet upstairs.'

Examples (222) - (225) show that the object of the postposition can not be relativized.

Relativization of an object of postposition: *sāṭhī* 'for'

(222)	*mī	(ø - sāṭhī)	āyuṣya	ghālawlelā	mulgā
	I	(ø - for)	life	spend-pst.part-sm	boy
	krutaghna	nighālā			
	thankless	turn out-pst-sm			

'The boy for whom I spent my life turned out to be thankless.'

Relativization of object of postposition: *pekṣā* 'compared to'

(223)	*he	ghar	(ø	tSyā	pekṣā)	lahān	aslelī
	this	house	ø	poss	than	small	be-pst.part-sf
	imārat						
	building-sf						

'The building which the house is smaller than . . '

Relativization of object of postposition: benefactive: *kaḍūn* 'by'

(224)	*tū	(ø	tSyā	kaḍūn)	pustak
	you		poss	by	book
	pāṭhawlelā		mānūs		
	send-pst.part-3sm		man		

'The man through whom you sent the book.'

Relativization of object of postposition: comitative: *barobar* 'with'

(225)	*tsor	(ø	tSyā	barobar)	ālelā
	thief		poss	with	come-pst.part-3sm
	polīs				
	policeman				

'The policeman who the thief came with'

1.1.2.3.7.2 *Constituents of the subordinate clause that can be relativized*

1.1.2.3.7.2.1 *Constituents of the subordinate clause that can be relativized by the sentential relative clause*

Any constituent of the subordinate clause may be relativized by the sentential relative clause. The following examples show (a) various types of subordinate clauses and (b) the range of constituents which can be relativized.

Relativization of the subject of a finite sentential complement:

(226)

ʤī	gāḍī	sũndar	āhe	asa	to
rel	car	beautiful	is	quot	he

mhaṇālā	tī	ṭoyoṭā	kresidā	āhe
say-pst-3sm	car	Toyota	Cressida	is

'The car which he said was beautiful, was a Toyota Cressida.'

Relativization of a direct object of a finite sentential complement:

(227)

ʤe	ghar	anūne	malā	sāŋgitle	kī
rel	house	Anu-ag	I-dat	tell-pst-3sn	comp

madhū-ne	wikle	te	pratāp	nagar	madhe
Madhu-ag	sell-pst-3sn	cor	Pratap	Nagar	in

āhe
is

'The house which Anu told me that Madhu sold is in Pratap Nagar.'

Relativization of an indirect object of a finite sentential complement of a noun:

(228)

ʤyā	mulīlā	hī	bātmī	kharī	āhe	kī
rel	girl-dat	this	news	true	is	comp

mī	paise	dile	tī	nāgpurlā	rāhte
I	money	give-pst-3pl.m	cor	Nagpur-dat	live-3sf

'The girl, to whom the news is true that I gave money, lives in Nagpur.'

Relativization of the object of the comparative postposition of a sentential complement:

(229)

ʤyā	mulāpekṣā	mohan	prāmāṇik	āhe
rel	boy-than	Mohan	honest	is

yāwar	madzhā	wiśwās	āhe	to	mulgā
this-on	I-poss-3sm	belief-3sm	is	cor	boy

ātā	ʤel	madhe	āhe
now	jail	in	is

'The boy who Mohan is more honest than in my belief, is now in jail.'

Relativization of the infinitival complement of a verb:

(230)

dzo	parwat	tsaḍhāylā	sagḷe	bhitāt	to
rel	mountain	climb-inf-dat	all	fear	cor

(parwat)	āmtSyā	gāwādzawaḷ	āhe
(mountain)	we-poss	town-close to	is

'The mountain which everyone is scared to climb is near our town.'

Relativization of object of a postposition/case marker in an adverb (participial) clause:

(231)

ʤyā	śetālā	dzātānā	āmhī	maitrīṇī	gāṇī
rel	farm-dat	go-adv.part	we	friends	songs

mhaṇat	asū	te	śet	babā̃nnī	wikla
sing-prog	be-pst-hab-1pl	cor	farm-3sn	father-ag	sell-pst-3sn

'Father sold the farm while going to which we friends used to sing songs.'

Relativization of the object of the gerundive subordinate clause:

(232)	dʒyā	gāwālā	madhū	gelyātsa	malā
	rel	town-dat	Madhu	go-pst-ger-poss-3sn	I-dat

kaḷla	te	gāw	phār	dūr	āhe
find-pst-	cor	town	very	far	is

'The town where I found out that Madhu went, is very far.'

1.1.2.3.7.2.2 *Constituents of subordinate clauses that can be relativized by the participial relative*

Although relativization of the constituents of the subordinate clause by using the participial relative clause is not as common as relativization by using a sentential relative clause, it is possible to use the SRC in the following contexts.

Relativizing into a finite sentential complement:

(233)	rām ne	pikle	āhet	sāŋgitlele
	Ram-ag	ripe	are	tell-pst.part-3pl.m

ā̃mbe	āmhī	wikat	ghetle
mangoes-3pl.m	we	buy	take-pst-3pl.m

'We bought the mangoes which Ram told us were ripe.'

Relativizing into the infinitival complement:

(234)	rām ne	sāŋgāylā	suruwāt	kelelī
	Ram-ag	tell-inf	beginning	do-pst.part-3sf

goṣṭa	manorandʒak	hotī
story-3sf	interesting	was-3sf

'The story which Ram began to tell was interesting.'

Relativizing into an adverbial conjunctive participle or a postpositional phrase:

(235)	kāl	mumbaīhūn	ālelyā	māṇsāne
	yesterday	Bombay-from	come-pst.part	man-ag

khūp	śodhūn	(/śodhlyāwar)	sāpaḍlela
a lot	search-conj.part	(/search-ger-on)	find-pst.part-3sn

ghar	ekā	tShoṭyā	gallīt	āhe
house	one	small	alley-loc	is

'The house which the man who came yesterday from Bombay found after searching a lot is in a small alley.'

Relativizing into an infinitival complement:

(236)	āīlā	ghaṭasphoṭ	dzhāleyā	mulītsa
	mother-dat	divorce	happen-pst.part-3s	daughter-poss-3sn

āwḍat	naslela	rātrī	uśīrā	parat	yeṇa
like	be-neg-perf.part	night-at	late	return	come-inf

māylekīntSyā	bhāṇḍaṇātsa	kāraṇ	dzhāla
mother-daughter-poss-3sn	conflict-poss-3sn	cause	become-pst-3sn

'The coming home late at night of the daughter who was divorced, which the mother did not like, became the cause of the conflict between the mother and the daughter.'

The reason for the infrequent occurrence of participial relatives in the case of relativization of the constituents of the subordinate clause is that (a) a participle requires obligatory deletion of the relativized noun phrase along with its case markers/postpositions and (b) there are no relative or correlative pronouns in a participial relative. This results in the loss of information about the thematic role/grammatical relation of the relativized noun (phrase), since the case markers/postpositions (either on the relativized noun or the relative or correlative pronouns) convey information about the thematic role of the relativized Np. For example in (237) the relativized noun *mulgā* is deleted in the subordinate clause. Therefore it is not clear whether the relativized Np is the recipient/subject of the fifteen thousand rupees or the indirect object in the matrix clause. Thus (237) can be interpreted as 'the boy who received fifteen thousand rupees' or as 'the boy whom *Ram* told that he *(Ram)* received fifteen thousand rupees.

Relativizing into a sentential complement of a noun:

(237) ??rām ne pandhrā hadzār rupaye miḷāle

??rām ne	pandhrā	hadzār	rupaye	miḷāle
Ram-ag	fifteen	thousand	rupees-3pl.m	receive-pst-3pl.m

aśī	bātmī	sāŋgitlelā	mulgā	itha	rāhto
comp	news	tell-pst.part-3sm	boy	here	live-pres-3sm

'The boy who Ram told the news that received fifteen thousand rupees lives here.'

Sentential relative clauses are preferred because they do not lead to the kinds of ambiguities mentioned above. Moreover, the position of the relative marker in the sentence is generally indicative of the thematic role of the relativized Np (237a). Thus, its absence results in the loss of a clue to the thematic role of the Np. For example, in (237), if the relativized Np is the recipient of the fifteen thousand rupees, the relative clause will be as follows:

(237a)

rām ne	ʤyālā	pandhrā	hadzār	rupaye
Ram-ag	rel-dat	fifteen	thousand	rupees

miḷāle	aśī	bātmī	sāŋgitlī	to
receive-pst-3pl.m	comp	news-3sf	tell-pst-3sf	cor

mulgā	itha	rāhto
boy	here	live-pres-3sm

'The boy who Ram told the news that received fifteen thousand rupees lives here.'

Note that in (237a) the relative marker *ʤyālā* has the dative case marker *-lā* which indicates the thematic role (recipient) of the deleted relativized Np. Moreover, the position of the relative pronoun *ʤyālā* immediately preceding the DO *pandhrā hadzār rupaye* 'fifteen thousand rupees', signals that the relativized Np is the recipient of the fifteen thousand rupees and that the relativized Np is a constituent of the subordinate clause. In contrast to this, if in (237) the relativized Np is the DO in the matrix clause, the sentential relative clause unambiguously indicates it by (a) an appropriate case marker/

postposition on the relative marker and (b) by the position of the relative marker in the sentence as illustrated in (237b).

(237b)	rām ne	pandharā	hadzār	rupaye	miḷāle
	Ram-ag	fifteen	thousand	rupees-3pl.m	receive-pst-3pl.m

aśī	bātmī	ʤyālā	sāŋgtlī	to
comp	news-3sf	rel-dat	tell-pst-3sf	cor

mulgā	itha	rāhto
boy	here	stay-3sm

'The boy whom Ram_i told that (he_i) received fifteen thousand rupees, lives here.'

1.1.2.3.7.3 *Elements of noun phrases that can be relativized*

Both possessor and possessed noun phrases can be relativized by using the sentential relative clause as in (238) and (239) respectively. In contrast to this, only the possessed and not the possessor noun phrase can be readily relativized by using the participial relative as in (240) and (241).

Relativization of the possessor Np (SRC):

(238)	ʤyātSyā	gharī	pārṭī	āhe	to	madzhā
	rel-poss	house-at	party	is	cor	my

mitra	āhe
friend	is

'He at whose house there is a party is my friend.'

Relativization of possessed Np (SRC):

(239)	tyātSī	ʤī	bahīṇ	amrāwatīlā
	he-poss-3sf	rel	sister	Amravati-dat

rāhte	tī	māʤhī	maitrīṇ	āhe
live-pres-3sf	cor	my-3sf	friend-3sf	is

'The sister of his who lives in Amravati is my friend.'

Relativization of possessor Np (PRC):

(240)	tudzha	māʤhyā	wāḍhdiwsālā	pāṭhawlela
	you-poss-3sn	my	birthday-at	send-pst.part-3sn

patra	khūp	āpulkītsa	āhe
letter-3sn	very	affectionate	is

'Your letter sent on my birthday is very affectionate.'

Relativization of possessor Np (PRC):

(241)	?/*gharāt	puṣkaḷ	māṇsa	asṇārā	mulgā
	house-loc	many	people	be-pres.part-3sm	boy

'The boy in whose house there are many people.'

Note that (241) is only marginally acceptable. However, when the possession is inalienable from the possessor, relativization of the possessor by using the strategy of the participial relative is readily acceptable as in (242).

Relativization of possessor Np (PRC):

(242)	ø	śarīrāt	tākad	aslelā	mulgā
		body-loc	strength	be-perf.part-3sm	boy

'The boy who has strength in (his) body'

Elements within a sentential relative clause can not be relativized either by using SRC or PRC as shown in (244) and (245).

Sentence containing a sentential relative clause:

(243)	ʤī	mulgī	ā̃mbe	wikte	tī	maʤhī
	rel	girl	mangoes	sell-pres-3sf	cor	my

śedzārīṇ	āhe
neighbor	is

'The girl who sells mangoes is my neighbor.'

Relativizing an element inside an SRC using the sentential strategy:

(244)	*[ʤe	ā̃mbe	[ʤī	mulgī	wikte]	tī
	rel	mangoes	rel	girl	sells	cor

māʤhī	śedzārīṇ	āhe]	goḍ	āhet
my	neighbor	is	sweet	are

'The mangoes which the girl who sells (them) is my neighbor are sweet.'

Relativizing an element inside SRC, using the participial strategy:

(245)	*[ʤī	mulgī	ø	wikte	tī	māʤhī	śedzārīṇ
	rel	girl	ø	sells	cor	my	neighbor

asṇāre]	ā̃mbe	goḍ	āhet
be-pres.part-3pl.n	mangoes-3pl.n	sweet	are

'The mangoes which the girl who sells them is my neighbor are sweet.'

However, a noun within a participial relative clause can be relativized by using the sentential relative clause as in (247).

Sentence with a participial relative clause:

(246)	[ā̃mbe	wikṇārī	mulgī	māʤhī
	mangoes	sell-pres.part-3sf	girl	my

śedzārīṇ	āhe
neighbor	is

'The girl who sells the mangoes is my neighbor.'

Relativizing an element inside PRC:

(247)	[ʤe	ā̃mbe	wikṇārī	mulgī	māʤhī
	rel	mangoes	sell-pres.part-	girl	my
				3sf	

śedzārīṇ	āhe]	te	(ā̃mbe)	goḍ	āhet
neighbor	is	cor	mangoes	sweet	are

'The mangoes which the girl who sells (them) is my neighbor are sweet.'

1.1.2.3.7.4 *Elements of postpositional phrases that can be relativized*

This has been discussed in sections 1.1.2.3.7.1.2 and 1.1.2.3.7.2.2.

1.1.2.3.7.5 *Elements of coordinate structures that can be relativized*

Elements within coordinate noun phrases may be relativized irrespective of the presence (248b) or absence (248a) of case-markers/postpositions after the noun phrases. This type of relativization is applicable to nonfinite constructions as well (249).

(248a)	ʤe	patra	āṇi	pen	ṭebalwar	hota
	rel	letter	and	pen	table-on	was

te	mī	lihila	hota
cor	I	write-pst-3sn	aux - be-pst-3sn

'The letter which and pen was on the table, was written by me' (lit: 'that I had written')

(248b)	ʤyālā	āṇi	malā	bakṣis	miḷāla
	rel-dat	and	I-dat	award-3sn	get-pst-3sn

to	mulgā	atiśay	huśār	āhe
cor	boy	extremely	intelligent	is

'The boy who and I got the award is extremely intelligent.'

(249)	dzyātsa	āṇi	mādzha	yeṇa
	rel-poss-3sn	and	I-poss-3sn	come-inf-3sn

tilā	āwaḍla	nāhī	to	mādzhā	bhāu	āhe
she-dat	like-pst-3sn	neg	cor	my	brother	is

'The one whose and my coming she did not like, is my brother.'

It should be noted here that in the case of lexically coordinated noun phrases, the relativized Np bearing ø marking for nominative cannot be deleted in the relative clause; rather, it is deleted in the matrix clause as in (248a). This restriction does not hold when the relativized noun phrase bears overt case-markers/postpositions for dative, possessive, etc. as in (248b). Moreover, repetition of the full relativized Np is more frequent in relativization of elements in coordinate structures as opposed to non-coordinate structures. This repetition is obligatory in those cases where the correlative pronoun may refer to either of the lexical nouns. The repetition of the relativized lexical noun unambiguously picks out the relativized lexical noun as in (250).

(250)	ʤe	patra	āṇi	pustak	ṭebalwar	āhe
	rel	letter-3sn	and	book-3sn	table-on	is

te	patra	mī	lihila	āhe
cor	letter-3sn	I	write-pst-3sn	is

'The letter which and a book is on the table is written by me.'

Note that in (250) the correlative pronoun may refer to *patra* 'letter' or *pustak* 'book'. However, the repetition of the noun *patra* 'letter' disambiguates the reference in (250).

Elements within coordinated verb phrases may not be relativized regardless of whether they are in the first (252) or the second conjunct (253).

Sentence containing conjoined verb phrases:

(251)	anūne	kapḍe	dhutle	āṇi
	Anu-ag	clothes	wash-pst-3pl.m	and

gāṇī	mhaṭlī
songs-3pl.n	sing-pst-3pl.n

'Anu washed clothes and sang songs.'

Relativization of an element inside the first conjunct of a coordinate verb phrase:

(252)	*anū ne	ʤe	kapḍe	dhutle	āṇi
	Anu-ag	rel	clothes	wash-pst-3pl.m	and

gāṇī	mhaṭlī	te	sutī	āhet
songs-3pl.n	sing-pst-3pl.n	cor	cotton	are

'The clothes which Anu washed and sang songs are (made) of cotton.'

Relativization of an element inside the second conjunct of a coordinate verb phrase:

(253)	*anū ne	kapḍe	dhutle	aṇi	ʤī
	Anu-ag	clothes	wash-pst-3pl.m	and	rel

gāṇī	mhaṭlī	tī	khūp	dzunī	hotī
songs-3pl.n	sing-pst-3pl.n	cor	very	old	were

'The songs which Anu washed clothes and sang were very old.'

Elements within coordinate sentences cannot be relativized as shown in (255) and (256).

Coordinate sentence (lexical):

(254)	madhū	sarkas	baghāylā	gelā	āṇī
	Madhu	circus	see-inf-dat	go-pst-3sm	and

rām	sinemā	baghāylā	gelā
Ram	movie	see-inf-dat	go-pst-3sm

'Madha went to see the circus and Ram went to see the movie.'

Relativization of an element inside a conjoined sentence (first conjunct):

(255)	*madhū	ʤī	sarkas	baghāylā	gelā	āṇi
	Madhu	rel	circus	see-inf-dat	go-pst-3sm	and

rām	sinemā	baghāylā	gelā	tī	nawīn
Ram	movie	see-inf-dat	go-pst-3sm	cor	new

hotī
was

'The circus which Madhu went to see and Ram went to see a movie, was new.'

Relativization of an element inside a conjoined sentence (second conjunct):

(256) *madhū sarkas baghāylā gelā āṇī rām
Madhu circus see-inf-dat go-pst-3sm and Ram

dzo sinemā baghāylā gelā to
rel movie see-inf-dat go-pst-3sm cor

agdī wāiṭ hotā
absolutely bad be-pst-3sm

'The movie, which Madhu went to see the circus and Ram went to, was absolutely bad.'

1.1.2.4 *Adverb clauses*

1.1.2.4.1 *Marking and position*

Adverb clauses are marked either by (a) the finite form of the verb or (b) by the non-finite form of the verb (i.e., participle, and infinitive forms). Finite adverb clauses can be placed pre- as well as post-sententially. However, the unmarked order of a non-finite adverbial clause is the preverbal position.

1.1.2.4.2 *Different types of adverb clauses*

1.1.2.4.2.1 *Adverb clauses of time*

Three types of adverb clauses are used to express a temporal sequence of actions in the subordinate (adverb) clause and the matrix clause respectively: (a) finite clauses with relative clause-like markers of time such as *dʒẽmwhā* 'when', *dʒyāweḷī* 'when (literally 'at the time')'; (b) participial (non-finite) adverbial constructions; and (c) infinitival constructions.

1.1.2.4.2.1.1 *Finite clauses with relative clause-like time markers*

Adverb clauses of time are generally signalled by time adverbials such as *dʒẽmwhā / dʒyāweḷī* 'when', *dʒẽmwhāpāsūn* 'since', *dzas* (followed by an appropriate vowel showing agreement with subject in number and gender) 'as soon as' *dzoparyanta* 'until'. Consider examples (257) - (260) below.

(257)

ʤẽmwhā	tī	ānandī	aste	(tẽmwhā)	tī	gāte
when	she	happy	is-3sf	(then)	she	sing-pres-3sf

'When she is happy, she sings.'

(258)

ʤẽmwhāpāsūn	to	itha	rāhāylā	lāglā
since	he	here	live-inf-dat	begin-pst-3sm

āmtSyā	āḷītlī	śā̃ntatā	naṣṭa	dzhālī
we-poss	neighborhood-adj-3sf	peace-3sf	disappear	happen-pst-3sf

'Since he began to live here, the peace in our neighborhood disappeared.'

(259)

dzasā	polīs	gharāt	śirlā
as soon as-sm	police-3sm	house-in	enter-pst-3sm

(tasā)	tsor	paḷūn	gelā
(then)	thief	run-conj.part	go-pst-3sm

'As soon as the police entered the house, the thief ran away.'

(260)

dzoparyā̃nta	to	parat	yet	nāhī
until	he	back	come	neg

(toparyā̃nta)	mī	ʤewṇār	nāhī
(till then)	I	eat-fut	neg

'Until he comes home, I will not eat.'

Notice that the time clauses in (257) - (260) are introduced by the adverbial markers *ʤẽmwhā* 'when' (257), *ʤẽmwhāpāsūn* 'since' (258), *dzas* + agreement vowel 'as soon as' (259), and *dzoparyā̃nta* 'until' (260). The adverb clauses in (257) - (259) have finite verbs which are inflected for tense and aspect. In (257) - (259) a temporal sequence of actions (in the past) is expressed, while in (260) the adverb clause expresses the time before which the action in the matrix clause will not take place in the future. Example (261) shows that the adverb clause with *ʤẽmwhā* can express simultaneous action as well.

(261)	ʤẽmwhā	to	dāḍhī	karto	(tẽmwhā)	to	gāto
	when	he	beard	do	(then)	he	sings

'When he shaves, he sings.'

The adverb clause of time generally precedes the matrix clause. However, it is possible to place it following the matrix clause as in (262).

(262)	tī	gāte	ʤẽmwhā	tī	ānandī	aste
	she	sings-3sf	when	she	happy	is-3sf

'She sings when she is happy.'

Generally, the adverb clause (relative) markers are not deleted. However, when the correlative markers are retained, their deletion is acceptable as in (263).

(263)	ø	to	gharī	ālā	tẽmwhā	rātra
	ø	he	home-loc	come-pst-3sm	then	night

dzhālī	hotī
happen-pst-3sf	be-pst-3sf

'When he came home, it had become dark (night).'

1.1.2.4.2.1.2 *Participial non-finite constructions*

Marathi uses a variety of non-finite participial adverb clauses of time which are of two types: (a) adverbial participles and (b) gerundive/infinitival constructions. The adverbial participles in (264) - (274) indicate the time at which the action expressed in the matrix clause takes place. The participles include both past (perfective) and present (progressive) aspect.

In (264) the progressive adverbial participle indicates simultaneity of actions/events denoted by the main verb and non-finite verb.

(264)	to	kām	kartānā	bolto
	he	work	do-pres.part	talk-pres-3sm
			(while doing)	

'While doing (his) work, he talks.'

In (265) another adverbial participle is used to indicate the period of time which separates the two events/actions denoted by the non-finite and finite verbs respectively. The participle is formed by adding the suffix *-ūn* to the verb stem. This participle is formally identical to the conjunctive participle. Also, the main verb in this type of construction is always *hoṇe* 'to be/ become'.

(265)

tyālā	itha	yeūn	khūp	diwas
he-dat	here	come-conj.part	many	day

dzhāle
happen-pst-3pl.m

'It has been many days since he has come.'

A conjunctive participle is used to indicate a temporal sequence of actions and the action expressed by the conjunctive participle precedes the action in the matrix clause as in (266).

(266)

madhū ne	pustaka	utslūn	kapāṭāt	ṭhewlī
Madhu-ag	book-3pl.n	pick up-conj.part	cupboard-loc	put-pst-3pl.n

'Having picked up the books, Madhu put (them) in the cupboard.' (i.e., Madhu first picked up the books and then he put them in the cupboard.)

The past (perfective) participle is used to indicate time of the occurrence of the action in the matrix clause.

(267)

rām	mumbaīlā	gelā	astānā
Ram	Bombay-dat	go-pst-3sm	be-part

tyātSyā	gharī	tsorī	dzhālī
he-poss	home-loc	theft-3sf	happen-pst-3sf

'When Ram had gone to Bombay his house was robbed.' (lit: 'When Ram had gone to Bombay, a theft occurred (at his house)).'

The reduplicated adverbial participial is used to indicate that the action expressed by the adverbial participle and the action expressed in the matrix clause are performed simultaneously as in (268).

(268)	pustak	wātstā	wātstā	to	śeŋgdāṇe
	book	read-part	read-part	he	peanuts
	khāt	hotā			
	eat-prog	be-3sm			

'While reading the book, he was eating peanuts.'

There is a set of gerundive constructions in Marathi which serve as time adverbial constructions. These are formed by adding a postposition or a suffix to the gerundive form of the verb. The verb remains invariant in its gerundive form.

gerund + dative suffix:

(269)	tyālā	itha	ālyālā	ek	mahinā	dzhālā
	he-dat	here	come-ger-dat	one	month	happen-pst-3sm

'It has been a month since he came.' (lit: 'A month has happened since he came.')

gerund + postposition/suffix *pāsūn* 'since':

(270)	itha	ālyāpāsūn	to	agdī	khūṣ	āhe
	here	come-ger-abl-since	he	absolutely	happy	is

'He is absolutely happy since he came here.'

(271)	kām	kelyāwar	to	gharī	gelā
	work	do-ger-after	he	home-loc	go-pst-3sm

'After doing the work, he went home.'

gerund + postposition *barobar* 'as soon as':

(272)	gharī	ālyābarobar	āī	mādʒhyāśī
	home-loc	come-ger-as soon as	mother	I-dat

kheḷte
play-pres-3sf

'Mother plays with me as soon as she comes home.'

It is to be noted here that in (269) - (272) the subject of the adverbial clause is coreferential and identical to the subject in the corresponding matrix clause and therefore is deleted in the adverbial clause. However, this coreferentiality or identity of the subjects is not necessary, as shown in (270a)-(272a). Note that the subject of the adverbial clause is not coreferential or identical to the subject in the corresponding matrix clause and as a result the subject of the adverbial clause is not deleted in (270a) - (272a).

(270a) mohan itha ālyāpāsūn sudhā agdī
Mohan here come-ger-since Sudha absolutely

khūṣ āhe
happy is

'Sudha is absolutely happy since Mohan came here.'

(271a) mīnā gharī ālyāwar mī dʒewto
Meena home-loc come-ger-after I eat-pres-1sm

'I eat after Meena comes home.'

(272a) bābā gharī ālyābarobar mula
father home-loc come-ger-as soon as children

śā̃nta dzhālī
quiet become-pst-3pl.n

'The children became quiet as soon as the father came home.'

The following set of adverbial constructions in Marathi are interesting because they involve invariant ('frozen') forms of the verb followed by a suffix (homophonous with past habitual suffix or progressive suffix) and a postposition or a noun (indicating time). It is important to note here that the aspectual meaning of the suffixes is totally lost in these constructions. Since these adverbial forms are derived from verbs, they are called participles in traditional grammars such as Damle (1966 [1911]).

verb stem + *-ī* (homophonous with the past habitual suffix) + *paryãnta* 'till':

(273)	anū	parat	yeīparyãnta	mī	dzhopṇār	nāhī
	Anu	back	come-till	I	sleep-fut	neg

'I will not sleep till Anu comes home.'

verb stem + progressive suffix *-tā* + *ts* 'as soon as':

(274)	to	gharāt	yetāts	tsor	paḷūn	gelā
	he	home-loc	come-as soon as	thief	run	go-pst-3sm

'As soon as he entered the house, the thief ran away.'

verb stem + *-t(ā)* + *kṣaṇī(ts)* 'at the very moment':

(275)	tyāne	dār	ughaḍtā	kṣaṇīts	tī	paḷūn
	he-ag	door	open	at the moment	she	run

geli
go-pst-3sf

'The moment he opened the door, she ran away.'

1.1.2.4.2.2 *Manner*

Manner clauses are structurally similar to adverbial relative clauses and participles expressing simultaneous actions. Clauses which express simultaneity of actions are generally ambiguous because they allow for manner readings as well.

1.1.2.4.2.2.1 *Relative clause-like manner adverbial clauses*

The relative clause-like marker *dzasa* 'as' (and its variants) is used to express the manner reading as in (276).

(276)	to	dzasa	sāŋgel	tasa	kām	kar
	he	as-rel	tell-fut-3sm	the same way-cor	work	do-imp-2s

'Do the work as he tells (you to do).'

1.1.2.4.2.2.2 *Participial constructions as manner adverbials*

Participles express the manner reading when they express simultaneous actions. Consider the following examples. In (277) the participle *gāṇī mhaṇat* 'singing' expresses the manner adverbial meaning.

(277)	to	gāṇī	mhaṇat	kām	karto
	he	songs	sing-prog.part	work	do-pres-3sm

'He does the work (while) singing.' (lit: 'He does the work singingly.')

In (278) the conjuctive participle expresses the manner adverbial reading.

(278)	to	hasūn	mhaṇālā
	he	laugh-conj.part	say-pst-3sm

'Smiling, he said' (lit: 'Laughingly, he said')

Negative manner is expressed by the use of the negative participle as in (279) and (280).

(279)	to	na	boltā	kām	karto
	he	neg	talk-prog.part	work	do-pres-3sm

'He does the work without talking.'

(280)	mādzha	bolṇa	na	samdzūn	to	mhaṇālā
	my-3sn	speech	neg	understand-conj.part	he	say-pst-3ms

'Without understanding my speech, he said ....'

1.1.2.4.2.3 *Purpose*

There are two ways of expressing purpose: (i) by using an infinitive clause and (ii) by using the quotative structure (along with the quotative marker *mhaṇūn).*

An infinitive clause followed by the postpositions *sāṭhī* and *kartā* 'for' can be used to express purpose. However, this usage is mostly restricted to formal contexts only (e.g., formal lectures, written expository discourse, etc.). The preferred form is the infinitive followed by the dative suffix *-lā*. Examples (281) and (282) illustrate the first and the second type respectively.

(281)	mī	mohanlā	bheṭṇyā {sāṭhī / kartā}
	I	Mohan-acc	meet-inf-for

mumbaīlā	gelo
Bombay-dat	go-pst-3sm

'I went to Bombay to meet Mohan.'

Infinitive + *-lā*:

(282)	mī	mohanlā	bheṭāylā	mumbaīlā	gelo
	I	Mohan-acc	meet-dat	Bombay-dat	go-pst-1sm

'I went to Bombay to meet Mohan.'

(282a)	mī	rāhullā	śikṇyāsāṭhī	bāsṭanlā	pāṭhawla
	I	Rahul-acc	study-for	Boston-to	send-pst-3sn

'I sent Rahul to Boston to study.'

The following example (283) shows the use of the quotative construction to express purpose. In this construction, the embedded clause is optative.

(283)	anūlā	bheṭāwe	mhaṇūn	mī	śikāgolā	gelo
	Anu-acc	meet-opt	quot	I	Chicago-dat	go-pst-1sm

'I went to Chicago to meet Anu.' (lit: "Let me meet Anu", saying (this) I went to Chicago.')

Additionally, a yes-no question may be used before the quotative to express purpose as in (284).

(284)	mītā	gharāt	āhe	kā	mhaṇūn	to
	Meeta	home-loc	is	Q	quot	he

ḍokāwūn	pāhāt	hotā
peep	see-prog	be-pst-3sm

'He was peeping to see if Meeta was home.'

When the subject of the embedded clause is different from the subject or the object of the matrix clause, the quotative is the only choice for expressing purpose as in (285). The infinitive construction requires that (a) the subjects of the matrix and the embedded clauses be coreferential (as in (281) and (282)) or (b) the object of the matrix clause and the subject of the embedded clause be coreferential (as in (282a)).

(285)	mula	ānandāt	rāhāwī	mhaṇūn	mī
	children	happiness-loc	live-opt-pl	quot	I

ghar	bā̃dhla
house-3sn	build-pst-3sn

'I built the house (so that) the children may live happily.'

1.1.2.4.2.4 *Cause*

Cause is generally expressed by the following: (i) finite clauses marked by *kāraṇ (kī)* 'because', or by the quotative *mhaṇūn* ; (ii) gerund; (iii) infinitive; (iv) participles; and (v) conjoining particle *āṇi* 'and'.

1.1.2.4.2.4.1 *Finite clause marked with kāraṇ 'because'*

Cause and effect sentences are juxtaposed and conjoined by the lexical conjoiner *kāraṇ* 'because' as in (286).

(286)	mītā	kāmāwar	ālī	nāhī	kāraṇ
	Meeta	work-on	come-pst-3sf	neg	because

tī	ādzārī	āhe
she	sick	is

'Meeta did not come to work because she is sick.'

Cause and effect clauses can also be conjoined by the quotative *mhaṇūn*. In this case, the clause of cause precedes the clause of effect and the quotative follows the clause of cause as in (287).

(287)	mulgī	gharī	ālī	mhaṇūn
	daughter	home-loc	come-pst-3sf	quot

āīlā	ānanda	dzhālā
mother-dat	happiness	happen-pst-3sm

'The daughter came home, therefore, the mother became happy.'

1.1.2.4.2.4.2 *Gerund*

Gerunds followed by instrumental case markers or postpositions such as *-ne* and *-muḷe* are frequently used to express cause. The gerunds are marked by the marker *-l,* preceded by aspectual/tense markers such as *-l* (perfective) or *-t* (progressive), or future *-ṇār* (followed by the auxiliary as 'to be'). Consider examples (288a) - (288c).

(288a)	madhū	ālyāne	/ ālyāmuḷe
	Madhu	come-ger-inst	/ come-ger-pp(because)

malā	khūp	ānanda	dzhālā
I-dat	a lot	happiness-3sm	happen-pst-3sm

'I became very happy because Madhu came.'

(288b)	auṣadh	ghet	rāhilyāne	/rāhilyāmuḷe
	medicine	take-prog	keep-ger-inst	keep-ger-pp

tyālā	bare	wāṭle
he-dat	good	feel-pst-3sn

'By taking the medicine continuously, he felt/got well.'

(288c)	gāḍī	yeṇār	aslyāne/aṣlyāmuḷe	rastā
	train	come-fut	be-ger-inst/be-ger-pp	train

banda	dzhālā	āhe
close	happen-pst-3sm	is

'The road is closed because the train is going to come.'

1.1.2.4.2.4.3 *Infinitive*

The infinitive + instrumental suffix/postposition is another device used to express cause as in (289).

(289)	(tyātSyā)	satat	prayatna
	(his)	continuously	effort

karṇyāne/karṇyāmuḷe	tyālā	yaś	miḷāla
do-inf-inst/do-inf-pp	he-dat	success	get-pst-3sn

'He became successful because of (his) continuous efforts' (lit: 'Because of (his) continuously trying, he became successful').

1.1.2.4.2.4.4 *Participles*

Conjunctive and progressive (reduplicated) participles are often used to express cause as in (290) and (291) respectively.

(290)	satat	tsālūn	to	thaklā
	continuously	walk-conj.part	he	tire-pst-3sm

'After walking continuously, he became tired.'

(291)	mī	diwasbhar	boltā	boltā
	I	day-whole	talk-prog.part	talk-prog.part

thakūn	dzāte
tire-conj.part	go-pres-1sf

'I get tired because of talking the whole day.'

1.1.2.4.2.4.5 *Conjunctive particle āṇi 'and'*

When two sentences involve a temporal sequence of the events expressed in them and are conjoined by *āṇi* 'and', they can be interpreted as cause and effect clauses respectively in that sequence as in (292).

(292)	yā	warṣī	pāūs	tsāŋglā	dzhālā	āṇi
	this	year-loc	rain	good	happen-pst-3sm	and

pīk	tsāŋgla	āla
crop-3sn	good-3sn	come-pst-3sn

'This year the rainfall was good and (there was) a good crop.' (Because of the good rainfall, there was a good crop this year.)

1.1.2.4.2.5 *Conditional and concessive clauses*

1.1.2.4.2.5.1 *Conditional clauses*

Condition clauses are marked by (i) the conjunction *dzar* 'if' - *tar* 'then', (ii) gerund + conditional suffix *-s*, and (iii) gerund + postposition *sārkhe*. The most productive device for expressing condition is the conjunction *'dzar - tar'* (if - then) as in (293a).

(293a)	dzar	tyāne	abhyās	kelā	tar	to
	if	he-ag	studying	do-pst-3sm	then	he

pās	hoīl
pass	be-fut-3s

'If he studies, he will pass (the exam).'

It is to be noted here that the occurrence of *dzar* 'if' is optional in conditional clauses such as (293a). The verb in the conditional clause may alternately be in the future tense as in (293b).

(293b)	dzar	to	abhyās	karel/karīl	tar	to
	if	he	studying	do-fut-3s	then	he

pās	hoīl
pass	be-fut-3s

'If he will study, he will pass'

A gerund is also used to express a condition. In this case the gerund (in various aspects/tenses) is followed by the suffix *-s* as in (294a) - (294c).

gerund:

(294a)	mohan	ālyās	madhū	paṇ	yeīl
	Mohan	come-ger-if	Madhu	also	come-fut-3s

'If Mohan comes, Madhu will come too.'

progressive + gerund:

(294b)	to	bolat	aslyās	mī	tSūp	rāhte
	he	talk-prog	be-ger-if	I	quiet	keep-pres-3sf

'If he is talking, I keep quiet.'

future + gerund:

(294c)	mītā	itha	yeṇār	aslyās	mī	itha
	Meeta	here	come-fut	be-ger-if	I	here

thā̃mbīn
wait-fut-1s

'If Meeta is going to come here, I will wait.'

A gerund + *sārkhe* (and its variants) is used to express a specific type of condition in a particular context. The gerund + *sārkhe* is used to express a condition which is already fulfilled at the time of the speech act. Thus gerund + *sārkhe* means, 'since X (action) has taken place'. In the rest of the sentence, the speaker expresses the hope that the expected result will occur as well. Example (295) illustrates this construction.

(295)	śikāgolā	gelyāsārkhā	manūlā	bheṭśīl
	Chicago-dat	go-ger- since	Manu-acc	meet-fut-2s

tar	bara	hoīl
then	fine	be-fut-3sn

'Since you are going to Chicago, it will be good if you meet Manu.'

Negative conditions are formed by using an appropriate form of (i) the negative verbs *nas/nāhī* following the main verb, and (ii) the conditional particles *dzar - tar* 'if - then'. Examples (296) - (298) illustrate this construction.

(296)	dzar	to	udyāparyānta	ālā	nāhī
	if	he	tomorrow-till	come-pst-3sm	neg

tar	mī	tyātSyāsāṭhī	thā̃mbṇār	nāhī
then	I	he - for	wait-fut	neg

'If he does not come by tomorrow, then I will not wait for him.'

(297)	dzar	to	ālā	nastā	tar
	if	he	come-pst-3sm	neg-pres-3sm	then

mī	sinemālā	gelo	nasto
I	movie-acc	go-pst-1sm	neg-1sm

'Had he not come, I would not have gone to the movie.'

(298)	dzar	to	udyā	yeṇār	nasel
	if	he	tomorrow	come-fut	neg-3s

tar	mī	paṇ	yeṇār	nāhī
then	I	also	come-fut	neg

'If he will not come tomorrow, then I will not come either.'

Another construction which expresses a stronger form of the negative conditional is illustrated in (299) where the negative polarity item *śiwāy* 'unless' is used. The meaning of the construction can be paraphrased in English as, 'unless X happens Y will not happen.' In this case, the negative verb *nāhī* (and its variants) occur in the main clause. The negative polarity item *śiwāy* 'unless' is attached to the gerundive form of the verb.

(299)	tyāne	witSārlyāśiwāy	mī	tyālā	hī
	he-ag	ask-ger-unless	I	he-dat	this

māhitī	deṇār	nāhī
information	give-fut	neg

'Unless he asks (me), I will not give this information to him.'

Counterfactual conditionals are formed by using (i) the past (perfective) aspect of the main verbs in the subordinate as well as main clause respectively; (ii) in both clauses the main verbs are followed by the auxiliary verb *as* 'to be', which is followed by the suffix *-tā* (and its variants); (iii) the negative form of the auxiliary (present tense) *as* (i.e., *-nas*) can not occur in both clauses, but it can occur either in the main or in the subordinate clause. Example (300) illustrates this construction.

(300)	amit	malā	bheṭlā	astā	tar	mī
	Amit	I-dat	meet-pst-3sm	be-cond-3sm	then	I

tyālā	hī	bātmī	sāŋgitlī	astī
he-dat	this	news-3sf	tell-pst-3sf	be-cond-3sf

'Had I met Amit, I would have told him this news.' (but I did not meet Amit and therefore I did not tell him the news either.)

On the basis of the above discussion, the tense/aspect possibilities and their combinations in conditional clauses can be summarized as follows:
(i) in the *dzar - tar* type conditional clauses, the verb in the conditional clause is either in the perfective aspect/past tense (293), or in future tense (293a). The verb in the main clause in both cases is in the future tense.
(ii) a conditional clause with a gerund is of the following four types:
(a) the verb in the conditional clause is a gerund followed by the suffix -s and the verb in the main clause is in the future tense (294a),

(b) the verb in the conditional clause is in the progressive aspect followed by a gerundive form of the verb *-as* 'be' with the suffix -s (294b),
(c) the verb in the conditional clause is in the future tense and it is followed by the gerundive form of the verb *-as* with the suffix -s (294c). The verb in the main clause is in the future tense, and,
(d) the verb in the conditional clause is in the gerundive form followed by *sārkhe* and the verb in the main clause is in the future tense (295).

In the negative conditional clauses, the possible combinations of tense/aspect of the verbs in the conditional and main clauses are given below:
(i) the verb in the conditional clause is in the past tense followed by the negative verb *nāhī* and the verb in the main clause is in the future tense (296).
(ii) the verb in the conditional clause is in the past tense followed by the negative verb *nas* with the present tense ending and the verb in the main clause is also in the past tense followed by the negative verb *nas* with the present tense ending. Both the main and the negative verbs agree with their respective subjects in each clause (297).
(iii) the main verb in the conditional clause is in future tense followed by the negative verb *nas* with future ending and the verb in the main clause is also in the future tense and it is followed by the negative verb *nāhī*. It should be noted here that in the examples in (296) - (298), the main clause may be affirmative even though the subordinate clause is negative.
(iv) when the lexical negative polarity item *śiwāy* is used in the conditional clause, the verb in the conditional clause is in its gerundive form followed by *śiwāy* 'unless' and the verb in the main clause is in the future tense followed by the negative verb *nāhī* (299).

1.1.2.4.2.5.2 *Concessive clauses*

Concessive clauses are generally formed by using the concessive markers *dzarī* 'although' (immediately preceding the concessive clause) and *tarī* (preceding the main clause). The main verb in the concessive clause is inflected for aspect/tense and is followed by the auxiliary *-as* 'to be', which takes the marker *-la* (and its variants). It is the auxiliary (and not the main verb) which agrees with the subject of the clause. The main clause does not have any specific markings (except for the concessive marker preceding it). Consider (301).

(301)	dzarī	tyāne	malā	bolāwla	asla
	although	he-ag	I-acc	invite-pst-3sn	be-conc

tarī	mī	dzāṇār	nāhī
even then	I	go-fut	neg

'Although he has invited me, I will not go.'

Examples (302) and (303) show that concessive clauses can be formed without the auxiliary *-as* 'to be'. In this case the concessive clause as well as the main clause are marked with *dzarī* and *tarī* respectively and the verb in the concessive clause is either in the perfective/past form (302) or is inflected with aspect and tense markers (303).

(302)	dzarī	umāne	āgraha	kelā
	even if	Uma-ag	insistence	do-pst-3sm

tarī	mī	yeṇār	nāhī
even then	I	come-fut	neg

'Even if Uma insists, I will not come.'

(303)	dzarī	tyātSyādzawaḷ	khūp	paise	nāhīt
	although	he-poss	lot	money	neg

tarī	to	khartSik	āhe
even then	he	spendthrift	is

Although he does not have a lot of money, he is a spendthrift.'

1.1.2.4.2.6 *Results*

Result clauses are not formally different from clauses of cause (as in 1.1.2.4.2.4). Additionally, result clauses (main clauses) may be introduced by *mhaṇūn* 'therefore' or *tyāmuḷe* 'because of that' as in (304).

(304)	hyāwarṣī	tsāŋglā	pāūs	paḍlā
	this-year-loc	good	rain	fall-pst-3sn

mhaṇūn/tyāmuḷe	pīk	tsāŋgla	āla
therefore	crop-3sn	good-3sn	come-pst-3sn

'This year the rainfall was good; therefore, the crop was good.'

1.1.2.4.2.7 *Degree*

1.1.2.4.2.7.1 *Clauses of comparative degree*

Clauses of comparative degree, though generally non-finite, may be finite as well.

non-finite:

(305)	gharī	dzopṇyāpekṣā	sinemālā	dzāṇa	bara
	home-loc	sleep-inf-compr	movie-to	go-inf	better-3sn

'It is better to go to a movie than sleeping at home.'

finite:

(306)	ajit	ḍɔkṭar	dzhālā	tyāpekṣā	to
	Ajit	doctor	become-pst-3sm	that-compr	he

śikṣak	dzhālā	astā	tar	bara
teacher	become-pst-3sm	be-cond-3sm	then	better-3sn

dzhāla	asta
become-pst-	be-cond-3sn

'Compared to (the fact that) Ajit became a doctor, it would have been better if he had become a teacher.'

(For further and detailed discussion of comparison see section 1.8 and sub-sections thereof.)

The object of comparison precedes the standard of comparison as in (307).

(307)	mohanpekṣā	sudhā	lahān	āhe
	Mohan-compared to (than)	Sudha	young	is

'Sudha is younger than Mohan.'

Example (308) shows that when the object of comparison follows the standard of comparison the outcome is an ungrammatical sentence.

(308)*	sudhā	lahān	mohanpekṣā	āhe
	Sudha	young	Mohan-compared to (than)	is

'Sudha is younger than Mohan.'

When the subordinate clause has a non-identical subject, then the subject of the subordinate clause takes the possessive case-marker which occurs on the infinitive form of the verb in the subordinate clause as in (309).

(309)	tyātSyā	wātsṇyāpekṣā	malā	gāṇa	āwaḍta
	he-poss	read-inf-than	I-dat	sing-inf	like-3sn

'I like to sing more than he likes to read.'

1.1.2.4.2.7.2 *Equative*

Equative clauses are formed by relative clauses introduced by the quantifiers *dʒitka/dʒewhḍha* 'as much as' and by lexical items such *barobarīne* 'equal' (310a). The quantifiers agree with the following noun in number and gender as in (310).

(310)	{dʒitke / dʒewhḍhe}	paise	malā	miḷtāt
	as much	money	I-dat	get-pres-3pl.m
	{titke / tewhḍhe}	anūlā	(paṇ)	miḷtāt
	that much	Anu-dat	(also)	get-pres-3pl.m

'Anu gets as much money as I get.'

(310a)	anūlā	mādʒyā	barobarīne	paise	miḷtāt
	Anu-dat	I-poss	equal	money	get-pres-3pl.m

'Anu gets as much money as I get.'

Note that in an equative construction as in (310b), the verb phrase in the main clause *miḷtāt* 'get' is deleted under identity with the verb phrase in the subordinate clause. Also, the object *paise* 'money' is also deleted in the main clause. The inclusive particle *paṇ* 'also' optionally occurs immediately following the subject-noun phrase of the main clause.

(310b) {ʤitke / ʤewhḍhe} ø malā ø
as much I-dat

{titke / tewhdḥe} anūlā (paṇ) miḷtāt
that much Anu-dat (also) get-pres-3pl.m

'Anu gets as much money as I get.'

Additionally, Marathi allows the equative construction to retain its structure in the same way as in the comparative construction. However the lexical quantifier *ewhḍha* 'this much' (and its variants) *itka* 'as much as' is substituted for the comparative marker *pekṣā* 'than'. Example (311) illustrates this construction.

(311) narmadā nadī gangeewhḍhī/itkī pawitra
Narmada river Ganges-equal to sacred

samadzlī dzāte
consider-pst-3sf go-pres-3sf

'The river Narmada is considered as sacred as the (river) Ganges.'

Another equative marker *sārkha* (and its variants) is attached to the object of comparison. While *ewhḍha* and *itka* 'this much' or *(ʤewhḍha - tewhḍha) ʤitka - titka* 'as much' express equality between the object of comparison and the subject of comparison (the thing/ person being compared) vis-a-vis the standard of comparison, the marker *sārkha* expresses only a close similarity and not exact degree or quantity between the two as in (312).

(312) madhū anūsarkhā prāmāṇik āhe
Madhu Anu-similar to honest is

'Madhu is as honest as Anu.'

It is interesting to note here that when the marker *sārkha* occurs before the standard of comparison (rather than being attached to the object or the subject of comparison), then it expresses the equality of the object and the subject of comparison vis-a-vis the standard of comparison.

In this case, *sārkha* is functionally similar to *ewhḍha/itka* or *dʒitka—titka*. Consider example (313).

(313)	madhū	āṇi	dīnū	sārkhe (ts)	huśār	āhet
	Madhu-3sm	and	Dinu-3sm	equal (emph)-3pl.m	intelligent-3pl.m	are be-pl

'Madhu and Dinu are equally intelligent.'

The difference between *ewhḍha/itka* and *dʒewhḍha—tewḍha* vs. *-sārkha* can be demonstrated in their respective paraphrases in English. The construction with the former set of markers can be paraphrased in English as "John is as intelligent as Bill" or "John is equal to Bill in (terms of) intelligence". On the other hand, the construction with *sarkha* can be paraphrased as, "John and Bill are equally intelligent."

1.1.2.4.3 *Non-finite comparative clauses*

Non-finite comparative clauses have already been discussed in sections 1.1.2.4.2.7.1 - 2.

1.1.2.5 - 1.1.2.5.1 *Sequence of tenses*

There is no requirement for a particular sequence of tense in the language. There are specific co-occurrence restrictions on the tense and aspect of non-finite forms and participles in adverbial clauses, which have been already discussed in the above sections. The tense of the finite subordinate clauses is determined with reference to the tense of the matrix clause rather than the time of the speech act. For example, if the verb in the subordinate clause is inflected for future tense, while the verb in the matrix sentence is the past tense, then the actions/events/states expressed in both the matrix and the subordinate clause are interpreted as having taken place in the past. The future tense inflection in the subordinate clause in this case indicates that the actions/events/states expressed in the subordinate clause occurred/would occur chronologically at a time later than those expressed by the matrix verb. Thus the tense of the subordinate clause is interpreted as relative to the tense in the matrix clause.

1.2 STRUCTURAL QUESTIONS

1.2.1 INTERNAL STRUCTURE OF THE SENTENCE

1.2.1.1 *Copular sentences*

Copular sentences have the verb *as* 'to be' or *ho* 'to happen/to become', which agrees with the subject and occurs sentence-finally as in (314) and (315).

(314)	te	itha	āhet
	they	here	are-3pl

'They are here.'

(315)	to	frānstsā	rādzā	hotā
	he	France-poss-3sm	king-3sm	was-3sm

'He was the King of France.'

(316)	to	ātā	ḍɔkṭar	dzhālā
	he	now	doctor	be-pst-3sm

'He has become doctor now.'

1.2.1.1.1-3 *Copular sentences with nominal, adjectival, and adverbial complements*

The complement of the copula may be a predicate noun, predicate adjective, participle, or a predicate adverb.

Predicate noun:

(317)	śiwādʒī	rādzā	āhe
	Shivaji	king	is

'Shivaji is a king.'

Predicate adjective:

(318) anū sũndar āhe
Anu beautiful is

'Anu is beautiful.'

Predicative (adverbial) participle:

(319) to dzaminīwar baslelā āhe
he floor-on sit-pst.part-3sm is

'He is sitting/seated on the floor.'

Predicate adverbial:

(320) tyātSī tsāl manda āhe
he-poss gait of walking slow is

'His speed of walking is slow.'

The unmarked order of constituents is subject-complement-copula.

1.2.1.1.4-5 *Retention and deletion of copula*

The copular verb is obligatorily retained in the positive/affirmative sentence. However, in a negative sentence, the copula is replaced by the negative verb *nāhī* as in (321).

(321) te huśār āhet
they intelligent are

'They are intelligent.'

(322) te huśār nāhīt
they intelligent are not

'They are not intelligent.'

(323) *te huśār nāhīt āhet
he intelligent are not are

'They are not intelligent.'

Note that when the copula is retained in the negative sentence, (323) is ungrammatical.

Similar to its positive counterpart, the negative copula verb also takes tense, person, and gender inflections as in (324) and (325).

(324) to śāḷet hotā
he school-loc be-pst-3sm

'He was in/at school.'

(325) to śāḷet nawhtā
he school-loc neg-be-pst-3sm

'He was not in/at school.'

1.2.1.1.6 *Different types of copula*

There are two copulas in Marathi: *as* 'to be' and *ho* 'to happen' or 'to become.' The first one expresses the existential/stative meaning while the second one expresses the inchoative meaning. Examples (314) - (325) involve the former *as* 'to be' copula, while the following (326) - (328) has the latter *ho* 'to happen/to become' copula.

(326) nokrī miḷālyāne to khūṣ dzhālā
job get-ger-inst he happy become-pst-3sm

'He became happy because he got the job.'

(327) hyā warṣī khūp pāūs dzhālā
this year-loc a lot rain happen-pst-3sm

'It has rained a lot this year.' (lit: 'A lot of rain happened this year.')

(328) puḍhtSyā warṣī to dɔkṭar hoīl
next-poss year-loc he doctor become-fut-3s

'He will become a doctor next year.'

The copula *ho* 'to become/happen' is additionaly used in a conjunct verb (a noun/adjective + copula sequence which functions as a single unit). Conjunct verbs form a large set in Marathi, similar to Hindi, Gujarati, and Punjabi and other South Asian languages. Some examples of conjunct verbs are:

(329a)	(X tse)	lagna	hoṇe	' for X to get married'
	(of X)	marriage	to happen	

(329b)	(X lā)	nafā	hoṇe	' for X to profit'
	(for X)	profit	to happen	

(329c)	(X lā)	dukkha	hoṇe	'for X to become unhappy'
	(for X)	sorrow	happen	

(329d)	bara	hoṇe	'to recover'
	good	become	

It is to be noted here that Marathi does not have single verbs as counterparts of conjunct verbs such as (329a) - (329d) above. Examples illustrating the use of conjunct verbs mentioned in (329a) - (329d) are given below in (330) - (333).

(330)	aruṇtsa	kāl	lagna	dzhāla
	Arun-poss	yesterday	marriage-3sn	happen-pst-3sn

'Arun got married yesterday.' (lit: 'Arun's wedding happened yesterday.')

(331)	wyāpārāt	malā	nafā	dzhālā
	bussiness-in	I-dat	profit-3sm	happen-pst-3sm

'I received profit in the business.' (lit: 'In business, profit happened to me.')

(332)	tī	bātmī	aikūn	tyālā	dukhkha
	that	news	hear-conj.part	he-dat	pain

hoīl
happen-fut-3s

'He will be sorry to hear that news.' (lit: 'After having heard the news, he will be sorry.')

(333)	to	ādzārī	hotā	paṇ	ātā	barā
	he	sick	was	but	now	fine-3sm

	dzhālā	ahe
	become-pst-3sm	is

'He was sick but now he has recovered.'

1.2.1.2 *Verbal sentences*

There are three types of verb groups based on their formal differences: (a) simple, (b) conjunct, and (c) compound. The first category selects only one verb root as in example (334a). The second type of verb comprises a noun/adjective/adverb + verb sequence (*kām* 'work') + *karṇe* 'do' = 'to work/to do work'. (For further details see 2.2.6.3.4.1). The last category consists of a sequence of verbs (For further details see 2.2.6.3.4.2).

1.2.1.2.1 *Subject*

All verbs generally have subjects overtly expressed in the sentence. However, omission of the subject is very common, since features of agreement on the verb provide information about the person, gender, and number of the subject. Omission of the subject is also extremely common under the following conditions: (i) when it is mentioned earlier in the discourse or recoverable contextually or pragmatically; (ii) in imperatives almost obligatorily (for details see section 1.1.1.3.1.1.1); (iii) in the impersonal construction.

The following examples illustrate situations in which omission of the subject is common/possible. In (334a) the intransitive verb has agreement markers (of gender and number of the subject). Hence it becomes possible to delete the subject as in (334b). The evidence for this deletion comes from the fact that if the deleted subject is assumed to be other than *to* 'he', as in (334c), the sentence becomes ungrammatical since the agreement features indicate that the implied subject is *to* 'he' (3sm) as in (334b).

(334a)	to	kāl	ālā
	he	yesterday	come-pst-3sm

'He came yesterday.'

(334b) ø kāl ālā
yesterday come-pst-3sm

'(He) came yesterday.'

(334c)* ø kāl ālā
yesterday come-pst-3sm

'she/they/it came yesterday.'

The subject (third person) of a transitive verb in the perfective aspect is marked with the postposition *-ne*. The first and the second person pronouns do not take *-ne*. However, the pattern of verb agreement is the same for the subject in all persons and genders. These are called ergative subjects, i.e., the verb does not agree with the subjects; rather, it agrees with the direct object (if it is not followed by any postposition). If the direct object is followed by a postposition, the verb remains in its unmarked form (i.e., third person, singular, neuter). The following examples illustrate this.

(335) mulgī itha ālī
girl here come-pst-3sf

'The girl came here.'

(336) mulīne[1] gāṇī mhaṭlī
girl-ag song-3pl.n sing-pst-3pl.n

'The girl sang songs.'

(337)* mulī ne ālī
girl-ag come-pst-3sf

'The girl came.'

(338)* mulgīø gāṇī mhaṭlī
girl song-3pl.n sing-pst-3pl.n

'The girl sang songs.'

---

[1] The deletion of *-g-* is a morpho-phonological deletion and is not relevant for determining the patterns of agreement.

Note that the subject of the transitive (336) and not the intransitive verb (335) takes *-ne*. Also notice (337) and (338). If the intransitive subject takes *-ne* , (337) is ungrammatical. Similarly, if the transitive (third person) subject fails to take *-ne*, (338) is ungrammatical. Note that in (335) the intransitive verb agrees with the subject, while in (336) the transitive verb agrees with the object *gāṇī*. Examples (339a) - (339b) show that the above pattern applies also to the pronouns. The first and second person pronouns do not take the postposition *-ne* (340b), while the third person pronoun does (339b). Also note that the verb in both (339a) and (339b) agrees with the object and not the subject.

(339a)	mī/āmhī/tū/tumhī	gāṇī	mhaṭlī
	I, we, you (sg), you (pl)	song-3pl.n	sing-pst-3pl.n

'I/we/you (sg)/you (pl) sang songs.'

(339b)	tyāne/tyā̃nnī/tine/tyā̃nnī	gāṇī	mhaṭlī
	he-ag/they (m)-ag/she-ag/they (f)-ag	song-3pl.n	sing-pst-3pl.n

'He/they (m)/she/they (f) sang songs.'

(340a)*	mīne/āmhīne/tūne/tumhīne	gāṇī	mhaṭlī
	I-ag/we-ag/you(s)-ag/you (pl)-ag	song-3pl.n	sing-pst-3pl.n

'I/we/you (s)/you (pl) sang songs.'

(340b)*	to/te/tī/tyā	gāṇī	mhaṭlī
	he/they (m) she/they (f)	song-3pl.n	sing-pst-3pl.n

'He/they (m)/she/they (f) sang songs.'

In Marathi, the subjects of the optative (section 1.1.1.3.1.1.2) (third person) and one type of obligative (section 1.1.1.3.1.1.4) optionally take the postposition *-ne*. The agreement pattern in this case is similar to the above. The interesting point to note here is that both intransitive and transitive subjects take *-ne* . In Pandharipande (1991b) it is shown that the emergence of the surface/partial ergative pattern can be attributed to the historical development and synchronic reinterpretation of non-progressive (present) structures (perfective, optative, obligative) in Marathi.

Additionally, it should be noted that some transitive verbs such as *bol* 'speak/tell, *bheṭ* 'meet', *samadz* 'understand' are exceptions, i.e., they do not take *-ne* in the perfective aspect.

(341) to mal̄a he boll̄a
*ty̆ane
he I-dat this tell-pst-3sm

'He told me this.'

(342) anū/*anūne mal̄a bheṭlī
Anu/*Anu-ag I-acc meet-pst-3sf

'Anu met me.'

Another class of subjects—generally known as dative/experiencer subjects—are marked by the dative postposition *-lā*. This construction generally involves psychological predicates such as *rāg yeṇe* 'to get angry', *wāṭṇe* 'to seem/to feel', *āwaḍṇe* 'to like', etc. Consider (343).

(343) āīlā rāg ālā
mother-dat anger come-pst-ms

'Mother became angry.'

Notice that dative subjects, like ergative subjects, fail to control verb agreement (for a detailed discussion of experiencer/dative subjects, see Pandharipande (1990b)).

There is a large class of non-volitional verbs which require the agent/subject to take the instrumental postposition *-ne* , where the verb agrees with the object instead of the subject as in (344).

(344) māʤyāne kap phuṭlā
I-inst cup-3sm break-pst-3sm

'I broke the plate (accidentally/not intentionally).'
(lit: 'The cup broke by me.')

It is important to note here that non-volitional verbs such as the one in (344) are not passivized in this construction; they are active verbs. In short, the agreement pattern is as follows: (a) the verb generally agrees with the subject of the sentence; (b) the verb agrees with the direct object (instead of the subject) if the subject is either followed by a postposition or occurs in the ergative (perfective, optative, or obligative constructions); (c) if the subject and the object both are followed by a postposition, the verb remains in its unmarked form.

As mentioned above, the deletion of the subject is possible only under those conditions in which it is recoverable through pragmatic, contextual, and syntactic clues. Marathi does not have dummy subjects.

1.2.1.2.2 *Direct object*

Verbs can be classified as intransitive and transitive on the basis of their ability to take objects. Intransitive verbs do not take a direct object, e.g., *bas* 'sit', *wāḷ* 'wither', etc.

(345)	tī	dzaminīwar	baslī
	she	floor-on	sit-pst-3sf

'She sat on the floor.'

A class of transitive verbs obligatorily occur with direct objects, e.g., *phek* 'throw', *toḍ* 'cut', etc.

(346)	tyāne	dzhāḍ	toḍle
	he-ag	tree-3sn	cut-pst-3sn

'He cut the tree.'

(347)	*tyāne	ø	toḍle
	he-ag		cut-pst-3sn

'He cut (the tree).'

Example (347) is not acceptable when the direct object is omitted, except when it is recoverable from contextual clues.

There is another class of verbs such as *haraw* 'get lost/lose' which can be used either with or without direct objects. These verbs are traditionally viewed as both transitive (when they take direct objects) and intransitive (when they do not take direct objects). Examples (348) and (349) illustrate this.

(348)	to	nawyā	śaharāt	harawlā
	he	new	city-loc	lose-pst-3sm

'He got lost in the new city.'

(349)	tyāne	pustak	śāḷet	harawla
	he-ag	book-3sn	school-loc	lose-pst-3sn

'He lost his book at school.'

The most productive process of transitivizing intransitive verbs involves adding the suffix *-aw* to the verb stem, e.g., *bas* 'sit', *bas-aw* 'make sit', *uṭh* 'get up', *uthaw* 'make (X) get up'. Similarly, a large class of transitive verbs are 'causativized' by adding the same suffix, though not iteratively (for further discussion see sections 2.1.3.1.3.1.1 and 2.1.3.1.3.2).

When the direct object is animate and/or definite, it is obligatorily marked by the accusative suffix *-lā* (and its variants). Consider example (350).

(350)	mī	dzhāḍ	pāhila
	I	tree-3sn	see-pst-3sn

(a) 'I saw a tree.'
(b) *'I saw the tree.'

In (350), the direct object *dzhāḍ* 'tree' is indefinite as is evident from (350b) in which *dzhāḍ* 'tree' is treated as the definite direct object, and the result is an ungrammatical sentence.

(351)	mī	mulīlā	pāhila
	I	girl-acc	see-pst-3sn

'I saw a/the girl.'

Note that in (351) the animate direct object *mulgī* 'girl' takes the accusative suffix *-lā* irrespective of whether it is a definite or an indefinite direct object (as is seen in the English translation which allows articles a/the. Marathi, similar to other Indo-Aryan as well as Dravidian languages, does not have any articles. Now consider example (352) below where the inanimate direct object is followed by the postposition *-lā*. The English translation of (352) clearly indicates that the direct object, in this case, is obligatorily interpreted as definite.

(352)	mī	dzhāḍālā	pāhila
	I	tree-acc	see-pst-3sn

(a) 'I saw the tree.'
(b) *"I saw a tree.'

In short, a definite object as well as an animate object obligatorily require the postposition *-lā*. Although, as shown above, animacy and definiteness are both relevant conditions in determining the *-lā*-marking, between the two, definiteness takes precedence over animacy. The evidence to support this comes from the fact that an inanimate definite direct object obligatorily takes *-lā*, and conversely, for many speakers, an indefinite animate direct object may not take the accusative marker *-lā* (although it can optionally take it) as in (353) and (354).

Definite direct object:

(353)	mī (ek)	bāī	pāhilī
	I (one)	woman	see-pst-3sf

'I saw a/*the woman.'

(354)	mī (ekā)	bāīlā	pāhila
	I (one)	woman-acc	see-pst-3sn

'I saw a/the woman.'

Since the *-lā* marking alone does not unambiguously express definiteness, the direct object is generally preceded by the demonstrative pronoun *tyā* (and its variants) to unambiguously express definiteness as in (355).

(355)	*mī*	*tyā*	*bāīlā*	*pāhila*
	I	that	woman-acc	see-pst-3sn

'I saw that/*a woman.'

A direct object may be omitted in sentences (with transitive verbs) if its presence is implied/understood contextually or pragmatically. For example, verbs such as *sā̃ŋg* 'tell', *mhaṇ* 'say', *witSār* 'ask', etc. can occur without overt direct objects as in (356).

(356)	āmhī	tyā̃nnā	sāŋgitla
	we	they-dat	tell-pst-3sn

'We told them.'

In cases such as (356), a generic neuter singular object is implied and the verb inflection indicates it. If a feminine object is introduced in (356), the resulting (356a) shows that the verb takes the feminine inflection.

(356a)	āmhī	tyā̃nnā	goṣṭa	sāŋgitlī
	we	they-dat	story-3sf	tell-pst-3sf

'We told them the story.

1.2.1.2.3 *Indirect object*

The indirect object is marked by the dative case suffix/postposition *-lā/-s*. The dative suffix *-te* of Old Marathi is almost extinct in the spoken variety and is used only occasionally in the religious poetry. The indirect object functions as (i) indirect object in ditransitive sentences (357) and (ii) underlying subject of 'ingestive' verbs in causative sentences (see also 2.1.3.1.3).

(357)	ādʒī	nātwālā	goṣṭa	sāŋgte
	grandmother	grandson-dat	story	tell-pres-prog
	āhe			
	is			

'Grandmother is telling a story to (the) grandson.'

(358)	āī	mulālā	dūdh	pādzte
	mother	child-dat	milk	drink-caus-pres-3sf

'Mother feeds milk to the child.'

1.2.1.2.4 *Other types of verbal arguments/oblique objects*

Various types of verbal arguments optionally occur such as instrumentals, comitatives, benefactives, locatives. Those arguments are marked by appropriate postpositions/suffixes (i.e., *-ne* (instrumental), *-barobar* (comitative), *-sāṭhī* (benefactive), and -V(owel) *-t* (locative)).

Instrumental:

(359)	anū	tsākūne	ā̃mbā	kāpte
	Anu-3sf	knife-inst	mango	cut-pres-3sf

'Anu cuts the mango with a knife.'

Comitative:

(360)	mī	sudhābarobar	dewḷāt	dzāīn
	I	Sudha-with	temple-loc	go-fut-1s

'I will go to the temple with Sudha.'

Benefactive:

(361)	tuʤhyāsāṭhī	mī	hā	śarṭa	wikat ghetlā
	you-for	I	this	shirt-3sm	buy-take-pst-3sm

'I bought this shirt for you.'

Locative:

(362)	ekṭa	rahṇyātSī	titSyāt	himmat	nāhī
	alone	live-inf-poss	she-loc	courage-3sf	neg

'She does not have the courage to live alone.' (lit: 'The courage to live alone is not in her.')

1.2.1.2.5 *Combination of arguments*

Though there is no restriction on the maximum number of arguments which can occur within the same sentence, the arguments strictly subcategorized by the verb must obligatorily be present. All of the objects may occur in the same sentence.

(363)	mī	anūlā	hī	bātmī	sāŋgṇyāsāṭhī
	I	Anu-dat	the	news-3sf	tell-inf-in order to

gharī	gelo
home-loc	go-pst-1sm

'I went home in order to tell this news to Anu.'

Note that the indirect and direct objects (*anū* and *bātmī* respectively) as well as the object of postposition *(sāŋgṇyāsāṭhī)* are present in (363).

1.2.1.2.6 *Order of arguments*

The unmarked word order is subject, indirect object, direct object, and verb. Adjectives or other nominal complements precede or follow the noun depending upon their attributive or predicative function. Adverbs generally immediately precede the verb. The word order of main arguments (i.e., subject, indirect object, direct object) and verb is more rigid compared to the word order of other optional arguments such as adverbs, complements, etc. The change in focus influences the change in word order in the main clause. In the subordinate clauses the unmarked word order of the main arguments and verb remains unchanged. (For further details see sections 1.1.2.1, 1.1.2.2.6 - 1.1.2.2.6.7).

1.2.1.3 *Adverbials*

Adverbs are assumed here to be elements which can modify adjectives, other adverbials or a sentence.

1.2.1.3.1 - 1.2.1.3.1.1-2 *Types of adverbials*

Adverbs can be classified according to their function and form. Adverbs can be categorized as follows according to their function: (i) adverbs of time: *kāl* 'yesterday', *ādz* 'today', *udyā* 'tomorrow', *sakāḷī* 'in the morning,' *punhā punhā* 'again and again'; (ii) adverbs of manner: *bharbhar* 'fast', *lawkar* 'quickly', *nīṭ* 'properly'; (iii) adverbs of place: *ithe* 'here', *bāher* 'outside', *āt* 'inside, etc.; (iv) adverbs of intensification: *khūp* 'a lot', *thoḍa* 'a little', *atiśay* 'too much/in abundance', *kamī* 'less', etc.

Adverbs can be categorized by their form, i.e., basic or derived. The above adverbs are basic, while derived adverbs are formed by adding case/postpositional suffixes to nouns, pronouns, infinitives, and gerunds, e.g.,: (i) noun + ne (*surīne* 'with knife'), (ii) pronoun + *muḷe (tyātSyāmuḷe* 'because of him), (iii) infinitive + *sāṭhī* (*karṇyāsāṭhī* 'in order to do (lit: 'for doing')', (iv) gerund + *war* (*ālyāwar* 'after coming'), etc.

Additionally, adjectives too can function as adverbs as in (364).

(364) tyāne kām tShān kela
he-ag work-3sn well-adj do-pst-3sn

'He did the work well.'

Participles can function as adverbs as in (365).

Conjunctive participle as manner adverbial:
(365) to tsorūn sigreṭ pito
he steal-conj.part cigarette drink-3sm

'He smokes stealthily.'

Additionally, perfective and progressive participles may also function as adverbs (see section 1.1.2.4.2.1.2).

Similar to other Indian languages (both Indo-Aryan and Dravidian), adverbs are reduplicated to express intensity, distribution, and frequency, as shown in (366) - (368) below.

(366) kām karūn karūn . . .
work having done having done

'Because of working too much . . .' (intensity)

(367) punhā punhā
again again
'Over and over again' (frequency)

(368) kuṭhe kuṭhe
where where

'(To) what all places?'

The particles *-ts,* (emphatic), and *hī/suddhā* (as well/even) are added to adverbs or nouns to express adverbial meaning, e.g., *āttā* 'right now + ts = *āttāts* 'right away', *ādz* 'today' + *hī* = *ādzhī/ādzsuddhā* 'even today'.

1.2.1.3.1.3 *Cases of noun phrases*

Nouns in instrumental, dative, ablative, and locative cases can express adverbial meaning, e.g., *surī-ne* (instrumental) 'with knife', *dupārlā* (dative) 'for the afternoon', *sandhyākāḷī* (locative) 'in the evening'.

1.2.1.3.1.4.1-2 *Adverbial clauses*

Various types of adverbial clauses—finite, as well as non-finite—have been discussed in sections 1.1.2.4 - 1.1.2.4.2.4.1.

1.2.1.3.2 *Position of adverbials*

Adverbials generally occur immediately preceding the verb. Non-finite adverbial clauses may precede the matrix clause or immediately precede the verb in the matrix clause. Adverbials generally do not occur post-verbally unless the adverbial provides only a piece of additional information as the result of the afterthought. All intensifier adverbs are placed to the left of the adjective they modify. This position of the intensifying adverb is fixed. If there is more than one intensifier, the preceding intensifier has scope over the one which follows it. Finite (relative) adverbial clauses either precede or follow the matrix clause. Lexical adverbs can occur in various positions without changing the meaning. In the following example (369), the lexical adverb *satat* 'continuously' can occur in any position, including post-verbally.

(369) maʤhī āī gharāt satat kām
my mother home-loc continuously work

karte
do-pres-3sf

'My mother continuously works in the house.'

1.2.1.3.3 *Optionality of adverbs*

Adverbials are optional, except when certain verbs are subcategorized for a locative argument, e.g., *rāh* 'live', or when an adverbial functions as a complement of a copula (see 1.2.1.1.1-3).

1.2.2 ADJECTIVE PHRASES

1.2.2.1 Definition

An adjective phrase in Marathi consists of (i) a 'basic' adjective (e.g., *tShān* 'good', *lā̃mb* 'long' etc.) and (ii) a derived adjective, i.e., a nominal + adjectivalizing suffix. Adjectives are derived from nominals by adding adjectivalizing suffixes *-wān/mān* 'having', *-wālā* 'having/belonging to, *-tsā* (possessive suffix), and *-t* (locative) + *lā* (adjectivalizing suffix). (iii) relative participles of verbs (discussed in 1.1.2.3.7.1.2, 1.1.2.3.7.2.2) are also examples of derived adjectives. Additionally, relative clauses (see sections 1.1.2.3.1, 1.1.2.3.2, 1.1.2.3.7.1.1, 1.1.2.3.7.2.1) also have adjectival function since they modify nouns. The following examples (370) - (373) illustrate adjectives derived by adding suffixes.

-wān:

(370a) *buddhī* 'intelligent' + *wān* = *buddhīwān* 'intelligent'
(lit: 'the one who has intelligence')

(370b) *buddhī* + *mān* = *buddhīmān* 'intelligent'

In (370a) and (370b) the adjectivalizing suffixes *-wān* and *-mān* respectively, are restricted to nouns inherited/borrowed from Sanskrit. *-wān* and *-mān* are possessive suffixes. Therefore, the derived adjective means 'x possessing the feature/quality expressed by the noun. The adjectivalizing suffix *-wālā* (which Marathi shares with Hindi and other Indo-Aryan languages) is functionally similar to the suffixes *-wān* and *-mān*. However, unlike *-wān* and *-mān*, *-wālā* is generally not used with nouns inherited or borrowed from Sanskrit but is restricted to native Marathi nouns or Persian/Persianized nouns in Marathi (for a detailed discussion on the distribution of suffixes see Pandharipande (1981a)). Consider example (371).

(371) *ghar-wālā* = 'the one with a house (householder)'
**gṛha-wālā*

Another adjectivalizing suffix which is quite frequently used in Marathi is *-tsā* (and its variants) which follows the postposition *war* 'on'. When these two (i.e., *war* and *-tsā*) are added to a noun, the derived form is an adjective which means 'the one which is on X (noun)'. Consider example (372).

(372)	dzhāḍāwartsa	phūl
	tree-on-adj-3sn	flower-3sn

'The flower which is on the tree.'

When a noun is followed by the locative suffix *-t* 'in', it is often adjectivized by adding the suffix *-lā* (and its variants). The derived adjective means 'the one in X' as in (373).

(373)	gharātla	ṭebal
	house-in-adj-3sn	table-3sn

'The table in the house'

In the above cases the adjectives derived from nouns modify/agree with the following noun in gender, number, and person.

1.2.2.1.1 *Operational definition of adjective phrases*

It is difficult to define adjective phrases since they are not morphologically distinguished from nouns. However, they can be distinguished from a noun phrase on the basis of their function, since they function as modifiers of nouns. Moreover, adjectives and adjective phrases unlike nouns, are not inherently marked for gender. Positionally, attributive adjectives/adjective phrases precede the noun which they modify and the predicative adjectives/adjective phrases follow the nouns. Thus the word order of an adjective/adjective phrase is determined vis-a-vis the noun which it modifies. The following examples illustrate this point.

(374) moṭhā mulgā
big-3sm boy

'Big boy'

(375) mulgā baslelā āhe
boy sit-pst.part-3sm is

'The boy is sitting' (lit: 'The boy is seated.')

An adjective/adjective phrase requires the noun/noun phrase it modifies to be present in the sentence.

1.2.2.2 *Adjectivals with arguments*

Basic adjectives and adjectives derived from nouns do not take arguments when used attributively. However, predicative adjectives may take an infinitival complement as in (376), or a conjunctive participial complement as in (377).

(376) to mulgā gharī dzāylā tayār āhe
that boy home-loc go-inf-dat ready is

'That boy is ready to go home.'

(377) ātā tī mulgī sāḍī nesūn
now that girl saree wear-conj.part

tayār āhe
ready is

'Having put on the saree, the girl is ready now.'

Note that in (376), the predicative adjective *tayār* 'ready' takes the complement *gharī dzāylā* 'to go home'.

Relative participles also take arguments similar to their corresponding verbs.

The order of the constituents in adjective phrase is as follows (as shown in (378) below):

Determiner - quantifier - adjective phrase - noun

(378)	kāhī	thoḍī	pikleli	phaḷa
	few	a bit	ripe	fruits

'A few somewhat ripe fruits'

1.2.2.3 *Adverbial modification of adjectives*

Intensifiers, which can modify adjectives, immediately precede adjectives. Intensifiers may be reduplicated in order to express a higher degree of intensification. A sample list of intensifiers is given in (379) below and their use is illustrated in (379a). More than one intensifier can occur as long as they are semantically compatible.

(379)	khūp	very
	phār	very
	dzarā	a little
	ati	very
	atyānta	extremely
	puṣkaḷ	quite/considerably

Consider example (379a).

(379a)	te	ghar	khūp/atyānta/dzarā/puṣkaḷ
	that	house	very/extremely/a little/considerably
	moṭha	āhe	
	big	is	

'That house is very/extremely/a little/considerably big.'

1.2.3 ADVERBIAL PHRASES

1.2.3.1 *Definition*

An adverbial phrase may consist of (i) a basic adverb, (ii) nouns (followed by suffixes) and adjectives which may also function as adverbs, (iii) postpositional phrases, (iv) adverbial participles of verbs, and (v) Verb$_{(infinitive)}$ + *lā* 'for doing V(erb)'. Examples of the above types are given below.

basic adverb:

(380)	to	bharbhar	tsālto
	he	fast	walk-pres-3sm

'He walks fast.'

noun + suffix as adverb:

(381)	to	sandhyākāḷī	dzhopto
	he	evening-loc	sleep-pres-3sm

'He sleeps in the evening.'

adjective as adverb:

(382)	tī	gāṇa	tsāŋgla	mhaṇte
	she	song-3sn	good-3sn	say-pres-3sf

'She sings well' (lit: 'She says song well').

postpositional phrase as adverb:
A postpositional phrase in this case may consist of a noun + postposition, an adjective + postposition, or an infinitive + postposition.

noun + postposition:

(383)	anū	+	muḷe
	Anu		because of

'Because of Anu'

adjective + postposition:

(384)	tsāŋglyā	+	tarhe-ne
	good-obl		manner-inst

'Properly'

infinitive + postposition:

(385)	dzāṇyā-kartā
	go-inf-obl-for

'In order to go'

participle as adverb:

(386)	kā̃m	kartā̃nā̃
	work	do-adv.part

'While doing work'

infinitive + *-lā̃* as adverb:

(387)	ʤewā̃ylā̃
	eat-inf-obl-dat

'In order to eat'

1.2.3.2 *Adverbial modifiers of adverbials*

Adverbials can be modified by intensifiers which also modify adjectives (see section 1.2.2.3). Intensifiers immediately precede the adverbs which they modify as in (388) and (389).

(388)	to	khūp	bharbhar	tsā̃lto
	he	very	fast	walk-pres-3sm

'He walks very fast.'

(389)	to	khūp	ā̃nandā̃ne	mhaṇālā̃ . . .
	he	very	happiness-with	say-pst-3sm

'He said very happily . . '

Reduplication of adverbials is also frequently used as a strategy to intensify the meaning expressed as in (390).

(390)	tū	lawkar	lawkar	parat	ye
	you	quickly	quickly	return	come-imp-2s

'You come back soon (as soon as possible).'

Adverbials can also be modified by comparative phrases as in (391).

(391)	madhū	anūpekṣā̃	ʤā̃sta	abhyā̃s	karto
	Madhu	Anu-compared to	more	study	do-pres-3sm

'Madhu studies more than Anu.'

1.2.4 - 1.2.4.3.5 POSTPOSITIONAL PHRASES

Postpositional phrases consist of a noun phrase followed by a postposition as in (392). (For a complete list of postpositions, see sections 2.2.6.1 - 2.2.6.2.4.)

(392) gharā-war
house-on
'On the house'

Postpositions can be simple, such as *āt* 'in', *bāher* 'outside', or derived from nouns by adding case-markers to the nouns as *hātāne* in (393).

(393)	madhūtSyā	hātāne
	Madhu-poss	hand-inst
	'Through Madhu (lit: 'By Madhu's hand')'	

All postpositions have an argument which is generally referred to as object or a complement which is a noun phrase. When a coordinate noun phrase occurs as the argument of a postposition, it appears that it has more than one argument. However, in this case, the coordinate noun phrase functions as a single unit as in (394).

(394)	mohan	āṇi	sudhā	barobar	to	sinemālā
	Mohan	and	Sudha	with	he	movie-to

gelā
go-pst-3sm

'He went to the movie with Mohan and Sudha.'

Marathi does not allow postpositions to be stranded. However, some postpositions function independently of noun phrases as adverbs. A partial list of independent postpositions is given below:

Postposition with an argument		Independent postposition	
- tSyā/ā (poss) + war	'on/above'	war	'above'
- tSyā (poss) + āt	'inside of'	āt	'inside'
- tSyā (poss) + puḍhe	'ahead of'	puḍhe	'ahead'
- tSyā (poss) + ādhī	'before'	ādhī	'first'

A large number of postpositions take relative participles, infinitive phrases, and gerunds as their arguments. Consider examples (395) - (396).

Relative participle as an argument:

(395)	arbānāt	rāhilelyā	baddal	to	bolat
	urbana-in	live-pst.part-poss	about	he	talk-prog

hotā
was

'He was talking about those living in Urbana.'

Infinitive phrase as an argument:

(396)	tyātSyā	mūmbaīlā	dzāṇyāmuḷe	āīlā
	he-poss	Bombay-to	go-inf-because	mother-dat

wāīṭ wāṭla
bad feel-pst-3sn

'Mother felt sad because of his going to Bombay.'

Gerundive phrase as an argument:

(397)	madhū	gharī	ālyāpāsūn	tī	khūṣ	āhe
	Madhu	home-loc	come-ger-since	she	happy	is

'She is happy since (the time) Madhu came home.'

1.2.4.4 *Cases governed by postpositions*

Postpositions govern the possessive case. The possessive case-marking *-tSā* (and its variants) is optionally present if the complement/argument is a noun, i.e., *madhū (tSyā) muḷe* 'because of Madhu'. However, if the complement/argument is a relative participle, an infinitive phrase, or a gerund, the case-marker is generally not present, (though its optional occurrence is not ruled out). It must be mentioned here that the occurrence of the possessive suffix *-tSyā* is much more readily accepted if the constituent is a noun as opposed to an infinitive, participial, or a gerundive phrase.

1.2.5 NOUN PHRASE (NOMINAL CONSTITUENT)

1.2.5.1 *Definition*

The minimal unit of a noun phrase can be a noun or a pronoun, which can be optionally preceded and/or followed by modifiers. A noun phrase functions as an argument (subject, direct object, indirect object) of the main verb in a sentence. Additionally, a noun phrase can function as an object of a postposition. A noun phrase may optionally have more than one modifier. Consider the following examples of a noun phrase.

Without a modifer:

(398) mulgā
'A/the boy'

Pronoun:

(399) te
'They'

Modifier (adjective):

(400)	tī	tShoṭī	khurtSī
	that	small	chair

'That small chair'

More than one modifier:

(401)	hī	tīn	pūrṇapaṇe	piklelī	rasraśīt	nāgpurī
	these	three	completely	ripe	juicy	Nagpur-from

sāntrī
oranges

'These three absolutely ripe, juicy oranges from Nagpur.'

Syntactically, noun phrases can act as subjects, direct objects, indirect objects, complements of copular sentences, and complements of postpositional phrases. As subjects (except for the ergative-like constructions), noun phrases control verb-agreement in person, gender, and number and serve as an antecedent of reflexives. They are marked for case, gender, and number. They can be replaced by pronouns. Noun phrases can be clausal in nature as well.

1.2.5.2 *Modifiers in noun phrases*

A nominal head may have a variety of modifiers.

1.2.5.2.1 *Attributive adjectives*

Adjectives precede the noun they modify.

(402) sũndar mulgī
beautiful girl

'Beautiful girl'

There is no grammatical restriction on the number of adjectives which may precede a noun.

1.2.5.2.2 *Relative clauses*

Participial and sentential relative clauses can modify a noun (See discussion in 1.1.2.3).

1.2.5.2.3 *Possessive adjectives*

In noun phrases, possessive adjectives precede the head noun as modifiers. The possessive suffix -*tsV*(owel) is added to the possessor noun (to derive the adjective) as in (403) or is incorporated into the derived possessive adjective as in (404).

(403) rā̃mtsā ghoḍā
Ram-poss-3sm horse-3sm

'Ram's horse'

(404) mā̃dzhā ghoḍā
my (I-poss) horse

'My horse'

1.2.5.2.4-5 *Articles and demonstrative objects*

Marathi does not have a separate category of articles. The function of the articles (i.e., of expressing indefiniteness and definiteness) is carried out by the numeral *ek* 'one' and the indefinite pronoun *koṇī* 'some (one)' as in (405) and the demonstrative pronouns as in (408). Definite noun phrases are generally unmarked.

(405) koṇī/ek mulgā
some/one boy

'Some/one/a boy'

It needs to be noted here that the choice of using *koṇī* 'some (one)' is restricted to nouns with animate referents as illustrated in (406).

(406) *koṇī ghar
some house

'Some/one/a house'

(407) ek ghar
one house

'Some/one/a house'

Demonstrative adjectives (which are homophonous with demonstrative pronouns) and ø-marking are used to mark a definite noun (phrase) as in (408).

(408) hā/to/ø mulgā
this/that/ø boy

'This/that/the boy'

1.2.5.2.6 *Quantifiers and numerals*

Various types of quantifiers and numerals (see section 2.1.6) are used to modify nouns. The quantifiers consist of the following co-occurring categories.

(409)	(approximate)	(cardinal)	(collective)
	(ordinal)	(multiplicative)	(measure)
			(fractional)

Some examples of the above are given below.

(410)	approximate:	dzawaḷ dzawaḷ 'approximate'
	ordinal:	pahilā 'first', dusrā 'second'
	cardinal:	ek 'one', don 'two'
	multiplicative:	duppaṭ 'twice', tippaṭ 'thrice'
	fractional:	pāw 'one fourth', ardhā 'half'
	collection:	dzoḍī 'pair', ḍadzhan 'dozen'
	measure:	kilo 'kilogram'

Some examples of noun phrase are given below.

Indefinite + cardinal + head noun:

(411)	dzawaḷdzawaḷ	āṭh	mulī
	approximately	eight	girls

'approximately eight girls'

Definite + ordinal + cardinal + head noun:

(412)	te	pahile	tSār	ṭrak
	those	first	four	trucks

'Those first four trucks'

Definite + ordinal + fractional + measure + head noun:

(413)	tī	pahilī	ardhā	kilo	ḍāḷ
	that	first	half	kilogram	lentils

'That first half kilo of lentils'

As seen in (409) - (413), quantifiers/numerals generally precede head nouns. However, quantifiers such as *sagḷV* (owel) 'all/whole', *thoḍV* (owel) 'a little' may alternatively follow head noun as in (414) and (415).

(414)	lok	sagḷe	āle	hote
	people	all	come-pst-3pl.m	be-pst-3pl.m

'All the people had come.'

(415)	mī	kām	ṭhoḍa	kela
	I	work	a little	do-pst-3sn

'I did a little work.'

If the head noun is a pronoun, the quantifiers generally follow the pronoun as in (416).

(416)	āmhī	sagḷe	kāl	ālo
	we	all	yesterday	come-pst-1pl

'We all came yesterday.'

1.2.5.2.7 *Adverbials*

Intensifiers, which are considered as adverbials by some of the traditional grammarians such as Damle (1966 [1911]), may be part of the noun phrase. However, they generally modify adjectives, rather than the head noun directly as in (417).

(417)	phār	tShoṭī	kholī
	a lot	small	room

'A very small room'

Adverbs such as *ithe* 'here', *tithe* 'there' modify nouns when they are followed by the suffix *-lā* (and its variants). The derived form precedes the head noun and functions as an adjective and agrees with the following noun as in (418) and (419).

(418)	ithla	dzhāḍ
	here-3sn	tree-3sn

'The tree over here'

(419)	tithle	lok
	there-3pl.m	people-3pl.m

'People over there'

1.2.5.2.8 *Emphatic markers and limiters*

Limiters such as *kewaḷ/phakta* 'only' precede, while emphatic particles such as *-ts* 'only', *paṇ* 'also'/*suddhā* 'as well' follow the noun phrase as illustrated below. (For further details on emphatic particles see 1.11.2.1.2.)

Limiter:

(420)	kewaḷ/phakta	don	kilo	ḍāḷ	āṇ
	only	two	kilos	lentil	bring-imp-s

'Bring only two kilograms of lentils'

Emphatic particle:

(421)	udyā	madhū<u>ts</u>	yeīl
	tomorrow	Madhu-emph	come-fut-3s

'Only Madhu will come tomorrow'

(422)	amit	paṇ/suddhā	mumbaīlā	gelā
	Amit	also/as well	Bombay-to	go-pst-3sm

'Amit also/as well went to Bombay.'

1.2.5.2.9 *Comparative/superlative/equative structures*

Marathi does not have morphological comparative, superlative, or equative structures. Some of the morphological superlative forms are borrowed from Sanskrit and are used in a stylized (highly Sanskritized) speech. Those forms are 'frozen' and the morphological (Sanskrit) devices are not productive in the current language. Some typical examples of borrowed forms are *sũndartam* (*sũndar* (beautiful) + *tam (a)* (most)) 'the most beautiful', *utStSatam* (*UtStSa* (high) + *tam(a)* (most)) 'the highest'. The most productive means of expressing comparative, superlative, and equative meaning is syntactic. The object of comparison takes the suffix *-pekṣā* 'compared to'. The object of comparison (along with the suffixes) may precede or follow the head noun as in (423) and (424), respectively.

(423)	anū	mītāpekṣā	ũntsa	āhe
	Anu	Meeta-compared to	tall	is

'Anu is taller than Meeta.' (lit: 'Anu is tall compared to Meeta.')

(423a)	mītāpekṣā	anū	ūntsa	āhe
	Meeta-compared to	Anu	tall	is

'Anu is taller than Meeta.'

(424)	Anū	sarwā̃npekṣa	ūntsa	āhe
	Anu	all-compared to	tall	is

'Anu is the tallest of all.' (lit: 'Anu is tall compared to all.')

(424a)	sarwā̃npekṣa	anū	ūntsa	āhe
	all-compared to	Anu	tall	is

'Anu is the tallest of all.'

1.2.5.2.10 *Other elements*

There are some nouns in Marathi such as *ranga* 'color', *wadzan* 'weight', *lā̃mbī* 'length' which can be used as classifiers. They occur immediately after nouns denoting color, measure of weight/length, respectively and they are optional. The following examples illustrate the use of these classifiers.

Color:

(425)	niḷyā	rangātSī	moṭar	/	niḷī	moṭar
	blue	color-poss	car	/	blue	car

'The blue-colored car/ the blue car'

Measure of weight:

(426)	tīn	kilo	(wadzanātSī)	bhādʒī
	three	kilogram	weight-poss	vegetable

'The vegetable weighing three kilograms/ three-kilogram vegetable'

Measure of length:

(427)	āṭh	fūṭ	(lā̃mbītSī)	tsaṭaī	āṇ
	eight	feet	long-poss	mat	bring-imp

'Bring a/the eight-feet (long) mat.'

1.2.5.3-4 *Co-occurrence and combination of modifiers*

Some modifiers such as demonstrative and interrogative adjectives, cardinal and ordinal numerals, quantifiers, emphatic particles, and classifiers can occur only once in a noun phrase. In contrast to this, there is no theoretical limit to the number of adjectives, relative clauses or possessive nouns that can occur in a noun phrase. When more than one possessive noun occurs in a noun phrase, each functions as a modifier of the one that immediately follows it, as illustrated in (428). That is to say, there may be several NPs with just one possessor per NP whereas a number of adjectives may occur in a single NP.

(428)	sudhātSyā	gharātSyā	samortsa	lāl
	Sudha-poss	house-poss	in front-poss	red
	tsāphyātSa	dzhāḍ		
	chapha-poss	tree		

'The red wild *chapha* tree in front of Sudha's house'

More than one numeral can occur; however in this case, they together function as a unit. When two numerals occur next to each other, approximation is indicated as in (429). Approximate number is also signalled by attaching the numeral *ek* to the numeral as in (430). Reduplication of a numeral indicates a distributive meaning as in (431). More than one intensifier can occur in the same sentence. In this case each modifies the one immediately following it as in (432).

(429)	pāts	sahā	mulī	ālyā
	five	six	girls	come-pst-3pl.f

'Approximately five or six girls came.'

(430)	pātsek	mulī	ālyā
	five-one	girls	come-pst-3pl.f

'Approximately five girls came.'

(431)

don	don	ãmbe	mulãnnã	de
two	two	mangoes	children-dat	give-imp

'Give two mangoes each to the children.'

(432)

agdī	khūp	sũndar	tSitra
absolutely	very	beautiful	picture

'A very, very beautiful picture'

Some combinatory constraints on modifiers do exist. For example, the combination of indefinite determiner and demonstrative pronoun is prohibited as in (433).

(433)

*koṇī	to	mulgā
some	that	boy

'Some that boy'

Similarly, a combination of a multiplicative and a collective quantifier is not allowed, as illustrated by (434).

(434)*

tippaṭ	ḍadzhan	ãmbe
thrice	dozen	mangoes

'Three times a dozen mangoes'

1.2.5.5 *Order of constituents in the noun phrase*

Except for some of the quantifiers, and limiters/emphatic particles ((414), (421) and (422)), other modifiers precede the head noun which they modify. The unmarked relative order of the modifiers in a noun phrase is as follows: demonstrative adjective; possessive adjective; quantifier; intensifier; adjective; relative clause; noun; head noun; emphatic particle. This order is illustrated in (435).

(435)

1	2	3	4	5
he	madʒhyā	bhãwãtse	don	atiśay
these	my	brother-poss	two	very

6	7	8	9
śrīmãnta	mumbaīt	rãhṇãre	mitra
rich	Bombay	live-rel.par	friends

'These two of my brother's very rich friends who live in Bombay.'

There is a certain degree of optionality in the placement of these constituents. There has not been any systematic study of the preferred order of the modifiers relative to one another. However, the following are some generalizations: (a) Demonstrative adjectives cannot be moved over numeral adjectives, (for example, (1) in (435) can not be moved over (4) in (435)). Thus, the following order is not allowed.

(436)	*don	he	mitra
	two	these	friends

'These two friends'

(b) Emphatic particles and limiters always follow (and never precede) the head noun (as in (420) and (421)). (c) The classifiers mentioned in (425) - (427) always follow (and never precede) the noun of color or measure. This follows from the general rule that classifiers occur after the noun. (d) Intensifiers immediately precede the noun. However, if the noun phrase contains one or more adjectives, then, the intensifier precedes the adjectives (which in turn precede the head noun) (recall example 379a).

1.3 COORDINATION

1.3.1.1 *Sentence coordination*

Marathi, similar to Dravidian languages such as Kannada, Tamil, and Telugu, prefers to use subordinate clauses instead of sentential coordination. However, devices of sentence coordination are available and will be discussed in the following sections.

Sentences can be coordinated by using one of the following devices: participialization, juxtaposition, and by using coordinating words such as *āṇi/wa* 'and', *kīmwā* 'or', and *paṇ/parãntu* 'but'. These devices differ in their formal, semantic and discoursal/pragmatic features, which are described in the following sections.

1.3.1.1.1 *'and' coordination*

'And' coordination is expressed by juxtaposing sentences or parts of sentences without the presence of the word *āṇi/wa* 'and'. This type of coordination is common in spoken and informal speech. Consider example (437) below:

(437)	mītā	gharī	gelī	mī	badzārāt
	Meeta	home-loc	go-pst-3sf	I	market-loc

gelo
go-pst-3sm

'Meeta went home and I went to the market.'

Any number of sentences can be coordinated in this manner. In written and formal speech as well as in spoken/informal speech, the word *āṇi* 'and' is placed after each coordinated element except the last to express 'and' coordination as in (438).

(438)	mohan	gāto	āṇi/wa	madhū	peṭī
	Mohan	sing-pres-3sm	and	Madhu	harmonium

wādzawto
play-pres-3sm

'Mohan sings and Madhu plays the harmonium'

When more than two sentences or constituents are coordinated, *āṇi/wa* usually occurs only before the last sentence/constituent as in (439).

(439)	madhū	gharī	ālā	anūne
	Madhu	home-loc	come-pst-3sm	Anu-ag

wāḍhle	āṇi/wa	sagḷe	(dzaṇ)	ʤewle
serve (food)-	and	all	(people)	eat-pst-3pl.m

'Madhu came home, Anu served the food, and everyone ate.'

Coordination of constituents using *āṇi* is illustrated in (440).

(440)

bābā̃nnī	āīlā	paise	āṇi
father-ag	mother-dat	money-3pl.m	and

sāḍī	dilī
saree-3sf	give-pst-3sf

'Father gave money and a saree to mother.'

When two or more sequential actions by the same agent are coordinated, the first occurrence of the subject/agent is retained and it is deleted from the other conjuncts as in (441).

(441)

anū	mumbaīlā	gelī	ø	madhūlā
Anu	Bombay-to	go-pst-3sf		Madhu-acc

bheṭlī	āṇī/wa	ø	paratlī
meet-pst-3sf	and		return-pst-3sf

'Anu went to Bombay, met with Madhu and returned.'

Alternatively, the coordination of sequential actions by the same agent is expressed by turning the main verbs of all but the last one into conjunctive participles as in (442). This strategy (as mentioned earlier) is preferred over the use of *āṇi.*

(442)

anū	mumbaīlā	dzāūn	Madhūlā
Anu	Bombay-to	go-conj.part	Madhu-acc

bheṭūn	paratlī
meet-conj.part	return-pst-3sf

'Anu, went to Bombay, met with Madhu and returned.' (lit: Anu, having gone to Bombay, having met Madhu, returned.)

1.3.1.1.2 *'but' coordination*

'But' coordination is expressed by the placement of the word *paṇ/parāntu* 'but' preceding the last coordinated element. Only sentences, not phrases, can be coordinated by using this strategy. While *paṇ* and *parāntu* are interchangeable, the use of *parāntu* is generally preferred in the formal/written language while *paṇ* is preferred in the informal/spoken language.

(443)	sudhīrdzawaḷ	paise	āhet	paṇ	ghar	nāhī
	Sudhīr-near	money-3pl.m	be-pres-3pl	but	home	not

'Sudhīr has money but not a home.'

(444)	tyālā	sarwā̃nnī	sā̃ŋgitla	paṇ	tyāṇe
	he-dat	all-ag	tell-pst-3sn	but	he-ag

aikla	nāhī
hear-pst-3sn	not

'Everybody told him but he did not listen.'

The use of paṇ before the last element:

(445)	dilip	bādzārāt	gelā,	rameś	sinemālā
	Dilip	market-loc	go-pst-3sm	Ramesh	movie-to

gelā	paṇ	rāʤū	gharī	rāhilā
go-pst-3sm	but	Raju	home-loc	stay-pst-3sm

'Dilip went to the market, Ramesh went to a movie, but Raju stayed home.'

When *paṇ* is attached to *tarī* 'even though/although' (which marks the concessive clause), it functions as a device to further emphasize the concessive meaning. In this case, the use of *paṇ* with *tarī* is optional. Moreover the use of *parā̃ntu* 'but' is prohibited in this case. Example (446) illustrates this use of *paṇ*.

(446)	rātrītse	bārā	wādzle	tarī(*parā̃ntu/paṇ)
	night-of	twelve	toll-pst-3pl.m	even then (but)

to	gharī	ālā	nāhī
he	home-loc	come-pst-3sm	not

'Although it was twelve o'clock at night (lit: of night), he did not come home.'

1.3.1.1.3 *'or' coordination*

'Or' coordination is expressed by using the words *kī* (only in questions)/*kīmwā/athwā* 'or' between the two members of the disjunctive set as in (447). When there are more than two members of the disjunctive set, then *kīmwā/athwā* are used immediately following each but the last member of the set as in (449) or only before the last member of the set as in (449a). While the use of *kīmwā* is more frequent in both informal/spoken and formal/written language, *athwā* is less frequently used and is largely restricted to the formal/written language.

(447)	madhū	āītSyā	śuśruṣesāṭhī	suṭṭī	
	Madhu	mother-of	looking-after-for	leave	

gheīl	kīmwā	tilā	hɔspiṭalmadhe	ṭhewīl
take-fut-3s	or	her	hospital-in	keep-fut-3s

'Madhu will take leave to take care of his mother or keep her in the hospital.'

(448)	tSandū	kīmwā	sudhā	udyāparyānta	yeīl
	Chandū	or	Sudha	tomorrow-by	come-fut-3s

'Chandu or Sudha will come by tomorrow.'

(449)	anū	kīmwā	madhū	kīmwā	sudhā
	Anu	or	Madhu	or	Sudha

itha	dupārparyānta	yeīl
here	afternoon-by	come-fut-3s

'Anu, or Madhu or Sudha will come here by the afternoon.'

(449a)	anū	ø	madhū	kīmwā	sudhā
	Anu		Madhu	or	Sudha

dupār-paryānta	yeīl
afternoon-by	come-fut-3s

'Anu, Madhu, or Sudha will come by the afternoon.'

1.3.1.2 - 1.3.1.2.3 *Number of coordinators*

In the case of *āṇi/wa* 'and', each coordinated element must have one instance of the coordinator. When more than two elements are coordinated, *āṇi* normally occurs before the last coordinated element. However, retention of as many instances of *āṇi* as there are coordinated elements minus one is not ungrammatical. In the case of the participial strategy all main verbs except for the last one are turned into conjunctive participles.

In a question, *kĩmwā/athwā* are replaced by *kī* as in (449b).

Disjunctive verbs:

(449b)	to	bādzārāt	gelā	kī/*kīmwā
	he	market-loc	go-pst-3sm	or
	gharī	(gelā) ?		
	home-loc	go-pst-3sm		

'Did he go to the market or did he go home?'

Disjunctive nouns:

(449c)	madhū	kī	mohan	ālā?
	Madhu	or	Mohan	come-pst-3sm

'Did Mohan or Madhu come?'

Paṇ 'but' occurs only once before the last coordinated element. *kĩmwā/athwā* occurs once (following the first member of the disjunctive set) if there are only two members of the disjunctive set. In cases where there are more than two members (of the disjunctive set), it is theoretically possible to retain one less coordinator than the number of coordinated elements (449). However, it is also possible to use *kĩmwā/athwā* once before the last coordinated element (449a).

1.3.1.3 *Coordination of major categories*

1.3.1.3.1 *'and' coordination*

The coordinator *āṇi,* in addition to being used to coordinate sentences, is used to coordinate nouns (subjects, direct, and indirect objects), verbs, adjectives, and adverbs.

Coordinate nouns:

(450)	bhārat	āṇi	kænaḍā	he	moṭhe
	India	and	Canada	these	big-pl.m

deś	āhet
countries	are

'India and Canada are big countries.'

Coordinate adjectives:

(451)	rādhā	sũndar	āṇi	suswabhāwī	āhe
	Radha	beautiful	and	good-natured	is

'Radha is beautiful and good-natured.'

Coordinate adverbials:

(452)	kāl	āṇi	parwā	mumbaīt	dange
	yesterday	and	day before yesterday	Bombay-loc	riots

dzhāle
happen-pst-3pl.m

'Riots occurred in Bombay yesterday and the day before yesterday.'

Coordinate verbs:

(453)	mī	gharī	āle	āṇi	dzhople
	I	home-loc	come-pst-1sf	and	sleep-pst-1sf

'I came home and slept.'

1.3.1.3.2 *'but' coordination*

In addition to verbs, adjectives as well as adverbs are coordinated by the coordinator *paṇ* 'but'.

Coordinate adjectives:

(454)	to	śrīmānta	paṇ	mūrkha	mulgā
	that	rich	but	foolish	boy

'That rich but foolish boy . . .'

Coordinate adverbs:

(455)	to	bharbhar	paṇ	spaṣṭa	bolto
	he	fast	but	clearly	speak-3sm

'He speaks fast but clearly.'

Coordinate verbs without negation:

(456)	to	ʤewlā	paṇ	bhukelā	rāhilā
	he	eat-pst-3sm	but	hungry-3sm	remain-pst-3sm

'He ate but (he) remained hungry.'

Coordinate verbs with negation:

(457)	. . .aikla	paṇ	lihila	nāhī. . .
	hear-pst-3sn	but	write-pst-3sn	neg

'. . .heard but did not write. . .'

(458)	. . .aikla	nāhī	paṇ	lihila. . .
	hear-pst-3sm	neg	but	write-pst-3sn

'. . did not hear but wrote. . .'

'But' coordination of nouns involves the addition of a negative particle following one of the adversative conjuncts. Consider examples (459) - (460).

(459)	. . .sudhā	paṇ	mohan	nāhī. . .
	Sudha	but	Mohan	neg

'. . . Sudha but not Mohan. . .'

(460)	. . .sudhā	nāhī	paṇ	Mohan. . .
	Sudha	neg	but	Mohan

'. . .not Sudha but Mohan. . .'

1.3.1.3.3 *'or' coordination*

The disjunctive markers *kīmwā* and *athwā* are used to disjoin nouns, adjectives, adverbs, and verbs. Consider the following examples.

Nouns:

(461)	anū	kīmwā/athwā	rādha
	Anu	or	Radha

'. . .either Anu or Radha. . .'

Adjectives:

(462)	sũndar	kīmwā/athwā	kurūp
	beautiful	or	ugly

'. . .either beautiful or ugly. . .'

Adverbs:

(463)	haḷū	kīmwā/athwā	bharbhar
	slowly	or	quickly

'. . .either slowly or quickly. . .'

Verbs:

(464)	tyāne	ā̃mbe	khālle	kīmwā	phekle. . .
	he-ag	mangoes	eat-pst-3pl.m	or	throw-pst-3pl.m

'Either he ate the mangoes or threw them (away).'

The disjunctive marker *kī* is used to disjoin nouns, adjective, adverbs and verbs as shown in the following examples. Note that *kī* always denote a choice or an alternative between two things.

Disjunctive nouns:

(465)	. . .anū	kī	kusum. . .?
	Anu	or	kusum

'. . .Anu or Kusum ? . . .'

Disjunctive adjectives:

(466)	. . .lahān	kī	moṭhā. . .?
	small	or	big

'. . .small or big?. . .'

Disjunctive adverbs:

(467)	. . .tsukūn	kī	muddām. . .?
	by mistake	or	deliberately

'. . by mistake or deliberately ?. . .'

Disjunctive verbs:

(468)	to	gharī	gelā	kī	sinemālā	gelā ?
	he	home-loc	go-pst-3sm	or	movie-to	go-pst-3sm

'Did he go home or did he go to a movie?'

Negative disjunction is expressed by substituting the negative particle *na* for *kīmwā/athwā* as in (469).

(469)	na	madhū	ālā	na	śyām
	neg	Madhu	come-pst-3sm	neg	Shyam

'Neither Madhu nor Shyam came.'

In the case of the disjoined nouns, the verb agrees with the nearest disjunct as in (470).

(470)	mādzhā	bhāū	kīmwā	bahīṇ	ālī
	my-3sm	brother	or	sister	come-pst-3sf

'My brother or sister came.'

(470a)	*madzhā	bhāū	kīmwā	bahīṇ	ālā
	my-3sm	brother	or	sister	come-pst-3sm

'My brother or sister came.'

(471)	madʒhī	bahīṇ	kīmwā	bhāū	ālā
	my-3sf	sister	or	brother	come-pst-3sm

'My sister or brother came.'

(471a)	*mādʒhī	bahīṇ	kīmwā	bhāū	ālī
	my-3sf	sister	or	brother	come-pst-3sf

'My sister or brother came.'

1.3.1.4 *Coordination and accompaniment*

Coordination and accompaniment are expressed by different devices. Accompaniment is expressed by means of a complex postposition *(-tSyā) barobar/-tSyā saha* 'with/in the company of'. Coordination and accompaniment are expressed in sentences (472) and (473) respectively.

(472)	madhū	āṇi	rām	āle
	Madhu	and	Ram	come-pst-3pl.m

'Madhu and Ram came.'

(473)	madhū	rām	(tSyā)	barobar/saha	ālā
	Madhu	Ram	(of)	company	come-pst-3sm

'Madhu came with Ram.'

Note that the verb in (472) has the plural agreement marker while the verb in (473) takes the singular agreement marker. While the coordinated elements form a single unit (472), the elements in accompaniment do not form a single unit. This explains why the pronoun *doghe* 'both' can be inserted in (472) but not in (473) as shown in (472a) and (473a) respectively.

(472a)	madhū	āṇi	rām	doghe	āle
	Madhu	and	Ram	both	come-pst-3pl.m

'Madhu and Ram both came.'

(473a)*	madhū	rām	(tSyā)	barobar/saha
	Madhu	Ram	(of)	company
	doghe	āle /	ālā	
	both	come-pst-3pl.m /	come-pst-3sm	

'Both Madhu came with Ram.'

The following examples show that coordinated elements (with *āṇi* 'and') do in fact form a unit; when an adverb is inserted inside the coordinated phrase, the result is an ungrammatical sentence (472b).

In contrast to this, the adverb can be readily inserted in phrases expressing accompaniment (473b).

(472b)*	madhū	gharī	āṇi	rām	āle
	Madhu	home-loc	and	Ram	come-pst-3pl.m

'Madhu and Ram came home.'

(473b)	madhū	gharī	rām	(tSyā)	barobar/saha
	Madhu-3sm	home-loc	Ram	(of)	company

āla
come-pst-3sm

'Madhu came home with Ram.'

The comitative postposition *(-tSyā) barobar/saha* always follows the noun of accompaniment. The coordinator *āṇi* and the comitative postposition *(-tSyā) barobar/saha* can both be used in the same sentence as in (474) below.

(474)	madhū	āṇi	rām	śyām	(tSyā)
	Madhu	and	Ram	Shyam	(of)

barobar/saha āle
company come-pst-3pl.m

'Madhu and Ram came with Shyam.'

1.3.1.5 *Structural parallelism and coordination*

Generally, members of the same class (e.g., noun, adjective, adverb, etc.) can be coordinated. If the members belong to different classes, their coordination is not acceptable as in (475), and (476) below.

Intensifier and adjective:

(475)*	to	phār	āṇi	tsāŋglā	mulgā	āhe
	he	very	and	good-3sm	boy	is

'He is very and good boy.'

Noun and adverb:

(476)*	mī	ā̃mbe	āṇi	lawkar	āṇle
	I	mangoes-3pl.m	and	quickly	bring-pst-3pl.m

'I brought mangoes and quickly.'

Some additional constraints on coordination will be discussed below.

1.3.1.5.1 *Adjectives and participial constructions*

Participles which function as adjectives can be readily coordinated with adjectives as in (477) and (478). However, in such coordinations, participles must precede adjectives.

Perfective/past participle and adjective:

(477)	dzhoplelā	(āṇi)	tShoṭā	mulgā	mādzhā
	sleep-perf.part	and	small	boy	my-3sm
	bhāū	āhe			
	brother	is			

'The small boy who (is) asleep, is my brother.'

Habitual participle and adjective:

(478)	to	khūp	kām	karṇārā	(āṇi)
	he	a lot	work	do-pres.part-3sm	and
	huśār	māṇūs	āhe		
	intellligent	man	is		

'He is an intelligent and hard-working man.'

The coordination of participles and adjectives by juxtaposition, without the use of the coordinator *āṇi* 'and', is preferred. However, its occurrence is perfectly acceptable.

The coordination of other participles (which do not function as adjectives) and adjectives is not acceptable as in (479) and (480).

Conjunctive participle and adjective:

(479)*	khūp	kām	karūn	āṇi	tsāŋglā	mulgā
	a lot	work	do-conj.part	and	good	boy

mādzhā	mitra	āhe
my-3sm	friend	is

'The boy who has done a lot of work and (is) good is my friend.'

Adverbial participle and adjective:

(480)*	tī	haḷu	boltānā	āṇi	sūndar
	she	slow	talk-adv.part	and	beautiful

mulgī	koṇ	āhe
girl	who	is

'Who is that girl slowly talking and beautiful?'

A finite relative clause cannot be coordinated with an adjective as shown in (481) and (482).

(481)*	dzo	śikāgolā	rāhto	āṇi	śrīmānta
	rel	Chicago-dat	live-pres-3sm	and	rich

'The one who lives in Chicago and rich. . .'

(482)*	śrīmānta	āṇi	dzo	śikāgolā	rāhto
	rich	and	rel	Chicago-dat	live-3sm

'The rich and who lives in Chicago. . .'

The coordination of a relative clause and adjective is possible only if the latter is part of a relative clause, which then would meet the condition of structural compatibility of the two elements in coordination.

1.3.1.5.2 *Nouns and nominalized constructions*

Nouns and nominalized constructions can be coordinated as in (483) and (484).

Noun and infinitive:

(483) tyālā sāŋgīt āṇi dzhopṇa āwaḍta
he-dat music and sleep-inf-3sn like-3sn

'He likes music and sleep.'

(484) tilā abhyās karṇa āṇi pustaka
she-dat study do-inf-3sn and book-3pl.n

āwaḍtāt
like-3pl.n

'She likes studying and books.'

Noun and gerund:

(485) hyā bātmīne āṇi tī gelyāne madhū
this news-inst and she go-ger-inst Madhu

nirāś dzhālā
depressed become-pst-3sm

'Because of this news and her departure, (lit: 'her leaving (going away)) Madhu became depressed.'

Nouns followed by postpositions/case markers cannot be coordinated with nouns which are not followed by postpositions/case markers as in (486).

(486)* mī myudzhiyammadhe mītālā āṇi
I museum-in Meeta-acc and

ek sũndar tSitra pāhila
one beautiful painting see-pst-3sn

'I saw Meeta and a beautiful painting in the museum.'

1.3.1.5.3 *Different types of adverbials*

Different types of adverbials can be coordinated.

Conjunctive participle and adverb:

(487)	tī	hasūn	āṇi	spaṣṭa	bollī
	she	laugh-conj.part	and	clearly	talk-pst-3sf

'She talked smilingly and clearly.'

Adverb and progressive participle:

(488)	tī	ɔfismadhe	āṇi	moṭar	tsālawtānā
	she	office-in	and	car	drive-prog.part
	kāmātsā	witSār	karte		
	work-of	thinking	do-pres-3sf		

'In the office as well as while driwing the car, she thinks about work.'

When two different types of adverbial participles are coordinated, the use of the coordinator *āṇi* is prohibited as in (489a). Consider example (489) in which the preceding adverbial participle modifies the following one and *āṇi* is absent.

Conjunctive and progressive participles:

(489)	bitShānyāwar	paḍūn	wātstānā	tyālā
	bed-on	lie-conj.part	read-prog.part	he-dat
	dzhop	lāglī		
	sleep-3f	attach-pst-3sf		

'While reading, lying down on the bed, he fell asleep.'

(489a)*	bitShānyāwar	paḍūn	āṇi	wātstānā
	bed-on	lie-conj.part	and	read-prog.part
	tyālā	dzhop	lāglī	
	he-dat	sleep-3f	attach-pst-3sf	

'While lying down on the bed and reading, he fell asleep.'

The following example (490) shows that when more than two different types of adverbial (participles and adverbs) are coordinated without using the coordinator *āṇi* 'and', each preceding adverbial modifies the following. There is no grammatical constraint on the number of adverbials coordinated by this process.

(490)	to	kāl	sakāḷī	bitShānyāwar
	he	yesterday	morning-loc	bed-on

paḍūn	wartamānpatra	wātstānā	ekdam
lie-conj.part	newspaper	read-prog.part	suddenly

uṭhūn	orḍūn	mhaṇālā. . .
get-up-conj.part	shout-conj.part	say-pst-3sm

'Yesterday morning, while he was reading the newspaper, lying on the bed, (after) suddenly getting up, (from the bed) shouting, he said. . .'

1.3.1.5.4 *Active and passive verbs*

Active and passive verbs can be coordinated using the coordinator *āṇi* 'and', as in (491).

(491)	tyāne	ghar	bā̃ndhla	āṇi	lagets
	he-ag	house-3sn	build-pst-3sn	and	immediately

(te)	wikla	gela
(that)	sell-pst-3sm	go(pass)-pst-3sn

'He built the house, and it was immediately sold.'

Although (491) is a perfectly grammatical sentence, Marathi speakers prefer the strategy of subordination (i.e., participialization of the first clause) over sentential coordination. Thus (491a), which is a counterpart of (491), is preferred to (491).

(491a)	(tyāne)	bā̃ndhlyābarobar	te	ghar
	(he-ag)	build-ger-as soon as	that	house-3sn

wikla	gela
sell-pst-3sn	go(pass)-3sn

'Soon after he built it, the house was sold.'

1.3.1.5.5 *Coordination of different categories of verbs*

Generally, verbs of the same category are readily coordinated. However, the coordination of active with passive, as well as affirmative with negative verbs, is also allowed. Similarly, conjunctive participles and progressive participles, when used as manner adverbials, can also be coordinated as in (489). Although coordination of verbs which require their subjects to take dative case markings and simple verbs (which require a nominative subject) is allowed, the frequency and acceptability of such coordination is definitely lower compared to that of the coordination of verbs of the same category, as illustrated in the following examples (492).

Dative and nominative verbs:

(492)	?tyālā	nokrī	miḷālī	āṇi	(to)	khūṣ	dzhālā
	he-dat	job-3sf	receive-pst-3sf	and	(he)	happy	become-pst-3sm

'He got the job and (he) became happy.'

Dative verbs:

(493)	tyālā	nokrī	miḷālī	āṇi	(tyālā)	āwaḍlī
	he-dat	job-3sf	receive-pst-3sf	and	(to-dat)	like-pst-3sf

'He got the job and (he) liked it.'

1.3.2.1 - 1.3.3.3 *Elements of the sentence that can be omitted under identity in coordination*

All major sentence elements can be omitted under identity in coordination.

Omission of subject:

(494)	anū	śikāgolā	gelī	paṇ	ø
	Anu-3sf	Chicago-dat	go-pst-3sf	but	

madhūlā	bheṭlī	nāhī
Madhu-acc	meet-pst-3sf	neg

'Anu went to Chicago but (she) did not meet Madhu.'

Omission of object:

(495)

Mohanne	ø	toḍle	āṇi	mī
Mohan-ag	ø	pick-pst-3pl.m	and	I

ā̃mbe	gharī	nele
mangoes-3pl.m	home-loc	take-pst-3pl.m

'Mohan picked (the mangoes) and I took the mangoes home.'

Omission of verb:

(496)

sudhā	mumbaīlā	ø	āṇi	mī
Sudha	Bombay-dat	ø	and	I

triwendramlā	dzāīn
Trivendram-dat	go-fut-1s

'Sudha (will go) to Bombay, and I will go to Trivendram.'

Omission of adverbial:

(497)

mā̃wśī	nāgpūrhūn	ø	ālī	āṇi	māmā
aunt	Nagpur from		come-pst-3sf	and	uncle

dillīhūn	diliptSyā	lagnālā	ālā
Delhi-from	Dilip-poss	wedding-for	come-pst-3sm

'Aunt came (for Dilip's wedding) from Nagpur and uncle came from Delhi for Dilip's wedding.'

Deletion of adjective:

(498)

thoḍī	barfī	āṇi	ø	khīr	khā
a little	barfī	and	ø	rice pudding	eat-imp-2s

'Eat a little *barfī* (Indian dessert) and (a little) rice pudding.'

1.3.3.4 *Verb agreement in coordination*

The rules of verb agreement in coordination of pronouns are as follows: (a) If one (or more) of the coordinated elements is the first person pronoun, then, regardless of the order of the pronouns, the verb takes first person plural markers as in (499).

(499)	mī, tū, āṇi	aruṇ	udyā	amrāwatīlā	dzāū
	I, you, and	Arun	tomorrow	Amravati-dat	go-fut-1pl

'Tomorrow, I, you and Arun will go to Amravati.'

(b) In the absence of the first person pronoun, the verb takes second person plural markers, if the second person pronoun is coordinated with other second or third person pronouns(s) as in (500). Similar to the pattern in the first person agreement, this agreement pattern is not sensitive to the order of the pronouns.

(500)	tū	āṇi	hī	mula	ekāts	wargāt
	you	and	these	boys	the same	class-loc
	āhāt	kā(y)?				
	are-2pl	Q				

'Are you and these boys in the same class?'

(c) In the case of the third person pronouns, the verb generally agrees with the last coordinated (immediately preceding) pronoun.

Agreement with the last coordinated pronoun:

(501)	te	tyā,	āṇi	te	āle
	it(n)	they(f)	and	they(m)	come-pst-3pl.m

'It, they(f), and they(m) came.'

(502)	te	to	āṇi	tyā	alyā
	they(m)	he,	and	they(f)	come-pst-3pl.f

'They(m), he, and they(f) came.'

(503)	te	to	āṇi	te	paḍla
	they(m)	he	and	it(n)	fall-pst-3sn

'They(m), he, and it(n) fell down.'

The pattern of verb agreement with coordinated nouns is identical to the pattern observed with the coordination of third person pronouns. The following examples illustrate this.

Masculine + feminine + neuter (nouns):

(504)	ghoḍā	moṭar	āṇi	skūṭar	āla
	horse-3sm	car-3sf	and	scooter-3sn	come-pst-3sn

'A horse, a car, and a scooter came.'

Neuter + masculine + feminine (nouns):

(505)	tyātsa	bolṇa,	tyātsā	āwādz	āṇi
	he-poss	speech-3sn	he-poss	voice-3sm	and
	tyātSī	lakab	malā	āwaḍlī	nāhī
	he-poss	style-3sf	I-dat	like-pst-3sf	neg

'I did not like his speech, (his) voice, and (his) style.'

Feminine + neuter + masculine (nouns):

(506)	ek	bāī	ek	mūl	āṇi	ek
	one	woman-3f	one	child-3n	and	one
	māṇūs	ālā				
	man-3m	come-pst-3sm				

'A woman, a child, and a man came.'

Note that in the above examples the coordinated nouns are subjects. If the coordinated nouns are objects, the verb still agrees with the last coordinated (immediately preceding) noun regardless of the gender, and number of the other noun(s). Consider the following examples.

Neuter (singular) + Neuter (plural):

(507)	tyāne	ek	ṭebal	āṇi	tīn	pustaka	āṇlī
	he-ag	one	table-3sn	and	three	books-3pl.n	bring-pst-3pl.n

'He brought one table and three books.'

Masculine + feminine (nouns):

(508)	mī	ek	sũndar	ghar,	ek	kutrā
	I	one	beautiful	house-3sn	one	dog-3sm

āṇi	ek	mulgī	titha	pāhilī
and	one	girl-3sf	there	see-pst-3sf

'There I saw a beautiful house, a dog, and a girl.'

Now consider (509) and (510) in which the order of the nouns in (507) and (508) is reversed. Note that the verb agrees with the last coordinated (immediately preceding) noun.

Neuter (plural) + Neuter (singular):

(509)	tyāne	tīn	pustaka	āṇi	ek	ṭebal	āṇla
	he-ag	three	books-3pl.n	and	one 3sn	table- 3sn	bring-

'He brought three books and a table.'

When the order of the nouns is reversed, the verb agreement changes accordingly.

Feminine + neuter + masculine (singular):

(510)	mī	ek	mulgī	ek	sũndar	ghar
	I	one	girl-3sf	one	beautiful	house-3sn

āṇi	ek	kutrā	titha	pāhilā
and	one	dog-3sm	there	see-pst-3sm

'There I saw a girl, one beautiful house, and a dog.'

When two nouns of different gender and number are coordinated, the pattern of verb agreement is the same as in (504) - (510). Consider the following examples.

Masculine + feminine (nouns):

(511)	madzhā	bhāū	āṇi	tSār	mulī	ālyā
	I-poss-3sm	brother	and	four	girls	come- 3pl.f

'My brother and four girls came.'

Feminine + masculine (nouns):

(512)	tSār	mulī	āṇi	mādzhā	bhāū	ālā
	four	girls	and	I-poss-3sm	brother	come-pst-3sm

'Four girls and my brother came.'

Masculine and neuter (nouns):

(513)	tīn	bail	āṇi	don	wāsra	ālī
	three	bulls-3pl.n	and	two	calves-3pl.n	come-pst-3pl.n

'Three bulls and two calves came.'

Although the general pattern of verb agreement in coordination is discussed above, the following variation is also possible. When two (or more) singular nouns of the same gender (masculine or feminine) are coordinated in the subject position, the verb may alternatively (i.e., in addition to conforming to the above pattern of agreeing with the last coordinated element) take plural endings of the same gender as shown in examples (514) and (515) below.

(514)	rām	(sudhīr)	āṇi	madhū
	Ram-3sm	(Sudhir-3sm)	and	Madhu-3sm
	āle	/	ālā	
	come-pst-3pl.m	/	come-pst-3sm	

'Ram, (Sudhir,) and Madhu came.'

(515)	sītā	(uṣā)	āṇi	mīnā
	Sita-3sf	(Usha-3sf)	and	Meena-3sf
	alyā	/	ālī	
	come-pst-3pl.f	/	come-pst-3sm	

'Sita, (Usha,) and Meena came.'

When a masculine singular and a feminine singular noun are coordinated in the subject position, the verb may alternatively (in addition to conforming to the pattern of agreement with the immediately preceding element) take masculine plural endings.

(516)

rām	āṇi	sītā	ālī	/	āle
Ram-3sm	and	Sita-3sf	come-pst-3sf	/	come-pst-3pl.m

'Ram and Sita came.'

When a masculine plural noun is coordinated with a masculine singular noun, the verb alternatively (i.e., in addition to the regular pattern mentioned above) may take masculine plural endings.

(517)

bhāū	āṇi	rām
brothers-3pl.m	and	Ram-3sm

ālā	/	āle
come-pst-3sm	/	come-pst-3pl.m

'Brothers and Ram came.'

This alternative is blocked if one of the nouns is modified by an adjective (phrase) as in (518).

(518)

sītā	āṇi	maʤhī	bahīṇ	mīnā
Sita-3sf	and	my-3sf	sister	Meena-3sf

ālī	/	*ālyā
come-pst-3sf	/	come-pst-3pl.f

'Sita and my sister Meena came.'

The alternative pattern of agreement mentioned above is blocked in the case of neuter nouns, as shown below in (519).

(519)

wāryāmuḷe	dukān,	(ghar)	āṇi	dzhāḍ
wind-due to	shop-3sn	(house)-3sn	and	tree-3sn

paḍla	/	*paḍlī
fall-pst-3sn	/	fall-pst-3pl.n

'Because of the wind, the shop, (the house,) and the tree fell down.'

When two clauses are conjoined, the verb agrees with the noun within the same clause, regardless of the gender and number of the other coordinated noun (recall example (437) and (439)).

1.4 NEGATION

1.4.1 SENTENCE NEGATION

Sentence negation is expressed by one of the following devices: (a) the negative particles *na* and *nāhī,* and (b) negative verbs such as (i) *nāhī* 'does not exist', (ii) prohibitive negative verbs *nako* (and its variants) 'do not do X', and naye 'should not do X' and (iii) the verb of the negation of identity nawhe 'X is not Y'.

In addition to the above, Marathi also has other negative elements such as negative participles, gerunds, negative modal, and negative prefixes. The distribution of the negative particles is discussed below.

Reduced or non-finite clauses (i.e., participles, gerunds, infinitives) are negated by using the negative particle *na.* Consider examples (520) - (524).

Negation of participle (habitual):

(520)	kām	na	karṇārā	mulgā
		*nāhī		
	work	neg	do-hab.part-3sm	boy

'The boy who does not work/does not do the work.'

Negation of participle (perfective):

(521)	na	wātslela	pustak
	*nāhī		
	neg	read-perf.part-3sn	book-3sn

'The book (which is) not read.' (lit: 'not read book')

Negation of gerund:

(522)

kāl	rātrabhar	na	dzhoplyāne	ādz
	*nāhī			
yesterday	night-all	neg	sleep-ger-inst	today

mādzha	ḍoka	dukhat	āhe
I-poss-3sn	head-3sn	hurt-prog	aux

'I have a headache today because I did not sleep at all last night.' (lit: 'Because I did not sleep all night yesterday, my head is hurting today.')

Negation of infinitive:

(523)

titsa	amerikelā	na/*nāhī	dzāṇa	malā	rutsla
her	America-dat	neg	go-inf-sn	I-dat	like-\ pst-3sn

'I liked it that she did not go to America.' (lit: 'I liked her not going to America.')

Note that *na* immediately precedes the negated element in (520)-(523). However, if the verb has more than one constituent, *na* immediately precedes the last constituent of the verb as in (524). Also note that the use of *nāhī* is prohibited in (520) - (523).

(524)

mumbaīlā	dzāṇār	naslelā	mulgā
Bombay-dat	go-fut	neg-be-perf-part-3sm	boy

'The boy who is not going to go to Bombay'

If *na* is placed after the negated element, the result is an ungrammatical phrase/clause as in (520a) - (523a) which are the counterparts of (520) - (523) respectively. Examples (520) - (523a) differ from (520) - (523) in only the placement of *na.*

(520a)*

kām	karṇārā	na	mulgā
work	do-hab.part-3sm	neg	boy

'The boy who does not work/the boy who does not do the work.'

(521a)*

wātslela	na	pustak
read-perf.part-3sn	neg	book-3sn

'The book (which is) not read.'

(522a)*

kāl	rātrabhar	dzhoplyāne	na
yesterday	night-all	sleep-ger-inst	neg

ādz	mādza	ḍoka	dukhat	āhe
today	I-poss-3sm	head	hurt-prog	aux

'I have a headache today because I did not sleep at all last night.'

(523a)*

titsa	amerkikelā	dzāṇa	na	malā	rutsla
her	America-dat	go-inf-sn	neg	I-dat	like-pst-3sn

'I liked it that she did not go to America.' (lit: 'I liked her not going to America.')

The other negative particle *nāhī* is used for constituent negation as shown in (526a) - (526d). However, it is also used as a negative response to an information question. In this case, it functions as a marker of sentential negation as in (525).

Negative answer to a yes/no question:

(525) Question:

mula	gharī	ālī	kā
children	home-loc	come-pst-3pl.n	Q

'Did the children come home?'

Answer:

nāhī	(mula	gharī	ālī	nāhīt)
neg	(children 3pl.n	home-loc	come-3pl.n	neg-be-pst-pl)

'No, (the children did not come home).'

Note that the sentence may be optionally repeated in the negative response to the information question in (525). The use of *na* is prohibited in this case. The negative particle *nāhī* is homophonous with the negative (modal) verb *nāhī* (present singular). The difference between the two is seen below in (526) where the negative verb is inflected for the plural number. In contrast to this, the examples (526a - (526d) show that the negative particle can not be inflected for the plural number.

(526)	te	kāl	bādzārāt	gele	nāhīt
	they	yesterday	market-loc	go-pst-3pl.m	neg-pl

'They did not go to the market yesterday.'

Negation of subject:

(526a)	te	nāhī	kāl	bādzārāt	gele
		*na			
		*nāhīt			
	they	neg	yesterday	market-loc	go-pst-3pl.m

'They did not go to the market yesterday (i.e., somebody else did).'

Negation of adverb (of time):

(526b)	te	kāl	nāhī	bādzārāt	gele
			*na		
			*nāhīt		
	they	yesterday	neg	market-loc	go-pst-3pl.m

'They did not go to the market yesterday (i.e., they went to market some other day).'

Negation of adverb (of place):

(526c)	te	kāl	bādzārāt	nāhī	gele
				*na	
				*nāhīt	
	they	yesterday	market-loc	neg	go-pst-3pl.m

'They did not go to the market yesterday (i.e., they went somewhere else).'

Sentential negation:

(526d)	?	nāhī	te	kāl	bādzārāt	gele
		*na				
		*nāhīt				
		neg	they	yesterday	market-loc	go-pst-3pl.m

'(Indeed, as I told you before), they did not go to the market.'

Examples (526a) - (526c) show that the negative particle *nāhī* negates the constituent when placed after it. Example (526d) shows that the sentence-initial position is not readily acceptable for *nāhī*. It is awkward but marginally acceptable as the repetition of an already confirmed negation as indicated by the English gloss in (526d).

1.4.1.1 *Negation as a finite/auxiliary verb*

In addition to the negative particles, Marathi uses negative verbs. Negative verbs are used for (a) sentential negation (b) constituent negation, and (c) negation of the identity of the referents of the two constituents. While *nāhī(t)* 'is/(are) not', *nako* 'do not want', and *nawhe* '(X) is not Y' are finite/main verbs, the auxiliary negative verbs are *nako* 'do not do X', *naye* 'should not'. The following example (527) shows the sentential negation with the negative verb *nāhīt* 'are not' which is the counterpart of the positive/affirmative existential verb *āhet* 'are'.

(527)	te	yethe	nāhīt
	they	here	are not (neg-pl)

'They are not here.'

Example (528) illustrates the use of the negative verb *nako* 'do not want' which is the negative counterpart of the verbs *hawa/pāhidʒe* 'want'.

(528)	tilā	ā̃mbe	nakot
	she-dat	mangoes	do not want (pl)

'She does not want mangoes.'

Unlike English and Hindi, Marathi uses the negative verb *nawhe* '(X) is not Y' to express the negation of the equivalence or identity of the referents of the two constituents. The negative verb, in this case, is placed sentence-finally, and is inflected for number agreement with the subject as in (529).

(529)	mī	tudʒhī	maitrīṇ	(Sudhā)	nawhe
	I	your-sf	friend-sf	(Sudha)	neg-s

'I am not your friend (Sudha). (i.e., do not mistake me for your friend Sudha, I am somebody else).'

Example (530) illustrates the use of the prohibitive imperative verb *nakā* (a variant of *nako*) 'do not do (X)', which is used as an auxiliary and not as the main verb. The form of the main verb in such cases remains invariant, i.e., verb stem followed by the suffix *-ū*. The agreement markers are placed on the negative (auxiliary) verb.

(530)	tumhī	gharī	dzāū	nakā
	you(pl)	home-loc	go	do not (pl)

'You (pl) do not go home.'

Another prohibitive (imperative) verb *naye* 'should not' is also used as an auxiliary. Similar to the case of *nako* the form of the main verb in this case too remains invariant - i.e., verb stem followed by -*ū*, and the agreement markers are placed on the negative (auxiliary) verb. Consider (531).

(531)	mulā̃nnī	ase	sineme	baghū	nayet
	children-ag	like these	movies	see	should not (pl)

'The children should not see movies like these.'

Note that in the above examples (i.e., (527) - (531)) the negative verbs are placed in the sentence-final position, and they negate the whole proposition. In contrast to this, when they are placed elsewhere in the sentence, they negate the constituent immediately preceding it. However, the prohibitive imperative *naye* is exception to this rule, i.e., *naye* can not occur in any position other than the sentence-final and thereby it can not be used for the constituent negation. Consider the following examples.

Constituent negation: *nāhīt* 'are not'

(532)	te	nāhīt	yethe
	they	are not (neg-pl)	here

'They are not here (somebody else is (here)).'

Constituent negation: *nako* 'do not want'

(533)	tyā̃nnā̃	nakot	ā̃mbe
	they-dat	do not want-pl	mangoes

'They do not want mangoes (somebody else may).'

Constituent negation: *nako* 'do not do (X)'

(534)	tumhī	gharī	nakā̃	dzāū̃
	you-pl	home-loc	do not (pl)	go

'You (pl) do not go home (go somewhere else).'

Constituent negation: *nawhe* '(X) is not Y'

(535)	mī	nawhe	tuʤhī	maitrīṇ	(sudhā)
	I	neg-s	your-sf	friend-sf	(Sudha)

'I am not your friend (Sudha) (somebody else could be).'

Constituent negation: *naye* 'should not'

(536)*	mulannī	nayet	ase	sineme
	children-ag	should not-pl	like these	movies
	baghū			
	see			

'Children should not see movies like these (others may).'

1.4.1.2 *Negation in modals*

Negation of modals/auxiliary verbs is discussed in 1.4.1.1 above.

1.4.1.3 *Negation and tense*

The tense is expressed in negative sentences by the form of the verb to which the negative element is attached. When the base form is infinitive, the sentence has the habitual meaning (537), when the base form is a gerund, the sentence has the past meaning (538). Similar to the tense, the aspect is also expressed by the base form of the verb. For example if the base form is perfective past participle the perfective aspect is signalled (539); if it is progressive, the progressive aspect is indicated (539).

Infinitive base: habitual meaning:

(537)	tyātsa	na	bolṇa	malā	botsta
	he-poss-3sn	neg	talk-inf-3sn	I-dat	hurt-pres-3sn

'His not talking (habitual) hurts me.'

(538)	tyāne	patra	na	lihilyāmuḷe	malā
	he-ag	letter	neg	write-ger-because of	I-dat

tyātSī	bātmī	kaḷlī	nāhī
he-poss-3sf	news-3sf	get-pst-3sf	neg-3s

'Since he did not write a letter, I did not get his news.'

Perfective (past)-participle base: perfective meaning:

(539)	anilne	pustak	wātslela	nāhī
	Anil-ag	book-3sn	read-perf.part-3sn	neg

'Anil has not read the book.'

1.4.2 CONSTITUENT NEGATION

As discussed earlier, the constituent negation is expressed both by using the negative particle *nāhī* (section 1.4.1) as well as the negative verb (section 1.4.1.1). Additionally, constituent negation may be expressed by the stress, in which case, the negative (auxiliary) verb *nāhī* (or its variant) occurs in the sentence-final position and the constituent which is to be negated, is stressed. The placement of the negative particle *nāhī* (after the constituent) is blocked in this case. Consider the following examples (540) and (541). The stressed constituent is in bold italics.

(540)	***sunandā***	sāḍyā	wikat	nāhī
	Sunanda	sarees-3pl.f	sell-pres	neg-3s

'Sunanda does not sell sarees (somebody else does).'

(541)	sunandā	***sāḍyā***	wikat	nāhī
	Sunanda-3f	sarees	sell-pres	neg-3s

'Sunanda does not sell sarees (i.e., she sells something else).'

Another (marked) device to express constituent negation is to place all the constituents after the verb phrase (i.e., main verb + *nāhī*) as in (542) and (543).

(542)	sunandā	wikat	nāhī	sāḍyā
	Sunanda	sell-pres	neg	sarees

'Sunanda does not sell sarees (i.e., somebody else sells them).'

(543)	sāḍyā	wikat	nāhi	sunandā
	sarees	sell	neg	Sunanda

'Sunanda does not sell sarees (i.e., she sells something else).' (lit: 'Sarees, Sunanda does not sell.')

When there is no constituent immediately before the verb phrase (i.e., when all the constituents are moved to post-verbal position), then the negative auxiliary *nāhī* negates the main verb itself as in (544).

(544)	wikat	nāhī	sunandā	sāḍyā
	sell	neg-3s	Sunanda	sarees

'Sunanda does not sell sarees (i.e., keeps them for herself or gives them away).'

1.4.3 MULTIPLE NEGATIVES

It is not uncommon to have two negatives in a sentence. In this case, usually, one of the negatives is in the subordinate (finite or participial) clause, and the other is in the main clause. If the subordinate clause is a finite clause, then the two negatives cancel each other out, yielding a positive sentence as in (545).

(545)	tyālā	hī	goṣṭa	māhit	nāhī
	he-dat	this	matter-3sf	know	neg-3s
	he	khara	nāhī		
	this-3sn	true-3sn	neg-3s		

'It is not true that he does not know this matter (i.e., He knows it.)'

In contrast to the above, when the negated subordinate clause is a participle, gerund, or an infinitive (and there is another negative in the main clause) the two negatives do not cancel each other out as in (546a) - (546b).

Negated participle:

(546a)	tyāne	na	toḍlela	dzhāḍ	mī
	he-ag	neg	cut-pst.part-3sn	tree-3sn	I

pāhila	nāhī
see-pst-3sn	neg-s

'I did not see the tree which he did not cut.'

Negated gerund:

(546b)	to	na	gelyātsa	malā	māhīt	nāhī
	he	neg	go-ger-poss-3sn	I-dat	know	neg-s

'I am not aware that he did not go.' (lit: 'I do not know of his not going.')

Negated infinitive:

(546c)	tyātsa	na	bolṇa	malā	āwḍat	nāhī
	he-poss-3sn	neg	speak-inf-3sn	I-dat	like	neg-s

'I do not like it that he does not say anything.' (lit: 'I do not like his not speaking.')

1.4.4 NEGATION AND COORDINATION

Negative elements can occur in the coordinator position. In this case the meaning of the coordinated sentences or constituents can be paraphrased in English as 'neither X nor Y . . .' (X and Y are sentences or constituents). Consider examples (547) and (548) below.

Coordinated sentences:

(547)	{na / nāhī}	tyāne	ā̃mbe	khālle
	neither	he-ag	mangoes-3pl.m	eat-pst-3pl.m

{na / nāhī}	ø	phekle
nor		throw-pst-3pl.m

'Neither he ate the mangoes nor did (he) throw them (away).'

Coordinated constituents:

(548)

na	anū	ālī	na	smitā	ø
neither	Anu	come-pst-3sf	neg	Smita	(come-pst-3sf)

'Neither Anu came nor Smita (came).'

In the constituent negation, the negative element may be placed before each of the negated constituents as in (549).

(549)

pūdʒesāṭhī	tyāne	na	phula	ø
worship-for	he-ag	neg	flowers-3pl.n	(bring-pst-3pl.n)

na	pāna	āṇlī
neg	leaves-3pl.n	bring-3pl.n

'He did not bring flowers or leaves for the worship ritual.' (lit: 'He brought neither flowers nor leaves for the worship ritual.')

In the cases, other than the above, the negated sentences are coordinated according to the general rules of coordination discussed in section 1.3.1.1 and sub-sections thereof.

1.4.5 NEGATION AND SUBORDINATION (NEG RAISING)

In the case of a small class of verbs (which express the opinion, belief, or perception) negation of a subordinate clause may optionally be expressed by negating the verb in the main clause. Consider the following examples (550) and (551).

wāṭ-ṇe 'to think/feel'

(550)

malā	wāṭat	nāhī	kī	to
I-dat	think-pres	neg	comp	he

ālā	āhe
come-pst-3sm	be-aux-3s

'I don't think that he has come.'

itStShā asṇe 'to wish'

(551)	mādʒhī	itStShā	nāhī	kī	tine
	I-poss-3sf	wish-3sf	neg-s	that	she-ag

amerikelā	dzāwa
America-dat	go-opt-3sn

'I do not want her to go to America.' (lit: 'My wish is not that she should go to America.')

1.4.6 UNIVERSAL NEGATION

Marathi expresses universal negation by using three types of strategies (a) by negating a question word, (b) by negating a quantifier, and (c) by using a question word with the verb (followed by the irrealis suffix *-ṇār*). The first strategy is commonly used in the Dravidian languages (Sridhar 1990:114), while the second (b) is commonly used in Hindi and other Indo-Aryan languages. The third strategy (i.e., (c) above) of using a question word (without a negative element) is also fairly common in Hindi and other Indo-Aryan languages. However, Hindi uses obligatory stress (on the question word) to make it a rhetorical question, and thus expresses universal negation by implication. Marathi uses an additional strategy. A combination of the question word + verb stem + *-ṇār* in Marathi also expresses universal negation. Examples (552a) - (555) illustrate these strategies.

Negation of question-word: *kadhī* 'when':

(552a)	to	kadhīts	rāgwat	nāhī
	he	when-emph	get angry	neg-s

'He never gets angry.'

The use of the emphatic particle *-ts* is obligatory.

Negation of question word: *koṇtī* 'which one':

(552b)	tyāne	koṇtīts	goṣṭa	malā
	he-ag	which-emph	story-3sf	I-dat

	sāŋgitlī	nāhī
	tell-pst-3sf	neg-s

'He did not tell me any story.'

The emphatic particle *-ts* alternates with another emphatic particle *-hī* in the cases such as (552a) and (552b). In the absence of the emphatic particle the sentences such as (552a) and (552b) are interpreted as questions.

The following example (553) shows the negation of the quantifier.

(553)	tyāne	malā	kāhīts/kāhīhī	sāŋgitla	nāhī
	he-ag	I-dat	something -emph	tell-pst-3sn	neg-s

'He did not tell me anything. (lit: 'He told me nothing.)'

Without the use of the emphatic particles, the sentence in (553) is ambiguous between constituent negation (i.e., negation of *kāhī* 'something' or universal negation (i.e., nothing)).

The strategy of expressing the universal negation by adding the question word with the suffix *-ṇār* to the verb stem is illustrated below. Notice that the negative element is <u>not</u> present in the sentence in this case (554a) and (554b). If the negative element occurs in this construction, it expresses affirmative meaning as illustrated in (555).

Negation without the negative element:

(554a)	aśā	māṇsālā	koṇ	āplī	mulgī
	like this-3sm	man-dat	who	refl-3sf	daughter

	deṇār ?
	give-irr

'Who would give one's daughter to a man like this ? (i.e., no one would)'

(554b)	to	kāy	aśā	praśṇātsa	uttar	deṇār
	he	what	like-this	question-poss-3sn	answer	give-irr

'What answer would he give to a question like this?' (i.e., 'It would not be possible for him to give any answer to a question like this.')

Negation with a negative element:

(555)	to	kā	nāhī	yeṇār ?
	he	why	neg	come-irr

'Why would he not come?' (i.e., 'He will certainly come.')

1.5 ANAPHORA

1.5.1 - 1.5.1.2 MEANS OF EXPRESSING ANAPHORA

Anaphoric relations are expressed by using one of two strategies: deletion and pronominalization. However, deletion is the preferred option. It is very common to delete the subject since the person, number, and gender features of the subject are marked on the verb (see section 1.2.1.2.1). Even when there is no marking on the verb, (as in the case of a direct or indirect object) noun phrases can be readily deleted when they are either mentioned earlier in the discourse or are recoverable from the context. Examples of both types of deletion are given below:

Deletion of the subject when the verb has agreement markers:

(556)	sudhā	kāl	mumbaīhūn	ālī	ø
	Sudha	yesterday	Bombay-from	come-pst-3sf	

maitriṇī	ø	bheṭylā
friends-3pl.f	ø	meet-pst-3pl.f

saglyānśī	bollī	ø	ʤewlī	ø
all-dat	talk-pst-3sf		eat-pst-3sf	

wartSyā	madzlyāwar	dzāūn	ø	dzhoplī
upper-poss	stairs-on	go-conj.part		sleep-pst-3sf

'Sudha came from Bombay, frineds met (her), (she) talked to everyone, ate, went upstairs, and slept.' (lit: 'Yesterday Sudha came from Bombay, friends met her, (she) talked to everyone and having gone upstairs went to sleep.')

Deletion of the subject in the imperative construction:

(557)	sandhyākāḷī	ye	mag	āpaṇ	sinemālā
	evening-at	come-imp-2s	then	we	movie-dat

dzāū	
go-fut-1pl	

'Come in the evening, then we will go to a movie.'

First person subjects are commonly deleted in a conversation as in (558). Note that the verb is marked for the first person in this case.

(558)		udyā	śetāwar	dzāīn
	ø	tomorrow	farm-on	go-fut-1s

'Tomorrow, (I) will go to the farm.'

The following example shows that the subject can be deleted in a narrative when it is recoverable from the context of the discourse regardless of whether or not the verbs agree with it.

(559)	kāhī	warṣānnī	aruṇ	bhāratāt
	some	years-after	Arun-3sm	India-loc

parat	ālā	ø	nokrī	ghetlī
back	come-pst-3sm		job-sf	take-pst-3sf

ø	ek	mulgī	āwaḍlī	mhaṇūṇ	ø
	one	girl	like-pst-3sf	therefore	

lagna	kela	āṇī	ø	amrāwatīlā
marriage-3sn	do-pst-3sn	and		Amravati-at

sthāyik	dzhālā
settle	become-pst-3sm

'After some years Aruṇ returned to India, took a job, (he) liked a girl and got married and settled down in Amravati.'

Note that the subject *Arun* is mentioned only in the first sentence and is deleted in the following sentences. The verbs in the second and the third sentence do not agree with *Arun*; rather they agree with the objects *nokrī* 'job' and *lagna* 'marriage', respectively. However, the deletion of the subject, *Arun,* is readily acceptable since it is recoverable from the context.

1.5.1.3 *Personal pronouns*

Once the participant (subject or object) is introduced, it is common to refer to it anaphorically through personal pronouns as in (560).

(560)	anū	gharī	ālī	āṇi	tine
	Anu	home-loc	come-pst-3sf	and	she-ag

bharbhar	kām	kela
quickly	work-3sn	do-pst-3sn

'Anu came home and she quickly finished the work.'

1.5.1.4 *Reflexive pronouns*

Reflexive pronouns (possessive and emphatic) are also used to express anaphora as in (561) and (562).

Possessive reflexive pronoun:

(561)	anū	āplyā	bhāwākaḍe	gelī
	Anu$_i$	refl-poss$_i$	brother-to	go-pst-3sf

'Anu went to her brother's (house).'

Emphatic reflexive pronoun:

(562)	anū ne	swatāhā	madhūlā	witSārle
	Anu-ag	self-emph.refl	Madhu-dat	ask-pst-3sn

'Anu herself asked Madhu.'

1.5.1.5-6 *Other means of expressing anaphora*

In addition to the above, Marathi has a number of words which function as anaphoric pronouns, adjectives, or adverbs: *saglạ* (and its variants) 'everything/entire', *saglẹ* 'all', *pahila* (and its variants) 'first', *dusra* (and its variants) 'second', etc., *itka* (and its variants) 'this much', *titka* (and its variants) 'that much', *asa* (and its variants) 'this way'/'like this', *tasa* (and its variants) 'that way'/'like that'. The interrogative counterparts are *kitī* 'how much'/'how many', *kasa* 'how' (lit: 'which way').

1.5.2 ANAPHORA IN DIFFERENT SYNTACTIC CONTEXTS

1.5.2.1 *Anaphora within the clause*

Anaphora within the clause is expressed by deletion or pronominalization.

Deletion:

(563)	rām-ne	baykolā	gharī	pāṭhawla
	Ram-ag	wife-acc	home-loc	send-pst-3sn

'Ram sent (his) wife home.'

In this sentence, 'home' refers to the wife's or *Ram's* or to the home which *Ram* and his wife share (which is the most unmarked reference). However, it is a pragmatic inference. The grammar would allow the deleted reference to refer to the subject's or the object's house. The strategy of pronominalization is used to disambiguate the reference as in (564).

Reflexive pronoun refers to the subject:

(564)	rām-ne	madhūlā	āpla	pustak	dila
	Ram-ag	Madhu-dat	refl-poss-3sn	book-3sn	give-pst-3sn

'Ram$_i$ gave Madhu his$_i$ book.'

Non-reflexive pronoun refers to the object:

(565)	rām ne	madhūlā	tyātsa	pustak	dila
	Ram-ag	Madhu-dat	his-poss-3sn	book-3sn	give-pst-3sn

'Ram gave Madhu$_i$ his$_i$ book.'

Note that the reflexive pronoun in (564) refers to the subject while the non-reflexive pronoun in (565) refers to the object.

1.5.2.2 *Anaphora in coordinate structures*

Anaphoric reference is expressed in coordinate structures through deletion or pronominalization. The strategy of deletion is used when (two or more) sentences are coordinated or when two or more clauses/participles are coordinated. The example of deletion in coordinated sentences is (559). Example (566) illustrates the strategy of deletion in the coordination of clauses/participles.

(566) sudhā mulīlā śāḷet potswūn ø
Sudha daughter-acc school-loc bring-conj.part ø

bādzārāt dzāūn ø phaḷa gheūn
market-loc go-conj.part ø fruit-3pl.n take-conj.part

gharī ālī
home-loc come-pst-3sf

'Sudha, after having brought (her) daughter to school, having gone to the market, having taken the fruit came home.'

In both (559) and (566), the coordinated sentences and clauses respectively share the same subject. Also notice that all occurrences of the subject except the first one are deleted. Thus the antecedents or referents of the deleted elements are generally in the earlier sentence(s) or clause(s). However, as seen in (567) and (568), they can occur in the following sentence(s) or clause(s) as well.

(567) ø gharī gelo āṇi mī dzhoplo
ø home-loc go-pst-1sm and I sleep-pst-1sm

'(I) went home and I went to sleep.'

(568) ø amerikelā dzāūn madhū-ne nawā
America go-conj.part Madhu-ag new-3sm

dhandā	surū	kelā
business-3sm	begin	do-pst-3sm

'Having gone to America, Madhu started a new business.'

Example (569) shows that anaphora within a coordinated noun phrase is obligatorily expressed through pronominalization. The strategy of deletion is prohibited in this case since it leaves the postposition stranded (which is not allowed in Marathi).

(569)	parī	āṇi	{ titsā / *ø (tsā) }	bhāū
	Parī	and	her/*ø (pp)	brother

ālā
come-pst-3sm

'Pari and her/* ø (of) brother came.'

Although deletion is the preferred strategy over pronominalization in coordinated sentences as well as clauses, pronominalization is also used alternatively as in (570).

(570)	sudhā	kāmāwar	gelī	āṇi	tine
	Sudha	work-on	go-pst-3sf	and	she-ag

diwasbhar	phon	kelā	nāhī
day-all	phone	do-pst-3sm	neg-s

'Sudha went to work and did not call (me) all day.'

In coordinated sentences, when the coreferential subject NPs have identical case markings as well, deletion of the subject in the second sentence is the only possibility (571a). When the coreferential subjects do not have identical case markings, pronominalization of the subject in the second sentence is obligatory (571b) except when one of the two subjects have *-ne* and the other has a zero (i.e., nominative) case marking (571c) in which case deletion (of the subject) is not ruled out.

subjects with identical case marking:

(571a)	aśok/ø/*to	gharī	ālā	āṇi
	Ashok/ø/he	home-loc	come-pst-3sm	and

dzhoplā
sleep-pst-3sm

'Ashok came home and slept.'

subjects with non identical case marking:

(571b)	tyālā	rāg	ālā	āṇi	tyāṇe/*ø
	he-dat	anger	come-pst-3sm	and	he-ag

pustak	phekūn	dīle
book-3sn	throw-conj.part	give-pst-3sn

'He got angry and he threw away the book.'

(571c)	tyāne	kām	kele	āṇi	to/ø
	he-ag	work-3sn	do-pst-3sn	and	he

gharī	gelā
home-loc	go-pst-3sm

'He did the work and he went home.'

1.5.2.3 *Anaphora between superordinate and subordinate clauses*

Anaphora is permitted between superordinate and subordinate clauses. Finite subordinate clauses (complements) follow, while non-finite (participles, infinitives, noun phrase complements) generally precede the superordinate clauses. Relative clauses may precede or follow the superordinate clauses (although their preferred position is before the superordinate clauses).

1.5.2.3.1 *Anaphora between a superordinate and a following subordinate clause*

Anaphoric reference between a superordinate and a finite subordinate clause is expressed by using deletion or pronominalization. However, pronominalization is preferred over deletion as in (572).

(572) āīne mulālā$_i$ sā̃ŋgitla kī
mother-ag son-dat tell-pst-3sn comp

tyāne$_i$/ø$_i$ amerikelā dzāū naye
ø$_i$/he-ag America-dat go should not

'Mother told her son not to go to America/that he should not go to America.'

Backward deletion or pronominalization is not possible in cases such as (572) as shown in (573).

(573) *āīne ø$_i$/tyālā$_i$ sā̃ŋgitla kī
mother-ag ø$_i$/he-dat tell-pst-3sn comp

mulāne$_i$ amerikelā dzāū naye
son-ag America-dat go should not

'Mother told ø$_i$/him that (her) son$_i$ should not go to America.'

1.5.2.3.2 *Anaphora between a superordinate and a preceding subordinate clause*

When a relative (subordinate) clause precedes a superordinate clause, both backward and forward deletion as well as pronominalization are possible strategies used to express anaphora as in the following sentences. Note that in the following examples, square brackets highlight the clause in which deletion or pronomalization occurs.

Backward deletion:

(574) [dzo ø ālā] to mulgā mādzhā
rel-ø come-pst-3sm cor boy my

bhāū āhe
brother is

'The boy who came is my brother.'

Forward deletion:

(575) [dzo mulgā ālā] to mādzhā bhāū āhe
rel boy come-pst-3sm cor my brother is

'The boy who came is my brother.'

Backward pronominalization:

(576)

[ʤẽmwhā	tī$_i$/ø,	mumbaīlā	gelī]	tẽmwhā
when	she$_i$/ø$_i$	Bombay-dat	go-pst-3sf	then

anū$_i$ne	samudra	pāhilā
Anu-ag	sea-3sm	see-pst-3sm

'When she$_i$ went to Bombay, Anu$_i$ saw the sea.'

Forward pronominalization:

(577)

[ʤẽmwhā	anū$_i$	mumbaīlā	gelī]
when	Anu$_i$	Bombay-dat	go-pst-3sf

tẽmwhā	tine$_i$/ø$_i$	samudra	pāhilā
then	she-ag$_i$/ø$_i$	sea	see-pst-3sm

'When Anu went to Bombay, she saw the sea.'

In both (576) and (577) pronominalization is favored over deletion.

When the subordinate clause is a noun phrase complement, then the anaphoric reference between the subordinate and the superordinate clause is expressed through pronominalization and not through deletion.

Pronominalization using a non-reflexive pronoun:

(578)

[to$_{i,j}$	khāṭik	āhe]	hī	goṣṭa
he$_{i,j}$	butcher	is	this	matter

rām$_i$lā	āwḍat	nāhī
Ram$_i$-dat	like	neg

'Ram$_i$ does not like the fact/matter that he$_{i,j}$ is a butcher.' (lit: 'That he$_{i,j}$ is a butcher (is) the matter that Ram$_{i,j}$ does not like.')

Pronominalization using a reflexive pronoun:

(579)

[āpaṇ$_i$	khāṭik	āhot]	hī	goṣṭa
refl-self$_i$	butcher	are-1pl	this	matter

rām$_i$lā	āwḍat	nāhī
Ram$_i$-dat	like	neg

'Ram does not like the fact that he is a butcher.' (lit: 'That (he) himself, is a butcher is the matter that Ram does not like.')

Deletion can not be used to express anaphoric reference in the sentences (578) and (579) as shown in (578a) and (579a).

Backward deletion:

(578a)	*[ø$_i$ khāṭīk	āhot]	hī	goṣṭa	rāmḷā
	butcher	are-1pl	this	matter	Ram-dat

āwḍat	nāhī
like	neg

'Ram does not like the fact/matter that he is a butcher.'

Forward deletion:

(579a)	*[rām$_i$	khāṭik	āhe]	hī	goṣṭa
	Ram$_i$	butcher	is	this	matter

ø$_i$	āwḍat	nāhī
ø$_i$	like	not

'Ram does not like the fact/matter that he is a butcher.'

1.5.2.3.3 *Anaphora between a non-finite subordinate clause and a superordinate clause*

The anaphoric reference between a superordinate and a non-finite clause (participle, infinitive, and gerund) is expressed through deletion of the coreferential constituent in the subordinate clause.

Participial (subordinate) clause:

(580)	mī	parīlā	[ø	kām	kartānā]	pāhila
	I	Pari$_i$-acc	ø$_i$	work	do-prog.part	see-pst-3sn

'I saw Pari$_i$ (while she was) doing$_i$ the work.'

Infinitive (subordinate) clause:

(581)	āīne	mulī$_i$lā	ø$_i$	śāḷet	dzāylā
	mother-ag	daughter-dat		school-loc	go-inf-dat

sāŋgitla
tell-pst-3sn

'Mother told the daughter to go to school.'

Gerundive subordinate clause:

(582)	madhū	sureś$_i$war	ø$_i$	weḷewar	na
	Madhu	Suresh-on		time-on	neg

ālyābaddal	rāgāwlā
come-ger-because of	get angry-pst-3sm

Madhu got angry at Suresh for not coming on time.'

Although deletion is the preferred strategy in sentences such as (580) and (582), the subject in the participial and the gerundive clause (respectively) is alternatively pronominalized as in (580a) and (582a) below. However, this alternative is not available in sentences with infinitival subordinate clause (581) as illustrated in (581a).

Pronominalization in the subordinate clause:

(580a)	mī	parīlā	[tī$_i$	kām	kartānā]
	I	Pari$_i$-acc	she$_i$	work	do-prog.part

pāhila
see-pst-3sn

'I saw Pari while she was doing the work.'

(581a)*	āīne	mulī$_i$lā	[tīlā$_i$	śāḷet
	mother-ag	daughter$_i$	she$_i$	school-loc

dzāylā]	sāŋgitla
go-inf-dat	tell-pst-3sn

'Mother asked (her) daughter to go to school.'

(582a)	madhū	sureś$_j$war	to$_j$	weḷewar	na
	Madhu	Suresh$_j$-on	he$_j$	time-on	neg

ālyābaddal	rāgāwlā
come-ger-because of	get angry-pst-3sm

'Madhu got angry at Suresh because he did not come on time.'

1.5.2.4 *Anaphora between different subordinate clauses*

Anaphora between successive subordinate clauses is expressed by (a) deleting the first occurrence of the coreferential noun (583 - 585), (b) backward pronominalization and (c) forward pronominalization.

Deletion:

(583)	malā	wāṭta	kī	[ø$_i$	diwasbhar	na
	I-dat	feel-pres-3sn	comp		day-all	neg

bolṇa]	sāŋgta	kī	[madhū$_i$	rāgāwlelā
speak-inf	tell-pres-3sn	comp	Madhu	get angry-past.part

āhe]
is

'I feel that (his) silence (literally: 'not saying anything') all day tells that Madhu is angry.'

Backward pronominalization:

(584)	malā	wāṭta	kī	[tyā$_i$tsa	diwasbhar	na	bolṇa]
	I-dat	feel-pres-3sn	comp	his$_i$	day-all	neg	speak-inf

sāŋgta	kī	[madhū$_i$	rāgāwlelā	āhe
tell-pres-3sn	comp	Madhu$_i$-3sm	get angry-perf.part-3sm	is

'I feel that his$_i$ not saying anything all day tells that Madhu$_i$ is angry.'

Forward pronominalization:

(585)	malā	wāṭta	kī	[Madhu$_i$tsa	
	I-dat	feel-pres-3sn	comp	Madhu$_i$-poss-3sn	
	diwasbhar	na	bolṇa	sãŋgta	kī
	day-all	neg	speak-inf	tell-pres-3sn	comp
	[to$_i$	rāgāwlelā		āhe	
	he$_i$	get angry-past.part-3sm		is	

'I feel that Madhu's not saying anything all day shows that he is angry.'

It should be mentioned here that in (584) and (585) the pronoun *to* 'he' is ambiguous between Madhu and someone else. However, the deletion in (583) unambiguously refers to Madhu. Also, forward deletion, though not very common, is acceptable.

1.5.2.5 *Anaphora between different sentences*

Anaphora between different sentences has already been illustrated in (559), (560), and (566).

1.6 REFLEXIVES

1.6.1 MEANS OF EXPRESSING REFLEXIVITY

Reflexivity is expressed by: (a) the reflexive pronouns *swatāhā* and *āpaṇ* that take different case forms, and (b) the compound reflexive pronoun *āpaṇ swatāhā* .

1.6.2 SCOPE OF REFLEXIVITY

The reflexive pronoun *swatāhā* is restricted to the simple sentence in which it occurs. In contrast to this, *āpaṇ* and *āpaṇ swatāhā* can be used to express sentential as well as intersentential reflexivity. Damle (1966 [1911]), Dalrymple (1990), Wali (1979), and Wali and Subbarao (1991) have discussed only *swatāhā* and *āpaṇ* and have not taken into account the compound reflexives *āpaṇswatāhā*. The following examples show the complex distribution of reflexives.

Reflexivity within a single clause:

(586)

sudhā	swatāhātSe/āple	pustak	phekte
Sudha	refl-poss-3sn	book-3sn	throw-pres-3sf

'Sudha$_i$ throws her$_i$ book.'

(586a)

sudhā	āpleswatāhātse		pustak	phekte
Sudha	refl-poss-3sn	refl-3sn	book-3sn	throw-pres-3sf

'Sudha$_i$ throws her$_i$ own book.'

(586b)

sudhā	āplyā	swatāhālā	sadzawte
Sudha	refl-obl	refl-acc	decorate-pres-3sf

'Sudha decorates herself.'

āpaṇ: reflexivity across clauses:

(587)

mohanlā	wāṭta	kī	āplyāwar	*swatāhāwar
Mohan-dat	feel-3sn	comp	refl-on	refl-on

kuṭumbātSī	dzabābdārī	āhe
family-poss-3sf	responsibility-3sf	is

'Mohan$_i$ feels that he$_i$ has the responsibility of the family.'

Similar to (586a) and (587b), *āpaṇ swatahā* can be alternatively used as a "long distance" reflexive as in (587a).

(587a)

mohanlā	wāṭta	kī	āplyā	swatāhāwar
Mohan-dat	feel-3sn	comp	self-obl	refl-on

kuṭumbātSī	dzabābdārī	āhe
family-poss-3sf	responsibility-3sf	is

'Mohan$_i$ feels that he$_i$ has the responsiblity for the family.'

Although the example in (586) shows that *āpaṇ* can alternate with *swatāhā* to express reflexivity within a clause, the following example (588) shows that this is not always the case.

(588)	anū	swatāhālā/*āplyālā	ārśāt	pāhte
	Anu	refl-acc/refl-acc	mirror-loc	see-pres-3sf

'Anu sees herself in the mirror.'

The distribution of the reflexives in Marathi can be adequately understood on the basis of the scope of the relationship between the antecedent and the reflexive. This relationship has been discussed in detail in Pandharipande (1990d) as follows.

Coreferentiality: (a) a reflexive is co-referential to the antecedent. This relationship is required for the occurrence of a reflexive in a (simple or complex) sentence in Marathi. The reflexives share this feature. None of the reflexives occurs by itself without an explicitly or an implicitly assumed coreferential antecedent. Although reflexives share this feature of coreferentiality with personal pronouns, unlike personal pronouns, reflexives do not occur by themselves. (b) In addition to coreferentiality, reflexives and their antecedents can hold a codependent relationship. A codependent relationship can be variously described as the one which holds between the antecedent and the reflexive: (i) when the antecedent and the reflexive are structurally subcategorized co-arguments of the same verb (example 590), (ii) when the antecedent and the reflexive have the same referent and they function as the source (antecedent) and goal (reflexive) respectively (example (591)), (iii) when the referent of the antecedent is a possessor and the referent of the reflexive is a permanent possession (example 592).

The following examples illustrate the above-mentioned distributional patterns of reflexives. Note that the relationship of coreferentiality does not have to entail codependency whereas codependency must entail coreferentiality. Coreferentiality between the antecedent and the reflexive is expressed by the reflexive *āpaṇ* and codependency by *swatāhā*.

It is important to mention here that the reflexives vary in their syntactic scope: the antecedent of *swatāhā* must be within the same clause in which they occur (see (586) and (587). In contrast, this condition does not apply in the case of *āpaṇ* and *āpaṇ swatāhā,* i.e., their antecedent may or may not occur within the same clause.

āpaṇ: obligatory with a "long-distance" antecedent

(589)	anūlā	wāṭta	kī	madhū	ne
	Anu-dat	feel-pres-3sn	comp	Madhu	ag

āplyālā/*swatāhālā/āplyāswatāhālā	phasawla
refl-acc/refl-acc/refl-acc	deceive

"Anu$_i$ feels that Madhu$_j$ deceived her$_i$/*himself$_j$.'

Swatāhā and *āpaṇswatāhā* can be used in (589) if their antecedent is within the same clause in which they occur (i.e., *Madhu* in this case). Thus (589) will be grammatical with *swatāhā* and *āpaṇ swatāhā* if the sentence means 'Anu feels that Madhu deceived himself.' However, (587a) shows that *āpaṇ swatāhā* can occur in the subordinate clause if the subject of the main clause is identical to the subject in the subordinate clause. Example (590) shows that if the antecedent and the reflexive (within the same clause) are codependent, (i.e., if they are arguments of the same verb), then, *āpaṇ* is blocked and *swatāhā* and *apaṇswatāhā* are the only choices (and *āpaṇ* is blocked in this case).

(590)	anū	swatāhālā/āplyā swatahālā/*āplyālā
	Anu	refl-acc / refl-acc / refl-acc

ārśāt	pāhte
mirror-loc	see-pres-3sf

Anu sees herself in the mirror.'

Example (591) below shows that when the antecedent and the reflexive are identical and are the source and the goal of the action (expressed by the verb) respectively, then, *swatāhā* or *āpaṇ swatāhā* is used and *āpaṇ* is blocked.

(591)	mīnā	swatāhālā/āplyāswatāhālā *āplyālā	sadzawte
	Meena	refl-acc	decorate-pres-3sf

'Meena decorates herself.'

In (591), the agent and the goal of the action of decorating is identical (i.e, *Meena*). While *swatāhā* and *āpaṇ swatāhā* are allowed, *āpaṇ* is blocked.

The following example (592) shows that when the referent of the antecedent is a possessor and the referent of the possessive is a possession which the possessor "owns", then *swatāhā* or *āpaṇswatāhā* is used. However, *āpaṇ* is blocked in this case.

(592)	anūtsa	he	swatāhātsa/*āpla/ āplaswatāhātsa	ghar	āhe
	Anu-poss-3sn	this	refl-3sn	house	is

'This is Anu's own house.'

In (592), it is implied that *Anu* owns the house (i.e., the house is a permanent possession) rather than rents it. Therefore, *swatāhā* or *āpaṇswatāhā* can be used alternatively. The use of *āpaṇ* is blocked in this case.

1.6.3 POSITION OF THE REFLEXIVE PRONOUN

Reflexive pronouns generally follow the noun phrase that has been reflexivized as shown in the sentences in section 1.6.2. However, the occurrence of the reflexive pronoun before the noun phrase is also acceptable when the subordinate clause with the reflexive is moved before the main clause (593). The placement of the reflexive before the antecedent does not convey any additional meaning.

(593)	āplyālā	kāy	pāhidʒe	he	tilā
	refl-dat	what	want-s	this	she-dat

samdzat	nāhī
understand	not

'She does not understand what she wants.'

The prenominal position is prohibited for the reflexive pronoun when the reflexive pronoun is followed by a possessive suffix and is the complement of the subject.

(594)*	he	{āplaswatāhātsa / swatāhātse}	
	this	refl-poss-3sn	
	ghar	anūtse	āhe
	house-3sn	Anu-poss-3sn	is

'This is Anu's own house.'

1.6.4-5 POSSIBLE RELATIONS BETWEEN ANTECEDENT AND REFLEXIVE

Generally, the subject of the sentence can be the antecedent of a reflexive as seen in (595), where the reflexive pronoun *āpaṇ* refers only to the subject *mī* and not to the object *tū* 'you'.

(595)	mī	tulā	āplyā	gharī	neīn
	I	you-acc	refl-obl	home-loc	take-fut-3s

'I will take you to my/*your house.'

The reflexives *swatāhā/āpaṇ/āpaṇswatāhā* may have a dative subject as their antecedent as in (596).

(596)	anūlā	swatāhātse/āple/āpleswatāhātse		
	Anu-dat	refl-poss-3sn		
	ghar	phārse	āwḍat	nāhī
	house	a lot	like	not

'Anu does not like her/her own/ house very much.'

Swatāhā/āpaṇ/āpaṇswatāhā can occur in the positions of the direct object, indirect object, or object of a postposition as shown in the examples below:

Swatāhā in the direct object position:

(597)	anū	swatāhālā/ *āplyālā/āplyāswatāhālā	sadzawte
	Anu	refl-acc	decorate-pres-3sf

'Anu decorates herself.'

Swatāhā in the indirect object position:

(598) prakāś swatāhālā phār
*āplyālā/āplyā swatāhālā
Prakash refl-dat a lot

mān deto
respect give-pres-3sm

'Prakash respects himself a lot.'

Swatāhā in the position of the object of a postposition:

(599) sudhā swatāhāwar/*āplyāwar/āplyāswatahāwar
Sudha refl-on

prem karte
love do-pres-3sf

'Sudha loves herself.' (lit: 'Sudha renders love on herself.')

āpaṇ in the direct object position:

(600) anūlā wāṭta kī
Anu-dat feel-3sn comp

āplyālā/*swatāhālā/āplyā swatāhālā sadzwāwa
refl-acc decorate-opt-3sn

'Anu feels that (she) should decorate herself.'

āpaṇ in the indirect object position:

(601) tyālā wāṭta kī āplyālā/*swatāhālā/
he-dat feel-3sn comp refl-dat

aplyā swatāhālā khūp paise miḷāwe
a lot money get-opt-3pl.m

'He feels that he should get a lot of money.'

āpaṇ in the position of the object of the postposition:

(602) aruṇlā samadzla kī
Arun-dat realize-pst-3sn comp

āplyāsāṭhi/*swatāhāsāṭhi/āplyāswatāhāsāṭhi	paise
refl-for	money

miḷawle	pāhidʒet
earn-perf-3pl.m	should-pl

'Arun realized that (he) should earn money for himself.'

Additionally, the reflexives can occur in the position of the subject complement.

(603)	tyātsa	swatāhātSyā/āplyā/āplyā swatāhātsyā
	his-3sn	refl-poss

paiśāne	bā̃ndhalela	ghar
money-with	build-pst-part-3sn	house-3sn

kāltSyā	purāt	wāhūn	gela
yesterday-poss	flood-loc	sweep-conj.part	go-pst-3sn

'The house built by him with his own money was swept away in yesterday's flood.'

Antecedent subject: reflexive modifier of direct object:

(604)	rāmne	swatātSī/āplī/āplīswatāhātSī	goṣṭa
	Ram-ag	refl-poss-3sf	story-3f

sāŋgitlī
tell-pst-3sf

'Ram$_i$ told his$_i$ story.'

Antecedent subject: reflexive modifier of indirect object:

(605)	śyām	swatāhatSyā/āplyā/āplyāswatāhātSyā
	Shyam	refl-poss

mulā̃nnā	paise	deto
children-dat	money	give-pres-3sm

'Shyam$_i$ gives money to his$_i$ children.'

Antecedent subject: reflexive modifier of subject complement:

(606)	rām	swatāhātSyā/āplyā/āplyāswatāhātSyā
	Ram	refl-poss

wargātsā	puḍhārī	dzhālā
class-poss-3sm	leader	become-pst-3sm

'Ram$_i$ became the leader of his$_i$ class.'

Antecedent subject: reflexive modifier of the object complement:

(607)	gurū	swahātSyā/āplyā/āplyāswatāhātSyā
	teacher	refl-poss-3sm

āwaḍtyā	śiṣyālā	widwān	banawto
like-nom-obl	student-acc	learned	make-pres-3sm

'The teacher makes (his) favorite student learned.'

Antecedent subject: reflexive object of adjective and modifer of such object:

(608)	tyālā	swatāhātsā/āplyāswatāhātsā	khūp	garwa	āhe
	he-dat	refl-poss-3sm	a lot	pride-3sm	is

'He is very proud of himself' (lit: 'He has a lot of pride of himself').

The following examples show that the reflexive can be the agent in the passive construction:

Antecedent subject: reflexive agent in passive construction.

(609)	to	swatāhākaḍūn/āplyāswatāhā kaḍūn/*āplyākaḍūn
	he	refl-inst (by)

phasawlā	gelā
deceive-pst-3sm	go-(pass)-pst-3sm

'He was deceived by himself.'

Additionally, the reflexive can be the modifier of the agent (610), or it can occur in the adpositional phrase as in (611) and (612).

Antecedent subject: reflexive modifier of agent in passive:

(610)

prakāś	swatāhātSyā/āplyā/āplyāswatāhātSyā
Prakash	refl-poss

mitrākaḍūn	marlā	gelā
friend-inst (by)	kill-pst-3sm	go-(pass)-pst-3sm

'Prakash$_i$ was killed by his$_i$ friend.'

Antecedent subject: reflexive element in other adpositional phrase:

(611)

anū	kuṇālā	swatāhāsāṭhī/āplyāsāṭhī/āplyāswatāhāsāṭhī
Anu	who-acc	refl-for

kām	karū	det	nāhī
work	do	give	neg

'Anu does not allow anyone to do work on her behalf (lit: 'for her').'

(612)

mī	arjunlā	swatāhātSyā/āplyā/āplyāswatāhātSyā
I	Arjun-acc	refl-poss

barobar	nāṭkālā	neṇyātsa	watSan	dila
with	drama-dat	take-inf-poss-3sn	promise-3sn	give-pst-3sn

'I promised to take Arjuna with me to the play.'

(613)

dilīp ne	swatāhābaddaltsa	pustak	malā	dila
Dilip-ag	refl-poss-3sn	book-3sn	I-dat	give-pst-3sn

'Dilip gave me the book about himself.'

1.6.6 REFLEXIVE RELATIONS WITHIN NOMINALIZED CLAUSES

The reflexive relations described in section 1.6.4-5 can exist within nominalized clauses as shown in example (614).

(614) tyātsa swatāhātSī stutī karṇa
he-poss-3sn refl-poss-3sf praise-3sf do-inf-3sn

lokãnnā agdī āwaḍla nāhī
people-dat absolutely like-pst-3sn neg

'People did not like his (act of) praising himself at all.'

1.6.7 REFLEXIVE RELATIONS WITHIN ORDINARY NOUN PHRASES

Reflexive relations do not exist within ordinary noun phrases.

1.6.8 REFLEXIVES WITHOUT OVERT ANTECEDENTS

Reflexives do not occur without overt antecedents (within or across clauses), except (a) in fixed idiomatic expressions, (b) when antecedents have been deleted in a discourse, and (c) when the agreement marker clearly indicates the antecedent (subject) as in (615). The idiomatic expressions are illustrated in examples (616) and (617).

Agreement markers as antecedent for the reflexives when the subject is not overtly present in the sentence:
(615) udyā swatāhātsyā/āplyā/āplyā swatāhātSyā
tomorrow refl-poss

gharī dzāīn
home-loc go-fut-1s

'(I) will go to my/my own home tomorrow.'

(616) āpla te mūl dusryãntsa te
refl-poss-3sn that-3sn child-3sn other-poss-3sn that

kārṭa
child (derogatory)

'(One always treats) one's own (child) as *mūl* (a term for 'child'), while others' as *kārṭa* (a derogatory term for child).'

(617)	dusryātSyā	ḍoḷyātla	kusaḷ	dista
	someone else's	eye-in-adj-3sn	blade of grass	see-pres-3sn

	pan̥	āplyā	ḍoḷyātla	musaḷ	disat	nāhī
	but	refl-pass	eye-in-adj-3sn	mortar	see	neg

'(One) sees (even) the blade of grass in someone else's eye, but not the mortar in one's (own) eye.' (It is easy to note even the minor faults of others but it is difficult to recognize one's own obvious (and/or) major faults.)

In the above cases, the implied subject is *lok* 'people'.

1.6.9 OTHER USES OF REFLEXIVE FORMS

1.6.9.1 *Reflexive pronouns as emphatic pronoun*

Example (618) below shows that while *swatāhā* or *āpaṇswatāhā* can be used for emphasis; *āpaṇ* is blocked in this case.

(618)	tī	swatahā/āpaṇswatāhā	ālī
	she	refl	come-pst-3sf

'She herself came.'

Examples (619) illustrates the use of *swatāhāhoūn/āpaṇhoūn*. These reflexives indicate that their antecedent performed the action (expressed by the verb) on his/her own accord and not by any other external coercion. Both *swatāhāhoūn* and *āpaṇhoūn* require their antecedent to be in the same clause in which they occur.

(619)	tyāne	āpaṇhoūn/swatāhāhoūn	malā	paise	diḷe
	he-ag	on his own accord	I-dat	money	give-pst-3pl.n

'He gave me money on his own accord (i.e., without anybody's coercion).'

1.6.9.2 *Reflexive as an adverb*

In section 1.6.2, it has already been shown that the reflexive pronoun is used to express the manner/attitude of the agent of the action in the sentence with the reflexive.

1.6.9.3 *Codependency of the coreferential referents*

As shown in section 1.6.2, reflexives are used to express the codependency of coreferential referents.

1.7 RECIPROCALS

Reciprocal relation is expressed by the following three expressions (a) *ekmek,* (b) *paraspar,* (c) *āp(āp)sāt.* All three can be used to express the reciprocal relation between two or among more than two participants. Therefore, they can be paraphrased as 'each other', or 'one another'. However, it is necessary to note here that *ekmek* can be freely used regardless of whether the participants are animate or inanimate as in (620) and (624) respectively. In contrast to this, *paraspar* and *āp(āp)sāt* are restricted only to animate participants as in (627) - (631). Moreover, *āp(āp)sāt* expresses exclusiveness of the reciprocal relation, i.e., the use of *āp(āp)sāt* indicates that the participants (two or more) interacted with each other/one another and excluded the others. *Ekmek* and *paraspar* do not express exclusiveness of the reciprocal relation. It should also be noted here that *ekmek* and *paraspar* obligatorily take a postposition which further indicates the nature of the reciprocal interaction as shown below in (620) - (628). Since *āp(āp)sāt* has the locative postposition *āt* 'in' built into it, it cannot take any other postposition.

The following examples illustrate the above-mentioned points about the reciprocals.

ekmek 'each other' followed by the accusative postposition:

(620)	prakāś	āṇi	anū	ekmekā̃nnā	bheṭle
	Prakash	and	Anu	each other-acc	meet-pst-3pl.m

'Prakash and Anu met each other.'

ekmek 'each other' followed by the dative postposition:

(621)

prakāś	ānī	anūne	ekmekā̃nnā
Prakash	and	Anu-ag	each other-dat

pustaka	dilī
books	give-pst-3pl.n

'Prakash and Anu gave books to each other.'

ekmek 'each other' followed by the postposition barobar 'with':

(622)

prakāś	āṇi	anū	ekmekā̃nbarobar
Prakaś	and	Anu	each other-with

kām	kartāt
work	do-pres-3pl.m

'Prakāś and Anu work with each other.'

ekmek 'one another' followed by the possessive postposition:

(623)

parikṣet	pās	dzhālelī	mula
examination-in	pass	become-pst-part-3pl.n	boys

ekmekā̃ntSe	abhinandan	karat	hotī
one another-	congratulations-3sn	do-prog	were

'The boys, who (had) passed the examination, were congratulating one another.'

ekmek 'one another' with inanimate participants:

(624)

wādaḷāt	sāpaḍlelī	dzhāḍa	ekmekā̃nwar
storm-in	catch-past-part-3pl.n	trees-3pl.n	one another-on

ādaḷat	hotī	āṇi	tuṭat	hotī
dash-prog	were	and	break-prog	were

'The trees caught in the storm were dashing against one another and breaking.'

paraspar with the dative postposition *-śī*:

(625)	anū	āṇi	rām	parasparā̃nśī	khūp	bolle
	Anu	and	Ram	each other-dat	a lot	talk-pst-3pl.m

'Anu and Ram talked a lot to each other.'

paraspar with the accusative postposition *-nā:*

(626)	anū	āṇi	rām	parasparā̃nnā	śobhtāt
	Anu	and	Ram	each other-acc	suit-pres-pl

'Anu and Ram suit each other.'

paraspar 'one another':

(627)	sankaṭātse	weḷī	lokā̃nnī	parasparā̃nnā
	disaster-poss	time-loc	people-ag	one another-dat
	madat	kelī	pāhidʒe	
	help	do-pst-3sf	should	

'In the time of disaster, people should help one another.'

Impossibiity of *paraspar* with inanimate participants:

(628)*	apghātāt	tSār	moṭarī	parasparā̃nwar
	accident-loc	four	cars	one another-on
	ādaḷlyā			
	dash-pst-3pl.f			

'In the accident, four cars dashed against one another.'

āpsāt 'among':

The participants in the reciprocal action can be two or more when *āpsāt* is used as indicated in (629) and (630), respectively.

(629)	tī	dogha	āpsāt	haḷūḷū	bolat
	those	two	among themselves	softly	talk-prog
	hotī				
	were				

'Those two were softly talking to each other' (i.e., they were whispering something to each other).

(630)	tyā	mulīntsa	āpsāt	bhāṇḍaṇ
	those	girls-poss	among themselves	fight-3sn

dzhāla
happen-pst-3sn

'Those girls had a fight among themselves' (i.e., no one else had anything to do with it).

āpsāt with inanimate participants:

(631)*	apghātāt	moṭārī	āpsāt	ādaḷlyā
	accident-in	cars	among	dash-pst-3pl.f

'The cars dashed against one another.'

In addition to the above, the following facts about the reciprocals need to be noted: (a) the reciprocals and their antecedents are always within the same clause, and (b) the reciprocals can never be used as subjects; they are always followed by a case-marker (other than nominative) or a postposition.

1.8 COMPARISON

1.8.1-3 MEANS OF EXPRESSING COMPARISON

Comparison of non-clausal sentence constituents is expressed by a comparative postposition *(-tSyā) pekṣā* or *-hūn* (ablative case-suffix) followed by the standard of comparison. The possessive postposition *(-tSyā)* which precedes *pekṣā/hūn,* is optional in the case of nouns but obligatory in the case of pronouns, and it follows the object of comparison. There are two possible orders of the elements:

(a) object of comparison + the standard of comparison + possessive case-marker (*-tSyā*) + comparative postposition + adjective or adverb (as in (632)).

(632)	anū	madhū (tSyā)	pekṣā/hūn	ũntsa	āhe
	Anu	Madhu poss	compr	tall	is

'Anu is taller than Madhu.'

(b) standard of comparison + possessive case-marker (*-tSyā*) + comparative postposition + object of comparison + adjective or adverb (as in (633)).

(633)	madhū	(tSyā)	pekṣā/hūn	anū	ūntsa	āhe
	Madhu	poss	compr	Anu	tall	is

'Anu is taller than Madhu.'

(c) if the object of comparison is a pronoun, the deletion of *-tSyā* is blocked.

(633a)	titSyā/*tī	pekṣā/hūn	to	huśār	āhe
	she-poss/*she	compr	he	intelligent	is

'He is more intelligent than her.'

Although both orders of the elements are grammatical and acceptable, the second order generally indicates emphasis on the standard of comparison and is generally accompanied by stress on the standard of comparison. The meaning of (633) can be expressed in English as 'As compared to X (standard of comparison), Y (the object of comparison) is (definitely) taller.

Comparison is also expressed as above through a clausal structure as in (634) and (635). The clause involved in this construction is generally non-finite as in (634). However, as shown in (635), a finite clause may also be used. The ablative case-suffix/postposition *-hūn* is also used alternatively in this case.

(634)	bhikāryālā	paise	deṇyāpekṣā	śāḷelā
	begger-dat	money	give-inf-compr	school-dat

	deṇa	bara
	give-inf-3sn	better

'It is better to give money to a school than to a beggar.'

(635)	to	sinemālā	gelā	tyāpekṣa	gharī
	he	movie-dat	go-pst-3sm	that-compr	home

gelā	astā	tar	bara
go-pst-3sm	be-cond-3sm	then	better

dzhāla	asta
happen-pst-3sn	be-cond-3sn

'He went to a movie, it would have been better had he stayed home.' (lit: 'He went to a movie. Compared to this his staying home would have been better.')

It should be mentioned here that the standard of comparison (in the case of finite/nonfinite clauses) may be optionally followed by the possessive postposition *(-tSyā)*. However, it is much more likely to be absent in the case of the clausal construction (as in (634) and (635)) than the phrasal one (as in (632) and (633)).

In addition to the above, the locative case-marker/postposition *-V(owel)-t/madhe* 'in' is used to express comparison under the following conditions:

(a) the object and the standard of comparison are nominals (and not clauses), (b) the nominals are conjoined by the particle *āṇi* 'and', and (c) one of the locative postposition/case-markers immediately follows the second member of the conjoined phrase.

The order of the elements is variable in this case. The following examples illustrate this construction.

(636)	sudhā	āṇi	dīpā	madhe	sudhā
	Sudha	and	Deepa	in	Sudha

sũndar	āhe
beautiful	is

'Between Sudha and Deepa, Sudha is beautiful.'

(637)	tyā	sarwān(tSyā)t	nikhil	huśār	āhe
	those	all-(poss)-in	Nikhil	intelligent	is

'Among all of them, Nikhil is intelligent.'

1.8.4 ELEMENTS THAT CAN BE OMITTED UNDER IDENTITY

Whenever more than one non-identical element is present in a subordinate clause, the verb can not be deleted even if this means it will be repeated. Consider examples (638) - (640). In (638) the verb is deleted in the subordinate clause where there is only one non-identical element. In contrast to this, in (639), there are two non-identical elements in the subordinate clause, and therefore the verb is retained. (640) shows that the deletion of the verb in this case results in an ungrammatical sentence.

(638)	sudhāpekṣā	anū	bharbhar	kām	karte
	Sudha-compr	Anu	fast	work	do-pres-3sf

'Anu does the work faster than Sudha.'

(639)	sudhātSyā	haḷūhaḥū	kām	karṇyāpekṣā	malā
	Sudha-poss	slowly	work	do-inf-compr	I-dat
	anūtsa	bharbhar	kām	karṇa	āwaḍta
	Anu-poss	fast	work	do-inf-3sf	like-3sn

'I like Anu doing the work fast (better) than Sudha doing the work slowly.'

(640)	*sudhātSyā	haḷūhaḥū	ø	pekṣā	malā
	Sudha-poss	slowly	ø	compr	I-dat.
	anūtsa	bharbhar	kām	karṇa	āwaḍta
	Anu-poss	fast	work	do-inf-3sf	like-3sn

'I like Anu doing the work fast (better) than Sudha doing the work slowly.'

1.8.5 TWO TYPES OF COMPARATIVE STRUCTURE

Two types of comparative structures (phrasal and clausal) are discussed in the previous section. While the case-markers/postpositions *pekṣā* and *-hūn* are used in both structures, the locative case-markers/postpositions *-V(owel) t* 'in' and *madhe* 'in' are restricted to phrasal structures. All comparative clauses are similar in that the nominal (phrasal or clausal) element is optionally (except for the personal pronoun where it is obligatory) followed by the possessive postposition *-tSyā* which is obligatorily followed by an appropriate comparative case marker/postposition.

1.8.6 CORRELATIVE COMPARISON

Correlative comparison is expressed by using the following pairs of relatives and correlatives in the subordinate and the main clause respectively.

	<u>Subordinate clause</u>	<u>Main clause</u>
amount:		
(a)	{ʤewhḍha / ʤitka} 'as much'	{tewhḍha / titka} 'that much'
manner:		
(b)	dzasa 'as'	tasa 'as'

The following example (641) illustrates the use of the above pairs.

(641)	tyālā	{ʤitke / ʤewhḍhe}	ʤāstā	paise	miḷāle
	he-dat	as much	more	money- -3pl.m	get-pst 3pl.m

{titkī / tewhḍhī}	tyātSī	hāw	wāḍhlī
that much	he-poss-3sf	greed-3sf	increase-pst-3sf

'The more money he got, the greedier he became.'

1.8.7 SUPERLATIVE

The superlative is expressed lexically. The universal quantifier *sagḷe* 'all', *sarwa* 'all' is used instead of, or in addition to a specific standard of comparison as in (642).

(642)	āmbā	sagḷyāt/sarwāt/sagḷyā	phaḷāt	swādiṣṭa
	mango	all-in/all-in/all	fruit-in	tasty

(phaḷ)	āhe
(fruit)	is

'Mango is the tastiest (fruit) of all fruits.'

Alternatively, the postposition *(tSyā) pekṣā* is used to express comparison as in (643).

(643)	āmbā	itar	sagḷyā/sarwa	phaḷān (tsyā)
	mango	other	all/all	fruits (poss)
	pekṣā	swādiṣṭa	(phaḷ)	āhe
	compr	tasty	(fruit)	is

'Mango is the tastiest of all fruits' (lit: 'Mango is tastier than all other fruits.').

1.9 EQUATIVES

Equatives are expressed by using the following strategies: (a) by adding the adverb *(tSya) itkV(owel)* 'so much' to the standard of comparison as in (644), (b) by adding the postposition *tSyā barobarīne* 'equal to' to the standard of comparison as in (645), and (c) by adding the postposition *(tSyā) sārkhV(owel)* to the standard of comparison as in (646).

(644)	kṛṣṇā	rām	(tSyā)	itkā(ts)	tākadwān	āhe
	Krishna	Ram	(poss)	eq (emph)	strong	is

'Krishna is as strong as Ram.'

(645)	japān	amerike	tSyā	barobarīne	puḍhārlelā
	Japan	America	poss	eq	developed
	deś	āhe			
	country	is			

'Japan is as developed a country as the U.S.'

(646)	sudhā	anū (tSyā)	sārkhī(ts)	ladzāḷū	āhe
	Sudha	Anu(poss)	similar to (emph)	shy	is

'Similar to Anu, Sudha is shy (indeed).'

The following points need to be noted regarding the above examples. First, the possessive suffix *-tSyā* is optional in the case of *itkV(owel)* 'so much' (644) and *(tSyā) sārkhV(owel)* 'similar to' (646). However, it is obligatory when the postposition *barobarīne* 'equal to' is used (645). Secondly, the emphatic particle *-ts* may optionally occur following the adverb *itkV(owel)* (644) and the postposition *(tSyā) sārkhV(owel)* (646) in positive sentences. However, its occurrence is blocked in negative sentences as in (647) and (648), respectively.

(647)*	kṛṣṇā	rām	(tSyā)	itkāts	tākadwān	nāhī
	Krishna	Ram	(poss)	eq-emph	strong	neg

'Krishna is not as strong as Ram.'

(648)*	sudhā	anū (tSyā)	sārkhīts	ladzāḷū	nāhī
	Sudha	Anu (poss)	similar to-emph	shy	neg

'Sudha is not as shy as Anu (is).'

Equatives can be used without standard of equation. In such cases, the standard appropriate for the task at hand or the topic of the discourse is implied (by the speaker). Consider example (649) below.

(649)	rāmū	titkā	wiśwāsū	naukar	nāhī
	Ramu	that much	trustworthy	servant	neg

'Ramu is not that trustworthy a servant.'

It is to be noted here that the equative *titkā* 'that much (3sm)' in (649) is a correlative adverb of comparison (recall section 1.8.6). The sentence (649) can have one of the following interpretations depending upon the context: (a) *Ramu* is not as trustworthy a servant as the job at hand requires him to be, or (b) *Ramu* is not as trustworthy as the person who is the topic of discussion. The deletion of the elements under identity in the equative construction is the same as discussed in sections on comparison (1.8.1 - 1.8.4). Although deletion of the elements under identity is more frequent, it is not obligatory. A sentence in which no elements are deleted (i.e., (650)) is perfectly grammatical and acceptable.

(650)	sureś	pohto	titkyā	wegāne	mohan
	Suresh	swim-pres-3sm	as much	speed-with	Mohan

paṇ	pohto
also	swim-pres-3sm

'Mohan swims with the same speed as Suresh swims.'

Equatives can be alternatively expressed by using full relative clauses. For example the relative clause in (644a) below is the counterpart of example (644) in which the equative is expressed by using the postposition *(tSyā)itkV(owel)* 'as much'.

(644a)	rām	dʒitkā	tākadwān	āhe
	Ram	rel-eq	strong	is

titkā(ts)	kṛṣṇā	tākadwān	āhe
cor-eq (emph)	Krishna	strong	is

'Krishna is as strong as Ram.'

1.10 POSSESSION

1.10.1 SENTENCE TYPES EXPRESSING POSSESSION

Possession is expressed by the following devices: (a) by the possessive marker *-tSyā* (and its variants) attached to the possessor noun followed by the noun of possession, (b) by the compound postposition *tSyā pāśī* or *tSyā dzawaḷ* 'near/close to' which is attached to the possessor noun followed by the noun of possession, and (c) by the dative subject construction in which the possessor noun is marked with the dative *-lā* and the noun of possession is in the nominative case.

The three patterns are illustrated below.

(651)	tyātsā	koṭ	niḷā	āhe
	he-poss-3sm	coat	blue	is

'His coat is blue.'

(652)

tyātSyā	dzawaḷ/pāśī	ādz	paise	āhet
he-poss	near	today	money-3pl.m	be-3pl

'Today he has money.' (lit: 'He has money near/with him today.')

(653)

malā	tīn	bhāū	āhet
I-dat	three	brothers	are

'I have three brothers.'

The first of the three (651) is an attributive construction which can be paraphrased in English as 'X's Y', while the second (652) can be paraphrased in English as 'X has Y'. Thus the second type of construction has an adverbial phrase which modifies the main verb as 'to be'. The third, dative subject/possessive construction is used with an overt copula which agrees with the noun of possession as in (653).

In addition to the above, there is a 'predicative possessive' in Marathi which is similar to the English construction, 'This book is mine.' In this construction, the noun or pronoun of possession is the subject, which is followed by the possessive form of a possessor noun or pronoun. In this case, the possessor noun functions as an adjective which agrees with the noun of possession in gender and number. The main verb in this construction is *as* 'to be' as in (654).

(654)

he	ghar	mādzha	āhe
this	house-3sn	I-poss-3sn	is

'This house is mine.'

It must be noted here that when the predicate nominal is non-human or inanimate, the meaning is not strictly possessive; rather, it can be paraphrased in English as 'belonging to' (as opposed to 'possessed by'). Example (655) illustrates this point.

(655)

āmhī	amrāwatītse	āhot
we	Amravati-poss-3sm	are

'We are from Amravati.'

1.10.2 ALIENABLE AND INALIENABLE POSSESSION

Alienable and inalienable possessions are not distinguished formally. Inalienable possession is indicated by the dative marking on the possessor noun as in (656).

(656)	malā	don	hāt	āhet
	I-dat	two	hands	are

'I have two hands.'

Use of the postpositional possessive is prohibited in this case as in (657).

(657)*	mādʒhyā	pāśī/dzawaḷ	don	hāt	āhet
	I-poss	near	two	hands	are

'I have two hands.'

An alienable possession is expressed by adding to the possessor noun the possessive marker *-tSyā* followed by the postposition *pāsī* or *dzawaḷ* 'near'.

(658)	tyātSyāpāsī/dzawaḷ	pāts	sāykalī	āhet
	he-poss-near	five	bicycles	are

'He has five bicycles.'

1.10.3 TEMPORARY AND PERMANENT POSSESSION

These two types of possessions are not formally distinguished.

1.10.4-5 POSSESSION OF DIFFERENT TYPES OF ENTITIES

Existential possession of relatives (kinship terms), friends, or of body parts (including mental faculties such as intelligence, ignorance, etc.) are expressed only through dative possessives (659) and not through postpositional possessives as in (660).

(659)	malā	don	bhāū	āhet
	I-dat	two	brothers	are

'I have two brothers.'

(660)*	mādʒhyā	pāśi/dzawaḷ	don	bhāū	āhet
	I-poss	near	two	brothers	are

'I have two brothers.'

Non-human but animate possession (i.e., pets) is expressed by using the postposition *(tSyā) pāśi* or *(tSyā) dzawaḷ* as in (660a).

(660a)	rām (tSyā)	dzawaḷ	ek	kutrā	āhe
	Ram (poss)	near	one	dog	is

'Ram has a dog.'

Additionally, when the noun of possession indicates an abstract possession which affects the body or mind (e.g., pain, happiness, anger, disease, fewer, cold, etc.), then the possessor noun obligatorily takes the dative marking. The postpositional possessive construction is blocked in this context. Consider the following examples.

(661)	malā	dukkha	āhe
	I-dat	pain	is

'I have pain.'

(662)*	madʒhyā	pāśī/dzawaḷ	dukkha	āhe
	I-poss	near	pain	is

'I have pain.'

(663)	madhūlā	khūp	tāp	āhe
	Madhu-dat	a lot	fever	is

'Madhu has a high fever.'

(664)*	madhū (tSyā)	pāśī/dzawaḷ	khūp	tāp	āhe
	Madhu (poss)	near	a lot	fever	is

'Madhu has a high fever.'

The above examples (660)-(664) show that inalienable possession—abstract or concrete—is expressed through the dative subject construction. It may be argued that relatives/friends are viewed as being like one's body parts—inseparable (emotionally in this case) from oneself. Therefore, the existential possession of relatives is expressed through the same (dative-subject) construction used with body parts or other abstract inalienable possesions in (660)-(664).

1.10.6 OTHER

In addition to the above, when the form of possession expresses inherent physical qualities or dispositional traits, the locative postposition -*Vowel + t /-madhe* 'in' is used.

(665)	tyātSyāt	himmat	āhe
	he-poss-loc	courage	is

'He has courage.' (i.e, 'He is courageous.')

(666)	rām madhe	tākad	āhe
	Ram-in	strength	is

'Ram has strength.' (i.e., 'Ram is strong.')

It must be noted here that in examples (665) and (666), the use of the dative (following the possessor noun) is also allowed. However, the dative possessive only indicates possession and is neutral about whether or not it is an inherent physical or dispositional quality of the possessor.

The discussion on the possessives points out that Marathi speakers distinguish alienable and inalienable possessions. The relationship between the possessor and the possession is indicated by the appropriate postpositions/case marking on the possessor. This correlation between the nature of the relationship between the possessor and the possession and the case marking or the postposition is shown below.

It is important to note here that all possessed entities that are human are viewed as inalienable while the rest of the animate beings (i.e., pets) as well as inanimate possessions are viewed as alienable.

(667) Inalienable possession:
(a) permanent/inherited
physical or dispositional - *-V(owel)t/madhe* 'in'
features (examples (665) and (666))

(b) body parts (example (656)) - *-lā* (dat)

(c) relatives/friends - *-lā* (dat)
(animate human possessions is perceived as inalienable)
(example (659))

(d) abstract/temporary - *-lā* (dat)
possessions (fever, anger, etc.) (examples (661) and (663))

Alienable possession:
(a) house, chair, money *-(tSyā) pāśī/dzawaḷ* (example (652))

(b) non-human animate *-(tSyā) pāśī/dzawaḷ*
possession (pets, etc.): (example (660a))

1.11 EMPHASIS

Emphasis is expressed through following devices: (a) intonation, (b) stress, (c) particles, (d) movement of the elements and (e) repetition. A combination of these devices indicates varying degrees of emphasis.

1.11.1 SENTENCE EMPHASIS

Sentence emphasis is expressed by using adverbs, particles, repetition, and intonation.

1.11.1.1 Non-contradictory emphasis

Non-contradictory sentence emhasis is generally expressed by using adverbs such as *nakkī* 'certainly', *dzarūr* 'definitely, *agdī / bilkul/awaśya* 'surely'. Consider the following sentence (668).

(668)	to	udyā	nakkī	parat	yeīl
	he	tomorrow	certainly	back	come-fut-3s

'He will certainly come back tomorrow.'

It is not uncommon to use more than one adverb to convey a higher degree of emphasis as in (669).

(669)	to	udyā	agdī	nakkī	parat	yeīl
	he	tomorrow	surely	certainly	back	come-fut-3s

'He will absolutely, certainly come back tomorrow.'

Additionally, sentence emphasis may be expressed by appending to the sentence a phrase such as *yāt sãuśay nāhī* 'there is no doubt in this' which is generally placed postverbally as in (670).

(670)	to	udyā	parat	yeīl	yāt	sãũśay
	he	tomorrow	back	come-fut-3s	this-in	doubt

	nāhī
	neg

'There is no doubt in that he will come back tomorrow.'

The negative polarity adverb *muḷīts* 'absolutely not' is used to emphasize a negative sentence as in (671).

(671)	to	udyā	parat	yeṇār	nāhī
	he	tomorrow	back	come-fut	neg

'He will not come back tomorrow.'

(672)	to	udyā	muḷīts	parat	yeṇār
	he	tomorrow	absolutely not	back	come-fut

	nāhī
	neg

'He will certainly not come back tomorrow.'

Noncontradictory sentence emphasis can also be expressed by using the emphatic particle *-ts* which is suffixed to the verb as in (673).

(673)	to	udyā	parat	yeīlats
	he	tomorrow	return	come-fut-emph

'He will certainly come back tomorrow.'

Note that in (673) the vowel */ā/* is inserted between the verb form *yeīl* 'will come' and the emphatic particle *-ts* to break the word-final consonant cluster (following the general rule of Marathi phonology).

Sentence emphasis is also conveyed by repeating the entire sentence. This device, though a little awkward, is used with stress on the verb in the second occurrence of the sentence as in (674).

(674)	to	udyā	parat	yeīl;	to	udyā
	he	tomorrow	back	come-fut	he	tomorrow

parat	yeīl
back	come-fut-3s

'He will come back tomorrow; he will come back tomorrow.'

In a sentence such as (674), the marker of an affirmative answer *ho* 'yes' can be inserted between the two occurrences of the same sentence. In this case, *ho* 'yes' functions as a connector of the two sentences.

Pitch is another device which is used to express noncontradictory sentence emphasis. In this case, the pitch on the verb (or verbal element) of a non-emphatic sentence is raised to the highest level.

(675)	to	udyā	parat	yeīl
	he	tomorrow	back	come-fut-3s

'He will certainly come back tomorrow.'

If the above sentence (with a high pitch on the verbal element) is preceded by the single or repeated affirmative answer *ho/ho ho,* the degree of emphasis is further enhanced in that order.

1.11.1.2 Contradictory emphasis

Contradictory emphasis is expressed by the repetition of the negative particle *nāhī* 'no' which precedes the negative sentence as in (676).

(676)	nāhī	nāhī	to	yeṇār	nāhī
	no	no	he	come-fut	neg

'No, no, he will not come.'

When the negative particle is placed immediately after a constituent, it indicates contradictory constituent emphasis as in (677).

(677)	anū	nāhī,	madhū	kām	karel
	Anu	neg,	Madhu	work	do-put-3s

'Madhu, not Anu, will do the work.'

Contradictory emphasis can also be expressed by using the particles (a) *khara* 'truly' and (b) *ṭhoḍV(owel).* The particle *khara* (similar to the Hindi particle *sahī* and Punjabi particle *saī* (see Bhatia 1993)), is placed in sentence-final (post-verbal) position and is generally preceded by another constituent contrastive particle *tar.*

Khara emphasizes the minimum negative condition to perform the act. A sentence with *(tar) khara* is generally accompanied by a warning tone which signifies that the speaker is using the sentence as a warning which is similar to the English expression 'dare not—or else. . .'

(677a)	tyālā	itha	yeū	de	tar	khara
	he-dat	here	come	give	emph	emph

'Let him (at least) come here.'

(Or 'When or if this condition is fulfilled, I will see what I can do.')

The particle *thoḍV(owel),* when used postverbally (or in sentence-final position), expresses sentential contradictory emphasis. It is homophonous with the adverb *thoḍV(owel)* 'a little' and agrees in gender and number with the subject. A sentence with *thoḍV(owel)* generally has an exclamation mark following it, and the use of the particle (in addition to adding emphasis) changes the polarity of the sentence. Thus the structurally positive sentence in (678) conveys negative meaning.

(678)	to	dzāṇār	thoḍā(ts)	āhe !
	he	go-fut	emph-3sm (emph)	is

'He is going to go (indeed)!' (He will certainly not go.)

Note that the particle *thoḍā* is optionally followed by another emphatic particle *-ts.*

Contradictory emphasis can also be conveyed by using the rhetorical question with the question word *kaśālā* 'why' as in (668).

1.11.2.1 *Constituent emphasis*

Constituent emphasis is expressed in a number of ways—by the use of stress, emphatic particles, movement, clefting, repetition or a combinaton of two or more of these devices.

1.11.2.1.1 *Emphatic stress*

Any element of a sentence may be emphasized by stressing it. The following sentence illustrates the difference in the readings of the sentence caused by the stress on different constituents of the sentence.

(679)	mī	kāl	madhūlā	pustak	dila
	I	yesterday	Madhu-dat	book-3sn	give-3sn

(a) I gave the book to Madhu yesterday.
(b) I gave the book to Madhu yesterday.
(c) I gave the book to Madhu yesterday.
(d) I gave the book to Madhu yesterday.
(e) I gave the book to Madhu yesterday.

In (679) the underlined constituents in the English sentence indicate that their respective corresponding Marathi counterparts are stressed yielding the contrastive emphasis vis-a-vis that particular constituent. In a non-emphatic sentence, all constituents generally bear equal stress.

1.11.2.1.2 *Emphatic particles*

The emphatic particles are *-ts* 'only', *hī* 'also', *suddhā* 'also/as well', *tar* 'indeed', *thoḍV(owel)* 'a little' (as discussed in (678)). Consider the following examples (680) - (693) which clearly illustrate the function of these particles:

-ts 'only' (exclusive):

(680)	don	piwḷyā	sāḍyā
	two	yellow	sarees

(681)	donats	pilwḷyā	sāḍyā
	two-emph	yellow-3pl.f	sarees-3pl.f

'only two yellow sarees (as opposed to more or less than two)'

(682)	don	piwḷyāts	sāḍyā
	two	yellow-emph	sarees

'only two yellow sarees (as opposed to sarees of any color other than yellow)'

(683)	don	piwḷyā	sāḍyāts
	two	yellow	sarees-emph

'only two yellow sarees (as opposed to any other clothes)'

hī 'also':

(684)	rāmne hī	pustak	wātsla
	Ram-ag-emph	book-3sn	read-pst-3sn

'Ram also read the book.'

(685)	rām ne	pustak hī	wātsla
	Ram-ag	book-3sn-emph	read-pst-3sn

'Ram read the book also.'

(686) rām ne pustak wātsla hī
Ram-ag book read-pst-3sn-emph

'Ram read the book as well.' (i.e., in addition to buying it)

suddhā 'as well':

(687) anū bhāṣaṇ dete
Anu talk give-pres-3sf

'Anu gives a talk.'

(688) anū suddhā bhāṣaṇ dete
Anu emph talk give-pres-3sf

'Anu as well gives a talk.'

(689) anū bhāṣaṇ suddhā dete
Anu talk emph give-pres-3sf

'Anu gives a talk as well.'

tar 'indeed':

(690) nokarī tar barī āhe
job emph all right is

'As far as the job is concerned, it is all right.'

(691) tyāne paise tar parat dile
he-ag money emph back give-pst-3pl.m

'As far as money is concerned, he gave it back (but did not give back anything else).'

(692) kāl to ɔfismadhe ālā tar
yesterday he office-in come-pst-3sm emph

hotā
be-pst-3sm

'He had come to the office yesterday (however, I do not know anything beyond this. I do not know whether or not he did his work,' etc.)

The use of the particle *thoḍV(owel)* has already been shown in (678) in the context of sentential constrastive stress. It is to be noted here that the particle *thoḍV(owel)* can express constituent emphasis as in (693).

(693)	to	mumbaīlā	thoḍā(ts)	gelā	hotā
	he	Bombay-dat	emph (emph)	go-pst-3sm	be-pst-3sm

'He did not go to Bombay.' ('He had gone some where else' or 'Contrary to the expectation he did not go to Bombay'.)

Emphatic particles may not co-occur if they are not semantically compatible. Thus, co-occurrence of the following particles is blocked.

(694) * hī ts
* ts hī

Note that *hī* is an inclusive emphatic particle while *ts* is an exclusive emphatic particle. When placed after the emphasized element X, they convey the following meanings respectively.

X hī 'X also', X ts 'only X'

Thus it is obvious that if they both are placed after the element (to be emphasized) the resulting sentence (694a) will be anomalous.

(694a)*	anū	{ts hī / hī ts}	asa	mhaṇālī
	Anu	emph-emph	this	say-pst-3sf

'Anu alone (and) also said this.'

(695) * suddhā ts
* ts suddhā

The co-occurrence of *suddhā* 'as well', and *ts* 'only' is also blocked since their co-occurrence would be semantically anomalous.

(696) * {suddhā / hī} thoḍV(owel)

* thoḍV(owel) {suddhā / hī}

The co-occurrence of *suddhā/hī* 'also' and *thoḍV(owel)* is blocked since *suddhā/hī* express the inclusive meaning while *thoḍV(owel)* expresses exclusive meaning. Consider (696a) and (696b).

(696a)*	anū	suddhā/hī	thoḍi (ts)	ālī
	Anu	emph emph	emph (emph)	come-pst-3sf

hotī
be-pst-3sf

'It was not only Anu also who had come.'

(696b)*	anū	ṭhoḍī	(ts)	hī/suddhā
	Anu	emph	(emph)	emph/emph

ālī   hotī!
come-pst-3sf   be-pst-3sf

'It was not only Anu also who had come!'

The emphatic particle *thoḍV(owel)* expresses negative polarity and additionally it identifies the specific element (exclusive) which is negated. Thus in (696a) and (696b) the particle *thoḍV(owel)* emphatically (and negatively) refers to *Anu*. In contrast to this, the emphatic particles *hī* and *suddhā* 'also' expresses the inclusive meaning. Therefore, when these two are juxtaposed with *thoḍV(owel)* the result is a semantically anomalous sentence.

The emphatic particles *ts* 'only' and *thoḍV(owel)* may co-occur since they are semantically compatible, i.e., while *ts* identifies the emphasized element exclusive of others and *thoḍV(owel)* negates the same element (exclusive of others) as in (696c).

(696c)	anūts	thoḍī	asa	mhaṇteḷ
	Anu-emph	emph	this	say-pres-3sf

'It is not only Anu who says this (i.e., others do too).'

(697) * hī suddhā
* suddhā hī

The co-occurrence of *hī* 'also' and *suddhā* 'also' is generally avoided because it is redundant (since both particles convey the same meaning). However, this co-occurrence does not present any semantic anomaly and therefore, is marginally acceptable for some speakers. For those (who accept the co-occurrence of these two) the function of the co-occurrence is to intensify the emphasis on the element immediately preceding them.

(697a) ??	anū	hī suddhā	ālī	hotī
	Anu	emph-emph	come-pst-3sf	be-pst-3sf

'Indeed, Anu also had come.'

It must be noted here that for those speakers who marginally accept (697a), the reverse sequence of the emphatic particles (i.e., *suddhā hī)* is completely unacceptable.

1.11.2.1.3 *Movement of emphasized element*

A constituent of a sentence can be emphasized by moving it to the left (post-verbally) as in (699) and (700).

(698)	sureś	kāl	badzārāt	gelā	hotā
	Suresh	yesterday	market-in	go-pst-3sm	be-pst-3sm

'Suresh had gone to the market yesterday.'

(699)	kāl	bādzārāt	gelā	hotā
	yesterday	market-loc	go-pst-3sm	be-pst-3sm

sureś
Suresh

'Suresh had gone to the market yesterday (as opposed to anyone else).'

(700)	sureś	badzārāt	gelā	hotā,
	Suresh	market-in	go-pst-3sm	be-pst-3sm,

kāl
yesterday

'Suresh had gone to the market yesterday' (as opposed to any other day, e.g., today or the day before yesterday, etc.).

1.11.2.1.4-5 *Clefting and pseudoclefting*

Clefting and pseudoclefting may also express emphasis by using (a) the exclusive emphatic particle *-ts* and (b) a relative clause/relative participle. Consider the following examples which show that various constituents of a sentence can undergo these processes.

Subject clefting:

(701)	śiwādʒī ne	marāṭhyā̃ntsā	mān	rākhlā
	Shivaji ag	Maratha-poss-3sn	pride-3sm	keep-pst-3sm

'Shivaji kept the pride of the Maratha (the Maratha community).'

Relative clause:

(702)	to	śiwādʒīts	hotā	dʒyāne
	cor	Shivaji-emph	was	rel-obl-ag

marāṭhyā̃ntsā mān rākhlā
Maratha-poss-3sm pride keep-pst-3sm

'It was Shivaji indeed who kept the pride of the Marathas.'

Object clefting:

(703)	to	marāṭhyā̃ntsāts	mān	hotā	dzo
	cor	Maratha-poss-3sm-emph	pride	was	rel

śiwādʒīne rākhlā
Shivaji-ag keep-pst-3sm

'It was the pride of the Marathas indeed which Shivaji kept.'

It is to be noted here that the clefted constituent in the above sentences in (702) and (703) is generally followed by the emphatic particle *-ts*. Clefting is possible without *-ts*. However, without *-ts*, this construction is indistinguishable from the relative clause construction and lacks emphasis.

Pseudo-cleft sentences involve relative clauses or relative participles as in (704) and (705) below.

(704)	ʤe	mī	kāl	pāhila	te	ek
	rel	I	yesterday	see-pst-3sn	cor	one

sũndar	phūl	hotā
beautiful	flower	was

'What I saw was a beautiful flower yesterday.'

Relative participle:

(705)	mī	kāl	pāhilela	sũndar	phūl
	I	yesterday	see-pst.part-3sn	beautiful	flower

'The beautiful flower which I saw yesterday . . .'

1.11.2.1.6 *Emphasis by dislocation*

A constituent can be moved out of its canonical position to the left or right of the sentence, with a pause separating it from the rest of the sentence. However, the functional difference between the rightward and the leftward movement is not clear. In addition to moving the elements to the sentence-initial or sentence-final position, certain constituents such as adjectives can be moved out of their position to the front of the noun phrase for emphasis.

(706)	hirwyā	rāŋgātSī	sũndar	ek
	green-obl	color-poss-3sf	beautiful	one

sāḍī	āṇ
saree-3sf	bring-imp

'Bring one beautiful saree of green color.'

In the above sentence (706), the adjective *sũndar* 'beautiful' and the postpositional phrase *hirwyā rā̃ŋgātSī* 'of green color' are moved to the front of the sentence for emphasis. Their normal position in the sentence is after the numeral (*ek* 'one' in this case) and before the nominal.

Any constituent can be placed in the sentence-initial position for emphasis. Consider the following examples:

Locative phrase:

(707)	gatStSīwar	rām	baslā	hotā
	terrace-on	Ram	sit-pst-3sm	was

'On the terrace, Ram was sitting.'

Verb:

(708)	baghitla	mī	tyālā	paise	tsortā̃nnā
	see-pst-3sn	I	he-acc	money	steal-adv.part

'I saw him stealing money.'

For a higher degree of emphasis, the dislocated verb (as in (708)) can be repeated as in (709).

(709)	baghitla,	baghitla	mī	tyālā	paise
	see-pst-3sn	see-pst-3sn	I	he-acc	money

tsortā̃nnā
steal-adv.part

'I saw him, I saw him stealing money.'

Constituents can be moved out of their normal positions and placed in the sentence-final position for emphasis, as illustrated in the following sentences. In the English translation below, emphasis is shown by underlying.

Subject:

(710)	sagḷa	kām	sampawla,	māʤhyā	bahiṇīne
	entire	work-3sn	finish-caus-pst-3sn	I-poss	sister-ag

'My sister finished the entire work.'

Object:

(711)	mī	sāgar	barobar	(tilā)	pāhila	warṣālā
	I	Sagar	with	(her)	see-pst-3sn	Varsha-acc

'I saw (her) with Sagar . . . Varsha.'

Adverb:

(712)	tīne	kām	karāylā	hawa	bharbhar
	she-ag	work	do-inf-dat	should-3sn	fast

'She should do the work fast.'

Adverbial phrase:

(713)	mī	tilā	sāŋgitla	gharī	dzāylā
	I	she-dat	tell-past-3sn	home-loc	go-inf-dat

'I told her to go home.'

Additionally, there seems to be some evidence for a preverbal (i.e., immediately preceding the verb) focus position.

(714)	presiḍenṭ	māʤhyā	gharī	āle
	president	I-poss	home-loc	come-pst-3pl.m

'The president came to my house.'

Preverbal focus:

(715)	māʤhyā	gharī	presiḍenṭ	āle
	I-poss	home-loc	president	come-pst-3pl.m

'It was the president who came to my house.'

1.11.2.1.7 *Repetition*

Adverbs and adjectives are generally repeated for emphasis.

(716)	tī	khūp	khūp	premaḷ	māwśī
	that	very	very	affectionate	aunt

'That extremely affectionate aunt.'

(717)	malā	tyātSyā	tShotyā	tShotyā
	I-dat	he-poss-3pl.f	small-3pl.f	small-3pl.f

goṣtī	āṭhawtāt
things-3pl.f	remember-pres-3pl.f

'I remember small, little things about him.'

Pronouns such as *sagḷa* 'whole', *sarwa* 'all' are repeated for emphasis. In this case the possessive suffix *tsā* (or one of its variants) is added to the first element of the pronominal phrase.

(718)	tyāne	sagḷa	tSyā	sagḷa	waraṇ
	he-ag	whole	poss-of	whole	lentil soup

piūn	ṭākla
drink	take-pst-3sn

'He drank up the whole of the lentil soup.'

1.11.2.1.8 *Inversion*

Inversion of the constituents of a compound verb indicates emphasis.

(719)	tū	he	patra	*phekūn*	de
	you	this	letter	throw	give-imp

'Throw away this letter.'

Inversion:

(720)	tū	he	patra	de	*phekūn*
	you	this	letter	give	throw

'Throw away this letter!'

Similarly, placement of the negation marker *nāhī* in the preverbal (as opposed to its normal, postverbal) position indicates emphasis.

(721)	dīpālī	abhyās	karat	nāhī
	Deepali	study	do-prog	not

'Deepali does not study.'

(722)	dīpālī	abhyās	nāhī	karat
	Deepali	study	not	do-prog

Deepali does not study at all.'

1.11.2.1.9 *Combinations of devices to express emphasis*

A combination of more than one device (of expressing emphasis) indicates a higher degree of emphasis. The pattern of possible combinations is illustrated in 1.11.2.1.2. Additionally, it is possible to use several devices together as in (723), which results in compounding the degree of emphasis.

(723)	saġḷe	tSyā	saġḷets	paise	tyāne
	whole	poss-of	whole-emph	money	he-ag
	uḍawle				
	spend-pst-3pl.m				

'He indeed spent the whole (amount) of money.'

In the above sentence, the pronoun *saġḷe* 'whole' is repeated, and the pronominal phrase (which functions as an adjectival phrase), along with the nominal *paise* 'money', has been moved out of its normal (post subject) position to the front of the sentence. Additionally, the emphatic particle *-ts* follows the pronominal phrase.

1.11.2.2.1 - 1.11.2.2.2.4 *Elements that may be emphasized*

Constituents of a main clause can be emphasized by any of the devices discussed above. However, certain devices are preferred over others for particular constituent-types. For example, noun phrases and adverbials are particularly flexible in terms of taking a wide variety of devices to mark emphasis, such as stress, rising intonation, clefting, dislocation, repetition, and emphatic particles. Verbs also are quite free to take the above devices although repetition of verbs is not as frequent as that of adverbs. Verbs are more sensitive to the movement, stress, and inversion of verbal elements (including the negative particle). The preferred strategies for emphasizing adjectives are repetition, emphatic particles and movement. There seem to be no particular restrictions on subordinate clause constituents that can be emphasized except that their movement must be clause-internal. They generally follow the pattern of the main clause. However, it must be noted here that the movement is much more readily possible for constituents of the main clause than for constituents of the subordinate clause.

In a coordinate construction, no constituent can be individually moved out of a coordinate phrase. However, the whole phrase can be moved for emphasis like any other constituent of a sentence. In the clausal coordination, no constituent can be moved out of its clause. However, its movement within the clause is allowed according to general movement rules.

1.11.2.2.2.5 *Emphasis of more than one constituent simultaneously*

There is no special restriction on the number of constituents that can be emphasized in a sentence as in (724).

(724)	anū	*swatāhāts*	tyālā	*punhā*	*punhā*	*tīts*
	Anu	refl-emph	he-dat	again	again	that

goṣta	*raḍūn*	*raḍūn*	sāŋgat	hotī
story	cry-conj.part	cry-conj.part	tell-prog	was

'Anu herself was telling him the same story, again again while crying continuously.'

The italicized constituent in the example and the underlined constituents in the English translation are emphasized in the sentence.

1.11.3 FOCUS OF YES-NO QUESTIONS

The focus of yes-no questions is emphasized by using the following strategies: (a) stress, (b) movement, i.e., fronting of the element in focus, (c) emphatic particle, and (d) alternative yes-no question. These devices are illustrated in the following examples.

Stress:

(725)	tū	udyā	*mādza*	kām	karśīl	kā?
	you	tomorrow	my	work	do-fut-2s	Q

'Will you do my work tomorrow?'

The underlined element is stressed and is the focus of the yes-no question in this sentence. Word stress always overrides intonation. Any constituent of the sentence can be brought under focus by stressing it.

Movement:

(726)	*mādza*	*kām*	tū	udyā	karśil	kā?
	I-poss-3sn	work	you	tomorrow	do-fut-2s	Q

'Will you do my work tomorrow?

In the above sentence, the object-phrase *mādzā kām* 'my work' is moved out of its normal position to the sentence-initial position and thereby is brought into focus.

Emphatic particle:

(727)	mādza	kām	tū	udyāts	karśil	kā?
	I-poss -3sn	work	you	tomorrow-emph	do-fut-2s	Q

'Will you do my work tomorrow itself?'

Again, the emphasized element *udyā* 'tomorrow' followed by the emphatic particle *-ts* is the focus of the yes-no question in (727).

Alternative yes-no question:

(728)	tū	mādza	kām	udyā	karśīl	kī
	you	I-poss-3sn	work	tomorrow	do-fut-2s	or
	udyā	karṇār	nāhīs?			
	tomorrow	do-fut	neg-2s			

'Will you do my work tomorrow or will you not do my work tomorrow?'

The element under focus is repeated with stress in the second clause.

1.12 TOPIC

1.12.1 MEANS OF INDICATING THE TOPIC OF A SENTENCE

There is no particular marker which exclusively marks the topic in Marathi. However, various strategies are used to indicate the topic of a sentence. The following examples indicate topicalization by leftward movement which places a constituent in the sentence initial position. In the unmarked SOV word order, the subject is treated as topic.

(729)	gharātSyā	tShaprāwar	to	baslā	hotā
	house-poss	roof-on	he	sit-pst-3sm	was

'On the roof of the house, he was sitting.'

(730)	tyātSī	bahīṇ	he	bara	dzhāla
	he-poss-3sf	sister	this	good	happen-pst-3sn

kī	amerikelā	gelī	nāhī
comp	America-acc	go-pst-3sf	neg

'His sister, it was good that she did not go to America.'

(731)	āilā,	hī	kāltSīts	goṣṭa	āhe
	Mother-acc	this	yesterday's-emph	matter	is

kī	rameś	dɔkṭarkaḍe	gheūn	gelā
comp	Ramesh	doctor-to	take	go-pst

'Mother, it is only yesterday's matter, that Ramesh took (her) to the doctor.'

Note that in (729) the locative phrase is moved to the sentence initial position. Examples (730) and (731) show that the elements in the subordinate clause can also be moved to the front of the matrix clause.

It must be noted here that some of the charecteristics of topic and emphasis are identical, especially, movement (of constituents) to sentence initial position and definiteness. Consequently, some of the markers of emphasis may also be used as topic markers as illustrated below.

The contrastive particle *tar* can also function as a topic-marker.

(732)

tudzha	ghaḍyāḷ	tar	mī
you-poss-3sn	watch-3sn	emph	I

kālats	tulā	parat	dila
yesterday-emph	you-dat	return	give-pst-3sn

'As for your watch, I returned (it) to you yesterday itself.'

(733)

tyātsa	nāgpūrlā	dzāṇa	tar
he-poss-3sn	Nagpur-dat	go-inf-3sn	emph

āwaśyak	hota
necessary	was

'As for his going to Nagpur, (it) was necessary.'

Additionally, a particle *mhaṇdze/mhaṇdʒe* is used to mark the topic. The particle *mhaṇdze/mhaṇdʒe* is an archaic form of the second person imperative of the verb *mhaṇ* 'say' (i.e., 'you say' (see Bloch 1970 for further discussion on the imperative in old Marathi)). When used as a topic-marker, it follows the element being topicalized and expresses the meaning 'As far as X (topic) is concerned ...' Consider the following example:

(734)

śiwādʒītSī	aurangdʒebāśī	bheṭ	mhaṇdʒe
Shivaji-poss-3sf	Aurangzeb-dat	meeting	topic-work

ek	phār	moṭhī	aitihāsik	ghaṭanā	hotī
one	very	important	historical	event-3sf	was

As for Shivaji's meeting with Aurangzeb, (it) was a very important historical event.'

It must be noted here that *mhaṇdʒe* can also function as a particle conjoining two sentences or as a verb in a sentence such as *king mhaṇdʒe rādzā* 'king (in English) mean *rādzā* (in Marathi)', etc. In the present context, we are not taking those functions into account.

The processes of infinitivalization as well as gerundivalization also can be viewed as devices of topicalization. In both cases the subordinate clause is generally nominalized and is moved to the front of the of the matrix sentence as in (735) and (736) respectively.

Infinitive:

(735)	tyātSyā	sahadz	hasṇyāmuḷe	mādzhā
	he-poss	natural	smile-inf-because of	I-poss-3sm
	rāg	nighūn	gelā	
	anger	away	go-pst-3sm	

'Because of his natural smile (lit: 'because of his natural smiling) my anger vanished (lit: went away).'

Gerund:

(736)	tilā	nokrī	miḷālyāmuḷe	tyālā
	she-dat	job	get-ger-because of	he-dat
	ānanda	dzhālā		
	happiness-3sm	happen-3sm		

'Because she got a job, he became happy.'

1.12.2 ELEMENTS THAT CAN BE TOPICALIZED

All elements may be topicalized by the devices discussed above.

1.12.3 OBLIGATORY / OPTIONAL STATUS OF TOPICALIZATION

Topicalization is an optional process in Marathi.

1.13 HEAVY SHIFT

1.13.1 HEAVY SHIFT PROCESSES

Heavy shift is the process which moves a structure with one head with many adjuncts or one or more complex adjuncts out of their normal or canonical position. Such movement can be optional or obligatory. Heavy shift is particularly difficult to define in the case of languages such as Marathi (also Hindi, Punjabi, and many other Indian languages), since there is considerable flexibility of word-order and, thereby, placement of structures in a sentence.

There is no instance of obligatory heavy shift in Marathi. However, there are many cases where heavy structures are moved from their normal position. Those cases typically involve right movement of the elements. Examples of this movement are given in section 1.13.2 below.

1.13.2 STRUCTURES SUBJECT TO HEAVY SHIFT

Adjective phrases, noun phrases and adverbial phrases, as well as most subordinate clauses (with a few exceptions) may undergo heavy shift.

1.13.2.1 *Adjective phrases*

Adjective (including relative clauses and relative participles) phrases generally occupy the prenominal position. Except for appositive relative clauses, adjective phrases are not subject to heavy shift.

(737)	kāl	bheṭlā	ʤyātSī	tumhī
	yesterday	meet-pst-3sm	rel-poss-3sf	you

khūp	tārīf	kelī	hotī	to
a lot	praise-3sf	do-pst-3sf	be-pst-3sf	he

'(I) met him yesterday - the one whom you had praised a lot.'

1.13.2.2 *Noun phrases*

Noun phrases are among the structures which are frequently subjected to heavy shift. These include the quotatives, infinitives, and gerundive complements.

Although the postverbal positioning of the quoted clause is an option available to all quotative constructions, in general, when a quoted clause is 'heavy', it is more likely to appear to the right of the verb than before it.

(738)

mī	udyā	yeīn	asa	tī
I	tomorrow	come-fut-1sn	quot	she

mhaṇālī
say-past-3sf

' "I will come tomorrow", she said.'

(739)

tī	mhaṇāḷī	kī	mī	udyā
she	say-pst-3sf	comp	I	tomorrow

yeīn	(asa)
come-fut-1s	(quot)

'She said, "I will come tomorrow." '

Note that the quoted clause may appear sentence-initially (738) or post-verbally (739). However, a heavy clause is more likely to appear post-verbally as in (740).

(740)

āī	mhaṇālī	kī	puḍhtSyā	āṭhawaḍī
mother	say-pst-3sf	comp	next-poss	weekly

bādzārāt	mī	tuʤhyāsāṭhī	tShān	bāŋgḍyā
market-in	I	you-for	nice	bracelets

gheīn
buy-fut-1s

' Mother said, "I will buy nice bracelets for you in the next weekly market (bazaar)." '

Moreover, there is a sylistic difference between the two clauses. The occurrence of the quotative to the right of the sentence is more frequently used in the written as opposed to the spoken style of Marathi.

It is not possible to unambiguously analyze (740) as 'heavy shifted' since the option of placing the quoted clause in the front of the matrix clause is available to the speaker.

Infinitival phrases can also be shifted to the post-verbal position as in (741).

(741)	malā	agdī	āwḍat	nāhī	tyātsa
	I-dat	absolutely	like	not	his

winākāraṇ	rāgāwṇa
without any reason	get angry-inf-3sn

'I absolutely do not like, his getting angry without any reason.'

The infinitival phrase would normally occupy the pre-verbal (object) position.

(742)	tyātsa	winākāraṇ	rāgāwṇa	malā
	his	without any reason	get angry-inf-3sn	I-dat

agdī	āwḍat	nāhī
absolutely	like	not

'I absolutely do not like his getting angry without any reason.'

Gerundive phrases, similar to infinitival phrases, can be moved to the post-verbal position (744). The normal position for the gerunds is immediately preceding the verb (743).

(743)	gelā	āṭhawḍābhar	satat	pāūs	ālyāmuḷe
	last	week-entire	continuously	rain	come-ger-because-of

gawat	agdī	hirawa	dzhālā	āhe
grass-3sn	absolutely	green	become-pst-3sn	is

'Because it has rained the entire past week, the grass has become absolutely green.'

(744)	gawat	āgdī	hirawa	dzhāla	āhe	gelā
	grass	absolutely	green	become-pst-3sn	is	last

āṭhawḍābhar	satat	pāūs	ālyāmuḷe
week-entire	continuously	rain	come-ger-because-of

'The grass has become absolutely green because it has rained continuously the entire past week.'

1.13.2.3 *Adverb phrases*

Adverb phrases of several types may be moved to the right of the main verb from their normal position, which is immediately preceding the main verb.

(745)	ek	diwā	tyā	nadīwartSyā	paḍkyā	dzunyā
	one	lamp	that	river-on-poss	dilapidated	old

gharāt	manda	manda	dzaḷat	hotā
house-in	dimly	dimly	burn-prog	was

'A lamp, in that old, dilapidated house on the river, was dimly burning.'

(746)	ek	diwā	manda	manda	dzaḷat	hotā
	one	lamp	dimly	dimly	burn-prog	was

tyā	nadīwartSyā	paḍkyā	dzunyā	gharāt
that	river-on-poss	dilapidated	old	house-in

'One lamp was dimly burning in that old, dilapidated house on the river.'

1.13.3-4 LANDING SITES OF HEAVY STRUCTURES

Although right movement of constituents is generally viewed as heavy shift, some occurrences of sentence-initial gerundival or infinitival phrases can also be treated as resulting from heavy shift, since sentence-initial position is not their normal or canonical position. Examples of this type of shift are given below.

Infinitive:

(747)	malā	titsa	punhā	punhā	nāgpurlā
	I-dat	her	again	again	Nagpur-acc

dzāṇa	āwḍat	nāhī
go-inf-3sn	like	not

'I do not like that she visits Nagpur over and over again.' (lit: 'I do not like her visiting Nagpur over and over again.')

Left-shift:

(748)	titsa	punhā	punhā	nāgpurlā	dzāṇa
	her	again	again	Nagpur-acc	go-inf-3sn
	malā	āwḍat	nāhī		
	I-dat	like	not		

'I do not like that she visits Nagpur over and over again.' (lit: 'Her visiting Nagpur over and over again (is what) I do not like.')

Gerundival phrases, similar to infinitival phrases, generally occur immediately before the verb (749). However, they can be moved to the front (sentence-initial) position (750).

Gerund:

(749)	madhū	tī	bātmī	aiklyābarobar	khuṣ
	Madhu,	that	news	hear-ger-as soon as	happy
	dzhālā				
	become-pst-3sm				

'As soon as he heard that news, Madhu became very happy.'

Left movement:

(750)	tī	bātmī	aiklyābarobar	madhū	khuṣ
	that	news	hear-ger-as soon as	Madhu	happy
	dzhālā				
	become-pst-3sm				

'As soon as he heard the news, Madhu became very happy.'

Although both left movement and right movement involve a shift, these two types of shifts are not functionally identical. Left movement topicalizes the shifted element(s) and thereby serves the discourse function of introducing the topic of the sentence. In contrast to this, the sentence-final occurrence (i.e., right movement) of the element has an attributive function similar to that of an adjective or a relative clause, which modify the content of the information already provided by the rest of the sentence. Similar functions of heavy shift are observed in Kannada (See Sridhar 1992:148-149).

1.13.5 HEAVY SHIFT WITH ELEMENTS ADJACENT TO COMPLEMENTIZERS

The head of the subordinate clause is always moved along with the rest of the clause. The following example shows that the lexical head of a noun phrase complement moves along with the complement.

(751) saglyā̃nnā hī goṣṭa māhīt āhe kī tī
all-dat this matter know is comp she

atiśay suswabhāwī mulgī āhe
very good-natured girl is

'Everyone knows the fact that she is a very good-natured girl.'

(752) tī atiśay suswabhāwī mulgī āhe hī
she very good-natured girl is this

goṣṭa saglyā̃nnā māhīt āhe
matter all-dat know is

'Everyone knows the fact that she is a very good-natured girl.'

Note that in (752) the lexical head *goṣṭa* 'matter/fact' is moved to the left of the verb along with its complement.

1.14 OTHER MOVEMENT PROCESSES

There are no other movement processes other than those described in the preceding sections.

1.15 MINOR SENTENCE TYPES

1.15.1 VOCATIVES

Vocatives can consist of (a) a proper name, or a common noun such as *mulā* 'boy!', *mulī* 'girl!'. Some vocative forms of nouns are given below in (753).

(753)

I	Masculine singular	Vocative	Gloss
(a)	ghoḍā 'horse'	ghoḍyā	'o, horse'
(b)	dhobī 'washerman'	dhobyā	'o, washerman'
(c)	tsākū 'knife'	tsākwā	'o, knife'
(d)	dew 'god'	dewā	'o, god'
II	Neuter singular	Vocative	Gloss
(a)	bāḷ 'child'	bāḷā	'o, child'
(b)	sukāṇū 'sail'	sukāṇwā	'o, sail'
(c)	pāṇī 'water'	pāṇyā	'o, water'
III	Feminine singular		
(a)	nadī 'river'	nadī	'o, river'
(b)	kalpanā 'imagination'	kalpane	'o, imagination'
(c)	bhinta 'wall'	bhintī	'o, wall'
IV	Plural	Vocative	Gloss
Masculine			
(a)	dhobī 'washerman'	dhobyā̃nno	'o, washermen'
(b)	dew 'gods'	dewā̃nno	'o, gods'
(c)	tsākū 'knives'	tsākwā̃nno	'o, knives'
Neuter:			
(a)	baḷa 'children'	baḷā̃nno	'o, children'
(b)	sukāṇwe 'sails'	sukāṇwā̃nno	'o, sails'
(c)	pāṇī 'water'	pāṇyā̃nno	'o, waters'
Feminine:			
(a)	nadyā 'rivers'	nadyā̃nno	'o, rivers'
(b)	kalpanā 'imaginations'	kalpanā̃nno	'o, imagination'
(c)	bhintī 'walls'	bhintī̃nno	'o, walls'

(b) Kinship terms are used as vocatives for relatives: *āī* 'mother', *bābā* 'father', *māmī* 'aunt', *ādʒī* 'grandma', etc. Kinship terms are used also for close friends who are viewed as members of the family. Therefore, the appropriate kinship terms (appropriate to the age of and the addressor's relationship to the addressee) are used for friends as well. For example, an older brother's friend is also addressed by the term *dādā* 'older brother', while a mother's friend is addressed as *māwśī* 'aunt', father's friend is addressed as *kākā* 'uncle', and so on. This tradition of adressing friends by kinship terms is commonly shared in most regions in India. When Marathi speakers use English, they generally transfer this pattern of their native speech to the English language as well. It is important to mention here that the above speech pattern functions as a means of establishing and recognizing an intimate bond between the speaker and the addressee. However, the same pattern is generally used when the addressee is a total stranger. In this case, the use of the kinship terms indicates respect for the addressee. The addressee in this case often belongs to a higher social class than the addressor. Thus the cab-drivers, vegetable vendors, or shopkeepers of small businesses generally address their customers by using kinship terms. In contrast to this, modern shopkeepers whose shops are in the westernized malls, generally avoid using kinship terms for their customers. They use "modern" terms such as *sāheb* 'sir', *bāī* 'lady' or *sir* or *madam*.

The use of kinship terms as address terms is largely restricted to informal contexts. In formal/professional contexts, kinship terms are avoided. Instead, one of the following conventions ((a) or (b)) is followed:

Modern Setting	Traditional Setting
(a) Mr. X/Mrs. X X bāī (for women)	(b) X rāw (for men)

Additionally, it is quite conventional to address a person by the name of his/her profession, i.e., *ḍɔkṭar* 'doctor'/ *ḍɔkṭar sāheb* 'doctor, sir', *dʒmādār* 'sweeper', *dhobī* 'washerman', *māstar* 'teacher', *māstarīṇ bāī* 'lady teacher', *polis* 'policeman', *bhādʒīwālā* 'vegetable vendor', *indʒīniyar sāheb* 'engineer sir', etc.

The traditional polite address term used by a wife for her husband is *aho*, while the address term used by a husband for his wife is *aga*. The terms *aho* and *aga* do not convey any particular meaning; rather, they can be viewed as attention-getters. Additionally, there are two types of attention-getters which are generally followed by the 'real' vocatives: (a) polite -*aho* 'sir, madam', (b) impolite/derogatory -*are*.

In traditional Maharastrian society in particular, and Indian society in general, the use of proper nouns is generally avoided. In the context of an intimate or close relationship between the addressee and addressor, the use of proper nouns is viewed as improper, since it fails to express the close relationship between the addressor and the addressee. In contrast to this, kinship terms express recognition of the relationship.

In a formal/professional context, the use of proper nouns (unaccompanied by the counterpart of *sir, madam*) is viewed as impolite, since such use fails to express recognition of the professional identity of the addressee, and, secondly, it fails to indicate the nature of the professional relationship between the two.

In a society where the identity of an individual is largely defined in terms of his/her relationship with the group (family, society, nation, etc.) it is not surprising that the vocatives manifest this very foundation of the identity of the individual. In order to understand the structure of the vocatives, it is essential to understand the conditions of appropriateness (*maryādā*) in the linguistic behavior of Marathi speakers. (For further discussion on *maryādā*, see Pandharipande 1991a, 1992c).

1.15.2 EXCLAMATIONS

There are diverse types of exclamations in Marathi which are used to express various emotions/mental states. Marathi shares some of these with the Dravidian languages (specially Kannada and Telugu) and some with the Indo-Aryan languages (especially Hindi, Gujarati, and Punjabi).

Exclamations expressing surprise:

(754) (a) ayyā! (restricted to women)
(b) are! (men and women)

shock:
(755) are bāpre! 'oh, father!'

pleasant surprise:
(756) oho!, ababa!, ahāhā!, aga baī!

pain:
(757) āī ga 'oh! mother!'

disapproval:
(758) tShe!, tShe! tShe!, tsa tsa!, tShaṭ!, haṭ!, tShī!, ũũ!, thū!

approval:
(759) hoy!, wāhwā!, bhale!, śābās!, phakkaḍ!, yāw!, khāśī mārū!

Gods' names:
(760) are dewā! 'o, god!', rāmā!, are kṛṣṇā! 'o, Kriṣṇā!', parameśwarā 'o, supreme god!'

Gods' names are used to express a wide range of emotional states of mind such as surprise, a response to an unexpected event, the feeling of helplessness, pain, disapproval, etc. In general, gods' names are used very often before starting work or after finishing it, before going to bed, soon after getting up, etc.

bashfulness:
(761) iśśya (restricted to women)

disgust:
(762) śī or śī śī

(763) thū (the sound of spitting)

Additionally, question words such as kāy 'what', *kitī* or *kittī* 'how much', *kasa* 'how', etc. are used as exclamations.

(764)	kāy	sũndar	gāṇa	mhaṇte	tī!
	what	beautiful	song	say-pres-3sf	she

'What a beautiful song she sings!' or 'How beautifully she sings!'

(765) tyāne kittī ā̃mbe āṇle!
he-ag how many mangoes bring-pst-3pl.m

'How many mangoes he brought!' (i.e., 'He brought a lot of mangoes!')

(766) kasa sũndar ʤangal hota te!
how beautiful forst was it

'What a beautiful forest it was!'

1.15.3 GREETINGS

Greetings are expressed variously according to the context of the situation or the social class. For example, the educated 'elite' class of Marathi speakers who are exposed to western ways of life (through western (English) education), generally use 'good morning!', 'good afternoon', and 'good night' as greetings at different times of the day. Banks, modern businesses (i.e., car dealers' shops, airports, western-style department stores and shops, etc.) are generally places where the use of greetings in English is becoming extremely fashionable.

In contrast to this, more traditional people, or in traditional contexts (family, friends or formal traditional gatherings, such as weddings, funerals, or any other traditional festivals) the most generally used greeting is *namaste* '(I) bow to you' or *namaskār* 'the action of prostrating (is being performed by me)'. Again, both *namaste* and *namaskār* are Sanskrit expressions and are used largely by people who belong to the middle to low middle class or to the traditional upper class. Farmers, workmen, vegetable vendors, etc. generally use the following expression to greet one another: *rām rām* 'Ram, Ram'.

1.15.4 TOPIC QUESTIONS

These are questions where only the topic is retained and the rest is deleted.

(767) sagḷa ṭhīk ?
everything all right

'Is everything all right ?'

(768) tsalāytsa ?
go-in-poss-3sn

'Should we go (now) ? (usually used as a suggestion).

(769) kām ?
work?

'What kind of work do you do ? (generally used when hiring laborers for manual labor)

(770) gāwātsa nāw ?
village-poss-3sn name-3sn

'What is the name of your village ?' (generally used while exchanging information regarding one's home-village)

(771) dʒewṇār ?
eat-fut

'Will you eat ?' (generally used when the speaker wants to find out whether the hearer would like to eat (dinner) or more specifically, whether the hearer would like to join the speaker in eating the meal).

1.15.5 SHORT ANSWERS

Short answers frequently consist of single words or phrases as in (772) - (772e).

(772)	madhū	gharī	ālā	kā ?
	Madhu	home-loc	come-pst-3sm	Q

'Did Madhu come home ?

Answers:

(772a) ho 'yes'
(772b) nāhī 'no'
(772c) māhit nāhī
know not

'I don't know.'

(772d) kuṇās ṭhāūk
who-dat know

'Who knows ?' (Nobody knows.)

(772e) nāhī, mumbaīlā gelā
neg, Bombay-to go-pst-3sm

'No, (he) went to Bombay.'

1.15.6 INFINITIVE SENTENCES

Infinitive clauses are generally subordinate clauses which are dependent on main clauses. However, they can be used as independent clauses in the following contexts.

(a) When formal instruction directions are given (These frequently appear at railway stations, on street signs, and in other public places):

(773) piṇyātse pāṇī
drin-inf-poss-3sn water-3sn

'Drinking water (is available here).'

(774) ʤewṇyātSī wa rāhṇyātSī uttam soy
eating-inf-poss-3sf and lodge-inf-poss-3sf excellent facility-3sf

'(There is) an excellent facility for lodging and boarding.'

1.15.7 NONCHALANT EXPRESSIONS

Expressions of unconcern or nonchalance generally consist of a pair of sentences conjoined by the particles *kīmwā/āthwā/wā* 'or'.

(775) to ālā kāy kīmwā gelā kāy
he come-pst-3sm Q or go-pst-3sm Q

'Who cares whether he comes or goes?'

(776)	to	dzago	wā̃/athwā̃	maro	(malā̃
	he	live-opt-s	or	die-opst-s	I-dat

	kā̃y	tyatsa)
	Q	it-poss-3sn

'He may live or die. (i.e., What do I care? lit: 'What is it to me ?')'

1.16 OPERATIONAL DEFINITIONS OF WORD CLASSES

1.16.1 NOUN

The noun is defined syntactically and morphologically. Syntactically, it can be:
(a) the head of a noun phrase, which may additionally contain other elements such as determiners, and adjectives.
(b) the head of a relative clause, infinitive participle or a gerund.

Morphologically, a noun can be followed by a case-suffix or a postposition, and, in the case of count nouns, a plural suffix, an honorific marker (generally, lexical item such as *-rāo* or *-pānta* (masculine) - *bāi* (feminine) (which are generally contextually determined). The verb generally agrees in person, gender, and number with the head noun if the head noun is not followed by any case marking or a postposition. Thus the verb does not agree with the head noun in the case of dative-subjects, where the dative subject is followed by the dative case-marker. Similarly, the so-called ergative subject does not control verb agreement if it is followed by the agent-marker *-ne* (i.e., in the case of the third person). However, in the case of first and the second person subjects of the ergative construction, the verb does not agree with the subject noun even when it is not followed by any case-marker or postposition (see 1.2.1.2.1).

1.16.2 PRONOUN

Pronouns consist of various types such as (a) personal, (b) demonstrative, (c) possessive, (d) reflexive. These differ from one another in terms of their lexical form and their distribution.

Syntactically, pronouns, similar to noun phrases can occur as subject, direct object, indirect object, complement, complement of a postposition, and head of a noun phrase, and modifiers of a noun.

1.16.3 VERB

The verb is the obligatory constituent of the predicate. In the imperative, as well as in affirmative sentences, it can be the only constituent. Both finite and non-finite verbs are marked for tense and/or aspect (For a detailed discussion of the verbal morphology and aspect, see sections 2.2.2, 2.2.2.1-5, 2.1.3.3 - 2.1.3.3.2.2.2).

1.16.4 ADJECTIVE

There are two types of adjectives—"true" or "basic" and "derived". The "true" adjectives are of the type *sũndar* 'beautiful', *moṭha* 'big', etc., and the "derived" adjectives are relative participles or adnominals, i.e., noun + adjectivalizing suffix of the following type—*gharātlā* (house-loc-adjectivalizing suffix) 'the one in the house' (for a detail discussion, see sections 1.2.2 - 1.2.2.3).

Syntactically, adjectives generally precede the noun which they modify. However, in a well-defined context, they may occur following the noun (see 1.2.2.1.1). They can be modified by adverbs of degree (see section 1.2.2.3).

Morphologically, adjectives can be divided into two groups—those which take the agreement markers of gender and number of the noun which they modify and those which do not take any agreement markers of the noun. Examples of the two types follow:

Adjective *tShoṭV*(owel) 'small':

(777) *tShoṭa* dzhāḍ
small-sn tree-3sn

'A small tree'

(777a) *tShoṭyā* mulī
small-pl.f girls

'Small girls'

Adjective sũndar 'beautiful':

(777b)	*sũndar*	dzhāḍ
	beautiful	tree

'A beautiful tree'

(777c)	*sũndar*	mulī
	beautiful	girls

'Beautiful girls'

1.16.5 POSTPOSITION

Postpositions are characterized by their position. They are bound morphemes and they immediately follow the noun phrase which they govern. Their complement nouns or noun phrases are generally marked by the possessive case, which is indicated by an optional, or in many cases obligatory (possessive), case-marker immediately following the noun (or the noun phrase). Examples of the two types are given below:

Optional:

(778)	gharā (tSyā)	dzawaḷ
	house-poss-	near

'Near the house'

Obligatory:

(779)	tyātSyā/*tyā	baddal
	he-poss he	about

'About him'

1.16.6 NUMERAL AND QUANTIFIER

Numerals and quantifiers do not have any specific morphological markers. They are generally defined semantically. They most commonly occur between demonstratives and classifiers.

(780)	tyā	kāhī	dzunyā	āṭhwaṇī
	those	few	old	memories

'Those few old memories'

However, some quantifiers, along with their classifiers, occur after the head noun as in (781) and (782).

(781)	te	tighe
	those	three-3pl.m

'those three (men/boys, etc.)

(782)	āmhī	pāts	dzaṇ(a)
	we	five	persons

'We five persons'

Numerals indicating more than a few can be modified by the lexical modifier *dzawaḷ dzawaḷ* or *dzawaḷ pās* (lit: 'near, near') or 'approximately'.

Numerals may occur in doublets to signify approximate quantity as in *pāts - sahā* 'five or six' (lit: 'five six').

A single repetition of a numeral indicates frequency (e.g., *pāts pāts minitãnnī* 'every five minutes) or distribution (of the objects, people, etc.) as in (783) and (784).

(783)	mī	pratyekālā	pāts	pāts	ãmbe	dile
	I	everyone-dat	five	five	mangoes	give-pst-3pl.m

'I gave everybody five mangoes each.'

(784)	dahā	dahā	lokãntSyā	ṭoḷīne	āmhī
	ten	ten	people-poss	batch-inst	we

parwatāwar	tsaḍhlo
mountain-on	climb-pst-1pl.m

'We climbed the mountain in batches of ten each.'

1.16.7 PARTICLE

Particles are attached freely to any constituent of the sentence or to the sentence (as a whole unit). They are not inflected. Some examples of the particles are as follows:

(a) the emphatic particle - *tsa* (attached to nouns, verbs, adjectives, adverbs and postpositions),

(b) the quotative *mhaṇūn* or *asa* (attached to the whole sentence),

(c) the emphatic reflexive *swatāhā* (attached to the specific constituent), and,

(d) the negative particle *na* which is used as a bound (in *naslelā* 'the one who is not') or free morpheme (*na ālelā* 'the one who (has) not come) morpheme). (For more discussion, see section 1.4 and sub-sections thereof).

MORPHOLOGY

2.1 INFLECTIONAL MORPHOLOGY

2.1.1 NOUN INFLECTION

2.1.1.1 *Means used to express syntactic and semantic functions of noun phrases*

The syntactic and semantic functions of noun phrases are expressed primarily by case-suffixes and postpositions. Word order does not play a role in determining grammatical relations except (a) where inanimate objects can not be distinguished from subjects (in a non-ergative construction) in terms of case-marking (since neither is case-marked with a suffix), and (b) where both the indirect and the direct object are marked with the homophonous postpositions *-lā* (dative and accusative, respectively).

Marathi uses case-markers and postpositions extensively for indicating syntactic and semantic functions. Case-markers are bound suffixes which are attached exclusively to noun phrases, and they immediately follow the noun or the noun phrase.

The following examples illustrate the various case-markers. It needs to be mentioned here that Marathi has three genders (masculine, feminine, and neuter). Nouns are divided into different classes according to gender as well as the phonological shape of their base-forms (e.g., vowel (*ā/ī*, etc.) ending, consonant ending, etc.). The following example (785) is of a consonant-ending masculine noun, *parwat* 'mountain'.

(785)	Case	Marker	Example
	Nominative	ø	parwat
	Accusative	-lā	parwatālā

Instrumental	-ne	parwatāne
Dative	-lā	parwatālā
Ablative	-(h)ūn	parwatāhūn
Possessive-genitive	-tsā/tSī/tse	parwatātsā
Locative	-t	parwatāt
Vocative	-ā	parwatā

Several points need to be made about the above paradigm in particular and all paradigms of noun phrases in general. First of all, not all case-markers are invariant; accusative, instrumental, dative, and locative markers have variant forms. Thus, the following remarks on variation in these case-markers are in order:

(i) The accusative/dative markers *-s* and *-te* are variants of the accusative/dative markers *-lā* (sg) and *-nā* (pl). The use of *-lā* (sg) and *-nā* (pl) is most frequent in written and spoken vareties of Standard Marathi (SM), while the use of *-s* was more widespread in Old Marathi (for further discussions on *-s*, see Bloch 1970). In SM the use of *-s* is restricted to the formal written register, specifically, to official memos. In the informal register of SM it is affixed to the name of the addressee in the beginning of a letter (e.g., *priya mādhurīs* 'Dear Madhuri'). In the Nagpuri variety of Marathi (NM), spoken on the northeastern border of Maharashtra, *-s* is used in the informal/spoken register. In this case, it marks the speaker as 'uneducated', as one who is not familiar with the Standard Marathi which is taught in school and is part of the speech of educated Marathi speakers in the Nagpur area).

(ii) *-te* is another variant of the dative suffix generally listed in the grammars of Marathi. This suffix was used in Old Marathi (especially, in Marathi poetry), and until the middle of the 20th century its use in the traditional religious/mythological poetry was quite acceptable (see Bloch: 1970 for discussion on *-te*). However, this suffix is not used at all in modern SM.

(iii) The instrumental suffixes *-ne* (sg) and *-nī* (pl) are used in all dialects and registers of Marathi. While *-śī* is recognized as an instrumental suffix by most speakers of Marathi, it is (alternatively) used only in the northeastern variety of Marathi spoken by the Marathi-speaking community which migrated to Madhyapradesh.

(iv) The locative suffix *-t* is most commonly used in all dialects/varieties of Marathi. However, some consonant-ending feminine stems take *-ī* as opposed to *-t* (e.g., *sakāḷī* (f) in the morning'/**sakāḷt.*) Some consonant-ending masculine stems also take the locative suffix *-ī* (as an alternative to *-t*). For example, *'hāt* 'hand' may take the suffix *-t* (i.e., *hātāt* 'in the hand') or the suffix *-ī* (i.e., *hātī* 'in the hand')). Similarly, some consonant-ending neuter stems such as *ghar* 'house' may take *-t* or *-ī*, alternatively, (i.e., *gharāt/gharī* 'in the house').

(v) There is no separate overt suffix to mark vocative singular nouns (masculine, feminine, and neuter). However, the form of the stem in this case is identical to the form which a noun-stem takes when a case-suffix or a postposition is added to it. Noun-stems in all genders in Marathi undergo certain changes when case-suffixes/postpositions are added. Those changes include insertion of an additional vowel/glide between the stem and the case-suffix. The changes are determined by the gender, number, and class of the noun. The paradigms of various noun-classes (see (786) - (806)) illustrate the changes in stems when case-suffixes are added. Those derived forms are traditionally called by grammarians *sāmānya rūpa* (literally, the common form of the stem followed by any case-suffix). We will refer to this form as the 'oblique' form of a stem. A singular oblique form (without any suffix following it) of a noun-stem is treated as the vocative singular form as well. The plural vocative suffix *-no* is affixed to the plural oblique forms of all noun-stems regardless of their gender and/or their morphological classes. (786) - (790a) are some examples of vocative forms of nouns in various genders and numbers.

		Stem	Oblique	Vocative
(786)	mas. sg.	dew 'god'	dewā	dewā 'o, god!'
(786a)	mas. pl.	dew 'god'	dewā	dewā̃nno 'o, gods!'
(787)	mas. sg.	ghoḍā 'horse'	ghoḍyā	ghoḍyā 'o, horse!'
(787a)	mas. pl.	ghoḍe 'horses'	ghoḍyā	ghoḍyā̃nno 'o, horses!'

(788)	neut. sg.	dzhād̤ 'tree'	dzhād̤ā	dzhād̤ā 'o, tree'
(788a)	neut. pl.	dzhād̤a 'trees'	dzhād̤ā̃nno	dzhād̤ā̃nno 'o, trees!'
(789)	neut. sg.	pillū 'young of an animal'	pillā	pillā 'o, cub! or 'o, kid!'
(799a)	neut. pl.	pilla 'young ones of an animal'	pillā	pillā̃nno 'o, cubs! or 'o, kids!'
(790)	fem. sg.	nadī 'river'	nadī	nadī 'o, river!'
(790a)	fem. pl.	nadyā 'rivers'	nadyā	nadyā̃nno 'o, rivers!'

Now let us consider the paradigms of various noun classes.

I. Masculine nouns:

(791) (a) *-ā* ending masculine nouns such as *ghod̤ā* 'horse'

	ghod̤ā 'horse' (singular)	*ghod̤e* 'horses' (plural)
nom	ghod̤ā	ghod̤e
acc	ghod̤yālā	ghod̤yā̃nnā
inst	ghod̤yā̃ne	ghod̤yā̃nnī
dat	ghod̤yāla	ghod̤yā̃nnā
abl	ghod̤yāhūn	ghod̤yā̃nhūn
poss/gen	ghod̤yātsā	ghod̤yā̃ntsā
loc	ghod̤yāt	ghod̤yā̃t
voc	ghod̤yā	ghod̤yā̃nno

(792) (b) *-ī* ending masculine nouns

	dhobī 'washerman' (singular)	*dhobī* 'washermen' (plural)
nom	dhobī	dhobī
acc	dhobyālā	dhobyā̃nnā
inst	dhobyā̃ne	dhobyā̃nnī
dat	dhobyāla	dhoyā̃nnā
abl	dhobyāhūn	dhobyā̃nhūn
poss/gen	dhobyātsā	dhobyā̃ntsā
loc	dhobyāt	dhobyā̃t
voc	dhobyā	dhobyā̃nno

(793) (c) *-ū* ending masculine nouns, *lāḍū* ' a kind of dessert'

	lāḍū 'a kind of dessert' (singular)	*lāḍū* 'pieces of a kind of dessert' (plural)
nom	lāḍū	lāḍū
acc	lāḍwālā	lāḍwā̃nnā
inst	lāḍwā̃ne	lāḍwā̃nnī
dat	lāḍwālā/lāḍūlā	lāḍwā̃nnā/lāḍū̃nnā
abl	lāḍwāhūn/lāḍūhūn	lāḍwāhūn/lāḍūhūn
poss/gen	lāḍwātsā/lāḍūtsā	lāḍwā̃ntsā/lāḍū̃ntsā
loc	lāḍwāt/lāḍūt/	lāḍwā̃t/lāḍū̃t
voc	lāḍwā/lāḍū	lāḍwā̃nno/lāḍū̃nno

(794) (d) *-a* ending masculine nouns, *mitra* 'friend'

	mitra 'friend' (singular)	*mitra* 'friends' (plural)
nom	mitra	mitra
acc	mitrālā	mitrā̃nnā
inst	mitrā̃ne	mitrā̃nnī
dat	mitrālā	mitrā̃nnā
abl	mitrāhūn	mitrā̃nhūn
poss/gen	mitrātsā	mitrā̃ntsā
loc	mitrāt	mitrā̃t
voc	mitrā	mitrā̃nno

(795) (e) *-u* ending masculine nouns, *śatru* 'enemy'

	śatru 'enemy' (singular)	*śatru* 'enemies' (plural)
nom	śatru	śatru
acc	śatrūlā	śatrū̃nnā
inst	śatrūne	śatrū̃nnī
dat	śatrūlā	śatrū̃nnā
abl	śatrūhūn	śatrū̃nhūn
poss/gen	śatrūtsā	śatrū̃ntsā
loc	śatrūt	śatrū̃t
voc	śatrū	śatrū̃nno

(796) (f) consonant-ending masculine nouns, *dew* 'god'

	dew 'god' (singular)	*dew* 'gods' (plural)
nom	dew	dew
acc	dewālā	dewā̃nnā
inst	dewā̃ne	dewā̃nnī
dat	dewālā	dewā̃nnā
abl	dewāhūn	dewā̃nhūn
poss/gen	dewātsā	dewā̃ntsā
loc	dewāt	dewā̃t
voc	dewā	dewā̃nno

It is to be noted here that the class of nouns (masculine, feminine, and neuter) ending in short vowels is very small in Marathi. Most nouns in this class are from Sanskrit, and final short vowels are lengthened in their oblique forms. In contemporary Marathi, there exists a variation in the written and spoken forms of these nouns, where they are alternatively written and pronounced with long vowels. There is a clear indication that these nouns are increasingly being interpreted as long vowel ending forms.

The following are patterns for feminine nouns in Marathi.

(797) (a) *-ā* ending feminine nouns, *śāḷā* 'school'

	śāḷā 'school' (singular)	*śāḷā* 'school' (plural)
nom	śāḷā	śāḷā
acc	śāḷelā	śāḷā̃nnā
inst	śāḷene	śāḷā̃nnī
dat	śāḷeḷā	śāḷā̃nnā
abl	śāḷehūn	śāḷā̃nhūn
poss/gen	śāḷetsā	śāḷā̃ntsā
loc	śāḷet	śāḷā̃t
voc	śāḷe	śāḷā̃nno

(798) (b) *-ī* ending feminine nouns, *nadī* 'river'

	nadī 'river' (singular)	*nadyā* 'rivers' (plural)
nom	nadī	nadyā
acc	nadīlā	nadyā̃nnā
inst	nadīne	nadyā̃nnī
dat	nadīlā	nadyā̃nnā

abl	nadīhūn	nadyā̃nhūn
poss/gen	nadītsā	nadyā̃ntsā
loc	nadīt	nadyā̃t
voc	nadī	nadyā̃nno

(799) (c) *-o* ending feminine nouns , *bāyko* 'wife'

	bāyko 'wife' (singular)	*bāykā*'wives' (plural)
nom	bāyko	bāykā
acc	bāykolā	bāykā̃nnā
inst	bāykone	bāykā̃nnī
dat	bāykolā	bāykā̃nnā
abl	bāykohūn	bāykā̃nhūn
poss/gen	bāykotsā	bāykā̃ntsā
loc	bāykot	bāykā̃t
voc	bāyko	bāykā̃nno

(800) (d) consonant-ending feminine nouns, *wāṭ* 'way'

	wāṭ 'way' (singular)	*wāṭā* 'ways' (plural)
nom	wāṭ	wāṭā
acc	wāṭelā	wāṭā̃nnā
inst	wāṭene	wāṭā̃nnī
dat	wāṭelā	wāṭā̃nnā
abl	wāṭehūn	wāṭā̃nhūn
poss/gen	wāṭetsā	wāṭā̃ntsa
loc	wāṭet	wāṭā̃t
voc	wāṭe	wāṭā̃nno

The class of consonant-ending feminine nouns in (801) differs from those in (d) in that the oblique forms in (e) are formed by suffixing *-ī* to the noun-stem, unlike those nouns in (d) (which take the suffix *-e* (for singular) and *-ā* (for plural) instead).

(801) (e) consonant-ending feminine nouns, *bahīṇ* 'sister'

	bahīṇ 'sister' (singular)	*bahiṇī* 'sisters' (plural)
nom	bahīṇ	bahiṇī
acc	bahiṇīlā	bahiṇī̃nnā
inst	bahiṇīne	bahiṇī̃nnī
dat	bahiṇīlā	bahiṇī̃nnā
abl	bahiṇīhūn	bahiṇī̃nhūn

poss/gen	bahīnītsā	bahiṇīntsā
loc	bahiṇīt	bahinīt
voc	bahiṇī	bahiṇīnno

There are no *-i* ending feminine nouns in contemporary Marathi. The Sanskrit *-i* ending feminine nouns such as *-mati* 'mind', *buddhi* 'intellect', etc. are pronounced with a long *-ī*, and are written with a long *-ī* as well. This development has taken place within the last thirty years or so, during which time the class of *-i* ending feminine nouns gradually merged (first in pronunciation and then in the written counterpart) with the class of *-ī* ending feminine nouns in (b).

There is a very small class of *-ū* ending feminine nouns such as *wāḷū* 'sand', *abrū* 'dignity', etc. The oblique form of these nouns remains the same as their stem.

(802) *-ū* ending feminine nouns:

	wāḷū 'sand' (singular)	*wāḷū* 'different types of sand' (plural)
nom	wāḷū	wāḷū
acc	wāḷūlā	wāḷū̃nnā
inst	wāḷūṇe	wāḷū̃nnī
dat	wāḷūlā	wāḷū̃nnā
abl	wāḷūhūn	wāḷū̃nhūn
poss/gen	wāḷūtsā	wāḷū̃ntsā
loc	wāḷūt	wāḷū̃t
voc	wāḷū	wāḷū̃nno

The following patterns represent the neuter nouns and their oblique forms with the case suffixes.

(803) (a) consonant-ending neuter nouns. This is the largest class of the neuter nouns in Marathi.

	dzhāḍ 'tree' (singular)	*dzhāḍa* 'trees' (plural)
nom	dzhāḍ	dzhāḍa/e
acc	dzhāḍālā	dzhāḍā̃nnā
inst	dzhāḍā̃ne	dzhāḍā̃nnī
dat	dzhāḍālā	dzhāḍā̃nnā
abl	dzhāḍāhūn	dzhāḍā̃nhūn
poss/gen	dzhāḍātsā	dzhāḍā̃ntsā

loc	dzhāḍāt	dzhāḍā̃t
voc	dzhāḍā	dzhāḍā̃nno

(804) (b) *-ū* ending neuter nouns, *pillū* 'young (animal)'

	pillū 'young' (singular)	*pilla* 'young ones of an animal' (plural)
nom	pillū	pilla/e
acc	pillālā	pillā̃nnā
inst	pillā̃ne	pillā̃nnī
dat	pillālā	plillā̃nnā
abl	pillāhūn	pillā̃nhūn
poss/gen	pillātsa	pillā̃ntsā
loc	pillāt	pillā̃t
voc	pillā	pillā̃nno

(805) (c) *-a/e* ending neuter nouns

	taḷa/e 'lake' (singular)	*taḷī* 'lakes' (plural)
nom	taḷa/e	taḷī
acc	taḷyālā	taḷyā̃nnā
inst	taḷyā̃ne	taḷyā̃nnī
dat	taḷyāḷā	taḷyā̃nnā
abl	taḷyāhūn	taḷyā̃nhūn
poss/gen	taḷyātsā	taḷyā̃ntsā
loc	taḷyāt	taḷyā̃t
voc	taḷyā	taḷyā̃nno

(806) (d) *-ī* ending neuter nouns

	pāṇī 'water' (singular)	*pāṇī* 'different types of water' (plural)
nom	pāṇī	pāṇī
acc	pāṇyālā	pāṇyā̃nnā
inst	pāṇyā̃ne	pāṇyā̃nnī
dat	pāṇyālā	pāṇyā̃nnā
abl	pāṇyāhūn	pāṇyā̃nhūn
poss/gen	pāṇyātsā	pāṇyā̃ntsā
loc	pāṇyāt	pāṇyā̃t
voc	pāṇyā	pāṇyā̃nno

As mentioned earlier, the noun-stems are augmented before case-suffixes/postpositions. Those augments vary according to the gender, number, and the morphological class of the nouns. The distribution of the augments is as follows:

(a) *-ā* is used for all masculine nouns (vowel - as well as consonant-ending singular as well as plural) except for *-u* ending (where the vowel *-u* is lengthened, see (795)). It is important to note that the noun-stems undergo additional changes before the augment (e.g., *-i* ending (792) and *-ā* ending (791) stems take a glide *-y* before *-ā* obligatorily, while *-ū* ending stems (793) take a glide *-w* before *-ā*.).

(b) *-e* is used for the *-ā* ending (797) and consonant-ending (800) feminine singular stems.

(c) other vowel-ending feminine singular stems ((798) and (799)) do not undergo any change and do not take any augment.

(d) Consonant-ending feminine nouns such as *bahīṇ* 'sister' (801), which have an *-ī* ending plural form, use the plural form as the oblique form of the stem.

(e) All feminine noun-stems use their corresponding plural forms as oblique plural forms. Additionally, the augment *-ā* is added to the plural oblique stem before case-suffixes are added. (See examples (797) - (801)).

(f) All neuter noun-stems (vowel- as well as consonant-ending singular and plural) use the augment *-ā* before the case-suffixes. Additional changes in the stem (i.e., glide *-y-* insertion before the augment *-ā*) are seen in (805) and (806).

(g) Plural oblique forms of all nouns, regardless of their gender and morphological class, take the *-n* augment, which occurs between the augment *-ā* and the instrumental, dative, possessive and vocative case-suffixes. In these cases, *-ā* is nasalized (see 3.1.2.2.1.3).

(h) As opposed to Standard Marathi examples in (791), in the South-Konkan dialect of Marathi, ablative, possessive and locative plural forms (of all class nouns) are pronounced with a nasalized vowel (*-ā̃*) which is not followed by a dental nasal *-n* before the ablative/possessive/locative suffixes, i.e., *ghoḍyā̃-hūn* (ablative), *ghoḍyā̃-tsā* (possessive), and *ghoḍyā̃-t* (locative).

(i) In the locative plural, the nasalization of the vowel (*-ā̃*) is lost and is only optionally retained in orthography in Standard Marathi.

Infinitive clauses behave like any noun phrase regarding case-forms. Gerundive clauses take instrumental, dative and possessive case-suffixes.

Case-markers are placed after the augments or suffixes (which derive the oblique forms of the noun) and before the clitics (e.g., *dzā̃ḍā̃-tsā̃-ts* 'of the tree indeed').

In addition to the case-markers, Marathi uses a large number of postpositions. The noun-stems undergo changes and take augments before postpositions, identical to those which they take before case-suffixes. The difference between case-suffixes and postpositions in Marathi needs to be studied, and a precise difference between the two needs to be characterized. However, one can say that postpositions are not as inalienable from the (noun) stem as case-suffixes. For example, some of the clitic particles can optionally intervene between the noun and a postposition (e.g., *dewā̃tSyā̃-ts-sā̃ṭhi* 'for the sake of the god alone'). However, a clitic particle *- ts* can not occur before the case-suffix (e.g., **dewā̃-ts-lā̃* 'for god alone'). Additionally, the semantic range of a postposition is wider than that of a case-suffix. Moreover, some of the postpositions can occur as independent morphemes (e.g., *madhe* 'in/inside/in the middle (of)', *dzawaḷ* 'nearby'). A number of clitics are used to express a variety of meanings such as emphatic, inclusive or exclusive. Clitics do not express the grammatical relation of a noun phrase with other constituents in the sentence.

2.1.1.2 *Expression of syntactic functions*

2.1.1.2.1 *Subject of intransitive verbs*

The subject of an intransitive verb (regardless of whether it is an agent) is a noun phrase. It is in the nominative case, which is its unmarked form. In the following examples, the unmarked nominative form is indicated by the ø-marking on it.

(807)	to	mā̃ṇūs	zhoplā̃
	that	man-ø	sleep-pst-3sm

'That man slept.'

(808)	to	mānūs	tSār	mail	tsāllā
	that	man-ø	four	miles	walk-pst-3sm

'That man walked four miles.'

(809)	to	mulgā	rāgāwlelā	āhe
	that	boy-ø	get angry-pst-part-3sm	aux-is

'That boy is angry' (i.e., that boy is in the state of anger).

2.1.1.2.2 *Subject of transitive verbs*

The subject of a transitive verb (which is generally an agent) is also unmarked or is in the nominative case except in the perfective, obligational, and optative aspects where it is marked by the postposition *-ne* .

(810)	mulī-ne	gāṇī	mhaṭlī
	girl-ag	song-3pl.n	sing-pst-3pl.n

'The girls sang songs.'

(811)	mulī	gāṇī	mhaṇtāt
	girls	song-3pl.n	sing-pres-3pl.f

'The girls sing songs.'

Note that the subject/agent in the perfective aspect (810) takes the postposition *-ne*, while it is unmarked when the aspect is not perfective (811) (see 2.1.3.3). Recall that the obligational and optative construction shows a different pattern from the perfective, i.e., both transitive and intransitive subjects take *-ne* in these constructions and the verb does not agree with the subject and remains in the unmarked form (see 1.1.1.3.1.1.2 and 1.1.1.3.1.1.4).

The unmarked subject (e.g., (811)) generally controls verb agreement and occurs sentence-initially. However, in the perfective aspect (regardless of the occurrence of *-ne*) it does not control verb agreement. It needs to be noted here that *-ne* is restricted only to nouns in the third person. The first and the second person nouns (which do not have any overt case-marking) in the perfective/obligational/optative constructions do not control verb agreement. (For further details, see Pandharipande 1981a).

2.1.1.2.3 *Subject of copular constructions*

The subject of a copular construction is also in the nominative or unmarked case.

(812)	ithe	khūp	phula	āhet
	here	a lot	flowers-ø	be-pres-3pl

'There are a lot of flowers here.'

2.1.1.2.3.1 *Subject of 'dative subject constructions'*

A large number of verbs expressing psychological or physical states or notions such as liking, wanting, possessing, feeling, etc. require their logical or semantic subject to take the dative case marking. In these cases this logical subject is the non-volitional experiencer and not an active agent of the action. In this case, the other noun phrase in the nominative functions as the surface subject in terms of the case-marking and verb agreement. (For details on dative subjects in Marathi, see Pandharipande 1990b).

(813)	mulālā	dukhkha	dzhāla
	boy-dat	sadness-3sn	happen-pst-3sn

'The boy became sad.' (lit: 'Sadness happened to the boy.')

(814)	tyālā	rāg	ālā
	he-dat	anger-3sm	come-pst-3sm

'He got angry.'

Dative subjects consistently take the dative marking across all tenses and aspects, and the postposition *-ne* is not used in this construction. The class of dative-subject verbs is very large in Marathi. These verbs can be included in the category of inchoative or stative verbs. In the case of these verbs, the subject is not an agent who actively performs the action, but, rather is an experiencer of the action expressed by the verb. The 'active' counterparts of dative-subject verbs are often substituted for dative-subject verbs when the subject is an active agent. Consider the following examples:

(815)	a) stative:	X - lā rāg asṇe (dative)	'for X to have anger'
	b) inchoative:	X-lā rāg yeṇe	'for anger to come to X' (for X to get angry)
	c) active:	X- ø rāgāwṇe	'for X to get angry'

Note that in the stative (815a) and the inchoative (815b), the subject (indicated by X) takes the dative postposition, while in the case of the active verb in (815c) the subject does not take it. The following examples illustrate this point.

(816a) stative:

tyālā	māzhā	rāg	āhe
he-dat	I-poss-3sm	anger-3sm	be-pres-3s

'He has anger toward me.'

(816b) incohative:

tyālā	mādzhā	rāg	ālā
he-dat	poss-3sm	anger-3sm	come-pst-3sm

'He got angry at me.' (lit: 'Anger toward me came to him.')

(816c) active:

to	māʤhyāwar	rāgāwlā
he	I-on	get angry-pst-3sm

'He got angry at (lit: 'on') me.'

Note that the subject of the active verb (816c) does not carry the dative marking.

The following examples ((817) and (818)) show that physical states which are involuntarily experienced are often expressed through the dative-subject construction.

(817)	tyālā	tāp	{ālā / hotā}
	he-dat	fever-3sm	come-pst-3sm be-pst-3sm

'He got/had fever.'

(818)	tyālā	apghātāt	dzakham	dzhālī
	he-dat	accident-in	injury-3sf	happen-pst-3sf

'He suffered an injury in the accident.'

Although the dative-subject does not control verb agreement, it demonstrates some of the properties of the nominative subject in Marathi. For example, it functions as an antecedent of reflexive pronouns as in (819), similar to a nominative subject as in (820).

Dative subject:

(819)	tyālā	āplyā	bhāwātsā	rāg	ālā
	he-dat	refl	brother-poss-3sm	anger-3sm	come-pst-3sm

'He$_i$ got angry at his$_i$ brother.'

Nominative subject:

(820)	to	āplyā	bhāwāwar	rāgāwlā
	he	refl	brother-on	get angry-pst-3sm

'He$_i$ got angry at his$_i$ brother.'

(For details on subject properties in Marathi, see Pandharipande 1981a.)

2.1.1.2.4 *Direct object*

The accusative marker *-lā* is homophonous with the dative marker *-lā*. The following points about the direct object need to be noted:

a) when the direct object is human it obligatorily takes the marker *-lā* as in (821).

(821)	polis	tsorālā/*tsor	mārto
	policeman	thief-acc/thief-ø	beat-pres-3sm

'The policeman beats the thief.'

(822)	mī	sudhālā/s	bheṭto
	I	Sudha-acc	meet-pres-1sm

'I meet Sudha.'

(823)	āī	mulīlā/*mulgī	sadzawte
	mother	daughter-acc/*daughter	decorate-pres-3sf

'The Mother decorates the daughter.'

b) Inanimate objects generally do not take the accusative postposition as in (824). When they do, they indicate specific referents as in (825).

(824)	to	ghara	sadzawto
	he	house-pl-ø	decorate-pres-3sm

'He decorates houses.'

(825)	to	gharānnā	sadzawto
	he	house-pl-acc	decorate-pres-3sm

'He decorates the houses.'

c) The (semantic) direct object in the dative subject construction typically lacks the accusative marking as in (826).

(826)	anūlā	mohan/*mohanlā	āwaḍto
	Anu-dat-3sf	Mohan-3sm/*Mohan-acc-3sm	like-pres-3sm

'Anu likes Mohan.'

In fact, in a dative-subject-construction such as that in (826), the (semantic) direct object controls verb agreement. The lack of marking and the control of verb agreement place the (semantic) direct object higher on the hierarchy of subjecthood compared to the dative subject. However, syntactic processes such as reflexivization (see 1.6 and sub-sections thereof), nominalization, etc. continue to treat the dative subject as subject as opposed to the (semantic) direct object. (For the relative status of the dative subject and direct object in the dative-subject construction, see Pandharipande 1981a, 1990b.)

d) Direct objects in the passive construction may optionally take the accusative postposition. When they lack it, they control verb agreement as in (827). In contrast to this, when they are marked with *-lā,* they fail to control verb agreement as in (828).

(827)	polisākaḍūn	tsorø	pakḍle
	policeman-by	thieves-3pl.m	catch-pst-3pl.m

gele
go-pass-pst-3pl.m
'The thieves were caught by the policeman.'

(828)	polisākaḍūn	tsorā̃nnā	pakaḍla	gela
	policeman-by	thieves-acc	catch-pst-3sn	go-pass-pst-3sn

'The thieves were caught by the policeman.'

On the basis of this evidence, Pandharipande (1981a) claims that the (semantic) direct-object in the passive construction in Marathi is higher on the scale of subjecthood properties compared to other objects, since it lacks the accusative marker which is generally placed after human direct objects.

e) Verbs such as (i) *sparśa karṇe* 'to touch' (lit: 'to do touch'), (ii) *bolawne* 'to call', (iii) tSikaṭṇe 'to stick' (intransitive) require an indirect oblique object. The following examples illustrate the obligatory use of the accusative marker after the direct object.

sparś karṇe 'to touch':

(829)	anū	dārālā/*dār-ø bāḷālā/*bāḷ-ø	sparśa	karte
	Anu	door-acc/*door-ø child-acc/*child-ø	touch	do-pres-3sf

'Anu touches the door/child.'

bolawṇe 'to call':

(830)	mī	tilā/*tī	bolawte
	I	she-acc/*she	call-pres-1sf

'I call her.'

tSikaṭṇe 'to stick' (intr):

(831)	dīŋkāmuḷe	tSitra	bhintīlā/*bhinta	tSikaṭta
	gum-due to	picture	wall-acc/*wall-ø	stick-pres-3sn

'Because of the gum, the picture sticks to the wall.'

f) Although the unmarked subject generally controls verb agreement, the unmarked direct object controls it under the following conditions: (i) when the verb is in the perfective, optative or obligative aspect as illustrated in (832) - (834) respectively.

Perfective:

(832)	mī	patra	lihilī
	I	letters-3pl.n	write-pst-3pl.n

'I wrote letters.'

(832a)	tyāne	gāṇī	mhaṭlī
	he-ag	song-pl-3pl.n	sing-pst-3pl.n

'He sang songs.'

Note that the direct object *patra* 'letters' in (832) and *gāṇī* 'songs' in (832a) control verb agreement regardless of the unmarked (832) or marked (832a) status of the agent in the sentence.

Optative:

(833)	mī	kāma	karāwī(t)
	I	jobs-3pl.n	do-opt-3pl.n

'I may do the jobs.'

(833a)	tyāne	kāma	karāwī(t)
	he-ag	jobs-3pl.n	do-opt-3pl.n

'He may do the jobs.'

Obligative:

(834)	mī	abhyās	karāylā	hawā
	I	study-3ms	do-inf-dat	should-3sm

'I should study.'

(834a)	tine	abhyās	karāylā	hawā
	she-ag	study-3sm	do-inf-dat	should-3sm

'He should study.'

Note that the verb in the optative ((833) and (833a)) and obligative ((834) and (834a)) agrees with the direct object regardless of the unmarked ((833) and (834)) and marked ((833a) and (834a)) status of the subject.

As mentioned earlier (in sections 1.1.1.3.1.1.2-4), the above three constructions constitute the ergative constructions in Marathi.

ii) The (semantic) direct object controls verb agreement when the subject is marked with a case-marker/postposition. The dative subject construction is one of the contexts where the subject is marked with a dative case marker/postposition *-lā* and the direct object is unmarked (see 1.2.1.2.1). Note that the verb in this case agrees with the direct object and not the (experiencer) subject. Another context where the subject takes the dative marker is the possessive construction illustrated in examples (835) and (836). Note that the verb in both examples agrees with the direct object and not the subject.

(835)	dzhāḍālā	phula	āhet
	tree-dat	flower-3pl.n	be-3pl

'The tree has flowers.'

(836)	malā	tSār	bhāū	āhet
	I-dat	four	brothers	be-3pl

'I have four brothers.'

In addition to the dative, the possessor-subject in Marathi can take the locative postposition *-madhe/-t* 'in'. In this case, the verb agrees with the direct-object of possession as shown in (837).

(837)	āmtSyāt/āmtSyāmadhe	śaktī	ālī
	we-loc-pl	strength-3sf	come-pst-3sf

'We got strength.' (lit: 'Strength came into us.')

2.1.1.2.5 *Indirect object*

The indirect object is primarily expressed by the dative postposition/case-marker *-lā* following a noun or a noun phrase. The use of *-lā* is obligatory in this case. Compound postpositions such as *(-tSyā) sāṭhī* / *(-tSyā) kartā* 'for' also mark an indirect object. Consider (838) and (839).

(838)	sudhālā	phula	de
	Sudha-dat	flowers	give-imp-2s

'Give flowers to Sudha.'

(839)	mī	sudhā (tSyā) sāṭhī/kartā	ek	sāḍī	āṇlī
	I	Sudha-for-(poss)	one	saree	bring-pst-3sf

'I brought one saree for Sudha.'

In (838) it is the dative postposition *-lā* which marks the indirect object, while in (839) the compound postposition *(-tSyā) sāṭhī/kartā* 'for' is used to express the indirect object.

It is necessary to note here that the dative postposition *-lā* expresses a wide variety of syntactic as well as semantic notions besides indirect object, such as purpose, goal, possession, location, etc. (For further discussion on the functions of the dative marker *-lā*, see Pandharipande 1990b).

Thus, it is necessary to note here that although the presence of the dative marker or postposition is obligatory in order to express the indirect object, it is not a sufficient condition. Moreover, the discussion in sections 1.2.1.2.1 and 1.2.1.2.2 has already pointed out that *-lā* can mark the (semantic) subject and the direct object respectively.

2.1.1.2.6 *Object of comparisons*

The object of comparison is either in the possessive case or oblique form followed by the comparative particle *pekṣā* 'than', or it is in the oblique form followed by the ablative suffix *-hūn* 'from'.

(840)	anū(tSyā)	pekṣā	sudhā	untsa	āhe
	Anu (poss)	compr	Sudha	tall	is

'Sudha is taller than Anu.'

(841)	anū-hūn	sudhā	untsa	āhe
	Anu-abl	Sudha	tall	is

'Sudha is taller than Anu.'

For more examples and morphological comparatives, see sections 1.8-1.8.7.

2.1.1.2.7 *Object of equation*

The object of equation is either in the possessive or oblique form followed by one of the following three postpositions: *itka* 'as much as/as many as, *sārkha* 'like', *barobarīne* 'equal'. Examples (842) - (844) illustrate the use of these postpositions.

itka 'as much as':

(842)	nyūyɔrk	madhe	śikāgo	itkī
	New York	in	Chicago	equal to-3sf
	thaṇḍī	paḍat	nāhī	
	cold-3sf	fall	neg-pres-3s	

'New York does not get as cold as Chicago.'

itka 'as many as':

(842a)	itha	śikāgo	itkī	dukāna	nāhīt
	here	Chicago	as many as	shop-3pl	neg-pres-3pl

'There are not as many shops here as in Chicago.'

sarkha 'like':

(843)	anū	mītā	sārkhī(ts)	suswabhāwī
	Anu-3sf	Meeta-3sf	like-3sf	good-natured
	(mulgī)	āhe		
	(girl)	is		

'Anu is a good-natured girl like Meeta.'

barobarīne 'equal to':

(844)	sureś	adʒittSyā	barobarīne	paisā	kamawto
	Suresh	Ajit-poss	equal to	money	earn-pres-3sm

'Ajit earns money equal to Suresh.'

The above postpositions are not always used interchangeably. *Itka* can be used to express equality/comparison in terms of quantity ((842) and (842a)), quality (843), and capacity (inherent or acquired) (844). However, the use of *sārkha* 'like' is restricted to expressing comparison in terms of quality. Thus *sārkha* can not replace *itka* ((842) and (842a)) or *barobarīne* (844). Similarly, *barobarīne* is restricted to comparison in terms of the capacity of the objects of comparison. Therefore, it can not replace *itka* (or *sārkha).*

In addition to the above, the pair of equative particles (*dʒitkā....titkā* 'as much as . . . so much as' may also be used to express comparison as in (845).

(845)	dʒitkā	paisā	rāmdʒawaḷ	āhe
	as much (rel-eq)	money	Ram-near	be-pres-3s
	titkā	(paisā)	madhūdzawaḷ	nāhī
	that much (cor-eq)	(money)	Madhu-near	neg-pres-3s

'Madhu does not have as much money as Ram (does).'

2.1.1.2.8 *Other objects governed by verbs*

Verbs such as *māgṇe* 'to ask/demand' can take either dative or ablative objects as in (846) and (847).

(846)	mī	āīlā/āīkaḍūn	paise	māgitle
	I	mother-dat/mother-abl	money	ask-pst-3pl.m

'I asked my mother for money/ I asked money from my mother.'

Certain verbs such as *kheḷṇe* 'to play', *bhāṇḍṇe* 'to fight', *bolṇe* 'to talk' take instrumental objects as in (847) and (848) or, alternatively, comitative objects as in the following:

(847)	sudhā	anūśī/barobar	kheḷte
	Sudha-3sf	Anu-inst-3sf/with	play-pres-3sf

'Sudha plays with Anu.'

(848)	mohan	dilīpśī/barobar	bhāṇḍto
	Mohan-3sm	Dilip-inst/with	fight-pres-3sm

'Mohan fights with Dilip.'

(849)	tū	rodz	anūśī/barobar	boltes
	you-sf	everyday	Anu-inst/with	talk-pres-2sf

'You talk to Anu everyday.'

Although instrumental as well as comitative markers are acceptable, the use of the instrumental marker in examples such as (847) - (849) is preferred over the comitative postposition. Additionally certain conjunct verbs determine the case-suffix/ postposition following their objects. The class of conjunct-verbs (a noun + verb sequence which functions as a single verb-unit) is very large in Marathi. For example, conjunct verbs such as *prātikṣā karṇe* 'to wait' (lit: 'to do waiting') *wāṭ pāhṇe* 'to wait' (lit: 'to stare at the path'), *stuti / praśaṃsā karṇe* 'to praise' (lit: 'to do praising'), *kāḷdʒī gheṇe* 'to take care' etc. require their objects to take the possessive postposition/case-markers as shown in (850) - (853) below.

(850)	mī	rodz	rātrī	parītSī	prātīkṣā
	I	everyday	night-loc	Pari-poss	waiting
	karte				
	do-1sf				

'I wait for Pari every night.'

(851)	mī	puḍhtSyā	warṣīparyānta	tuʤhī	wāṭ
	I	next	year-till	you-poss-3sf	path-3sf
	pāhīn				
	see-fut-1s				

'I will wait for you till the next year.'

(852)	waḍīl	mulātSī	nehmīts	stutī/praśaṃsā
	father	son-poss-3sf	always	praise-3sf
	kartāt			
	do-pres-3pl.m			

'Father always praises his son.'

(853)	āī	bāḷātSī	khūp	kaḷʤī	ghete
	mother	child-poss-3sf	a lot	care-3sf	take-pres-3sf

'Mother takes a lot of care of the child.'

Another class of conjunct verbs and simple verbs require their objects to take the locative postposition *-war* 'on'. Example (854) illustrate the use of the conjunct verb *prem karṇe* 'to love' (lit: 'to do love'), while (855) shows that simple verbs such as *sopawṇe* 'to entrust', also require their objects to take the postposition *-war* 'on'.

(854)	to	āplyā	kuṭumbāwar	prem	karto
	he	refl-obl	family-on	love	do-pres-3sm

'He loves his family.'

(855)	mī	anūwar	dzabābdārī	sopawlī
	I	Anu-on	responsibility-3sf	entrust-pst-3sf

'I entrusted the responsibility to Anu.'

Certain other conjunct verbs take dative objects as in (856) and (857).

madat karṇe 'to help' (lit: 'to do helping'):

(856)	tū	malā	madat	karśīl	kā ?
	you	I-dat	help	do-fut-2s	Q

'Will you help me ?'

protsāhan deṇe 'to encourage' (lit: 'to give encouragement'):

(857)	tyāne	malā	bhāratāt	rāhṇyātsa
	he-ag	I-dat	India-loc	live-inf-poss-3sn

protsāhan	dila
encouragement-3sn	give-pst-3sn

'He encouraged me to live in India.'

A comprehensive study of conjunct verbs in Marathi in particular and verb agreement in general is needed to determine the (syntactic, and semantic) conditions which determine the choice of postposition in the context of various verbs.

2.1.1.2.9 *Complement of copula constructions*

Marathi does not formally distinguish between defining and identitying functions of copulas. The complement of the copula is a noun phrase in the nominative case in all contexts and occupies preverbal position in the sentence. The following examples (858) - (859) illustrate the various functions and the position of the complements of the copula verb.

Defining:

(858)	to	rākṣas	āhe
	he	demon	is

'He is a demon.'

Identifying:

(859)	tī	mulgī	gāyikā	āhe
	that	girl	singer	is

'That girl is a singer.'

(860)	to	nyāyādhīś	āhe
	he	judge	is

'He is a judge.'

In addition to the above, the copular verbs such as *hoṇe* 'to become', *banṇe* 'to be made/become' also take complements which are also placed in the pre-verbal position and are in the nominative case.

(861)	to	meyar	dzhālā
	he	mayor	become-pst-3sm

'He became the mayor.'

(862)	to	nokar	banlā
	he	servant	become-pst-3sm

'He became the servant.'

The verbs *hoṇe* 'to become' and *banṇe* 'to become' are not semantically identical. While the use of *hoṇe* indicates that the speaker is making a statement about the event in the real world (861), the use of *banṇe* generally indicates the event (862) takes place in the ficticious/make believe world (i.e., play, dream, etc.). Thus the event in (861) is interpreted to be a statement of fact, while the event in (862) is interpreted to be an event in a play.

2.1.1.2.10 *Subject complement*

Subject complements are not distinguished from the copular complements discussed in 1.2.1.1. Copular verbs are not passivized in Marathi.

2.1.1.2.11 *Object complement*

The object complement is generally in the accusative case, which is expressed with the ø-marking (and it is not followed by any postposition). Consider the following examples.

(863)	tī	malā	mulgī	mānte
	she	I-acc	daughter-ø	consider-pres-3sf

'She considers me (to be her) daughter.'

Sentences such as (863) are related to the complex sentence (864).

(864)	tī	mānte	kī	mī	titSī
	she	consider-pres-3sf	comp	I	her-3sf

mulgī	āhe
daughter	is

'She considers that I am her daughter.'

The above construction in (863) is restricted to certain verbs of mental states, (*dzāṇne* 'to know') cognition, or judgement (*mānṇe/samadzṇe* 'to consider', *oḷakhṇe* 'to recognize'). Moreover, it is necessary to note here that the embedded sentence in this case is always a copular sentence as in (864).

The object complement of verbs other than the above is generally in the accusative (ø-marked) and is generally followed by the quotative marker *mhaṇūn* as in (865).

(865)	sabhāsadā̃nnī	śrī	dzośyā̃nnā	kamiṭītse
	members-ag	Mr.	Joshi-acc	committee-poss-3pl.m

adhyakṣa	mhaṇūn	nemle
president	quot	appoint-pst-3sn

'The members appointed Mr. Joshi as the president of the committee.'

This feature of using the quotative marker after the object complement is shared by Dravidian languages (see Sridhar 1990:163).

2.1.1.2.12 *Objects governed by adjectives*

A number of adjectives and/or predicate nominals require their objects to be marked with specific case-suffixes or postpositions. For example, *khūṣ* 'happy', *phidā* 'attracted', etc. take the locative (*war)* 'on' (866); while *huśār* 'clever', *agresar* 'expert, leader', *nipuṇ* 'skilled' (generally indicating superlative degree) take the locative *-t* 'in' (867) and *śobhṇārā* 'befitting' (present participle), *lāgṇārā* 'necessary' (present participle), etc., take dative objects (868). The following examples illustrate the use of the above case-suffixes/ postpositions.

khūṣ 'happy':

(866)	to	āplyā	nokrīwar	khūṣ	āhe
	he	refl-obl	job-on	happy	is

'He is happy with his job.'

Note the use of the locative postposition *-war* 'on'; following the object *nokrī* 'job' in (866).

agresar 'expert/leader':

(867)	adʒit	sāŋgītāt	agresar	āhe
	Ajit	music-in	{expert / leader}	is

'Ajit is the expert/leader in music.'

Note the use of the locative suffix *-t* in this example.

śobhṇārā 'befitting/deserving':

(868)	anūlā	śobhṇārā	nawrā	kuṭha
	Anu-dat	befitting-pres.part-3sm	husband	where

miḷel ?
get-fut-3s

'Where would (one) find a suitable husband for Anu ?'

Note the dative marker *-lā* in (868). It is necessary to note here that the case-suffixes or postpositions (following the objects of participles/predicate nominals) are determined by the basic verbs from which the predicate nominals are derived. For example, the basic verb in the participle *śobhṇārā* 'befitting' (868) is *śobhaṇe* 'to befit', which requires the subject to take the dative marker *-lā*. Thus, the derived participle also requires its object *anū* to take the same (dative) marker.

2.1.1.2.13 *Agent in passive/pseudopassive/impersonal constructions*

The use of the passive in Marathi is not as frequent as its non-passive/active counterpart in spoken and informal registers of Marathi. However, the written and formal registers of Marathi use the passive construction quite frequently. The newspaper registers of Marathi and the language of official correspondences are the two contexts where the passive construction is frequently used. In the spoken and/or informal register of Marathi, the passive construction is used to express the capability of the agent to carry out the action expressed by the passive verb. This usage of the passive construction is commonly shared by other Indo-Aryan languages such as Hindi, Kashmiri, Nepali, and Punjabi. (For a detailed discussion on the syntax and semantics of the passive construction in these languages, see Pandharipande 1981a). Pandharipande (1981a) also points out that this semantic feature of the passive is not shared by Kannada and other Dravidian languages.

Consider example (869) which illustrates the use of the passive construction in the formal and written registers of Marathi.

(869)	pradhān	māntryā	dwārā/kaḍun	hā
	prime	minister	by/by	this

ādeś	dilā	gelā	kī	. . .
order-3sm	give-pst-3sm (passive)	go-pst-3sm	that	. . .

'The order was issued by the prime minister that . . .'

It should be noted here that the use of the postposition *dwārā* 'by/through' is preferred over *kaḍūn* 'by' in the formal register.

Now consider the use of *kaḍūn* in the informal and spoken registers of Marathi:

(870)	mādʒhyā	kaḍūn/*dwārā	kām	kela
	I-obl	by	work	do-pst-3sn

gela	nāhī
go-pst-3sn (passive)	neg

'The work was not done by me.' (I was unable to do the work.)

Pandharipande (1981a) shows that the use of *kaḍūn* in (870) is justified in sentences such as (870) for the following two reasons: (a) *kaḍūn* 'by' marks the direct agency of the agent in performing the act while *dwārā* generally marks the indirect agency of the agent. Therefore, in (870) *kaḍūn* (and not *dwārā*) is used. In contrast to this, *dwārā* 'by/through' generally marks the indirect agency or instrumentality of the agent in performing the act. (for example, it is used in sentences such as 'I sent the parcel by/through the post-office.' (*mī posṭādwārā parsal pāṭhawla*)). Thus in sentences such as (869) where the instrumentality, rather than the direct agency of the prime minister in issuing the order is in focus (since the action of actually issuing the order is the job of the personnel office of the prime minister), the use of the postposition *dwārā* is preferred over *kaḍūn*. When the prime minister's direct agency is to be emphasized, the use of *kaḍūn* is preferred; (b) the capabilitative meaning of the passive sentence is restricted to *kaḍūn* and is blocked for *dwārā*. Therefore, only *kaḍūn* (and not *dwārā*) is used in (870). (For further discussion on the semantics of *kaḍūn* see Pandharipande 1981a.) The agent does not appear in the personal construction as in (871).

(871)	kāltSya	dangyāt	barīts	ghara
	yesterday's	riot-loc	many	houses-3pl.n

dzāḷlī	gelī
burn-pst-3pl.n	go-pst-3pl.n (passive)

'Many houses were burnt in yesterday's riot.'

Note that the agent of the passive verb *dzāḷṇe* 'to burn' is not present in (871). However, this impersonal passive construction is not semantically identical to the other impersonal (non-passive) construction in (872) where the verb is intransitive and the agent is not present.

(872)	kāltSyā	dangyāt	barīts	ghara
	yesterday's	riot-loc	many	houses-3pl.n
	dzaḷlī			
	burn (intr)-3pl.n			

'Many houses got burnt in yesterday's riot.'

Although the agent is not present in either (871) or (872), the action of burning denoted by the intransitive verb *dzaḷṇe* 'to burn' is interpreted to be an intentional act in (871) while it is not in (872). In other words, a passive sentence always (with or without the overtly expressed agent) expresses an intentional act. The absence of the overt agent in this case may be due to one or more of the following reasons:

(i) it is not known to the speaker,
(ii) it is not the topic of conversation, or
(iii) the object is in focus.

In contrast to the above, no agent is implied in (872). The action of burning is viewed as non-intentional. This is why when arson is suspected in the burning of a house, the impersonal passive construction (871) is used in Marathi. (For further discussion on this topic, see Pandharipande 1981a). There is no pseudopassive construction in Marathi.

2.1.1.2.14 *Topic*

There is no specific marker for topic in Marathi. It was already mentioned in section 1.12.1 that Marathi does not distinguish between subject and topic. Occasionally, the particles *-ta(r)* and *mhaṇdʒe* are used to mark the topic as in (873).

(873)	mī	ta(r)	gelo	nawhto
	I	emph	go-pst-3sn	neg-pst-3sm

'As for me, I had not gone.'

(874)	to	malā	mhaṇʤe	muḷīts	paise
	he	I-dat	pt	absolutely	money
	det	nāhī			
	give-pres	neg-pres-3s			

'As to me, he absolutely does not give money.'

2.1.1.2.15 *Emphasized elements*

Emphasized elements in a sentence are marked by stress, particle, movement, dislocation and repetition (For details, see section 1.11 and sub-sections thereof).

2.1.1.3 - 2.1.1.3.4 *Syntactic functions in non-finite or nominalized constructions*

Syntactic functions such as subject, object, etc. in non-finite constructions are expressed in the same manner as in finite constructions. However, the subject of the non-finite embedded clause differs from the subject of the main clause in that it is either deleted under identity with a matrix subject (as in 875) or appears with a possessive/genitive postposition as in (876).

Deleted embedded subject:

(875)	mī	ø	gharī	dzaṇyātsā	witSār
	I	ø	home-loc	go-inf-poss-3sm	thinking-3sm
	karto	āhe			
	do-prog-1sm	aux			

'I am thinking of going home.'

Possessive embedded subject:

(876)	titsa	atSānak	dzāṇa	yogya
	she-poss-3sn	suddenly	go-inf-3sn	appropriate

āhe	kā ?
is	Q

'Is it appropriate for her to suddenly leave?' (lit: 'Is her suddenly leaving appropriate ?')

All other syntactic relations remain the same as in finite clauses. Nominalized verb forms take nominal suffixes/postpositions (see section 1.1.2.2.2.2).

2.1.1.4 *Means of expressing non-local semantic functions*

2.1.1.4.1 *Benefactive*

The benefactive meaning is expressed by (a) the dative case-suffix or by postpositions *(-tSyā) kartā* 'for', *(-tSyā) sāṭhī* 'for'; (b) compound verbs. The optional suffix in the above is the possessive oblique suffix. The following examples illustrate the use of suffixes and postpositions.

Dative:

(877)	tyāne	anūlā	paise	pāṭhawle
	he-ag	Anu-dat	money-3pl.m	send-pst-3pl.m

'He sent money to Anu.'

kartā :

(878)	mī	tuʤhyākartā	kāy	karṇār	nāhī ?
	I	you-for	what	do-fut	neg

'What will I not do for you ?'

sāṭhī :

(879)	tyāne	deśāsāṭhī	ʤīw	dilā
	he-ag	country-for	life-3sm	give-pst-3sm

'He gave (his) life for his country.'

Compound verbs with the explicators *gheṇe* 'to take' and *deṇe* 'to give' refer to subject and object benefactives respectively (see also sections 2.1.3.3.2.1.1.5 and 2.1.3.3.2.1.1.3).

2.1.1.4.2 ***Source***

Source is primarily expressed by the following: (a) instrumental/ablative postposition - ***kaḍūn*** 'by/from'; (b) ablative case marker ***hūn*** 'from' or the ablative postposition ***-pāsūn*** 'from'; (c) the locative case marker *-t* 'in' + ablative case marker *-ūn* 'from' 'from inside'. Consider the following examples.

kaḍūn :

(880)	malā	rām	kaḍūn	bātmī	kaḷlī
	I-dat	Ram	from	news-3sf	{findout / get}-pst-3sf

'I got the news from Ram.'

hūn:

(881)	mī	amrāwatīhūn	ālo
	I	Amravati-from	come-pst-1sm

'I came from Amravati.'

pāsūn:

(882)	bhāratāt	kāndamuḷānpāsūn	kitītarī
	India-loc	roots (of trees)-from	many
	auṣadha	banawtāt	
	medicines	make-cause-pres-3pl.m	

'In India (people) make a lot of medicines from roots (of trees).'

locative + ablative (*-t* + *-ūn*):

(883)	to	mātītūn	tel	kāḍhū	śakto
	he	dirt-loc-abl	oil	extract	can-pres-3sm

'He can extract oil from dirt.' (i.e., he can accomplish a seemingly impossible task)

Alternatively, the morphological locative *madhe* followed by the ablative suffix *-ūn* (i.e., *madhūn* 'from within') is used to indicate source as in (883a).

(883a) gāḍīmadhūn lok bāher yet hote
train-from people out come-prog be-pst-3pl.m

'People were coming out of the train.'

In addition to the above, the possessive case-marker *-tsā* is used to express the regional identity of a person or an object. In this case, the name of the region (country, state, or city) is followed by the possessive case-marker and the derived element functions as an adjective and agrees with the noun in gender and number as in (884)-(886). This device of expressing regional identity is commonly shared by other Indo-Aryan languages such as Gujarati, Hindi, Punjabi, etc.

(884) hāruko ʤapāntSī āhe
Haruko-f Japan-poss-3sf be-pres-s

'Haruko is from Japan.'

(885) mī gudzrāth-tsā āhe
I Gujarat-poss-3sm be-pres-s

'I am from Gujarat (state).'

(886) te madrāstse āhet
they Madras-poss-3pl.m be-pres-pl

'They are from Madras.'

It should be noted here that in addition to the above, similar to most Indo-Aryan languages, Marathi uses adjectives derived from the place name to indicate the origin (identity) of a person or the source of an object. The following examples are the counterparts of examples (884) - (886) respectively.

(884a) hāruko ʤapānī āhe
Haruko Japan-adj be-pres-3s

'Haruko is Japanese.'

(885a)	mī	gudzrāthī	āhe
	I	Gujarat-adj	be-pres-3s

'I am a *Gujaratī* (the one from Gujarat).'

(886a)	te	madrāsī	āhet
	they	Madras-adj	be-pres-3pl

'They are *Madrāsī* (those from Madras).'

In (884a) - (886a), adjectives are derived from place-names by adding the suffix *-ī* to the noun stems (of the place names). It should be noted here that this process of derivation is restricted only to place-names whose noun stems are consonant-ending. In the cases of vowel-ending stems, the process of adding the possessive suffix is the only option available.

Interestingly, Marathi uses another device for expressing people's regional identity. In this case the expression *-kaḍtsā* (and its variants) 'from' (lit: 'of the side') is added to the place-name (vowel as well as consonant-ending) as in (887).

(887)	tumhī	nāgpūrkaḍtse	āhāt
	you-pl	Nagpur-side-poss-pl.m	be-pl

'You are from the Nagpur region.'

This device of using the morpheme *-kaḍ* (abbreviation of the word *kaḍe* 'in the direction of') is similar to the one in the Dravidian languages. (See Sridhar 1990:167.) Thus Marathi has two types of expressions to express similar meanings (origin or regional identity) - one shared with Indo-Aryan and the other with Dravidian languages. However, these two are not always used interchangeably in Marathi. The one with possessive postposition and the derived adjective is used to express the specific location ((884) - (886a)) of a person or an object, while the one with the directional morpheme *-kaḍtsā* is used to express non-specific or general location (887).

2.1.1.4.3 *Instrumental*

Instrumentality is expressed by the case-marker *-ne*, which is also used to mark cause. Additionally, the postpositions *kaḍūn* 'by', and *-tSyā dwārā* or *-tSyā mārfat, karwī, -tSyā, hātī* 'through' are used to express instrumentality. Consider the following examples.

-ne (instrumental):

(888)	mī	sābṇāne	hāt	dhutle
	I	soap-inst	hands	wash-pst-3pl.m

'I washed (my) hands with the soap.'

-ne (cause):

(889)	wāryāne	ḍzhāḍa	tuṭṭāt
	wind-inst	trees-3pl.n	break (intr)-pres-3pl.n

'Trees break because of the wind.'

(889a)	to	ālyāne	malā	ānānda
	he	come-ger-inst	I-dat	happiness-3sm

dzhālā
happen-pst-3sm

'I became happy because he came.' (lit: 'Because of his coming, I became happy.')

kaḍūn (instrumental):

(890)	anū	madhū	*kaḍūn/dwārā/* (tSyā)
	Anu	Madhu	by/through

mārfat/tSyā hātī	paise	pāṭhwate
through/at the hands of	money	send-pres-3sf

'Anu sends money by/through/at the hands of Madhu.'

The negative instrumental is expressed by adding the postposition (-*tSyā*) *śiwāy/winā* '(poss) without' to the instrument noun as in (891).

(891)	yogya	hatyārān(tSyā)	śiwāy/winā	yuddha
	proper	weapons (poss)	without	war-3sn

ʤīŋktā	yet	nāhī
win	come-pres	neg-3s

'It is not possible to win a war without proper weapons.'

2.1.1.4.4 *Comitative*

The postpositions *(-tSyā) barobar* 'with' and *(-tSyā) saha* 'with' are used to express comitativity as in (892).

(892)	mī	rāhul (*tSyā*)	barobar/saha
	I	Rahul (poss)	with

bɔsṭanlā	dzāīn
Boston-to	go-fut-1s

'I will go to Boston with Rahul.'

Negative comitativity is expressed by means of the postpositions (-*tSyā) śiwāy/winā* in the same way as negative instrumentality (see previous section) as in (893).

(893)	mī	rāhul (tSyā)	śiwāy/winā	bɔston
	I	Rahul (poss)	without	Boston

lā	dzāṇār	nāhī
to	go-fut	neg-s

'I will not go to Boston without Rahul.'

It must be noted here that the use of the above postposition *(-tSyā) śiwāy* 'without' is not obligatory. Thus the sentence in (892) may be negated by retaining the postposition *(-tSyā) barobar* 'with' and adding the negative auxiliary verb *nāhī* immediately following the verb as shown in (892a) below.

(892a)	mī	rāhul (tSyā)	barobar	bɔston
	I	Rahul (poss)	with	Boston

lā	dzāṇār	nāhī
to	go-fut	not-s

'I will not go to Boston with Rahul.'

Note that (893) and (892a) are not semantically identical. Example (892a) is ambiguous regarding whether or not the speaker is going to Boston.

In the Nagpuri variety of Marathi, instead of the postposition *(-tSyā) barobar,* the postpositions *(-tSyā) sāŋga/(-tSyā) sobat* 'with' are used. These are semantically as well as syntactically identical to the postposition *(-tSyā) barobar* 'with'.

2.1.1.4.5 *Circumstance*

Circumstance is expressed by means of one of the following devices: (a) perfective/habitual participles, (b) postposition *wālā,* (c) possessive marker, (d) locative marker. Consider the following examples ((894) - (897)) which illustrate the use of these devices.

Perfective participle:

(894)	ṭopī	ghātlelā	māṇūs . . .
	cap	wear-perf.part-3sm	man

'The man with a cap . . . '

Postposition *wālā :*

(895)	tShatrīwālī	bāī	. . .
	umbrella-pp	woman	

'The woman with an umbrella . . .'

Possessive marker:

(896)	kāḷyā	koṭātsā	māṇūs	. . .
	black	coat-poss-3sm	man	

'The man in the black coat . . .'

In order to identify the location of an object (+ or - human), the locative suffix *-t* or the morphological locative *-madhe* 'in' is added to the noun of location. The suffix *-lā* is added following the locative suffix. The element expresses adjectival meaning, i.e., 'the one who is in X . . .' and agrees with the noun in number and gender as shown in section 2.2.3.4.

Locative marker:

(897)	tyā	kholītla/kholīmadhla	sāmān
	. . .		
	that-obl	room-loc-adj-3sn	luggage-3sn

'The luggage in that room . . . '

2.1.1.4.6 - 2.1.1.4.6.3 *Possessive*

Possession is expressed by the possessive, dative, and locative suffixes (for a detailed discussion, see sections 1.10.1-6). It should be noted here that the noun of possession controls agreement within the possessive phrase and functions as the syntactic head of the possessive phrase. In the possessive phrase, the possessor noun precedes the noun of possession. The following example illustrates the most commonly used possessive phrase in Marathi. Other ways of expressing possession are discussed in detail in sections 1.10.1-6.

(898)	anūtSī	pustaka
	Anu-poss-3pl.n	books-3pl.n

'Anu's books'

2.1.1.4.7 *Possessed*

The possessed noun phrase is unmarked.

2.1.1.4.8 *Quality*

Quality is expressed by the following devices: (a) by an adjective, (b) by an adjective derived from a noun, (c) by an adjective derived from an adverb, and (d) by a nominal functioning as the complement of a dative subject.

Adjective:

(899)	sũndar	mulgī
	beautiful	girl

Adjective derived from a noun by adding the native Marathi suffix *-ḷū* to the noun:

(900a) lāz 'shyness' —> lādzāḷū 'shy'

(900b) dzhop 'sleep' —> dzhopāḷū 'the one who sleeps a lot'

In addition to the above suffix, suffixes such as *-wān/mān* are added to a noun to derive an adjective. These are suffixes from Sanskrit and their use is generally restricted to Sanskrit nouns (which are either borrowed or inherited from Sanskrit into Marathi).

(901) buddhi (Skt.) 'intelligence' - buddhiwān (Skt) 'intelligent'
buddhimān (Skt)

buddhī (M) buddhiwān (M)
buddhimān (M)

Note that the word final *-i* of Sanskrit feminine nouns is lengthened in Marathi. The Sanskrit form with word final short *-i* is used when a suffix is added (see section 3.4.1.3.5) and which explains *-ī/i* alternation in the forms *buddhī/ buddhiwān/ buddhimān* in Marathi.

Nouns of Perso-Arabic origin (e.g., *akkal* 'intelligence', and *himmat* 'courage') generally do not take the above Sanskrit suffixes; instead, those nouns take the possessive adjectival postposition *-wālā* as in (902a) and (902b).

(902a) akkalwālā 'intelligent'

(902b) himmatwālā 'courageous'

It should be noted here that the restriction on the suffixes *-wān* and *-mān* is gradually disappearing from Marathi. In the grammar of Damle (1966 [1911]) their use is shown to be restricted to Sanskrit nouns, while in the current spoken variety of Marathi their use with the above nouns of Perso-Arabic origin is acceptable. However, the degree of acceptability of these suffixes (with Perso-Arabic nouns) varies according to register (i.e., it is higher in spoken as opposed to written language), as well as according to regional variety of Marathi (i.e., it is higher in the Marathi spoken in the Puṇe region (western variety) as opposed to the Nagpur region (eastern variety)).

Adjective derived from a verb: (suffix *-āū*)
(903) ṭākṇe 'to throw, abandon'

(903a) ṭāk-āū —> ṭākāū 'that which deserves to be thrown away'

(904) wikṇe 'to sell'

(904a) wik-āū —> wikāū 'that which is for sale'

Other suffixes such as *-īt* and *-īl/el* are added to verb stems to derive adjectives as in (905) and (908a).

(905) lakhlakh-ṇe ' to dazzle'

(905a) lakhlakhīt 'dazzling' (that which dazzles)

(906) khaṇkhaṇ-ṇe 'to sound (loudly)'

(906a) khaṇkhaṇīt 'that which sounds loudly'

In general, the suffix *-īt* is added to onomatopoeic verbs or verbs with reduplicated syllables (see example (905) - (906a)). The suffix *-īl/el* is also used to derive an adjective from a verb as in (907a), and (908a).

(907) tShāp-ṇe 'to print'

(907a) tShāpīl 'that which is printed'

(908) saḍ-ne 'to be spoiled/rotten'

(908a) saḍel/saḍīl 'rotten'

A nominal functioning as a complement of a dative subject:

(909)	tilā	madanātSī	bādhā	dzhālī
	She-dat	Cupid-poss-3sf	affliction-3sf	happen-pst-3sf

āhe
be-3s

'She is in love.' (lit: 'She is afflicted by Cupid.')

Negative quality is expressed by adding a negative prefix or suffix to the noun or adjective as in (910) and (911).

(910)	nākhūṣ neg-happy	'unhappy'
(911)	buddhihīn/buddhiwihīn intelligence-without	'foolish'

The suffix *-wihīn* is borrowed/inherited from Sanskrit. Additionally Marathi has several negative adjectives from Sanskrit which express negative quality.

Reference quality is expressed by the possessive form as in (912).

(912)	radʒātsa	śaurya
	king-poss-3sn	valor-3sn

'the valor of the king'

2.1.1.4.9 *Quantity*

Quantity is expressed in the following ways: (a) numeral + unit of measure (classifier, terms of weight, length) + possessive as in (913) - (915), (b) noun indicating the measure of volume followed by the measure noun *bhar*. In general, the traditional measures of volume (*pāsrī*, *pāylī*, etc., used for measuring grain) have been replaced by measures of weight such as kilograms, milligrams, etc. In modern Marathi, the count noun *-bhar* 'full' (indicating quantity) may be placed after a noun which the speaker uses to indicate volume (quantity) as in (916) - (918).

(913)	sahā	kilotsā	ḍabā
	six	kilo-poss-3sm	box-3sm

'a box of six kilograms'

(914)	tīn	fūṭāntSī	dorī
	three	feet-poss-3sf	rope-3sf

'three feet of rope' (lit: 'a rope of three feet')

(915)	don	ekrāntSī	dzamīn
	two	acre-poss-3sf	land-3sf

'two acres of land' (lit: 'the land of two acres')

In cases such as the above, the nouns indicating measure may be optionally inserted between the numeral of measure and the possessive suffix as in (913a) and (914a).

(913a) sahā kilo wadznātsā ḍabā
six kilo weight-poss-3sm box-3sm

'a box of the weight of six kilos'

(914a) tīn fūṭ lā̃mbītSī dorī
three feet lenght-poss-3sf rope-3sf

'a rope of the length of three feet'

Quantity indicated by the use of *-bhar:*

(916) kapāṭbhar kapaḍe
closet-full clothes

'closet-full of clothes' (i.e., clothes which can fill up a whole closet)

(917) kapbhar ras
cup-full juice

'a cup-full of juice'

Reference quantity is expressed by placing the quantity phrase (which generally consists of a numeral + noun) before the noun expressing the element being modified as in (918).

(918) dahā kilo gahū
ten kilogram wheat

'ten kilograms of wheat'

2.1.1.4.10 *Material*

Material is expressed by the possessive as in (919).

(919)	wiṭāntSī	bhinta
	bricks-poss-3sf	wall-3sf

'a wall of bricks' (i.e., a brick wall)

Another way of expressing material is to use an adjective derived from the noun of material as in (920).

(920) dagaḍ 'stone' (noun) —> dagḍī 'made of stone' (adjective)

(920a) dagḍī pāyryā 'steps (made) of stone'

Negative material is commonly expressed by (*-tSyā* - possessive) + *śiwāy* 'without' which follows the noun of material as in (921).

(921)	dudhā (tSyā)	śiwāy	kelelā	tSahā
	milk	without	do-perf-past-3sm	tea-3sm

'tea (which is) made without milk'

2.1.1.4.11 *Manner*

Manner is expressed by using one of the following strategies: (a) by an adjective or adverb which is placed immediately preceding the verb as in (922) and (923), (b) by a present, conjunctive participle expressing manner as in (924), (c) by the instrumental marker, (925), (d) by a postposition of comparison, i.e., (*-tSyā*) *sārkha* 'like X' (926), (e) by use of the postpositions *pāsūn* 'from', *lāwūn* 'having applied' (927) and (928).

Adjective of modification:

(922)	to	patra	tsāŋglī	lihito
	he	letters	well	write-pres-3sm

'He writes letters well.'

adverb of modification:

(923)	rām	bharbhar	tsālto
	Ram	fast	walk-pres-3sm

'Ram walks fast.'

Present/conjunctive participle:

(924)	anū	hasat/hasūn	mhaṇālī
	Anu	smile-prs-part/smile-conj.part	say-pst-3sf

'Anu said smiling.'

Instrumental marker:

(925)	tyāne	madzhe	ādarāne	swāgat	kele
	he-ag	I-poss-3sn	respect-inst	greeting-3sn	do-pst-3sn

'He greeted me with respect.'

Postposition: X (tSyā) *sārkha* 'like X'

(926)	tū	āīsārkhīts	hastes
	you	mother-like-emph	smile-pres-2s

'You smile like (your) mother.'

(927)	to	manāpāsūn	kām	karto
	he	heart-from(com)	work	do-pres-3sm

'He works whole-heartedly.' (lit: 'from the bottom of his heart')

(928)	to	nehmī	man	lāwūn	kām	karto
	he	always	heart	having applied	work	do-pres-3sm

'He always works whole-heartedly.' (lit: 'by applying his heart to the work')

gerund:

(929)	to	bitShānyāwar	paḍlyā	paḍlyā
	he	bed-on	lie-ger	lie-ger

pustak	wātsto
book	read-pres-3sm

'He reads the book lying on the bed.'

Negative manner is expressed by the postposition (*-tSyā) śiwāy* or by the negative particle *-na*.

(930)

oraḍlyā	śiwāy	tulā	boltā	yet
shout-ger	without	you-dat	talk	come-pres

nāhī	kā?
neg-pres-3s	Q

'Can you not talk without shouting?'

(931)

ātā	na	boltā	kām	kar
now	neg	talk	work	do-imp-2s

'Now do the work without talking.'

2.1.1.4.12 *Cause*

Cause is expressed in one of the following ways: (a) the instrumental case-marker *-ne*, (b) the postpositon *muḷe*, (c) a noun *kāraṇ* (cause) followed by the instrumental case-marker *-ne* (i.e., *kārṇāne* 'because of'), and (d) conjunctive participle. The following examples illustrate the use of the above devices to express cause.

Use of the instrumental case-marker *-ne :*

(932)

purāne	ghara	wāhūn	gelī
flood-inst	house -3pl.n	sweep-conj.part	go-pst-3pl.n

'The houses got swept away because of the floods.'

muḷe :

(933)

mulgā	yuddhāhūn	parat	ālyāmuḷe
son	war-from	return	come-ger-because of

āīlā	ānānda	dzhālā
mother-dat	happiness-3sm	happen-pst-3sm

'The mother became happy because (her) son returned home from the war.'

kārṇāne :

(934)	diwasbhar	kām	kelyākārṇāne	tī	thaklī
	day-whole	work	do-ger-because of	she	tired
	āhe				
	is				

'She is tired because she worked all day.'

conjunctive participle:

(935)	bandukitSī	goḷī	lāgūn	to	melā
	gun-poss-3sf	bullet-3sf	hit-conj.part	he	die-pst-3sm

'He died of the gunshot.' (lit: 'bullet from the gun')

2.1.1.4.13 *Purpose*

Purpose is expressed by (a) the dative case-marker *-lā* (following the infinitive form of the verb), (b) the postposition *kartā/sāṭhī* (following a noun or an infinitive form of the verb), (c) an optative sentence followed by the quotative marker *mhaṇūn*. The following examples illustrate the use of the above devices to express purpose.

dative case-marker *-lā :*

(936)	to	amerikelā	śikāylā	gelā
	he	America-dat	study-inf-dat	go-pst-3sm

'He went to America to study.'

kartā/sāṭhī (following a noun):

(937)	to	kuṭumbā {kartā / sāṭhī}	kaṣṭa	karto
	he	family-for	hardwork	do-pres-3sm

'He works hard for the sake of (his) family.'

kartā/sāṭhī (following the infinitive form of a verb):

(938)	tulā	bheṭṇyā {kartā / sāṭhī}	mī	bhāratāt	dzāīn
	you-dat	meet-inf-for	I	India-loc	go-fut-1s

'I will go to India to meet you.'

optative followed by the quotative *mhaṇūn* :

(939)	paise	miḷwāwe	mhaṇūn	to	amerikelā
	money	earn-opt-3pl.n	quot	he	America-dat
	gelā				
	go-pst-3sm				

'He went to America so that he may earn money.' (lit: '(I) may earn money, saying this, he went to America.')

2.1.1.4.14 *Function*

Function is expressed by using the quotative marker *mhaṇūn* or by the compound postposition (*-tSyā* (poss) *sārkhā* 'like').

mhaṇūn :

(940)	mādzhā	bhāū	sofā	palang	mhaṇūn	wāparto
	my	brother	sofa	bed	quot	use-pres-3sm

'My brother uses the sofa as bed.'

(*-tSyā*) *sārkhā* :

(941)	anū	sāḍī	śālīsārkhī	pāŋgharte
	Anu	saree	shawl-like	wrap-pres-3sf

'Anu wraps the saree like a shawl.'

2.1.1.4.15 *Reference*

Reference is expressed by the postpositions (*-tSyā*) *bābat/bābtīt* '(poss) about', (*-tSyā*) *baddal* '(poss) about', (*-tSyā*) *wiṣayī* '(poss) about', (*-tSyā*) *sāmbandhī* '(poss) about'.

The above postpositions are added to a noun or an infinitive form of a verb as in (942) and (943) respectively. *Sāmbandhī* can be used in both (942) and (943).

(942)	mī	bhāratā (tSyā)	wiṣayī	bolat	hote
	I	India- (poss)	about	talk-prog	was-3sf

'I was talking about India.'

(943)	mī	bhāratālā	dzāṇyābaddal	bolat	hote
	I	India-dat	go-inf-about	talk-prog	was-3sf

'I was talking about going to India.'

2.1.1.4.16-17 *Essive and translative*

Essive is expressed by the expressions (a) *-tSyā rūpāt* 'in the form of/as', (b) *-tSyā weṣāt* 'in the garb of/as'.

-tSyā rūpāt:

(944)	malā	wāṭla	kī	dew	tuʤhyā
	I-dat	feel-pst-3sn	comp	god-3sm	your
	rūpāt	malā	bheṭlā		
	form-loc	I-dat	meet-pst-3sm		

'I felt that God met me in your form.'

-tSyā weṣāt:

(945)	polīs	dukāndārātSyā	weṣāt	bhaṭkat
	policeman	shopkeeper-poss	garb-loc	wander-prog
	hotā			
	was			

'The policeman was wandering in the garb of a shopkeeper.'

Translative is marked by the quotative *mhaṇūn* in informal speech (as in (946)). In formal speech, it is marked by the expression *-tSyā padāwar* 'in the position of' as in (947).

mhaṇūn:

(946)	presiḍenṭ ne	tyālā	sekreṭarī	mhaṇūn	nemle
	president-ag	him	secretary	quot/trans	appoint-pst-3sn

'The president appointed him secretary.'

-*tSyā padāwar* 'in the position of':

(947)	presiḍenṭ ne	tyālā	sekreṭarī	tSyā	padāwar
	president-ag	him	secretary	poss	position-on

nemle
appoint-pst-3sn

'The president appointed him secretary.' (lit: 'in the position of secretary')

2.1.1.4.18 *Part-whole*

Part-whole relations are expressed by the possessive marker*tsā* (sm), or one of its variants -*tSī* (sf), -*tse* (sn/pl.m), -*tSyā* (pl.f), -*tSī* (pl.n)) suffixed to the noun (or the noun phrase) referring to the whole. The noun phrase referring to a part follows the noun phrase referring to the whole as in (948) and (949).

(948)	kawitetSī	pahilī	oḷ
	poem-poss-3sf	first-3sm	line-3sf

'the first line of the poem'

(949)	hātātsa	ek	boṭ
	hand-poss-3sn	one	finger

'one finger of the hand'

Occasionally, part-whole relationship is expressed by the adjective derived from the noun expressing the whole, with the noun expressing a part following it as in (950).

(950)	gharātlī	kholī
	house-loc-adj-3sf	room-3sf

'the room inside the house/the room of the house'

It must be noted here that (950) is ambiguous between the room inside (as opposed to outside) the house vs. the room of the house. In contrast to this, the use of the possessive postposition makes (951) unambiguous.

(951)	gharātSī	kholī
	house-poss-3sf	room-3sf

'the room of the house'

2.1.1.4.19 *Partitive*

The partitive-non-partitive distinction is not always expressed the same way as in English. For example, for English expressions such as 'two of his sisters', 'one of his sons', 'some of his brothers', etc., Marathi does not generally use the partitive expression. Rather, the Marathi counterparts of the above are 'his two sisters', 'his one son', 'his some brothers' respectively, as in (952), (953), and (954).

(952)	tyātSyā	don	mulī
	his	two	sisters

'his two sisters (two of his sisters)'

(953)	tyātsā	ek	mulgā
	his	one	son

'his one son (one of his sons)'

(954)	tyātse	kāhī	bhāū
	his	some	brothers

'his some brothers (some of his brothers)'

Partitive meaning is expressed by one of the following two devices: (a) suffixing the compound postposition (*-tSyā) paikī* 'among' to the noun followed by the partitive numerals or quantifiers, and (b) suffixing the locative postposition *-t* (along with the adjectivalizing suffix *-l* V(owel) to the noun followed by partitive numerals or quantifiers.

(-tSyā) paikī 'among':

(955)	tyātSyā	mulīn(*tSyā*)	paikī	don
	his	daughers (poss)	among	two

(mulī) alyā
daughters come-pst-3pl.f

'Two of his daughters came.' (lit: 'Among his daughters, two came.')

(-tSyā) paikī + quantifier:

(956) sabhāsadā̃n (*tSyā*) paikī kāhī (sabhāsad)
members (poss) among some (members)

āle
come-pst-3pl.m

'Some of the members came.' (lit: 'Among the members, some came.')

-locative + *lV(owel)* + numeral:

(957) śā̃mbhar widyārthyā-t-le pāts (widyarthī)
one hundred students-loc-adj-3pl.m five (students)

āle
come-pst-3pl.m

'Five of the hundred students came.'

-locative + *lV(owel)* + quantifier:

(958) sahā bhāwāt-le kāhī (bhāū) āle
six brothers-loc-adj some (brother) come-pst-3pl.m

'Some of the six brothers came.'

2.1.1.4.19.2 & 2.1.1.4.19.4 *Non-partitive numerals and quantifiers*

Non-partitive numerals and quantifiers precede the noun, which is unmarked.

(959) tīn/kāhī dzhāḍa
'three/some trees'

2.1.1.4.19.5 *Partitive negative quantifiers*

Marathi lacks morphological negative quantifiers; instead the following devices used simultaneously convey negative quantification: (a) a question word *kuṇī/koṇī* followed by the emphatic particle *hī/ts/suddhā* , (b) negation in the verb phrase, (c) the noun modified by the quantifier preceding the quantifier and is followed by the compound postposition (*-tSyā) paikī* 'among'.

(960)	tyãntSyā	mulãnpaikī	koṇīhī/ts/suddhā	itha
	their	children-among	who-emph	here
	rāhāt	nāhī		
	live	neg		

'None of their children lives here.'

With non-count nouns, the word *thoḍV*(owel) 'a little' is used followed by one of the emphatic particles *hī* or *suddhā* as in (961).

(961)	tyāne	thoḍīsuddhā/hī	sattā	gamāwlī	nāhī
	he-ag	a little - emph	power	lose-pst-3sf	neg

'He did not lose even a little bit of power.'

2.1.1.4.19.6 *Non-partitive negative quantifier*

Non-partitive negative quantification is expressed by using the word for the numeral one, *ek* , followed by the emphatic particle *hī.* The noun modified by the quantifier precedes the numeral and is followed by the postposition *(-tSyā) paikī* 'among'. A negative verb must be used in this case.

(962)	tyãntsyāpaikī	ekahī	(māṇūs)	ālā	nāhī
	they-among	one-emph	person	come- pst-3sm	neg-s

'Not a single person among them came.'

2.1.1.4.20 *Price*

Price is expressed by the dative.

(963)

mī	śãmbhar	rupayãnnā	tī	khurtSī
I	one hundred	rupees-dat	that	chair

ghetlī
take-pst-3sf

'I bought that chair for one hundred rupees.'

(964)

tū	he	pen	kitīlā	ghetla ?
you	this	pen-3sn	how much-dat	take-pst-3sn

'For what price did you buy this pen ?'

2.1.1.4.21 *Value*

Value is expressed by the possessive postposition or by the expression *kimmat* 'worth' which follows the value expression.

(965)

pandhrā	lākhãntSā	ghar
fifteen	lakhs-poss-3sf	house-3sn

'a 15-lakh house' (one lakh = 100,000)

Note that the possessive agrees with the following noun 'house' in number, gender, and person.

(966)

ek	lākhātse	dāgine
one	lakh-poss-3pl.m	jewelry-3pl.m

'jewelry worth one lakh of rupees'

2.1.1.4.22 *Distance*

Distance is expressed by (a) the optional adverb *dūr* 'distance' following the expression of distance in the nominative case, and (b) the noun *ãntar* 'distance'.

(967)

śikāgo	ithūn	ekśe	wīs	mail
Chicago	here-abl	one hundred	twenty	miles

(dūr)	āhe
(distance)	is

'Chicago is one hundred twenty miles from here.'

It should be noted here that when the distance between two points is expressed, as in (967), the use of *dūr* 'distance' is optional. Distance can be also expressed by the noun *ãntar* 'distance'as in (968).

(968)	arbānā	āṇi	śikāgo	madhe	ekśe
	Urbana	and	Chicago	between	one hundred

wīs	mailā̃ntse	ãntar	āhe
twenty	miles-poss.3sn	distance-3sn	is

'The distance between Urbana and Chicago is one hundred and twenty miles.'

2.1.1.4.23 *Extent*

Extent is expressed by a classifier (*lā̃mb* 'long', *rũnda* 'wide', *ũntsa* 'tall', *khol* 'deep') following the phrase describing the extent.

(969)	...tīs	fūṭ	lā̃mb	dor...
	thirty	feet	long	rope

'...a thirty foot long rope...'

(970)	...tīn	fūṭ	rũnda	kapḍā
	three	feet	wide	cloth

'...the three foot wide cloth...'

(971)	...sahā	fūṭ	ũntsa	mulgā...
	six	feet	tall	boy

'...a six foot tall boy...'

(972)	...nawwad	fūṭ	khol	wihīr...
	ninety	feet	deep	well

'...a ninety foot deep well...'

Extent may be expressed also by a prenominal modifier which is derived by adding the possessive suffix to the noun of extent. In this case, the modified noun follows the modifier as in (973).

(973)	...tīn	fūṭ	rundī-tsā	kapḍā
	three	feet	width-poss-3sm	cloth-3sm

'...the three foot wide cloth...' (lit: 'the cloth of three feet width...')

2.1.1.4.24 *Concessive*

Concessive is expressed only syntactically by (i) the pair of conditionals (*dzarī*) X . . . *tarī* Y ...Y' (i.e., despite X, Y takes place), (ii) conjunctive participle + emphatic particle *hī* (975), (iii) gerund + postposition *war* + emphatic particle *hi* or *suddhā* (976), and (iv) adverbial participle + *hi* or *suddhā* (977).

(974)	(dzarī)	to	ādzārī	hotā	tarī
	(though)	he	sick	was	even then

to	kāmāwar	ālā
he	work-on	come-pst-3sm

'Although he was sick, he came to work.'

(975)	pustak	vātsūn	hī/suddhā	to	kāhī
	book	read-conj.part	emph	he	anything

śiklā	nāhī
learn-pst-3sm	neg

'Even after reading the book, he did not learn anything.'

(976)	tSahā	piūn	hī/suddhā	to	dzhopūn
	tea	drink-adv.part	emph	he	sleep

gelā
go-pst-3sm

'He dozed off even after drinking tea.'

2.1.1.4.25 *Inclusion*

Inclusion is expressed by the postpositional phrase *lā dharūn* 'including X' following the noun of inclusion. The postpositional phrase is comprised of the accusative case-marker/postposition *-lā* followed by the conjunctive participle of the verb *dharṇe* 'to hold/to include', or by the postposition *sahit* 'with' following the noun as in (978).

(977)	anūlā	dharūn	āṭh	mulī	ālyā
	Anu-acc	include-conj.part	eight	girls	come-pst-3pl.f

hotyā
be-pst-3pl.f

'Including Anu, eight girls had come.'

(978)	anūsahit	tīn	mulī	ālyā
	Anu-with	three	girls	come-pst-3pl.f

'Including Anu, three girls came.'

Additionally, the inclusive particles *hī* 'also', and *suddhā* 'also' express the function of inclusion (see section 1.11.2.1.2).

2.1.1.4.26 *Exclusion*

Exclusion is expressed by one of the following devices: (a) by using the postpositional phrase X *tSyā śiwāy* 'besides/without X...', (b) by the conjunctive participle of the verb *soḍṇe* 'to leave', (c) by using the negative form of the phrase of inclusion, X *lā na dhartā* 'not including X . . .'. The following example illustrates the use of the above devices.

X tSyā śiwāy 'besides/without X':

(979) mādʒhyā śiwāy/malā soḍūn/malā
I-poss-besides/I-acc leave-conj.part/I-acc

na	dhartā	pāts	bāykā	yetīl
neg	including	five	women	come-fut-3pl.f

'Besides me/leaving me/not including me, five women will come.'

2.1.1.4.27 *Addition*

Addition is expressed by the postpositional phrase X *(tSyā) śiwāy* / X *(tSyā) kheridz...*' without/besides' when the subject is either modified by the adverb of degree *āṇkhī* 'more' or followed by the particles *paṇ/hī/suddhā* 'also'.

(980) mohan (tSyā) śiwāy/(tSyā) kherīdz
Mohan-(poss)-besides/(poss)-without

āṇkhī	sahā	mitra	titha	hote
more	six	friends	there	were

'In addition to Mohan, six more friends were there.'

The conjunctive participle expression of exclusion X *lā soḍūn* (as in 2.1.1.4.26) 'leaving X' is also used to express addition, when the subject is either followed by the particle of inclusion *hī/suddhā* or is modified by *āṇkhī* 'more' as in (981).

(981)	malā	soḍūn	āṇkhī	dahā	widyārthī
	I-acc	leave-conj.part	more	ten	student-3pl.m

āle
come-pst-3pl.m

'Besides me, ten more students came.'

2.1.1.4.28 *Vocative*

Vocative is expressed by (a) the oblique form of singular masculine, feminine, and neuter nouns, and (b) by the oblique form of plural nouns followed by the suffix *-no* (see the discussion on the vocative form in section 1.15.1).

Additionally, there are vocative particles which precede or follow proper or common nouns or names of professions, but are not obligatory. Vocatives such as *sāheb* 'sir' and *bāī* 'madam' are polite vocatives which may occur by themselves or before nouns as in (982) and (983) respectively.

(982)	a)	sāheb!	'respectable sir!'
	b)	dzośī sāheb	'Mr. Joshi' (polite)

(983)	a)	bāī!	'respectable madam!'
	b)	dzośī bāī !	'Mrs. Joshi' (polite)

The forms of the vocative particles and the contexts in which these are used are given below:

(984)	a)	are	male addressee intimate to the speaker or of inferior status to the speaker
	b)	aga	female addressee, intimate to the speaker or of inferior status to the speaker
	c)	aho	addressee: husband (polite) (in this case, *aho* is used by itself, not with husband's name)
	d)	aho	addressee: male or female, polite or casual speech
	e)	aga	addressee: wife (in this case, *aga* is used by itself, not with wife's name)

The choice of vocative particles is determined by conditions of appropriateness according to the sex, age, and social status of the addressee relative to that of the speaker (for further discussion on the conditions of appropriateness see Pandharipande 1991a). The following examples note the co-occurrence of various nouns (kinship terms, terms for professions, etc.) and vocative particles.

	Vocative particle	+	Nouns
(985)	aho		(a) kinship terms - *bābā* 'father', *māmā* 'uncle', *ādzobā* 'grandfather', etc.

		(b) terms of profession - *dɔkṭar* 'doctor', *māstar* 'teacher', etc. (c) last names of unfamiliar persons - *deśpande* 'Deshpande', *āpte* 'Apte', etc. (d) generic terms of politeness: *sāheb* 'sir', *bāī* 'madam'
(986)	are	(a) kinship terms - *dādā* 'older brother' (b) terms of profession - *dhobi* 'washerman', *telī* 'oil-seller (c) common nouns indicating intimacy - *mitra/dost* 'friend', *dew* 'god' (in religious discourse)
(987)	aga	(a) kinship terms - *āī* 'mother', *tāī/ākkā* 'elder sister, *māmī* 'aunt', etc. (b) terms of profession - *bhāʤīwālī* 'vegetable vender (female)', *molkarīṇ* 'maid' (c) terms indicating intimacy - *maitrīṇ* 'friend', *dewī* 'goddess' (in religious discourse)

Several points need to be mentioned here regarding (985) - (987). First, *aho* is used to indicate politeness, regardless of the gender of the addressee (985); second, *are* and *aga* are used with male and female addressees respectively; third, pragmatic conditions on politeness may vary according to the context. For example, *aho* is generally used to indicate politeness to an addressee who is older than the speaker (985a) or of respectable social status (985b) or not intimate with the speaker (985c). However, when the addressee is older than the speaker but is intimate with him/her, then the use of *are* (male) or *aga* (female), is more appropriate and preferred to *aho*. This explains why the vocative particles *are* and *aga* are used for god and goddess/mother respectively. In other words, the relationship between the speaker and the addressee (i.e., intimate vs. non-intimate) overrules the pragmatic conditions of age and respect. (For further discussion on the conditions of appropriateness, see Pandharipande 1991a.)

2.1.1.4.29 *Citation form*

The citation form is nominative singular for nouns and the imperative singular for verbs, e.g., *nadī* 'river', *dzā* 'go'.

2.1.1.4.30 *Label form*

The nominative form is generally used for shop signs, labels of parcels, etc., e.g., *sāykal sṭoar* 'cycle store'. The names of shops fall in the following categories:

(a) proper or common nouns (which do not refer to the merchandise sold in the shops). For example, *alaṃkār* (lit: 'jewelry') can be the name of a saree-shop, restaurant, pottery shop, etc. The noun of the name of the shop is in the nominative case.

(b) common nouns indicating the merchandise sold in the shop. In this case, Marathi chooses one of two strategies: the noun which is the name of the merchandise is in the possessive case, followed by the Marathi noun for shop, i.e., *dukān: kirāṇyā-tse dukān* 'grocery-store', (lit: 'shop of grocery'), *kapḍyā-tse dukān* 'cloth-store' (lit: 'shop of cloth').

(c) common nouns in Marathi or English (in the nominative case) followed by the term for shop (i.e., *sṭoar* 'store') borrowed from English, i.e., *sāḍī sṭoar* 'saree-shop', *sāykal sṭoar* 'cycle-shop'.

In addressing a specific person or institution in a letter, the address label bears the name of the person or institution in the nominative case as in (988). The designation or title of the person generally follows the name of the person. Also, the honorific nouns *śrī (mān)* (lit: 'prosperous male') and *śrī (matī)* (lit: 'prosperous female') generally precede proper nouns, i.e., *śrī(mān) Mohan Joshī.* The honorific nouns are used for married or elder people. For unmarried or young, the honorific nouns are *kumār* (for a male) and *kumārī* (for a female). However, *śrī(mān)* and *śrī (matī)* are replacing *kumār* and *kumarī* respectively in contemporary language.

Another convention which is mostly restricted to the rural varieties (as opposed to the cities) is of placing honorific titles such as *pānta* (for *Brāhmin* males) and *rāo/sāheb* (for males of all castes including the *Brāhmins*) and *bāī* for women (of all castes) following the first name of the addressee.

(988)	śrī	madhukar-pānta/rāo/sāheb	gogṭe
	Mr.	Madhukar-honor	Gogṭe

'Mr. Madhukar Gogṭe'

(989)	śrīmatī	sudhābaī	gogṭe
	Mrs.	Suddhā	Gogṭe

'Mrs. Sudha Gogṭe'

Note that the simultaneous use of honorifics preceding and following the first name is acceptable as in (988) and (989).

2.1.1.5 *Local Semantic functions*

Local semantic functions are expressed by case-suffixes and postpositions.

2.1.1.5.1 *General location*

General location is expressed by (a) the locative suffixes *-ī* or *-t* which follow the noun of location, (b) the locative postpositions *(-tSyā) madhe* 'in/in the middle of', *-tSyā* (poss) *āt* 'in' (lit: 'inside of'). The following examples illustrate the use of these case-suffixes and postpositions.

-ī/-t :

(990)	to	ādz	gharī/gharāt	nāhī
	he	today	home-loc at/home-loc-in	neg-3s

'He is not at home/in the house today.'

madhe 'in the middle of':

(991)	tyāne	rastyā(tSyā)	madhe	gāḍī
	he-ag	street (poss)	in the middle of	car-3sf

thāmbawlī
stop-pst-3sf

'He stopped the car in the middle of the street.'

-tSyā āt 'in':

(992)	śāḷetSyā	āt	ek	moṭhī	lāyabrarī	āhe
	school-poss	inside	one	big	library	is

'There is a big library inside the school.'

Motions to and from are expresed by the dative *-lā* and locative *- ī* (993) and the ablative (994) respectively. It should be noted here that the use of the dative *-lā* (in (993)) is common in all varieties of Marathi and is not determined by the morphological form of the noun. In contrast to this, the locative suffix *-ī* is used only with consonant-ending nouns and is more commonly used in western/southern Maharashtra as opposed to eastern and northern Maharashtra.

dative *-lā* /locative *-ī* (motion to):

(993)	to	gāwālā/gāwī	gelā
	he	village-dat/village-loc	go-pst-3sm

'He went to the village.'

ablative (motion from):

(994)	mī	kāl	mumbaī-hūn	ālo
	I	yesterday	Bombay-abl	come-pst-3sm

'Yesterday, I came from Bombay.'

Motion past is expressed by (a) the postposition *madhe* 'in the middle' followed by the ablative case-suffix *-ūn* (i.e., *madhūn* 'through'), (b) the compound postposition *-tSyā bādzūne* 'by the side of', (c) the compound postposition *-tSyā dzawaḷūn* 'by the side of' (lit: 'from the close proximity of'), (d) *-lā tSakkar mārūn* 'going around' (lit: 'by taking a round around a particular location'), (e) the postposition *-tSyā paryānta* 'up to but not beyond'. The use of the above postpositions is exemplified in (995) - (999) below.

madhūn 'through':

(995)	pūrṇā	nadī	gāwā-madhūn	wāhte
	Purna	river-3sf	village-through	flow-pres-3sf

'The river Purna flows through the village.'

-tSyā bādzūne 'by the side of':

(996)	mandirātSyā	bādzūne	dzā
	temple-poss	side-inst	go-imp-2s

'Go by the side of the temple.'

-tSyā dzawaḷūn 'from the close proximity of':

(997)	bus	nāmbar	tīn	mādʒhyā	gharātSyā
	bus-3sf	number	three	I-poss	home-poss
	dzawaḷūn	dzāte			
	close-abl	go-pres-3sf			

'Bus number three goes by my home.'

-lā tSakkar mārūn 'going around':

(998)	gāḍī	parwatālā	tsakkar	mārūn
	train	mountain-dat	round/circle	strike-conj.part
	puṇyālā	dzāte		
	Pune-dat	go-pres-3sf		

'The train goes to Pune after circling the mountain.'

(-tSyā) paryānta 'up to':

(999)	amit	nāgpūr (*tSyā*)	paryānta	gelā
	Amit-3sm	Nagpur (poss)	up to	go-pst-3sm

'Amit went up to Nagpur.'

2.1.1.5.2 *Proximate location*

Proximate location is expressed by the compound postpositions (a) *-tSyā dzawaḷ/-tSyā pāśī* 'near', (b) *-tSyā bādzūlā* 'by the side of', (c) *-lā lāgūn* 'next to'. The following examples illustrate the use of the above postpositions.

(-tSyā) dzawaḷ/(-tSyā) pāśī 'near':

(1000)	mādʒhyā	gharā (tSyā)	dzawaḷ/pāśī	ek
	I-poss	house-poss	near/near	one

waḍātsa	dzhāḍ	āhe
banayan	tree	is

'There is a banayan tree near my house.'

-tSyā bādzū-lā 'by the side of':

(1001)	dukānātSyā	bādzūlā	ek	pārk	āhe
	shop-poss	side-dat	one	park	is

'There is a park by the side of the shop.'

-lā lāgūn 'next to':

(1002)	mandirā-lā	lāgūn	ek	talāw	āhe
	temple-dat	attach-conj.part	one	lake	is

'There is a lake next to the temple.'

Motion 'near to' and 'from near something' are expressed by the compound postposition *(-tSyā) dzawaḷ/(-tSyā) pāśī* and *(-tSyā) dzawaḷ* followed by the ablative case-suffix *-ūn* 'from' respectively (as in (1003) and (1004)).

(-tSyā) dzawaḷ / (-tSyā) pāśī 'near to':

(1003)	dupārī	don	wādztā	to
	afternoon-in	two	o'clock	he

gāwādzawaḷ/gāwāpāśī	potslā
village-near/village near	reach-pst-3sm

'At two o'clock in the afternoon, he reached near the village.'

(-tSyā) dzawaḷ-ūn 'from near':

(1004)	bāgetSyā	dzawaḷūn	harīṇ	dhāwat	gele
	garden-poss	near-abl	deer	run-prog	go-pst-3sn

'The deer went running by the garden (lit: 'from near the garden').

When proximate direction is to be expressed, the postpositions *-tSyā bādzūne* 'from the direction of' (lit: 'from the side of') or *-tSyā* *diśene* 'from the direction of' are used as illustrated in (1005) and (1006) respectively.

(1005)	bɔmbtsā	āwadz	gharātSyā	bādzūne
	bomb-poss	noise-3sm	home-poss	side-inst
	ālā			
	come-pst-3sm			

'The noise of the bomb came from the direction of the house.'

(1006)	bɔmbtsā	āwādz	gharātSyā	diśene
	bomb-poss	noise-3sm	home-poss	direction-inst
	ālā			
	come-pst-3sm			

'The noise of the bomb came from the direction of the house.'

Proximate motion past is expressed by the compound postposition *(-tSyā) wār* 'on' followed by the ablative case-suffix *-ūn* (i.e., *-tSyā warūn*) as seen below.

(1007)	gāḍī	amarāwatīwarūn	ākolyālā	dzāte
	train-3sf	Amravati-on-abl	Akola-dat	go-pres-3sf

'The train goes to Akola via Amravati.'

2.1.1.5.3 *Interior*

Interior location is expressed by the locative case-suffix *-t* or the compound postposition *(-tSyā) āt* and *(-tSyā) madhe* as discussed in 2.1.1.5.1. Directional motion 'from' is expressed by the above-mentioned locative suffix and postpositions as in (1008). Additionally, the postpositions *āt* 'in' and *madhe* 'in/in the middle of' (*ātmadhe* 'into') preceded by the optional possessive suffix *-tSyā* express motion 'into' as in (1009) and (1010).

(1008)	gharātSyā	ātūn	āwādz	ālā
	house-poss	in-from	sound-3sm	come-pst-3sm

'The sound came from inside the house.'

case-suffix/postpositions 'into':

(1009) tsor gharāt/gharātSyāāt/gharāmadhe
thief-3sm home-loc/house-poss-in/house in

śirlā
enter-pst-3sm

'The thief entered the house.'

-tSyā ātmadhe 'into':

(1010)	polīs	tyā	imāratī-tSyā	ātmadhe
	policeman-3sm	that-obl	building-poss	into

ghuslā
dash-pst-3sm

'The policeman dashed into the building.'

Specific location 'inside' is also expressed by an adjective derived by adding the dative suffix *-lā* to the postpositional phrase *-tSyā āt* 'inside of'. The derived adjective precedes the noun and agrees with it in gender and number as in (1011).

(1011)	śāḷetSyā	āt-lyā	kholyā	lahān	āhet
	school-poss	in-dat-3pl.f	rooms-3pl.f	small	are

'The rooms inside the school are small.'

Locations 'out of' and 'through' are expressed by adding the locative suffix *-t* or the postpositions *-tSyā-āt / -tSyā madhe,* followed by the ablative suffix *-ūn* as in 'out of' (from inside):

(1012) mandirā-t-ūn/mandirā-tSyā āt-ūn/mandirā-madh-ūn
temple-loc-abl/temple-poss in-abl/temple-inside-abl

ārtītsā	āwādz	yet	hotā
prayer-poss	sound-3sm	come-prog	be-pst-3sm

'The sound of the prayer was coming from inside the temple.'

(1013) bas gāwātūn/gāwātSyā-at-ūn/gāwā-(tSyā)
bus-3sf village-loc-abl/village-poss-in-abl/village-(poss)

madh-ūn dzāte
inside-abl go-pres-3sf

'The bus goes through (the middle of) the village.'

The location 'up to inside' is expressed by the compound postposition *-tSyā āt* 'inside of' followed by the adverb *paryānta* 'up to' as in (1014).

(1014) ...mandirā-tSyā āt-...paryānta...
temple-poss inside-up to

'... up to the inside of the temple ...'

2.1.1.5.4 *Exterior*

Exterior location is expressed by the postposition *(-tSyā) bāher* 'outside' which follows the noun as in (1015).

(1015) ...dukānā(tSyā) bāher...
shop - (poss) outside

'...outside the shop...'

Directional motion 'up to' is expressed by the same postposition as in (1015). Consider (1016).

(1016) rādʒāne tsorālā deśā(tSyā) bāher pāṭhawle
king-ag thief-dat country(poss) outside send-pst-3sn

'The king sent the thief outside the country.' (i.e., beyond the limits of the country)

Exterior motion past is expressed by the postposition *(-tSyā) bāher* followed by the ablative case-suffix *-ūn* (i.e., *(-tSyā) bāherūn* 'from the outside of') as in (1017).

(1017) śatrūtsa sainya gāwā(tSyā)-bāher-ūn
enemy-poss army-3sn village-(poss)-outside-abl

nighūn gela
away go-pst-3sn

'The army of the enemy went past the village.'

Exterior motion 'up to' is expressed by the postposition *-tSyā bāher* 'outside of' followed by the adverb *paryānta* 'up to' as in (1018).

(1018) tī āg śaharā-tSyā bāher-paryānta
that fire-3sf city-poss outside-up to

potslī hotī
reach-pst-3sf was-3sn

'That fire had spread up to the outskirts of the city.'

2.1.1.5.5 *Anterior*

Anterior location is expressed by one of the following postpositions.

(a) *(-tSyā) samor* 'in front of'
(poss) front

(b) *(-tSyā) puḍhe* 'ahead of'
(poss) ahead

(c) *-tSyā puḍhyāt* 'in front of/opposite of'
poss ahead-loc

(d) samortSyā bādzūlā 'to the front side of'
front-poss side-dat

(e) puḍhtSyā bādzūlā 'to the front side of'
ahead-poss side-dat

Consider the following examples:

(-tSyā) samor 'in front of':

(1019)	anūtSyā	gharā	(tSyā)	samor	bāg	āhe
	Anu-poss	house	(poss)	front	garden	is

'There is a garden in front of Anu's house.'

-tSyā puḍhe 'ahead of':

(1020)	śāḷetSyā	puḍhe	ek	moṭhe	maidān	āhe
	school-poss	ahead	one	big	field	is

'There is a field in front of the school.'

-tSyā puḍhyāt 'in front of/opposite of':

(1021)	tī	dhāwat	ālī	āṇi	mādʒhyā
	she	run-prog	come-pst-3sf	and	I-poss
	puḍhyāt	baslī			
	ahead-loc	sit-pst-3sf			

'She came running and sat in front of me.'

samortSyā bādzūlā 'to the front side of':

(1022)	mādʒhyā	gharātSyā	samortSyā	bādzūlā	
	I-poss	house-poss	front-poss	side-dat	
	ek	sarkārī	kāryālay	āhe	
	one	government	office	is	

'There is a government office in front of my house.'

puḍhtSyā bādzūlā 'to the front side of/ahead of':

(1023)	śṭeśantSyā	puḍhtSyā	bādzūlā	ek	dukān
	station-poss	ahead-poss	side-dat	one	shop
	āhe				
	is				

'There is a shop in front of (lit: 'ahead of') the station.'

Anterior at rest as well as motion to are expressed simply by the above postpositions. Motion from is expressed by the ablative *(-tSyā) samorūn* 'from the front of' or *(-tSyā) puḍhūn* 'from ahead of', and by the instrumental *samortSyā bādzūne/puḍhtSyā bādzūne* 'by the front side of' as in (1024 - 1027) below.

'motion to':

(1024)	to	vaḍilāntSyā	samor/puḍhe	gelā
	he	father-poss	front/ahead	go-pst-3sm

'He went in front of/ahead of the father.'

'motion from':

(1025)	gāḍī	dukānā (tSyā)	samorūn/(tSyā)	puḍhūn
	car	shop (poss)	from-abl/(poss)	ahead
	ālī			
	come-pst-3sn			

'The car came from the front of the house.'

(1026)	gāḍī	gharātSyā	samortSyā	
	car-3sf	house-poss	front-poss	
	bādzūne /	puḍhtSyā	bādzūne	ālī
	side-inst /	ahead-poss	side-inst	come-pst-3sf

'The car came from the front of the house.'

2.1.1.5.6 *Posterior*

Posterior location is expressed by *(-tSyā) māge* 'in back of' or *(-tSyā) māgtSyā bādzūlā* 'in the back side of'. Posterior at rest and motion to are expressed by simply using the postpositions *(-tSyā) māge* 'in the back of' and *(-tSyā) māgtSyā bādzūlā* 'in the back side of'. Motion from and motion past are expressed by the ablative *-tSyā māgūn* 'from behind', or by the instrumental *māgtSyā bādzūne* 'from the back side of'. The following examples illustrate the use of the above postpositions.

Posterior location:

(1027)	tī	dārā (tSyā)	māge	laplī
	she	door (poss)	behind/back	hide-pst-3sf

'She hid behind the door.'

(1028)	tī	dārā	tSyā	māgtSyā	bādzūlā
	she	door	poss	back-poss	side-dat

lāplī
hide-pst-3sf

'She hid behind the door.'

'motion to':

(1029)	to	dukānā(tSyā)	māge	gelā
	he	shop (poss)	behind/back	go-pst-3sm

'He went to the back of the house.'

(1030)	to	dukānā (tSyā)	māgtSyā	bādzūlā	gelā
	he	shop (poss)	back (poss)	side-dat	go-pst-3sm

'He went to the back side of the house.'

'motion from/motion past':

(1031)	tī	śāḷetSyā	māg-ūn	dhāwat	ālī
	she	school-poss	back-abl	run-prog	come-pst-3sf

'She came running from the back of the house.'

2.1.1.5.7-8 *Superior and superior-contact location*

Superior contact/surface location is marked by the postposition *war* 'on'. Superior non-contact location is marked by *-tSyā wār* 'on' or by *-tSyā wartSyā bādzūlā* 'on the upper side of'. Consider the following examples.

-*war* 'on':

(1032)	dzhāḍātSyā	phā̃ndī	war	popaṭ
	tree-poss	branch	on	parrot-3sm

baslā āhe
sit-pst-3sm is

'The parrot is sitting on the branch of the tree.'

-tSyā war/-tSyā war tSyā bādzūlā 'above':

(1033)	ṭeblā-tSyā		war/ṭeblātSyā		wartSyā
	table-poss		on/table-poss		on-poss
	bādzūlā	ek	moṭhe	ghaḍyāḷ	āhe
	side-dat	one	big	clock	is

'There is a big clock above the table.'

Note that in the case of superior non-contact, the noun of location is followed by the possessive suffix *-tSyā*; optionally, the noun *bādzū* followed by the dative suffix *-lā* may also be added after the possessive suffix *-tSyā* 'of' as in (1033).

Motion from is expressed by the suffix *-ūn* added to noun + *war* 'on'. Motion past is expressed by either the ablative suffix *-ūn* (1034) or instrumental suffix *-ne* added to the noun *bādzū* 'side' as in (1035). Motion to is expressed by adding the dative suffix *-lā* to the noun *bādzū* as in (1036).

warūn 'from off':

(1034)	to	gatStSī-varūn	mādʒhyāśī	bollā
	he	terrace-on-abl	I-dat	speak-pst-3sm

'He talked to me from the terrace.'

wartSyā badzūne 'from above'

(1035)	āmtSyā	gharātSyā	{vartSyā bādzū-ne / varūn}
	our	house-poss	on-poss side-inst/on-abl
	wimān	dzāta	
	aeroplane	fly-pres-3sn	

'The aeroplane flies over (lit: 'from above') our house.'

wartSyā bādzūla 'over/across':

(1036)	pakṣī	mandirātSyā	wartSyā	bādzūlā	uḍālā
	bird-3sm	temple-poss	on-poss	side-dat	fly-pst-3sm

'The bird flew to the upper side of the temple.'

Motion up to is expressed by adding the adverb *paryānta* 'up to' to the postposition *war* as in (1037). The use of *-tSyā wartSyā badzūlā* 'to the upper side of' is not allowed in this context.

warparyānta 'up to/on':

(1037)	to	gharatSyā	war	paryānta	tsaḍhlā
	he	house-poss	on	up to	climb-pst-3sm

'He climbed up to the top of the house.'

2.1.1.5.9-10 *Inferior and inferior-contact location*

Inferior and inferior contact-location are expressed by adding the postposition (*-tSyā*) *khālī* 'under' or *-tSyā khāltSyā bādzūlā* 'to the side below' as in (1038) and (1039). While *(-tSyā) khālī* expresses both inferior contact (1038) as well as non-contact locations (1039), *-tSyā khāltSyā bādzūlā* 'to the side below' is restricted to the inferior contact-location (1040).

(-tSyā) khālī 'under' (Inferior contact):

(1038)	anūtSyā	gharā	(*tSyā*)	khālī
	Anu-poss	house	(poss)	under
	taḷghar	āhe		
	basement	is		

'There is a basement under Anu's house.'

(-tSyā) khālī 'under' (Inferior non-contact):

(1039)	mī	thakūn	tyā	dzhāḍā-khālī
	I	tire-conj.part	that	tree-under
	khūp	weḷ	basle	
	long	time	sit-pst-1sf	

'Being tired, I sat under the tree for a long time.'

-tSyā khāltSyā bādzūlā 'to the side below' (Inferior contact):

(1040)	tShparā(tSyā)	khāltSyā	bādzūlā	ek	moṭhe
	roof (poss)	under-poss	side-dat	one	big

poḷe	hote
bee-hive	was

'There was a big bee-hive {under / below} the roof.'

Motion up to expressed by adding the adverb *paryãnta* 'up to' to the postposition *(-tSyā) khālī* 'under' as in (1041).

(1041)

pāwsātsa	pāṇī	gharātSyā	khāl-paryãnta
rain-poss	water-3sn	house-poss	under-up to
potsla			
reach-pst-3sn			

'The rain water reached (up to) below the house.'

The postposition *-tSyā khaltSyā bādzūlā* 'to side below' is not allowed in this context. Motion from below is expressed by adding the instrumental suffix *-ne* to the postposition *khāltSyā bādzū.*

(1041a)

ʤinyātSyā	khāltSyā	bādzūne	āwādz
staircase-poss	below-poss	side-inst	sound-3sm
ālā			
come-pst-3sm			

'The sound came from below the staircase.'

2.1.1.5.11-12 *Lateral and lateral-contact location*

Both lateral and lateral contact location are expressed by adding one of the following postpositions to the noun of location: (a) *(-tSyā) pāśī* 'close to', (b) *(-tSyā) dzawaḷ* 'near', (c) *(-tSyā) śedzārī* 'next to'. It should be noted here that these three postpositions are generally interchangeable. However, the degree of proximity expressed by *(-tSyā) pāśī* and *(-tSyā) śedzārī* is higher than the degree of proximity expressed by *(-tSyā) dzawaḷ.* The following examples illustrate the use of the three postpositions:

(-tSyā) pāśī 'near':

(1042)	śāḷe(tSyā)	pāśī	ek	dawākhānā	āhe
	school (poss)	close to	one	clinic	is

'There is a clinic close to the school.'

(-tSyā) dzawaḷ 'near':

(1043)	mādʒhyā	gāwā (*tSyā*)	dzawaḷ	tudzha
	I-poss	village (poss)	near	you-poss
	gāw	āhe		
	village	is		

'Your village is near my village.'

(-tSyā) śedzārī 'next to':

(1044)	madhū	dhāwat	ālā	āṇi
	Madhu	run-prog	come-pst-3sm	and
	mādʒhyā	śedzārī	baslā	
	I-poss	next to	sit-pst-3sm	

'Madhu came running and sat next to me.'

Motion rest is expressed in (1041) - (1044). Motion to and motion up to are expressed exactly as in (1041) - (1044). Motion from is expressed by adding the ablative suffix *-ūn* to the postpositions *(-tSyā) dzawal* and *(-tSyā) śedzārī* as illustrated in (1045) - (1047) below. The use of *(-tSyā) pāśi* is not possible in this context.

(-tSyā) dzawaḷūn 'from near':

(1045)	tī	moṭar	mādʒhyā	dzawaḷ-ūn	gelī
	that-3sf	car	I-poss	near-abl	go-pst-3sf

'The car went past me (lit: 'went from near me').'

(-tSyā) śedzārūn 'from near':

(1046)	dūdhwālā	rodz	āmtSyā	gharā	śedzārūn
	milkman	everyday	our	house	next to

dzāto
go-pres-3sm

'The milkman goes right past our house every day.'

2.1.1.5.13-14 *Citerior and citerior-contact location*

Citerior location at rest is expressed by adding the postposition *-tSyā hyā badzū* 'side' followed by the dative postposition *-lā* to the noun as in (1047). Motion to is expressed in exactly the same manner as in (1047) except that in the case of 'motion to', the motion-verb is used as in (1048). Consider these examples:

-tSyā hyā bādzū-lā 'to this side of ':

(1047)	dõŋgrātSyā	hyā	bādzū-lā	ek	sũndar
	mountain-poss	this	side-to	one	beautiful

nadī āhe
river is

'There is a beautiful river by this side of the mountain.'

-tSyā hyā bādzū-lā 'to this side of ':

(1048)	dukānātSyā	hyā	bādzū-lā	dzā
	shop-poss	this	side-to	go-imp-2s

'Go to the side of the shop.'

Motion from is expressed by adding the instrumental postposition to the noun *bādzū* 'side' as in (1049).

-tSyā bādzū-ne 'from this side of':

(1049)	bail	gādī	nadītSyā	hyā	badzū-ne
	bullock	cart-3sf	river-poss	this	side-inst

gelī
go-pst-3sf

'The bullock cart passed by this side of the river.'

Motion past is expressed by adding the dative postposition *-lā* to the noun *bādzū̩* 'side'.

-tSyā bādzūla 'on this side of':

(1050)	to	dukānātSyā	hyā	bādzūlā	ālā
	he	shop-poss	this	side-to	come-pst-3sm

'He came to this side of the shop.'

There is no formal distinction made between citerior and citerior-contact locations.

2.1.1.5.15-16 *Ulterior and ulterior-contact location*

Ulterior location is expressed by replacing the proximate demonstratives *hyābādzūlā/alikaḍe* 'this side' by the remote demonstratives *tyā bādzūlā/palikaḍe* 'that side', respectively. It follows the pattern of citerior location.

2.1.1.5.17-18 *Medial location*

Medial location is expressed by (a) the postposition *(-tSyā) madhe* (variant *-madhye* 'middle'), or (b) the locative suffix *-t* 'in'. Both (a) and (b) are used interchangeably to express the notions 'between' and 'among'.

(1051)	to	āmhā	doghā̃n	(*tSyā*)	madhe/madye/-t
	he	we-obl	two	(poss)	middle/between

	yeūn	baslā
	come-conj.part	sit-pst-3sm

'After coming, he sat between the two of us.'

(1052)	tī	ekṭīts	puruṣā-t	dzāūn	baslī
	she	alone-emph	men-loc	go-conj.part	sit-pst-3sf

'She alone, having gone (there) sat among the men.'

2.1.1.5.19 *Circumferential location*

Circumferential location is expressed by the postposition *(-tSyā) bhowatī* 'around'.

(1053)	śāḷe (tSyā)	bhowatī	maidān	āhe
	school (poss)	around	ground	is

'There is ground/open field around the school.'

2.1.1.5.20 *Citerior-anterior location*

Citerior-anterior location is expressed by (a) the postposition (*-tSyā*) *samor* 'in front of', (b) *(-tSyā) samortSyā bādzūlā* 'to the front (opposite) side of' and (c) *(-tSyā) puḍhyāt* 'in front of /opposite side of' (see also 2.1.1.5.5).

(1054)	tyātSyā	gharā	(tSyā)	samor/samortSyā
	he-poss	house	(poss)	in front/front-poss

bādzūlā/puḍhyāt	ek	pārk	āhe
side-dat/opposite	one	park	is

'There is a park opposite his house.'

2.1.1.5.21-29 *Motion past long objects*

There are no special forms to express motion past a long object in the direction of its length. The postposition (*tSya*) *tūn* 'through' or (*-tSyā*) *madhūn* 'through' are used to express motion through as in (1055) below.

(1055)	hyā	tarāntūn	saglyā	gāwālā
	this-obl	wires-through	the whole	village-dat

wīdz	purawilī	dzāte
electricity-3sf	supply-pst-3sf	go-pres-3sf

'Electricity is supplied to the whole village through these wires.'

(1056)	lagnātSī	warāt	gāwā(tSyā)	madhūn
	wedding-poss	procession-3sf	village (poss)	through
	gelī	āṇi	sṭeśanwar	potslī
	go-pst-3sf	and	station-on	reach-pst-3sf

'The wedding procession went through the village and reached the station.'

2.1.1.5.30 *Other directional locations*

Other directional markers of location are: *(-tSyā) pūrwelā* 'to the east of; *(-tSyā) paśtSīme lā* 'to the west of', *(-tSyā) uttarelā* 'to the north of', and *(-tSyā) dakṣiṇelā* 'to the south of', (1057). Location to the right or to the left is expressed by adding the postpositions *-tSyā udzwīkaḍe* 'to the right (direction) of', or *-tSyā ḍāwī kaḍe* 'to the left (direction) of' as in (1058).

(1057)	...gharātSyā	pūrwelā/paśtSimelā/uttarelā/dakṣiṇelā
	house-poss	east-dat/west-dat/north-dat/south-dat

'...to the east/west/north/south...'

(1058)	...mandirātSyā	udzwīkaḍe/ḍāwīkaḍe
	temple-poss	right-direction/left-direction

'...to the right (direction) / left (direction) of the temple'

It should be noted here that the postposition *-tSyā kaḍe* expresses direction and therefore can be used with nouns of direction (i.e., east, west, north and south) to express the direction of a location vis-a-vis a particular point.

2.1.1.5.31 *Locational precision*

Locational/directional precision is expressed in one of the following three ways: (a) by the emphatic particle following the locational expression/postposition, (b) by repeating the locational marker, (c) by repeated locational markers with intervening possessive postposition *-tSyā* as in (1059) - (1060) respectively.

(1059) ...dukānātSyā ātats ...
shop-poss inside-emph

'...right inside the shop...'

(1060) ...kholītSyā madhomadh/ ātlyāāt ...
room-poss middle-intens-middle/inside-intens

'...right in the middle/inside the room...'

In (1060), the form of locational marker *madhomadh* 'right in the middle' is 'frozen' (derived from *madhe + madhe*). This derivation is not applicable to other locational markers, i.e., **ātoāt* (*āt + āt*) 'right inside'. The other derivation in (1060), (*ātlyā āt* 'right inside') is a productive one and is applicable to all location markers / nouns of location) with the locative suffix *-t*. The adjectivalizing suffix *-lā* is added to the locative suffix and the derived form is in the oblique form. The repeated locational marker/noun is also followed by the locative suffix *-t*. The following examples illustrate this derivation.

(1061) ...kholī-t-lyā kholī-t...
room-loc-adj-obl room-loc

'... right inside the room...'

(1062) ...dakṣiṇe-t-lyā dakṣiṇe-t...
south-loc-adj-obl south-loc

'...right in the south ...'

The following examples illustrate another process, which is commonly used in the context of all locational markers.

(1063) ...bāher-tSyā bāher...
outside-poss outside

'...right (from the) outside...'

(1064) ...māg-tSyā māge...
behind-poss behind

'...right behind...'

(1065) ...kholī-tSyā kholī-t...
room-poss room-loc

'...right inside the room...'

2.1.1.6 *Location in time*

2.1.1.6.1 *General time expression*

Time is expressed by using one of the following strategies: (a) noun in the nominative case (without any marking), e.g., *kāl* 'yesterday', *udyā* 'tomorrow', etc., (b) dative marker *-lā* or the locative *-ī* added to the noun.

somwār 'Monday':
(1066) somwār-lā 'on Monday'
somwār-ī 'on Monday'

In addition to the above, there are a number of general time expressions such as:

(a) *-tSyā ādhī/pūrwī* 'before'
(b) *-tSyā nāntar* 'after'
(c) *ādz* 'today'
(d) *ādzkāl* 'now-a-days'
(e) *sadhyā* 'at present'
(f) *aśāt / alikaḍe* 'recently'
(g) *-tSyā ādhitsā* 'the (time) before'
(h) *-tSyā nāntartsā* 'the (time) after'
(i) *śewaṭtsā* 'the last (time)'
(j) *-tSyā weḷī* 'at the time'

2.1.1.6.1.1 *Time of day*

Punctual/exact time of day is expressed by a phrase with the following structure. The first element is the noun indicating morning, afternoon, evening or night. The second element is the numeral followed by a fixed expression *wadztā* 'at' which is an adverbial participle of the verb *wādz* 'toll'. Consider the following example.

(1067) ...dūpārī tSār wādztā...
afternoon-loc four o'clock

'... at four o'clock in the afternoon...'

Parts of an hour are expressed by inserting the fractional expression before the numeral indicating the hour as in (1068).

(1068)	...sawwā/sāḍe/pāwṇe	tīn	wādztā...
	quarter after/half past/quarter to	three	o'clock

'...quarter after/half past/quarter to three...'

The time expressions *dīḍ* 'one-and-a half' and *aḍīts* 'two-and-a-half' do not allow the use of the numerals one and two with them respectively.

(1069)	*ek	dīḍ
	one	one-and-a-half

(1069b)	*don	aḍīts
	two	two-and-a-half

Expressions indicating minutes after the hour have the following structure: the first element is a numeral for the hour; the second element is the conjunctive participle of the verb *wādz* 'toll'; the third element is the numeral of minutes, and the fourth element is the noun *miniṭa* 'minutes'. Consider (1070) below.

(1070)	sahā	wādzūn	wīs	miniṭa/e
	six	toll-conj.part	twenty	minutes

'... twenty minutes past six...'

The expression of minutes before the hour consists of the following elements: the first element is a numeral for the hour; the second element is the infinitive of the verb *wadz* 'toll', followed by the dative marker *-lā* 'to', the third element is the numeral of minutes and the fourth element is the word for minute *miniṭa* 'minutes' as in (1071).

(1071)	...tīn	wādzāylā	pāts	miniṭa
	three	toll-inf-dat	five	minutes

'...five minutes to three ...'

The following examples (1072) and (1072a) illustrate the use of the fractional phrases in (1075) and (1076) respectively.

(1072)	ātā	āṭh	wādzūn	dahā	miniṭa
	now	eight	toll-conj.part	ten	minutes-3pl.n

	dzhālī	āhet
	happen-pst-3pl.n	are

'It is now ten minutes past eight.'

(1072a)	ātā	tīn	wādzāylā	bāwīs	miniṭa
	now	three	toll-inf-dat	twenty-two	minutes

āhet
are

'It is twenty two minutes to three.'

The most common question for asking time is as follows.

(1073)	kitī	wādzle	(āhet)?
	how many	toll-pst-3pl.n	(are)

'What time is it? (lit: 'How many (times) did the bell toll?)'

2.1.1.6.1.2 *Period of day*

The following expressions are used to indicate the period of day: *sakāḷ* 'morning', *dupār* 'afternoon', *sandhyākāḷ* 'evening', *rātra* 'night.' The locative suffix *-ī* is added to the above time expressions to convey the meaning 'in' or 'at' (e.g., 'in the morning', 'in the afternoon', 'at night,' etc.), i.e., *sakāḷ-ī* 'in the morning', *dupār-ī* 'in the afternoon', *sandhyākāḷ-ī* 'in the evening', *rātr-ī* 'at night'. Alternatively, nouns of time expressions are followed by the possessive suffix *-tse* or *-tSyā* which is followed by the noun of time and the locative suffix *-weḷ + ī* (locative) i.e., *sakāḷ-tse-weḷī/sakāḷ-tSyā weḷī* 'in the morning' (lit: 'in the time of morning'), *dupār-tse-weḷ-ī/dupārtSyā-weḷ-ī* 'in the afternoon' (lit: 'in the time of afternoon'), *sandhyākāḷ-tse-weḷ-ī/sandhyākāḷ-tSyā-weḷ-ī* 'in the evening' (lit: 'in the time of evening'), and *rātrī-tse-weḷ-ī/ratrī-tSyā-weḷ-ī* 'at night' (lit: 'at the time of night').

2.1.1.6.1.3 *Day of the week*

The day of the week is indicated by a compound word which consists of the name of the day of the week and the fixed morpheme *-wār* 'day', i.e., *som-wār* 'Monday', *māŋgaḷ-wār* 'Tuesday', etc. The names of the other days of the week are *budh-wār* 'Wednesday', *guru-wār* 'Thursday', *śukra-wār* 'Friday', *śani-wār* 'Saturday', and *rawi-wār* 'Sunday'. In order to express location in time, the locative suffix *-ī* is added to the noun of the day of the week, i.e., *somwār-ī* 'on Monday. Alternatively, the noun of the day of week is followed by the possessive suffix *-tse* or *-tSyā* which is followed by the noun of the day and the locative suffix *-diwaś-ī.* Those derivations are illustrated below:

(1074) (a) somwār-ī/somwār-tse/tSyā diwaś-ī 'on Monday'

(b) māŋgaḷwār-ī/māŋgaḷwār-tse/tSyā diwś-ī 'on Tuesday'

(c) budhwār-ī/budhwār-tse/tSyā diwś-ī 'on Wednesday'

(d) guruwār-ī/guruwār-tse/tSyā diwś-ī 'on Thursdsay'

(e) śukrawār-ī/śukrawār-tse/tSyā diwś-ī 'on Friday'

(f) śaniwār-ī/śaniwār-tse/tSyā diwś-ī 'on Saturday'

(g) rawiwār-ī/rawiwār-tse/tSyā diwś-ī 'on Sunday'

2.1.1.6.1.4 *Month of the year*

Months of the year are expressed either by the English loan-words or by the Sanskrit words for the months. The locative markers *-t/madhe* 'in' are added to the names of the months as shown below:

English loans:	Sanskrit:
(a) janewārī-t/madhe 'in (the month of) January'	(a) tSaitrā-t/cairā-madhe 'in (the month of) tSaitra'
(b) Februwārī-t/madhe 'in (the month of) February'	(b)Waiśākhā-t/waiśākhā-madhe 'in (the month of) Waiśākh'

Alternatively, the name of the month (English-loan or Sanskrit) is followed by the noun *mahinā* 'month' which takes the locative suffix *-t/-madhe* 'in'. The possessive suffix is optionally added to the name of the month.

(1075)	jānewāri (tSyā)	mahinyā-t/mahinyā-madhe
	January-loc (poss)	month-loc/month-in

'In the month of January'

2.1.1.6.1.5 *Year*

The year is expressed by the locative marker *madhe*, i.e.,

(1076) ...ekoṇīs-śe-nawwad-madhe....
ṇineteen-hundred-ninety-in

'...in the year 1990...'

2.1.1.6.1.6 *Festivals*

There are two ways of referring to festivals: (a) one referring to the festival period (in this case, the name of the festival is followed by the dative suffix *-lā*) and (b) the other referring to the specific day of the festival (in this case, the name of the festival is in the possessive case followed by the word *diwas* with the locative suffix *-ī* (i.e., *diwśī*). Consider the following examples.

(1077)	aruṇ	diwāḷī-lā	gharī	yeīl
	Arun	Diwali-dat	home-loc	come-fut-3s

'Arun will come for Diwali.'

(1078)	diwāḷī-tSyā	diwśī	asa	raḍū	naye
	Diwali-poss	day-loc	like this	cry	should not

'(One) should not cry on the Diwali-day.'

2.1.1.6.1.7 *Seasons*

Location in a season is expressed in one of two ways: (i) the name of the season followed by the locative marker *-t* (1079) or (ii) the name of the season followed by the possessive suffix *-tSyā* which is followed by the word *diwas* 'day' with the locative suffix *-t* (1080).

(1079)	mī	pāwsāḷyāt	bhāratālā	dzāīn
	I	rainy-season-loc	India-dat	go-fut-3s

'I will go to India in the rainy season.'

(1080)	unhāḷyā-tSyā	diwsāt	āmhī	gatStSīwar
	summer-poss	season-loc	we	terrace-on
	dzhopto			
	sleep-pres-1pl			

'We sleep on the terrace in the summer season.'

2.1.1.6.2 *Frequentatives*

Frequentative expressions are marked by the word *pratyek/dar* 'every' preceding the time expression as in (1081).

(1081)	pratyek/dar	śukrawār-ī	āmhī	mandirāt	dzāto
	every	Friday-loc	we	temple-loc	go-pres-1pl

'We go to the temple every Friday.'

Additionally, time expressions relating to the days of the week, month or year express frequency when they are followed by the possessive suffix *-tSyā* followed by the same (repeated) time expression with either the locative suffix *-ī/-t* or the dative suffix *-lā* as in (1082).

(1082)	to	mahinyātSyā	mahinyālā	kirāṇā	āṇto
	he	month-poss	month-dat	groceries	bring-pres-3sm

'He brings (i.e., buys) groceries once every month.'

(1083)	to	rawiwār-tSyā	rawiwār-ī	āmtSyā	gharī
	he	Sunday-poss	Sunday-loc	our	house-loc

yeto
come-pres-3sm

'He comes to our house every Sunday.'

2.1.1.6.3 *Punctual future*

The locative suffix *-t* or the adverbial suffix *-nnī* 'after' is added to a time expression to express the meaning of punctual future as in (1084).

(1084)	mādhurī	tīn	tāsāt/tāsānnī	nāgpurlā
	Madhuri	three	hours-loc/-after	Nagpur-dat

potsel
reach-fut-3s

'Madhuri will reach Nagpur in three hours /after three hours.'

2.1.1.6.4 *Punctual past*

The postposition *(-tSyā) pūrwī/ādhī* 'before' is added to a time expression to convey the meaning of punctual past as in (1085).

(1085)	tSār	diwasān(tSyā)	pūrwī/ādhī	tī
	four	days (poss)	before	she

amrawatīlā	gelī
Amravati-dat	go-pst-3sf

'She went to Amravati four days ago.'

The punctual past may also be expressed by a phrase in which the first element is the agent followed by the dative suffix *-lā;* the second element is the gerund of the verb expressing the action past followed by the dative suffix *-lā;* the third element is the time expression and the last element is the appropriate form of the verb *hoṇe* 'to happen'.

(1086)	ãmhãlã	mumbaīlã	gelyãlã	don
	we-dat	Bombay-dat	go-ger-dat	two

warṣa	dzhãlī
years-3pl.n	happen-pst-3pl.n

'It has been two years since we went to Bombay.' (lit: 'Two years have passed (happened) for us to have gone to Bombay.')

2.1.1.6.5 *Duration*

The adverbial expression *paryãnta* 'up to' following a time expression expresses the duration of time as in (1087).

(1087)	mī	ãṭh	warṣa	paryãnta	tuʤhī	wãṭ
	I	eight	years	up to	your	way-3sf

pãhilī
see-pst-3sf

'I waited for you for eight years.'

Duration may also be expressed without the adverbial *paryãnta* if the time expression itself is explicit/specific as in (1087). However, when duration is expressed by a time expression such as '...till X comes...' the use of *paryãnta* is obligatory as in (1088).

(1088)	tū	amerikehūn	parat	yeī-paryãnta/*yeī
	you	America-from	back	come-till

mī	tuʤhī	wãṭ	pãhīn
I	your	way	see-fut-1s

'I will wait for you till you return from America.'

2.1.1.6.6-7 *Anterior duration-past and future*

The postposition *paryãnta* 'up to' or *pãwtar* 'up to' following a time expression in the possessive expresses anterior duration. The difference between past and future is conveyed by the verb tense.

(1089)

tyāne	don	wādzeparyānta/pāwtar
he-ag	two	toll-up to

kām	kele
work	do-pst-3sn

'He worked (lit: 'did the work') till 2 o'clock.'

(1090)

to	don	wādzeparyānta/pāwtar	kām	karel
he	two	toll-up to	work	do-fut-3s

'He will work (lit: 'do the work') till 2 o'clock.'

2.1.1.6.8 *Posterior duration-past*

Both past and future posterior duration are expressed by the postposition *pāsūn* 'from, since' following a time expression in oblique form which is optionally followed by the possessive suffix *-tSyā*. The verb tense indicates past duration.

(1091)

mī	kāl (tSyā)	pāsūn	ithe	kām
I	yesterday (poss)	from	here	work-3sn

surū	kela
start	do-pst-3sn

'I started working here yesterday.'

If the reference to the past is relative to a particular point in time, then *pāsūn* is preceded by the word *ādhī* 'before' as in (1092).

(1092)

tyāne	somwār tSyā	don	diwas	ādhī
he-ag	Monday-poss	two	days	before

pāsūn	patra	lihāylā	suruwāt	kelī
from	letter	write-dat	beginning-3sf	do-pst-3sf

'He began to write the letter two days before Monday.'

2.1.1.6.9 *Posterior duration-future*

The postpositions *(-tSyā̃) nā̃ntar* or the adverbial suffix *-nnī* 'after' expresses posterior future duration. The time expression in this case is in the oblique case and is optionally followed by the possessive postposition *(-tSyā̃)* as in (1093).

(1093)	to	pā̃ts	diwasā̃nnā̃ntar	/ diwasā̃nnī	kā̃m
	he	five	days-after		work

surū	karel
begin	do-fut-3sm

'He will start working after five days.'

When a specific point in time (from which action is going to start) is noted, the postposition *-pā̃sūn* is used and it follows the time expression as in (1094).

(1094)	to	somwā̃r-pā̃sūn	kā̃m	surū	karel
	he	Monday-from	work	begin	do-fut-3sm

'He will start working from Monday.

2.1.1.6.10 *Anterior-general*

Anterior-general is expressed by one of the following postpositions: (a) *(-tSyā̃) ā̃dhī* 'before', (b) *(-tSyā̃) pūrwī* 'prior to', (c) *(-tSyā̃) pahile* 'before'. The postposition follows the noun phrase of time as in (1095).

(1095)	moṭar	somwā̃r-tSyā̃	ā̃dhī/pūrwī/ā̃dhī
	car-3sf	Monday-poss	before

amrā̃watīlā̃	potslī
Amravati-dat	reach-pst-3sf

'The car reached Amravati before Monday.'

2.1.1.6.11 *Posterior-general*

Posterior-general is indicated by the use of the postposition *(-tSyā) nāntar* 'after' following the noun of time as in (1096).

(1096)	tyālā	ek	tārkhe	(tSyā)	nāntar
	he-dat	first	date	(poss)	after
	pagār	miḷel			
	salary	get-fut-3s			

'He will get the salary after the first (day of the month).

2.1.1.6.12 *Point in period-past*

Point or points in period-past are expressed by one of two devices: (a) the locative suffix *-t* 'in/within', or (b) the postposition *(-tSyā) madhe* 'in/within'. The period past is indicated by the adverb *māgtSyā* 'past' or *gelyā* 'last' (lit: 'gone') which precedes the time expression as well as by the verb tense as in the following example (1097).

(1097)	māgtSyā/gelyā		tīn	warṣāt	anū
	past/last		three	years-loc	Anu-3sf
	phakta	ekdāts	madʒhyā	gharī	ālī
	only	one-emph	my	house-loc	come-pst-3sf

'In the last three years, Anu came to my house only once.'

2.1.1.6.13 *Point in period-future*

The only distinction between point or point in period-future and point or point in period-past lies in the verb tense. The verb tense in (1098) is future.

(1098)	tīn	warṣāt	anū	bhāratālā	parat
	three	years-loc	Anu	India-dat	back
	dzāīl				
	go-fut-3s				

'Anu will go back to India within three years.'

2.1.1.7 *Double case-marking*

There is no double case-marking in Marathi. A noun in attributive relationship to another head noun carries only its own case marking/postposition and does not agree with the head noun in its case.

2.1.1.8.1 *The number-marking system in nouns*

The number-marking system distinguishes between singular and plural. The distribution of the singular and plural suffixes was already discussed in 2.1.1.1.1, which clearly shows that different classes of nouns behave differently with regard to the marking of singular and plural number.

2.1.1.8.2-3 *The extent to which the system of number-marking is obligatory*

Except for masculine kinship terms, number marking is obligatory for nouns even if it is redundant, i.e., even when the number is indicated by numerals or pronouns. The following example (1099a) illustrates this point. However masculine kinship terms do not bear plural case marking (see (1103) and (1104)).

(1099a) ...pandhrā sāḍyā...
fifteen saree-3pl.f

'...fifteen sarees...'

(1099b) *pandhrā sāḍī
fifteen saree-3sf

'...fifteen sarees...'

(1100a) ...anek dzhāḍa...
many tree-3pl.n

'... many trees ...'

(1100b)	*...anek	dzhāḍ...
	many	tree-3sn

'...many trees...'

Number marking is also obligatory in the case of oblique forms of the nouns. (For details, see section 2.1.1.1.)

	Direct:	
(1101)	dzhāḍ 'tree' (neut.sg.)	dzhāḍa 'trees' (neut.pl)
	Oblique:	
(1102)	dzhāḍā	dzhāḍā

masculine kinship terms:

(1103)	(a)	ek	māmā	'one maternal uncle'
		one	uncle-3sm	
	(b)	don	māmā	'two maternal uncles'
		two	uncle-3sm	
	(c)	*don	māme	'two maternal uncles'
		two	uncle-3pl.m	

(1104)	(a)	ek	ādzobā	'one grandfather'
		one	grandfather-3sm	
	(b)	don	ādzobā	'two grandfathers'
		two	grandfathers	
	(c)*	don	ādzobe	'two grandfathers'
		two	grandfathers	

2.1.1.8.4 *Collective and distributive plural*

There is no formal distinction between a collective and a distributive plural.

2.1.1.8.5 *Collective nouns*

Collective nouns can be grouped under three classes: (a) inherent collectives such as *kuṭumba* 'family', *dzhāḍī* 'grove', *gardī* 'crowd', *thawā* 'flock of birds', *meḷā* 'a festive gathering', (b) collective nouns derived by using the noun *lok* 'people', i.e., *pākistānī lok* 'people from Pakistan', (c) echo words: *mulgā bilgā* 'boy and others'.

Collective nouns can be both singular and plural. While *lok* 'people', is always plural, collective nouns such as *thawā* 'flock of birds', *kuṭumba* 'family, *dzhāḍī* 'grove' can be treated as singular and take plural markings as in (1105).

(1105)		singular		plural	
	(a)	thawā	'a flock'	thawe	'flocks'
	(b)	kuṭumba	'a family'	kuṭumbe	'families'

Nouns such as *gahū* 'wheat', *tā̃ndūḷ* 'rice' are treated both as plural (distributive) nouns (i.e., the verb takes plural marking when it agrees with those nouns) and as singular collective nouns (i.e., the verb takes singular marking when it agrees with those nouns).

2.1.1.8.6 *Manner of realization of the number distinction*

See section 2.1.1.8.1.

2.1.1.8.7 *Number-marking of foreign words*

Marathi has borrowed words from Sanskrit, Persian, and English. Nativized loans from these three languages are inflected for the Marathi number-system. For example, *pustak* (n) (Sanskrit) 'book' and *ṭebal* (n) (English) 'book', and *takrār*(f) 'complaint' (Persian), are inflected like the native Marathi words *dzāḍ* 'tree', *kurhāḍ* 'axe (f)', for example *ṭebla* 'tables' (similar to *dzhāḍa* 'trees'), *pustaka* 'books', and *takrārī* 'complaints' (similar to *kurhāḍī* 'axes'). Non-nativized loans are pluralized by using numerals preceding the nouns, i.e., *don dɔkṭar* 'two doctors'. Occasionally, English loan words may take the English plural suffix i.e., *ṭebals* 'tables'.

2.1.1.9 *Noun classes*

2.1.1.9.1 *Gender*

There are three genders (i.e., masculine, feminine, and neuter) in Marathi. The gender system is neither semantically nor morphologically determined. Gender is purely conventional. For example, *parwat* 'mountain' is masculine, *nadī* 'river' is feminine, and *dzhāḍ* 'tree' is neuter; *āg* 'fire' is feminine, *māsā* 'fish' is masculine, and *bhādʒī* 'vegetable' is feminine.

The distribution of noun classes according to their gender is discussed in 2.1.1.1. It should be noted here that noun forms are sensitive to gender, number, and case. See sections 2.1.1.8.1-5 for plural formation. See also sections 2.1.1.9.3-4 for further details.

2.1.1.9.2 *Meaning of noun classes*

Based on the semantic criterion, nouns can be grouped as count and mass, which can be further grouped as animate/inanimate, and concrete/abstract as shown below.

Nouns

A. <u>Count Nouns</u>

animate	inanimate	concrete	abstract
mā̃ndzār	*dagaḍ*	*ghar*	*kalpanā*
'cat'	'rock'	'house'	'imagination'

B. <u>Mass Nouns</u>

animate	inanimate	concrete	abstract
lok	*pāṇī*	*dūdh*	*prem*
'people	'water'	'milk'	'love'

2.1.1.9.3-4 *Classifiers*

A small closed set of nouns are used as classifiers with certain semantic classes of nouns when elaboration is involved. These nouns (used as classifiers) specify the semantic category to which the noun belongs. The classifier nouns include *ā̃ntar* 'distance', *wadzan* weight', *dzaṇ* 'people', *rā̃ŋga* 'color', *diwas* 'season' (lit: 'day'), and *weḷ* 'time'. The following examples illustrate the use of these classifiers.

(1106a)	tīn mailā̃ntse ā̃ntar	'the distance of three miles'
(1106b)	pā̃ts kilō̃tse wadzan	'the weight of five kilos'
(1106c)	niḷyā rā̃ŋgā̃tse ghar	'the house of black color'
(1106d)	unhāḷyā tSyā diwasā̃t	'in the summer time'

2.1.1.9.5 *Assignments of loan words to noun classes*

Most loan words are assigned a gender on the model of the gender of their native Marathi semantic counterpart. Thus a borrowed noun takes the morphological suffixes which are appropriate for the semantic class of nouns to which the Marathi noun belongs. The following examples illustrate this point vis-a-vis English borrowings in Marathi.

	Borrowed		Marathi		
	noun	gender	noun	gender	gloss
(1107a)	kār	feminine	gāḍī	feminine	'car'
(1107b)	būṭ	masculine	dzoḍā	masculine	'shoe'

If there is no native Marathi semantic counterpart of the borrowed noun, then, the borrowed noun is assigned the gender of nouns which are perceived to belong to a semantic category similar to that of the borrowed noun. For example, the English nouns *television (ṭelewidʒan), telephone, (ṭelifon), fax (fæx),* etc., which are borrowed into Marathi, have no native Marathi semantic counterparts. All of these nouns are consonsant-ending and thereby can be assigned any of the three genders (since Marathi has consonant-ending masculine (*pahāḍ* 'mountain'), feminine (*āg* 'fire'), as well as neuter (*dzāḍ* 'tree') nouns). The choice of masculine as opposed to the other genders does not seem to be determined merely by the phonetic shape of the noun. On the other hand, it seems to be plausible to assume that the choice is made on the basis of the perception of Marathi speakers that nouns referring to electronically operated gadgets should be assigned the masculine gender. Although the older borrowings such as *radio (reḍiyo/reḍio* in Marathi) and perhaps the most recent one *computer* (*kampyuṭar* in Marathi) support the above hypothesis in that they are both assigned the masculine gender, the conditions which determine the choice are far from clear. A systematic study of borrowings is necessary to provide a conclusive statement.

2.1.1.10 - 2.1.1.10.6 *Definiteness marking in noun phrases*

There is no separate marker for indicating definiteness in noun phrases. However, there are various strategies which are used by speakers to express definiteness. For example, absence of any marking on the noun indicates a definite noun phrase about which both the speaker and the hearer have prior knowledge.

Definiteness can also be expressed by the use of a demonstrative morpheme preceding the noun (phrase) as in (1108) and (1109).

(1108)	te	dzhāḍ	sũndar	āhe
	that-3sn	tree-3sn	beautiful	is

'That tree is beautiful.'

(1109)	hī	pustaka	wāts
	this-3pl.n	books-3pl.n	read-imp-2s

'Read these books.'

The demonstrative morphemes *he* 'this' and *te* 'that' are homophonous with the demonstrative pronouns. However, the demonstrative morphemes in (1108) and (1109) should be treated as demonstrative adjectives as opposed to pronouns because (a) unlike the demonstrative pronouns, which may precede or follow the noun, they always precede and never follow the noun and (b) they can never be used as substitutes for nouns. The demonstrative adjective *he* 'this' expresses proximity/closeness of the noun phrase to the speaker in space, time, or mind (i.e., psychological proximity of the noun to the speaker), while the demonstrative adjective *te* 'that' expresses remoteness of the noun phrase from the speaker. Similar to other adjectives, the demonstrative adjective agrees with the following noun in gender and number as in (1108) and (1109).

Demonstrative adjectives are used also with proper nouns as well as to indicate distance as in (1110) and (1111).

(1110)	he	amrāwatī	śahar	orisātlyā
	the	Amravati	town	Orissa-in-adj

amrāwatī	pekṣā	khūp	lahān	āhe
Amravati	compared to	very	small	is

'This town of Amravati is much smaller than the Amravati in the state of Orissa.'

(1111)	te	audārya	ʤagāweg!a	hota
	that	generosity	world-different	was

'That generosity was out of this world.'

It should be noted here that there are several processes in Marathi by which adjectives are derived from verbs, nouns, adjectives, and adverbs which function as definiteness markers. Some examples of these processes are given below.

Participle:

(1112)	khālī	paḍlele	ā̃mbe
	down	fall-pst.part-3pl.m	mangoes-3pl.m

'mangoes (which are) fallen down'

Adjectives derived from nouns:

(1113a)	ghartSī	goṣṭa
	home-poss-3sf	matter-3sf

'the family matter' (lit: 'the matter of the family')

(1113b)	gharā-t-lī	māṇsa
	home-in-adj-3pl.n	people-3pl.n

'The people in the home' (i.e., relatives or people gathered in the house)

Adjectives derived from adverbs:

(1114a)	ithla	dzhāḍ
	here-adj-3sn	tree-3sn

'the tree (which is) here'

(1114b)	kāltsa	patra
	yesterday-poss-3sn	letter-3sn

'Yesterday's letter'

2.1.1.11 - 2.1.1.11.6 *Indefiniteness marking on noun phrases*

Indefiniteness is generally expressed by using the numeral *ek* 'one' preceding a singular count noun. Plural and mass and count nouns are marked for indefiniteness by the quantifiers *kāhī* 'some', *kiṃtSit* 'a little', *thoḍe* 'a little/a few'.

(1115)	gāḍīt	wātsāylā	malā	ek	pustak
	train-in	read-inf-dat	I-dat	one	book

	de
	give-imp-2s

'Give me a book to read on the train.'

(1116)	malā	thoḍa	waraṇ	hawa
	I-dat	a little-3sn	lentil soup-3sn	want-3sn

'I want a little lentil soup.'

(1117)	kāhī	pāhuṇe	udyā	yetīl
	some	guests	tomorrow	come-fut-3pl

'Some guests will come tomorrow.'

It should be noted here that indefiniteness marking (similar to definiteness marking) is not obligatory in Marathi. The lack of marking on the noun phrase can result in a vague reading of the noun phrase regarding definiteness as in (1118).

(1118)	kholīt	khurtSī	āhe
	room-in	chair-3sf	are-3s

'There is a/the chair in the room.'

In the situation of vagueness, pragmatic factors such as the speaker's/hearer's knowledge of the noun phrase, the context of the conversation, etc., disambiguate the reading of the noun phrase.

2.1.1.12 - 2.1.1.12.4 *Referential and non-referential indefiniteness*

Referential indefiniteness is expressed by the use of the numeral *ek* 'one' preceding the noun, as in (1119). Non-referential indefiniteness is indicated by a question word *koṇ* 'who' to which the indefinitizing marker *-ī* is attached as in (1120), or *kuṭhe* 'where', *koṇta* 'which', *kadhī* 'when', followed by the suffix *-tarī* to express a higher degree of indefiniteness (1121).

ek 'one':

(1119)	ek	maṇūs	tulā	bheṭāylā
	one	man	you-dat	meet-inf-dat
	ālā		hotā	
	come-pst-3sm		be-pst-3sm	

'A man had come to meet you'

koṇī/kuṇī :

(1120)	*koṇī/kuṇī*	he	kām	karīl	kā ?
	who-indef	this	job	do-fut-3s	Q

'Will anyone do this job ?'

kuṭhe-tarī :

(1121)	mī	paise	gharāt	kuṭhetarī	ṭhewle
	I	money-3pl.n	home-in	where-indef	keep-pst-3pl.n

'I kept the money somewhere in the house.'

2.1.1.13 - 2.1.1.13.2 *Genericness*

Genericness is expressed by a singular noun phrase without any marking as in (1122).

(1122)	ghoḍā	pāḷīw	dzanāwar	āhe
	horse	domestic	animal	is

'The horse is a domestic animal.'

Although the use of singular nouns is more common, plural nouns are also used to express genericness as in (1123).

(1123)	mogryātSī	phula	pāwsāḷyāt	phultāt
	jasmine-poss-3pl.n	flowers-3pl.n	rainy season-loc	bloom-pres-3pl.n

'Jasmine flowers bloom in the rainy season.'

The non-copular habitual conjugation of the verb *asṇe* 'to be' exclusively expresses genericness as in (1124a). However, the copular conjugation of the verb *asṇe* 'to be' does not express genericness (1124b).

non-copular construction:

(1124a)	śaharātlyā	mulī	dhīṭ	astāt
	city-loc-adj-3pl.f	girls	bold	be-pres-hab-3pl.

'City-girls (girls from a city) are generally bold.'

(1124b)	śaharātlyā	mulī	dhīṭ	āhet
	city-loc-adj-3pl.f	girls	bold	be-pres-3pl

'The city girls are bold.'

In (1124a) the subject *śahrātlyā mulī* 'city girls' is a generic subject where *astāt* is not a copular form. It is a habitual form. In contrast to this, in a copular construction such as (1124b), the subject *śahrātlyā mulī* is a definite (subject) noun.

2.1.1.14 - 2.1.1.14.4 *Degree of importance of actors*

There are no morphemes which distinguish more important noun actors from less important actors. However, honorific particles and titles can be used to express the importance of the actors.

2.1.2 PRONOUNS

2.1.2.1 *Personal pronouns*

The paradigm of personal pronouns is given below. Note that gender distinction is maintained only in the third person. Also note that the third person pronouns are separated by the parameter of proximity and remoteness. Plural forms of the pronouns are used to express politeness or respect. Reflexive pronouns (both emphatic and anaphoric) occur with all pronouns in all persons.

Person	Prox/Rem	Gender	Number			
			S	Pl	Incl	Excl
First	-- --	-- -- --	mī	āmhī	āpaṇ (you+I)	
Second	-- --	-- -- --	tū	tumhī/		āpaṇ
Third	Proximate	mas	hā	he		
		fem	hī	hyā		
		neut	he	hī		
	Remote	mas	to	te		
		fem	tī	tyā		
		neut	te	tī		
Reflexive	emphatic		swatāhā/ āpaṇswatāhā			
	anaphoric		āpaṇ (with the case endings)			

In the second person pronouns, *āpaṇ* (plural) is used to express a high degree of deference to the addressee (due to the addressee's age, profession, or social status). While *tumhī* and *āpaṇ* both are second person plural pronouns, only *āpaṇ* obligatorily implies deference towards the addressee (whereas *tumhī* may or may not do so). Traditionally, *āpaṇ* has been used for older in-laws, teachers, kings, government officials, priests, etc. However, in contemporary India, the use of *tumhī* is favored over *āpaṇ* in almost all contexts.

2.1.2.1.1 *Free pronouns*

Free pronouns occur in the language in all positions: subject, direct object, indirect object, object of a postposition, object of a comparative particle, etc. Pronouns are not obligatory in any of the persons if they are subjects of finite clauses, since they are traceable from the verb which bears the gender, number, and person markings of the subject. In this case, pronouns are generally dropped (1125). However, in the perfective (transitive), optative, and obligative constructions (see sections 1.1.1.3.1.1.2-4), where the subject is marked with the so-called "ergative" ending *-ne* and the verb does not agree with the subject, but rather with the object, pronouns are generally retained (1126). Consider the following examples.

(1125)	ø	gāwālā	gelī
		town-dat	go-pst-3sf

'(She) went to town.'

Pronoun retained:

(1126)	tyāne	kām	kele
	he-ag	work-3sn	do-pst-3sn

'He did the work.'

When pronouns are non-subjects or subjects of non-finite clauses and are not identical to the subjects of the main clause, they are generally retained. Note the obligatory occurrence of the pronoun in infinitival (1127) and gerundive clauses (1128).

(1127)	tudzha	ugitsats	rāgāwṇa
	you-poss-3sn	without reason	get angry-inf-3sn
	malā	āwḍat	nāhī
	I-dat	like-pres	neg

'I do not like you getting angry (lit: 'your getting angry') without any reason.'

(1128)	tyālā	ithūn	gelyālā	khūp
	he-dat	here-from	go-ger-dat	many
	diwas	dzāle		
	days-3pl.m	happen-pst-3pl.m		

'Many days have passed since he left from here.'

The free pronoun subject does not occur with infinitival and participial clauses (see sections 2.1.3.5.1 and 2.1.3.5.2.1-3) since it is recoverable from the subject of the main clause.

2.1.2.1.1.1 - 2.1.2.1.1.5 *Obligatory/optional status of pronouns*

Old, as well as modern, grammars (Damle 1966 [1911], Apte 1962) do not discuss the obligatory vs. optional status of pronouns. In addition to the contexts discussed in the preceding section, pronouns are optional in other grammatical positions when discourse conditions allow their deletion in the sentence. Generally, their deletion is favored when they are recoverable through the context of the discourse. The discourse structure of the language has not yet been adequately researched, and, therefore, discourse conditions on the deletion of pronouns is one of the topics which remains to be explored in further detail. However, it is beyond doubt that Marathi, similar to other modern Indo-Aryan (Bhatia 1993, Kachru 1980) and Dravidian languages (Sridhar 1990), favors deletion as an anaphoric strategy rather than pronominalization. In particular, if the subject of the discourse remains the same in a set of consecutive sentences, then it is deleted in all but the first sentence. Free pronouns in other positions such as direct and indirect objects and objects of a postposition are also deleted under similar conditions. In the following narrative, the sites where free pronouns are omitted are indicated by ø in the Marathi text. The omitted pronouns are given in parentheses in the English translation.

(1129) ā̃ṭh warṣā̃nnī mohan amerikehū̃n
eight years-after Mohan America-from

parat ālā. ø barobar bā̃yko āṇī
return come-pst-3sm with wife and

mula paṇ hotī. ø gharī yeū̃n
children also were home-loc having come

ø nātewāīkā̃nnā bheṭlā. ø don
relatives-acc meet-pst-3sm two

diwsā̃nnī bā̃dzārā̃t ā̃tSā̃nak ek dzunā
days-after market-loc unexpectedly one old

mitra ø bheṭlā. ø tyālā gharī
friend meet-pst-3sm he-acc home-acc

gheūn	ālā.	ø	khūp	gappā
having brought	come-pst-3sm		a lot	chatting-3pl.f

kelyā;	ø	bākītSyā	mitrāntSī
do-pst-3pl.f		other	friends-poss-3sf

tsaukaśī	kelī	ø	sandhyākāḷparyānta	ø
inquiry-3sf	do-pst-3sf		evening-till	

thāmbawūn	ghetla	āṇi	ø	punhā	bheṭṇyātsa
make stay-conj.part	take-pst-3sn	and		again	meet-inf-poss-3sn

āśwāsan	gheūn	ø	gharī	potsawla
promise	take-conj.part		home-loc	reach-caus-pst-3sn

'After eight years, Mohan returned from America. (His) wife and children were with (him). After coming home, (he) met (his) relatives. After two days (he) unexpectedly met (his) old friend in the market. (He) brought him home. (He) chatted a lot (with him). (He) inquired about other friends. (He) made (him) stay till the evening. And having made (him) to promise to meet again the next day, (he) dropped (him) home.'

Note that the subject of the sentences in this narrative is Mohan. Therefore, the reference to Mohan in all the sentences (except the first one) is indicated by the empty pronominal anaphor. In the third sentence the *friend* of Mohan is introduced. In the fourth sentence the reference to the friend is conveyed by the pronoun *tyālā* 'him'. In all of the succeeding sentences, the reference to the friend (as well as to the subject *Mohan*) is conveyed by the empty pronominal anaphor.

Generally, free pronouns occur in contrastive and emphatic contexts only. In particular, in imperatives, cleft sentences, or in answer to a question, free pronouns are used.

In imperatives, the second person pronoun is generally omitted. However, example (1130) shows that when a contrast is to be conveyed, the second person pronoun is retained in an imperative sentence.

(1130)	tū	ithe	bas	āṇī	anū	tithe	basel
	you	here	sit-imp-2s	and	Anu	there	sit-fut-3s

'You sit here, and Anu will sit there.'

Pronouns are used as answers to questions as in (1131) below.

(1131a)	bāher	koṇ	āhe ?
	outside	who	is

'Who is outside ?'

(1131b)	mī
	I

'It is I.'

Clefting the pronoun to the postverbal position for emphasis:

(1132)	āītsā	apmān	kelā	tyāne
	mother-poss-3sm	insult-3sm	do-pst-3sm	he-ag

'It was he who insulted mother.'

Clefting the pronoun to the sentence-initial position for emphasis followed by the question word *kā* :

(1133)	tyālā	kā	kāl	polisne	pakaḍla ?
	he-acc	Q	yesterday	police-ag	catch-pst-3sn

'Was it he whom the police caught ?'

There are no reduced pronouns in the language. The contrast between emphatic and unemphatic contexts is indicated by the use of higher stress or the emphatic particle with the pronoun. However, there is no syntactic or phonological difference between the use of pronouns in emphatic and non-emphatic contexts.

2.1.2.1.2 - 2.1.2.1.3.7 *Person distinctions in pronouns*

The pronominal system distinguishes pronouns according to first, second, or third person. Except for the first person plural pronoun *āpaṇ* 'we' (you+I), the pronominal system does not have any distinction between inclusive versus exclusive pronouns. *Āpaṇ* 'we' in the first person, is inclusive of the speaker and the hearer, and thereby is in contrast with *āmhī* 'we' which is exclusive of the hearer as shown in (1134a) and (1134b). When used in the second person, *āpaṇ* is exclusive of the speaker and only refers to the hearer.

(1134a)	āmhī	udyā	mumbaīlā	dzāū
	we-excl	tomorrow	Bombay-dat	go-fut-1pl

'We (exclusive of the hearer) will go to Bombay tomorrow.'

(1134b)	āpaṇ	udyā	mumbaīlā	dzāū
	we (incl)	tomorrow	Bombay-dat	go-fut-1pl

'We (you and I) will go to Bombay tomorrow.'

2.1.2.1.4 - 2.1.2.1.5.2 *Number marking in pronouns*

Similar to nouns, pronouns are obligatorily marked for singular or plural number (see the paradigm in sections 2.1.2.1 and 2.1.2.1.1). Additionally, pronouns may be associated with numerals which immediately follow them as in (1135) and (1136).

(1135)	te	tSār	dzaṇ	dzhāḍāwar	tsaḍhle
	they-3pl.m	four	people-3pl.m	tree-on	climb-pst-3pl.m

'Those four people climbed up the tree.'

(1136)	tyā	tighīnnī	gāṇī	mhaṭlī
	those	three person-3pl.f	song-3pl.n	sing-pst-3pl.n

'Those three persons (women) sang songs.'

Collective plurals are not distinguished from distributive plurals. There is no marking of the relative status of the referents of third person pronouns.

2.1.2.1.6 - 2.1.2.1.6.1 *Proximity marking in pronouns*

The third person pronouns are obligatorily distinguished from each other on the basis of proximity/remoteness of the referent of the pronoun to the speaker (in space, time, and the psychological context). The proximate pronouns begin with *h-* while the remote pronouns begin with *t-*. The remote forms are used in the unmarked cases.

2.1.2.1.7 *Special anaphoric pronouns*

There are no special anaphoric third person pronouns. The deictic forms are used for this purpose (see section 1.5.1.3 for examples).

2.1.2.1.8 *Gender distinctions in pronouns*

Three genders (masculine, feminine, and neuter) are distinguished only in the third person pronouns in both singular and plural, that is , the first and the second person pronouns are not distinguished for genders (see section 2.1.2.1 and sub-sections thereof). The gender of the first and the second person pronouns can be inferred from the gender agreement markers on the finite verb forms.

2.1.2.1.9 - 2.1.2.1.9.1 *Other relationships*

There are no special pronominal forms to indicate tribal, sectional, family relationships of referents.

2.1.2.1.10 *Lists of pronominal forms*

See 2.1.2.1 above.

2.1.2.1.11 *Tense marking in pronouns*

There is no tense marking on pronouns.

2.1.2.1.12 *Status distinctions in pronouns*

With the exception of the second person plural form *āpaṇ* 'you (honorific)' no other pronoun is specifically marked for status. Plural forms are generally used to indicate the higher status of the referent and deference to her/him.

Persons of higher status are generally addressed with plural forms of the second person *tumhī/āpaṇ*. Between *tumhī* and *āpaṇ*, the latter is viewed as "extra polite" or extremely deferential and is reserved for a small set of referents such as priests, teachers, in-laws, or speakers at a formal occasion. People of higher status are referred to with plural forms of the third person pronouns. Plural forms are also used for strangers, while singular forms are generally used for familar and/or intimate persons. Singular forms are used for persons of lower status. When the status hierarchy is not clear, plural forms are generally used.

The choice of pronouns in Marathi is determined by the "power" relationship between the speaker and the addressee or referent. Chronological age is one of the determinants of "power". Older people are generally addressed or referred to with plural forms, while younger people are addressed or referred to with singular forms.

Until recently, caste was considered to be the determiner of the choice of the form of pronouns. Plural forms have been used for the "upper" castes. This tradition continues to hold in smaller cities or villages in present day Maharashtra. However, for both address and reference, the "caste" is being rapidly replaced by the class or "profession" of the referent. Doctors, lawyers, merchants, business executives, college/university and school teachers require the use of the plural forms of pronouns. In contrast to this, sweepers, cleaners, rikshaw/(cart)-pullers, barbers, cooks, maids and other servants and laborers are addressed or referred to with the singular form of pronouns.

It is important to note here that intimacy overrides power in the context of kinship: grandmother, grandfather, mother, aunts, older siblings, uncles, are addressed/referred to with the singular forms of pronouns in many families. There exists a great deal of variation in this context. In a large number of families, female relatives (older in age) are addressed/referred to with singular pronouns, while male relatives (older in age) are addressed/ referred to with the plural forms of pronouns. God is generally addressed/referred to (in prayers, benedictions, etc.) with singular forms of pronouns.

There exist asymmetries in Maharashtrian society (which are commonly shared by Indian society at large) which are observed in the above discussion on variations in the use of the forms of pronouns. Additionally, a husband generally uses a singular pronoun for addressing/referring to his wife. However, a wife generally addresses/refers to her husband with the plural form of the pronoun. However, there exists tremendous variation in the "norm" or "standard" for the usage of plural vs. singular forms of pronouns in diverse groups in the Marathi-speaking community. In middle class urban society (such as that in Bombay, Puṇe, Nagpur, Sholapur, etc.) at present, in the younger generation (between the ages 20-25), both husband and wife address/refer to each other with the singular form of the pronoun.

Persons of high spiritual character such as priests, religious leaders, saints, mystics, etc. are addressed/referred to with the plural forms of pronouns.

2.1.2.1.13-14 *Special non-specific indefinite pronouns*

There are no special non-specific indefinite pronouns like "one" in English. This function is carried out by using one of the following strategies: (a) by using the second person pronoun *tū* 'you' (sg) as in (1137), (b) by the third person plural pronoun *lok* 'people' which is generally omitted, as in (1138), (c) by using generic nouns such as *māṇūs* 'human being', *wyakti* 'person or individual' (as in (1139)), and (d) by using the indefinite pronoun *koṇī* 'who', *koṇītarī* 'whoever', in a rhetorical or negative sentence (as in (1140a) and (1140b)).

(1137)

tulā	koṇī	śeṇ	khā	asa
you-dat	someone	cowdung	eat-imp-2s	thus

mhaṭla	tar	tū	khāśīl	kā ?
say-pst-3sn	then	you	eat-fut-2s	Q

'If someone tells you (someone) to eat cowdung, will you (someone) eat it ?

(1138)

asa	mhaṇtāt	kī...
thus	say-3pl	that

'(They) say that ... ' (It is said that ...)

(1139)

māṇsālā	satat	mānasik	tāp
human being-dat	continuous	mental	strain-3sm
nako	asto		
not-want	be-pres-3sm		

'A human being does not want continuous mental stress.'

(1140a)

koṇī/koṇītarī	asa	bolel	kā?
who/whoever	thus	speak-fut-3s	Q

'Who will talk like this ? '(lit: 'Will anyone talk like this ?')

(1140b)

koṇī	āplyā	āīlā	asa
someone	refl	mother-acc	like this/thus
phaswat	nāhī		
deceive	neg		

'No one deceives one's mother like this.'

2.1.2.1.15 - 2.1.2.1.15.3 *Special emphatic pronouns*

There are no special emphatic pronouns. Pronouns are made emphatic by adding the emphatic particle *-ts* to them, i.e., *tots* 'he' (as opposed to anyone else), *tyāts* 'they (fem)' (as opposed to anyone else), etc. There is an emphatic reflexive pronoun *swatāhā* 'self'.

2.1.2.1.16 *Complex pronouns*

There are no special complex pronouns in the language. As noted in sections 1.6.1 and 2.1.2.2 - 2.1.2.2.7, a combination of two reflexive pronouns, *āpaṇ swatāhā*, is used to express a particular kind of anaphoric relationship.

2.1.2.1.17 *Pronoun-noun constructions*

The pronoun-noun construction, where a noun is in opposition to a pronoun (i.e., where both the noun and the pronoun have the same referent), is fairly common in Marathi. Pronouns of all person participate in this construction as seen in the following examples (1141 - 1143).

(1141)

āmhī	bāyakā	nehmīts	āplyā
we	women	always-emph	refl

kutumbā̃n	sāṭhī	khapto
families	for	work hard-1pl

'We women always work hard for the sake of our families.'

(1142)

tumhī	rāʤpūt	deśāsāṭhī	prāṇ
you-pl	Rajput	country-for	life

dyāylā	sadaiwa	tayār	astā
give-inf-dat	always	ready	are-2pl

'You Rajputs are always ready to sacrifice (your) life for the country.'

(1143)

he	bhāratīya	(lok)	masālyā̃n
these	Indians	(people)	spices

śiwāy	swaypāk	karat	nāhīt
without	cooking	do	neg-3pl

'These Indians (people) do not cook without spices.'

2.1.2.1.18 *Pairs of pronouns*

Construction of the type "we (and) the priests" with the meaning "I and the priest" do not occur in the language.

2.1.2.1.19 *Secondary pronoun system*

There is no secondary pronoun system.

2.1.2.1.20 - 2.1.2.1.20.1.5 *Case system in pronouns*

Pronouns take the same case-suffixes as nouns. The occasional variation in the case forms of pronouns is due to historical and/or morphophonemic factors. The following paradigms are representative of pronouns in the three persons.

(1144a)

1st person:

cases	singular forms	plural forms
nom	mī	āmhī/āpaṇ
acc	ma-lā	āmhā-lā/āpyā-lā
inst	māʤhyāne	āmtSyā-ne/āplyā-ne
dat	ma-lā/māʤhyā-śī	āmhā-lā/āmtSyā-śī/āplyāśī
abl	māʤhyā-hūn	āmtSyā-hūn/ālyā-hūn
poss	mādzha (and its variants)	āmtsa (and its variants) āpla (and its variants
loc	māʤhyā-t	āmtSyā-t/āplyāt

(Case forms of the inclusive first person plural pronoun *āpaṇ* 'we (you + I)' are the same as those of *āpaṇ* (2nd person plural pronoun in 1144b.)

(1144b)

2nd person:

cases	singular forms	plural forms
nom	tū	tumhī/āpaṇ
acc	tu-lā	tumhālā/{āpaṇā-lā āplyā-lā}
inst	tuʤhyā-ne	tumtSyā-ne/āplyā-ne
dat	tu-lā	tumhālā/{āpṇālā āplyālā}
abl	tuʤhyā-hūn	tumtSyā-hūn/{āpṇā-hūn āplyā-hūn}
poss	tudza (and its variants)	tumtsa/āpla (and their variants)
loc	tuʤhyā-t	tumtSyā-t/{āpṇā-t āplyā-t}

(1144c)

3rd person (proximate):

cases	singular forms			plural forms		
	mas	fem	neut	mas	fem	neut
nom	hā	hī	he	he	hyā	hī
acc	hyā-lā	hi-lā	hyā-lā	hyā̃nnā		
inst	hyā-ne hyātSyā-ne	hitSyā-ne	hyātSyā-ne	{hyā̃nnī / hyā̃ntSyā-ne}		
dat	hyā-la hyātSyāśī	hi-lā hitSyā-śī	hyā-lā hyātSyāśī	{hyā̃nnā / hyā̃ntSyā-śī}		
abl	hyātSyā-hūn	hitSyā-hūn	hyātSyā-hūn	{hyā̃ntSyā-hūn}		
poss	hyātsa	hitsa (and their variants)	hyātsa (and its variants)	{hyā̃ntSa}		
loc	hyā-t/ hyātSyā-t	hitSyā-t	{hyāt / -hyātSyāt}	{hyāt / hyā̃ntSyā-t}		

Third person remote pronouns are derived by substituting *t-* for word-initial *h-* in the above forms in (1144c).

Some points need to be noted regarding the pronominal case system: (a) The case-forms of the first person plural (inclusive) pronoun *āpaṇ* 'I + you', are the same as those of the homophonous second person plural exclusive pronoun *āpaṇ* 'you (honorific)'. However, the second person pronoun has alternative forms as well. (b) The nominative case-forms of 3rd person singular/plural pronouns are distinguished from one another by gender. However, the distinction is neutralized among the rest of the masculine singular and neuter singular case forms. Only masculine-neuter and feminine case forms are distinguished. (c) The gender distinction in plural case forms is neutralized in the third person. (d) Gender distinction is not maintained in first and second person case forms. (e) The possessive pronouns agree in gender and number with the noun of possession.

Variants of possessive forms are marked by change in the final vowel of the possessive case-form, i.e., *mādzha* 'my (sn)', *mādzhā* 'my (sm)', *madʒhī* 'my (sf)', *madʒhī* 'my (pl.n)', *mādzhe* 'my (pl.m)', *mādʒhyā* 'my (pl.f)'. (f) All pronouns, similar to nouns, take postpositions to express various semantic relations such as 'with', 'on', 'like', etc. (e.g., *mādʒhyā-barobar* 'with me', *tudʒhyā-war* 'on you', *tyātSyā-sārkhā* 'like him', etc.). The ergative postposition is added only to the third person pronouns and the resulting forms are given below:

singular forms			plural forms		
mas	fem	neut	mas	fem	neut
to	tī	te	te	tyā	te
tyāne	tine	tyā̃nnī	tyā̃nnī	tyā̃nnī	tyā̃nnī

2.1.2.2 - 2.1.2.2.7 *Reflexive pronouns*

Reflexive pronouns are discussed in sections 1.6 - 1.6.9.3. There are two types of reflexives: emphatic (*swatāhā*) and possessive (*āpaṇ*). Neither of the reflexive pronouns occur without an antecedent. Both take the full range of case-forms as shown below:

(1145a) ***Swatāhā:***

Cases	Singular and Plural
nom	swatāhā
acc	swatāhā-lā
inst	swatāhā-ne
dat	swatāhā-lā
abl	swatāhā-hūn
poss	swatāhā-tsa (and its variants)
loc	swatāhā-t

(1145b) ***āpaṇ:***

Cases	Singular and Plural
nom	āpaṇ
acc	āplyā-lā
inst	āplyā-ne
dat	āplyā-lā
abl	āplyā-hūn

poss	āpla (and its variants)
loc	āplyā-t

It is evident from (1145a) and (1145b) that the singular and plural case forms of the reflexive pronouns are identical. The complex reflexive pronoun *āpaṇ swatāhā* has the same case-ending as *swatāhā*. Its function is discussed in detail in section 1.6. Subcategories such as inclusion, obviation, proximity, gender, kinship or tribal affiliation, status, etc. are not distinguished. As mentioned in section 1.6, reflexives are governed by the clausal/sentential subject. There are two additional complex reflexive-like morphemes: *āpoāp* (historically *āpaṇ-āpaṇ*) 'by itself' and *āplaāpaṇ* 'by oneself'. The former is used exclusively with inanimate subjects while the use of the latter is restricted to animate subjects. Both of these function as adverbs as in (1146) and (1147) respectively.

āpoāp:

(1146)	gāḍī	āpoāp	ruḷāwarūn	ghasarlī
	train	by itself	track-from	slip-pst-3sf

'The train slipped from the track by itself.'

āplaāpaṇ:

(1147)	ādzobā	gharātlī	sagḷī
	grandfather	home-loc-adj-3pl.n	all-3pl.n

kāma	āplīāpaṇ	karūn	ghetāt
job-3pl.n	refl-3pl.n	do-conj.part	take-pres-3pl

'Grandfather manages to do all of the household jobs by himself.'

Note that the first part of the complex reflexive-like morpheme *āplīāpaṇ* in (1152), agrees with the direct object *kāma*. *Āpoāp* and *āplaāpaṇ* are not treated as reflexives in traditional Marathi grammars (most notably, Damle 1966 [1911]). They are treated as adverbs in grammars and are listed as adverbs in dictionaries. However, their phonological forms as well as their function are very similar to those of the reflexives in Marathi. An alternate means of expressing reflexivity (i.e., implicitly) is the use of the explicator verb (*gheṇe* 'to take') in a compound verb construction. The reflexive *āpaṇ* is homophonous with the first person inclusive (speaker + hearer) as well as the second person plural (honorific) pronouns.

2.1.2.3 *Reciprocal pronouns*

There are no reciprocal pronouns in the language. Reciprocity is expressed by the means described in section 1.7.

2.1.2.4 - 2.1.2.4.11.1 *Possessive pronouns*

Personal pronouns, when marked with the possessive case, express possessive meaning. Possessive pronouns are not distinguished from genitive pronouns. For other ways of expressing possession, see section 1.10.

2.1.2.5 - 2.1.2.5.8.1 *Demonstrative pronouns*

The third person personal pronouns (cf. 2.1.2.1) function also as demonstrative pronouns. These are formally indistinguishable from the demonstrative adjectives. There are two forms of each of the demonstrative pronouns: proximate, beginning with *h-* ; and remote, beginning with *t-*. The proximate and remoteness distinction is based on the spatial, temporal, as well as psychological distance of the referent of the pronoun from the speaker, and not from the hearer. For example, if the referent is close to the speaker, it is referred to with the proximate form even if it is far away from the hearer. If two referents are at equal distance from the speaker and one of two is relatively further from the hearer, the speaker will refer to one with the proximate form and the other with the remote form. If the referents are closer to the hearer than to the speaker, the speaker will use the remote forms of the pronouns. As mentioned earlier in sections 2.1.2.1.6 - 2.1.2.1.6.1, the distance can be spatial, temporal, and psychological. However, psychological distance takes precedence over spatial and or temporal distance. A remote referent (in time and/or space) can be referred to with a proximate form of a pronoun if it is psychologically close to the speaker.

2.1.2.6 - 2.1.2.6.1 *Interrogative pronouns*

There are two types of interrogative pronouns—general and specific. The general forms are used when the speaker does not have any knowledge of the referents with regard to sex, number, social status, etc. Thus the general interrogative pronouns are used in unmarked contexts to get basic information about the referent. In contrast to this, the specific interrogative pronouns are used when the speaker is inquiring about or seeking more information about one or more presupposed referent(s). The general interrogative pronouns are *koṇ* 'who' (for animate referents), and *kāy* 'what' (for inanimate referents).

The selective interrogative pronouns are *koṇtā* 'which-he (i.e., 'who' sm)', *koṇtī* 'which she (i.e., 'who' sf)', *koṇta* 'which-it' (i.e., sn), *koṇte* 'which-they' (i.e., 'which' pl.m), *koṇtyā* 'which-they' (i.e., 'which' pl.f), and *koṇtī* 'which-they' (i.e., 'which' pl.n).

Selective interrogative pronouns, similar to nouns and personal pronouns, take gender and number markings and are inflected for case as shown below.

(1148) *koṇtā* (sm)/*koṇte* (pl.m)

Cases	Singular	Plural
nom	koṇtā	koṇte
acc	koṇālā/kuṇālā	koṇā-lā/kuṇā-lā
inst	koṇātSyā-ne	koṇātSyā-ne
dat	koṇā-lā/kuṇā-lā	koṇā-lā/kuṇā-lā
abl	koṇā-hūn	kuṇā-hūn
poss	koṇā-tsa (and its variants)	koṇā-tsa (and its variants)
loc	koṇā-t/kuṇāt	koṇāt/kuṇāt

Note that the above interrogative pronoun has identical singular and plural case forms.

The selective interrogative pronouns function as adjectives and therefore do not take case-endings; rather, they agree in gender and number with the following noun (explicitly mentioned or implicitly assumed) when the noun is in the nominative case (1149a). However, when the noun (which immediately follows the interrogative pronoun) is followed by a case-suffix (acc-loc), the interrogative pronoun remains in its oblique form (1149b).

(1149a)	Interrogative Pronoun	Noun
	koṇtī	mulgī
	which-3sf	girl-3sf
	'which girls'	
(1149b)	koṇtyā	mulīlā
	which-obl	girl-dat
	'to which girl'	

Selective interrogatives are generally followed by a noun; they do not occur by themselves. In a conversational discourse, however, it is possible to delete a noun about which the speaker and hearer have prior knowledge, as in (1150) below.

(1150)	A:	bhūkãmpāt	kāhī	ghara	dzaḷlī
		earthquake-in	some	houses	burn-pst-3pl.n
		'Some houses (got) burnt in the earthquake.'			
	B:	koṇtī (ghara)?			
		which-3pl.n (house-3pl.n.)			
		'Which (houses)?'			

2.1.2.6.2 *Other question words*

There are question words other than those discussed earlier. They include adverbs, adjectives and quantifiers. They all begin with *-k*.

(1151)	a.	kitī	'how much, how many' (quantity), (number)
	b.	kewhḍha (and its variants)	'what size'
	c.	kuṭhe/a	'where'
	d.	kasa (and its variants)	'what kind/manner'
	e.	kẽmwhā/kadhī	'when'
	f.	kaśālā	'why'

g.	kuṭhūn	'from where'
h.	kitīdā	'how many times'

2.1.2.7 - 2.1.2.7.3 *Relative pronouns*

An elaborate set of relative pronouns exists in the language. These relative pronouns are used to introduce a relative (subordinate) clause and modify the head noun phrase. They agree with the head noun in gender and number. They do not function as substitutes for nouns and do not occur in a finite clause. The list of relative nouns is given below. (See also 1.1.2.3.)

(1152)	a.	ʤẽmwhā	'when'
	b.	ʤewhḍha (and its variants)	'as much'
	c.	ʤītka (and its variants)	'as many'
	d.	ʤithe/a	'where'
	e.	ʤikḍe	'in which direction'
	f.	dzasa (and its variants)	'which kind of'

The relative pronouns function as adverbs (1152a, 1152d and 1152e) or adjectives (1152b, 1152c and 1152f). Remote third person demonstrative pronouns are used as correlative pronouns in relative clauses (for further details see section 1.1.2.3.1). Relative participles involve deletion of the head noun, rather than the use of pronouns.

2.1.3 VERB MORPHOLOGY

2.1.3.1 *Voice*

2.1.3.1.1 - 2.1.3.1.1.1.3 *Passive*

Passive is defined variously in the grammar/descriptions of Marathi. A traditional grammarian such as Damle (1966 [1911]) define passive exclusively on the basis of the verb agreement. Therefore, the passive construction, according to Damle, is the one in which the verb does not agree with the subject or the agent (*kartā*), but rather, with the object (*karma*).

In contrast to this, Pandharipande (1981a) defines passive as the construction in which the agent is "downgraded" (see Pandharipande 1981a for details)—morphologically, syntactically, and semantically. Moreover, Pandharipande (1981a) claims that in the passive construction, the main verb (which is passivized), always expresses a volitional act. Additionally, it is argued in Pandharipande (1981a) that the passive construction expresses the capabilitative meaning (i.e., the capability of the agent to perform/not perform the action expressed by the verb).

While both definitions commonly share the assumption that the subject/agent does not have prominence in the passive construction; they differ from each other in many significant ways: (a) Damle's passive includes all the constructions in Marathi where the subject/agent is marked with a case-suffix (e.g., dative-subject/ experiencer-subject construction, instrumental-subject constructions) or with the postposition *kaḍūn* 'by'. In contrast to this, Pandharipande labels only those constructions as passive in which the agent is followed by the postposition *kaḍūn* 'by' (b) while Damle's definition captures a broad generalization, namely that when the subject agent is followed by a case-suffix or a postposition, its status as the subject/agent is lowered and the verb morphology/verb agreement indicates it (i.e., the verb fails to agree with the subject/agent which is followed by the case-suffix and/or postpositions), this definition however does not take into account the fact that morphological prominence (or "downgrading" of a noun phrase) does not always imply the same level of syntactic/semantic prominence (or downgrading of a noun phrase). In Pandharipande (1981), it is shown that noun phrases followed by different postpositions indicate different levels of syntactic/semantic "downgrading" (c) Moreover, each of these constructions expresses a particular semantic relationship between the subject and the verb. For example, in the dative-subject construction (see section 2.1.1.2.3.1) the subject is the experiencer of the action/state expressed by the verb (and it is not an agent). Also, this construction expresses a non-volitional act. In contrast to this, in a construction where the subject is followed by the postposition *kaḍūn,* 'by', it is assumed that the subject not only is an agent but also that he/she volitionally performs the action (expressed by the verb). Pandharipande's definition treats these constructions as being separate from one another on the basis of their morphological, syntactic and semantic properties and points out the following four characteristics of the passive construction in Marathi:

(a) the passive subject/agent is followed by the postposition *kaḍūn* 'by',

(b) the main verb is in the perfective form and is followed by the verb *dzā* 'go'. Both verbs agree with the direct object.

(c) the passive construction (with the agent) expresses a volitional act, and

(d) with the agent present in the sentence, a passive sentence expresses capabilitative meaning. A typical example of the passive construction is given below.

(1153)	rāmkaḍūn	pustak	wātsla	gela
	Ram-by	book-3sn	read-pst-3sn	go-pass-pst-3sn
	nāhī			
	neg-s			

'The book was not read by Ram.' (i.e., Ram was unable to read the book.)

Note that in (1153) the verb agrees with the direct object (derived subject) *pustak* and not with the basic subject/agent *Ram* (which is followed by the postposition *kaḍūn* 'by').

Several features of the passive construction need to be mentioned here: (a) the passive is a productive construction in Marathi, (b) only the direct object and no other constituent can become a derived subject, (c) only transitive verbs are passivized in Marathi. (Marathi, unlike Indo-Aryan languages, shares this feature with Dravidian languages such as Kannada and Telugu), (d) the agentive phrase may be absent. In this last case, the passive sentence does not express capabilitative meaning, but rather expresses a volitional act performed by an implied agent. Pandharipande (1981a) has demonstrated that the capabilitative meaning is expressed by the passive construction in other Indo-Aryan languages such as Hindi, Kashmiri, Nepali, and Punjabi as well. Moreover, the passive construction expresses the capability of the agent (in performing the act) which is determined by agent-internal (physical or psychological) conditions. Thus in (1153), it is assumed that it was due to a headache, or a state of mind that Ram was incapable of reading the book and that it was not the case that for example, there was not enough light for reading a book or the book had very small type (which made it difficult to read). The passive construction also expresses prescriptive meaning under the following conditions: (a) when there is no overt agent in the sentence and the implied agent is generic (i.e., people) and (b) when the verb is in the present tense, imperfect aspect, and is marked for third person singular/plural. The following example (1154) illustrates this function of the passive.

(1154)	ā̃dzobā̃nśī	asa	bolla	dzāt
	grandfather-dat	like this	talk-pst-3sn	go-pass-pres
	nāhī			
	neg			

'It is not talked like this with grandfather.' (i.e., One does not talk like this with grandfathers.)

The passive construction (without an overt agent) is also used in the newspaper as well as other formal registers (e.g., official correspondence, reports, etc.).

Newspaper:

(1155)	kāl	māhīmlā	wīs	tsor
	yesterday	Mahim-acc	twenty	thieves
	pakḍle	gele		
	catch-pst-3pl.m	go-pass-pst-3pl.m		

'Yesterday twenty thieves were caught at Mahim.'

Official letter:

(1156)	udyāparyānta	sarwa	adhikāryā̃nnā	māntryā̃ntSyā
	tomorrow-till	all	officers-dat	ministers-poss
	kāryakramātSī	māhītī	kaḷwilī	dzāwī
	program-poss-3sf	information-3sf	inform-pst-3sf	go-pass-opt-3sf

'By tomorrow, all officers may be informed about the program (i.e., schedule) of the ministers.'

When the authority and not necessarily the direct agency of the agent is to be expressed in a formal register, the agent of the passive sentence is followed by the postposition *dwārā* 'through/by' instead of *kaḍūn* 'by'.

(1157)

pradhān	māntryāntSyā	dwārā	hā
prime	minister-poss	through	this

ādeś	dilā	gelā	kī. . .
order	give-pst-3sm	go-pass-pst-3sm	that. . .

'The order was issued by the prime minister that . . .'

It must be noted here that the postposition *kaḍūn* 'by' expresses direct agency while *dwārā* 'through/by' expresses indirect agency in causatives as well. The direct causee gets the postposition *kaḍūn* , while the indirect causee gets the postposition *dwārā* .

Another type of passive construction is formed by (a) adding the instrumental suffix *-ne* to the agent, and (b) placing the main verb in the infinitive form followed by the auxiliary verb *ho* 'to happen' (which agrees with the infinitive).

(1158)

tyātSyāne	dahā	wādzeparyānta
he-ag	ten	o'clock-until

uthṇa	hot	nāhī
get up -inf-3sm	happen-pres	neg

'He cannot get up till ten o'clock.' (lit: 'Getting up does not happen by him till ten o'clock.')

The above sentence differs from the earlier passive construction in that (a) it requires the agent to be present in the sentence, (b) transitive as well as intransitive verbs can participate in this construction, (c) it expresses the speaker's attitude (positive or negative) toward the agent of the sentence. For example in (1158) the speaker implies that the agent is lazy; i.e., does not get up in the morning before 10 a.m.

Similar to this construction, Marathi has another construction which is also treated as passive in the traditional grammars (Damle 1966 [1911]: 761). In this construction, the agent/subject is followed by either the instrumental suffix *-ne* or the dative suffix *-lā,* and the verb (transitive or intransitive) is followed by the suffix *-aw* (which is homophonous with the causative suffix). The transitive verb agrees with the direct object and the intransitive verb remains in the unmarked form, i.e., third person, singular, neuter. Example (1159) illustrates this construction.

(1159)	tyātSyā-ne/tyā-lā	he	kām	kar-aw-te
	he-inst/he-dat	this	job	do-able to-pres-3sn

'He is able to do the job.'

2.1.3.1.1.2 - 2.1.3.1.2.3 *Impersonal passive*

As example (871) in section 2.1.1.2.13 shows, the passive construction may not have a surface agent/subject. Another construction which expresses a passive-like meaning, i.e., 'the work got done' is illustrated in (1160a). The construction most commonly lacks the surface subject/agent and the verb is invariably *hoṇe* 'to happen'; which agrees with the (semantic) direct object. When the main verb is other than *hoṇe* 'to happen', it occurs in the conjunctive participial form (followed by the appropriate form of *hoṇe* as in (1160b).

(1160a)	sagḷī	mahatwātSī	kāma	dzhālī
	all	importance-poss-3pl.n	jobs-3pl.n	happen-pst-3pl.n

'All the important jobs got done.'

(1160b)	patra	lihūn	dzhālī
	letters	write-conj.part	happen-pst-3pl.n

'The letters got written.' (lit: 'The writing of letters happened.')

When the appparently agentive phrase occurs in this construction, it is generally followed by the instrumental suffix *-ne* as in (1161).

(1161)	tyāṭSyāne	sagḷī	kāma	dzhālī
	he-inst	all-3pl.n	jobs-3pl.n	happen-pst-3pl.n

'All the jobs got done because of him.'

In (1161) the agent has the status of an instrument in getting the jobs done. The instrumental suffix *-ne* in the construction (shown in 1161) is readily replaceable by the postposition of cause *muḷe* 'because of'.

2.1.3.1.2 - 2.1.3.1.2.2 *Means of decreasing the valency of a verb*

The valency of a verb can be decreased by the following strategies: (a) by choosing an intransitive counterpart of the transitive verb. The following sample of pairs of transitive and intransitive verbs illustrates this point. Except for (iii), the rest of the pairs are semantically (lexically) related.

	Transitive	Intransitive
(i)	toḍ-ṇe 'to break'	tuṭ-ṇe 'be broken'
(ii)	phoḍ-ṇe 'to break'	phuṭ-ṇe 'be broken'
(iii)	mār-ṇe 'to hit, kill'	mar-ṇe 'to die'
(iv)	soḍ-ṇe 'to leave X'	suṭ-ṇe 'be left'

Consider the following examples which show the contrast between the transitive and intransitive verb.

(1162a)	rām	dzhāḍa	toḍto
	Ram-3sm	trees-3pl.n	break-3sm

'Ram breaks the trees.'

(1162b)	wādaḷāt	dzhāḍa	tuṭṭāt
	storm-loc	trees-3pl.n	break-3pl.n

'Trees break (are broken) in the storm.'

(b) by using the (agentless/subjectless) passive construction as in (1154) and (1155), and (1156), (c) by chosing other agentless/subjectless constructions as shown in (1160a) and (1160b), and (d) by choosing a conjunct verb with the auxiliary *hoṇe* 'to happen'. There are conjunct verbs in Marathi which have two constituents, a noun plus the auxiliary *hoṇe* 'to happen'/*karṇe* 'to do'. With the auxiliary *hoṇe* 'to happen', the conjunct verb is intransitive and lacks a surface agent/subject. The auxiliary verb agrees with its object noun as in (1163).

swaypāk hoṇe 'for the cooking to get done':

(1163)	swaypāk	dzhālā
	cooking-3sm	happen-pst-3sm

'The cooking got done'

With the auxiliary *karṇe* 'to do' the conjunct verb is transitive and the agent is present in the sentence. The verb *karṇe* 'to do' agrees with the object in this case as in (1164).

(1164)	tine	swaypāk	kelā
	she-ag	cooking-3sm	do-pst-3sm

'She cooked.' (lit: 'She did the cooking.')

Some verbs have dual valency; therefore, they can be used either transitively or intransitively. These verbs allow their direct objects to be dropped, thus decreasing their valency. Thus the verbs in this case are used intransitively, and, as a consequence of this, the ergative/agentive postposition *-ne* is not used with subjects/agents in the perfective aspect, third person. A list of such verbs is given below.

(a) śikṇe 'to study (in a college, school)
(b) bolṇe 'to speak, tell'
(c) ʤĩŋkṇe 'to win'
(d) samdzṇe 'to understand'
(e) tsāwṇe 'to bite'

2.1.3.1.3 *Means of increasing the valency of a verb*

2.1.3.1.3.1.1 *Verbal causativization*

There are two types of causatives—morphological and periphrastic. The former is neutral regarding the attitude of the causer and the causee, while the latter expresses coercion of the causee by the causer to perform the act expressed by the verb. Let us consider the process of (morphological) causativization. Intransitive, transitive, and ditransitive verbs undergo causativization. The causative suffix *-aw* is used to derive the first causative (i.e., the transitive verb from its intransitive counterpart). The suffix *-aw* is also used for deriving causatives from transitive verbs (which is generally called the process of deriving the second causative).

The suffix *-aw* is used to derive causatives from both intransitive as well as transitive verbs as shown in (1165) and (1166).

(1165)	Intransitive	First causative
	basṇe 'to sit'	bas-aw-ṇe 'to seat'
	dzhopṇe 'to sleep'	dzhop-aw-ṇe 'to put to sleep'
	uṭhṇe 'to get up'	uṭh-aw-ne 'to make (X) to get up'

(1166)	Transitive	Second causative
	karṇe 'to do'	kar-aw-ṇe 'to make (X to) do'
	aikṇe 'to hear'	aik-aw-ṇe 'to make (X to) hear'
	lihiṇe 'to write'	lih-aw-ṇe 'to make (X to) write'

Intransitive:

(1167)	rām	khūrtSīwar	baslā
	Ram-3sm	chair-on	sit-pst-3sm

'Ram sat on the chair.'

Causative:

(1167a)	anū-ne	rām-lā	khurtSīwar	bas-aw-la
	Anu-ag	Ram-acc	chair-on	sit-caus-pst-3sn

'Anu made Ram sit on the chair.'

Transitive:

(1168)	sudhāne	patra	lihilī
	Sudha-ag	letters-3pl.n	write-pst-3pl.n

'Sudha wrote letters.'

Causative:

(1168a)	aīne	sudhā kaḍūn	patra	lihaw(i)ilī
	mother	Sudha-by (inst)	letters-3pl.n	write-caus-3pl.n

'Mother made Sudha write letters.'

The following example illustrates the process of causativization of ditransitive verbs.

Ditransitive:

(1169)	kumud	mīnālā	pustak	dete
	Kumud-3sf	Meena-dat	book-3sn	give-pres-3sf

'Kumud gives the book to Meena.'

Causative:

(1169a)	anū	kumudkaḍūn	mīnālā	pustak
	Anu-3sf	Kumud-by	Meena-dat	book-3sn

dewaw(i)te
give-caus-pres-3sf

'Anu makes (causes) Kumud to give the book to Meena.'

The examples in (1167a), (1168a), and (1169a) differ from (1167), (1168), and (1169) respectively in that they have an additional argument.

The examples also show that when intransitive verbs are causativized, the subject of the intransitive verb becomes the direct object in its causative counterpart (1167a). In contrast to this, the subject of a transitive (i.e., mono and di) sentence becomes the instrumental agent in its causative counterpart and takes the instrumental postposition *-kaḍūn* (1169a). (For futher discussion on the comparative syntax and semantics of causatives in Hindi, Kannada, Kashmiri, Nepali, Marathi and Punjabi, see Pandharipande 1981a.)

It should be noted here that in Marathi, there is a small class of transitive verbs which are distinguished from their respective intransitive counterparts by the length of the stem vowel. These transitive verbs can be viewed as causatives derived from their intransitive counterparts. However, this process of deriving causatives (by lengthening the stem vowel) is not productive in the language. It is restricted only to a small class of verbs. The following examples illustrate the process.

(1170)	Intransitive	Transitive/First causative
	marṇe 'to die'	mārṇe 'to kill'
	paḍṇe 'to fall'	pāḍṇe 'to fell'
	tarṇe 'to go over'	tārṇe 'to take across'

(1171)	anū	dzhāḍāwarūn	paḍlī
	Anu-3sf	tree-on-from	fall-pst-3sf

'Anu fell down from the tree.'

(1171a)	prakāś-ne	anūlā	dzhāḍāwarūn	pāḍla
	Prakash-ag	Anu-acc	tree-on-from	fall-caus-pst-3sn

'Prakash made Anu fall from the tree.'

Note that the suffix *-ā* is added to the verb (*paḍṇe* 'to fall') in the causative sentence (1171a). Thus the derived causative verb is *pāḍṇe* 'to fell'. Also note that the subject of the intransitive verb *Anu* (1171) becomes the direct object of the causative sentence and takes the accusative suffix *-lā* (1171a). The derived causative sentence (1171a) may also be passivized.

The coercive causative construction in Marathi can be illustrated as follows: (a) the coercive causative has a periphrastic form, i.e., it is a sequence of the main verb followed by the verb *lāw* 'attach' (which is the marker of the causative), (b) the main verb is in its infinitive form followed by the dative suffix *-lā,* (c) the verb *lāw* takes the agreement markers of gender, number, and person, (d) the causee takes the accusative suffix *-lā* regardless of whether the causativizing verb is transitive or intransitive, (e) similar to the other causative construction, the coercive causative construction derives causatives both from intransitive as well as transitive verbs as in (1172a) and (1173a).

Intransitive:

(1172)	amit	khurtSīwar	baslā
	Amit-3sm	chair-on	sit-pst-3sm

'Amit sat on the chair.'

(1172a)	rāmne	amitlā	khurtSīwar
	Ram-ag	Amit-acc	chair-on
	basāylā	lāwle	
	sit-inf-dat	attach (caus)-pst-3sn	

'Ram forced Amit to sit on the chair.'

Transitive:

(1173)	anū	sāḍī	neslī
	Anu-3sf	saree-3sf	wear-pst-3sf

Anu wore a saree.'

(1173a)	mī	anūlā	sāḍī	nesāylā	lāwla
	I	Anu-acc	saree	wear-inf-dat	attach-caus-pst-3sn

'I forced Anu to wear a saree.'

The coercive causatives are formed from both consonant-ending as well vowel-ending transitive and intransitive verbs. In fact, this is the most productive process of forming causatives in Marathi. Causatives from vowel-ending verbs (except for *deṇe* 'to give' which allows causative to be formed by either process) are coercive periphastic causatives. The process of forming causatives by adding *-aw* is blocked in this case. Examples are given below.

(1174)	Verb stem	Causative
	khā 'eat'	khāylā lāwṇe 'to make eat' *khāwṇe/*khāwawṇe
	ye 'come'	yāylā lāwṇe 'to make come' *yāwṇe/*yewawṇe
	dzā 'go'	dzāylā lāwṇe 'to make go' (pāṭhawṇe 'to send') *dzāwṇe/*dzāwawṇe
	dhu 'wash'	dhuwāylā lāwṇe 'to make wash' *dhuwawṇe

2.1.3.1.3.2 *Agentivity of the causee*

Agentivity is crucial for determining case-assignment in causative sentences. As is evident from the examples in section 2.1.3.1.3.1.1, the causee is generally an agent. It is important to note here that direct vs. indirect agency of the causee in carrying out the act expressed by the verb is indicated by the suffix/postposition. For example, if the agency of the causee is direct, then the causee takes the accusative suffix *-lā* or the instrumental postposition *kaḍūn* 'by'. The indirect agency of the causee is indicated by the postposition *dwārā* 'through' as in (1175).

(1175)	mī	mohan (tSyā)	dwārā	kām
	I	Mohan (poss)	through	work-3sn
	karawle-3sn			
	do-caus-pst-3sn			

'I got the work done through Mohan.'

(For further discussion on the syntax and semantics of postpositions in causatives, see Pandharipande 1981a.)

It is crucial to remember that the causee's agency or ability (to carry out the act expressed by the verb) is implied in a causative sentence. The postpositions *-lā, kaḍūn,* and *dwārā* indicate that the causee is the agent (direct or indirect) of the act. However, when the causee is non-volitional (either because it is inanimate or lacks control of the action (i.e., she/he is merely an experiencer)), the above postpositions are blocked and the verbs do not undergo causativization. Thus, dative-subject verbs (where the subject is the experiencer and takes the dative postposition *-lā*) do not undergo the process of causativization as in (1176).

(1176)*	mī	tyālā/tyātSyākaḍūn/tyātSyādwārā	rāg
	I	he-acc/he-poss-by/he-poss-through	anger
	yewawto/yāylā	lāwto	
	come-caus-1sm/come-inf-dat	attach (caus)-1sm	

'I make him get angry.'

The only alternative construction (which is marginally acceptable) is one where the dative suffix is retained on the experiencer subject and the verb of coming (*yeṇe* 'to come') is replaced by the verb *āṇṇe* 'to bring'.

(1176a)	mī	tyālā	rāg	āṇto
	I	he-dat	anger	bring-1sm

'I make him get angry.' (lit: 'I bring anger to him.')

2.1.3.1.3.3 *Omission of causee*

The causee is omitted in the causative sentences such as (1175) whenever it is recoverable by means of context or shared knowledge (pragmatic, social, etc.). If the causee can not be known on the basis of knowledge shared between the speaker and the hearer or by means of context, it may not be omitted.

2.1.3.2 *Tense*

Tense is marked by a suffix, which immediately follows the verb stem and precedes all other suffixes. The agreement markers for person, number, and gender are different in different tenses. Additionally, the verbs *asṇe* 'to be', *rāhṇe* 'to be/to stay', and *dzāṇe* 'to go' are widely used to indicate various aspects and tenses. Aspectual and tense markers are not always separate (e.g., the perfective marker *-l* indicates past time reference).

It should be noted here that there is not always a correlation between the morphological tense forms and the time reference indicated by them. For example, present and past tense markers may be used to express future time (see sections 2.1.3.2.1 - 2.1.3.2.1.3.2). The verb form (with the tense/aspect markers) in the matrix sentence or the main clause provides the time reference for the entire sentence (including the subordinate/embedded clause). For example, the main as well as the subordinate clause in (1177) below refer to past tense/time regardless of the fact that the embedded subordinate clause is in the present tense.

(1177)	anū	mhaṇālī	kī	manʤū
	Anu	say-pst-3sf	comp	Manju
	hindī	śikawte		
	Hindi	teach-pres-3sf		

'Anu said that Manju taught Hindi.'

Similarly, the verb in the matrix clause determines the tense or the time reference in a conditional sentence regardless of the tense conveyed by the verb (and the tense markers) in the conditional clause, as in (1178) below.

(1178)	dzar	to	ālā	tar	mī	sinemālā	dzāīn
	if	he	come-pst-3sm	then	I	movie-to	go-fut-1s

'If he comes (lit: 'came'), then I will go to the movie.'

The tense, aspect and mood system of Marathi is extremely complex due to the following facts: (a) tense and aspect markers often merge, (b) several explicator verbs carry the function of aspect/tense markers, and (c) time reference is not always determined by tense markers on a verb within the same clause.

2.1.3.2.1 *Tenses distinguished formally*

Three tenses—present, past, and future—are formally distinguished. These tenses are marked by the following suffixes:

(1179)

Tense	Marker	Example	Gloss
Present	-t	basto	'he sits'
Past	-l	baslā	'he sat'
Future	vowel + l/n	basel	'he will sit'

As far as the present, past, and future tense markers are concerned, there are no irregular verbs in Marathi.

2.1.3.2.1.1 *Universal time reference*

Universal time reference is signalled by the present tense form of the verbs as in the following examples.

asṇe 'to be':

(1180)	manuṣya	swārthī	prāṇī	āhe
	man	selfish	animal	is

'Man is a selfish animal/being.'

(1181)	ameriketse	lok	māns	khātāt
	America-poss-3pl.m	people	meat	eat-pres-3pl.m

'American people eat meat.'

(1182)	keraḷāt	khūp	pāus	paḍto
	Kerala-loc	a lot	rain-3sm	fall-pres-3sm
	'It rains a lot in Kerala.'			

Note that the present tense form is used in (1181) and (1182) to indicate universal time reference. However, the habitual meaning (which is expressed by the present tense form) is not ruled out in these cases.

2.1.3.2.1.2 *Present*

The present tense is formed with the suffix *-t* , which is the same as the imperfective aspectual marker, followed by the vowel-suffix of gender and number. The complete paradigm is illustrated in (1183).

(1183) *yeṇe* 'to come':

	Singular		Plural	
	mas	fem	mas	fem
1p	yeto	yete	yeto	yeto
2p	yetos	yetes	yetā	yetā
3p	yeto	yete	yetāt	yetāt

karṇe 'to do':

	Singular		Plural	
	mas	fem	mas	fem
1p	karto	karte	karto	karto
2p	kartos	kartes	kartā	kartā
3p	karto	karte	kartāt	kartāt

Note that the gender distinction is neutralized in the plural form. Also note that the first and the third person singular forms are identical.

Damle (1966 [1911]) points out that the present tense forms of verbs are used to indicate an immediately following quote. Consider the following examples from Damle (1966 [1911]: 685).

(1184a)	tukārām	mhaṇto . ..
	Tukaram	say-pres-3sm

'Tukaram says . . .'

(1184b)	kṛṣṇaśāstrī	lihitāt. . .
	Krishnashastri	write-pres-3pl

'Krishnashastri writes . . .'

Additionally, Damle (1966 [1911]: 685) correctly observes that present tense forms are used to express a future action when (a) the certainty of the action is to be indicated, and (b) the action is expected to occur almost immediately, as in (1185), (1186).

(1185)	tyatSī	prakṛtī	itkī	bighaḍlī
	he-poss-3sf	health-3sf	so much	deteriorate-pst-3sf

āhe	kī	ātā	to	marto
is	comp	now	he	die-pres-3sm

'His health/is deteriorated so much that he is going to die now.' (lit: 'Now he dies')

(1186)	tsalā	mī	tumhās	ek
	come-imp-3pl	I	you-(pl)-dat	one

maudz	dākhawto
interesting-3sf	show-pres-3sm

'Come, I (will) show you something interesting.'

2.1.3.2.1.3 - 2.1.3.2.1.3.2 *Past*

Past tense indicates a state or action which has occurred before the speech. The past tense suffix *-l* is homophonous with the perfective aspectual suffix. Past habitual and past progressive are the only non-perfective aspects in Marathi, i.e., there is no independent past imperfective in Marathi. In this respect, Marathi is similar to other Indo-Aryan languages such as Hindi, Gujarati, Punjabi, etc. The suffix *-l* immediately follows the verb stem and precedes the agreement suffixes of person, gender, and number. The pattern of verb agreement in the past tense differs from that in the present tense. In the past tense, the intransitive verb agrees with the subject, while the transitive verb agrees with the direct object (for further discussion, see section 1.2.1.2.1). Marathi shares this "ergative" pattern with other Indo-Aryan languages. (For the ergative pattern in Hindi, see Pandharipande 1991b, and for Punjabi, see Bhatia 1993.) However, Marathi differs from Hindi and Punjabi in that in Hindi and Punjabi the agentive/ergative suffix *-ne* marks the agent (in all persons) of the transitive verb in the past tense. In contrast to this, in Marathi, the agent of transitive verb is marked with *-ne* only in the third person. The agreement pattern of transitive verbs in the past tense with second person (agent) is complex, since the verb bears double marking, i.e., it agrees with the direct object in gender, person, and number and bears additional agreement marking for the agent as in (1188). (For further discussion, see Pandharipande 1991b.)

Consider the paradigms of transitive and intransitive verbs in the past tense.

(1187) Transitive verb *karṇe* 'to do'

	Singular	Plural
Masculine	kelā	kele
Feminine	kelī	kelyā
Neuter	kela	kelī

It is assumed in the above paradigm that the agreement is with the direct object and the subject is either in the first or in the third person. With a second person subject, the agreement pattern will be as follows.

(1188)

	Singular	Plural
Masculine	kelā-s	kele-t
Feminine	kelī-s	kelyā-t
Neuter	kela-s	kelī-t

Note that the verb forms in (1187) do not have subject agreement markers on the verb. In contrast to this, the verb forms in (1188) show subject agreement markers (*-s* for singular and *-t* for plural), in addition to the gender and number markers of the object.

It should be further noted that the double (subject and object) marking is consistently maintained in Puṇe Marathi (spoken in western Maharashtra), while it is optional in Nagpuri Marathi (spoken in eastern Maharashtra), where the subject marking is optionally maintained.

(1189) Intransitive verb *basṇe* 'to sit':

	Singular		Plural	
	mas	fem	mas	fem
1p	baslo	basle	baslo	baslo
2p	baslās	baslīs	baslāt	baslāt
3p	baslā	baslī	basle	baslyā

Past tense forms are also used to indicate time in the immediate future as in (1190).

(1190)

tumhī	ātā	nighā;	mī	pāts
you-pl	now	leave-imp-pl	I	five

miniṭāt	ālo(ts)
minutes-within	come-pst-1sm (emph)

'You leave now; I will certainly come (i.e., I will be there) within five minutes.'

There are no morphological markers to indicate the degree of remoteness in the past tense. Copular forms are used to indicate the distinction between immediate vs. remote past. Present tense copular forms (which immediately follow verbs marked with past tense, gender, number and person markers) indicate proximate past, and the past tense copular forms indicate remote past. The future-in-past (future perfect) is also expressed by the copular form. The following examples illustrate the use of copular forms to indicate the degree of remoteness. No distinction exists between the past tense marking of the finite verb in the main clause and complement clause.

(1191) *Proximate past /present perfect tense :*

mī	patra	lihile	āhe
I	letter-3sn	write-pst-3sn	is

'I have written the letter.'

(1192) *Remote past (pluperfect tense):*

anek	warṣā̃npūrwī	mī	amrāwatīlā
many	years-ago	I	Amravati-dat

rāhilo	hoto
stay-pst-3sm	was

'Many years ago, I had stayed at Amravati.'

(1193) *Future-in-the-past (future perfect):*

udyāparyānta	tyāne	kām
tomorrow-by	he-ag	work-3sn

sampawla	asel
finish-pst-3sn	be-fut-3sn

'He will have finished the work by tomorrow.'

2.1.3.2.1.4 *Future*

Although *-l* is described as the future tense marker (in the traditional grammars), there exists variation in the marking of the future tense in different persons as seen in example (1194).

(1194) *pāhṇe* 'to see':

	Singular		Plural	
	mas	fem	mas	fem
1p	pāhīn	pāhīn	pāhū	pāhū
2p	pāhśīl	pāhśīl	pahāl/pāhāl	pahāl/pāhāl
3p	pāhīl	pāhīl	pāhtīl	pāhtīl

The following points are immediately observed in the above paradigm: (a) There exists variation in the future tense marker; i.e., the first person is marked differently from the second and third person. While *-n* is the marker of the future for first person singular, *ū* is the marker of the future for first person plural. The rest of the verb forms (the second and the third person) bear the future tense marker *-l*. (b) The vowel preceding the *-l* marker also varies according to number. For example, in the second person singular and third person (singular and plural) it is *-ī*, while in the second person plural it is *-ā*. (c) The consonant *-ś* immediately follows the verb stem and precedes other markings in the second person singular form of the verb. (d) Gender-distinction is not indicated by any morphological markers. (e) Examples (1195) and (1195a) below show that the vowel preceding the future tense marker *-n* (in the first person singular form of the verb) is variable (i.e., either *-e* or *-ī*) for most of the consonant-ending verbs. The verb *pāhṇe* 'to see' is an exception where only *-ī* is allowed. In the case of vowel-ending verbs the vowel preceding the future tense marker *-n* is consistently *-ī*. Consider examples (1195), (1195a), and (1195b) which illustrate the future tense marking for the first person.

(1195) *karṇe* 'to do':

	singular	plural
1p	karen/karīn	karu

(1195a) *basṇe* 'to sit':

	singular	plural
1p	basen/basīn	basū

(1195b) *dzāṇe* 'to go':

	singular	plural
1p	dzāīn	dzāū

2.1.3.2.3 *Absolute/relative tense*

The tense is absolutive in main and relative clauses, i.e., the tense indicated by the tense suffix is the tense of the clause. In contrast to these, the tense in subordinate and conditional clauses is relative, i.e., it is determined by the matrix clause, irrespective of the morphological tense-marking on the verb in those clauses (see discussion in section 2.1.3.2). Non-finite clauses (e.g., infinitives, gerunds, etc.) are not marked for tense. They have the same time-reference as subordinate clauses (for further details, see sections 2.1.3.5.1 and 2.1.3.5.2).

2.1.3.3 *Aspect*

2.1.3.3.1 *Perfective aspect*

2.1.3.3.1.1-2 *Form of perfective aspect*

The perfect aspect which indicates completion of an action or the resultant state is expressed by the suffix *-l* (which is homophonous with the past tense suffix). The suffix *-l* (unlike the future marker *-l* which is the final element of the verbal complex) immediately follows the verb stem and precedes person, number, and gender (agreement) suffixes. When a verb marked with *-l* (and the other agreement suffixes) is not followed by any auxiliary verb, it expresses past tense (see section 2.1.3.2). However, when it is followed by the auxiliary *as* 'to be', it expresses perfect aspect. Various tense-forms of *as* 'to be' express the perfect aspect in different tenses—present, past, and future. The following examples illustrate these three types of perfect aspect.

(1196) *present perfect:*

mītā	śāḷet	gelī	āhe
Meeta	school-loc	go-perf-3sf	be-pres-3s

'Meeta has gone to school.'

(1197) *past perfect:*

mohan	kāl	dewḷāt	gelā
Mohan	yesterday	temple-loc	go-perf-3sm

hotā
be-pst-3sm

'Mohan had gone to the temple yesterday.'

(1198) *future perfect:*

tū	yeśīl	to	paryānta	mī
you	come-fut-2s	then	by	I

amrāwatīlā	gelī/e	asen
Amravati-dat	go-perf-1sf	be-fut-1sf

'By the time you come (lit: 'you will come'), I will have gone to Amravati.'

It must be noted here that the form of the perfect aspect discussed above is similar to the same form in other Indo-Aryan languages such as Hindi, Punjabi, etc. However, in addition to the above, the perfect aspect is also expressed in Marathi by using the past/perfective participial form of the verb followed by the auxiliary verb (which indicates the tense). Marathi shares this feature of perfect aspect with the Dravidian language Kannada (see Sridhar 1990: 228-229). The following examples illustrate the participial form of the verb in the perfect aspect.

(1199) *present perfect:*

tyāne	kām	kelela	āhe
he-ag	work-3sn	do-perf.part-3sn	be-pres-3s

'He has done the work.'

(1200) *past perfect:*

tyāne	kām	kelela	hota
he-ag	work-3sn	do-perf.part-3sn	be-pst-3sn

'He had done the work.'

(1201) *future perfect:*

tū	yeśīl	tēmwhā	tyāne
you	come-fut-2s	at that time	he-ag

kām	kelela	asel
work-3sn	do-perf.part-3sn	be-fut-3sn

'When you come (lit: 'when you will come'), he will have done the work.'

The past tense form and the perfective form of the verb are interchangeable in the perfect aspect.

2.1.3.3.1.3 - 2.1.3.3.1.3.4 ***Situations indicated by the perfect aspect***

The perfect aspectual form can indicate a number of situations as follows:

(a) Present result of a past situation:

(1202)

auṣadhāmuḷe	titSī	tabyet
medicine-because of	her-3sf	health-3sf

sudhārlī	āhe
improve-perf-3sf	be-pres-3s

'Because of the medicine, her health has improved.'

(b) A situation that has held at least once in the period leading up to the present:

(1203)	tū	kadhī	nāgpurlā	gelī	āhes	kā?
	you	ever	Nagpur-dat	go-perf-3sf	be-pres-2s	Q

'Have you ever been to Nagpur ?'

(c) A situation that began in the past and is still continuing:

(1204)	tī	tSār	tās	itha	tyatSī
	she	four	hours	here	he-poss-3sf

wāṭ	pāhat	baslī	āhe
wait	-prog	sit-perf-3sf	be-pres-3s

'She has been sitting here (lit: 'she has seated here'), waiting for him for four hours.'

(d) A situation which was completed a short time ago:

(1205)	tī	sāḍī	neslī	āhe
	she	saree-3sf	wear-perf-3sf	be-pres-3s

'She has put on a saree.'

(e) A situation that will shortly be completed:

(1206)	tū	ṭæksī	stænḍwar	potseparyānta	mī
	you	taxi	stand-on	reach by the time	I

titha	ālelo/ālelā	asen
there	come-perf.part-1sm/come-perf-3sm	be-fut-1s

'By the time you reach the taxi-stand, I will have come there.'

2.1.3.3.1.4 *Similarity between expression of perfect aspect and recent past tense*

As mentioned in sections 2.1.3.2.1.3 - 2.1.3.2.1.3.2 and 2.1.3.3.1.3 - 2.1.3.3.1.3.4, the perfective suffix *-l* is homophonous with the recent past tense suffix, and the verb marked with the suffix *-l* (followed by person, number, and gender markers) expresses recent past tense. When the above verb form is followed by the auxiliary *as* 'to be', it expresses the perfect aspect (for details, see section 2.1.3.3.1.1-2).

2.1.3.3.2 *Aspect and duration*

2.1.3.3.2.1 *Nature of marking*

The following distinctions are marked regularly on all verbs where applicable.

2.1.3.3.2.1.1 *Perfective*

A perfective situation (indicating the completion of an action or a state) is expressed either by the suffix *-l* as discussed earlier in section 2.1.3.3.1.1-2, or by several aspectual auxiliary verbs (see Pandharipande 1990c, 1992a) which are also called vector verbs or explicators. These auxiliary verbs may convey attitudinal meanings in addition to the completion of the action expressed by the main verb. Some of these verbs also function as main verbs in finite clauses. However, they are partially or completely 'bleached' of their lexical meaning when they function as explicators or auxiliary verbs. Some of the typical explicators or auxiliary verbs are listed below along with their functions (for further details on the use of explicators in compound verbs, see section 2.2.6.3.4.2).

(1207)

Explicator/auxiliary	Lexical meaning	Aspectual meaning
dzā	'to go'	completion, finality, unexpectedness or suddeness, unintended mistake

pāh/bagh	'to see'	attemptive
de	'to give'	completion, action intended for someone other than the agent, unwillingness of the agent in performing the action
ṭāk	'to drop'	completion, undesirable action, completion of the action in order to finish it off
ghe	'to take'	completion, self-benefactive, self-initiated action, reflexive
tsuk	'to make a mistake'	completion, undesirable action

Examples of the above verbs are given in the following sections.

2.1.3.3.2.1.1.1 *dzā 'to go'*

The aspectual auxiliary *dzā* 'to go' follows the conjunctive participial forms of the verb and indicates completion of the action. Additionally, it indicates that the agent (of the action) performed the action unintentionally and unexpectedly, or mistakenly. Consider the following example.

(1208)	kāl	gappāntSyā	oghāt	to	lāts
	yesterday	chat-poss	course-loc	he	bribe
	ghetlyātSī	goṣṭa	bolūn	gelā	
	take-ger-poss-3sf	matter-3sf	say-conj.part	go-pst-3sm	

'During the course of chatting, he blurted out the matter of accepting a bribe.' (lit: 'He talked about the matter of taking a bribe.')

2.1.3.3.2.1.1.2 *pāh/bagh 'to see'*

The verbs *pāh/bagh* are used to express the experimental nature of the action. Thus the verbs *pāh/bagh* 'to see' indicate the meaning 'try'.

(1209)	ekdā	alāskāt	rāhūn	pāhā/bagh
	once	Alaska-loc	live-conj.part	see-imp-2s

'Try living in Alaska once.'

2.1.3.3.2.1.1.3 *de 'to give'*

De 'to give' is used to indicate an action which the agent performs for someone other than the agent himself/herself. Moreover, it expresses actions which are carried out to their completion. It also has the overtone of unwillingness on the part of the agent toward performing the action.

(1210)	mī	tyātsa	saga	kām	karūn
	I	he-poss-3sn	whole-3sn	work	do-conj.part
	dila				
	give-pst-3sn				

'I did all of his work (for him).'

2.1.3.3.2.1.1.4 *ṭāk 'to drop'*

The use of the explicator *ṭāk* 'to drop' indicates that the action is carried out to its completion. Additionally, it indicates that the action is performed in order to get rid of the responsibility of performing it. Consider example (1211).

(1211)	mī	auṣadh	piūn	ṭākla
	I	medicine-3sn	drink-conj.part	drop-pst-3sn

'I drank the medicine' (in order to get rid of the obligation of drinking it!)

2.1.3.3.2.1.1.5 *ghe 'to take'*

(1212)

wikat	gheṇyā	pūrwī	ghar	ekdā
buy	take-inf	before	house	once

nīṭ	pāhūn	ghe
properly/carefully	see-conj.part	take-imp-2s

'Carefully examine the house (for yourself) (lit: 'look at the house') before buying it.'

2.1.3.3.2.1.1.6 *tsuk 'to make a mistake'*

When used as an auxiliary, the verb *tsuk* expresses completion of the action and, additionally, conveys a sense of finality. However, the verb in this context is almost completely 'bleached' of its lexical meaning.

(1213)

tī	mukeślā	lagnātsa	watSan
she	Mukesh-dat	wedding-poss-3sn	promise-3sn

deūn	tsuklī	āhe
give-conj.part	perf-pst-3sf	be-pres-3s

'She has already promised Mukesh to marry him.' (i.e., she has made a commitment of marriage to Mukesh) (lit: 'She has given a promise to Mukesh of marrying him.')

2.1.3.3.2.1.2 *Imperfective aspect*

The imperfective aspect marker *-t* follows the verb stem and is followed by person, number, and gender suffixes. Examples of the imperfective aspect are given in section 2.1.3.2.1.2. The imperfective aspectual marker *-t* is homophonous with the present tense marker. The imperfective marker indicates habitual aspect as well. There are no morphologically marked past or future imperfectives.

2.1.3.3.2.1.3 *Habitual aspect*

There is no separate marker of the present habitual aspect. Past habitual acts are indicated by adding the past form of the copula *as* 'to be' to the verb stem with the imperfective present aspect marker *-t*. In this case, the main verb has an invariant form with *-t* marking, and the agreement markers are added on the copula verb. Consider the following examples of present and past habitual action respectively.

(1214) *present habitual:*

to	śāḷet	dzāto
he	school-loc	go-imperf-3sm

'He (habitually) goes to school.'

Note that no auxiliary is present in (1214).

(1215) *past habitual:*

to	śāḷet	dzāt	ase
he	school-loc	go-imperf	be-pst-3s

'He (habitually) used to go to school.'

It should be noted here that it is possible to use a present tense form of the copula *as* 'to be' in sentences such as (1214). However, in this case, it expresses habitual progressive aspect as in (1216).

(1216) *habitual progressive :*

mī	ʤẽmwhā	ʤẽmwhā	tyātSyā	gharī
I	when	when	he-poss	house-loc

dzāto	tẽmwhā	tẽmwhā	to	bāsrī
go-imperf-1sm	then	then	he	flute

wādzwat	*asto*
play -imperf	be-pres-3sm

'Whenever I go to his house, he is playing the flute.'
(lit: 'When I go to his house, then he is playing the flute.')

In order to express the habitual progressive aspect in the past tense, the suffix *-ts* is added to the infinitive form of the copula *as*. The suffix *-ts* is further followed by an appropriate vowel suffix which marks person, number, and gender agreement. The following example illustrates this type of habitual aspect.

(1217)	rodz	sandhyākāḷī	tī	gāṇa
	everyday	evening-loc	she	song-3sn

mhaṇat	asāytSī
sing-imperf	be-inf-hab-3sf

'Every evening, she used to be singing a song.'

In addition to the above, the habitual aspect is also expressed by using the copula *as* 'to be' (with appropriate tense markers) immediately following the past perfective participial form of the main verb, as in the following examples:

(1218) *habitual (present) perfect aspect:*

to	diwasbhar	dukānāt	baslelā	asto
he	day-entire	shop-loc	sit-perf.part-3sm	be-pres-3sm

'He is sitting (lit: 'seated') in the shop all day.'

(1219) *habitual (past) perfect aspect:*

to	diwasbhar	dukānāt	baslelā
he	day-entire	shop-loc	sit-perf.part-3sm

ase/asāytsā
be-pst-3s/be-inf-3sm

'He used to be sitting (lit: 'seated') in the shop all day.'

2.1.3.3.2.1.4-5 *Continuous and progressive aspects*

The non-habitual/progressive aspect is expressed by using the existential form of the copula *as* 'to be' (refer to verb morphology section), which immediately follows the imperfective form of the verb (marked with *-t*).

(1220) *present progressive:*

anū	āŋghoḷ	karīt/karat/karte	āhe
Anu	bath-3sf	do-prog	is

'Anu is taking a bath.'

Note that the vowels *-ī* and *-a* in the imperfective form of the verb are used interchangeably. The third alternative is the present/imperfect form *karte* which is marked with the third person, singular number, and feminine gender. In the spoken language, the progressive aspect marker (i.e., the copular verb *āhe*) merges with the imperfective form of the main verb, yielding the form *kartey* where the imperfective form *karte* (which carries the agreement marker *-e*) wins over the other two and *-y* expresses the progressive aspect. Example (1221) shows that the merger of the copular with the main verb is possible in the third person plural form of verbs as well.

(1221)

pudʒārī	ganget	āŋghoḷ
priests	Ganges-loc	bath

karīt/karat/ø	āhet/*kartāhet*
take-imperf/ø	be-pres-pl/do-imperf-pres-pl

'The priests are bathing (lit: 'taking a bath') in the Ganges.'

The above merger is possible in the rest of the forms as well.

It should be noted here that there is a dialectal variation in the progressive aspect marker in Marathi. While the above verb form in the progressive aspect belongs to "Standard Marathi" (or Puṇe Marathi), the Marathi spoken in the northeast of Maharashtra and known as Nagpuri Marathi uses a different progressive verb form. Nagpuri Marathi, which is influenced by Hindi (spoken in the contiguous areas), shares with Hindi the progressive marker—the auxiliary verb *rāh* 'to live'. The constituents of the verb in the progressive aspect can be described as follows: (conjunctive participial form of the main verb) + (*rāh* + perfective aspect marker *-l* + person, number, and gender markers) + (the copula *as* 'to be' + tense + number markers).

(1222)

mula	śāḷetSyā	maidānāt
children-3pl.n	school-poss	ground-loc

kheḷūn	rāhilī	āhet
play-conj.part	prog-perf-3pl.n	be-pres-3pl

'The children are playing on the school ground.'

The habitual progressive aspect was already discussed in section 2.1.3.3.2.1.3.

Additionally, the auxiliary verb *bas* 'to sit' may be substituted for the copula in order to express a incessant/continuous action for a long period of time. Consider the following example (1223).

(1223)	tī	dupārbhar	sweṭar	wiṇat	baste
	she	afternoon-entire	sweater	knit-imperf	sit-pres-3sf

'She keeps knitting a sweater all afternoon.'

(For a detailed discussion on the progressive construction in Nagpuri Marathi, see Pandharipande (1986a).)

2.1.3.3.2.1.6 *Ingressive aspect*

Ingressive aspect is expressed by the explicator *lāg* 'begin' following the dative-infinitive form of the main verb. The tense, person, number, and gender markings are added to the explicator verb *lāg*.

(1224)	nirmalā	gāylā	lāglī
	Nirmala-3sf	sing-inf-dat	begin-pst-3sf

'Nirmala began to sing.'

Marathi shares the use of the auxiliary verb *lāg* 'begin' with other Indo-Aryan languages such as Hindi, Punjabi, and Gujarati, etc.

2.1.3.3.2.1.7 *Terminative aspect*

Terminative aspect is expressed by the auxiliary *tsuk* 'to complete' following the conjunctive participial form of the main verb.

(1225)	mī	sagḷa	tulā	sāŋgūn
	I	everything	you-dat	tell-conj.part
	tsukle	āhe		
	complete-pst-3sf	be-pres-3s		

'I have finished telling you everything.'

2.1.3.3.2.1.7.1 *Prior completion*

The verb *asṇe* 'to be', with a past/perfective participle, expresses the completion of another situation prior to the situation being described. Consider the following example (1226) of this type.

(1226)	mī	tyālā	rāmwiśayī	sāŋgitlela
	I	he-dat	Ram-about	tell-perf.part-3sn
	āhe			
	be-pres-3sn			

'I have already told him about Ram.'

2.1.3.3.2.1.8 *Iterative aspect*

Marathi makes a distinction between regular and intermittent habitual (frequent) action. Frequentative actions are expressed by means of simple as well as compound verb constructions. In the present tense the verb is marked with the present tense marker *-t* , which is homophonous with the habitual marker. In this case, the 'habitual' action refers to regular action performed with a higher frequency (as in 1227), compared to the compound verb construction (as in 1228), which consists of the main verb followed by *as* 'to be'.

(1227)	to	śāḷet	dzāto
	he	school-loc	go-pres-3sm

'He goes to school regularly (i.e., habitually).'

(1228)	to	śāḷet	dzāt	asto
	he	school-loc	go-pres	be-pres-3sm

'He goes to school frequently.'

As discussed in section 2.1.3.3.2.1.3, the construction in (1228) is also used to express progressive habitual aspect.

Frequency of actions in the past is expressed by two distinct constructions, one of which involves compound verbs and the other a suffix on the verb. Those constructions are illustrated in the examples below. Note that in the first construction in (1229), the main verb stem is followed by the present tense marker *-t* , and the auxiliary *as* 'to be' follows the main verb. The frequency of action expressed by this construction is lower than that expressed by the construction shown in (1230).

(1229) lahanpaṇī / childhood-loc · to / he · mādʒhyābarobar / I-with

ṭenis / tennis · kheḷat / play-pres · ase / be-pst-3s

'He used to play tennis with me in (our) childhood.'

Now consider the following example (1230), in which the infinitive form of the main verb is marked with the suffix *-ts* followed by person, number, and gender markers.

(1230) lahānpaṇī / childhood-loc · to / he · mādʒhyābarobar / I-with

ṭenis / tennis · kheḷāytsā / play-inf-hab-(pst)-3sm

'He used to play tennis with me in (our) childhood.'

2.1.3.3.2.1.9-10 *Semelfactive and punctual aspects*

There is no special marking to signal semelfactive or punctual aspect. Regular tense forms are used in these situations.

2.1.3.3.2.1.11 *Durative aspect*

There is no specific marker for indicating the durative aspect, which signals situations or actions which take place over a long period of time. However, the following explicators (following main verbs marked with the present tense marker *-t*) convey the durative aspect: (a) *dzā* 'to go', (b) *ye* 'to come', (c) *bas* 'to sit', and (d) *rāh* 'to remain/to live'. Consider the following examples:

(a) *dzā* 'to go':

(1231)	to	don	āṭhawaḍe	rodz
	he	two	weeks	everyday

bhagwadgītā	wātsat	dzāīl
Bhagavadgita	read-pres	go-ft–3sm

'He will read the Bhagavadgita everyday for the next two weeks.'

(b) *ye* 'to come':

While the explicator *dzā* 'to go' can be used in the past, present, and future tenses, *ye* 'to come' is used exclusively to indicate duration from the past to the present. Consider example (1232).

(1232)	to	ādzparyānta	khara	bolat
	he	today-up to	truth	speak-pres

ālā (āhe)
come-pst-3sn (be-pres-3s)

'He has been telling the truth till today.'

(c) *bas* 'to sit':

The explicator *bas* 'to sit' can be used in all three tenses to express continuation of the action expressed by the verb. Additionally, it expresses the undesirability of such continuous action as in (1233).

(1233)

tī	gāyikā	dzawaḷ	dzawaḷ
that-3sf	singer-3sf	near	near

tīn	tās	gāt	baslī
three	hours	sing-pres	sit-pst-3sf

'That female singer went on singing for three hours.'

(d) *rāh* 'to remain':

In contrast to *bas* 'to sit', *rāh* 'to remain' is neutral regarding the attitude of the speaker toward the continuous action expressed by the verb.

(1234)

tī	gāyikā	dzawaḷ	dzawaḷ	tīn
that-3sf	singer-3sf	near	near	three

tās	gāt	rāhīlī
hours	sing-pres	remain-pst-3sf

'That female singer kept singing for three hours.'

2.1.3.3.2.1.12 *Simultaneous aspect*

There are no formal simultaneous or telic aspect markers. Simultaneity of one action with another is expressed by the use of the adverbial (invariable) form of the verb in the embedded/ subordinate clause as in (1235).

(1235)

dewālā	dzātānā	to	prārthanā	mhaṇto
god-dat	go-adv.part	he	prayers	recite (say)-pres-3sm

'On the way to the temple (lit: 'god') he recites prayers.'

Additionally, simultaneity is signalled by repeating the adverbial present participial form (without the syllable *-nā*) as in (1236).

(1236)

āī	āmtSyāśī	boltā	boltā
mother	we-dat	talk-adv.part	talk-adv.part

sweṭar	wiṇat	ase
sweater	knit-pres	be-pst-3s (habitual)

'Mother used to knit a sweater while talking to us.'

Another device which expresses simultaneity is the conjunctive participial form of a stative verb.

(1237)

anū	nehmī	bitShānyāwar
Anu-3sf	always	bed-on

paḍūn	wātste
lie down-conj.part	read-pres-3sf

'Anu always reads lying down on the bed.'

In addition to the above, there is a construction in Marathi which is used to express simultaneity of two actions. However, the use of this construction is restricted to the meaning 'when the body is in the state X, action y takes place.' The verb expressing the physical state of the body (e.g., *basṇe* 'to sit', *paḍṇe* 'to lie down', *dzhopṇe* 'to sleep', etc.) is the gerundive form as in (1238) below.

(1238)

rāhul	sofyāwar	paḍlyā	paḍlyā
Rahul	sofa-on	lie down-ger	lie down-ger

tī	whī	pāhto
T.	V.	see-pres-3sm

'Rahul watches T.V. lying down on the sofa.'

Note that the gerundive form of the verb is repeated, and the subject of two actions (i.e., lying down and watching T.V.) is coreferential.

2.1.3.3.2.1.13 *Other aspects*

The verb is not marked to indicate distinctions such as telic and atelic aspect. This distinction is expressed by the use of an explicator verb as in (1239a) and (1239b) below. Note that in (1239a) the explicator verbs indicate that the action must come to an end when two pieces of bread are consumed. No such indication is given in (1239a), where the explicator verb is absent.

(1239a)	ātā	tū	don	poḷyā	khāūn
	now	you	two	breads	eat-conj.part

ghe/ṭāk
take-imp-2s/drop-imp-2s

'Now you eat two pieces of bread (and that's all).'

(1239b)	ātā	tū	don	poḷyā	khā
	now	you	two	breads	eat-imp-2s

'Now you eat two pieces of breads.'

2.1.3.3.2.2.2 *Restriction on the combination of different aspectual values*

The following aspectual values are not combined: the progresssive aspect cannot be combined with stative verbs:

(1240)*	to	khurtSīwar	basat	āhe
	he	chair-on	sit-prog	is

*'He is sitting on the chair.'

Similarly, the following combinations of aspectual meanings are not allowed in Marathi:

(a) Durative + iterative
(b) Completive + iterative
(c) Ingressive + completive
(d) Terminative + habitual

2.1.3.4 *Mood*

Marathi has a large range of modal forms which are expressed by (a) the marking(s) on the verb, (b) the use of the modal auxiliaries, and (c) a combination of both (a) and (b). Moods such as indicative, conditional, imperative, optative, intentional, debitative, etc., express conditions as well as goal(s) of the action (expressed by the verb).

2.1.3.4.1 *Indicative*

Indicative is the unmarked mood which is a statement of fact (at least from the perspective of the speaker).

(1241)	te	amrāwatīlā	gele
	they	Amravati-dat	go-pst-3pl.m

'They went to Amravati.'

2.1.3.4.2 *Conditional*

Conditional is expressed by (a) the present tense form of the verb *-asṇe* 'to be'; and (b) *-asṇe* 'to be' marked with *-lā* (and its variants). While the form in (a) refers to the condition in the past, the form in (b) refers to the condition in the future. In both cases the main verb precedes the auxiliary *-as ṇe* and can occur in the perfect, imperfect, progressive, perfective participle, and potential aspect. The following examples (1242a) and (1242b) of the verb *śikṇe* 'to learn/to study' illustrates those forms.

(1242a)	Past conditional perfect	śiklā astā
	Past conditional imperfect progressive	śikat astā
	Past conditional perfect participle	śiklelā astā
	Past conditional potential	śikṇār astā
(1242b)	Conditional perfect	śiklā aslā
	Conditional imperfect progressive	śikat aslā
	Conditional perfect participle	śiklelā aslā
	Conditional potential	śikṇār aslā

It should be noted here that the form *-aslā* in (1242b) may be replaced by the future tense form *asel* of the verb *asṇe* 'to be'. In all four cases, the meaning expressed by the conditional clause is 'If the condition expressed in the conditional clause is met, then the action in the following clause is likely but not certain to happen.' (For illustrations see section 1.1.2.4.2.5.1.)

2.1.3.4.3 *Imperative*

The use of the imperative is discussed in sections 1.1.1.3 and sub-sections thereof. The first person and the third person imperative are discussed in section 2.1.3.4.4 on subjunctive/optative.

The second person, singular imperative form of the verb is the same as the stem. However, the rising intonation of the imperative distinguishes it from the stem. The plural as well as polite (second person) forms are marked by the suffix *-ā* , which follows the stem as shown in (1243) below.

(1243)

	verb stem/ imperative singular		plural/polite imperative plural
(a)	kar	'do'	karā
(b)	ho	'be'	whā
(c)	toḍ	'break'	toḍā
(d)	ye	'come'	yā
(e)	ghe	'take'	ghyā
(f)	dzā	'go'	dzā

In (1243), (a) and (c) are consonant-ending stems while (d) - (f) are vowel-ending stems. While *-ā* ending stems such as *dzā* in (f) do not change their form in the plural, *-e* ending stems in (d) and (e) undergo phonological changes when they are followed by the plural/polite suffix *-ā*.

In order to express a higher degree of politeness, optative forms are substituted for plural forms as in (1244).

(1244)

	plural/polite		optative/extra polite
(a)	karā	'please do'	karāwe
(b)	whā	'please be'	whāwe
(c)	toḍā	'please break'	toḍāwe
(d)	yā	'please come'	yāwe
(e)	ghyā	'please take'	ghyāwe
(f)	dzā	'please go'	dzāwe

2.1.3.4.4 *Subjunctive/optative*

The subjunctive, which is also called optative, or hortative, is used to express suggestion, demand, and obligation. It is formed by adding the suffix *-wa* (and its variants) to the verb stem (for further discussion, see Pandharipande 1990b).

Suggestion/demand:

(1245)	tyāne	ātā	gharī	dzāwe
	he-ag	now	home-loc	go-opt-3sn

'He may go home now.'

Obligation:

(1246)	mulānnī	āīwaḍilānnā	sāmbhāḷāwa
	children-ag	mother-father-acc-pl	take care-3sn

'Children should take care of their parents.'

Additionally, the optative is used to express a strong wish (e.g., blessing or curse, etc.). In this case, the verb is marked with the suffix *-o* immediately following the verb stem as in (1247) and (1248) below.

Blessing:

(1247)	mulā,	tudʒhī	bharbharāṭ	howo
	child,	you-poss-3sf	prosperity–3sf	happen-opt-3s

'Child, may you be prosperous!' (lit: 'Child, may your prosperity happen!')

Curse:

(1248)	tudzhā	satyānāś	howo
	you-poss	destruction-3sm	happen-3sm

'May you perish.' (lit: 'May your destruction happen.')

2.1.3.4.5 *Intentive*

There is no morphologically distinct suffix to express the intentive. However, the subjunctive/optative (cf. 2.1.3.4.4) and indicative (cf. 2.1.3.4.1) are often used to express intentionality. Additionally, verbs such as *witSār asṇe* or *irādā asṇe* 'to have intention' are used to express intention as in (1249). The verb in this case is in the infinitive form followed by the possessive suffix.

(1249)	ādz	dupārī	mādzhā	dzhopṇyātsā
	today	afternoon-be	I-poss-3sm	sleep-inf-poss-3sm

	witSār/irādā	āhe
	intention-3sm/intention-3sm	is

'Today, I intend to sleep in the afternoon.'

2.1.3.4.6 *Debitive*

Obligation is expressed by the use of modal verbs. There is a hierarchy of degree of obligation as shown below:

lower ↓	(a) verb - inf - poss + *as*
	(b) verb - dat + *hawa*
	(c) verb - pst-3sn + *pāhidʒe*
higher	(d) verb - opt + *lāg*

Since (a) indicates internal compulsion, therefore it is viewed as the lowest on the hierarchy of obligation (since it is interpreted as closest to the intention of the agent and least burdensome).

In contrast to (a), (b) and (c) are stronger in terms of the obligational force. These are neutral regarding internal vs. external compulsion; rather, they mean 'it is necessary to perform the action'. The construction in (d) indicates the strongest obligation and clearly indicates external compulsion. The meaning conveyed by this construction can be paraphrased in English as, 'I will have to do X even if I do not want to.' Consider the following examples (1250) - (1252), which illustrate (a) - (c) respectively.

(1250)	malā	bhāratālā	dzāytsa	āhe
	I-dat	India-dat	go-inf-poss	is

'I need to go to India.' (also, 'I do want to go to India.')

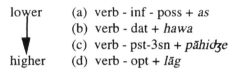

(1251a)	malā	bhāratālā	dzāylā hawa	
	I-dat	India-dat	go-inf-dat	should

'I should go to India.' (or, 'It is necessary for me to go to India.')

(1251b)	malā	bhāratālā	gela	pāhidʒe
	I-dat	India-dat	go-pst-3sn	should

'I should go to India.' (or, 'It is necessary for me to go to India.').

(1252)	malā	bhāratālā	dzāwa	lāgel
	I-dat	India-dat	go-opt-3sn	must-fut-3s

'I will have to go to India (i.e., even if I do not want to go).'

2.1.3.4.7 *Potential*

Potential is expressed in various ways by using auxiliaries as well as suffixes. Inherent ability is distinguished from acquired ability. Similarly, ability/inability determined by agent-internal factors is distinguished from that determined by external/situational factors.

The modal *śak-ṇe* 'can/able to' expresses the ability of a person to perform the action expressed by the main verb (1253a-1253d). It is neutral regarding the factors which determine ability. Ability acquired after a lot of effort is expressed by the auxiliary verb *dzam-ṇe* which follows the main verb (1254). Learned ability is expressed by the auxiliary *ye-ṇe* 'to come' which follows the main verb (1255). The passive construction is used to express ability determined by agent-internal factors (see section 2.1.3.1.1 - 2.1.3.1.1.1.3). The suffix *-aw*, when added to the main verb, expresses ability of the agent determined by agent-internal factors. The agent in this case is typically followed by either the instrumental case-marker *-ne* or the dative case-marker *-lā* (1256). Examples are given below.

verb stem + *ū* + śak:

śak-ṇe 'can/able to' - inherent ability:

(1253a)	to	te	dzaḍ	bhāṇḍa	utslū	śakto
	he	that-3sn	heavy	pot-3sn	lift	can-pres-3sm

'He can lift that heavy pot.'

śak-ṇe 'can/able to' - acquired ability:

(1253b)	to	bāŋgālī	bolū	śakto
	he	Bengali	speak	can-pres-3sm

'He can speak Bengali.'

śak-ṇe 'can/able to' - ability determined by agent-external factors:

(1253c)	ādz	sakāḷī	apghātāt	sāpaḍlyāmuḷe
	today	morning-loc	accident-loc	get caught-ger-because of

tī	kāmāwar	yeū	śaklī	nāhī
she	work-on	come	can-pst-3sf	not

'She could not come to work today because she got into an accident (or, got caught in an accident)'

śak-ṇe 'can/able to' - ability determined by agent-internal factors:

(1253d)	mādzha	ḍoka	dukhat	aslyāmuḷe
	my-3sn	head-3sn	hurt-prog	be-ger-because of

mī	abhyās	karū	śaklo	nāhī
I	study-3sm	do	can-pst-3sm	neg

'I could not study because I had a headache (lit: 'My head was hurting.').'

dzam-ṇe 'to be able to' - ability acquired after a lot of effort:

(1254)	don	warṣānnī	śewṭī	{ tyātsa / his-3sn // tyālā / he-dat }
	two	years-after	finally	

itha	{ yeṇa / come-inf-3sn / yāylā / come-inf-dat }	dzamla
here		able to-pst-3sn

'After two years, finally he could come here/managed to come here.'

verb stem + *tā* + *ye-ṇe* 'to come' - learned ability:

(1255) tilā ingradʒī boltā yeta
she-dat English-3sn speak come-pres-3sn

'She knows how to speak English' (i.e., she has native/native-like competence in English.)

verb stem + (causative) suffix *-ā* / *-aw* - ability determined by agent-internal conditions:

(1256) alikaḍe mhātārpaṇāmuḷe titSyāne/tilā
these days old age-because of she-inst/she-dat

bharbhar tsālwāt nāhī
fast walk-able to neg

'Nowadays/these days she cannot walk fast due to (her) old age.'

2.1.3.4.7 - 2.1.3.4.7.1 *Potential and permission*

The modal *śak-ṇe* 'can/able to' is always used with the potential form of the main verb (see example (1253a) - 1253d)). When *śak-ṇe* is inflected for the present tense, it can be ambiguous between a potential and permissive reading.

(1257) andʒū ātā gharī dzāū śakte
Anju now home-loc go can-pres-3sf

'Anju can go home now.'

2.1.3.4.8 *Degree of certainty*

Degree of certainty is expressed by the use of adverbs (*nakkī* 'definitely/certainly', *agdi* 'surely, *dzarūr* 'decidedly'), the emphatic particle *-ts* immediately following the verb form (with tense and aspectual markers), as well as by auxiliaries with various aspectual markers. The adverbs and the emphatic particle express a higher degree of certainty compared to that expressed by the auxiliaries with aspectual markers. The auxiliaries with different aspectual markers express varying degrees of certainty—the auxiliary *asṇe* 'to be' with the perfective aspect expresses the highest degree of certainty without relying on adverbs or the emphatic particle. The next form in degree of certainty is the "presumptive" *-as* used with the future tense marker. Even less certain is the assertion formed with the auxiliary *-as* with the optative marker. The auxiliary in all of the above three cases immediately follows the main verb. Again, in all of these cases, the main verb in the perfective form expresses a higher degree of certainty than the main verb in the non-perfective form. Consider the following examples of varying degrees of certainty expressed by auxiliaries with various aspectual markers.

present perfective:

(1258)	tyāne	kām	kela	āhe
	he-ag	work	do-perf-3sn	is-3s

'He has done the work.'

In this sentence the perfective/past form *kela* 'did' can be replaced by the perfective participle form *kelela* 'done (3sn)'.

perfective + *as* + future:

(1259)	tyāne	kām	kela	asel
	he-ag	work	do-perf–3sn	be-fut-3s

'He must have done the work.'

perfective + *as* + optative:

(1260)	tyāne	kām	kela	asāwa
	he-ag	work	do-perf-3sn	be-opt

'He might have done the work.'

In general, perfective aspect markers convey a higher degree of certainty compared to non-perfective markers. Thus in the above examples, if the perfective form of the verb is replaced by its non-perfective form, the degree of certainty is lowered.

2.1.3.4.9 *Authority for assertion*

In order to negate any responsibility for the truth-value of a statement, the speaker generally embeds the statement under a matrix sentence such as *malā asa wāṭta kī* 'I feel that. . .', *asa ɛkiwāt āhe kī,* '(They) say that . . .'. In contrast to this, the speaker asserts his/her authority for assertion by explicitly pointing out his/her authoritative (social, professional) position vis-a-vis the hearer. The following examples illustrate this point.

(1261) mī, tuʤhī āī tulā sāŋte
I your mother you-dat tell-prog

āhe kī . . .
be-1s that

'I, your mother, am telling you that. . .'

(1262) mī, tudzhā ḍɔkṭar mhaṇto kī
I your doctor say-pres-3sm that . . .

'I, your doctor, say that. . .'

Additionally, authority for assertion is also expressed by using warning expressions such as *khabardār* 'beware', or the imperative second person singular form preceded by the main verb in the conjunctive participial form and the conditional particle *tar.*

(1263) khabardar titha gelās tar . . .
beware there go-cond if

'Beware, if you go there. . .'

(1264) titha dzāūn tar bagh
there go-conj.part if see-imp-2s

'Go there, and see . . .!'

2.1.3.4.10 *Hortatory*

A discussion on the hortatory (encouraging or suggesting someone to perform actions) has been presented in section 2.1.3.4.4.

2.1.3.4.11 *Monitory*

Monitory mood (for giving warnings) is expressed by (a) using the expression illustrated in (1263), (b) using the emphatic particle *-ts* following the verb (with tense and aspectual markers), followed by one of the auxiliary verbs *pāhidʒe* 'should' (invariant form) or *hawa* (and its variant forms) 'should' (1265 and 1266), (c) using the reduplicated forms of the imperative (1267), and (d) using the "frozen" (invariant) warning expressions *bara* (lit: 'O.K.'), *pāhū* (lit: 'let us see'), *baghū* (lit: 'let us see') immediately following the main verb (1268).

pāhidʒe 'should':

(1265)	tū	śikāgolā	gelats	pāhidʒe
	you	Chicago-dat	go-pst-3sn-emph	should

'You must (i.e., you have no choice) go to Chicago.'

hawa 'should':

(1266)	tulā	śikāgolā	dzāylāts	hawa
	you-dat	Chicago-dat	go-inf-emph	should

'You must go to Chicago.'

reduplication of the imperative form:

(1267)	dzā,	dzā	ātā
	go-imp-2s	go-imp-2s	now

'Go, go now!'

warning expressions:

(1268)	ātā	tū	dzā	bara/pāhū/baghū
	now	you	go–imp-2s	better!

'Now you better go!'

Note that the verbs *pāhidʒe* and *hawa* express a higher degree of compulsion with the emphatic particle *-ts* added to the main verb. Therefore, these verbs are translated in English as 'must' and not as 'should'.

2.1.3.4.12-13 *Narrative and consecutive*

There are no separate morphological suffixes for expressing these moods.

2.1.3.4.14 *Contingent*

The contingent is expresed by (i) the optative or by (ii) the future tense form of the auxilliary verb *asṇe* 'to be'. The aspect, in this case, is expressed by the aspect marker on the main verb, which immediately precedes the main verb, which in turn immediately precedes the auxilliary. The examples of (i) and (ii) are given below.

Optative:

(1269)	tyāne	udyāparyānta	kām	sampawāwa
	he-ag	tomorrow-by	work-3sn	finish-opt

'He may finish the work by tomorrow.'

Future:

(1270)	to	ātā	gharūn	nighālā	asel
	he	now	hom-from	leave-perf -3sm	be-fut-3s

'He must have left home by now.'

Note that the main verb has the perfective marker *-l* (*nighālā*). The following example shows the present marker on the verb.

(1271)	to	ātā	gharūn	nighat	asel
	he	now	home-from	leave-pres	be-fut-3s

'He must be leaving home now.'

The optative construction indicates lower degree of certainty/possibility of action compared to the future construction.

2.1.3.5 *Finite and nonfinite forms*

Marathi makes a clear distinction between finite and nonfinite forms. Finite forms can be used independently as the main verb in a simple or complex sentence as well as in embedded clauses. Nonfinite forms are used only in subordinate clauses (with the exception of the past participial form, which can be used as the main verb in spoken/colloquial Marathi of Bombay (for example, in the sentence *mī te ghar pāhilela* (past participle-3sn) meaning 'I have seen that house', the auxiliary verb *āhe* is deleted.)). The derived nonfinite forms are infinitives, gerunds, and participles. Infinitives and gerunds are not inflected for tense, voice, aspect, mood, etc. However, the participles (present, past, and future) maintain their aspectual reference. The finite forms have already been discussed in detail in the previous chapter. The derivations of nonfinite forms are illustrated below.

2.1.3.5.1 *Infinitive*

Infinitive forms are derived by adding the suffix *-ṇa/-ṇe* to the stem. The derived form is treated as a noun and takes the full range of case suffixes and postpositions. The complete paradigm is given below. When case-suffixes/postpositions are added, the infinitive forms, similar to noun stems, change to their oblique forms (i.e., *dzāṇa/dzāṇe* (direct) —> *dzāṇyā* (oblique)) except in the dative where *ṇ* and the final *-ā* of the oblique infinitive are omitted. This omission is obligatory in the dative while it is optional in the genitive.

(1272) *dzā* 'to go'
Infinitive - *dzāṇa* 'the action of going'

	(a) case-forms	(b) postpositions
nom	dzāṇa/dzāṇe	dzāṇyā-sāṭhī 'for the purpose of going'
acc	dzāṇa/dzāṇe	dzāṇyā-baddal 'about going'
inst	dzāṇyā-ne	
dat	dzāy-lā	
abl	dzāṇyā-hūn	
poss/gen	dzāṇyā-tsa	
loc	dzāṇyāt	

The infinitive is used in purpose clauses and modals (obligatives, capabilities, desideratives).

2.1.3.5.2 *Gerund*

Gerunds are formed by adding the suffix *-yā* 'to the perfective/past tense form of the verb. There are no gerunds in the nonperfective forms. The gerunds are used in complementation and with postpositions. Examples are given below.

(1273)	*bas-ṇe*	'to sit'
	bas-lyā	'sitting'
	sit-perf-ger	
(1273a)	baslyā-barobar	'as soon as sitting took place'
	sit-perf-ger-pp	
(1273b)	baslyā-baddal	'about sitting'
	sit-perf-ger-pp	

Gerunds are used as subordinate clauses and require their subject/agent to be deleted under identity with the subject/agent of the matrix clause. If the subject/agent of the matrix clause is not identical to that of the gerund, the subject/agent of the latter is not deleted. Gerunds are used to express time (as in 1273a) or a condition, as in (1274), or the manner adverbial meaning as in (1275) below.

(1274)	to	ālyās	malā	sāŋg
	he	come-ger-cond	I-dat	tell-imp-2s

'If he comes, inform me.'

(1275)	tī	bitShānyāwar	paḍlyā	paḍlyā
	she	bed-on	lie-ger	lie-ger
	wātsat	hotī		
	read-prog	was		

'She was reading (while) lying in bed.'

2.1.3.5.2.1 *Relative participles*

Marathi has a large range of relative participles (past, present, and future; see section 1.1.2.2.6 for details) which are typically formed by adding *-l* (past) *-ta* , *-ṇārā* (present), and *-ṇār as* (future). The participles function as adjectives. They agree with the noun which they modify in gender and number and express tense/aspect, and voice distinction. These are used as subordinate clauses except for the past participle, which can be used as the main verb in spoken/colloquial Marathi in Bombay as exemplified in (1276).

(1276)	mī	te	ghar	baghitlela
	I	that	house-3sn	see-pst.part-3sn

'I have seen that house.'

In cases such as (1276), the auxiliary *āhe* 'is' (which follows the participles in Standard Marathi) is absent. However, the meaning of the present perfect (as indicated by the English translation) is still maintained. This use of the participle as main verb is not found in any other variety of Marathi.

2.1.3.5.2.2 *Adverbial participles*

Similar to the adjectival participles discussed in the previous section, adverbial participles are formed by adding *tān(n)ā-tāts* to the verb stem. They express aspect, tense and voice distinctions. They are used in subordinate clauses to indicate time, manner, and conditional meaning. (For details, see sections 1.1.2.4.2.1-5).

2.1.3.5.2.3 *Conjunctive/absolutive participles*

Conjunctive/absolutive participles are discussed in detail in section 1.1.2.4.2.1.2. These are formed by adding *-ūn* to the verb stem and are used to express a temporal sequence of actions in which all except the last are indicated by conjunctive/absolutive participles. Additionally, they are used in compound verbs where the main verb is in the conjunctive/absolutive participle form. As indicated earlier (cf. 1.1.2.4.2.1.2), the conjunctive participles are always used in subordinate clauses. Generally, the subject/agent of the conjunctive participle is identical or coreferential to the subject/agent of the matrix clause and is obligatorily deleted. However, there are cases where a causal relation between the two agents is to be emphasized, and the agents of the matrix and the participial clauses can be different and are maintained in the complex sentence. Consider the example given below.

(1277)	pāūs	paḍūn	dhānya	pikla
	rain	fall-conj.part	crop-3sn	grow-pst-3sn

'The rain having fallen, the crop grew.' (i.e., The crop grew (well) due to the rainfall.)

(For further details on conjunctive participles, see Pandharipande 1993).

2.1.3.5.2.4 *Agentive participle*

The agentive participle is formed by adding the marker *-wālā* to the noun. The derived possessive adjective agrees with the noun in gender, and number (see sections 2.1.1.4.5 and 2.2.3.5).

2.1.3.6 *Agreement*

2.1.3.6.1-2 *Categories which must / may be coded in the verb*

In general, subjects must be encoded in the verb by means of gender, number, and person suffixes. If the subject is marked with a postposition, the direct object becomes a candidate for verb agreement (cf. 1.2.1.2.1, 2.1.1.2.2, and 2.1.3.2.1.3 - 2.1.3.2.1.3.2). If the direct object is also followed by a postposition, the verb does not agree with any element in the sentence. In this case, it takes the neuter, third person, singular marking, i.e., the default agreement. The case-markers (instrumental, dative, ablative, possessive, and locative) on the subject block the verb's agreement with it. The so-called "ergative"/agentive postposition (in the perfective, optative, and obligative) following the third person agent, blocks verb agreement (see sections 1.1.1.3.1.1.2 and 1.1.1.3.1.1.4) (for exceptions see section 2.1.3.6.3).

2.1.3.6.3 *Conditioning factors*

(a) Factors such as word order and topic-comment, etc. do not affect verb agreement. (b) Omission of the subject (or object) generally does not affect verb agreement. However, with verbs such as *dʒīŋk ṇe* 'to win, *har-ṇe* 'to be defeated', *khā̃-ṇe* 'to eat', omission of the object (as in (1278)) affects verb agreement as shown in the following examples.

(1278)	mī	ek	tāsāpūrwī	khālla
	I	one	hour-before	eat-pst-3sn

'I ate an hour ago.'

(1279)	mī	ek	tāsāpūrwī	ā̃mbā	khāllā
	I	one	hour-before	mango-3sm	eat-pst-3sm

'I ate a mango an hour ago.'

(c) The use of plural agreement with singular subjects indicates respect toward the subject. (d) Definiteness and animacy together with the semantic categorizatiin of the verb play an important role in the selection of the postposition of the direct object (see sections 2.1.1.2.4 and 2.1.1.10 - 2.1.1.10.6). (e) In the so-called "ergative" constructions, the verb does not agree with the subject/agent despite the fact the subject/agent is not followed by the ergative/agentive postposition *-ne*. Instead, the verb agrees with the object. Also it has already been shown (see section 2.1.3.2.1.3 - 2.1.3.2.1.3.2) that in the variety of Marathi spoken around Puṇe, the second person (verb) agreement marker (which indicates agreement with the object) is accompanied by the additional subject agreement markers *-s* (second person, singular) and *-t* (second person plural). (f) The status of the statement (e.g., direct assertion vs. indirect "hearsay") is also indicated by the use of agreement markers. (see section 2.1.3.4.9)

2.1.3.6.4 *Features of subject coded in verb*

The person, number and gender of the subject are coded in the verb. Gender distinction is not coded in the future tense, imperative, or optative agreement markers.

2.1.3.6.5 *Effect on coding of incompatible features*

2.1.3.6.5.1 *Discrepancies between syntactic and semantic features*

Discrepancies between syntactic and semantic features which might affect verb agreement are usually not allowed. The exceptions are noted below:

(a) Experiencer (dative), passive, and "ergative" subjects, which are logical subjects, do not control verb agreement.

(1280)	tyālā	ghar	āwaḍla
	he-dat	house-3sn	like-past-3sn

'He liked the house.'

(1281)	tyāntSyā	kaḍūn	sagḷī	patra
	they	by	all	letter-3pl.n
	pāṭhawlī	gelī		
	send-pst-3pl.n	go-pst-3pl.n		

'All letters were sent by them.'

Although the dative, passive, and ergative agents/subjects do not control verb agreement, other processes such as reflexivization are clearly controlled by these subjects and thereby express subject properties (for a detailed discussion on the subject properties, see Pandharipande 1981a).

(b) In a coordinate noun phrase, the verb agrees in gender and number with the nearest noun, regardless of the gender and number of the other noun. Consider the following examples.

(1282)	ek	mulgā	āṇī	ek	mulgī	ālī
	one	boy	and	one	girl	come-pst-3sf

'One boy and one girl came.'

(1283)	tSār	puruṣ	āṇi	don	bāykā	titha	hotyā
	four	men	and	two	women	there	were-3pl.f

'Four men and two women were there.'

2.1.3.6.6 *Environment in which there is no verb agreement*

When the subject and the object are both followed by a postposition or a case-marker, there is no verb agreement. In such cases, the verb remains in its unmarked form (i.e., third person, singular, neuter). Non-finite verb forms (infinitives, gerunds, etc.) do not agree with either the subject or with the object of the subordinate clause.

2.1.3.6.7 *Identity between subjects of different verbs*

No specific marker is used to express identity between the subjects of different verbs. However, when two verbs or clauses with agents are connected with participles, the participial form of the verb is used only if its subject is identical to the subject of the matrix sentence (see section 1.1.2.4.2.1.2). In this case, the subject of the participle is obligatorily absent. If the subjects of the nonfinite and matrix verbs are not identical, both are obligatorily retained.

(1284)	ø	ʤewūn	to	gharī	gelā
		eat-conj.part	he	home-loc	go-pst-3sm

'Having eaten, he went home.'

(1285)	anū	gharī	ālyāwar	mī	dzhople
	Anu	home-loc	come-ger-on	I	sleep-pst-3sf

'I went home to sleep after Anu came home.'

Another case where the identity of the subject of a verb and that of a preceding verb is implied is the infinitival construction. When the main verbs of certain clauses which express an attempt, wish, want, etc. occur as finite verbs in sentences with subordinate clauses, the subjects of the two clauses must be identical, and the verb in the subordinate clause is changed into an infinitive. In this case, the subject of the subordinate clause is obligatorily deleted.

(1286)	amit	anūlā	bheṭāylā	gelā
	Amit	Anu-dat	meet-inf-dat	go-pst-3sm

'Amit went to see Anu.'

2.1.3.6.8-9 *Reflexive form of the verb*

There is no morphologically distinct reflexive or reciprocal form of the verb. For means of expressing reflexivity or reciprocity, see section 1.5.1.4 and sub-sections thereof.

2.1.3.6.10 *Orientation of actions and incorporation*

There is no special morphological form of the verb to indicate actions oriented toward the speaker. There is no incorporation of nouns, adjectives, or any other category in the verb. The use of the explicator verb *ye-ṇe* 'to come' and *dzā ṇe* 'to go' in the compound verb construction express the notions "toward" and "away" from the speaker respectively.

2.1.3.7 *Change or loss of features in a string of verbs*

In compound verbs, tense, mood, and aspectual information is attached to the explicator rather than to the main verb (see sections 2.1.3.3.2.1.1 - 2.1.3.3.2.1.1.6 and 2.2.6.3.4.2).

2.1.4 ADJECTIVES

There are three major types of adjectives: (a) Simple Adjectives such as *sũndar* 'beautiful', *niḷā* 'blue', *moṭhā* 'big', etc., (b) Derived Adjectives (see sections 2.2.3 - 2.2.3.5) which are derived from nouns and adverbs, such as the following.

(1287)	Nouns	Adjectives
	a) buddhī 'intelligence'	buddhi-mān/buddhi-wān 'intelligence'
	b) puruṣ 'man'	puruṣ-ī 'masculine'
	c) lādz 'shyness'	lādzā-ḷū 'shy'
	d) madʒā 'enjoyment'	madʒe-dār 'interesting
	e) himmat 'courage'	himmat-wālā 'courageous'
	Adverbs	Adjectives
	f) mãnda 'slow'	mãnda 'slow'
	g) dzawaḷ 'near'	dzawaḷ-tsā 'close'
	h) āt 'inside'	āt-lā 'the one who/which is inside'

(c) Participial Adjectives: Participial adjectives are derived by adding suffixes to verbs. Marathi has a large range of participles (see section 1.1.2.2.6 - 1.1.2.2.6.7) which are distinguished according to aspect and tense. Some examples are *gelelā* '(the one who has) gone', *tsālat aslelā* '(progressive) '(the one who is) walking', *dzāṇār aslelā* (future) '(one who is) going to go'. Participles can be used attributively as well as predicatively, with no morphological distinction between the two.

Adjectives can be vowel-ending or consonant-ending. Except for the *-ā*-ending adjectives, all adjectives remain in their invariable form. Thus, with respect to agreement (with a noun), adjectives can be divided into two groups, *-ā* ending and those which do not end in *-ā*. A sample of the inflected forms of the *-ā* ending adjectives is given below.

(1288)

Case	I Masculine		II Feminine	
	Singular	Plural	Singular	Plural
Direct	moṭhā	moṭhe	moṭhī	moṭhyā
Oblique	moṭhyā	moṭhyā	moṭhyā	moṭhyā

	III Neuter	
	Singular	Plural
Direct	moṭha	moṭhī
Oblique	moṭhyā	moṭhyā

No other factors such as the deletion of a noun or the position of a noun influence the agreement of adjectives with nouns. The ordinals, participles (both past and present), possessive nouns, and the particle *wālā*, which end in *-ā*, behave like adjectives ending in *-ā*, i.e., they agree with the following nouns (for further details, see section 1.1.2.2.6 - 1.1.2.2.6.7, 2.1.6.2, 2.1.6.4-5, 2.2.3.3, and 2.2.3.5).

There are no native Marathi suffixes which mark comparative adjectives. The Sanskrit comparative suffixes *-tara* (comparative), and *-tama* (superlative) are added to Sanskrit adjectives which are retained in Marathi. Some examples are given below.

(1289)	laghu	'small'
	laghu-tar(a)	'smaller'
	laghu-tam(a)	'smallest'

Adverbs of degree such as *khūp* 'very', *thoḍa* 'little' are used to indicate the degree of the adjectives such as *lahān* 'small', *lā̃mb* 'long', etc. (For further details, see section 1.2.2.3).

2.1.5 -2.1.5.4 POSTPOSITIONS

Postpositions are discussed in detail in sections 1.2.4 - 1.2.4.3.5, and 2.1.1.1. Marathi does not have prepositions. Postpositions are generally invariable. However, some postpositions/ suffixes are exceptions. For example, the possessive/genitive postposition/suffix *-tSā* agrees with the following noun in gender and number. (See section 2.1.1.4.6 - 2.1.1.4.6.3) Similarly, the postposition *(-tSyā) sārkhā* 'similar to' also agrees with the following noun. Postpositions are neither combined with personal pronouns nor with articles to form series of personal forms or postpositional articles. Simple, as well as compound, postpositions are found in Marathi (For details, see sections 2.2.6.1-2).

2.1.6 NUMERALS/QUANTIFIERS

2.1.6.1 *Forms of numerals*

The cardinal numerals are as follows.

1	ek	11	akrā
2	don	12	bārā
3	tīn	13	terā
4	tSār	14	tsaudā
5	pāts	15	pandhrā
6	sahā	16	soḷā
7	sāt	17	satrā
8	āṭh	18	aṭhrā
9	naū	19	ekoṇīs
10	dahā	20	wīs
21	ekwīs	31	ektīs
22	bāwīs	32	battīs
23	tewīs	33	tehtīs

24	tSowīs	34	tsautīs
25	pañtSwīs	35	pastīs
26	sawwīs	36	tShattīs
27	sattāwīs	37	sadotīs/sadatīs
28	aṭṭhāwīs	38	aḍhotīs/aḍhtīs
29	ekoṇtīs	39	ekoṇtSāḷīs
30	tīs	40	tSāḷīs
41	ekketSyāḷīs	51	ekkāwan
42	betSāḷīs	52	bāwan
43	tretSāḷīs	53	trepan
44	tsauretSāḷīs	54	tSaupan
45	pañtsetSāḷīs	55	pāntsāwan
46	śehetSāḷīs	56	tShappan
47	sattetSāḷīs	57	sattāwan
48	aṭṭhetSāḷīs	58	aṭṭhāwan
49	ekoṇpannās	59	ekoṇsāṭh
50	pannās	60	sāṭh
61	eksaṣṭ(a)	71	ekāhattar
62	bāsaṣṭ(a)	72	bāhattar
63	treaṣṭ(a)	73	tryāhattar
64	tsausaṣṭ(a)	74	tsauryāhattar
65	pāsaṣṭ(a)	75	pañtSyāhattar
66	sahāsaṣṭ(a)	76	śahāttar
67	sadusaṣṭ(a)	77	sattyāhattar
68	aḍhusaṣṭ(a)	78	aṭṭhyāhattar
69	ekoṇsattar	79	ekoṇainśī
70	sattar	80	ainśī
81	ekyānśī	91	ekyāṇṇaw
82	byānśī	92	byāṇṇaw
83	tyānśī	93	tyāṇṇaw
84	tsauryānśī	94	tsauryāṇṇaw
85	pañtSyānśī	95	pañtSyāṇṇaw
86	śahyānśī	96	śahāṇṇaw
87	sattyānśī	97	sattyāṇṇaw
88	aṭṭhyānśī	98	aṭṭhhyāṇṇaw
89	ekoṇnawwad	99	nawhyāṇṇaw
90	nawwad	100	śāmbhar

100 up to 1000:

200	donśe	600	sahāśe
300	tīnśe	700	sātśe
400	tSārśe	800	āṭhśe
500	pātsśe	900	naūśe
		1000	hadzār

1000 up to 100,000,000:

2000	don hadzār	20,000	wīs hadzār
3000	tīn hadzār	30,000	tīs hadzār
4000	tSār hadzār	40,000	tSāḷīs hadzār
5000	pāts hadzār	50,000	pannās hadzār
6000	sahā hadzār	60,000	sāṭh hadzār
7000	sāt hadzār	70,000	sattar hadzār
8000	āṭh hadzār	80,000	ainśī hadzār
9000	naū hadzār	90,000	nawwad hadzār
10,000	dahā hadzār	100,000	lākh

100,000 up to 10,000,000:

1,000,000		dahā lākh
2,000,000		wīs lākh
etc.		
10,000,000		karoḍ/koṭī
10 karoḍ/koṭī	=	1 abʤa
10 abʤa	=	1 kharwa
10 kharwa	=	1 nikharwa
10 nikharwa	=	1 mahāpadma
10 mahāpadma	=	1 śāŋku
10 śāŋku	=	1 ʤaladhī
10 ʤaladhī	=	1 āntya
10 āntya	=	1 madhya
10 madhya	=	1 parārdha

It is clear from the list above that the numerals from 11 to 18 are 'n(umeral 1-8) + 10', 19 is twenty minus one. Multiples of 10 from 20 to 90 are 'n(umeral 2-9) x 10'. Multiples of 100 from 100 to 900 are 'n(umeral 2-9) x 100'. Multiples of 1000 are 'n x 1000' and so on.

An example of complex numerals is given below.

(1290)	sawwīs	hadzār	sātśe	bāwīs
	26	1000	7 + 100	2 + 20

'26,722'

In the rural areas of Mahārashtra, people use 20 (wīs) as the base unit of counting. Multiples of 20 are formed by n x 20, *don wīs* = 2 x 20 = 40, *tīn wīs* = 3 x 20 = 60, etc. The remaining numbers are derived either by adding to or subtracting from *wīs*.

(1291)	don	wīs	āṇi	tīn	= 43
	2	20	and	3	

(1292)	tSār	wisālā	ek	kamī	= 79
	4	20-to (dat)	one	less	

As is evident from the above examples, the number to be added is preceded by the conjunction marker *āṇi* 'and' (as in (1291)) which follows the number 20. The number to be subtracted also follows the number 20 (*wīs*) with the dative marker *-lā*. The word *kamī* 'less' follows the number which is subtracted (as in 1292). Thus the whole expression can be paraphrased in English as 'n times 20 plus or minus X'.

2.1.6.2 *Cardinal numerals as attributes*

All the numeral forms given above are used as attributes.

2.1.6.3 *Counting different kinds of objects*

The counting system described above in section 2.1.6.1 is used regardless of the nature of the objects being counted.

2.1.6.4-5 *Ordinal numerals*

The ordinal numerals are: *pahilā* 'first', *dusrā* 'second', *tisrā* 'third', *tsauthā* 'fourth', and *pātswā* 'fifth'. The rest of the numerals including the complex numbers (such as 254) follow the pattern of five, i.e, they are formed by adding the suffix *-wā* to a cardinal number, for example, *donśe tSaupanna* 'two hundred and fifty four' —> *donśe tSaupannāwā* 'two hundred and fifty fourth'. When cardinals are used as attributes, they function as adjectives ending in *-ā,* and agree with the following noun in number and gender.

2.1.6.6 *Quantifiers*

The following quantifiers are used: *kāhī* 'some', *khūp* 'a lot', *thoḍa* 'a little', *dzarāsa* 'a bit', *ʤāsta* 'much', *puṣkaḷ* 'many', *kintSit* 'a little', *sagḷa* 'all/whole', *sarwa* 'all', *pratyek* 'each/every'. Aggregative quantifiers are derived by the addition of the emphatic particle *-hī* to the cardinal numerals:

don + *hī* = *donhī* 'both'
tīṇ + *hī* = *tinhī* 'all three'
tSār + *hī* = *tSārhī* 'all four'
pāts + *hī* = *pātsahī* 'all five'
aṭh + *hī* = *āṭhahī* 'all eight'

Note that the emphatic particle is combined with the cardinal numeral in the case of the numerals 1 through 4. However, starting from the numeral 5, the particle is separated from the numeral stem by inserting the vowel *-a* between the particle and the numeral stem. Negation incorporated particles are not found in Marathi. (For constituent negation, see section 1.4.2). Negative polarity items are formed by suffixing the emphatic particles *-ts* or *hī* to the interrogative pronouns for who, how many/how much, where, and how respectively. When the emphatic particles are used with who (*koṇ*) and where (*kuṭhe*) in negativized sentences, they express the meaning of negative quantifiers. Consider the following examples.

(1293) koṇīts/koṇīhī kuṇits/kuṇihī gela nāhī

who-emph go-pst-3sn neg

'No one went.'

(1294) te kuṭhets/kuṭhehī gele nāhīt
they where-emph go-pst-3pl.m neg-pl

'They did not go anywhere.'

While *koṇ* 'who' and *kuṭhe* 'where' can take *-ts* or *-hī* alternatively, *kitī* 'how many/much' and *kasa* 'how' take only *-hī*. Also, it must be noted that *kitī* and *kasa*, when followed by *-hī* , occur only in subordinate clauses. The meaning expressed by them can be paraphrased in English as 'regardless of /no matter how much . . .' (in the case of *kitī*) and 'regardless of/no matter how . . .' (in the case of *kasa*).

(1295)

mī	kitīhī	sāŋgitla	tarī
I	how much-emph	tell-pst-3sn	even then

tyālā	paṭla	nāhī
he-dat	agree-pst-3sn	neg

'Regardless of how much I told him, he did not agree.'

(1296)

mī	kasahī	kām	kela	tarī
I	how-emph	work	do-pst-3sn	even then

tyālā	te	āwaḍat	nāhī
he-dat	that-3sn	like-pres	neg

'Regardless of how I do the work, he does not like it.'

Other examples of quantifiers are:

(1297)

malā	ṭhoḍīśī	sākhar	de
I-dat	a little bit-3sf	sugar-3sf	give-imp-2s

'Give me a little bit of sugar.'

(1298)

tyātsa	man	khūp	moṭha	āhe
he-poss-3sn	heart	a lot	big	is

'He has a very big heart (i.e., he is a very generous person).'

(1299)

warṇāt	mīṭh	kintSit	kamī	āhe
lentil soup	salt	just a little	less	is

'The salt is just a little bit less (than required) in the lentil soup.'

2.1.6.6.1-2 *Quantifier compounds and other means of quantification*

Quantifiers can be compounded as in the following fashion:
(a) quantifier plus numeral: *dar* 'every' *tīn* 'three' *diwasā̃nnī* 'days after',
(b) quantifier + *tarī*: The quantifer *kā̃hī* 'some' is combined with the suffix *-tarī*, i.e., *kā̃hītarī* 'something' (indefinite). The suffix *-tarī* is used with interrogative pronouns as well, e.g., *koṇītarī* 'someone (indefinite)', *kuṭhetarī* 'somewhere' (indefinite),
(c) relative pronoun plus indefinite pronoun: *dzo* 'who' (relative) + *koṇī* 'someone' = *dzo koṇī* 'whoever',
(d) reduplication: Numerals, quantifiers, indefinite pronouns and nouns undergo the process of reduplication to express sequential, distributive, exhaustive intensified meaning.

Sequential:

(1300)	ek	ek	karūn	sagḷe	nātewāīk
	one	one	do-conj.part	all	relative
	āle				
	come-pst-3pl.m				

'One by one, all of the relatives came.'

Distributive:

(1301)	gharā	gharāt	diwe	dzaḷat
	house	house-loc	lamp-3pl.m	burn-prog
	hote			
	be-pst-3pl			

'Lamps were burning in every house.'

Exhaustive:

(1302)	maṇsā	māṇsālā	hī	bātmī	kaḷlī
	man	man-dat	this	news-3sf	come to know-pst-3sf

'Everyone came to know this news.'

(e) Reduplicated quantifiers with intervening *nā/na* 'neg': The quantifiers *koṇī* 'someone' and *kāhī* 'something' are reduplicated, and the negative particle is inserted between the two, e.g., *koṇī-nā/na koṇī* 'someone or other', *kāhī nā/na kāhī* 'something or other'. Question words such as *kuṭhe* 'where', and *kadhī* 'when' also participate in this construction. e.g., *kuṭhe nā/na kuṭhe* 'somewhere' (i.e., if not here) *kādhī nā/na kadhī* 'some other time' (i.e., if not now). Although a phrase with a reduplicated quantifier/interrogative pronoun expresses indefiniteness/unspecificity, similar to phrases with *-tarī* (see (b) above), these two differ from each other in the degree of certainty, i.e., the phrase in (b) expresses a lower degree of certainty compared to the reduplicated phrase. Thus *koṇītarī* means 'someone' whereas *koṇī-na-koṇī* means 'someone or other'.

2.1.7 - 2.1.7.2.4 ADVERBS

See sections 1.1.2.4, 1.2.1.3 - 1.2.1.3.3, 1.2.3, and 1.2.3.2.

2.1.8 CLITICS AND PARTICLES

There are no clitics in Marathi. Particles are discussed in sections 1.16.7 and 1.11.2.1.2.

2.2 DERIVATIONAL MORPHOLOGY

Affixation (both prefixation and suffixation) is the most productive device in Marathi for word-formation. Derivation takes place by adding affixes to stems or derived stems of major word classes. While the process of suffixation is equally applicable to both nouns and verbs, the process of prefixation is largely restricted to nouns and is very rarely applicable to verbs. In Marathi, the derivational process generally does not affect the transparency of the stem and the suffix/prefix. The derivational history of the word can be traced in a straightforward manner through the sequence of morphemes.

It should be noted here that Marathi has affixes borrowed from Sanskrit and Persian. Although borrowed affixes are largely restricted to vocabulary borrowed from the same language (i.e., Sanskrit prefixes are restricted to Sanskrit nouns, Persian suffixes are restricted to Persian nouns, and so on), there is some crossover as well. (For further discussion, see Pandharipande 1979).

2.2.1 DERIVATION OF NOUNS

2.2.1.1 *Nouns from nouns*

In the following examples, unless otherwise noted, Sanskrit affixes are added to the Sanskrit stems and Persian affixes are added to the Persian stems. The relevant sections in which a given morphophonemic alternation has been explained, are at times indicated in parentheses right after/below the examples.

(i) *-wãnta/wān:*

The Sanskrit suffix *-wãnta/wān* is attached to Sanskrit nouns in order to derive personal nouns expressing the meaning 'one who has X'.

(1303)	buddhī (f) 'intelligence'	buddhiwãnta 'intelligent' buddhiwān (cf. 3.4.1.3.5)
(1304)	witSār (m) 'thought'	witSārwãnta 'thoughtful'
(1305)	bal (n) 'strength'	balawãnta 'strong' balawān

Note that this suffix is added to nouns of all genders. The suffixes *-wãntā* and *-wān* can be replaced by the Sanskrit suffixes *-mãnta,* and *-mān* respectively. These two sets are semantically identical. Although the derived nouns are masculine in Sanskrit, these are gender neutral in Marathi; i.e., they can have masculine, or feminine referents though the verb agrees in gender and number of the actual referent.

(ii) *-ār:*

The suffix *-ār* derives a noun expressing the professional identity of the person related to the noun (to which the suffix is added). According to Damle (1966 [1911]: 520), the suffix *-ār* is the reduced form of the Sanskrit suffix *-kār.*

(1306) kumbha 'pot' (m) kumbhār 'potter'

(1307) loha 'iron' (n) lohār 'blacksmith'

(1308) sona 'gold' (n) sonār 'goldsmith'

For deletion of stem final *a* before the suffix *-ār* in (1306) - (1308), see section 3.4.4.1.2.

(iii) *-āḷū*

Personal nouns are derived by adding the suffix *-āḷū* to abstract nouns.

(1309) krupā/dayā 'mercy/kindness' (f) krupāḷū/dayāḷū 'kind person'

(1310) dzhop 'sleep' (f) dzhopāḷū 'the person who sleeps a lot'

(1311) kaṣṭa 'hardwork' (pl.m) kaṣṭāḷu 'hardworker'

For deletion of stem final *ā* in (1309) and of *a* in (1311), see section 3.4.4.1.3 and 3.4.4.1.2, respectively.

(iv) *-ī:*

The suffix *-ī* can be added to masculine or neuter nouns to derive diminutive feminine nouns.

(1312) ḍabā (m) 'box' ḍabī (f) 'small box'

(1313) pīṭh (n) 'flour' piṭhī (f) 'finely ground flour'

(1314) dāṇḍā (m) 'a big stick' dāṇḍī (f) 'a small stick'

For deletion of stem final *ā* in (1312) and (1314), and for *ī/i* alternation in (1313), see sections 3.4.4.1.3 and 3.4.1.3.1.1 respectively.

(v) *-īṇ:*

The suffix *-īṇ* is added to a masculine noun indicating a profession to derive its feminine counterpart.

(1315) mãstar (m) 'teacher' mãstarīṇ 'female teacher'

(1316) dhobī (m) 'washerman' dhobīṇ 'washerwoman'

See sections 3.4.1.3.1.1 and 3.4.4.1.6 for deletion of stem final *ī* before the suffix in (1316).

(vi) *-ãrī:*

The suffix *-ãrī* is used to derive a noun indicating an action pertaining to the primary noun stem.

(1317) pãn 'belal leaf' pãnãrī 'one who sells belal leaves'

(1318) phũl 'flower' phulãrī 'flower-seller'

(1319) pũdʒã 'worship' pudʒãrī 'worshipper'

See section 3.4.1.3.1.1 for *ũ/u* alternation in (1318) and (1319).

(vii) *-twa:*

-twa is a Sanskrit suffix and is restricted to Sanskrit nouns. It is used to derive an abstract noun.

(1320) pitã (Skt. stem: pitṛ) 'father' pitrutwa 'fatherhood' (M. stem: pitru)

(1321) alpa 'a little' alpatwa 'smallness'

(1322) strī 'woman' strītwa 'womanhood'

(viii) *-ī:*

Suffix *-ī* is added to cardinal numbers to derive abstract nouns.

(1323) *wīs* 'twenty' *wiśī* 'twenty-some years'

(1324) *tSãḷīs* 'forty' *tSãḷiśī* 'forty-some years' or 'reading glasses' (which are generally required at the age of forty)

See section 3.4.1.3.1.1 for *ī/i* alternation in (1323) and (1324).

(ix) *-uklī:*

This suffix derives a feminine diminutive noun from feminine nouns.

(1325) dhanū (f) 'bow' dhanuklī (f) 'small bow'

(1326) tSindhī (f) 'a piece of cloth' tSindhuklī (f) 'a small piece of cloth'

See sections 3.4.1.3.1.1 and 3.4.4.1.6 for deletion of stem final vowels before the suffix in (1325) and (1326). The use of this suffix is restricted to a very small group of nouns.

(x) *-karī:*

The suffix *-karī* is used to derive a personal noun as shown below.

(1327) deṇe 'debt' deṇekarī 'debtor'

(1328) gā̃w 'village' gā̃wkarī 'villager'

(1329) bhāḍe 'rent' bhāḍekarī 'tenant'

(1330) śet 'farm' śetkarī 'farmer'

(xi) *-kī:*

Abstract nouns are derived by adding *-kī* to a noun.

(1331) māṇūs 'human being' māṇuskī 'humanity'

(1332) māstar 'teacher' māstarkī 'teachership'

(1333) sutār 'carpenter' sutārkī 'carpentership'

See section 3.4.1.3.1.1 for *ū/u* alternation in (1331).

(xii) *-ka:*

The suffix derives a diminutive neuter noun from a noun.

(1334) puḍā (m) 'package' puḍka (n) 'small package'

(1335) hoḍī (f) 'boat' hoḍka (n) 'small boat'

(1336)	ḍhol (m) 'drum'	ḍholka (n) 'small drum'

See section 3.4.4.1.3 for deletion of stem final *ā* before the suffix in (1334) and sections 3.4.1.3.1.1 and 3.4.4.1.6 for deletion of stem final *ī* in (1335).

(xiii) *-paṇā*

The suffix *-paṇā* is used to derive abstract nouns from common nouns.

(1337)	tsor	'thief'	tsorpaṇā	'thievery'
(1338)	manuṣya	'human being'	'manuṣyapaṇā 'humanity'	

(xiv) *-dār:*

This suffix is borrowed from Persian, and it derives personal nouns (and adjectives) from common nouns.

(1339)	dzamīn (f) 'land'	dzamindār /dzamīndār	'landlord'
(1340)	abrū (f) 'honor'	abrudār/abrūdār	'honorable

This suffix is added to nouns borrowed from Perso-Arabic sources such as the above, and also to native Marathi nouns.

(xv) *-dān:*

The Persian suffix *-dān* expresses the meaning of 'holder (that which holds)', and derives masculine, neuter (with *dān*) and feminine (with *-dāṇī*) nouns.

(1341)	kalam (f) 'pen'	kalamdān 'penholder'
(1342)	attar (n) 'perfume'	attardāṇī 'perfume bottle'
(1343)	pān (m) 'betal leaf'	pāndān 'the tray which holds *'pān'* and other spices'

(xvi) *-khānā:* 'house'

This Persian suffix denotes the meaning 'house of' and derives masculine nouns, as shown in the following examples:

(1344)	diwāṇ 'sofa' (m)	diwāṇkhānā 'living room'
(1345)	khāṭik 'butcher' (m)	khāṭikkhānā 'butcher's house'

(xvii) *-gār*

The Persian suffix *-gār* derives nouns bearing an agentive relationship to the root nouns. This suffix is restricted to Persian words. The alternation between *-gār* and *-gar* is lexical and not morphophonemic.

(1346)	saudā (m) 'trade'	saudāgar (m) 'trader'
(1347)	gunhā (m) 'crime'	gunhegār 'criminal' (cf. 3.4.3)
(1348)	ʤādū (f) 'magic'	ʤādūgār/ʤādugār 'magician' (cf. 3.4.1.3.1.1)

Prefixes:

(i) *swa-/ātma-* 'self':

These Sanskrit prefixes are added to nouns (mostly Sanskrit).

(1349)	śaktī (f) 'strength'	swaśaktī 'self-strength'
(1350)	rāʤya (n) 'kingdom'	swarāʤya 'self government'
(1351)	wiśwās (m) 'confidence'	ātmawiśwās 'self confidence'
(1352)	hatyā (f) 'killing'	ātmahatyā 'suicide' (lit: 'self-killing')

Although *swa-* and *ātma-* can be used alternatively in the above contexts, their distribution is conventionalized in some cases such as *ātmahatyā* 'suicide' and *swarāʤyā* 'self government'. Therefore, the substitution of *swa-* and *ātma-* (respectively) in these cases will be unconventional, though not ungrammatical.

(ii) *a-/be-* 'absence of/negation':

The prefix *-a* (from Sanskrit) and *-be* (from Persian) are used to derive negative nouns as shown below:

(1353)	dharma (m) 'religion/duty'	adharma (m) 'unrighteousness'
(1354)	nām (m) 'name'	anām (m) 'nameless'
(1355)	ʤñān 'knowledge'	aʤñān 'ignorance'

Sanskrit prefixes are restricted to Sanskrit nouns as shown above. The Persian prefix is restricted to Persian nouns as shown below:

(1356)	adbī (f) respect	beadbī (f) 'disrespect'
(1357)	idzdzat (f) 'honor'	beidzdzat (f) 'dishonor'
(1358)	fikir (f) 'worry'	befikirī (f) 'the state of mind devoid of worry' (*-i* is a nominalizing suffix)

The following Sanskrit prefixes (iii - v) derive the negative counterparts of nouns.

(iii) *apa- :*

(1359)	mān (m) 'honor'	apamān (m) 'insult'
(1360)	śakun (m) 'good omen'	apaśakun (m) 'bad omen'
(1361)	yaś (n) 'victory'	apayaś (n) 'defeat'

(iv) *ku-:*

(1362)	buddhī (f) 'inclination/thought'	kubuddhī (f) 'wrong inclination/thought'
(1363)	karma (n) action	kukarma (n) 'wrong action'

(v) *dur-:*

(1364)	din (m) 'day'	durdin (m) 'bad times'
(1365)	ʤan (pl.m) 'people'	durʤan (pl.m) 'evil people'

Other Sanskrit prefixes are used to derive nouns with a wide variety of meanings as in (vi) - (xiii) below:

(vi) *upa-* 'near', 'sub':

(1366)	kulagurū 'chancellor'	upakulagurū 'vice-chancellor'
(1367)	bhāg (m) 'section'	upabhāg (m) 'sub-section'
(1368)	māntrī 'minister'	upamāntrī 'deputy minister'

(vii) *pra-* 'intensity':

(1369)	śikṣan (n) 'education'	praśikṣan (n) 'special training'
(1370)	bhāw (m) 'emotion'	prabhāw (m) 'effect'
(1371)	gatī (f) 'speed'	pragatī (f) 'progress'

(viii) *su-* 'good':

(1372)	kanyā 'daughter'	sukanyā 'good daughter'
(1373)	lakṣaṇ (n) 'feature/ characteristics	sulakṣaṇ 'positive/ auspicious 'feature'

(ix) *prati-* 'reaction to/reflection of/every'

(1374)	din (m) 'day'	pratidin (m) 'everyday'
(1375)	kriyā (f) 'action'	pratikriyā (f) 'reaction'
(1376)	bimba (n) 'form'	pratibimba (n) 'reflection'

(x) *wi-* 'specific/particular/away'

(1377)	bhāg (m) 'section'	wibhāg (m) 'special section'
(1378)	dʒñān (n) 'knowledge'	widʒñān (m) 'analytical knowledge/science'

(xi) *punar-* 'again':

(1379)	wiwāha (m) 'marriage'	punarwiwāha (m) 'remarriage'
(1380)	dʒanma (m) 'birth'	punardʒanma (m) 'rebirth'

(xii) *sama-* 'equal':

(1381)	druṣṭī (f) 'outlook/view'	samadruṣṭī (f) 'same outlook/view'
(1382)	śaktī (f) 'strength'	samaśaktī (f) 'equal strength'

(xiii) *para-* 'other/for other's'

(1383)	strī 'woman'	parastrī 'someone else's wife'
(1384)	upkār (m) 'good/ virtuous deed'	paropkār (m) 'a good/ virtuous deed for others'

In (1384), the alternation is due to the sandhi rule (i.e., *a* + *u* = *o*) of Sanskrit.

2.2.1.2 *Nouns from verbs*

In the following examples, unless otherwise noted, all affixes and the stems/words to which they are added belong to the native Marathi lexicon. The process of suffixation is very commonly used to derive nouns from verbs. The most productive suffix used is *-ṇe/ṇa* , which is the native Marathi infinitive marker.

(i) *-ṇe/ṇa* infinitive marker:

When the infinitive marker *-ṇe/ṇa* is added to the verb stem, the derived noun is marked for third person neuter, singular.

	Stem	Infinitive Nouns
(1385)	ye 'come'	yeṇe/yeṇa 'arrival'
(1386)	wāts 'read'	wātsṇe/wātsṇa 'reading'
(1387)	dukh 'hurt/pain'	dukhṇe/dukhṇa 'disease/pain'

Pairs of verb stems in their infinitive forms also function as nouns.

deṇa - gheṇa (n) 'obligation' (lit: 'give take')
give-inf take-inf

khāṇa - piṇa (n) 'food and drink'
eat-inf - drink-inf

yeṇa - dzāṇa (n) 'relationship/exchange of visits'
come-inf - go-inf

(ii) *-īkaraṇ:*

The Sanskrit suffix *-īkaraṇ* (originally derived from the Sanskrit verb *kṛ* 'to do') is added to nouns to derive process nouns. This very productive process in Marathi is borrowed from Sanskrit. In the contemporary Marathi, the following nouns in (1388) - (1390) are derived as follows: noun + *ī* + *kar* (Marathi verb 'to do') + *aṇ*.

(1388)	nagar (n) 'city'	nāgarīkaraṇ (n) 'urbanization'
(1389)	brāhmaṇ (m)/'brāhmaṇ'	brāhmaṇīkaraṇ (n) 'Brāhmaṇization'
(1390)	bhārat (m) 'India'	bhāratīkaraṇ (n) 'Indianization'

The vowel alternation in (1388) is due to the *vṛddhi* rule (i.e., a—> ā) of Sanskrit.

(iii) *-aṇ*

The suffix *-aṇ* is added to verb stems to derive abstract or common nouns.

	Stem	Abstract Nouns
Intransitive verbs:		
(1391)	ghaḍ 'shape'/'be designed'	ghaḍaṇ (f) 'shape'
(1392)	tsaḍh 'climb'	tsaḍhaṇ (f)
(1393)	utar 'descend'	utaraṇ (f) 'slope'
(1394)	loḷ 'roll'	loḷaṇ 'rolling'
(1395)	waḷ 'turn'	waḷaṇ 'turn'

Transitive verbs:

(1396)	śimp 'sprinkle'	śimpaṇ (n)	'the process of sprinkling'
(1397)	daḷ 'grind'	daḷaṇ (n)	'that which is to be ground'
(1398)	nāŋgar 'plough'	nāŋgraṇ (n)	'the process of ploughing'
(1399)	ʤew 'eat'	ʤewaṇ (n)	'food/meal'
(1400)	kāṇḍ 'pound'	kāṇḍaṇ	'the material for pounding'
(1401)	bhāṇḍ 'fight'	bhāṇḍaṇ	(n) 'fight'

(iv) zero suffix:

A large number of intransitive and transitive verbal stems yield abstract nouns.

	Stem (intransitive)	*Abstract nouns*
(1402)	pots 'reach'	pots (f) 'extent of reaching'
(1403)	dzā 'go' /ye 'come'	dzā-ye (f) 'traffic'

(1404)	upadz 'grow/sprout'	upadz (f) 'growth'
(1405)	dzhop 'sleep'	dzhop (f) 'sleep'
(1406)	oraḍ 'shout'	oraḍ (f) 'shouting'
	Stem (transitive)	Abstract Noun
(1407)	samadz 'understand'	samadz (f) 'understanding'
(1408)	wisar 'forget'	wisar (f) 'forgetting'
(1409)	ṭhew 'keep'	ṭhew (f) 'item given for keeping'
(1410)	mār 'beat'	mār (m) 'beating'
(1411)	dzāṇ 'know'	dzāṇ (f) 'knowledge'
(1412)	phek 'throw'	phek (f) 'throw'

Pairs of verb stems can also function as nouns. The class of such nouns is restricted to the following pairs:

dhar - soḍ (f) hold leave	'ficklemindedness'
dhāw - paḷ (f) run run away	'hustle bustle'
ye - dzā (f) come go	'traffic'
toḍ - phoḍ (f) break break/crack	'destruction'
paḍ - dzhaḍ (f) fall break	'breaking and falling of trees'
āḍaḷ - āpaṭ (f) drop throw down	'the act of dropping and throwing things'

(v) *-āw:*

Process nouns are formed by adding the suffix *-āw* to the stem.

	Stem	Process Nouns
(1413)	dzam 'get together'	dzamāw (m) 'gathering'
(1414)	uṭh 'get up'	uṭhāw (m) 'upheaval/ raised structure'
(1415)	ṭhar 'resolve' (intr)	ṭharāw (m) 'resolution'
(1416)	pāḍ 'fell'	pāḍāw (m) 'defeat'
(1417)	dab 'to be pressed'	dabāw (m) 'pressure'

(vi) *-āṭ*

Abstract masculine nouns are formed by adding the suffix *-āṭ* to verbal reduplicated stems.

	Stem	Abstract Nouns (Masculine)
(1418)	lakhlakh 'shine'	lakhlakhāṭ 'dazzle'
(1419)	khaḍkhaḍ 'rattle'	khaḍkhaḍāṭ 'rattle'
(1420)	gaḍgaḍ 'thunder'	gaḍgaḍāṭ 'thunder of the clouds'

(vii) *-āī*

The suffix *-āī* derives abstract feminine nouns from verb stems and conveys the meaning 'payment for the action expressed by the verb'.

	Stem	Abstract Nouns (Feminine)
(1421)	khod 'dig'	khodāī 'payment for digging'
(1422)	tsar 'graze'	tsarāī 'payment for grazing cattle'
(1423)	tShāp 'print'	tShapāī 'printing' (cf. 3.4.1.3.1.2)
(1424)	kāp 'cut'	kapāī 'payment for cutting' (cf. 3.4.1.3.1.2)

(viii) *-ī:*

The suffix *-ī* derives a large number of abstract process (feminine) nouns from verb stems.

	Stem	Abstract Feminine Nouns of Process
(1425)	buḍ 'sink'	buḍī 'dive'
(1426)	tsor 'steal'	tsorī 'theft'
(1427)	bol 'speak'	bolī 'speech'
(1428)	ukaḷ 'boil'	ukḷī 'state of boiling' (cf. 3.4.4.1.6)

Instrumental nouns:

	Stem	Feminine Nouns
(1429)	kātar 'cut'	kātarī/kātrī 'scissors' (cf. 3.4.4.1.6)
(1430)	khurap 'weed'	khurpī 'weeding instrument' (cf. 3.4.4.1.6)
(1431)	hā̃ntar 'spread'	hā̃ntarī/hā̃ntrī 'rug' (cf. 3.4.4.1.6)

(ix) *-ārī:*

Agentive nouns are derived from verb stems.

	Stem	Agentive Nouns
(1432)	ranga 'color'	rangārī 'painter' (cf. 3.4.4.1.6)
(1433)	tSitār 'paint'	tSitārī 'painter'
(1434)	luṭ 'rob'	luṭārī / luṭārū 'robber'
(1435)	pindz 'card'	pindzārī 'carder'

(x) *-ā:*

The suffix *-ā* derives various types of masculine nouns from verb stems.

	Stem	Abstract Nouns (Masculine)
(1436)	piḷ 'wring'	piḷā 'the cloth which has been wrung'
(1437)	ghoṭāḷ 'move randomly'	ghoṭāḷā 'confusion'
(1438)	pukār 'call'	pukārā 'call'
(1439)	gher 'surround'	gherā 'encircling'
(1440)	ulgaḍ 'unfold'	ulgaḍā 'unfolding'

Common nouns:

	Stem	Nouns (Masculine)
(1441)	bharaḍ 'pound'	bharḍā 'pounded (object)' (cf. 3.4.4.1.6)
(1442)	tsār 'feed'	tsārā 'feed'
(1443)	ṭhew 'keep'	ṭhewā 'objects for safe keeping'
(1444)	tsur 'to pulverize'	tsurā 'powder'
(1445)	bhurak 'sip'	bhurkā 'sip' (cf. 3.4.4.1.6)

Onomatopoeic nouns:

	Stem	Nouns (Masculine)
(1446)	ṭhok 'bang'	ṭhokā '(sound of a) bang'
(1447)	bhurak 'sip'	bhurkā '(sound of a)sip' (cf. 3.4.4.1.6)
(1448)	has 'laugh'	haśā '(sound of) laughter'

In (1448), *s* changes to *ś* to maintain the contrast between the imperative *hasā* 'you (pl.) laugh' and *haśā* '(sound) of laughter'

Agentive nouns:

	Stem	Nouns (Masculine)
(1449)	dzhar 'flow'	dzharā 'that which flows' (i.e., spring)
(1450)	oḍh 'pull'	oḍhā 'pull/attraction'

Abstract nouns expressing the state resulting from the action:

	Stem	Nouns (Masculine)
(1451)	pasar 'spread' (intr)	pasārā 'mess'
(1452)	ukaḍ 'warm' (tr)	ukāḍā 'heat'

In examples such as (1451) and (1452), the vowel *a* of the verb stem, instead of being deleted is lengthened to maintain the morphological contrast in the language. For example, *pasrā* 'stretch yourself!' and *ukḍā* '(You) warm up (something)!' will neutralize the contrast between the plural imperative forms and the abstract nouns.

(xi) *-ū:*
The suffix *-ū* also derives agentive nouns from verb stems.

	Stem	Agentive Nouns
(1453)	utar 'descend'	utārū 'passenger'
(1454)	dzhāḍ 'sweep'	dzhāḍū 'broom'
(1455)	khā 'eat'	khāū 'snack for children'
(1456)	tsāṭ 'lick'	tsāṭū 'flirt'
(1457)	bhiḍ 'connect'	bhiḍū 'partner'

In example (1453), the vowel *a* is lengthened, instead of being deleted to maintain the morphological contrast between *utrū* 'we will descend' and *utārū* 'passenger'.

-ū is added to conjunct verbs to derive nouns (as well as adjectives).

	Stem	Nouns
(1458)	māthā 'head/mind' phir 'to wander'	māthephirū 'crazy' (cf. 3.4.3) 'for head to whirl'
(1459)	gaḷā 'neck' kāp 'to cut'	gaḷekāpū 'killer' (cf. 3.4.3) someone's neck/kill
(1460)	khisā 'pocket' kāp 'cut'	khisekāpū 'pickpocket' (cf. 3.4.3)

(1461)	poṭ 'stomach' bhar 'fill stomach'	poṭbharū 'one who somehow manages to live' (i.e., fill his stomach)

Abstract nouns are derived by adding the suffix *-ū* .

	Stem	Nouns (Neuter)
(1462)	has 'laugh'	hasū 'laughter'
(1463)	raḍ 'cry'	raḍū 'cry'

(xii) *-kī:*

The suffix derives abstract nouns and agentive adjectives from a limited group of verbs.

	Stem	Nouns (Feminine)
(1464)	ḍul 'nod'	dulkī 'nap'
(1465)	phir 'move/wander'	phirkī 'revolving lid'
(1466)	unāḍ 'to goof off'	unāḍkī 'goofing off'
(1467)	mār 'to beat'	mārkī (adj) 'the one who attacks'

(xiii) *-ṇī:*

The suffix *-ṇī* derives a variety of feminine nouns from verb stems.

	Stem	Abstract Nouns
(1468)	kāp 'cut'	kāpṇī 'the act of cutting the crop'
(1469)	pāh 'see'	pāhṇī 'examine'
(1470)	rāh 'live'	rāhṇī 'lifestyle'
(1471)	wāṭ 'distribute'	wāṭṇī 'distribution'

Object nouns:

	Stem	Nouns
(1472)	per 'sow'	perṇī 'process of sowing'
(1473)	puraw 'supply'	purawṇī 'supplement'

Instrumental nouns:

	Stem	Nouns
(1474)	rokh 'obstruct'	rokhṇī 'barricade'
(1475)	tsāḷ 'sift'	tsāḷṇī 'instrument for sifting'
(1476)	kis 'grate'	kisṇī 'grating instrument'
(1477)	gāḷ 'strain'	gāḷṇī 'strainer'

Locative noun:

	Stem	Noun
(1478)	nhā 'bathe'	nhāṇī 'bathing place'

(xiv) *-ṇūk:*

Abstract process nouns are derived from verbs by adding the suffix *-ṇūk* to the verb stem.

	Stem	Nouns (Feminine)
(1479)	niwaḍ 'elect'	niwaḍṇūk 'election'
(1480)	miraw 'to display/show off'	mirawṇūk 'procession'
(1481)	phasaw 'be deceive'	phasawṇūk 'deception'

(xv) *-tī:*

The suffix *-tī* derives abstract feminine nouns from verb stems. The use of this suffix is limited to a small class of verbs.

	Stem	Nouns
(1482)	gaṇ 'count'	gaṇtī 'count'
(1483)	phir 'wander'	phirtī 'travel related to job/work'
(1484)	bhar 'fill' (intr)	bhartī 'tide'
(1485)	suk 'dry (intr)'	suktī 'web'
(1486)	pāw 'receive'	pāwtī 'receipt'

(xvi) *-(a)nā:*

This is a Sanskrit suffix which derives abstract (feminine) nouns from Sanskrit verb stems.

	Stem	Nouns
(1487)	ghaṭ 'happen'	ghaṭanā 'event'
(1488)	prārth 'pray'	prārthanā 'prayer'

(xvii) *-ak:*

The suffix-*ak* (Sanskrit) derives agentive nouns (and adjectives) from Sanskrit and Marathi verb stems.

	Stem	Nouns
(1489)	(Skt) rakṣ 'protect'	rakṣak 'protector'
(1490)	(M) gā 'sing'	gāyak 'singer' (cf. 3.4.4.2.2)

(xviii) *-paṭṭī:*

The suffix *-paṭṭī* is added to a small number of verb stems to derive abstract nouns and expresses excess of action.

	Stem	Nouns
(1491)	uḍhaḷ 'spend excessively'	uḍhaḷpaṭṭī 'excessive spending'
(1492)	māṛ 'beat'	māṛpaṭṭī 'excessive beating'
(1493)	kharaḍ 'scold'	kharaḍpaṭṭī 'excessive scolding'

(xix) *-ḍā:*

The suffix *-ḍā* derives abstract process nouns from verb stems.

	Stem	Nouns (Masculine)
(1494)	ghasar 'slip'	ghasarḍā 'slippery spot'
(1495)	hãmbar 'cry loudly'	hãmbarḍā 'loud cry'
(1496)	ukar 'scratch'	ukarḍā/ukirḍā 'garbage heap'

(xx) *-āwaṭ:*

This suffix is used in the variety of Marathi spoken around Nagpur. It is borrowed from Hindi, and its use is restricted to verb stems which are also borrowed from Hindi or which Marathi shares with Hindi. Abstract (feminine) nouns are derived by this suffix.

	Stem (shared with Hindi)	Nouns (Feminine)
(1497)	thak 'be tired'	thakāwaṭ 'fatigue'
(1498)	sadz 'decorate'	sadzāwaṭ 'decoration'

	Stem (borrowed from Hindi)	Nouns (Feminine)
(1499)	ban 'make'	banāwaṭ 'makeup'
(1500)	rok 'obstruct'	rukāwaṭ 'obstruction'

In the derivation *rukāwat* 'obstruction' the *o* of the stem is changed to *u*. This is a regular change in Hindi.

2.2.1.2.1 *Syntax of deverbal nouns and non-derived nouns*

The syntax of the deverbal nouns is the sams as that of non-derived/basic nouns. Deverbal nouns, similar to non-derived nouns, are marked for gender, number and case (1501). They can be modified by adjectives/modifiers and they determine the gender and number of the modifier (1501). Also, deverbal nouns control verb agreement and have the SOV word order of the elements in the subordinate clause. However, the deverbal noun differs from the non-derived noun in one respect, i.e., if the subject of the embedded clause of the deverbal noun (infinitive) is present, it is followed by the possessive postposition as in (1502).

(1501)	hyā	warṣī	kāpsātSī	upadz
	this	year-loc	cotton-poss	growth-3sf

tsāŋglī dzhālī
good-3sf happen-pst-3sf

'This year, the cotton-crop was good (lit: 'This year, the growth of the cotton was good.')

(1502)	bāḷātSyā	niṣpāp	hasṇyāne	āītsā
	child-poss	innocent	smile-inf-inst	mother-poss
	thakwā	adʒibāt	gelā	
	fatigue-3sm	absolutely	go-pst-3sm	

'Mother's fatigue absolutely vanished (lit: 'went') by the child's innocent smile.'

It should be noted here that the word order in the deverbal noun clause cannot be changed as in (1504).

(1503)	tyātsa	patra	lihiṇa . . . .
	he-poss-3sn	letters	write-inf-3sn
	'His writing letters'		
(1504)*	patra	tyātsa	lihiṇa
	letters	he-poss-3sn	write-inf-3sm
	'His writing letters . . . .'		

2.2.1.3 *Nouns from adjectives*

Suffixation is the only process used to derive nouns from adjectives.

(i) *-ī:*

The most productive means of deriving abstract feminine nouns from adjectives is the addition of the suffix *-ī.*

	Adjective (consonant-ending)	Abstract Nouns (Feminine)
(1505)	lā̃mb 'long'	lā̃mbī 'length'
(1506)	lāl 'red'	lālī 'redness'
(1507)	khūṣ 'happy'	khuṣī 'happiness' (cf. 3.4.1.3.1.1)
(1508)	garam 'hot'	garmī 'heat' (cf. 3.4.4.1.6)
(1509)	huśār 'intelligent/clever'	huśārī 'intelligent/clever'

(1510)	imāndār 'honest'	imāṇdārī 'honesty'
(1511)	untsa 'tall'	untSī 'height' (cf. 3.4.4.1.2 and 3.4.1.1.1.3)
	Adjective (-ā ending)	Abstract/Concrete Nouns (Feminine)
(1512)	niḷā (sm) 'blue'	niḷāī 'blueness'
(1513)	(consonant ending) udhār 'on credit'	udhārī 'credit'

(ii) *-paṇā:*

The suffix *-paṇ/paṇā* derives abstract masculine nouns from adjectives. Again, this is a very productive process in Marathi.

	Adjective (Masculine Singular)	Abstract Nouns (Masculine)
(1514)	moṭhā 'big'	moṭhepaṇ/moṭhepaṇā 'largeness (of an object, of heart or prestige/pride)' (cf. 3.4.3)
(1515)	mhātārā (sm) 'old'	mhātārpaṇ/mhātārpaṇā 'old age' (cf. 3.4.4.1.3)
(1516)	sabhya 'gentleman'	sabhyapaṇā 'gentlemanliness'
(1517)	krūr 'cruel'	krūrpaṇā 'cruelty'
(1518)	duṣṭa 'evil'	duṣṭapaṇa 'evil'
(1519)	nādzuk 'delicate'	nādzukpaṇā 'delicateness'

(iii) *-tā:*

The Sanskrit suffix *-tā* is added exclusively to Sanskrit adjectives to derive feminine nouns.

	Adjectives	Abstract Feminine Nouns
(1520)	udār 'kind'	udārtā 'kindness'

(1521)	namra 'polite'	namratā 'politeness'
(1522)	udāsīn 'sad'	udāsīntā 'sadness'
(1523)	pātra 'worthy'	pātratā 'worthiness'

(iv) *-twa:*

The Sanskrit suffix *-twa* is added to adjectives from Sanskrit to derive abstract neuter nouns.

	Adjective	Abstract Neuter Nouns
(1524)	sama 'equal'	samatwa 'equality'
(1525)	laghu 'small'	laghutwa 'smallness'
(1526)	utStSa 'high'	utStSatwa 'height'
(1527)	dīrgha 'long'	dīrghatwa 'length'

(v) *-kī:*

Abstract feminine nouns are derived by adding the suffix *-kī* to adjectives.

	Adjective	Abstract Feminine Nouns
(1528)	labāḍ 'naughty'	labāḍkī 'naughtiness'
(1529)	ṭawāḷ 'vagabond'	ṭawāḷkī 'vagabondness'
(1530)	kutsāḷ 'gossip-monger'	kutsāḷkī 'gossip'

(vi) *-īk:*

A small set of abstract feminine nouns are derived by adding the suffix *-īk* to adjectives.

	Adjective (Masculine Singular)	Abstract Feminine Nouns
(1531)	soyrā 'relative'	soyrīk 'relation' (cf. 3.4.4.1.3)
(1532)	mokḷā 'free'	mokḷīk 'freedom' (cf. 3.4.4.1.3)

(1533)	weg!ā 'different'	weg!īk 'difference' (cf. 3.4.4.1.3)

(vii) *-girī:*

This Persian suffix is added to the native Marathi adjectives to derive abstract feminine nouns. The class of these derived nouns is very small.

	Adjective (Masculine Singular)	Abstract Feminine Nouns
(1534)	lutStSā 'deceitful'	lutStSegirī 'deceit' (cf. 3.4.3)
(1535)	sāwadh 'cautious'	sāwadhgirī 'caution'
(1536)	bhāmṭā 'untrustworthy/ dishonest/vagabond'	bhāmṭegirī 'dishonesty/ vagabondness' (cf. 3.4.3)

(viii) *-ya:*

The Sanskrit suffix *-ya* is added to Sanskrit adjectives to derive abstract neuter nouns.

	Adjective	Abstract Neuter Nouns
(1537)	durbal 'weak'	daurbalya 'weakness'
(1538)	krūr 'cruel'	krauraya 'cruelty'
(1539)	sūndar 'beautiful'	saūndarya 'beauty'

The alternation between *u, ū/au* in (1537) - (1539) is due to the *vṛddhi* rule in Sanskrit.

2.2.1.4 *Nouns from adverbs*

There are very few nouns which are derived from adverbs. Examples are given below:

	Adverb	Nouns
(1540)	dzawaḷ 'near/close by'	dzawaḷik (f) 'closeness'
(1541)	dzarūr 'certainly'	dzarūrat (f) 'need'

(1542) dūr 'far away' durāwā (m) 'the state of being far away' (cf. 3.4.1.3.1.1)

2.2.1.5 *Nouns from other categories*

2.2.1.5.1 *Postpositions*

A large class of nouns are derived from nouns, adjectives, or adverbs by adding the postposition *wālā* to them. *Wālā* can be treated as a postposition because it requires the preceding noun to be in its oblique form. Some examples are given below:

(1543) paise-wālā 'rich' (one who possesses money)

(1544) bhādʒī-wālā 'vegetable vendor' (one who has vegetables)

(1545) bāsrī-wālā 'flute-player' (one who has the flute)

The derived words can be used as nouns as well as adjectives.

2.2.1.5.2 *Reflexive pronoun*

An abstract masculine noun can be derived from the reflexive pronoun *-āpaṇ* 'self'.

(1546) āple-paṇa 'intimacy'

It should be noted here that in this context, the pronoun *āpaṇ* is in its possessive case and oblique form (i.e., *āple*).

2.2.2 DERIVATION OF VERBS

2.2.2.1 *Verbs from nouns*

(i) *zero* affix:

A large number of words in Marathi are used both as verbs and nouns.

(1547) bol 'speak'

(1548) tsaḍh 'ascend/ascent'

(1549) dzhop 'sleep'

(1550) tsāl 'walk'

(1551) misaḷ 'mix'

(1552) pakaḍ 'catch'

(ii) *nouns as verbs:*

A large number of nouns can be used as verbs. In this case, the noun-stems (unlike those in (i)) undergo some changes: (a) the penultimate vowel *-ū* is shortened (1553), (b) the stem-final vowel is deleted(1554) and (1555), (c) the suffixes *-āṭ* or *-aw* or *-āḷ* are added to the stems as in (1556), (1558) and (1557) respectively.

	Noun	Verb
Vowel-shortening:		
(1553)	phūl 'flower'	phulṇe 'to flower' (cf. 3.4.1.3.1.1)
Stem-final vowel deletion:		
(1554)	surkutī 'wrinkle'	surkut-ṇe 'to wrinkle' (cf. 3.4.1.3.1.1 and 3.4.4.1.6)
(1555)	pisārā 'plumage'	pisār-ṇe 'to open plumage' (cf. 3.4.4.1.3)
-aṭ-insertion:		
(1556)	tSīk 'gum'	tSik-aṭ-ṇe 'to stick' (cf. 3.4.1.3.1.1)
-āḷ-insertion:		
(1557)	hāt 'hand'	hātāḷ-ṇe 'to handle'
-āw-insertion:		
(1558)	ḍoka 'head'	dok-āw-ṇe 'to peep' (cf. 3.4.4.1.2)
(1559)	sukh 'happiness'	sukh-āw-ṇe 'to be happy'

(iii) *Conjunct verbs:*

One of the highly productive processes used to derive verbs from nouns is the formation of conjunct verbs, e.g., *kṣamā* 'mercy' *karṇe* 'do' - 'to forgive'. This process is used to assimilate borrowings from English, Persian, and Sanskrit.

	English noun	Marathi verb	Conjunct verb
(1560)	śɔk 'shock'	bas-ṇe 'to sit'	śɔk basṇe 'to get a shock'
	Sanskrit noun	Marathi verb	Conjunct verb
(1561)	niśtSay 'decision'	kar-ṇe 'to do'	miśtSay karṇe 'to decide'
(1562)	Persian noun	Marathi verb	Conjunct verb
	takrār 'complaint'	kar-ṇe 'to do'	takrār karṇe 'to complain'

2.2.2.2 *Verbs from verbs*

(i) *-aw:*

The two causative suffixes *-aw* and *-ā* are commonly used to derive verbs from verbs (see the discussion on transitivization and causativization in 2.1.3.1.3 and 2.1.3.1.3.1.1). Some examples are given below.

(1563)	bas 'to sit'	basaw-ṇe 'to make sit'
(1564)	mar 'to die'	mār-ṇe 'to kill'

(ii) Compound verbs/verb serialization:

The formation of compound verbs is another device for deriving verbs from verbs. In this case, verbs are juxtaposed to form a single unit. (For further discussion on compound verbs, see 2.1.3.3.2.1.1 - 2.1.3.3.2.1.1.6 and 2.2.6.3.4.2.)

2.2.2.3-5 *Verbs from other categories*

Nouns, adverbials, adjectives, and pronouns may all occur as the first constituent in a conjunct verb in Marathi.

noun + verb:

(1565) dhakkā 'push' (n) + deṇe 'give' = 'to push'

	adverb + verb:
(1566)	(gup)tSup 'quietly' + bas 'sit' = 'to be quiet'
	adjective + verb:
(1567)	ādzārī 'sick' (adj) + paḍṇe 'face' = 'to get sick'

2.2.3 DERIVATION OF ADJECTIVES

2.2.3.1 *Adjectives from nouns*

(i) *-ī:*

One of the most productive processes of deriving adjectives from nouns is the addition of *-ī* to nouns.

	Noun	Adjective
(1568)	sūt 'cotton'	sutī 'made of cotton' (cf. 3.4.1.3.1.1)
(1569)	sarkār 'government'	sarkārī 'pertaining to government'
(1570)	lokhaṇḍa 'iron'	lokhaṇḍī 'made of iron' (cf. 3.4.4.1.2)
(1571)	andhār 'darkness'	andhārī 'dark'
(1572)	gulāb 'rose'	gulābī 'pink'
(1573	gudzrāth 'Gujarat'	gudzrāthī 'one who lives in the state of Gujarat'
(1574)	lākūḍ 'wood'	lākḍī 'wooden' (cf. 3.4.1.3.1.1 and 3.4.4.1.6)

(ii) *-āḷ:*

In order to express the meaning 'full of/filled with' (i.e., to express abundance of an entity), the suffix *-āḷ* is added to a noun to derive an adjective.

	Noun	Adjective
(1575)	dūdh 'milk'	dudhāḷ 'full of milk (an adjective used for a cow)' (cf. 3.4.1.3.1.1)

(1576)	kes 'hair'	kesāḷ 'hairy'
(1577)	barpha 'snow'	barphāḷ 'snowy' (cf. 3.4.4.1.2)
(1578)	khaḍak 'rock'	khaḍkāḷ 'rocky' (cf. 3.4.4.1.6)
(1579)	ras 'juice'	rasāḷ 'juicy'

(iii) *-kar:*
The suffix *-kar* derives agentive adjectives from nouns.

(1580)	kheḷ 'game/sport'	kheḷkar 'playful'
(1581)	hit 'benefit'	hitkar 'beneficial'

(iv) *-āḍī/āḍyā:*
These two suffixes also derive agentive adjectives from nouns:

	Noun	Adjective
(1582)	nāw 'boat'	nāwāḍī/nāwāḍyā 'boatman'
(1583)	wāṭ 'path'	wāṭāḍī/wāṭādyā 'guide'
(1584)	sõng 'funny'	sõŋgāḍī/sõŋgāḍyā 'clown' appearance'

It must be noted here that the derived adjectives in (1582) - (1584) above can be used as nouns as well.

(v) *-elā:*
When added to a noun, the suffix *-elā* derives a personal adjective expressing the possession of the state indicated by the noun.

	Noun	Adjective
(1585)	tahān 'thirst'	tahānelā 'thirsty'
(1586)	bhūk 'hunger'	bhukelā 'hungry' (cf. 3.4.1.3.1.1)

It should be noted here that adjectives derived in this way take the agreement markers of the noun as follows.

(1587a) tahānelā (sm)
(1587b) tahānele (pl.m)
(1587c) tahānelī (sf)
(1587d) tahānelyā (pl.f)
(1587e) tahānela (sn)
(1587f) tahānelī (pl.n)

(vi) *dār:*

The possessive suffix *-dār* derives adjectives (as well as nouns) from nouns. This suffix is borrowed from Persian.

	Noun	Adjective
(1588)	tsaw 'taste'	tsawdār 'tasty'
(1589)	pāṇī 'water/power'	pāṇīdār 'watery/powerful'
(1590)	nok 'sharp point'	nokdār 'one with sharp point'
(1591)	pailū 'angle'	pailūdār 'with many angles/ multifaceted)

(vii) *-bādz:*

Another Persian suffix which is quite productive in Marathi is *-bādz*, which derives personal adjectives expressing excessive habitual behavior vis-a-vis the referent of the noun.

	Noun	Adjective
(1592)	dārū 'alcohol'	dārūbādz 'drunkard'
(1593)	dagā 'betrayal'	dagābādz 'betrayer'
(1594)	tSain 'luxury'	tSainbādz 'fond of luxurious lifestyle'

(viii) *-nawīs:*

Agentive personal adjectives are derived by adding the Persian suffix *-nawīs* 'writer' to nouns.

	Noun	Adjective
(1595)	tSiṭṭhī 'letter'	tSiṭṭhīnawīs 'one who writes letters'
(1596)	potah 'expenditure'	pot(ah)nawīs 'accountant'

(1597)	kārkhānā 'factory'	kārkhānnawīs/kārkhānīs 'accountant for a factory' (cf. 3.4.4.1.3)

Although the suffix *-nawīs* is recognized by speakers, it is not productive in contemporary language.

(ix) *be-* 'without':

The Persian prefix *be-* is used to derive adjectives from Persian (borrowed) nouns.

	Noun	Adjective
(1598)	dʒān 'life'	bedʒān 'lifeless'
(1599)	tSain 'comfort'	betSain 'uncomfortable'
(1600)	hoś 'consciousness'	behoś 'unconscious'

(x) *-āspad:*

The Sanskrit suffix *-āspad* is added to Sanskrit nouns to derive adjectives which express the meaning 'capable of/worthy of'.

	Noun	Adjective
(1601)	ghruṇā 'disgust'	ghruṇāspad 'capable of/worthy of creating disgust'
(1602)	sãũśay 'doubt'	saũśayāspad 'worthy of creating doubt/doubtful'
(1603)	mān 'honor/respect'	mānāspad 'respectable/honorable'

(xi) *-may:*

The Sanskrit suffix *-may* is added to abstract nouns. The derived adjective indicates the meaning 'full of/endowed with'.

	Noun	Adjective
(1604)	krupā 'mercy'	krupāmay 'merciful'
(1605)	prabhā 'light'	prabhāmay 'bright'
(1606)	lāwaṇya 'beauty'	lāwaṇyamay 'beautiful'

(xii) *-yogya:*

This Sanskrit suffix conveys the meaning 'worthy' and derives an adjective from a Sanskrit noun.

	Noun	Adjective
(1607)	sewā 'service'	sewāyogya 'worthy for service'
(1608)	ādar 'respect'	ādarāyogya 'deserving respect'

In (1608), the increment vowel *-ā* is inserted between the noun-stem and the suffix.

(xiii) *-īya:*

This Sanskrit suffix is used to derive adjectives meaning 'pertaining to' from Sanskrit and Marathi nouns.

	Noun	Adjective
(1609)	(Skt) bhārat 'India'	bhāratīya 'Indian'
(1610)	(M) parkā 'other'	parkīya 'other's' (cf. 3.4.4.1.3)
(1611)	(M) dzāt 'caste'	dzātīya 'related to caste'

(xiv) *-śīḷ:*

This Sanskrit suffix conveys the meaning 'one who has the characteristic of'.

	Noun	Adjective
(1612)	prayatna 'effort'	prayatnaśīl 'one who always tries'
(1613)	wiwek 'conscience'	wiwekaśīl 'conscientious'
(1614)	dharma 'religion'	dharmaśīl 'religious'

(xv) *yukta:*

This Sanskrit suffix derives adjectives from nouns. The derived adjective indicates the possession of the quality expressed by the noun.

	Noun	Adjective
(1615)	śaktī 'strength'	śaktiyukta 'strong' (cf. 3.4.1.3.5)

(1616)	bhaktī 'devotion'	bhaktiyukta 'full of devotion' (cf. 3.4.1.3.5)

(xvi) *-dāyī:*

The suffix *-dāyī* is from Sanskrit and expresses the meaning of 'giver/bestower of'.

	Noun	Adjective
(1617)	ānānda 'joy'	ānāndadāyī 'bestower of joy'
(1618)	dukhkha 'pain'	dukhkhadāyī 'painful'
(1619)	widyā 'knowledge'	widyādāyī 'bestower of knowledge'

(xviii) *-ik(a):*

This Sanskrit suffix conveys the meaning 'pertaining to'.

	Noun	Adjective
(1620)	buddhī 'intelligence'	bauddhik 'pertaining to intelligence'
(1621)	dharma 'religion'	dhārmik 'religious'
(1622)	mās 'month'	māsik(a) 'monthly'
(1623)	mūl 'origin'	maulik(a) 'original'
(1624)	khartsa 'expenditure'	khartSik 'spendthrift'

The vowel alternations *u/au* (1620, 1623) and *a/ā* (1621) are due to the *vṛddhi* rule in Sanskrit. Note that this rule is not applicable to the Persian noun *khartsa* in (1624). Also note that the Sanskrit suffix *-ik* is used with the Persian borrowing *khartsa* 'expenditure'. This is a rare example. As noted before, Sanskrit suffixes are not normally added to Perso-Arabic loans; they are restricted to the Sanskrit and Marathi lexicon. (For details, see Pandharipande 1981c.)

(xviii) *-ādhīn:*

This Sanskrit suffix expresses the meaning 'dependent on'.

	Noun	Adjective
(1625)	kāl time'	kālādhīn 'dependent on time'
(1626)	daiwa 'fate'	daiwādhin 'dependent on fate' (cf. 3.4.4.1.2)
(1627)	par 'other'	parādhīn 'dependent on others'
(1628)	swa 'oneself'	swādhīn 'dependent on oneself (independent)' (cf. 3.4.4.1.2)

The vowel alternation *a/ā* is due to the regular *sandhi* rule in Sanskrit.

(xix) *-ākrānta:*

This suffix from Sanskrit expresses the meaning 'afflicted with':

	Noun	Adjective
(1629)	tSintā 'worry'	tSintākrānta 'afflicted with worry' (cf. 3.4.4.1.3)
(1630)	bhay 'fear'	bhayākrānta 'frightened'
(1631)	lobh 'greed'	lobhākrānta 'extremely greedy'
(1632)	nidrā 'sleep'	nidrākrānta 'attacked by sleep' (very sleepy) (cf. 3.4.4.1.3)

(xx) *-kar:*

This Sanskrit suffix derives agentive adjectives from Sanskrit nouns.

	Noun	Adjective
(1633)	prabhā 'light'	prabhākar 'giver of the light/the sun'
(1634)	hit 'welfare'	hitakar 'benevolent'

(xxi) *-ʤanak:*

This Sanskrit suffix conveys the meaning 'causing the event/state expressed in the noun.'

	Noun	Adjective
(1635)	yaś 'victory'	yaśadʒanak 'causing victory' (cf. 3.4.4.2.4)
(1636)	sãntoṣ 'satisfaction'	sãntoṣadʒanak 'satisfactory' (cf. 3 .4.4.2.4)

(xxii) *-dhārī:*

The Sanskrit suffix *-dhārī* , when added to a noun, derives an agentive adjective expressing the meaning 'the one who holds'.

	Noun	Adjective
(1637)	krupāṇ 'sword'	krupāṇdhārī 'wielder of sword'
(1638)	sattā 'power'	sattādhārī 'wielder of power'

(xviii) *-hīn:*

This Sanskrit suffix indicates the lack of the quality expressed by the noun.

	Noun	Adjective
(1639)	buddhī 'intelligence'	buddhihīn 'fool (without intelligence)' (cf. 3.4.1.3.5)
(1640)	āśā 'hope'	āśāhīn 'without hope'
(1641)	tSakṣu 'eye'	tSakṣuhīn 'blind'

(xxiv) In addition to the above, there are Sanskrit suffixes such as *-arha* 'worthy of' (*nindārha* 'worthy of being criticized'), *-dʒña* 'knower of' (*sarwadʒña* 'the one who knows everything'), etc. which are not very productive in Marathi.

2.2.3.2 *Adjectives from verbs*

(i) Adjectives are derived from verbs by the use of the relative participles (see section 2.1.3.5.2.1 for detailed discussion on the processes of deriving participles).

(ii) *-kā:*

The suffix *-kā* (and its variants with agreement markers) derives adjectives from verb stems.

	Verb stem	Adjective
(1642)	paḍ 'fall'	paḍkā (sm) 'fallen/dilapidated'
(1643)	tuṭ 'break'	tuṭkā (sm) 'broken'
(1644)	phāṭ 'tear (intr)'	phāṭkā (sm) 'torn'
(1645)	bas 'sit'	baskā (sm)
(1646)	bol 'speak'	bolkā (sm) 'one who talks a lot'

(iii) *-tā:*

Agentive adjectives are derived by adding the suffix *-tā* to the verb stem.

	Verb stem	Adjective
(1647)	has 'smile/laugh'	hastā (sm) 'the one who is laughing'
(1648)	khā-pī 'eat/drink'	khātā-pitā (sm) 'one who eats/drinks/one who is healthy and fine'
(1649)	kheḷ 'play'	kheḷtā (sm) 'one who is playing'

(iv) *-rā:*

When added to a verb stem, the suffix *-rā* expresses a habitual action/state on the part of the agent who is the referent of the derived adjective.

	Verb stem	Adjective
(1650)	tsāw 'bite'	tsāwrā 'one (dog) who is in the habit of biting'
(1651)	nāts 'dance'	nātsrā 'one who always dances'
(1652)	bots 'prick'	botsrā 'one which always pricks' (e.g., nail, pin, etc.)
(1653)	has 'smile'	hasrā 'always smiling'

(1654)	lādz 'be bashful'	lādzrā 'bashful'

(v) *-kaṭ:*

When the beginning of the action (but not quite its completion) is to be indicated in its source/location, the suffix *-kaṭ* is added to the verb stem to derive an adjective.

	Verb stem	Adjective
(1655)	maḷ 'become dusty/dirty	maḷkaṭ 'almost dusty'
(1656)	pus 'be wiped off'	puskaṭ 'almost wiped off/ blurry'
(1657)	dzaḷ 'burn (intr)'	dzaḷkaṭ 'almost burnt'
(1658)	kudz 'be spoiled (intr)'	kudzkaṭ 'almost spoiled (food)'

(vi) *-īt:*

The suffix *-īt* indicates the possession of the quality/state expressed by the verb.

	Verb stem	Adjective
(1659)	lakhlakh 'shine'	lakhlakhīt 'shining, dazzling'
(1660)	tsurtsur 'become crisp'	tsurtsurīt 'crispy'

(vii) *-āū:*

The suffix *-āū* expresses the meaning 'suitable for' the action expressed by the verb.

	Verb stem	Adjective
(1661)	dzaḷ 'burn (intr)'	dzaḷāū 'suitable for burning (e.g., gas, wood, coal, etc.)
(1662)	ṭik 'last'	ṭikāū 'durabale, long-lasting'
(1663)	wik 'sell'	wikāū 'for sale'

2.2.3.3 *Adjectives from adjectives*

(i) Some suffixes, such as the following, are added to adjectives of specific colors. The function of these suffixes is to intensify the meaning already conveyed by the adjective. It is interesting to note that these suffixes are not interchangeable across all adjectives of colors.

	Adjective	Adjective
(1664)	lāl 'red'	lāl-bhaḍak 'very red'
(1665)	piwḷā 'yellow'	piwḷā-dhamak/-dzarda 'very yellow'
(1666)	hirwā 'green'	hirwā-gār 'very green'
(1667)	niḷā 'blue'	niḷā-garda 'very blue'
(1668)	kāḷā 'black'	kāḷā-kṣār/kāḷā-kuṭṭa 'very black'
(1669)	pāṇḍhrā 'white'	pāṇḍhrā-phaṭphatīt 'very white'

(ii) *-sar:*

In contrast to the suffixes in (i), the suffix *-sar* lowers the degree of intensity of meaning conveyed by the adjective.

	Adjective of color	Adjective
(1670)	lāl 'red'	lāl-sar 'reddish'
(1671)	piwḷā 'yellow'	piwaḷ-sar 'yellowish' (cf. 3.4.4.1.3 and 3.4.4.2.3)
(1672)	niḷā 'blue'	niḷ-sar 'bluish' (cf. 3.4.4.1.3)
(1673)	maū 'soft'	mau-sar 'softish' (cf. 3.4.1.3.1.1)
(1674)	weḍā 'crazy'	weḍ-sar 'a bit crazy' (cf. 3.4.4.1.3)
(1675)	goḍ 'sweet'	goḍ-sar 'a bit sweet'
(1676)	bhoḷā 'naive'	bhoḷ-sar 'a bit naive' (cf. 3.4.4.1.3)

(iii) *-aṭ/-sā:*

These suffixes are similar to *-sar* in that they also lower the degree of intensity when added to adjectives.

	Adjective	Adjective
(1677)	lā̃mb 'long'	lā̃mbaṭ 'longish'
(1678)	ũntsa 'tall'	{ũntsaṭ / ũntsasā} 'tallish'
(1679)	rũnda 'narrow'	rũndasā 'narrowish'
(1680)	moṭhā 'big'	moṭhāsā 'biggish'
(1681)	lahān 'small'	lahānsā 'smallish'

(iv) *-(h)erī:*

When added to cardinal numerals, this suffix conveys the meaning 'with x numbers of strands' (of the object indicated by the noun). The alternations between cardinal numerals and their corresponding adjectival forms in (1683) - (1684) are lexical in nature.

	Cardinal Adjective	Adjective
(1682)	ek 'one'	ekerī 'with one strand' (of rope, thread, etc.)
(1683)	don 'two'	duherī 'with two strands'
(1684)	tīn 'three'	tiherī 'with three strands'

(v) *-wā:*

This suffix derives ordinal adjectives from cardinal adjectives (numerals). Note that this suffix appears as *-lā* in *pahilā* 'first', as *-rā* in *dusrā* 'second' and *tisrā* 'third', and as *-thā* in *tsauthā* 'fourth'.

	Cardinal Adjective	Ordinal Adjective
(1685)	ek 'one'	pahilā 'first'
(1685b)	don 'two'	dusrā 'second'
(1685c)	tīn 'three'	tisrā 'third'
(1685d)	tSār 'four'	tsauthā 'fourth'

(1685e)	pāts 'five'	pātswā 'fifth'
(1685f)	sahā 'six'	sahāwā 'sixth'
(1685g)	sāt 'seven'	sātwā 'seventh'

The alternations in (1685) - (1685d) are lexical. The rest of the ordinal adjectives are derived by adding *-wā* to their corresponding cardinal adjectives. As usual, the derived adjectives are treated as *-ā* ending adjectives which agree in gender and number with their corresponding nouns.

(vi) *-āḍ:*

The suffix *-āḍ* , when added to an adjective, expresses excess, and therefore undesirability, of the quality of the possessor.

	Adjective	Adjective
(1686)	moṭhā 'big'	moṭhāḍ 'too big' (cf. 3.4.4.1.3)
(1687)	thor 'large/big'	thorāḍ 'too large'
(1688)	ũntsa 'tall'	ũntsāḍ 'too tall' (cf. 3.4.4.1.2)

(vii) *gair- :*

The Persian prefix *gair-* derives adjectives which indicate the absence of the quality indicated by the corresponding adjective.

	Adjective	Adjective
(1689)	hadzar 'present'	gairhadzar 'absent'
(1690)	sāwadh 'aware'	gairsāwadh 'unaware'

Again, a Persian prefix is added to an adjective of Sanskrit origin (*sāwadh* 'one who is aware of'). This cross-application of affixes (Sanskrit-Perso-Arabic) indicates that some of the borrowings (affixes/lexical items) are old and have been completely assimilated into the native Marathi grammar.

Prefixes:

(i) *nir-:*

This Sanskrit prefix derives negative adjectives from their corresponding adjectives.

	Adjective	Adjective
(1691)	aparāḍhī 'criminal'	niraparādhī 'innocent'
(1692)	doṣ 'flaw'	nirdoṣ 'flawless/innocent'
(1693)	ʤan 'people'	nirʤan 'deserted (place)'

(ii) *a-:*

The Sanskrit prefix *a-* also derives negative adjectives from their corresponding adjectives.

	Adjective	Adjective
(1694)	ʤñānī 'learned'	aʤñānī 'ignorant'
(1695)	yogya 'deserving'	ayogya 'unworthy'
(1696)	krutrim 'artificial'	akrutrim 'natural'
(1697)	nyāyī 'just'	anyāyī 'unjust'
(1698)	purā 'complete'	apurā 'incomplete'

(iii) *nā-:*

The Persian prefix *nā-* derives negative adjectives.

	Adjective	Adjective
(1699)	khūṣ happy'	nākhūṣ 'unhappy'
(1700)	māndzūr 'acceptable'	nāmāndzūr 'unacceptable'
(1701)	lāyak 'worthy'	nālāyak 'unworthy'

(iv) *ati-:*

The Sanskrit prefix *ati-* intensifies the meaning expressed by the Sanskrit and Marathi adjectives.

	Adjective	Adjective
(1702)	(Skt) sūndar 'beautiful'	atisūndar 'very beautiful'
(1703)	(M) samanʤas 'reasonable'	atisamanʤas 'very reasonable'

(1704)	(P) tSalākh 'clever'	atitSalākh 'very clever'

It is interesting to note here that the Sanskrit prefix is added to a Persian adjective, *tSalākh* 'clever'. However, this is an exception; Sanskrit suffixes and prefixes are generally not added to Persian words.

2.2.3.4 *Adjectives from adverbs*

(i) *-tsā* possessive:

The possessive suffix *-tsā* and its variants derive adjectives from adverbs.

(1705)	ghar 'house'	(a) ghartsā (sm) 'pertaining to a house' (b) ghartse (pl.m) (c) ghartSī (sf) (d) ghartSyā (pl.f) (e) ghartse/tsa (sn) (f) ghartSī (pl.n)
(1706)	dūr 'far away location'	dūrtsā 'of a faraway place' (and its variants)
(1707)	dzawaḷ 'near'	dzawaḷtsā 'of a nearby place' (and its variants)
(1708)	kāl 'yesterday'	kāltsā 'of yesterday' (and its variants)
(1709)	nāgpūr 'Nagpur ' (name of city)	nāgpūrtsā 'pertaining to Nagpur' (and its variants)

This is the most productive means of deriving adjectives from adverbs.

(ii) -īl:

The suffix *-īl* , when added to an adverb, derives an adjective.

	Adverb	Adjective
(1710)	āt 'in'	ātīl 'that which '

(1711)	khālī 'down'	khālīl 'one which is down/below' (cf. 3.4.1.3.1.1 and 3.4.4.1.4)
(1712)	war 'up'	warīl 'one which is up/above'
(1713)	bāher 'outside'	bāherīl 'one which is outside'
(1714)	{puḍhe / samor} 'in front'	{puḍhīl / samorīl} 'one which is in the front' (cf. 3.4.4.1.4)

(iii) *-lā:*
-lā is another suffix which derives adjectives from adverbs.

	Adverb	Adjective
(1715a)	āt 'inside'	ātlā 'that which is inside'
(1715b)	madhe 'inside/ in the middle of'	madhlā 'that which is inside/in the middle of'
(1716)	māge 'behind'	māglā 'the one which is behind'
(1717)	puḍhe 'in front'	puḍhlā 'the one in front'
(1718)	ikḍe 'in this direction'	ikaḍlā 'the one which is in this direction'
(1719)	ithe 'here'	ithlā 'the one which is here'
(1720)	tikḍe 'in that direction'	tikaḍlā 'the one in that direction'
(1721)	tithe 'there'	tithlā 'the one there'

For stem-final vowel /*e*/ deletion in (1716), (1717), (1718), (1719) and (1721) and *a* insertion in (1718) and(1720), see sections 3.4.4.1.4 and 3.4.4.2.3 respectively.

(iv) *-sārkhā:*
The postposition *(-tSyā) sārkhā / lyā sārkhā* (for locatives only) 'like/similar to' derives adjectives from adverbs.

	Adverb	Adjective
(1722)	ādz 'today'	ādz(tSyā)sārkhā 'like today'
(1723)	parwā 'the day before yesterday'	parwā(tSyā)sārkhā 'like the day before yesterday'
(1724)	ithe 'here'	iṭhlyāsārkhā 'like here' (cf. 3.4.4.1.4)
(1725)	āt 'inside'	ātlyāsārkhā 'like inside'

2.2.3.5 *Adjectives from other categories*

-wālā

(i) postposition:

Adjectives are derived from adjectives by adding the postposition *wālā*. In this case, the postposition *wālā* serves as a marker to pick out one (identified by the postposition *wālā*) from a group.

	Adjective	Postposition	Adjective
(1726)	piwḷī 'yellow' (sf)	wālī (sf)	piwḷīwālī 'the yellow one'
	piwḷā (sm)	wālā (sm)	piwḷāwālā
(1727)	tSoṭī 'small' (sf)	wālī (sf)	tSoṭīwālī 'the small one'
	tSoṭā (sm)	wālā (sm)	tSoṭāwālā

The Perso-Arabic postposition *mand* formerly was fairly commonly used in Marathi (see Damle 1966 [1911]). However, it is not a productive postposition any more in contemporary Marathi. Adjectives derived from nouns by adding this postposition are now viewed as basic adjectives.

	Noun	Postposition	Adjective
(1728)	akkal 'brain/ intelligence'	mand	akkalmand 'intelligent'
(1729)	daulat 'wealth'	mand	daulatmand 'rich'
(1730)	fāydā 'profit'	mand	fāydemand (cf. 3.4.3)

(ii) pronoun:

The Possessive form of the reflexive pronoun *āpaṇ* functions as an adjective.

(1731)	(a)	āplā 'one's own' (sm)
	(b)	āple (pl.m)
	(c)	āplī (sf)
	(d)	āplyā (pl.f)
	(e)	āpla (sn)
	(f)	āplī (pl.n)

2.2.4 DERIVATION OF ADVERBS

2.2.4.1 *Adverbs from nouns*

(i) The most productive process of deriving adverbs from nouns is by the addition of the instrumental suffix *-ne* .

	Noun	Simple Adverb
(1732)	ghāī (f) 'hurry'	ghāīne 'hurriedly'
(1733)	bhaktī (f) 'devotion'	bhaktīne/bhaktine 'with devotion'
(1734)	rāg (m) 'anger'	rāgāne 'angrily'
(1735)	prem (n) 'love'	premāne 'lovingly'
(1736)	dukhkha 'pain'	dukhkhāne 'painfully'
		Instrumental Adverb
(1737)	hāt (m) 'hand'	hātāne 'by hand'
(1738)	toṇḍ (n) 'mouth'	toṇḍāne 'by mouth'
(1739)	dzhāḍū (m) 'broom'	dzhāḍūne 'with broom'
(1740)	posṭ 'post'	posṭāne 'through the post'

The vowel alternations in (1734) - (1740) are due to the regular process of insertion of an increment vowel before a case suffix to derive the oblique form from the stem. (For further discussion, see section 2.1.1.1).

(ii) *-(ā)t/ī:*
The locative suffixes *-(ā)t/-ī* derive adverbs from nouns.

	Noun	Adverb
(1741)	ghar 'house'	gharāt/gharī 'in/to the house'
(1742)	dukān 'shop'	dukānāt 'in/to the shop'
(1743)	śāḷā 'school'	śāḷet 'in/to the school'

Alternations in (1741) - (1743) are because of the stem changing to its oblique form before case suffixes and postpositions.

(iii) *-lā*
The suffix *-lā,* when added to nouns, derives an adverb.

	Noun	Adverb
(1744)	sakāḷ 'morning'	sakāḷlā 'in the morning'
(1745)	rātra 'night'	rātrīlā 'at night'
(1746)	ādz 'today'	ādzlā 'today'

Once again, stems change to their respective oblique forms before the suffix *-lā* in (1744) - (1746).

(iv) *-tahā*
The Sanskrit suffix *-tahā* 'with'/'through' derives adverbs from Sanskrit nouns.

	Noun	Adverb
(1747)	ãnśa 'part'	ãnśatahā 'part-by-part'
(1748)	yatna 'effort'	yatnatahā 'by/through effort'

(v) Special nouns in the pre-verbal position: Certain nouns, when placed immediately preceding the verb, function as adverbs.

(1749)	to	khara	dagaḍ	bolto
	he	truth	rock	tell-pres-3sm

'He tells the truth! Impossible!' (i.e., it cannot possibly be true that he tells the truth)

The word *dagaḍ* 'rock' is used metaphorically to indicate that the proposition cannot possibly be true. The word *mātī* 'dirt' or *khāk* 'ashes' can be alternatively used in place of *dagaḍ* in (1749) above to convey the same meaning.

(vi) Postposition/case suffix incorporation: Case-suffixes/ postpositions are added to nouns to create adverbs. Some examples are given below. As mentioned before, stems change to their corresponding oblique forms before case suffixes and postpositions.

Case-suffix incorporation:

	Noun	Adverb
(1750)	gāw (sn) 'village'	(a) gāwā-lā (dative) 'to the village'
		(b) gāwā-hūn (ablative) 'from the village'
		(c) gāwā-t (locative) 'in the village'

Postposition incorporation:

(d) gāwā-sāṭhī 'for the village'
(e) gāwā-paryānta 'up to the village'
(f) gāwā-mūḷe 'because of the village'

(vii) Adverbs indicating frequency are derived from certain time-measurement nouns by adding the Persian prefix *dar-*.

	Noun	Adverb	
(1751)	diwas 'day'	dardiwaśī every-day-loc	'every day'
(1752)	mahinā 'month'	darmahinyā-lā every-month-dat	'every month'

(1753) warśa 'year' darwarśī 'every year'
every-year-loc

In the examples above, the locative suffixes (*-ī/-lā*) follow the nouns which change to their oblique forms.

(viii) *-tsā:*
The suffix *-tsā* derives an adverb when added to a noun expressing the time of day.

	Noun	Adverb
(1754)	sakāḷ 'morning'	sakāḷtsā 'in the morning'
(1755)	sandhyākāḷ 'evening'	sandhyākāḷtsā 'in the evening'

It must be noted here that the derived elements can be used both as adverbs and adjectives:

Adverb:

(1756)	tū	sakāḷtsā	ye	mhaṇdʒe	āpaṇ
	you	morning-of	come-imp-2s	so that	we
	śāḷelā	barobar	dzāū		
	school-to	together	go-fut-1pl		

'Come in the morning so that we will go to school together.'

Adjective:

(1757)	sakāḷtsa	wartamānpatra	adzūn
	morning-of-3sn	newspaper-3sn	even now
	āla	nāhī	kā ?
	come-3sn	not	Q

'Has the morning newspaper not come yet ?'

(ix) Sanskrit suffixes
Some Sanskrit suffixes ((a) - (e)) and prefix *-ā* (f) are commonly used to derive adverbs from Marathi nouns.

(a) -pūrwak 'with'
(b) -druṣṭyā 'from the point of view'
(c) -waśāt 'due to'

(d) -anusār 'according to'
(e) -anurūp 'suitable for'
(f) ā- 'up to'

Examples:

pūrwak:

	Noun	Adverb
(1758)	nyāy 'justice'	nyāypūrwak 'justly'
(1759)	prem 'love'	prempūrwak 'with love'

-druṣṭyā:

	Noun	Adverb
(1760)	śāstra 'science'	śāstradruṣṭyā 'scientifically/ according to the scripture'
(1761)	samādʒ 'society'	samādʒdruṣṭyā 'from the point of view of the society'

-waśāt:

	Noun	Adverb
(1762)	daiwa 'fate'	daiwawaśāt 'due to fate'
(1763)	kāl(a) 'time'	kāl(ā)waśāt 'due to time'

-anusār:

	Noun	Adverb
(1764)	śikṣak 'teacher'	śikṣakānusār 'according to the teacher'
(1765)	patra 'letter'	patrānusār 'according to the letter'

-anurūp:

	Noun	Adverb
(1766)	guṇ 'qualities'	guṇānurūp 'suitable to the qualities'
(1767)	prasāŋga 'occasion'	prasangānurūp 'suitable for the occasion'

In examples in (1764) - (1767), nouns change to their oblique forms before Sanskrit suffixes.

ā-:

	Noun	Adverb
(1768)	maraṇ 'death'	āmaraṇ 'until death'

These suffixes and prefix are restricted to nouns borrowed from Sanskrit.

2.2.4.2 *Adverbs from verbs*

(i) A common strategy used to derive adverbs from verbs is the process of participialization. Both present and past participles function as adverbs. The formation of participles was already discussed in section 2.1.3.5.2.2. Some examples of participles (as adverbs) are given below.

-t progressive participles:

(1769)	to	hasat	kam	karto
	he	smile-prog	work	do-pres-3sm

'He does the work smiling.'

-tānā - participle:

(1770)	to	pustak	wātstānā	tSahā	pito
	he	book	read-perf.part (while)	tea	drink-pres-3sm

'He drinks tea while reading the book.'

perfective (or past) participle:

(1771)	mī	tilā	dzhoplela	pāhila
	I	she-dat	sleep-perf.part-3sn	see-pst-3sn

'I saw her asleep (i.e., while she was asleep).'

(1772)	tī	hasūn	mhaṇālī
	she	*smile-conj.part*	*say-pst-3sf*

'Smiling, she spoke.'

-t participle:

The present participle (i.e., *-t* participle) is repeated to indicate the manner or time (or both) of the action expressed by the main verb.

Time:

(1773)	to	kā̃m	kartā	kartā	gā̃t
	he	work	do-pres.part	do-pres.part	sing
	hotā				
	was				

'He was singing while doing the work.'

(1774)	to	bolat	bolat	kā̃m	karat	holā
	he	talk-pres.part	talk-pres.part	work	do-op	was

'He was working as he was talking.'

Note that the participle in (1773) is inflected with the suffix *-ā* , while it is not in (1774), where the vowel *-a* occurs between the stem and the participial suffix *-t*. The difference between these two is that in (1773) the repeated participle emphasizes the time of the singing (the action expressedby the main verb), while in (1774) it emphasizes the manner in which the work was done. This difference between the two becomes clear in the following sentences. When it is to be indicated that he stopped in the middle of doing the work, only the *-tā* participle is allowed (1775). In contrast to this, if the question "How was he working?" is to be answered, only the *-at* is allowed (1775b).

(1775)	to	kā̃m	kartā	kartā	thā̃mblā
			*karat	karat	
	he	work	do-pres.part	do-pres.part	stop-pst-3sm

'He stopped in the middle of doing the work.'

(1775a)	Q:	to	kā̃m	kasa	karat	hotā ?
		he	work	how	do	was

'How was he working ?'

(1775b)	Answer:	bolat	bolat
		*bolatā	boltā
		talk-pres.part	talk-pres.part

'While talking'

2.2.4.3 *Adverbs from adjectives*

(i) word order:

Adjectives placed immediately preceding verbs function as adverbs.

(1776)	mat	tsāŋgla	samadzṇa . . .
	opinion	good-3sn	understand-inf-3sn

'. . . understanding the opinion properly'

(ii) *-dā*

The suffix *-dā* is added to numerals to derive adverbs which indicate the frequency of the action expressed by the verb.

	Numeral	Adverb
(1777)	ek 'one'	ekdā 'once'
(1778)	don 'two'	dondā 'twice'
(1779)	sahā 'six'	sahādā 'six times'

(iii) *-rītīne* 'by the manner'

The postposition *-rītīne* 'by the manner' may be added to some adjectives in oblique form to derive adverbs of manner which explains the morphonemic alternation in the forms in (1780) - (1781).

	Adjective	Adverb
(1780)	tsāŋglī 'good (sf)'	tsāŋglyārītīne 'properly/nicely'
(1781)	sopī 'easy (sf)'	sopyārītīne 'easily'

(iv) *-ne:*

The suffix *-ne,* when added to adjectives (in their oblique forms ending in *-yā*), derives adverbs.

	Adjective	Adverb
(1782)	pahilā 'first (sm)'	pahilyāne 'first time'
(1783)	moṭhā 'big (sm)/ loud'	moṭhyāne 'loudly'
(1784)	mukāṭ 'quiet'	mukāṭyāne 'quietly'

(v) The suffix *-paṇe* when added to adjectives derives adverbs.

(1785)	niśtSit 'certain'	niśtSitpaṇe 'certainly'
(1786)	sāwadh 'cautious'	sāwadhpaṇe 'cautiously'

2.2.4.4 *Adverbs from adverbs*

(i) *-ūn*

The suffix *-ūn* is added to adverbs to derive other adverbs.

	Adverb	Adverb
(1787)	war 'on'	warūn 'from the top'
(1788)	khālī 'down'	khālūn 'from the down side' (cf. 3.4.1.3.1.1 and 3.4.4.1.6)
(1789)	āt 'in'	ātūn 'from inside'
(1790)	bāher 'onto'	bāherūn 'from outside'

(ii) *-war*

The suffix *-war* is added to adverbs of time and place to indicate time/space limitations.

	Adverb	Adverb
(1791)	ādz 'today'	ādzwar 'till today'
(1792)	yethe 'here'	yethwar 'up to here' (cf. 3.4.4.1.4)
(1793)	tethe 'there'	tethwar 'up to there' (cf. 3.4.4.1.4)

(iii) *-śī*

The suffix *-śī* is added to adverbs of time and place to derive emphatic adverbs (which emphasize/intensify the adverbial meaning conveyed by their counterparts).

	Adverb	Adverb
(1794)	maghā 'a little while ago'	maghāśī 'indeed, a little while ago'
(1795)	ithe 'here'	itheśī 'here indeed'

(iv) *-diśī*

The suffix *-diśī* is added to adverbs which involve onomatopoeic words expressing the manner of action. An adverb with this suffix intensifies the meaning conveyed by its counterpart without it.

	Adverb	Adverb
(1796)	ṭuṇṇa 'with a sudden upward movement'	ṭuṇṇadiśī 'with a sudden upward movement'
(1797)	{tsaṭ / dzhaṭ} 'quick'	{tsaṭdiśī / dzhaṭdiśī} 'quickly'

It should be noted here that the suffix *-diśī* can be replaced by the suffix *-kan*. Both *-diśī* and *-kan* carry the function of intensifying the meaning of the adverb. Two adverbs are paired together to convey metaphorical meanings as in following examples.

(1798)	māge behind	puḍhe in front	pāhṇe see/look	'to be hesitant' (lit: 'to look behind and forward')
(1799)	ikḍe here	tikḍe there	pāhṇe look	'to lack concentration' (lit: 'to look here and there')
(1800)	ādz today	udyā tomorrow		'in the near future'
(1801)	kāl yesterday	parwā day before yesterday		'in the recent past'

2.2.4.5 *Adverbs from other categories*

Adverbs are derived from pronouns by addition of the suffixes *-the, -kaḍe,* and *-sa* to derive locative adverbs, directional adverbs, and manner adverbs, respectively. The demonstrative pronouns *he* 'this', *te* 'that', and the relative *dzo* participate in this derivation. The alternations in (1802) - (1810) are lexical in nature.

	Pronoun	Adverb (locational)
(1802)	he 'this (sn)'	ithe/yethe 'here'
(1803)	te 'that (sm)'	tithe/tethe 'there'
(1804)	dze/ʤe 'which (sn)'	ʤithe/ʤethe 'where (relative)'

	Pronoun	Adverb (directional)
(1805)	he 'this'	ikḍe 'in this direction'
(1806)	te 'that'	tikḍe 'in that direction'
(1807)	dze/ʤe 'who'	ʤikḍe 'in which (relative) direction'

	Pronoun	Adverb (manner)
(1808)	he 'this'	asa 'like this/in this manner'
(1809)	te 'that'	tasa 'like that/in that manner'
(1810)	dze/ʤe 'which'	dzasa 'in which manner (relative)'

2.2.5 POSTPOSITIONS

Postpositions such as (*-tSyā) kaḍe* 'in the direction (of)' and *(-tSyā) dzawaḷ* 'close (to)' take the suffix *-ūn* to derive adverbs as follows.

	Postposition	Adverb
(1811)	X (*tSyā)* kaḍe	X (*tSyā*) kaḍūn 'from X'
(1812)	X (*tSyā*)dzawaḷ	X (*tSyā*)dzawaḷūn 'from close to X'

2.2.5.1 *Order of suffixes*

The derivational suffixes follow inflectional suffixes:

	Masculine noun	Feminine noun	Feminine plural
(1813)	dhobī 'washerman'	-ṇ *dhobīṇ* 'washerwoman/ washerman's wife	-ī *dhobiṇī* 'washerwomen'
(1814)	tsor 'thief'	-ī tsorī 'theft'	-ā *tsoryā* 'many thefts'

Postpositions follow inflectional suffixes (which change nouns to their oblique forms):

(1815a) kutrā 'dog'

(1815b) kutre 'dogs'

(1815c) kutryā̃*tSyā* 'of the dogs'

2.2.6 DERIVATION OF POSTPOSITIONS

2.2.6.1 *Complex postpositions*

Complex postpositions are derived by adding case markers—especially locative, ablative, and possessive—to postpositions.

(i) simple postposition + case marker:

(1816a) war 'above'

(1816b) warūn (abl) 'from above'

(1816c) wartsā (poss) 'of the above'

(1817a) khālī 'down/below'

(1817b) khālūn (abl) 'from below'
(alternation due to oblique stem before case-suffixes/ postpositions)

(1818a) puḍhe 'ahead'

(1818b) puḍhyāt (loc) 'in front of'
(alternation due to oblique stem before case-suffixes/ postpositions)

(ii) Compound postpositions:

The possessive postposition -*tSyā* (and its variants) is commonly used with postpositions. Those postpositions are historically derived from nouns and adverbs.

(1819) X (tSyā) samor 'ahead of/in front of'

(1820) X (tSyā) kaḍe 'toward X'

(1821) X (tSyā) sārkhā 'like X'

(1822) X (tSyā) toḍītsā 'equal to X'

Note that the possessive suffix -*tSyā* occurs only optionally in these cases. Note that (1819), (1820), (1821)) are de-adverbial postpositions, and (1822) is a de-nominal postposition derived from the nominal *toḍ* 'comparison' (f).

2.2.6.2 *Simple derived postpositions*

2.2.6.2.1 *De-nominal*

A number of postpositions are derived from nouns by the addition of case markers to their respective oblique forms.

	Noun	Derived postposition
(1823)	hāt 'hand'	hātī/hātāne 'through'
(1824)	uttar 'north'	uttarelā 'to the north'
(1825)	pūrwa 'east'	pūrwelā 'to the east'

2.2.6.2.2 *De-verbal*

The conjunctive participial as well as progressive present participial forms of the verb are used as postpositions.

(1826) soḍūn 'excepting/excluding' (conjunctive particple of *soḍ* 'leave')

(1827) dharūn 'including' (conjunctive particple of *dhar* 'to include or hold')

(1828) kartā 'for' (present progressive participle of *kar* 'to do')

2.2.6.2.3 *De-adjectival*

There are no postpositions derived from adjectivals.

2.2.6.2.4 *De-adverbial*

Adverbs are frequently used as postpositions. Since they are formally identical, it is not possible to identify one as basic and the other derived. Some examples are given below.

(1829) war 'above/on'

(1830) khālī 'below/down'

(1831) dzawaḷ 'near'

(1832) māge 'behind'

(1833) puḍhe 'in front'

2.2.6.3 *Compound morphology*

Compounding is one of the most productive processes of word-formation in Marathi. Traditional grammars of Marathi discuss and categorize this process on the basis of the meaning of the components of the compound. However, the formal features of the compounds are not dealt with extensively.

2.2.6.3.1 *Nouns*

2.2.6.3.1.1 *Noun-noun compounds*

Noun-noun compounding is of the following types: Nouns which belong to the same semantic class may be compounded, with the derived compound syntactically behaving as a conjunct, plural noun phrase. The sequence of the nouns in a compound like this is not always interchangeable. This type of compounding is extremely common in Sanskrit, where the compounds are called *dwandwa* 'pair'. Some examples are given below.

(1834) āī- {bāp / vaḍīl}
mother-father — 'parents'

(1834a) *bāp/waḍīl-āī

(1835) warṣā-rutu — 'rainy season'
rain- season

(1835a) *rutu-warṣā

(1836) nāk-ḍoḷe — 'facial features'
nose-eyes

(1836a) *ḍoḷenāk

(1837) {rātran divas / night-day}
'continuously/ uncessantly'
{divasrātra / day-night}

-*n* after *rātra* in (1837) is the contracted form of *an* 'and'. Note that, except in (1837), the sequence of the components is not allowed to change. In contrast to the above, pairs of semantically contrastive nouns (antonyms) are also observed in Marathi.

(1838) sukha-dukhkha 'happiness'
happiness-pain

(1839) utStSa-nītS 'high or low'
high-low

(1840) pāp-puṇya 'sin or merit'
sin-merit

2.2.6.3.1.2 *Superordinate compounds*

This class of compounds consists of two nouns which belong to the same semantic class but are never antonyms. Together, they signify a superordinate semantic class.

(1841) hāt-pāy 'body'
hand-feet

(1842) baykā-pora 'family'
women/wives-children

(1843) tikhaṭ-mīṭh 'spices'
pepper-salt

(1844) nāk-ḍoḷe 'facial features'
nose-eyes

(1845) tūṭ-phūṭ 'destruction'
break-breaking (of glass)

The following features of the above compounds should be noted:

(a) both members of such compounds are 'heads' or are of equal significance in their semantic interpretation, i.e., there is no hierarchical head-embedding relationship between the two;
(b) neither member undergoes any morphophonemic change in the process of compounding;
(c) the order of the two is generally fixed;
(d) the meaning of the derived nominal phrase is generally transparent (i.e, derived from the meaning of its constituents in a straightforward fashion), and
(e) the derived compound is treated as a plural noun-phrase.

2.2.6.3.1.3 *Complex compounds*

This class of compounds involves a noun + noun combination in which there is no hierarchical relationship between the two members, and neither member acts as a semantic head. The nouns often have overlapping semantic features. Moreover, the meaning of the derived compound is not transparent, i.e., it cannot be derived by conjoining the meaning of the constituent members of the compound.

Some examples are given below:

(1846) khāṇa-piṇa 'lifestyle'
eating-drinking

(1847) hawā-pāṇī 'climate'
air-water

(1848) poṭ-pāṇī 'livelihood'
stomach-water

(1849) dew-ghew 'dealings'/'transaction'
giving-taking

(1850) ghar-dār 'entire property/estate'
house-door

Complex compounds with three nouns are not very common, but they do exist.

(1851) tan man dhan 'devotion' (*tan* 'body', *man* 'mind', and *dhan* 'money')

2.2.6.3.1.4 *Hyponymous compounds*

In an hyponymous compound, the first member is a hyponym of the semantic class of the second noun. Thus, the second noun functions as a semantic head, as shown in the following examples.

(1852) gangā nadī 'river-Ganges'
ganges river

(1853)	kamal lotus	puṣpa flower	'lotus-flower'
(1854)	tSãndan sandalwood	udbattī incense-stick	'incence-stick with sandalwood scent'
(1855)	pālā(e) leaf	bhāʤī vegetable	'leafy vegetable'

2.2.6.3.1.5 *Attributed compounds*

In an attributed compound, the first member functions as an attribute of the second member. The first member, though always in the nominative case, bears an accusative, locative, possessive, or dative relationship with the following noun.

Accusative attributive:

(1856) kām - tsor 'work thief' (one who shirks work)
work - thief

Locative attributive:

(1857) ḍāḷ-wāŋga 'eggplant, cooked in lentil soup'
lentil soup-eggplant

Possessive attributive:

(1858) rāʤ-wāḍā 'royal palace'
king-palace

(1859) bhāʤī-bādzār 'vegetable market'
vegetable-market

Dative attributive:

(1860) wasatī-gṛha 'boarding house'
residence-house

(1861) swaypāk-ghar 'kitchen'
cooking-house/place

2.2.6.3.1.6 *Emphatic compounds*

This type of compound involves two synonymous nouns. This process of compounding intensifies/emphasizes the meaning of the first noun by expressing the same meaning by the use of a synonym. The nouns in this type of compound can be drawn from one language (Marathi, Hindi, Sanskrit) or from two different languages, i.e., Marathi and Hindi.

(1862)	tsūk-bhūl	'mistake (M) - mistake (H)'	'mistake'
(1863)	ker-katsrā	'garbage (M) - garbage (M)'	'garbage'
(1864)	bāg-bagītSā	'garden (M) - garden (M)'	'garden'
(1865)	śāk-bhāʤī	'vegetable (H) - vegetable (M)'	'vegetable'
(1866)	ʤīw-ʤāntu	'animate(S) - animate (S)'	'living/ animate beings'
(1867)	por-bāḷ	'child (M) - child (M)'	'child'

2.2.6.3.1.7 *Reduplicative compounds*

Repetition of a noun derives a reduplicated noun compound. Reduplicated compounds express exhaustive and intensified meaning.

(1868)	mī	tyātsā	paisā	paisā	tsukawlā
	I	his-3sm	penny-3sm	penny-3sm	return-pst-3sm

'I returned his every penny.' (i.e., I returned all the money I owed him.)

Reduplicative compounds convey classificatory as well as reciprocal meaning.

Classificatory reduplicative compounds:

(1869)	noṭā	noṭā	itha	ṭhew	āṇi
	bills	bills	here	keep-imp-2s	and

nāṇī	nāṇī	tikḍe	ṭhew
coins	coins	there	keep-imp-2s

'Keep all the bills here and the coins there.'

Reciprocal reduplicative compounds:

(1870)	bāyakā	bāykāntSyā	goṣṭī . . .
	women	women	talks-3pl.f

'The talks among women . . .' (i.e., women to women talks)

2.2.6.3.1.8 *Echo-words/Partially reduplicative compounds*

These are formed by reduplicating the stem and replacing the first syllable with *bi.* The compound functions as an indefinitizer. This process applies to all major lexical categories.

(1871)	sāḍī (noun)	sāḍībiḍī	'sarees and the like'
	tuṭka (adj)	tuṭkābiṭkā	'broken (adj) and the like'
(1872)	war (adv)	warbir	'above or something'
(1873)	tsuklā (pst.part)	tsuklābiklā	'he made a mistake or something'
(1874)	paḍlā (pst 3sm)	paḍlābiḍlā	'he fell or something'

Note that in the above examples the first syllable (or only CV of a monosyllabic word) of the first member of the compound is replaced by *bi* in the reduplicated (second) member. Also note that the syllable *bi* does not undergo any phonological changes, regardless of the phonological shape of the syllable which it replaces. In Nagpuri Marathi, *gi,* instead of *bi,* is used to replace the first syllable of the first member of the compound. There is also a small class of compounds in which *s* + vowel replaces the first syllable of the first member of the compound. In this case, the choice of vowel is determined by the final vowel of the syllable which is being replaced, i.e., the final vowel in the replacing syllable is the same as the final vowel in the syllable which is replaced.

(1875)	lahān 'small'	lahānsahān 'small and the like'

(1876) ulaṭ 'wrong' ulaṭsulaṭ 'wrong and the like'

(1877) bhaltā 'strange', 'wrong' 'inappropriate' bhaltāsaltā 'strange/wrong and the like'

There is a related class of compounds in which the first nominal member is followed by a phonologically related (semantically empty) morpheme. This type of compound differs from the reduplicative compounds discussed above in that the phonological shape of the second member in these compounds varies from compound to compound and is not predictable on the basis of any regular phonological rule.

(1878) śedzārī 'neighbor' śedzārīpādzārī 'neighbors and the like'

(1879) oḷakh 'familiarity' oḷakhpāḷakh 'familiarity and the like'

(1880) daṇā 'grain' dāṇāduṇā 'some grain/or grain or the like'

(1881) moḍkā 'broken' moḍkātoḍkā 'broken and the like'

(1882) phāṭkā 'torn' phāṭkātuṭkā 'torn and the like'

In these compounds it is the first member which generally conveys meaning and the second member which is semantically empty. However, there are examples below where it is the second member which expresses meaning while the first member is empty.

(1883) khuṇā 'signals' khāṇākhuṇā 'signals and the like'

(1884) padośī 'neighbor' aḍośīpadośi 'neighbors and the like'

2.2.6.3.1.9 *Adjective-noun compounds*

In these compounds, the first member is an adjective which modifies the meaning of the following noun. The second member is the semantic head. This type of compound is commonly found in most modern Indian languages, such as Hindi, Punjabi, Gujarati, Kannada, etc. Some examples are given below.

(1885)	mahā-mūrkha great-fool	'a very foolish person'
(1886)	pīta-āmbar (pītāmbar) yellow-clothing	'yellow dress'
(1887)	tāmbaḍ-mātī red-clay	'red clay'
(1888)	piṭhī -sākhar powdered-sugar	'powdered sugar'
(1889)	sāḍe-tSār half-four	'four and a half'
(1890)	sawwā sāt quarter seven	'seven and a quarter'
(1891)	gawtī- tSahā grass-of tea	'tea made of a special kind of grass'

2.2.6.3.1.10 *Noun + gaṇīk*

This type of compound involves a sequence of a noun followed by the morpheme *ganīk* which is a distributive marker as shown below.

māṇūs 'person':

(1892)	māṇsā-gaṇīk person-every	'every person'

rastā 'street':

(1893)	rastyā-gaṇīk	'every street'

śahar 'city'

(1894)	śahrā-gaṇīk	'every city'

In the above examples, the noun is in its oblique form,which indicates that *gaṇīk* functions as a postposition.

2.2.6.3.2.1 *Noun-verb compounds*

The first member of this compound is a noun, and the second member is a verb stem. The derived compound functions as a noun.

(1895)	ghar-phoḍ house-break	'house-breaking'
(1896)	ḍoḷe-dzhāk eyes-close	'closing the eyes' (i.e., purposely ignoring something)
(1897)	wāṭ-tsāl way/path-walk	'walking on a path'

There is another set of compounds consisting of noun + verb stem. In this case, the verb stem is followed by the suffix *-ū* and the derived compound is an adjective.

(1898)	khise-kāp-ū pockets-cut	'pickpocket' (the one who cuts pockets)
(1899)	māthe-phir-ū heads-twist (intr)	'crazy' (the one whose mind is twisted)

Note that in the above compounds the nouns are in their plural form.

(Additional examples of noun + verb (derivational) compounds were already discussed in sections 2.2.2.3.5 and 2.2.6.3.4.1.)

2.2.6.3.2.2 *Participle-noun compounds*

(1900)	pikla-pān ripe (withered)-leaf-pst.part	'withered leaf' (old person)
(1901)	kruta - karma do-pst.part action	'done-action' (action which is already done)
(1902)	mruta-deha die-pst.part-body	'dead body'

In this type of compound the first member is generally a Sanskrit past participle (as in *kruta* 'done', and *mruta* 'dead'), and the second member is a Sanskrit noun. However, native Marathi counterparts of this compound (as in *pikla* 'ripe/withered'), though not very common, are also found.

2.2.6.3.3.1 *Adjective-numeral compounds*

A large number of compounds derived from a numeral-noun + adjectival suffix are also observed in Marathi. The derived compound functions as an adjective. The numeral may occur in its complete or partial form in this case.

(1903) du-toṇḍ-yā 'double-mouthed (person)' (one who speaks for both (conflicting sides))
two-mouth-adj

(1904) tīn-māh-ī/timāhī 'three-monthly'
three-month-adj

(1905) pā̃ntSa-wārṣa-ik-(pañtsawārṣik) 'five-yearly' (that which is done for/every five years)
five-year-adj

2.2.6.3.3.2 *Reduplicated and echo-compounds*

Reduplicated and echo-compounds involving adjectives are very common in Marathi. This type of compound expresses a variety of meanings.

(1906) ā̃ndhaḷā-ā̃ndhaḷā 'every-blind (person)'
blind-blind

(1907) ũntsa-ũntsa 'every tall (person)'
tall-tall

The reduplication of adjectives intensifies the meaning expressed by the adjective.

(1908) goḍ-goḍ 'very sweet'
sweet-sweet

(1909) moṭhe-moṭhe 'very big'
big (pl.m) - big (pl.m)

(1910) halka-halka 'very light'
light (sn) - light (sn)

It should be noted here that in the above compounds the adjective may be inflected for the gender and number of the following noun. Additionally, the last syllable may be optionally dropped as in the following examples.

(1911a) bhaltā-bhaltā 'very strange'
strange (sm) - strange (sm)

(1911b) bhal-bhalta 'very strange'

(1912a) nirāḷā-nirāḷa 'very different'
different (sm) - different (sm)

(1912b) nir-nirāḷā 'very different'

The second member of the echo compound adjective functions as an intensifier. The second member (or intensifier in this case), is not used as an independent adjective (for further details, see section 2.2.3.3). Some examples are given below.

(1913) kāḷā-kṣār 'deep black'
black-intens

(1914) lāl-tsuṭuk 'deep red'
red-intens

(1915) hirawā-gār 'deep green'
green-intens

In the following echo compounds adjective, the second member retains only one of the consonants of the first member and, again, serves as an intensifier as in the following examples.

(1916) laṭṭha-muṭṭha 'very fat'
fat-intens

(1917)	kāḷā-kuṭṭa black-intens	'deep black'
(1918)	lā̃mb-latsak long-intens	'very long'
(1919)	ṭhengṇa-ṭhuskā short-intens	'very short'

The second member is never used as an independent adjective elsewhere in the language.

2.2.6.3.4 *Verbs*

2.2.6.3.4.1 *Conjunct verbs*

Conjunct verbs are formed by adding verbs such as *as/hoṇe* 'to be', *karṇe* 'to do', *wāṭṇe* 'to feel', *deṇe* 'to give', *gheṇe* 'to take' to preceding nouns, adjective, pronouns, and adverbs. This process is extremely productive in Marathi. A number of vocabulary items borrowed from English and Sanskrit participate in this construction.

Noun-Verbs:

		Action	*Stative*	*Inchoative*
(1920)	āṭhwaṇ	āṭhwaṇ-karṇe	āṭhwaṇ-asṇe	āṭhwaṇ-yeṇe
	'memory'	'to remember'	'to remember'	'to remember'
(1921)	kāḷʤī	kāḷʤī-karṇe	kāḷʤī-asṇe	kāḷʤī-wāṭṇe
	'worry'	'to worry'	'to worry'	'to get worried'
(1922)	dukhkha	dukhkha-karṇe	dukhkha-asṇe	dukhkha-hoṇe
	'pain'	'to suffer'	'to have pain'	'to get pain'

Pronoun-verbs:

		Action	*Stative*	*Inchoative*
(1923)	āpla 'self'	āpla(sa)-karṇe 'to make one's own'		āpla(sa)-hoṇe 'to become one's own'

Adjective-verbs:

		Action	*Stative*	*Inchoative*
(1924)	bara 'all right'	bara-karṇe 'to make all right/ 'to cure'	bara-wāṭṇe/ 'to be all right'	bara-hoṇe 'to become all right'
(1925)	ghāī 'hurry'	ghāī-karṇe 'to rush'	ghāī-asṇe 'to be in a hurry'	ghāī-hoṇe 'to be in a hurry'

In addition to the above, Marathi also has conjunct verbs formed with verbs such as *basṇe* 'to sit' (to indicate a sudden/unexpected action), *wāṭṇe* 'to feel' (indicative of the state of mind), *deṇe* 'to give', *gheṇe* 'to take', *miḷṇe* 'to receive' (to indicate an intentional action).

	Noun	Conjunct verb	
(1926)	dhakkhā 'shock'	dhakkā-basṇe shock-sit	'to get a shock'
(1927)	āśtSarya 'surprise'	āṣtSarya-wāṭṇe surprise-feel	'to be surprised'
(1928)	wāīṭ 'bad'	wāīt-wāṭṇe bad-feel	'to feel bad'
(1929)	bhāṣaṇ 'lecture'	bhāṣaṇ-deṇe lecture-give	'to give lecture'
(1930)	suṭṭī 'leave'	suṭṭī-gheṇe leave-take	'to take leave'

(1931)	sandhī 'chance'	sandhī-miḷṇe chance-receive	'to get a chance'

Note that the verbs *karṇe* 'to do', *deṇe* 'to give', and *gheṇe* 'to take' express a volitional act and therefore indicate the agent's control over the action. The subject/agent of these actions is in the nominative case. In contrast to this, the verbs *asṇe/hoṇe* 'to be/to become', *wāṭṇe* 'to feel', *yeṇe* 'to come', *bas* 'to sit', express a state or a non-volitional act on the part of the subject of the verb. In this case, the subject of the verb is in the dative case (for further discussion on dative-subjects, see Pandharipande 1992a).

2.2.6.3.4.2 *Verb-verb compounds/serial verbs*

As discussed earlier in section 2.1.3.3.2.1.1, compound verbs primarily involve a sequence of two verbs. The first is a primary/main verb and the second verb is a verb which is variously termed the explicator, vector, operator, or auxiliary. The primary meaning of this verb-verb compound is determined by the lexical meaning of the main verb. The explicator verb adds a special/additional meaning to the meaning of the main verb. It is the explicator verb which receives the tense and aspectual marking, while the main verb remains in its conjunctive participial form. The following examples illlustrate the compound verbs.

(1932)	tyāne	patra	lihūn	ṭākla
	he-ag	letter-3sn	write-conj.part	drop-pst-3sn

'He wrote off the letter' (to get rid of the responsibility of writing it!).

(1933)	to	asa	bolūn	baslā
	he	like this	speak-conj.part	sit-pst-3sm

'He spoke like this (inadvertently/inappropriately).'

Note that in (1932) and (1933) the main verbs are *lihiṇe* 'to write', and *bolṇe* 'to speak' respectively, which are in their conjunctive participial forms, and they determine the primary meaning of the sentences. The explicator verbs *tākṇe* 'to drop', and *basṇe* 'to sit' contribute additional meanings as illustrated in the English translations of the sentences.

There is a small class of explicator verbs in Marathi. The following explicators are frequently used in Marathi.

(i) *deṇe* 'to give'
Expresses the benefactive meaning. The beneficiary is generally other than the subject of the action. In the case of verbs such as *raḍṇe* 'to cry', *hasṇe* 'to laugh', the explicator *deṇe* expresses an overt and/or sudden action.

(ii) *yeṇe* 'to come'
Indicates action toward the subject or the focal point.

(iii) *dzāṇe* 'to go'
Indicates action away from the subject or the focal point. It also indicates action performed inadvertently.

(iv) *gheṇe* 'to take'
Expresses action which is beneficial to the subject. When used with the main verb *radṇe* 'to cry' or *hasṇe* 'to laugh', it expresses an introvert action.

(v) *ṭākṇe* 'to drop'
Conveys that the action is performed by the subject to get rid of the responsiblity of performing it.

(vi) *basṇe* 'to sit'
Indicates that the action is performed inadvertantly and/or inappropriately by the subject.

(vii) *dākhawṇe* 'to show'
Indicates determination on the part of the subject to perform and/or complete the action.

(viii) *soḍṇe* 'to leave'
Indicates determination on the part of the subject to pursue the action till its completion/conclusion.

Modal verbs such as *tsukṇe* 'to complete', *śakṇe* 'to be able to' are also treated as explicators in Marathi grammars (see sections 2.1.3.3.2.1.1.7 and 2.1.3.4.7 for details and examples). The following combinations of verbs are also treated as compound verbs in the grammars of Marathi, since they involve a sequence of verbs.

(i) infinitive (main verb) + dative + *pāhidʒe* 'should'
or
have 'should'
or
lāg 'have to'

(For further details on obligational constructions see sections 1.1.1.3.1.1.2-5.)

(ii) infinitive (main verb) + dative + *lāgṇe* 'to begin to'

(iii) main verb + *ū* + *deṇe* 'to allow'

(iv) main verb + perfective (*l*) + *as* 'completion of the action'

(v) main verb + progressive (*t*) + *as* 'progressive aspect' (action in progress)

(vi) main verb + progressive (*t*) + *as* (pst) 'habitual aspect'

(For discussion on the complete range of serial verbs indicating various aspectual meanings, see section 2.1.3.3 and subsections thereof.)

2.2.6.3.4.3 *Reduplicative verb compounds*

Various types of reduplication are observed in Marathi.

(i) Reduplication of verbs intensifies the meaning of the verb as well as the aspect.

(1934) present progressive:

kām	karat	karat . . .
work	do-prog	do-prog

'while continuously doing the work'

(1935) conjunctive participle:

...kām	karūn	karūn	thaklā
work	do-conj.part	do-conj.part	tire-pst-3sm

'He got tired of doing the work.'

(ii) Another type of verbal reduplication involves the repetition of the verb stem, which intensifies the meaning of the verb.

(1936)	tī	raḍ	raḍ	raḍlī
	she	cry	cry	cry-pst-3sf

'She cried a lot.'

(1937)	tī	bol	bol	bollī
	she	talk	talk	talk-pst-3sf

'She talked a lot.'

In this case the stem of the main verb is repeated twice, and the main verb takes the tense and aspectual markers.

(iii) The third type of verb-compounding is observed in the repetition of the future first person (singular or plural) form of the verb. The compound is placed in a quote and indicates the uncertainty of the action expressed by the verb.

(1938)	to	yeīn	yeīn	(asa)
	he	come-fut-1s	come-fut-1s	(thus)

mhaṇto
say-pres-3sm

'He says, "I will come, I will come." '

(1939)	tyā	mulī	paise	deū
	those	girls	money-pl.m	give-fut-3pl

deū	(asa)	mhaṇtāt
give-fut-3pl	(thus)	say-pres-3pl.f

'Those girls say, "we will give money, we will give money." '

(iv) Another type of verb-compounding is used to express the meaning 'as soon as . . . '. In this case the gerundive form of the verb is repeated, as in the following sentence:

(1940)	anū	gharī	ālyā	ālyā	dzhopte
	Anu	home-loc	come-ger	come-ger	sleep-pres-3sf

'Anu goes to sleep as soon as she comes home.'

2.2.6.3.5 *Hybrid compounds*

A large number of hybrid compounds are found in both spoken and written varieties of Marathi. While Sanskrit-Marathi compounds have been extensively used all through the history of Marathi, a renewal of these compounds has been motivated by the process of modernization of Marathi. There is a strong drive among government administrators, as well as speakers, to "purge" Marathi of the extensive influence of English (which has lasted for over 200 years) by substituting Sanskrit vocabulary for English counterparts. This process has created a large number of new Sanskrit-Marathi compounds. Some representative examples are given below.

(1941) satSiw-ālay 'secretariat'
secretary-house

(1942) pradhān-māntrī 'prime minister'
prime-minister

(1943) wāta-anukūlit 'air-conditioned'
(wātānukūlit)
air-conditioned

Interestingly enough, the process of modernization is also attested to in new hybrid Engish-Marathi compounds in Marathi.

(1944) kirāṇā-ṣtoar 'grocery store'
grocery-store

(1945) bhadʒī-mārkeṭ 'vegetable market'
vegetable-market

(1946) pustak-kampanī 'book-company'
book-company

(1947)	rāṣṭrīya-bank national-bank	'national bank'

These two apparently conflicting currents of Sanskritization and Englishization in Marathi indicate the speakers' ambivalent attitude toward the English language. It is viewed as the symbol of "modernity" (which explains its borrowing into Marathi in order to modernize the language), as well as the language of the colonizers (which explains why it is being replaced by Sanskrit vocabulary). At present, these two processes are distributed in different domains, i.e., Sanskritization is largely restricted to the official/formal/and written register of Marathi, while Englishization is largely restricted to the spoken variety, especially in the scientific/business registers of Marathi. A large number of conjunct verbs (English noun/adjective + Marathi auxiliary) are frequently used in the spoken variety of Marathi.

(1948)	apɔiṇṭmenṭ-gheṇe appointment-take	'to take/make an appointment'
(1949)	risīw-karṇe receive-do	'to receive'
(1950)	inwīṭeśan-deṇe invitation-give	'to invite'

PHONOLOGY

3.1 PHONOLOGICAL UNITS (SEGMENTAL)

The pulmonic egressive airstream mechanism is involved in the production of all phonetic segments of the language.

3.1.1 DISTINCTIVE SEGMENTS

The distinctive segments of Standard Spoken Marathi are the following:

Table 1

Vowels and Diphthongs

	Front	Central	Back
High: tense/long	i		u
lax/short	I		U
Mid	e		o
Mid Low	əi, *æ	ə	əu, *ɔ
Low		a	

[* occurs only in words borrowed from English.]

The vowel segments /i/, /I/, /e/, /əi/, /æ/, /ə/, /a/, /u/, /U/, /o/, /əu/ and /ɔ/ are transcribed as /ī/, /i/, /e/, /ai/, /æ/, /a/, /ā/, /ū/, /u/, /o/, /au/ and /ɔ/, respectively. Also, it is important to mention here that the precise difference between ə and *a* is not very clear at this point. Hence in the Table 1 above, though on the basis of distributional properties I have characterized these two vowels as qualitatively different, based on the general nature of morpho-phonemic alternations in Marathi, I have treated them as differing in quantity as well. More research is needed to resolve this ambiguity.

For a list of consonants in Marathi, see Table 2 on the next page.

3.1.2 DESCRIPTION OF DISTINCTIVE SEGMENTS

3.1.2.1 *Non-syllabics (consonants)*

3.1.2.1.1 *Plosives and affricates*

(i) *stops*

[p] is a voiceless unaspirated bilabial (labio-labial) stop. *pãn* 'leaf', *āpaṇ* 'we', *dzhop* 'sleep'.

[ph] is a voiceless aspirated bilabial (labio-labial) stop. *phaḷ* 'fruit', *saphal* 'successful', *ḍaph* 'drum'

[b] is a voiced unaspirated bilabial (labio-labial) stop. *baḷ* 'strength', *sāban* 'soap', *kharāb* 'bad'

[bh] is a voiced aspirated bilabial (labio-labial) stop. *bhay* 'fear', *kumbhār* 'potter', *amitābh* 'the sun' (the one of infinite light)

[t] is a voiceless unaspirated dental stop. *tās* 'hour', *utār* 'descent', *mat* 'opinion'

[th] is a voiceless aspirated dental stop. *thãmb* 'stop!', *uthaḷ* 'shallow', *sāth* 'epidemic'

[d] is a voiced unaspirated dental stop. *dār* 'door', *ādar* 'respect', *pad* 'position'

[dh] is a voiced aspirated dental stop. *dhar* 'hold', *udhār* 'loan/debt', *śodh* 'discovery'

[ṭ] is a voiceless unaspirated retroflex stop. *ṭīmba* 'dot', *tSiṭak* 'to stick', *dzhaṭpaṭ* 'fast'

Table 2

Consonants

		Labial	Dental	Alveolar	Retroflex	Alveo-palatal	Velar	Glottal
Stop	vl. unasp.	p	t		ṭ		k	
	vl. asp.	ph	th		ṭh		kh	
	vd. unasp.	b	d		ḍ		g	
	vd. asp.	bh	dh		ḍh		gh	
Nasal		m	n		ṇ			
Flap						r		
Lateral					ḷ	l		
Affricate	vl. unasp.			ts		tS		
	vl. asp.			-		tSh		
	vd. unasp.			dz		ʤ		
	vd. asp.			dzh		ʤh		
Fricative	vl.	* f	s		ṣ	ś		h
	vd.	* v						
Semi vowels		w				y		

[* occurs only in words borrowed from English or Persian/Arabic.]

[ṭh] is a voiced aspirated retroflex stop. *ṭhets* 'injury (of the toe)', *baiṭhak* 'living room', *uṭh* 'get up'

[ḍ] is a voiced unaspirated retroflex stop. *ḍabā* box', *kaḍak* 'hard', *ughaḍ* 'open'

[ḍh] is a voiced aspirated retroflex stop. *ḍhekar* 'burp', *kaḍhaī* 'wok', *oḍh* 'pull'

[k] is a voiceless unaspirated velar stop. *kũmpaṇ* 'fence', *pakaḍ* 'hold/catch', *ṭok* 'point/edge'

[kh] is a voiceless aspirated velar stop. *khāraṭ* 'salty', *tSikhal* 'mud', *oḷakh* 'familiarity/acquaintance'

[g] is a voiced unaspirated velar stop. *gāṇa* 'song', *rāgīṭ* 'angry', *āg* 'fire'

[gh] is a voiced aspirated velar stop. *ghār* 'eagle', *ughḍā* 'open', *ogh* 'course of water'

(ii) *Affricates*

[ts] is a voiceless unaspirated alveolar affricate. *tsamtsā* 'spoon', *utsal* 'pick up', *pots* 'reach'

[tS] is a voiceless unaspirated alveo-palatal affricate. *tSahā* 'tea', *vatSan* 'promise', *nītS* 'vile/evil'

[tSh] is a voiceless aspirated alveo-palatal affricate. *tShān* 'nice/good', *bitShānā* 'bed'

[dz] is a voiced unaspirated alveolar affricate. *dzar* 'if', *ādzār* 'disease', *ādz* 'today'

[dzh] is a voiced aspirated alveolar affricate. *dzharā* 'spring (of water)', *ozha* 'burden', *wāndzh* 'childless'

[ʤ] is a voiced unaspirated alveo-palatal affricate. *ʤalad* 'fast', *uʤāḍ* 'forsaken (place)', *saroʤ* 'lotus' [ʤh] is a voiced aspirated alveo-palatal affricate. *ʤhirapṇe* 'to trickle', *māʤhī* 'my (fem.sg.)'

3.1.2.1.2 *Fricatives*

[f] is a voiceless labio-dental fricative found only in loan words from English or Perso-Arabic sources. *fī* 'fee' (English), *kafnī* 'a long dress worn by a Muslim monk (Perso-Arabic), *tārīf* 'praise' (Perso-Arabic)

[v] is a voiced labio-dental fricative restricted to vocabulary borrowed from English, e.g., *VCR*, *Vote*, etc. Its use is marginal, and Marathi speakers tend to replace it with [w] .

[s] is a voiceless apico-dental sibilant. *sāt* 'seven', *basūn* 'having seated', *bas* 'sit/enough'

[ṣ] is a voiceless retroflex (apico-post-alveolar) sibilant. *ṣatkon* 'hexagon', *poṣaṇ* 'rearing', *doṣ* 'drawback'. This sound is largely restricted to Sanskrit vocabulary.

[ś] is a voiceless palatal (lamino-palatal) sibilant. *śãŋkā* 'doubt', *viśāl* 'expansive', *pāś* 'attachment (i.e., binding force)'

[h] is a voiced glottal fricative. *hiwāḷā* 'winter', *pahāṭ* 'early morning', *kalah* 'conflict'

3.1.2.1.3 *Nasals*

Nasals are bilabial, apico-dental, and retroflex.

[m] is a bilabial voiced nasal stop. *mī* 'I', *amar* 'immortal', *kām* 'work'.

[n] is a dental (apico-dental) nasal stop. *nāk* 'nose' It is realized as dental before dental consonants , [t] and [d]: *ãnta* 'end', *kãnda* 'root'. It is realized as alveo-palatal before palatal affricates: *tSãñtSal* 'unstable/constantly moving', *gũñʤan* 'sound of singing', and as velar before velar consonants [k], [g]: *ãŋkur* 'sprout', *ãŋga* 'body'.

It should be noted here that [n] can occur in all positions, i.e., word-initial, medial, and final. However, its alveo-palatal or velar counterparts occur only in medial position. Moreover, neither [ŋ], nor [ñ] occurs as an independent phoneme.

[ṇ] is a retroflex (sublamino-post-alveolar) nasal stop. It does not occur initially. *pāṇī* 'water', *tāṇ* 'stretch'

3.1.2.1.4 *Liquids*

[l] is a voiced dental lateral. *lahar* 'whim', *gulāb* 'rose', *phūl* 'flower'

[ḷ] is a retroflex lateral. It does not occur initially. *bāḷ* 'child', *taḷa* 'lake'

[r] is an alveo-palatal flap or short trill. *ras* 'juice', *śarad* 'autumn', *ghar* 'house'

3.1.2.1.5 *Semi vowels*

[y] is a voiced palatal glide. It occurs in all positions. *yaś* 'success/victory', *gāyan* 'singing', *gāy* 'cow'

[w] is a voiced bilabial glide. *wārā* 'wind', *diwā* 'lamp', *kāsaw* 'tortoise'

3.1.2.2 *Syllabics*

3.1.2.2.1 *Vowels*

The vowels are described here in the order in which they are written in the *Devanāgrī* alphabet.

[a] is a short mid-low central unrounded vowel. It occurs in all positions: *apār* 'a lot', *dzawaḷ* 'near', *dzāḍa* 'trees'.

This vowel is lengthened word-finally when it occurs as a free variant of the vowel /e/. (See section 3.4.1.3.4 for details.)

[ā] is a long low central unrounded vowel which occurs in all positions: *āṭh* 'eight', *pasārā* 'mess', *śāḷā* 'school'

[i] is a short high front unrounded vowel. It occurs in all positions: *itha* 'here', *tSitra* 'picture', *gati* 'speed'

It should be noted here that word-final [i] in contemporary Marathi is replaced by [ī]. However, it is still maintained in the orthography in the formal Sanskritized register of Marathi. Words with word-final [i] are in most cases borrowings from Sanskrit.

[ī] is a long high front unrounded vowel. It occurs in all positions: *īrṣā* 'jealousy', *bāwīs* 'twenty-two', *bhitī* 'fear'

[u] is a short high back rounded vowel which occurs in all positions: *upaṭ* 'uproot', *surī* 'knife', *paśu* 'animal'

[ū] is a long high back rounded vowel. It occurs in all positions: *ūs* 'sugarcane', *vartaṇūk* 'behavior', *pātsū* 'emerald'

[e] is a mid front unrounded vowel which occurs in all positions. *ekṭī* 'alone' (fem.sg.), *anek* 'many', *ā̃mbe* 'mangoes'

[æ] is a mid-low front unrounded vowel used primarily in words borrowed from English. *bænk* 'bank', *hæt* 'hat', etc. It is also found in the exclamation *hæa!* which indicates disagreement with the speaker's statement and expresses a distinctly derogatory tone. It can be paraphrased in English as 'Come on, it is just not true!'.

[o] is a mid-high back rounded vowel that occurs in all positions. *ola* 'wet', *koṇ* 'who', *bāyko* 'wife'

[ɔ] is a mid-low back rounded vowel which is restricted to words borrowed from English. *dɔkṭar* 'doctor', *ɔthar* 'author', *ɔmlet* 'omlet', etc.

3.1.2.2.1.2 *Diphthongs*

[ai] is a mid-low front central unrounded diphthong, and it occurs in the initial and medial positions: *aik* 'listen', *gairhadzar* 'absent'

[au] is a mid-low back rounded diphthong which occurs in the initial and medial positions: *auṣadh* 'medicine', *haus* 'hobby/interest'

3.1.2.2.1.3 *Nasal vowels*

There are no inherently nasal vowels in contemporary Marathi. Vowels are nasalized before a nasal consonant, e.g., *ā̃mbā* 'mango', *tõṇd* 'month', *gā̃mmat* 'joke/an interesting matter'. Kelkar (1958: 12) claims that vowels are semi-nasalized before a nasal. An in-depth analysis of the nasalization of vowels is necessary.

Although nasalization of vowels is predictable in contemporary Standard Marathi, the question of the phonemic contrast between oral and nasal vowels is controversial in Marathi and in other Indo-Aryan languages (see Masica 1991: 117 for further details). In contemporary Standard Marathi, the nasal vowels of Old Marathi are realized either as a sequence of a nasalized vowel and a nasal consonant homorganic with the following consonant (see the plural forms of nouns in examples (791) - (806) in section 2.1.1.1 for example) or simply as an oral vowel (see the locative plural forms of nouns in examples (791) - (806)).

Although nasalization is not phonemic in Standard Marathi, as mentioned earlier in section 2.1.1.1, South-Konkani and some other dialects of Marathi do maintain this phonemic contrast. The adverbs of Old Marathi, *kẽwhā̃* 'when', *tẽwhā̃* 'then', *dʒẽwhā̃* 'when' (rel), have lost the nasalization on the final vowel. In these examples there is alternation between /ẽ/ and /e/ in the contemporary Marathi. It should be noted here that those speakers who pronounce a nasal /ẽ/ in *kẽwhā*, *tẽwhā*, and *dʒẽwhā* add a nasal consonant /m/ after it and also tend to retain the nasality on the final vowel. Thus the pronunciation of these words in this case is *kẽmwhā̃*, *tẽmwhā̃*, and *dʒẽmwhā̃* or alternatively, *kẽw̃w̃hā̃*, *tẽw̃w̃hā̃*, and *dʒẽw̃w̃hā̃* where /m/ is replaced by a nasalized glide /w̃/. Although in orthography there is a free alternation between

/ẽ/ and /e/, the word final /ã/ of Old Marathi words is always represented as /ā/

3.1.2.2.2 *Nasal diphthongs*

Marathi has a nasal diphthong /ãũ/ which is restricted to loan words from Sanskrit. Historically, this nasal diphthong is a result of *aṃ* changing to *ãũ*. This change is restricted to Sanskrit loans. The deletion of /ṃ/ takes place only before sibilants and liquids. Examples are given below.

Sibilants:

(1951)	haṃs	—>	hãũs	'swan'
(1952)	daṃś	—>	dãũs	'bite'

Liquids:

(1953)	saṃrakṣan	—>	sãũrakṣaṇ	'protection'
(1954)	saṃlakṣaṇ	—>	sãũlakṣan	'good quality'

Affricates:

(1955)	saṃtSālan	—>	sañtSālan	'operation'

Stops:

(1956)	saṃkramaṇ	—>	sãŋkramaṇ	'a major change in the direction of a movement/ operation'
(1957)	saṃpradān	—>	sãmpradān	'act of giving'

Note that before stops and affricates the nasal vowel /ṃ/ of Sanskrit loans is replaced by a homorganic nasal in accordance with the following stop/affricate. Although this process of diphthongization (and nasalization) has not been discussed in the grammars, it is clearly the loss of /ṃ/ which causes this change. This change is predictable because Marathi allows only homorganic nasals before consonants. Since there are no homorganic nasals for the sibilants and liquids, the nasal /ṃ/ drops and, consequently, the preceding vowel is nasalized.

3.1.2.2.3 *Nasalization of glides*

/y/ and */w/* are nasalized when followed by a nasalized vowel.

(i) tyā-tsa 'his'
he-poss-3sn

(ii) t͠yā̃n-tsa 'their'
they-poss-3sn

3.1.2.2.4 *Vowel assimilation*

Vowels are nasalized before nasal consonants.

(1958) mũŋgus 'mongoose'

(1959) t͠yā̃ntsā 'their-3sm'

(1960) ʤī̃ŋkṇe 'to win'

(1961) tSãndra 'moon'

(1962) ʤhē̃ṇḍā 'flag'

(1963) dõŋgar 'mountain'

3.1.2.3 *Consonants and vowels occurring in loan words*

The following consonants/vowels are restricted to loan words from Persian or English. The consonant */f/* occurs only in Persian and English words.

(1964) fikir 'worry' (Persian)

(1965) foṭo 'photograph' (English)

Similarly the vowels */æ/* and */ɔ/* are restricted to English loans.

(1966) kɔnṭrækṭ 'contract'

(1967) dɔkṭar 'doctor'

Moreover, these sounds (i.e., */æ/* and */ɔ/*) are restricted to the speech of educated Marathi speakers who wish to retain the English pronunciation.

3.1.2.4 *Restrictions on phonological segments by grammatical categories*

The sounds in loan words discussed in section 3.1.2.3 do not occur in postpositions, articles, pronouns and numerals (except English ones). They occur mostly in nouns and, to a lesser extent, in verbs, adjectives and adverbs.

3.2 PHONOTACTICS

3.2.1 DISTRIBUTION OF SEGMENTS

3.2.1.1 *Word-final consonants*

Except */tSh/* and */ʤh/*, all consonant segments, including borrowed ones, occur word-finally.

3.2.1.2 *Word-initial consonants*

All consonants except */ṇ/* and */ḷ/* occur word-initially.

3.2.2 CONSONANT CLUSTERS

3.2.2.1 *Distribution of consonant clusters*

Marathi has word-initial consonant clusters. A large number of consonant clusters occur in words inherited (*tatsama*) or derived (*tadbhava*) from Sanskrit.

(1968) strī 'woman'

(1969) krūr 'cruel'

(1970) bhramar 'bee'

However, in uneducated speech, initial consonant clusters (from Sanskrit) are absent, since either the Marathi equivalent is used instead, or the cluster is placed in the medial position by inserting a vowel word-initially; or the cluster is broken up by placing a vowel between the two consonants.

	Sanskrit	Marathi	
(1971)	strī	istrī	'woman'
(1972)	spaṣṭa	sapaṣṭa	'clear'

Similarly, word-initial consonant clusters, which occur in English loans in educated speech, are simplified in uneducated speech.

	English		Marathi	
(1973)	sṭeśan	'station'	iśṭeśan/ṭhesan	'station'

Consonant clusters freely occur in the medial position. In contrast to other modern Indian languages such as Hindi, Kashmiri and Punjabi, Marathi has a relatively small number of word-final consonant clusters. Marathi shares this feature with Dravidian languages, e.g., Kannada and Telugu.

3.2.2.2 *Possible consonant clusters*

3.2.2.2.1 *Possible word-initial consonant clusters*

The following consonant clusters occur word-initially:

pr	prem 'love'
br	brāhmaṇ 'priestly caste'
bhr	bhramar 'bee'
kr	krūr 'cruel'
gr	grahaṇ 'eclipse (of the sun or the moon)'
ghr	ghrāṇendriya 'nose' (lit: 'the organ of smelling')
dr	drūṣṭī 'eyesight'
tr	trāṇ 'strength'
ṭr	ṭrak 'truck'
sr	srot 'spring'
sp	spaṣṭa 'clear'
sk	skarṭ 'skirt'
śl	ślok 'a verse'

kl	kleś 'suffering'
st	stom 'hypocrisy'
sth	sthān 'place'
khy	khyātī 'fame'
py	pyālā 'glass'/'drank (3sm)'
by	byād 'nuisance'
bhy	bhyālā 'got scared' (3sm)
my	myān 'sheath'
ty	tyālā 'to him'
dy	dyūt 'game of dice'
dhy	dhyān 'meditation'
ny	nyāy 'justice'
ly	lyālā 'he wore'
wy	wyāpār 'business'
hy	hyālā 'to this one'
mh	mhais 'buffalo'
kw	kwatSit 'rarely/infrequently'
sw	swatāhā 'self'
dw	dweṣ 'envy'
nh	nhāṇī 'bathroom'

As mentioned earlier, these clusters are simplified in the rural/uneducated speech. Geminates never occur word-initially.

3.2.2.2.2 *Possible word-medial consonant clusters*

Various combinations of consonant clusters occur in the word-medial position. These can be divided into the following groups:

Geminates:

stops:		
kk	akkal	'intellect'
khkh	makhkha	'foolish'
ṭṭ	ghaṭṭa	'tight'
pp	gāppā	'casual conversation'
affricates:		
tsts	katstsā	'raw/unripe'
tStS	gatStSī	'terrace'

liquids:		
ll	gallī	'alley'
rr	bharrkan	'quickly'
nasals:		
nm	anna	'food'
mm	gãmmat	'amusing event/matter'

Non-geminates:

stop + stop:		
ṭk	paṭkan	'quickly'
kḍ	pakḍūn	'having caught'
stop + liquid:		
pl	āplā	'one's own'
tr	tShatrī	'umbrella'
affricate + stop:		
tsk	utskī	'hiccup'
fricative + stop:		
st	nustā	'only'
sk	nāskā	'spoiled'
ṣṭ	śiṣṭa	'proud'
fricative + liquid:		
sl	baslā	'sat down'
śr	āśram	'hermitage'
liquid + stop:		
lk	bolkā	'one who talks a lot'
rk	garka	'immersed'
lṭ	ulṭā	'reverse'
liquid + fricative:		
ḷś	āḷśī	'lazy'
rs	ārsā	'mirror'

liquid + nasal:

rm	karma	'action/fate'
rṇ	bharṇā	'overcrowding'
lṇ	salṇa	'hurt (mf)'

liquid + liquid:

rl	kārla	'bitter melon'
lr	balrām	'boy's name'

liquid + semivowel:

rw	garwa	'pride'
ly	ṭoplyā	'baskets'

nasal + stop:

nṭ	ghāṇṭā	'bell'
mbh	ārāmbha	'beginning'

nasal + semivowel

my	sāmya	'resemblance'
ny	anya	'other'

Marathi does have tripartite clusters, but the class of these is very small.

The sequence of nasal + stop + *r* is common, as in *sãntrī* 'oranges', *mãntrī* 'minister'. A few other commonly used tripartite clusters are the following:

kõmbḍā	'rooster'
ghõŋgḍa	'blanket made of rough fiber'
ṭoplyā	'baskets'
āmtSyā	'ours'

Affixation, suffixation, and the schwa syncope rule are primarily responsible for creating a large number of tripartite word-medial clusters in the language.

(1974)	pradān 'give'	sãm-pradān 'special gift' special-gift
(1975)	dzãmbhūḷ 'a kind of fruit'	dzãmbhḷ-ā-lā 'to the fruit' fruit-incr-dat

(For further discussion, see section 3.4.4.1 and sub-sections thereof.)

3.2.3 DISTRIBUTION OF VOWELS

3.2.3.1 *Word-final vowels*

All vowels occur freely in word-final position. However, the occurrence of */i/* and */u/* word-finally is rather limited (e.g., *āṇi* 'and', *parãntu* 'but'). It should be noted here that word-final short high vowels in Sanskrit nouns (borrowed, derived or inherited), such as *mati* 'intellect', *kṛti* 'action', *kīrti* 'fame', *guru* 'teacher', *madhu* 'honey', etc. are pronounced as long vowels although they may be represented as short vowels orthographically.

3.2.3.2 *Word-initial vowels*

There is no restriction on the occurrence of word-initial vowels.

3.2.3.3 *Sequences of (syllabic) vowels*

The following sequences of syllabic vowels occur in Marathi:

[iī]	piī 'used to drink'
[eī]	deī 'used to give'
[eū]	deū 'will give'
[aī]	tsaṭaī 'mat'
[āī]	āī 'mother'
[āū]	wikāū 'an object for sale'
[uī]	suī 'needle'

Sequences such as [*ie*], [*īe*], [*uo*], [*ūo*], [*iu*], [*īu*], [*iū*], [*īū*], are not found in the basic or derived vocabulary. The [*ie*] sequence across word-boundaries is broken up by the semivowel */y/*, while the sequence of [*uo*] is broken up by the semivowel */w/*.

3.2.4 CORRESPONDENCE BETWEEN THE STRUCTURE OF LEXICAL MORPHEMES AND WORD STRUCTURE

The structure of the lexical morphemes is the structure of their citation form to some extent. Noun forms occur in their citation forms in the nominative case. Also, the citation forms do occur at the syntactic level as well. Therefore, the possibilities for word structure do not exclude the structure of lexical morphemes. Verb stems (in their citation forms) are used as separate words (in the case of the imperative singular).

3.2.5 SYLLABLES

3.2.5.1 *Assignment of medial clusters to syllables*

Single medial consonants are assigned to the succeeding syllable. The first consonant of two-consonant clusters is assigned to the first syllable, while the second consonant is assigned to the next, e.g., *bhak* + *ta* —> *bhakta* 'devotee' (+ indicates syllable boundary). If there is a triple cluster in the medial position, in a bisyllabic word the first consonant is assigned to the first syllable, while the other two consonants are assigned to the second syllable, e.g., *san* + *tra* —> *santra* 'orange'.

3.2.5.2 *Canonical Syllable*

A canonical syllable type consists minimally of a single vowel, which may be short or long, preceded by up to three consonants, and which may be followed by a single consonant.

(C) (C) (C) V (V) (C)

3.2.6 RESTRICTIONS BETWEEN CONSONANTS AND VOWELS

3.2.6.1 *Restrictions between syllable-initial units and following vowels*

There are no restrictions between syllable-initial segments and following vowels.

3.2.6.2 *Restrictions between word/syllable-final units and preceding vowels*

There seems to be no restriction between consonants that might occur word- or syllable-finally and the vowels that precede them.

3.2.6.3-5 *Restrictions between syllable-initial and syllable-final units*

There are no constraints on the possible syllable-initial units or clusters or syllable-final units or clusters. Similarly, there are no restrictions on the units or clusters in the next syllable. There is neither vowel nor consonant harmony in Marathi.

3.2.6.6 *Phonotactic patterns in different word classes*

/f/, */æ/*, */ɔ/* occur in words borrowed from Persian and English. Similarly, */ṣ/* is restricted to *tatsama* words in Marathi.

3.3 SUPRASEGMENTALS

3.3.1 DISTINCTIVE DEGREES OF LENGTH

3.3.1.1-2 *Vowels*

Three pairs of vowels are distinguished according to length: */i/*, */ī/*; */u/*, */ū/*; and */a/ /ā/*.

(1976)		short vowels	long vowels
	/i/	pik 'split'	pīk 'crop'
	/u/	pur 'bury!'	pūr 'flood'
	/a/	paḷ 'run!'	pāḷ 'take care!/nourish!'

The length contrast is absent in other vowels.

Semivowels, liquids, nasals, fricatives, stops and affricates can contrast in length. The minimal pairs are often hard to find. The list of these double consonants is given in section 3.1.2.2. Some minimal pairs are given below:

3.3.1.3 *Semivowels*

(1977) tawā 'pan' sawwā '$1^{1}/_{4}$'

(1978) bāyā 'women' hiyyā 'courage'

3.3.1.4 *Stops*

(1979) śikā 'you (honorific) learn' śikkā 'stamp'

(1980) patī 'husband' pattī 'leaves'

3.3.1.5 *Liquids*

The lateral consonants /l/, /ḷ/ contrast in length.

(1981) kalā 'art' kallā 'loud noise'

(1982) gar 'pulp' garra 'whirling motion'

3.3.1.6 *Nasals*

Nasals also contrast in length.

(1983) suna 'quiet/silent' sunna 'blank/depressed'

3.3.1.7 *Affricates*

Affricates contrast in length.

(1984) khats 'heap' khatstsa 'a lot'

(1985) gatSī 'neck' gatStSī 'terrace'

3.3.1.8 *Fricatives*

Fricatives contrast in length.

(1986) ghusā 'you (pl) enter!' ghussā 'anger'

3.3.2 STRESS

Stress is not a prominent feature of Marathi. Moreover, it is perhaps one of the least investigated areas of Marathi phonology. Therefore any statement about the role of stress is tentative at this point. The stress patterns can be described as follows.

The distinction between light and heavy syllables is based on the length of the vowel and the coda consonant, if any. Thus, CV is a light syllable and CVV and CVC are heavy and CVV(C) is super heavy. [ī], [ū], [ā], [e], and [o] are treated as VV and [a], [i], and [u] are treated as V.

Stress rules:

(i) In a word, if there is only one heavy or a super heavy syllable, it is always stressed regardless of its position. In the following examples, bold and underlined letters show the locus of the main/primary stress in a word.

Word-final heavy:
(1987) kuṭh**e** 'where'

Word-initial heavy:
(1988) dzh**ā**ḍa 'trees'

First light syllable with coda:
(1989) d**u**ṣṭa 'evil/wicked person'

Heavy syllable in the medial position:
(1990) sam**a**sta 'entire'

Super heavy syllable gets stressed:
(1991) mhāt**ā**rpaṇa 'old ages'

(ii) In bisyllabic words, if both syllables are heavy, then the initial syllable gets stressed.

(1992) t**ā**rā 'star'

(1993) ś**ā**ḷā 'school'

(1994) m**ū**rtī 'statue'

(iii) In bisyllabic words, if both syllables are light, then the first is stressed.

(1995) ph**a**ḷa 'fruit (pl)'

(1996) mu̱ḷa 'roots'

(1997) ba̱ra 'all right!'

(1998) I̱ntSa 'inch'

(1999) bhi̱nta 'wall'

(2000) su̱ta 'threads'

(iv) There are no trisyllabic words in which all syllables are light.

(v) When the first two syllables of a trisyllable word are heavy, the first syllable is stressed.

(2001) dhI̱rāna 'courageously'

(2002) bha̱wātsa 'brother's'

(vi) In a trisyllabic word, if all syllables are heavy, the stress falls on the first syllable.

(2003) a̱ḍhāwā 'estimate'

(2004) mha̱tārā 'old man'

(2005) a̱dzārī 'sick'

(2006) pa̱wsāḷā 'rainy season'

(vii) In a trisyllabic word, if the second and the third syllables are heavy, the stress is on the second syllable.

(2007) tSala̱khī 'cleverness'

(2008) sama̱dhī 'the state of transcendence from the phenomenal world'

(2009) pudʒa̱rī 'priest/worshipper'

(viii) In a trisyllabic word, if only the last syllable is heavy, the stress is on that syllable.

(2010) garib**I** 'poverty'

(2011) dzawaḷ**I**k 'intimacy'

(2012) atSãmb**a** 'surprise'

(2013) dhaḍpaḍy**a** 'an active but clumsy man'

(ix) In a trisyllabic word, if the middle syllable is heavy, the stress is on that syllable.

(2014) im**a**rat 'building'

(2015) duk**a**na 'shops'

(2016) suk**a**ṇu 'sail'

The stress rules are equally applicable to nouns and verbs.

Heavy syllable in the final position:
(2017) kar**a** '(you-pl) do!'
do-do-2pl

Heavy syllable in the initial position:

(2018) dh**u**tla 'washed'
wash-pst-3sm

Both heavy syllables:
(2019) dh**a**wā '(you-pl) run!'
run-2pl

Both light syllables:
(2020) p**i**ṇa 'to drink'
drink-inf

Trisyllabic word (verb):

Initial heavy syllable:

(2021) th**a**mbawṇe 'to cause someone to stop'
stop-caus-inf

Heavy syllable in the middle position:

(2022) kar**a**wṇe 'to make someone do'
do-caus-inf

Heavy syllable in the final position:

(2023) basawl**a** 'to make X(mas-sg) to sit'
sit-caus-pst-3sm

Second and the third syllables heavy:

(2024) dhar**a**wā '(X) may be held'
hold-opt-3sm

The first and the last syllables heavy:

(2025) p**a**thawlā 'sent X(mas-sg)'
send-pst-3sm

3.3.3 TONES/PITCH

Marathi does not have tones, and pitch is not distinctive in the language.

3.3.4 INTONATION

There has been no systematic study of the patterns of intonation in Marathi. Therefore, the following discussion is tentative and needs further investigation.

3.3.4.1 *Major intonation patterns*

Yes-no questions have a final rising intonation.

(2026)	rām	tudzhā	mitra	āhe	kā ?
	Ram	your	friend	is	Q

'Is Ram your friend ?'

(2027)	tyālā	pohāylā	yeta	kā ?
	he-dat	swim-inf-dat	come	Q

'Can he swim ?'

Statements have a final falling intonation.

(2028)	to	ādz	amrāwatīlā	gelā
	he	today	Amravati-dat	go-pst-3sm

'He went to Amravati today.'

(2029)	mānʤū	śāḷet	dzāte
	Manju	school-loc	go-pres-3sf

'Manju goes to school.'

Information questions also have a final falling intonation.

(2030)	to	kuṭhe	gelā ?
	he	where	go-pst-3sm

'Where did he go ?'

Tag questions have a final rising intonation.

(2031)	tū	sukhī	āhes,	na ?
	you	happy	be-2s,	tag

'You are happy, aren't you ?'

Reconfirmation questions (in which the focused constituent is fronted) have final rising intonation.

(2032)	to	kā	rāgāwla ?
	he	Q	angry-pst-3sm

'Was it he who got angry ?'

Echo questions have a final rising intonation.

(2033)	pandhrā	ā̃mbe ?
	fifteen	mangoes

'Fifteen mangoes ?'

Imperatives have a final falling intonation.

(2034)	tū	ātā	gharī	dzā
	you	now	home-loc	go-imp-2s

'Now, you go home.'

Blessings and curses have a level intonation.

(2035)	sadā	sukhī	rāhā
	always	happy	be-2s

'May you always be happy.'

(2036)	tudzhā	satyānāś	howo
	your	destruction	be-opt-3s

'May you be destroyed!'

Similarly, repeated affirmative responses (*ho, ho* 'yes, yes') or negative responses (*nāhī nāhī* 'no, no') have a level intonation.

Doubt is expressed by falling intonation on the question word.

(2037)	khara	kā ?
	true	Q

'Is it true ?'

The process of extra vowel lengthening is used to express emphatic intonation. In the examples below, underlined vowels are extra long.

(2038)	mādzha	tyātSyāwar	khūp	prem	āhe
	I-poss-3sn	he-on	a lot	love	is

'I love him a lot.'

(2039)	mī	dzāṇār	nāhī
	I	go-fut-emph	not

'I will certainly not go.'

The extra length of a vowel in orthography is generally indicated by the use of the symbol *s* (which Marathi has retained from Sanskrit) after the vowel. This symbol is repeated to express increased emphasis.

Contrastive stress may be used to shift the peak of intonation to the stressed syllable or to create an additional intonation peak. The underlined words bear contrastive and/or emphatic stress in the following examples.

(2040)	to	huśār	mulgā	āhe
	he	intelligent	boy	is

'He is an intelligent boy. (as opposed to dumb)'

(2041)	to	mādzhā	praśṇa	āhe
	that	my	question	is

'It is my (as opposed to anyone else's) question.'

Vowel-lengthening is also used to indicate persuasion.

(2042)	tū	mādzha	he	kām	karśīl	kā?
	you	my	this	work	do-fut-2s	Q

'Will you do this work for me ?' (lit: 'Will you do this work of mine ?')

3.4 MORPHOPHONOLOGY (SEGMENTAL)

3.4.1 ALTERNATIONS

3.4.1.1 *Assimilatory processes*

3.4.1.1.1 *Consonant assimilation*

The following assimilatory processes are found in Marathi: nasalization, retroflexion, and palatalization.

3.4.1.1.1.1 *Nasal assimilation*

Stops become homorganic nasals before nasals (+ denotes a morpheme boundary in the following examples):

(2043) bhagawat + nām —> bhagawannām 'god's name'
god + name

(2044) ṣaṭ + mās —> ṣaṇmās 'six months'
six + month

3.4.1.1.1.2 *Retroflexion*

(i) /l/ becomes /ḷ/ after /ḷ/.

(2045) dzaḷ-l-a —> dzaḷḷa 'it burnt'
burn-pst-3sn

(ii) /t/ becomes /ṭ/ after /ṭ/

(2046) dāṭ-tānā —> dāṭṭānā 'while scolding'
scold-adv.part

(2047) phāṭ-tānā —> phāṭṭānā 'while being torn'
tear-adv.part

3.4.1.1.1.3 *Palatalization*

(i) Alveolar affricates are palatalized before the high front vowel and the palatal glide.

(2048) sudhā-ts-ī —> sudhātSī 'Sudha's (3sf)
Sudha-poss-3sf

(2049) dzo-ā —> ʤyā 'who' (obl)
who-obl

(ia) s is palatalized before /i/, /y/.
kas-i → kaśi 'how, what kind of?' (fsg)
khis-yāt → khiśāt 'in the pocket'

(ii) The dental stop */t/* is palatalized before a palatal affricate.

(2050)	tat	+	tSaritra —> tatStSaritra 'that/his character'
	that/he	+	character

(2051)	sat	+	ʤan —> saʤʤan 'good people/person'
	good	+	people/person

(iii) A dental sibilant is palatalized before a palatal sibilant.

(2052)	as	+	śīl	—> aśśīl 'you will be'
	be	+	fut-2s	

(2053)	bas	+	śīl	—> baśśīl 'you will sit'
	sit	+	fut-2s	

(iv) The dental aspirate stop */th/* becomes */ts/* before */ts/* in the Nagpuri variety of Marathi. In (2054) and (2055) the stem final */e/* is deleted before suffixes.

(2054)	tithe	+	tsā —>	tith-tsā —>	titstsā 'one who/
	there	+	poss-3sm	there-poss-3sm	which is there'

(2055)	kuṭhe	+	tsā —>	kuṭh-tsā —>	kutstsā 'of
	where	+	poss-3sm	where-poss-3sm	where?'

3.4.1.2 *Dissimilatory processes*

There are no dissimilatory processes in Marathi.

3.4.1.3 *Other alternations between segments*

3.4.1.3.1 *Vowel shortening*

3.4.1.3.1.1 High vowel shortening

High vowels */ī/, /ū/* are shortened to */i/* and */u/* respectively, when followed by either a vowel-initial or consonant-initial suffix. This rule of high vowel shortening though applicable to high vowels in all environments, may fail to apply in derivations involving Sanskrit (e.g., (1522) and (1527)) and Persian stems and affixes (e.g., (1339) and (1340)).

(2056) pī 'drink' —> pi-īn 'I will drink'
drink-fut-1s

(2057) dhū 'wash' —> dhu-ūn 'having washed'
wash-conj.part

(2058) dhū 'wash' —> dhu-to 'he washes'
wash-pres-3sm

(2059) bhī 'to fear' —> bhi-ṇe 'the act of getting scared'

(2060) bahīṇ 'sister' —> bahiṇ-ī 'sisters'

(2061) bahīṇ 'sister' —> bahiṇ-ī-lā 'to the sister'
sister-incr-dat

Note that in both of the last two examples (i.e., vowel-initial plural suffix and the consonant-initial dative suffix *-lā*) the noun stem is followed by the long vowel *-ī.* In example (2061), */ī/* is an increment vowel which is inserted before a postposition or a suffix (including a case suffix) to derive an oblique form of a feminine noun-stem. (for details see section 2.1.1.9). The following example is of a neuter noun with a long high vowel which is shortened when a suffix/postposition is added.

(2062) mūl 'child' —> mul-a 'children'

(2063) mūl 'child' —> mul-ā-lā 'to the child'
child-incr-dat

(2064) mūl 'child' —> mul-ā-sāṭhī 'for the child'
child-incr-for

In examples (2063) and (2064), */ā/* is an increment vowel inserted before a suffix to derive the oblique form *mulā.*

For other examples of high vowel shortening, see examples (1313), (1318), (1319), (1323), (1324), 1331), (1348), and (1542) in section 2.2 and sub-sections thereof.

3.4.1.3.1.2 *Low vowel shortening*

Non-final /ā/ becomes /a/ before the suffix *-āī* (recall examples (1423) and (1424) in section 2.2).

3.4.1.3.2 *Glide formation*

(i) Stem final /ī/ and /ū/ change to /y/ and /w/ respectively before /ā/.

(2065) dhobī-ā-lā —> dhobyālā 'to the washerman'
dhobī-incr-dat

(2066) lāḍū-ā-lā —> lāḍwālā 'to the desert (lāḍū)'
lāḍū-incr-dat

(2067) telī-āt —> telyāt 'in the oilman'
oilman-loc

(2068) tsorī-ā —> tsor-y-ā 'thefts'
theft-pl

(2069) dorī-ā —> doryā 'ropes'
rope-pl

(ii) The above process of glide formation (followed by metathesis) is observed in the following cases as well, where /o/ changes to /w/ when it is preceded by /h/ and followed by a syllable consisting either of /ā/ only or of a consonant and /ā/.

(2070) na-ho-tā —> nawhtā 'he was not' (*nahwtā)
not-be-pst-3sm

(2071) ho-ā —> whā 'be!' (*hwā)
be-imp-pl

Note that in (2070) and (2071) metathesis (hw —> wh) has occured in addition to /o/ replaced by /w/.

(iii) /o/ changes to /y/ when followed by the suffix /ā/.

(2072) to-ā —> t-y-ā 'he (obl)'
he-incr

(2073) dzo-ā —> ʤyā 'who (obl)'
who-incr

(iv) */e/* changes to */y/* when followed by */ā/*.

(2074) te-ā —> t-y-ā 'they (obl)'
they-incr

(v) */āe/* after a vowel changes to */y/* as in the following:

(2075) karto-ā(h)e —> karto-y 'I am doing (it)'
do-1sm-be-s

(vi) */ū/* between a vowel and a consonant change to */w/* when followed by a vowel-initial suffix.

(2076) pāūs 'rain' pāw-s-āt 'in the rain'
rain-in (loc)

(2077) deūḷ 'temple' dewḷ-āt 'in the temple'
temple-in (loc)

3.4.1.3.3 *Vowel raising*

There is no vowel raising in Standard Marathi. However, in the Nagpuri variety of Marathi, the first person singular feminine agreement suffix */e/* (used for the subject of intransitive verbs in past tense) as well as the agentive marker *-ne* (in perfective) have a morphological variant */ī/*, as in the following example.

(2078) āle —> ālī 'I came'
come-pst-1sf

(2078a) tyā-ne —> tyānī 'he'
he-ag

3.4.1.3.4 *Vowel lowering*

Vowel lowering is absent in Standard Marathi. However, in the Nagpuri variety of Marathi, the neuter plural (past tense) suffix */ī/* has a morphological variant */e/* as in the following example.

(2079)	dzhāḍe paḍlī	—>	dzhāḍa	paḍle
	trees-fall-pst-3pl.n		trees	fall-pst-3pl.n
			'trees fell'	

The marker /e/ in *dzāde* is optionally lowered to /a/ (pronounced as a lengthened schwa). Historically the /e/ marker was nasalized. In the variety of Marathi spoken in Konkan and Goa the nasalized /ẽ/ is still maintained. In other varieties (i.e., Puṇe, Bombay, Nagpurī and Khāndeśī), the nasalization is maintained only in the speech of old people (i.e., over 60 years old). This loss of nasalization (except in the speech of the people in Konkan and Goa) is a widespread phenomenon in Marathi, and it may be observed elsewhere as well. In orthography, the marker of nasalization (i.e., *anusvāra* indicated by the dot above the horizontal line on the consonant) is still maintained on the final consonant, although it functions as the marker of the phonetically lengthened vowel /a/ in contemporary Marathi. The following examples illustrate the process.

Neuter third person plural:

(2080) mulẽ —> mula/mule 'children'

(2081) dukānẽ —> dukāna/dukāne 'shops'

(2082) dzhādẽ —> dzhāda/dzhāde 'trees'

Neuter third person singular:

(2083) kheḷṇẽ —> kheḷṇa/kheḷṇe 'toy'

(2084) bhāṇḍẽ —> bhāṇḍa/bhāṇḍe 'pot'

(2085) bolṇẽ (inf) —> bolṇa/bolṇe 'talking'

Neuter third person singular verb suffix:

(2085a) kelẽ —> kela/kele 'did (3sn)'

Note that *bolṇe* 'talking' is the infinitive form of the verb *bol* 'talk'. The infinitive functions as a neuter noun in Marathi and therefore is marked with the neuter third person singular marker /e/.

Pronouns/adverb:

(2086) kasẽ —> kasa/kase 'how'

(2087) dzasẽ —> dzasa/dzase 'relative pronoun'

(2088)	tasẽ	—> tasa/tase 'correlative pronoun'
(2089)	barẽ (adv)	—> bara/bare 'all right'
(2089a)	ithẽ (adv)	—> itha/ithe 'here'

3.4.1.3.5 *Vowel lengthening*

(i) Word-final short vowel */i/* is lengthened in words inherited or borrowed from Sanskrit

(2090) mati —> matī 'intellect'

(2091) gati —> gatī 'speed'

It is important to note that suffixes are added to the non-lengthened or original Sanskrit forms of stems only.

(ii) In compounds, a sequence of two identical short vowels across a morpheme boundary results in a long (vowel) counterpart of the short vowels.

(2092) śiwa-artSanā —> śiwārtSanā 'worship of god Śiva'
Śiwa-worship

(2093) ati-indriya —> atīndriya 'beyond sense perceptions'
beyond-senses

3.4.2 METATHESIS

When *ho* and *hū* are followed or preceded by the vowel */a/* or */ā/*, the */o/* and */u/* change to */w/*, and */h/* and */w/* are metathesized to yield the */wh/* sequence. Consider the following examples.

(2094) na-hotā —> nawhtā 'was not'
not-be-pst-3sm

(2095) ho-ā —> whā 'be!'
be-imp-2pl

(2096) gahū-ā-tsa —> gawhātsa 'of the wheat'
wheat-incr-poss-3sm

3.4.3 COALESCENCE AND SPLIT

A large number of *-ā* ending nominals change to their oblique forms, ending with *-yā* before suffixes and suffix like morphemes. This *-yā* of oblique stems coalesces to *-e* (recall examples (1458) - (1460), (1534), (1536) in section 2.2). There are no examples of split in Marathi.

3.4.4 DELETION AND INSERTION

3.4.4.1 *Deletion processes*

The following types of deletion processes are observed:

(i) degemination
(ii) word-final vowel deletion
(iii) deletion of a long vowel in a non-final syllable
(iv) deletion of /a/, /u/, and /i/ in a non-final syllable.

3.4.4.1.1 *Degemination*

Geminates, which always occur intervocalically in Marathi, become degeminated when a following vowel is deleted because of suffixation.

(2097) gā̃mmat-ī-ne —> gamtīne 'jokingly'
joke-incr-inst

(2098) hīmmat-ī-ne —> himtīne 'courageously'
courage-incr-inst

(2099) tippaṭ-ī-ne —> tipṭīne 'three times'
three times-incr-inst

3.4.4.1.2 *Word-final schwa deletion*

To date there is no systematic account of this process available. A large number of noun-stems borrowed from Sanskrit lose their word-final schwa.

(2100) widʒaya (Skt) —> widʒay (M) 'victory'

(2101) śikṣaka (Skt) —> śikṣak (M) 'teacher'

However, Marathi retains the word-final schwa of Sanskrit stems if deletion would result in the occurrence of a consonant cluster word-finally ((2102) and (2103) below) or a non-permissible consonant cluster medially ((1440), (1445) etc.). Also, schwa deletion may fail to apply in a few *tatsama* words (i.e., words inherited from Sanskrit) ((1521), (1523), (1524), (1526), (1527) etc.). In fact, this may be considered one of the characteristic features of the sanskritized register of modern Marathi.

(2102) hasta (Skt) —> hasta (M) 'hand'

(2103) bhakta (Skt) —> bhakta (M) 'devotee'

3.4.4.1.3 *Stem-final /ā/ deletion*

Stem final *-ā* is deleted before vowel-initial or consonant-initial suffixes (recall examples (1319), (1334) etc.).

3.4.4.1.4 *Stem-final /e/ deletion*

The stem final vowel */e/* is optionally deleted before */ī/*.

(2104) de-īn —> deīn/dīn 'I will give'
give-fut-is

(2105) ghe-īn —> gheīn/ghīn 'I will take'
take-fut-1s

3.4.4.1.5 *Deletion of long high vowels in non-final position*

A long vowel in a final syllable is deleted when a suffix with a long vowel is added.

(2106) parīṭ-ā-lā —> parṭālā 'to a washerman'
washerman-incr-dat

(2107) kārbhārīṇ-ī-lā —> kārbhārṇīlā 'to the mistress of the house'
mistress of the house -incr-dat

(2108) kāpūs-ā-t —> kāpsāt 'in the cotton'
cotton-incr-loc

It is important to note here that the rule of high vowel deletion mentioned above is actually the combined result of two related and sequentially interacting rules. One is the rule of High vowel shortening (cf. section 3.4.1.3.1.1) and the other is the rule of short vowel deletion (cf. 3.4.4.1.6), which deletes short vowels in non-initial open syllables .

3.4.4.1.6 *Deletion of short vowels*

When a suffix/postposition is added, deletion of the short vowels /a/, /i/, and /u/ in open (including the stem final) but non-initial syllable is a common process in Marathi

(2109) dagaḍ- ā-lā —> dagḍālā 'to the rock'
rock-incr-dat

(2110) kaṇik-e-lā —> kaṇkelā 'for the bread-flour'
flour-incr-dat

(2111) ṭeŋguḷ - ā-tsa —> ṭeŋgḷātsa 'of the bump on the forehead'
bump-incr-poss

(2112) gavat-ā-var —> gavtāvar 'on the grass'
grass-incr-on

(2113) kamaḷ-ā-t —> kamḷāt 'in the lotus'
lotus-incr-loc

Note that in the above examples, */ā/* is an increment vowel. Also, this rule may fail to apply in words pertaining to marked vocabulary items, such as, kinship terms, numerals etc. (recall examples (1324), (2060), (2061) etc.).

3.4.4.2 *Insertion processes*

3.4.4.2.1 *The increment vowel*

An increment vowel is inserted between nominal, infinitival, adjectival, and participial stems and the case-suffixes or postpositions. The distribution of increment vowels is determined by the gender, number, and shape of the stems. (See section 2.1.1.1).

3.4.4.2.2 *Glide insertions*

The environments for glide insertion are described below.

(i) */y/* is inserted between */ī/* and */ā/* and */w/* is inserted between */ū/* and */ā/*.

(2114) bī - ā —> bi-y-ā 'seeds'
seed-pl

(2115) dhū - ā —> dhu-w-ā 'wash (imp-pl)'
wash-conj.part

(ii) */w/* is inserted when */e/* and */o/* are followed by */ū/*.

(2116) ho-ūn —> howūn 'having become'
be-conj.part

(2117) ghe-ūn —> ghewūn / gheūn 'having taken'

(iii) The glide */y/* is inserted before the vowel */æ/* in words borrowed from English.

(2118) cat(E) —> kyæṭ (M) 'cat'

(2119) hat (E) —> hyæṭ (M) 'hat'

(iv) The glide */y/* is inserted between */ā/* and */a/* (recall (1490)).

3.4.4.2.3 *Vowel insertion for cluster simplification*

Word-initial consonant clusters are simplified by the insertion of a vowel between the two consonants. The strategy of inserting a vowel before or after the cluster is also frequently used to move the cluster to the medial position. Also, non-permissible three consonant clusters (in any position) are broken by *-a-* insertion (e.g., (1671), (1718), etc.). These three strategies are illustrated in the following examples.

(i) Vowel-insertion between consonants:

(2120) pyālā —> piyālā 'he drank'
drink-pst-3sm

(2121) bhyālo —> bhiyālo 'I was frightened'
fear-pst-1sm

(2122) trās —> tarās 'trouble'
trouble

(2123) prasāŋga —> parsāŋga 'occasion'
occasion

It should be noted here that this type of vowel-insertion is characteristic of uneducated speech and is blocked in educated speech.

(ii) Vowel-insertion in initial position:

A vowel is inserted before a consonant cluster in word-initial position. This insertion is observed in borrowings from English and Sanskrit.

(2124) strī (Skt) —> istrī (M) 'woman'
woman

(2125) steśan (E) —> isṭeśan (M) 'station'
station

(iii) Word-final vowel-insertion:

A vowel is inserted word-finally to move the consonant cluster to the medial position.

(2126) durust —> durusta 'repaired'
repaired

(2127) mast —> masta 'happy and joyful'
happy and joyful

In order to avoid word-final consonant clusters, final vowels in borrowed Sanskrit vocabulary are retained in Marathi (e.g., *mukta* 'free', *aṣṭa* 'eight', *puṣpa* 'flower', etc.)

(iv) In order to avoid consonant clusters word finally, -*a* vowel is inserted between the two consonants.

(2128)	satat - ts always - emph	—> satatats 'always indeed!'
(2129)	tsālat - ts walk - emph	—> tsālatats 'walking, indeed!'

3.4.4.2.4 *Apparent schwa insertion*

When a Sanskrit stem with stem-final */a/* is used for suffixation, it results in apparent */a/* insertion, which is just that (recall examples (1635) and (1636)).

3.4.4.2.5 *Gemination*

When /ū/ and /ī/ are followed by /w/ and /y/ respectively, the process results in glide gemination, as shown in the following examples.

(2130)	naū - wārī nine - yards	—> nawwārī 'a nine yard (saree)'
(2131)	nāhī - yet neg - come-pres	—> nāhyyet 'does not come'

3.4.5 REDUPLICATION

As mentioned earlier, reduplication is an extremely productive process in Marathi, and it is applicable to nouns, adjectives, adverbs, and verbs. For a detailed discussion on the reduplication of partial/complete units, see sections 1.11.2.1.7, 2.2.6.3.1.7-8, 2.2.6.3.2, and 2.2.6.3.4.3).

3.5 MORPHOPHONOLOGY (SUPRASEGMENTAL)

Stress and tonal structure are not affected by morphological processes.

IDEOPHONES AND INTERJECTIONS

4.1 IDEOPHONES

bhū-bhū (nn)	dogs' barking
taṭ-taṭ (adv)	sound of breaking sticks
dhag-dhag (nf)	sound of blazing fire
phus-phus (nf)	whisper/hissing sound of a snake
tSiw-tSiw (nf)	twitter
rim-ʤim (nf)	sound of rain
tsaṭ-paṭ (adv)	quickly/fast
dzhapādzhap (adv)	fast
ghaṇ-ghaṇ (adv)	sound of a bell
ṭip-ṭip (nf)	sound of trickling water
ṭap-ṭap (adv)	sound of horse-step
huśśya (interjection)	sound of a sigh of relief
tsa (K) - ts(a)K (adv)	sound of disapproval
dhappa (adv)	sound of falling
tsarra (adv)	sound of burning

ruṇ-dzhuṇ (nf)	sound of anklets
kir-kir (nf) kur-kur (nf)	sound of complaint
ghar-ghar (nf)	sound of the breathing of a person about to die
tuṇṇa (adv)	sound of a jump
sū̃-sū̃ (adv)	sound of blowing wind
rip-rip (nf)	sound of continuous light rain
ṭaṇatkār (nm)	sound of a bow-string
dzhā̃ŋkār (nm)	sound of a string (of a musical instrument)
dzhuḷ-dzhuḷ (adv)	sound of a gently flowing stream
daṇ-daṇ (adv)	sound of thumping steps
kal-kalāṭ (nm)	collective sound of a flock of birds/young children
kuhū-kuhū (nf)	sound made by a cuckoo
ku-kūtS-kū (adv)	sound made by a rooster
kil-bil (nf)	pleasant, soothing sounds of the chirping of birds
gaṭ(ā)-gaṭā (adv)	sound of fast gulping of liquid
gar-gar (adv)	whirling motion
thū-thū (nsf)	sound of spitting
thar-thar (adv)	sound/motion of trembling

oksā-bokśī (adv)	sound of profuse crying
taṭ-taṭā (adv)	sound of breaking a thread
sar-sar (adv)	quickly/fast
tsaṭṭā-maṭṭā (nm)	sound of licking the pots to the last grain of food
wāhwā-wāhwā (interjection)	bravo! well done!
khad-khad (nf)	sound of boiling lentils
ũ hũ (interjection)	sound of disapproval
tāḍ-tāḍ (nf)	sound of beating
thay-thay (adv)	sound of dancing steps
hur-hur (nf)	sound of anxiety
gur-gur (nf)	growl
hãmbar-ṇe (v)	cow's bellow
myā̃w (nn)	cat's purr
miṇ-miṇ (nf)	dim light
ṭhaṇ-ṭhaṇāṭ (nm)	loud noise
dzhag-magāṭ (nm)	dazzle
śuk-śukāṭ (nm)	sound of silence
dhaḍak-ṇe (v)	to arrive unexpectedly
lakh-lakhāṭ (nm)	dazzling light
suḷ-suḷāṭ (nm)	overabundance
ayyā (interjection)	sound of surprise

iśśya (interjection)	embarassment, bashfulness
naṭṭā-paṭṭā (nm)	lavish/glamorous make-over
hũndaḍ-ṇe (v)	sound of aimless jumping/ wandering
guḷ-guḷīt (adj)	smooth
taḷ-taḷāṭ (nm)	anger
tsaktsakīt (adj)	shining/absolutely spotless
dzhaṇ-dzhaṇīt (adj)	spicy hot
gar-garīt (adj)	full/round
tuḍ-tuḍīt (adj)	energetic
phaḍ-phaḍ (adv)	sound of fluttering
dzaḷ-dzaḷ (nf)	burning sensation
kaḷ-kaḷ (nf)	great concern
taḷ-maḷ-ṇe (v)	to be in pain
dzaḷ-phaḷāt (nm)	jealousy
tsaḷ-tsaḷā (adv)	sound of shaking/trembling
tsuṭ-puṭ (nf)	uneasiness
kudz-būdz (nf)	sound of whispering
baṭ-baṭīt (adj)	with loud colors
khus-khuśīt (adj)	crisp (food)
tar-tarīt (adj)	fresh/energetic healthy
dhusphus-ṇe (v)	'to grumble'

ḍhas-ḍhasā (adv)	sound of loud crying
bhus-bhuśīt (adj)	soft (soil, ground)
guṭ-guṭīt (adj)	healthy/chubby baby/child
phaṭ-phaṭīt (adj)	pale/white
laṭ-laṭ (adv)	manner of trembling/shaking
phus-phus (nf)	secretive talk
suṭ-suṭīt (adj)	easy to manage
rakh-rakhīt (adj)	scorching/intense (heat)
tak-takīt (adj)	shiny
tsar-tsarīt (adj)	sharp (edge)
waḷ-waḷ (adv/nf)	constant movement
ḍhaḷ-ḍhaḷīt (adj)	absolutely clear/transparent
bhaḷ-bhaḷ(ā) (adv)	constant flow of blood from an injury
haḷ-haḷ (nf)	sadness
ṭarra (nf)	the act of making fun (of somebody)
dzhir-dzhirīt (adj)	transparent
gaḍ-gaḍāṭ (nm)	sound of thunder
saṇ-saṇīt (adj)	sound of a slap
{bhaṇ-bhaṇ (nf) kaṭ-kaṭ (nf)}	bother
tsaṇ-tsaṇ (nf)	scarcity

ṭāp-ṭīp (nf)	neat and tidy
ṭhaṇ-ṭhaṇīt (adv)	loud and clear sound
daṇ-daṇīt (adv)	forceful sound
katsā-kats (adv)	completely full

4.2 INTERJECTIONS

Interjections are discussed in section 1.15.2.

LEXICON

5.1 STRUCTURED SEMANTIC FIELDS

5.1.1 KINSHIP TERMINOLOGY

The kinship terminology of Marathi is quite extensive. In the traditional extended families (which are common even today in many parts of India), specific kinship terms are used to indicate specific relationships (e.g., *kākā* 'father's brother', *māmā* 'mother's brother', etc.). Three parameters are used in the system—age, laterality (relations on mother's side or father's side), and relation by blood or marriage.

There is no difference in reference between a natural and an adopted child. Therefore, step-mother, step-brother, son/daughter, father are referred to as mother, brother, son/daughter, and father, respectively. However there exists an adjective *sāwatra* 'step' which is used to indicate the real/biological vs. step mother, father, etc. in the legalistic context as well as in the context where the referent is absent and a reference is being made to him/her.

The terms given below are reference terms and not necessarily address terms.

5.1.1.1 *Kin related by blood*

5.1.1.1.1 *Own generation*

brother, elder	dādā/aṇṇā
sister, elder	ākkā/tāī

5.1.1.1.2 *First ascending generation*

father	bābā, āppā, waḍīl
mother	āī
father's brother	kākā
father's sister	ātyā
mother's brother	māmā
mother's sister	mawshī

5.1.1.1.3 *Second ascending generation*

father's father	ādzobā
father's mother	āʤī
mother's father	ādzobā
mother's mother	āʤī
father's grandfather	paṇdzobā
father's grandmother	paṇʤī
mother's grandfather	paṇdzobā
mother's grandmother	paṇʤī

5.1.1.1.4 *First descending generation*

son	mulgā
daughter	mulgī

5.1.1.1.5 *Second descending generation*

son's son	nātū

son's daughter	nāt
daughter's son	nātū
daughter's daughter	nāt

5.1.1.1.6 *Other relatives*

father's brother's son	tsulat bhāū
father's brother's daughter	tsulat bahīṇ
father's sister's son	ate bhāū
father's sisters's daughter	ate bahīṇ
mother's brother's son	māme bhāū
mother's brother's daughter	mame bahīṇ
mother's sister's son	māwas bhāū
mother's sister's daughter	māwas bahīṇ
brother's son	bhātsā
brother's daughter	bhātSī
sister's son	bhātsā
sister's daughter	bhātSī

5.1.1.2 *Kin by partial blood*

half-brother/step brother, elder	dādā/aṇṇā
half-sister/step sister	ākkā/tāī

It should be noted here that the above reference terms for cousins are used only when the referents are absent. In their presence the regular terms for brothers and sisters are used to refer to them or to address them. The underlying assumption here is that cousins are to be treated as real brothers and sisters in an extended family.

half-brother	sāwatrabhāu step/half brother

half-sister	sāwatra bahīṇ step/half sister
stepfather	sāwatra waḍīl
stepmother	sāwatra āī

Again, these terms are used only in the absence of the referents. In their presence or to address them the regular terms for brothers and sisters are used.

5.1.1.3 *Kin by marriage*

wife	bāyko/patnī
co-wife	sawat
husband	nawrā/patī
father's brother's wife	kākū
father's sister's husband	ātobā
mother's brother's wife	māmī
mother's sister's husband	mawsā
elder's brother's wife: younger's brother's wife	wahinī bhāwdzay
sister's husband	mehuṇā/mewhṇā
wife's brother	mewhṇā/sāḷā (borrowed from Hindi)
wife's sister	mewhṇī/sāḷī (borrowed from Hindi)
husband's father husband's mother husband's brother husband's sister	sāsrā/māmañʤī sāsū dīr/bhāuʤī naṇand/wansa

wife's brother's wife	—
wife's sister's husband	sāḍū
husband's brother's wife	dzāu
husband's sister's husband	mehuṇā/dzāwaī
son's wife	sūn
son's wife's father	wyāhī
son's wife's mother	wihīṇ
daughter's husband	dzāwaī
daughter's husband's father	wyāhī
daughter's husband's mother	wihīṇ
neice's husband	dzāwaī (son-in-law)
nephew's wife	(bhatse) sūn (daughter-in-law of nephew)
granddaughter's husband	nāt-dzāwaī
grandson's wife	nāt-sūn

5.1.1.4 *Kin by adoption*

stepfather	bābā/aṇṇā/waḍīl
stepmother	āī
stepson	dattak putra/mulgā
stepdaughter	dattak kanyā/mulgī

5.1.1.5 *Kin by fostering*

foster father	mānlele waḍil
foster mother	mānlelī āī
foster son	mānlelā mulgā
foster daughter	mānlelī mulgī
foster brother	mānlelā bhāū
foster sister	mānlelī bahīṇ

5.1.2 COLOR TERMINOLOGY

The following color terms are used in the language.

color	rãŋga
white	pāṇḍhrā
black	kāḷā
red	lāl/tā̃mbḍā
green	hirwā
yellow	piwḷā
blue	niḷā
brown	tapkirī
orange	keśrī
purple	dzā̃mbhḷā

Additionally, some color terms are derived from the names of the flowers bearing the color indicated by the terms as given below.

gulāb 'rose'	—>	gulābī 'rose-pink'
abolī 'a kind of flower'	—>	abolī 'peach'
gulbākṣī 'a kind of flower'	—>	gulbākṣī 'magenta'

Also, some color terms refer to the objects or elements which bear that color, as in the following examples.

ākāś 'sky'	—>	ākāśī 'sky-blue'
asmān 'sky'	—>	asmānī 'sky-blue'
śendūr 'vermillion'	—>	śendrī 'vermillion-orange'

tsṭṇī 'chutney' —> tsaṭṇī 'chutney-green'

All color terms are treated as adjectives and are inflected as such. When the color terms are used as modifiers, they agree with nouns in gender and number. The color terms are optionally followed by the noun *rāŋga* 'color' as shown in the following examples.

(2132)	pāṇdhrī	sāḍī	'a white saree'
	white-3sf	saree-3sf	

(2133)	pāṇdhryā	rangātSī	sāḍī
	white-obl.	color-poss-3sf	saree-3sf

'a white-colored saree'

5.1.3 BODY PARTS

A number of terms for body parts are borrowings from Sanskrit. Those are indicated by S in the parenthesis.

body	deha (S) śarīr (S)
head	ḍoka
face	tSehrā, mukha (S)
hair	kes, keś (S)
forehead	mastak, kapāḷ
eye	ḍoḷā, netra
eyebrow	bhuwaī
eyelash	pāpṇī
ear	kān, karṇa (S)
nose	nāk
mouth	toṇḍ

lip	oṭh
tooth	dāt
jaw	dzabḍā
tongue	ʤībh
cheek	gāl
chin	hanuwaṭī
moustache	miśī
beard	dāḍhī
neck	mān
throat	gaḷā/ghasā
chest	tShātī
breast	stan (S)
nipple	stanāgra (S)
heart	hṛday/man
shoulder	khā̃ndā
arm	hāt
armpit	kākh
elbow	kopar
forearm	hāt
hand	hāt
wrist	mangaṭ

palm	taḷhāt
finger	boṭ
thumb	ãŋgṭhā
nail	nakh
stomach	poṭ
liver	ʤaṭhar
intestines	ātaḍa/ātaḍī
naval	bembī
penis	śisna (S), linga (S)
pudenda	yonī (S)
testicle	wruśana (S)
buttock	nitãmba (S)/ḍhuŋgaṇ
thigh	mãnḍī
knee	guḍghā
leg	pāy
foot	pāy
toe	boṭ
heel	ṭāts
sole of foot	taḷpāy
back	pāṭh
bone	hāḍ

skin	twatSā (S)/kātaḍa/kātaḍī
skull	kawṭī
brain	mendu
lung	phephḍe
rib	bargaḍī

5.1.4 COOKING TERMINOLOGY

5.1.4.1 *Methods of cooking*

śidzawṇe	'to cook'
bhidzawṇe	'to soak'
garam karṇe	'to heat'
misaḷṇe	'to mix'
paratṇe	'to sautee'
wāṭṇe	'to grind'
ḍhawaḷṇe	'to stir'
ukaḍṇe/wāphawṇe	'to steam'
ukaḷṇe	'to boil'
bhādzṇe	'to roast'
taḷṇe	'to fry'
kāpṇe	'to cut'
tSirṇe	'to chop (vegetables)'
śekṇe	'to toast over open fire'
sukawṇe	'to dry'
āṭawṇe	'to heat and stir (milk) in order to reduce the water content in it'
kisṇe	'to grate'
phoḍṇī deṇe	'to season with hot oil, and other spices'
niwaḍṇe	'to clean grain by taking out the small stones and other s poiled grain'
pākhaḍṇe	'to clean grain in a tray made of cane'
otṇe	'to pour'
laṭṇe	'to roll (the bread)'

tsotsawṇe	'to finely chop (a cucumber or raddish)'
thāpṇe	'to spread (dough or a mixture) with the palm'
kuṭṇe	'to pound'
wāḷawṇe	'to dry (in the sun)'
kālawṇe	'to mix ingredients with/in liquid'
pāk karṇe	'to make syrup'
gāḷṇe	'to strain'
piḷṇe	'to squeeze'
maḷṇe	'to knead'

5.1.4.2 *Cooking implements*

tāṭ	'big plate/dinner plate made of metal'
tāṭlī	'small plate'
pelā	'glass'
wāṭī	'metal bowl for soup/desserts'
tsūl	'clay oven'
śegdī	'coal-oven'
gæs-sṭow	'gas stove'
tsamtsā	'spoon'
battā	'metal/wooden or stone object for pounding/grinding'
khal	'metal, wooden or stone pot in which ingredients are pounded or ground
dzāta	traditional mill for grinding the grain'
pātela	'big or small metal pot'
bhāṇḍa	'pot'
tasrāḷa	'a shallow metal pot with a large flat bottom'
kaḍhaī	'round metal pot with round bottm and a round metal rings to lift it' (generally used for deep frying)
tawā	'pan (used for roasting breads)'
poḷpāṭ	'rolling base'
lāṭṇa	'rolling pin'
ḍabā	'metal box'
pāḷa	'spice box'
barṇī	'clay or glass can to store cooking ingredients' (e.g., lentils, flours, etc.) and pickles

parāt	'metal tray for kneading dough'
tā̃mbyā	'metal jug'
pāṭā	'stone-base for grinding'
warwanṭā	'stone for grinding'
gāḷṇī	'strainer'
dzārā	'metal ladle with holes'
ulathna	'metal ladle with flat head (used for stir-fry cooking)'
kisṇī	'grater'
wiḷī	'traditional half-circle shaped knife fixed on a wooden base (used for cutting vegetables)'
surī	'knife'
dzhākaṇ	'lid'
dzhakṇī	'small lid'
sūp	'tray-like object made of cane used for cleaning grain'
paḷī	'ladle for stirring and serving liquid'
kukar	'pressure cooker'
hā̃ṇḍā	'huge metal pot'

5.1.4.3 *Typical dishes*

poḷī/tsapātī	'bread roasted on a metal pan'
phulkā	'thin bread roasted on open fire'
parāṭā	'bread pan-fried'
purī	'deep-fried bread'
thālīpīṭh	'spicy pancake made by spreading the dough on the pan'
bhākrī	'bread (thick) roasted on open fire'
dhirḍa	'spicy pancake made of grain flour (or a mixture of flours) mixed with water and spices'
bhādʒī	'vegetable'
waraṇ	'lentil soup'
āmṭī	'lentil soup of a special kind'
bhāt	'rice (plain)'
pulāw	'spicy rice (with vegetables and/or meat)'
kośimbīr	'salad with or without yogurt'

tsaṭṇī	'dry or liquid mixture of various spices blended with water/lemon juice/yogurt or tamarind paste'
khīr	'milk pudding of various kinds'
śrīkhāṇḍa	'a special yogurt dish'
lāḍū	'dessert of various kinds generally made with flour'
waḍī	'dessert made of various milk products, flours'
purṇātSī poḷī	'a special dessert of bread stuffed witih cooked lentil and sugar'
sābuḍāṇyāte waḍe	'a spicy snack made of tapioca and potatoes'
puḍātSī waḍī	'a spciy pastry made of green corriander'
tSiroṭā	'a dessert pastry soaked in sugar syrup'

5.1.5 AGRICULTURE

5.1.5.1 *Crops grown in the area*

kāpūs	cotton
gahū	wheat
harbhare	garbanzo
ūs	sugar cane
maṭar	pea
tā̃nḍūḷ	rice
tūr	a kind of lentil
mūg	a kind of lentil
makā	corn
ʤwarī	a kind of grain
bādzrī	a kind of grain

5.1.5.2 *Agricultural implements*

aut ɔt/nāŋgar	plough
śet	farm
bī	seed
khurpa	shovel
bail	ox
gāy	cow

bailgāḍī	bullock cart
dzū	yoke
pāta (nāŋgrātsa)	blade (of plow)
kudaḷ	hoe
phāwḍa	shovel

5.1.5.3 *Agricultural activities*

nāŋgarṇe	'to plough'
perṇe	'to sow'
wakharṇe	'to weed'
kāpṇe	'to cut the crop/harvest'

5.2 BASIC VOCABULARY

1.	all	sarwa/sagḷa
2.	and	āṇi
3.	animal	dzanāwar
4.	ashes	rākh/bhasma
5.	at	wādztā (time), - the (place: i.e., *ithe* 'here', *tithe* 'there', etc.), or *-t* (locative, e.g., *ghar* - 'house' —> *gharāt* 'at home')
6.	back	pāṭh (of body), māge (behind)
7.	bad	wāīṭ, kharāb
8.	bark (of tree)	sāl
9.	because	kāraṇ (kī)
10.	belly	poṭ
11.	big	moṭhā
12.	bird	pakṣī
13.	bite	tsāwā (n) tsāwṇe (v)
14.	black	kāḷā
15.	blood	rakta (s)
16.	blow	uḍṇe (v)
17.	bone	hāḍ
18.	breast	stan (s)
19.	breathe	śwās gheṇe
20.	burn	dzaḷṇe (v.intr)
21.	burn	dzāḷṇe (v. tr)
22.	child	mūl
23.	cloud	ḍhag

24.	cold	thaṇḍī
25.	come	yeṇe
26.	count	modzṇe
27.	cut	kāpṇe
28.	day	diwas/wār
29.	die	marṇe
30.	dig	khodṇe
31.	dirty	ghāṇerḍa/maḷḷela
32.	dog	kutrā
33.	drink	piṇe (v), peya (n)
34.	dry	sukawṇe (v), wāḷawṇe (v) suklela/wāḷḷela (part.adj), suka (adj)
35.	dull	kanṭāḷwāṇa
36.	dust	dhūḷ
37.	ear	kān
38.	earth	dzamīn, pṛthwī (s)
39.	eat	khāṇe (v)
40.	egg	aṇḍa
41.	eye	ḍoḷā
42.	fall	paḍṇe (v)
43.	far	dūr
44.	fat/grease	tSarbī/med (s)
45.	father	waḍīl
46.	fear	bhitī, bhay (s)
47.	feather	pāŋkha
48.	few	thoḍa, wiraḷ
49.	fight	laḍhṇe (v), laḍhāī (n)
50.	fire	āg
51.	fish	māsā
52.	five	pāts
53.	float	tarāŋgṇe (v)
54.	flow	wāhṇe (v)
55.	flower	phūl
56.	fly	uḍṇe
57.	fog	dhuka
58.	foot	pāy
59.	four	tSār
60.	freeze	goṭhṇe (v)
61.	fruit	phaḷ
62.	full	bharlela (part. adj.)
63.	give	deṇe

64.	good	tsāŋgla
65.	grass	gawat
66.	green	hirwa
67.	guts	huśārī (cleverness)
68.	hair	kes
69.	hand	hāt
70.	he	to
71.	head	ḍoka
72.	hear	aikṇe
73.	heart	hṛday (S) /man
74.	heavy	dzaḍ
75.	here	ithe/yethe
76.	hit	mārṇe, (beat), dzhoḍapṇe (beat up), baḍawṇe (beat up)
77.	hold/take	pakaḍṇe
78.	horn	śinga
79.	how	kasa
80.	hunt	śikār karṇe (lit: 'to do hunting')
81.	husband	nawrā
82.	I	mī
83.	ice	barpha
84.	if	dzar
85.	in	āt
86.	kill	mārṇe, mārūn, ṭākṇe
87.	knee	guḍghā
88.	know	dzāṇṇe, māhit asṇe
89.	lake	talāw
90.	laugh	hasṇe
91.	leaf	pān
92.	left side	ḍāwī bādzū
93.	leg	pāy
94.	lie	khoṭa bolṇe (lit: 'to tell a lie')
95.	live	rāhṇe, dzagṇe
96.	liver	kāḷīdz
97.	long	lā̃mb
98.	louse	ū
99.	many	khūp, puṣkaḷ
100.	meat/flesh	mā̃ūs
101.	moon	tSāndra
102.	mother	āī
103.	mountain	parwat
104.	mouth	tõṇḍ

105.	name	nāw
106.	narrow	arūnda
107.	near	dzawaḷ
108.	neck	mān
109.	new	nawīn
110.	night	rātra
111.	nose	nāk
112.	not	nāhī/na
113.	old (animate)	mhātārā
	old (inanimate)	dzunā
114.	one	ek
115.	other	dusrā/bākītse
116.	person	māṇūs/manuṣya (s)/wyakti (s)
117.	play	kheḷ (n), kheḷṇe (v)
118.	pull	oḍhṇe (v), oḍh (n)
119.	push	ḍhakalṇe (v), dhakkā deṇe (to give a push)
120.	rain	pāūs
121.	red	lāl/rakta (s)/tāmbḍā
122.	right/correct	barobar/khara/yogya
123.	right side	udzwī bādzū
124.	river	nadī
125.	road	rastā/saḍak
126.	root	mūḷ
127.	rope	dor
128.	rotten	saḍlela/saḍkā
129.	round	gol
130.	rub	tsoḷṇe/ghāsṇe
131.	salt	mīṭh
132.	sand	retī
133.	say	bolṇe/mhaṇṇe
134.	scratch	orbāḍṇe
135.	sea	samudra (s)
136.	see	pāhṇe
137.	seed	bī
138.	sew	śiwṇe
139.	sharp	tīkṣṇa (s)/dhārdār
140.	short (in height)	ṭheŋgṇā
141.	sing	gāṇe
142.	sit	basṇe
143.	skin	twatSā (s)/tsāmḍī
144.	sky	ākāś

145.	sleep	dzop (n), dzopṇe (v)
146.	small	lahān/tSoṭā
147.	smell	wās (n)/wās gheṇe (v)
148.	smooth	maū/tSikṇā
149.	smoke	dhūr (n)/sigreṭ oḍhṇe or sigreṭ piṇe (v) (lit: 'to pull a cigarette', or 'to drink a cigarette')
150.	snake	sāp
151.	snow	barfa
152.	some	kāhī
153.	spit	thunkṇe (v), thunkī (n)
154.	split	phāḍṇe/tSirṇe
155.	squeeze	piḷṇe/dābṇe
156.	stab/pierce	bhosakṇe
157.	stand	ubha rāhṇe
158.	star	tārā/tsā̃ndaṇī
159.	stick	kāṭhī
160.	stone	dagaḍ
161.	straight	saraḷ
162.	suck	tsokhṇe
163.	sun	sūrya (s)
164.	swell	sudzṇe
165.	swim	pohṇe
166.	tail	śepūṭ/śepṭī
167.	that	to (mas), tī (fem), te (neut)
168.	there	tethe/titha
169.	they	te (mas), tyā (fem), tī (neut)
170.	thick	ghaṭṭa
171.	thin	pātaḷ/bārīk/roḍ
172.	think	witSār karṇe (lit: 'to do thinking')
173.	this	hā (mas), hī (fem), he (neut)
174.	thou	tū
175.	three	tīn
176.	throw	phekṇe
177.	tie	bā̃dhṇe
178.	tongue	ʤībh
179.	tooth	dāt
180.	tree	dzhāḍ
181.	turn	waḷaṇ (n), waḷṇe (v)
182.	two	don
183.	vomit	okṇe/ulṭī karṇe/ulṭī hoṇe

184.	walk	tsāḷṇe 'to walk' phirāylā dzāṇe 'to go for a walk'
185.	warm	garam
186.	wash	dhuṇe
187.	water	pāṇī
188.	we	āmhī/āpaṇ (you + I)
189.	wet	olā
190.	what	kāy
191.	when	kẽmwhā
192.	where	kuṭhe
193.	white	pā̃ṇḍhrā
194.	who	koṇ
195.	wide	rũnda
196.	wife	bāyko/pātnī (s)
197.	wind	wārā
198.	wing	pāŋkha
199.	wipe	pusṇe
200.	with	(tSyā) barobar/(tSyā) saha
201.	woman	bāī, strī (s)
202.	woods	ʤāŋgal, dzhāḍī
203.	worm	kiḍā
204.	yes	ho
205.	year	warṣa (s)/sāl
206.	yellow	piwḷā

BIBLIOGRAPHY

Agnihotri, D. H. [1983] *Abhinav Marathi-Marathi Śabdakoś.* Poona: Venus Publishing House.

Akolkar, G. V. [1970] *Marāṭhītse Adhyāpan.* Pune: Venus Prakashan.

Apte, M. L. [1962] *A Sketch of Marathi Transformational Grammar.* Ph.D. Dissertation. Madison: University of Wisconsin.

Arjunwadkar, K. S. [1987] *Marathi Vyākaraṇ: Vād āṇi Pravād.* Pune: Sulekha Prakashan.

Ballentine, J. R. [1839] *A Grammar of the Mahratta Language.* Edinburgh: n.p.

Banahatti, S. N. and B. Dharmadhikari. [1968] *Sugam Marathi Śabdakoś.* Nagpur: Suvichar Prakashan Mandal.

Banahatti, S. N., et al. [1977] *Nawe Marathi Vyākaraṇ wa Lekhan (Part II).* 6th edition. Pune: Suvichar Prakashan.

Beams, J. [1872-1879a] *Comparative Grammar of the Modern Aryan Languages of India.* 3 vols. London: Trübner & Co.

________. [1872-1879b] *Outlines of Indian Philology.* Calcutta: Rupabani Press.

________. [1872] *A Comparative Grammar of Modern Languages of India.* Delhi: Munshiram Manoharlal. [Reprint 1966]

Berntsen, M. [1973] *The Speech of Phaltan: A Study in Sociolinguistics.* Ph.D. Dissertation. Philadelplhia: University of Pennsylvania.

________, and J. Nimbkar. [1975] *A Marathi Reference Grammar.* Philadelphia: University of Pennsylvania, South Asia Regional Studies.

________, and J. Nimbkar [1982] *Marathi Structural Patterns, Book One.* New Delhi: American Institute of Indian Studies.

Bhagwat, S. V. [1961] *Phonemic Frequencies in Marathi and Their Relation to Devising a Speed-Script.* Pune: Deccan College.

Bhatia, T. K. [1993] *Punjabi: A Cognitive Descriptive Grammar.* London: Routledge.

Bhide, V. V. [1918] *Marāṭhī Bhāṣetse WākpratSār wa Mhaṇī.* Pune: Chitrashala.

Bloch, J. [1920] *La Formation de la Langue Marathe.* (English translation [1970] *The Formation of the Marathi Language,* by D. R. Chanana.) Delhi: Motilal Banarsidass.

Bright, W. [1960] Linguistic Change in Some Indian Caste Dialects. In *Linguistic Diversity in South Asia.* C. Ferguson and J. J. Gumperz, eds. Bloomington: Indiana University Press, 19-26.

Burgess, E. [1854] *A Grammar of the Marathi Language.* Bombay: American Mission Press.

Caldwell, R. [1856] *A Comparative Grammar of the Dravidian or South Indian Family of Languages.* [3rd edition, 1961] Revised and edited by J. L. Wyatt and R. Ramakrishna Pillai. Madras: University of Madras.

Cardona, G. [1974] Indo-Aryan Languages. *Encyclopedia Britannica.* 15th edition. Vol. 9: 439-450.

Carey, W. [1805] *A Grammar of the Mahratta Language.* Serampur: The Mission Press.

Chatterji, S. K. [1926] *The Origin and Development of the Bengali Language.* London: George Allen and Unwin Ltd. [Reprint 1970]

________. [1942] *Indo-Aryan and Hindi.* Ahemadabad: Gujrat Vernacular Society.

________. [1960] Mutual Borrowing in Indo-Aryan. *Bulletin of the Deccan College* 20: 50-62.

Chauhan, D. V. [1969] Origin of the Consecutive Conjunction *ki* in Marathi: An Historical Search. *Indian Linguistics* 30: 85-89.

Chiplunkar, K. [1893] *Marathi Vyakaranavar Nibandha.* Pune: Chitrashala.

Chitnis, V. [1964] *The Khandeshi Dialect as Spoken by Farmers in the Village of Mohadi in the Dhulia Taluka.* Ph.D. Dissertation. Poona: University of Poona.

________. [1979] *An Intensive Course in Marathi.* Mysore: Central Institute of Indian Languages.

Chomsky, N. [1957] *Syntactic Structures.* The Hague: Mouton.

Comrie, B. and N. Smith, eds. [1977] Lingua Descriptive Studies: Questionnai -re. *Lingua* 42.1: 1-72.

Dalrymple, M. [1990] *Syntactic Constraints on Anaphoric Binding.* Ph.D. Dissertation. Stanford: Stanford University.

Damle, M. K. [1911] *Śāstrīya Marathi Vyākaraṇ*. Pune: Damodar Sawalaram ani Company. [1965 edition]

Dange, C. and I. Indapurkar. [1963] *Māybolītse Adhyāpan: Tattva āṇi Paddhatī*. Pune: Chiranjiva Grantha Prakashan.

Darby, A. [1933] *A Primer of the Marathi Language for the Use of Adults*. Bombay: n.p.

Das Gupta, B. B. and T. Pandit. [1975] *Marathi Self-taught*. 2nd edition. Calcuta: Das Gupta Prakashan.

Date, Y. R. et al. [1932-1950] *Mahārāṣṭra Śabdakoś* (1-7 vols.). Pune: Maharashtra Kosh Mandal.

Date, Y.R. and C. G. Karveteds. [1942, 1947] *Mahārāṣṭra Vāksampradāy Koś*. Pune: Maharashtra Kosh Mandal.

Deshpande, A. [1876] *Gramatica da Lingua Maratha*. Nova Goa: n.p.

________. [1879] *Maharashtra-Portuguese Koś*. Goa: n.p.

Deshpande, A. N. [1966] *PrātSīn Marathi Vaŋgmayātsā itihās*. Pune: Venus Prakashan.

________. [1966-1977] *Ādhunik Marathi Vaŋgmayātsā itihās*. 4 vols. Pune: Venus Prakashan.

Dhongde, R. V. [1974] *Tense, Aspect, and Mood in English and Marathi*. Ph.D. Dissertation. Poona: University of Poona.

________. [1976] Modality in Marathi. *Indian Linguistics* 37.2: 91-101.

________. [1979] From Verbal Stems to VP in Marathi. *Indian Linguistics* 40.2: 102-109.

________. [1983] *ArwātSīn Marathi*. Pune: Continental Prakashan.

Dikshit, P. N. [1980] *Marathi Vyākaraṇ: Kāhī Samasyā*. Kolhapur: Phadke Booksellers.

Emeneu, M. B. [1956] India as a Linguistic Area. *Language* 32.1: 3-16.

Gajendragadkar, S. N. [1969] Postpositions in Marathi: A Controlled Study. *Indian Linguistics* 30: 93-103.

Ghatge, A. M. [1963] *A Survey of Marathi Dialects*. Bombay: Maharashtra State Literature and Culture Board.

________. [1970] Marathi of Kasargod. *Indian Linguistics* 31.4: 138-144.

Godbole, K. S. [1867] *Marathi Bhāṣetse Nawīn Wyākaraṇ*. (1895 edition: *A New Grammar of the Marathi Language*.) Bombay: n.p.

Gosavi, R. R. and S. Vaidya. [1976] *Marathitse Aitihāsik Bhāṣāśāstra*. Pune: Moghe Prakashan.

Govilkar, L. [1974] *Marāṭhītse Wyākaraṇ.* Pune: Swadhyay Mahavidyalay Prakashan.

Gramopadhye, G. B. [1941] *Peśwe Daptarātīl Marāthī Bhāṣetse Swarūp.* Pune: Nerlekar.

________. [1964] *Bhāṣā-witSār āṇi Marathi Bhāṣā.* Pune: Venus Prakashan.

Grierson, G. A. [1905] *Linguistic Survey of India, Vol. VII.* Delhi: Motilal Banarsidass. [Reprint 1967]

Gulahti, S. P. [1992] *Encyclopedia of India, Vol. VII: Maharashtra.* P. N. Chopra, ed. New Delhi: Rima Publishing House.

Gumperz, J. [1971] Convergence and Creolization: A Case from the Indo-Aryan/Dravidian Border in India. In *Language in Social Groups: Essays by John J. Gumperz.* A. Dil, ed. Stanford: Stanford University Press, 251-273.

Gunjikar, R. B. [1867-1890] Marathi Wyākaraṇāwar Wichar. *Wiwidhajñānawistar.* (Published as *Sankalit Lekh.* [1942] Bombay: R. K. Tatnis.)

Gupte, S. M. [1975] *Relative Constructions in Marathi.* Ph.D. Dissertation. Ann Arbor: Michigan State University.

Hock, H. H. [1986] *Principles of Historical Linguistics.* New York: Mouron de Gruter.

Hook, P. E. [1977] The Distribution of the Compound Verb in the Languages of North India and the Question of Its Origin. *International Journal of Dravidian Linguistics* 6.2: 336-349.

________. [1987] Differential s-marking in Marathi, Hindi-Urdu and Kashmiri. *Chicago Linguistic Society* 23.

________. [1990] Experiencers in South Asian languages: A gallery. In *Experiencer Subjects in South Asian Languages.* M. Verma and K. P. Mohanan, eds. Stanford: The Center for the Study of Languages and Information, Stanford University, 319-334.

Indapurkar, C. D. [1989] *Marathi Bhāṣā, Wyawasthā, āṇi Adhyāpan.* Pune: Continental Prakashan.

Jahagirdar, R. V. [1930] Influence of Kanarese on Marathi Syntax. *Annals of Bhandarkar Oriental Research Institute 9.* (M.A. Dissertation. London: University of London. 1928)

Jha, A. [1966] *An Outline of Marathi Phonetics.* Pune: Deccan College.

Joshi, L. [1973-1985] *Marathi Wiśwakoś.* Mumbai: Maharashtra Rajya Sahitya Samskruti Mandal.

Joshi, P. N. [1963] *Marathi Vyākaraṇ.* Pune: Venus Prakashan.

________. [1970] *Ādarśa Marathi Śabdakoś.* Pune: Vidarbha Marathwada Book Company.

Joshi, R. B. [1889] *Prauḍhbodh Marathi Vyākaraṇ.* Pune: n.p. (In English. *A Comprehensive Marathi Grammar.* [1900] Pune: Arya Bhushana Press.)

________. [1918] *Marathi BhāṣetSī Ghaṭanā.* [2nd edition, 1923] Pune: n.p.

Joshi, V. S. [1981] *Bhāṣā wa Sahitya.* Pune: Maharashtra Sahitya Parishad.

Junghare, I. [1969] A Generative Approach to Marathi tadbhava Phonology. M.A. Dissertation. Bulletin of Deccan College Research Institute.

________. [1972] The Perfect Aspect in Marathi, Bhojpuri, and Maithili. *Indian Linguistics* 33.2: 128-134.

________. [1973] Restrictive Relative Clauses in Marathi. *Indian Linguistics* 34.4: 251-262.

________. [1983] Markers of Definiteness in Indo-Aryan. *Indian Linguistics* 44: 43-53.

Juvekar, P. [1973] *Descriptive Analysis of Indore Marathi Speech Dialect.* Ph.D. Dissertation. Indore: University of Indore.

Kachru, Y. [1979.] The Quotative in South Asian Languages. *South Asian Languages* 1: 63-78.

________. [1980] *Aspects of Hindi Grammar.* New Delhi: Manohar Publications.

________, and R. Pandharipande. [1978] On Ergativity in Selected South Asian Languages. *Studies in Linguistic Sciences* 8.1: 111-127.

________, and R. Pandharipande. [1980] Toward a Typology of Compound Verbs in South Asian Languages. *Studies in Linguistic Sciences* 10.1: 113-124.

________, B. Kachru and T. K. Bhatia. [1976] On the Notion of "Subjecthood" in Hindi, Punjabi and Kashmiri. In *On the Notion of Subject in South Asian Languages.* M. K. Verma, ed. Madison: University of Wisconsin, 79-108.

Kale, K. and A. Soman. [1986] *Learning Marathi.* Pune: Vishvakala Prakashan.

Kalelkar, N. G. [1955] *DhwanivitSār.* Pune: Deccan College.

________. [1962] *Bhāṣā āṇi Sāũskruti.* Mumbai: Mauz Prakashan.

________. [1964] *Bhāṣā Itihās āṇī, Bhūgol.* Mumbai: Mauz Prakashan.

Kanade, M. S., ed. [1979] *Marāthītsā Bhāṣik Abhyās.* Pune: Shrividya Prakashan.

Karandikar, M. A. [1966a] Drāwiḍ Bhāṣāsangha wa Marathi Bhāṣā. In *Marāṭhī Sāśodhana*, Part 1. A. K. Priyolkar, ed. Mumbai: Mumbai Marathi Granthasamgrahalay, 65-88.

________. [1966b] Marathi Bhāṣetīl Ingradʒī Apabhraṣṭa Śabda. In *Marāṭhī Sāśodhana*, Part 2. A. K. Priyolkar, ed. Mumbai: Mumbai Marathi Granthasamgrahalay, 2-54.

Karve, I. [1965. *Kinship Organization in India*. 2nd edition. New York: Asia Publishing House.

Katenina, T. E. [1963a] *Ocherk Grammatiki Iazyka Maratkhi*. Moscow: Izd. Lit. na Inostranykh Iazykakh.

________. [1963b] *Yazyk Marathi*. Moscow: n.p.

Katre, S. M. [1944] *Some Problems of Historical Linguistics in Indo-Aryan*. Bombay: University of Bombay.

Katre, S. [1966] *The Formation of Konkani*. Poona: Deccan College.

Kavadi, N. and F. C. Southworth. [1965] *Spoken Marathi, Book 1: First-year Intensive Course*. Philadelphia: University of Pennsylvania Press.

Kelkar, A. R. [1958] *The Phonology and Morphology of Marathi*. Ph.D. Dissertation. Ithaca: Cornell University.

________. [1965] Marathi VyākaraṇātSī Nawī Diśā. *Satyakathā*. January: 19-31.

________. [1973] Relative Clauses in Marathi: A Plea for a Less Constricted View. *Indian Linguistics* 34.4: 274-300.

________. [1977] Marathi Dewanāgarī Warṇakramī: Ek Tipaṇ. *Maharashtra Sahitya Patrika*, Vol. 202. In *Vaikharī: Bhāṣā āṇi Bhāṣāvyavahār*. [1983] Mumbai: Majestic Bookstall.

________. [1985] Bhāṣaśikṣaṇ. *Marathi Wiśwakoś*. Bombay: Maharashtra Rajya Marathi Vishvakosh Nirmiti Mandal.

Kelkar, G. H. [1966] *Marathi VyākaraṇātSī Mūlatative*. 4th edition. Pune: City Book Stall.

Khaire, V. [1979] *Marathi Bhāṣetse Mūḷ*. 5th edition. Mumbai: Marathi Sauśodhan Mandal.

Kher, A. K. [1895] *A Higher Marathi Grammar*. Poona: n.p.

Khokle. V. [1969] *Two Models of Phonological Distinctive Features: An Evaluation as Applied to Marathi*. Ph.D. Dissertation. University of Minnesota, Minneapolis.

Konow, S. [1903] Maharashtri and Marathi. *Indian Antiquary* 32: 180-192.

________. [1934] A Marathi Idiom. *Indian Linguistics* 4: 263-272.

Kulkarni, K. P. [1949] *Marathi Wyutpattī Koś: Aitihāsik wa Taulanik*. Mumbai: K. B. Dhavle.

________. [1969] *Marathi Bhaṣā Udgam va Vikās.* Pune: Modern Bookdepo Prakashan.
Kulkarni, S. B. [1966] Marāṭhītsī Wyākaraṇ-paramparā. In *Maraṭhi Wyākaraṇatsī Mūlatattve.* 4th edition. G. H. Kelkar, ed. Pune: City Book Stall, 289-298.
________. [1969] An Experiment in Estimating Transfer of Information Among Some Marathi Dialects. *Indian Linguistics* 30: 73-76.
Kulkarni, S. R. [1970] *Prātsīn Marathi Gadya: Preraṇā āṇi Paramparā.* Mumbai: Sindhu Prakashan.
________. [1974. *Powarī Bolī.* Nagpur: Nagpur Vidyapith.
Kundale, M. B. [1974] *Marāṭhītse Adhyāpan.* Pune: Shri Vidya Prakashan.
Kuznetsov, B. I. [1971] *Ocherk Grammatikhotglago l'nykh Imen Yazyka Maratkhi.* Ph.D. Dissertation. Leningrad: University of Leningrad.
Laddu, S. [1983] *Marāṭhītsyā Pramāṇ Bhāṣetse Swarūp.* Pune: Maharashtra Vidyapitha Granthanirmiti Mandalasathi Kontinentala Prakasana.
________. [1962] Prerequisites of a Comparative Dictionary of the Dialects of Marathi. *Journal of the University of Poona, Humanities.* No. 15.
Laddu, T. K. [1911] Genitive Accusative in Marathi. *Journal of the Royal Asiatic Society.* London.
Lambert, H. M. [1943] *Marathi Language Course.* Calcutta: Oxford/Humphrey Milford.
Lloyed, J. A. and S. G. Kanhere. [1928] The Pronunciation of Marathi. *Bulletin of the School of Oriental Studies,* 791-801.
Maharashtra Government. [n.d.] *Śāsanwyawahārāt Marathi.* [Bombay]: Bhasha Sanchalanalay.
Mangrulkar, A. [1964] *Marāṭhītsyā Vyākaraṇātsā PunarvitSār.* Pune: Pune Vidyapith.
________, and K. S. Arjunvadkar. [1958] *Marathi Ghaṭanā, RatSanā, Paramparā.* Pune: Deshmukh Prakashan.
Marathe, S. M. [1972] *The Marathi Verb.* M.A. Dissertation. Cardiff: University of Wales.
Masica, C. P. [1976] *Defining a Linguistic Area: South Asia.* Chicago: University of Chicago Press.
________. [1991] *The Indo-Aryan Languages.* New York: Cambridge University Press.

Master, A. [1957] Some Marathi Inscriptions, A.D. 1060-1300. *Bulletin of the School of Oriental and African Studies* 20: 417-435.

________. [1967] *A Grammar of Old Marathi.* Oxford: Clarendon Press.

Miranda, R. V. [1978] Caste, Religion, and Dialect Differentiation in the Konkani Area. *International Journal of the Sociology of Language* 16 (*Aspects of Sociolinguistics in South Asia.* B. B. Kachru and S. N. Sridhar, eds., 77-91).

Mishra, M. [1990] Dative/Experiencer Subjects in Maithili. In *Experiencer Subjects in South Asian Languages.* M. K. Verma and K. P. Mohanan, eds. Stanford: The Center for the Study of Language and Information, 105-118.

Modak, G. K. [1932] *Marāṭhītse Antarangadarŋśan.* Pune: Lekhak.

Molesworth, J. T. [1857] *A Dictionary of Marathi and English.* 2nd edition. Bombay: Bombay Native Education Society Press.

Mone, M. S. [1927a] *Marathi Bhāṣetse Wyākaraṇkār wa Wyā Karanprabandhakar.* Pune: Chitrashala.

________. [1927b] *Wyākaraṇkār āṇi Wyākaraṇprabandhakār.* Pune: Chitrashala.

Nadkarni, M. V. [1975] Bilingualism and Syntactic Change in Konkani. *Language* 51: 672-683.

Navalkar, G. [1925] *The Student's Marathi Grammar.* Poona: Scottish Mission Press.

Pandharipande, R. [1979] Passive as an Optional Rule in Hindi, Marathi, and Nepali. *South Asian Languages Analysis* 1: 89-106.

________. [1981a] *Syntax and Semantics of the Passive Construction in Selected South Asian Languages.* Ph.D. Dissertation. Urbana: University of Illinois at Urbana–Champaign.

________. [1981b] Transitivity in Hindi. *Studies in Linguistic Sciences* 11.2: 161-180.

________. [1981c] Nativization of Lexicon: The Case of Marathi. *Linguistics* 19: 987-101.

________. [1982a] Counteracting Forces in Language Change: Convergence vs. Maintenance. *Studies in Linguistic Sciences* 12.2: 97-116.

________. [1982b] Volitionality: More Evidence for Constraints on Passive in Hindi. In *South Asian Review, Vol. 3.* P. J. Mistry, ed., 89-103.

________. [1982c] Linguistics and Written Discourse in Particular Language. Contrastive Studies: English and Marathi. *Annual Review of Applied Linguistics* 3: 118-136.

________. [1985] The Impact of Relational Grammar on Empirical Studies. In *Relational Grammar.* D. P. Pattanayak and Y. Kachru, eds. Mysore: Central Institute of Indian Languages, 42-88.

________. [1986a] Language Contact and Language Variation: Nagpuri Marathi. In *South Asian Languages: Structure, Convergence, and Diglossia.* Bh. Krishnamurti, C. Masica, and A. Sinha, eds. Delhi: Motilal Banarsidass, 219-231.

________. [1986b] Modernity, Religion and Regional Identity: Contexts and Conflicts in Language and Power. *Sociolinguistics* 16.1: 35-45.

________. [1987] On Nativization of English. *World Englishes* 6.2: 149-158.

________. [1990a] Formal and Functional Constraints on Code-mixing. In *Codeswitching as a Worldwide Phenomenon.* R. Jacobson, ed. New York: Peter Lang, 15-32.

________. [1990b] Experiencer (dative) NPs in Marathi. In *Experiencer Subjects in South Asian Languages.* M. K. Verma and K. P. Mohanan, eds., 161-180.

________. [1990c] The Serial Verb Construction in Marathi. In *When Verbs Collide: Papers from 1990 Ohio State Mini-Conference on Serial Verbs.* B. D. Joseph and A. M. Zwicky, eds. Columbus: The Ohio State University, 178-199.

________. [1990d] Reflexives in Marathi: Issues and Implications. Presented at International Seminar on Anaphora: Form and Function. Delhi University, Delhi, India.

________. [1991a] A Grammar of Politeness in Marathi. Presented at the South Asian Language Analysis Roundtable. University of Illinois at Urbana-Champaign.

________. [1991b] Some Issues Related to Ergativity in Marathi. Presented at the 20th Annual Conference on South Asia. In *Verb Agreement in South Asian Languages* (Conference Proceedings of 20th Annual Conference on South Asia). [in press] M. K. Verma, ed. Madison: University of Wisconsin.

________. [1992a] Complex Predicates in Marathi. In *Complex Predicates in South Asian Languages.* M. K. Verma, ed. New Delhi: Manhar Publications, 177-195.

________. [1992b] Marathi. In *Oxford Encyclopedia of Linguistics*. W. Bright, ed. New York: Oxford University Press, 386-389.

________. [1992c] Defining Politeness in Indian English. *World Englishes* (Special Issue on the Extended Family: English in Global Bilingualism. Studies in Honor of Braj. B. Kachru) 11.2/3: 241-250.

________. [forthcoming] *Sociolinguistic Dimensions of Marathi: Multilingualism in Central India.* Delhi: Manohar.

________. [forthcoming] Is Genetic Connection Relevant in Code-Switching?: Evidence from South Asian Languages. In *Code-Switching Worldwide*. R. Jacobson, ed. Mouton de Gruyter.

________, and Y. Kachru. [1977] Relational Grammar, Ergativity and Hindi-Urdu. *Lingua* 41: 217-38.

Pandit, P. B. [1972] *India as a Sociolinguistic Area.* Poona: Poona University Press.

Pangarkar, L. R. [1932] *Marathi Vañgmayātsā Itihās.* Mumbai: K. B. Dhawle. [Reprint 1972]

Panse, M. G. [1953] *Linguistic Peculiarities of Jnāneshwarī.* 2 vols. Pune: Deccan College.

Pareira, J. [1971] *Konkaṇī: A Language (A History of the Konkaṇī Marathi Controversy).* Dharwad: Karnatak University.

Pathan, Y. M. [1973] *Marathi Bakharītīl Fārsīce Swarūp.* Aurangabad: Marathwada Vidyapith Prakashan.

Prabhudesai, V. B. [1963] *Satrāwyā Śatakātīl Gomantakī bolī.* Mumbai: Mumbai Vishvavidyalay.

Priyolkar, A. K. [1932] *Grānthik Marathi āṇi Koṇkaṇī Bolī.* Pune: Pune Vidyapith.

________. [1966a] Kānārī, Kõnkaṇī: BhāṣāvātSak Śabda. In *Marāṭhī Sāśodhana*, Part 2. A. K. Priyolkar, ed. Mumbai: Mumbai Marathi Granthasamgrahalay, 69-88.

________, ed. [1966b] *Marāṭhī Sāśodhana.* Part 1 and 2. Mumbai: Mumbai Marathi Granthasamgrahalay.

Raeside, I. M. P. [1958] The Marathi Compound Verb. *Indian Linguistics* (Turner Volume), 237-248.

Rajwade, V. K. [1909] *Shri Jñāneswarītīl Marathi Bhāṣetsa Vyākaraṇ.* Dhulia: n.p. (Reprint 1979. S. G. Tulpule, ed. Mumbai: Maharashtra Rajya Sahitya Mandal.)

________. [1967] *Rajwade Lekh Saṃgraha.* 2nd edition. L. S. Joshi, ed. Mumbai: Popular Prakashan.

Ranade, N. B. [1916] *The Twentieth Century English-Marathi Dictionary.* Bombay: Western India Co. (Reprint in 2 vols. [1977] Pune: Shubhada Saraswat.)

Sabnis, M. P. [1951] *Adhunik Marathice Uchchatar Vyakaran.* Bombay: n.p.

Sardesai, V. N. [1930] Some Problems in Nasalization of Marathi. *Journal of the Royal Asiatic Society,* 337-365.

Schwartzberg, J. E. [1978] *A Historical Atlas of South Asia.* Chicago: University of Chicago Press.

Shapiro, M. C. and H. C. Schiffman. [1981] *Language and Society in South Asia.* Delhi: Motilal Banarsidass.

Sote, D. G. [1974] *Vaidarbhī Bolītsā Śabda-koś.* Wardha: Sote Sahitya Prakashan.

Southworth, F. C. [1961] The Marathi Verbal Sequences and Their Co-occurrences. *Language* 37.2: 201-208.

________. [1971] Detecting Prior Creolization: An Analysis of the Historical Origins of Marathi. In *Pidginization and Creolization of Languages.* Dell Hymes, ed. Cambridge University Press, 255-276.

________. [1974] Linguistic Stratigraphy of North India. *International Journal of Linguistics* 3.2: 201-223.

________. [1976] The Verb in Marathi-Konkani. *International Journal of Dravidian Linguistics* 5.22: 298-326

Sridhar, S. N. [1990] *Kannada.* London: Routledge.

Stevenson, J. [1841] An Essay on the Vernacular Literature of the Marathas. *Journal of the Bombay Branch Royal Asiatic Society* 1.1: 1-2.

________. [1983, 1868] *The Principles of Murathee Grammar.* Bombay: n.p.

Tarkhadkar, D. P. [1836 (1937)] *Mahārāśṭra Bhāṣetse Wyākaraṇ.* 2nd edition. Mumbai: B.S. Tarkhad.

Tulpule, S. G., ed. [1960] *An Old Marathi Reader.* Pune: Venus Prakashan.

________. [1973] *Yadawkālīn Marāṭhī Bhāṣā.* Pune: Venus Prakashan.

________. [1979] *Classical Marathi Literature.* Weisbaden: Otto Harrassowitz.

Turner, R. L. [1916] The Indo-Germanic Accent in Marathi. *Journal of the Royal Asiatic Society* 1: 203-251.

Varhadpande, V. K. [1972] *Nāgpurī Bolī: Bhāṣāśāstrīya Abhyās.* Nagpur: Indira Prakashan.

Wali, K. [1976] *Two Marathi Reflexives and Their Implication for Causative Structure.* Ph.D. Dissertation. Syracuse: Syracuse University.

________. [1979] Two Marathi Reflexives and the Causative Structure. *Studies in Language* 3.3: 405-438.

________. [1980] Oblique Causee and Passive Explanation. *Linguistic Inquiry* 11.1: 258-260.

________. [1981] Cause, Causer, and Causee: A Semantic Perspective. *Journal of Linguistics* 17: 289-308.

________. [1982] Marathi Correlatives. In *South Asian Review,* Vol. VI:3. P. J. Mistry, ed. Fresno: California State University, 78-88.

________. [1988] A Note on Marathi and Kashmiri - WH Questions. *Cornell University Papers in Linguistics* 8, 161-180. Ithaca: Cornell University Department of Modern Languages and Linguistics.

________. [1989] *Marathi Syntax: A Study of Reflexives.* Patiala: Indian Institute of Language Studies.

________, and K. V. Subbarao. [1991. On Pronominal Classification: Evidence from Marathi and Telugu. *Linguistics* 29: 1093-1110.

Walimbe, S. G. [1964] *Descriptive Analysis of Mang Marathi (Malwa).* Ph.D. Dissertation. Poona: University of Poona.

Zograph, G. A. [1983] *Languages of South Asia.* London: Routledge and Kegan Paul.

INDEX

Adjectives 450-2
- adjective phrases 141-4
- adjective-noun compounds 524-5
- adverbial modification of 144
- adverbs from 511-12
- and classifiers 24-6
- and conjunct verbs 487
- and demonstrative pronouns 391
- and emphasis 245-6
- and heavy shift 255
- as anaphora 198
- attributive 143-4
- coordination of 163-7
- demonstrative 80-1, 151, 158, 371-2
- derivation of 480-4
- nouns from 480-3
- numerals as 455-7
- operational definition 269-70
- participles as 170-1
- possessive 150
- predicative 142-3
- quantifiers as 456-7
- simple 450
- types of 269-70, 450
- with arguments 143-4

Adverbials 139-41
- adverbial phrases 144-6
- definition of 138
- position of 140-1
- types of 138-40

Adverbs
- and concessive 119-20
- and conditional 115-9
- and emphasis 234-6
- and participles 139, 146, 445
- and postpositions 139
- and verbs 124
- basic 139
- comitative 137, 310
- derived 139
- and finite clauses 103-5, 140-1
- formation of 139
- of cause 112
- of location 138-9
- of manner 138
- of purpose 111-2
- of result 120-1
- of time 103, 138
- operational definition of 138, 269-70
- position of 234-5, 237-8, 247
- reduplication of 139, 146

Adversative *See* Coordination

Agent
- and causee 398, 401-5, 405-7
- and causer 401-5
- and subject 403
- in passive constructions 301-3
- of ergative construction 48-51, 130

Agentless sentences 399-400

Ambiguity
- in anaphora 198
- in direct and indirect speech 2-7
- in negation 194
- in reflexivization 198

Anaphora 195-200
- and superordinate clauses 201-6
- between non-finite subordinate clauses 204-6
- between successive subordinate clauses 206-7
- between superordinate and subordinate clauses 202-6
- by deletion 195-7
- by pronominalization 198-9
- by reflexivization 197
- in coordinate structures 199-201
- within the clause 198-9
- zero 376-80, 443-4, 445-6

Animacy 13, 135, 219-222, 230, 232-4, 273, 369, 390, 392, 406, 447
- and postposition/case-marking 135-6

Answers 10, 37-42, 184-6, 266-7
- minimum 38-9
- to leading questions 10
- to question-word-questions 41-2
- to yes-no questions 40

Articles 135, 150, 452

Aspect 414-31 (*See also* Ergativity)
- and compound verbs 418
- and duration 418-31
- and tenses 414
- and time reference 414
- durative 48, 428-9
- habitual 422-3
- imperfective 421
- ingressive 425
- iterative 426-7
- marking of *See* Marking
- other aspects 430-1
- perfective 414-19
- progressive 423-5
- punctual 427
- restriction on the combination of aspectual values 431
- semelfactive 427
- simultaneous 429-30
- terminative 425-6

Basic vocabulary 596-601

Case 273-83
- accusative 134-6
- dative 136-7
- double 366

function of 282
instrumental 319-20
locative 282, 340, 351
marking of *See* Marking
nominative 283-5
oblique 275-6
and postpositions 270
suffixes 273
vocative 275

Causee (*See also* Verb: causative)
and agentivity 405-7
deletion of 407
marking of *See* Marking
non-volitional 406-7

Circumstance 311-2

Citation form 334

Classifiers 24, 369

Clause (*See also* Subordination)
marking of
finite clause 103-4, 112-3
gerundive clause 21
infinitival clause 21
matrix clause 1-7
non-finite clause 21
participial clause 21
subordinate clause 5-6, 61-2

Cleft construction 244-5

Coalescence 570

Comitative 310-11

Comparison 222-7
and deletion 223-5
correlative 226
markers of 222, 224-6
means of expressing 222-4
object of 222-4
by clausal structure 223-4
of non-clausal constituents 222-3
and order of the elements 222-3
superlative 226-7

Complement clause *See* Subordination

Complements
and verb agreement 65
kī "that" 2, 61-2, 65-7
marking of *See* Marking
object 299-300
of a copular 125-6, 297-8
of gerunds 66-7
of infinitives 66-7
of participles 66-7
of verbs 65-6
subject of 298

Compound
adjective-noun 524-5
attributed compounds 521
complex 520
echo compounds 527-9
emphatic compounds 521-2
hybrid 535-6
hyponymous compounds 520
intensifier 527-9
noun and *ganik* 525
noun-noun 518-9
noun-verb compounds 529-31

participle and noun 526-7
possessive
reduplicative 522-3
superordinate 519
verb-verb 531-3

Concessives 119-20, 329

Concessive clauses 119-20

Conditional 115-9, 432
adverb clause 115-9
counterfactual 118-9
negative 117
tense/aspect possibilities in 118-9

Conjunct verb 295-7, 401, 529-31
and loan words 536

Consonant clusters 547-51

Consonants
affricates 538-41
assimilation of 562-3
cluster simplification of 573-4
distribution of glides 572
liquids 542
stops 538-40

Constraints
on aspectual values 431
on combination of consonants 549-51
on combination of consonants and vowels 553
on coordination 168-74
on emphatic particles 241-3
on passivization 396-7
on phonological segments 547
on question 31
on relativization 89-91
on tense marking 21, 119, 189, 407
on verb agreement 130-5, 176-82, 412, 446-9
on word order 157-9, 183, 211-2
semantic 47-51, 53, 209, 436-7, 448
syntactic 18-20, 29, 89, 96, 99, 102, 157, 163, 171-2, 202, 204, 213, 221, 223, 241-3

Contingent 442

Coordination 29-31, 158-82
"and" 159-60
and accompaniment 168-9
and agreement 176-82
and negation 191-2
and questions 29-31
and reflexivization
and relativization 101-3
"but" 160-1, 164-5
adjective and participial constructions in 170-2
deletion in 175-6
means of 29, 158
number of coordinators in 163
of active and passive verbs 174
of adjectives and participles 170-1
of adverbials 172-4
of major categories 163-7
of noun and nominalized 171-2

"or" 165-7
order of conjuncts 160
structural parallelism in 169-70
verb agreement in 176-82

Copula 125-9 (*See also* Verb)
complement of 125-6
retention and deletion of 126-7
types of copular sentences 127-9

Coreferentiality
and deletion 75-6, 200, 204-6
and reflexivization 209
and relativization 76-9
and subordination 67-8, 76-7, 109, 112, 204-6
in coordination 200
object-subject 212
subject-subject 203-4

Counter nouns 315-6, *See also* Classifiers

Dative (*See also* Case)
and gerund 66, 107, 361
and infinitive 111, 425
of kinship 231-3
of possession 312
subjects 212, 229-30, 233, 285-7

Definiteness 135, 370-2

Degemination 570-1

Deixis 395

Deletion
anaphoric 202-4
and identity 228-9, 304
backward 202-4
and coreferentiality 76-7, 108, 204-6
forward 202-4
in comparatives 222-4
in coordination 199-201
in discourse 217
in equatives 123, 228
in gerunds 444
in infinitives 443
in non-finite adverb clauses 108
in participles 445-6
in relative clauses 78-80, 84-7, 89, 93, 100-1, 202
of imperative subject 57, 196-7
of postposition 270
of subjects 32-4, 37, 42, 75, 129, 133, 195-7

Derivation
of adjectives 487-504
of adverbs 504-514
of nouns 460-84
of postpositions 515-36
of verbs 484-7

Determiner *See* Noun phrase; Pronouns; Relative clause

Diphthongs 544

Direct and indirect speech 1-7, 67-9

Dislocation 245-7

Duration 362-4 (*See also* Aspect)

anterior 366-8
future 369
past 368
posterior 366-8

Emphasis 234-51
by adverbs 234-5
by clefting 244-5
by constituent 238
by dislocation 245-7
by inversion 248-9
by movement 243-4
by particles 235-6, 239-43
by pitch 236
by pseudo-clefting 245
by repetition 247-8
by stress 238-9
choice of devices and constituent types in 249
combinatory 249
contradictory 237-8
non-contradictory 234-7
of more than one constituent and focus 250

Equatives 122-4, 227-9
backward deletion in 123, 229
by adding adverb 227
by adding postpositions 227
deletion possibilities in 228
forward deletion in 122
in relative clauses 122-4
phrasal 123
sentential 229

Ergativity
and obligative 131-2
and optative 131-2
and perfective aspect 130
and verb agreement 130-1
marking of subject 129-33

Essive 322-3

Exclamation 263-5

Explicator verbs *See* Verb: compound; Aspect: equative

Expression (Semantic)
of cause 319-20
of concessive 329
of distance 327-8
of essive 222-3
of exclusion 300-1
of extent 328-9
of function 321
of inclusion 330
of location 335-9
of manner 317-9
of material 316-7
of price 326-7
of purpose 320-1
of quality 312-5
of reference 321-2
of source 306-8
of value 327

Focus
and emphasis 245-7
and heavy shift 254-260
and movement 85-6, 243-4
and repetition 247-8
and stress 238-9
and topicalization 252-4
and word order 138
contrastive 237-8, 253, 379-80
and inversion 248-9
marking of *See* Marking
of yes-no questions 250-1

Gender 368-9
  and nouns 273-83
  and participles 445
  and pronouns 375-6, 382, 391-2
  and tense 407-8
  marking of *See* Marking

Gerund 72-3, 113-4
  as verbal complement 66-7
  formation of 444

Glide
  formation of 566
  insertion 573-5

Greeting 265

Heavy shift 254-60
  landing sites of 258-60
  of adjective phrases 255
  of adverb phrases 258
  of complementizers 260
  of gerundive phrases 257-8
  of infinitival phrases 257
  of noun phrases 255-8
  structures subject to 255-8
  and complementizers 260

Identity *See* Coreferentiality

Ideophones 577-82

Imperative 42-61, 53-4, 187-8, 196, 433-441-2
  by other means 57-61
  contingent forms as imperatives 59
  degrees of 53-4
  degrees of politeness in direct 42-4
  indirect optative as 44-7
  negative 55-7
  obligative as 48-52
  omission of subjects in 196
  polite 42-4
  prohibitive as 55-7
  suggestive as 47-8

Impersonal construction 129, 301-3, 399-400

Imprecative 59-60

Indefiniteness 373

Indicative mood 432

Indirect commands 71-2

Indirect object *See* Object

Indirect questions 69-71

Infinitive 21, 114, 443-4
  and agreement 72-3
  and relativization 93-5
  as noun 469
  as verbal complement 66-7
  formation of 443-4
  oblique of 443

Interjection 263-5

Intonation
  contrastive stress 562
  doubt 561
  emphasis 561-2
  functions of 559-62
  in affirmative sentences 561
  in questions 559-60
  in tag questions 560

of persuasion 562
patterns of 559
Kannada 61, 158, 260, 263, 301, 396, 403, 416, 525

Length 318

Lexicon 583-601
agricultural 595-6
basic 596-601
body parts 589-92
color terms 588-9
cooking terms 592-5
kinship 583-7

Liquids 545, 549-50, 555

Loan words 368, 370, 486, 529-30

Location 335-355
in time 355-66

Marathi
dialects of xxxviii, xliii-iv, 424
grammatical tradition of xxxix-xliii
history of xxxv-xxxvii, xliii-xlv
literature of xlii-iii
nativization in xliii-iv
standard xxxviii, xli, xlv
writing system of xxxviii

Marking
in passives 394-400
of adverbial 138-9
of aspectual 418-30
of case 273-5
of causative 401-2
of compliments 62-3
of focus 303-4
of gender 276-83
of gerund 444
of infinitives 443-4
of mood 431-42
of nouns 273-83, 368-9, 373-5
of number 366-7
of numerals 455
of object 134-6
of participles 445-6
of person 129-31, 375-6, 381-2, 387-9, 396-7, 409-14, 433, 447 433
of relative clause 76-80
of subject 129-33
of tense 362-5, 382, 407-14

Material 316-7

Metathesis 566, 569

Minor sentence types 260-8
conditions of appropriateness in 262
exclamations as 263-5
greetings as 265
kinship terms as 262-3
vocatives 261-3

Modals *See* Verb

Mood 431-2
and aspect 414-31
conditional 432
contingent 442
debitive 435-6
degree of certainty 439-40
hortatory 441
imperative 443
indicative 432

intentive 438
monitory 441-2
potential 436-8
potential and permission 448
subjunctive/optative 444

Movement 243-4

Nasalization 544-6, 568

Negation 182-95
and coordination 191-2
and reduplication 459
and subordination 192-3
and tense 188-9
emphasis in 235
emphatic particles in 237-8, 456
multiple negatives in 190-2
negative answers in 184-6
negative verb in 186-8
of adverb 185
of constituent 183, 187-8
of gerund 183
of infinitive 183
of participle 182
of sentence 185-6
sentential 185
universal 193-5

Nominalization 22-3, 70, 171-2, 216-7, 253-4, 304-5

Noun phrases 149-58
and loan words 370
and noun-noun compounds 518-9
and noun-verb compounds 526
and reduplication 458
and reflexive pronouns 217
definiteness marking in 370-2
function of 149
genericness in 374-5
indefiniteness marking in 373
movement of 255-8
non-finite 64-5
of finite complements 63-5
operational definition of 268
order of constituents in 157-8
participial 73-6
participle-noun compounds 526-7
structure of 154-5
types of 22-3

Nouns
and gender marking 368-9
and verb agreement 284-5, 394-8, 400, 411
and verb formation 484-5
as adjectives 480-3
as adverbs 483-4
basic 268
classes of 368-70
collective 367-8
derivation of nouns from
adjectives 480-3
nouns 460-8
other categories 484
postpositions 484
verbs 468-79
deverbal 479-80
infinitives as 443-4
marking of *See* Marking
possessor 312

Number 366-7
and verb agreement 404-17, 421-7
collective 367-8
distributive 367
dual 369
marking of *See* Marking
marking of foreign words 368
plural 366
singular 366

Numerals 151-3, 452-9
and indefiniteness 151-2
approximate 151-2
as adjectives 151-3
cardinal 452-4
collective 151-2
fractional 151-2
marking of *See* Marking
multiplicative 151-2
ordinal 455-6

Object
and verb agreement 394-6, 399, 401, 410-2
animate 135
definite 134-6
deletion of 136
direct 133-6
inanimate 134
indefinite 134-5
indirect 136
marking of *See* Marking
of a postposition 147-50
of passive verbs 394-5

Obligatives 45-52, 291
and ergative 47-8
and postpositions 48-52
and verb agreement 49-50
as imperatives *See* Imperatives
future obligative 51-2

Optatives 44-7, 434
and ergative 131-2
and postposition 45
and verb agreement 44-5
as indirect imperatives 46

Particle
and questions 7-11, 38-41
and warnings 441-2
combination of emphatic particles 249
contrastive 253
disjunctive 165-7
emphatic 239-43
hi 140, 239-43
negative 9-10, 37-41, 182-6, 237-8
of exclusion 239-43
of inclusion 243, 330
suddha 239-43
ts 238-43, 329
vocative 331-4

Passive
agent in 301-3
agentless 301
and agreement 394-6
capabilitative 301
formation of 394-400
function of 301-3, 397-9
object marking in 396
postpositions in 394-400
subject marking in 396

Persian xxxv, xlii-v, 141, 368, 459-60, 464-6, 483,

489-90, 492, 499-501, 506, 546, 554, 564

Person
- and ergative marking 130
- marking of *See* Marking

Politeness
- and imperative 43, 46, 53-4, 433
- and plurals 376, 383-4
- and question 71
- and vocatives 262-3

Possession 229-34
- alienable/inalienable 231-4
- and verb agreement 230
- means of expressing 229-30
- of abstract qualities/traits 233
- of animate/inanimate 230-232
- of temporary/permanent 231
- predicative 230

Possessive
- adjectives 150, 312
- and infinitives 22-3
- postpositions/case-suffixes in 64, 66-7, 141, 148, 150, 295, 305, 308, 323, 327, 357-65
- pronouns 391
- reflexives 389-91

Postpositions (*See also* Case)
- ablative 223, 306
- accusative 219, 221, 288-9, 330
- adjectives from 503
- and adverbs 139, 145
- and verb agreement 446
- as nouns 518-25
- complex 168, 515-6
- dative 47-52, 132, 221, 351
- deletion of 89, 95
- derivation of 147, 515-36
- ergative 48-50, 133, 389, 446
- for time reference 107-9
- in causative sentences 401-7
- in comparative clause 222-4
- in passive sentences 394-6, 398
- incorporation of 506
- instrumental 113-4, 308-10
- invariable 452
- locative 225-6, 292, 296, 335-7
- object of 17, 22, 90-1, 147-8
- of purpose 111-2, 320-1
- operational definition 270
- order of suffixes and 515
- possessive 148, 229, 231-4, 516
- simple 147, 517
- syntactic and semantic functions of 147-8
- transitive subjects and 48-50, 401
- variable 452

Pragmatic factors
- and degree of certainty 439-40
- and possession 233-4, 320-4
- and pronouns 383-4
- and reflexives 209, 219

in compound verbs 418-21, 531-3
in imperatives 45-54
in imprecatives 60-1
in optatives 46
in passives 301-3, 369-9
in relative clauses 83-4
in vocatives 332-4

Pronominalization 198-207

Pronouns
anaphoric 375-6
and number 375-6
and politeness 375-6
case-system in 387-9
complex 385
deletion of 378-80
demonstrative 391
emphatic 385
emphatic reflexive 385
free 376-7
gender distinction in 375-6
generic 374-5
in imperative 379-80
indefinite 384-5
interrogative 391-3
number marking in 381-2
obligatory/optional status of 378-80
of exclusion 381
of inclusion 381
operational definition of 268-9
pairs of 386
possessive 391
pronominal forms 386, 383
proximate 382
reciprocal 391
reflexive 218, 376, 211-4
relative 394
remote 382
secondary 386
special anaphoric pronouns 382
status distinctions in 383-4

Punjabi xxxiv, 61, 65, 128, 237, 255, 263, 301, 307, 396, 403, 410-1, 416, 425, 525, 548

Purpose 320-1

Quality 312-5

Quantifiers 151-3, 270-1, 323-6, 456-9
aggregative 456
as adjectives 151-3, 456-9
indefinite 152, 373
means of quantification 458-9
negative 456
quantifier compounds 458-9
questioning of 393-4
reduplicated 458-9
universal 226

Questions 7-61, 112, 163, 193-5, 250-1, 264-5
adjectival 14-6
alternative 11, 250-1
as imperatives 57-8, 61
echo 32-7
leading 8-10, 40-1
negative 8-9, 36, 39-40, 57-8, 184-6
pronominal 11-4
question-word 11-6, 35, 41-2, 58, 70, 193

questioning possibilities 16-32
in main clause 16-20
in coordinate structures 29-31
in echo question 36-7
in finite subordinate clauses 20-1
in nominalized clauses 22-3
in non-finite clauses 21
in noun phrase 23-8
in participial clauses 22
in postpositional phrase 28-9
in relative clause 27-8
tag 60-1
yes-no 7-11, 32-4, 36-40, 57-8, 61, 112, 250-1

Reciprocals 219-22

Reduplication
and emphasis 39, 146, 527-9, 533-5
for distributive meaning 139, 156, 458
for expressing meanings 458-9
in answers 39-40
of adverb 139-46
of nouns 458, 522-3
of participles 114-5
of particle 39-40
of pronouns 458
of question words 459
of verb 314, 472, 533-5
of verbal compounds 533

Reflexives 197, 207-19, 389-91, 484
as adverb 219
as emphatic pronouns 197, 218
choice of 208-10
coreferentiality and codependency in 209-10, 219
in nominalized clauses 216-7
in noun phrases 217
position of 211-2
position of head noun in 84
relations between antecedent and 212-6
scope of 207-11
without overt antecedents 217-8

Reflexivization 207-19
across clauses 208-9
types of antecedent 209-10
within a single clause 208

Relative clauses 76-105, 150
deletion in 77-80
derivation of 76-84
finite 88-9, 103-5
headless 86-7
marking of *See* Marking
non-finite 74-6
participial 94-7
position of relativized element 85-6
relativization of
adverbial 90
direct object 88-92
indirect object 88, 92-3
infinitival complement 93, 95

instrumental phrase 90
object of postposition 91-3
object of sentential complement 92-4, 96
subject 88-90
restrictive and non-restrictive 80-4
sentential 76-80

Relativization possibilities 84-103
and deletion 84-5
in coordinate structures 100-3
in main clause 88-94
in noun phrase 97-9
in postpositional phrase 100
in subordinate clause 92-7

Repetition 247-8

Retroflexion 538-9, 541-2, 563-4

Sanskrit xxxvi-vii, xxxix-xlv, 141, 154, 265, 278, 284, 313, 315, 358-9, 368, 451, 459-62, 466-7, 469, 478, 481-3, 486, 490-4, 499-500, 505, 507-9, 518, 522, 527, 529, 535-6, 541, 543, 545, 547-8, 552, 562, 564, 570-1, 574-5

Semivowels 542, 551-2

Sentence types 1-61
agentless 302-3
conditional 115-9
coordinate 29-31, 100-3, 158-82, 191-2, 199-201-250
copular 125-9
direct speech and indirect speech 1-7
equational 122-4, 227-9
infinitive 267
interrogative 7-37
minor *See* Minor sentence-types
questions 7-37, 57-8, 61
verbal 129

Stress 555-9
and intonation 561

Subject 129-30
and agreement 132-3
and reflexivization 212, 214-5
as topic 252
coordinate 175-82
dative 132, 285-7
definite 370-2
deletion of 129-30
dummy 133
embedded 71, 111-2
ergative 132-3
experiencer 285-6
indefinite 374-5
intransitive 130-1, 283, 4
marking of *See* Marking
nominative 287
of active sentence 129
of gerund 441
of participles 445-6
possessive 229-30
relativization of 88-9, 92
transitive 129-31, 284-5

Subordination 61-2

adverbial 61, 103-25
and negation 192-3
and noun phrase complements 64-5
and reflexivization 209-12
and tense 124-5
markers of 61-2
verbal complements 65-7

Suffix
ablative 293, 306, 346, 349
causative 401-2
dative 66-7, 107, 111, 136, 274, 359-61, 398, 404, 406
derivational 515
instrumental 66-7, 114, 504
locative 73, 142, 275, 282, 300, 311-2, 335-6, 339-40, 351, 354, 357, 359-60, 365
morphological 505, 507
number marking 366-7
order of 515
tense 407-14
vocative 275

Suffixation 459-60

Suprasegmentals 576

Syncope 551

Tense
and agreement marking 407-14
and aspect 414-31
and gerunds 113-4, 444
and infinitives 114, 443-4
and negation 188-9
and participles 114-5, 445-6
and time reference 408-9
future 413-4
in conditionals 118-9, 432
in matrix clauses 407-8
in subordinate clauses 124-5
marking of *See* Marking
past and perfective 415-8
present 409-10
sequence of 124-5

Time
anterior-general 364
days of the week 358
festivals 359
frequentative 360-1
month of the year 358-9
of the day 355-7
period of day 357
points in period-future 365-6
points in period-past 365
posterior general 365
seasons 359-60

Topic 252-4
and subject 252
and topic question 265-6
by gerundivalization 254
by infinitivalization 254
by movement 252-3
by particles 253

Verb
active 394-9
agreement 446-50
and aspect 414-31
and ergativity 411
and exclusion 330-1
and inclusion 330

and tense 407-14
auxiliary 47, 52, 64, 113, 118-20, 186-8, 310, 398, 400-1, 415-9, 421-32, 436, 439, 441-2, 443, 445
causativization 401-5
compound/serial 486-7, 531-6
conjunct 486-7
copular 412-3
dative-subject 285-7, 531
definition of 269
derivation of 484-7
finite 443
gerund 444, 113-4
inchoative 127-9, 285-6
infinitive 114, 443-4
modal 184, 188, 431, 435-6, 438, 444, 532
nature of marking 418-31
negation of *See* Negation
non-volitional 132-3
of experience 132, 285, 395, 400, 448
of motion 336-53
of psychological states 285-7
of speaking 3-6
of wanting 47-8, 66
passive 394-400
performatives 59
reduplication 533-5
transitive 133-6
valency 400-7
volitional 395-6, 531

Verb phrase (*See also* Participles, Infinitives and Gerunds)
coordination of 29-31
relativization in 100-3
verb compounds 526, 531-6

Vowels
deletion 570-2
distribution of 552
insertion 565-6, 572-5
length 554-6,
lengthening 542, 561, 568
lowering of 567-9
nasal 544-5, 551, 554-555, 567
oral 554
raising 566
sequence 551-2, 544, 552
shortening 564-5

Word compounding 517-36

Word order 138
and emphasis 16, 186, 223, 234, 242
and focus 3, 85-6, 243-4
and heavy shift 254-60
and negative particles 9
and topicalizaiton 252-3
and verb agreement 446-7
in adjectival pharse 269
in adverbial participles 449
in causatives 404
in comparative clauses 121-2
in coordination 28-31
in copular clauses 125
in equatives 154
in main clauses 23
in non-finite noun clauses 75-6
in question-word questions 11-6
in questions 8-16
in quotatives 2-3

in reflexives 211-2
in relative clauses 80-7
in subordination 61

Made in the USA
Monee, IL
23 December 2021

86987259R00374